HANDBOOK OF RESEARCH METHODS AND APPLICATIONS IN POLITICAL SCIENCE

HANDBOOKS OF RESEARCH METHODS AND APPLICATIONS

Series Editor: Mark Casson, *University of Reading, UK*

The objective of this series is to provide definitive overviews of research methods in important fields of social science, including economics, business, finance and policy studies. The aim is to produce prestigious high quality works of lasting significance. Each *Handbook* consists of original contributions by leading authorities, selected by an editor who is a recognised leader in the field. The emphasis is on the practical application of research methods to both quantitative and qualitative evidence. The *Handbooks* will assist practising researchers in generating robust research findings that policy-makers can use with confidence.

While the *Handbooks* will engage with general issues of research methodology, their primary focus will be on the practical issues concerned with identifying and using suitable sources of data or evidence, and interpreting source material using best-practice techniques. They will review the main theories that have been used in applied research, or could be used for such research. While reference may be made to conceptual issues and to abstract theories in the course of such reviews, the emphasis will be firmly on real-world applications.

Titles in the series include:

Handbook of Research Methods and Applications in Urban Economies
Edited by Peter Karl Kresl and Jaime Sobrino

Handbook of Research Methods and Applications in Empirical Finance
Edited by Adrian R. Bell, Chris Brooks and Marcel Prokopczuk

Handbook of Research Methods and Applications in Empirical Macroeconomics
Edited by Nigar Hashimzade and Michael Thornton

Handbook of Research Methods and Applications in Entrepreneurship and Small Business
Edited by Alan Carsrud and Malin Brännback

Handbook of Research Methods and Applications in Spatially Integrated Social Science
Edited by Robert J. Stimson

Handbook of Research Methods and Applications in Economic Geography
Edited by Charlie Karlsson, Martin Andersson and Therese Norman

Handbook of Research Methods and Applications in Environmental Studies
Edited by Matthias Ruth

Handbook of Research Methods and Applications in Social Capital
Edited by Yaojun Li

Handbook of Research Methods and Applications in Transport Economics and Policy
Edited by Chris Nash

Handbook of Research Methods and Applications in Heterodox Economics
Edited by Frederic S. Lee and Bruce Cronin

Handbook of Research Methods and Applications in Happiness and Quality of Life
Edited by Luigino Bruni and Pier Luigi Porta

Handbook of Research Methods and Applications in Political Science
Edited by Hans Keman and Jaap J. Woldendorp

Handbook of Research Methods and Applications in Political Science

Edited by

Hans Keman

*Professor Emeritus of Comparative Political Science,
Department of Political Science and Public Administration,
Vrije Universiteit Amsterdam, the Netherlands*

Jaap J. Woldendorp

*Department of Political Science and Public Administration,
Vrije Universiteit Amsterdam, the Netherlands*

HANDBOOKS OF RESEARCH METHODS AND APPLICATIONS

Cheltenham, UK • Northampton, MA, USA

Published by
Edward Elgar Publishing Limited
The Lypiatts
15 Lansdown Road
Cheltenham
Glos GL50 2JA
UK

Edward Elgar Publishing, Inc.
William Pratt House
9 Dewey Court
Northampton
Massachusetts 01060
USA

A catalogue record for this book
is available from the British Library

Library of Congress Control Number: 2016944285

This book is available electronically in the **Elgar**online
Social and Political Science subject collection
DOI 10.4337/9781784710828

MIX
Paper from
responsible sources
FSC   FSC® C013056
www.fsc.org

ISBN 978 1 78471 081 1 (cased)
ISBN 978 1 78471 082 8 (eBook)

Typeset by Servis Filmsetting Ltd, Stockport, Cheshire

Printed and bound in Great Britain by TJ International Ltd, Padstow, Cornwall

Contents

Contributors

Klaus Armingeon is a Full Professor for European and Comparative Politics at the University of Bern. He worked on institutions in comparative and historical perspective, such as corporatism, consociational democracy or the welfare state.

Dirk Berg-Schlosser has been Professor and Director of the Institute of Political Science and Dean of the Faculty of Social Sciences and Philosophy, Philipps-University, Marburg/Germany. He was Chair of the European Consortium for Political Research (ECPR), and from 2006 to 2009 Vice-President of the International Political Science Association (IPSA). He is currently the coordinator of the IPSA Summer Schools on Research Methods at the universities of Sao Paulo, Singapore and Ankara.

Robin E. Best is an Associate Professor in the Department of Political Science at Binghamton University (State University of New York – SUNY). Her research focuses on political parties, elections, electoral rules, voting behavior, and representation in democratic systems of government. Her work has been published in journals such as *Comparative Political Studies, Electoral Studies,* the *European Political Science Review, Government and Opposition, Party Politics,* and *Political Analysis.*

Nicole Bolleyer is Professor of Comparative Politics at the University of Exeter, UK. Her most recent monograph, *New Parties in Old Party Systems,* came out in 2013 with Oxford University Press. Her work appeared in journals such as the *European Journal of Political Research, Governance, European Political Science Review, West European Politics* and *Party Politics.*

Sarah Butt is a Research Fellow in the Centre for Comparative Social Surveys at City, University of London. Part of the Core Scientific Team for the European Social Survey (ESS) since 2012, she is involved in all aspects of survey design and implementation. Prior to joining the ESS, Sarah worked at NatCen Social Research where she was involved in the International Social Survey Programme and was co-director of the British Social Attitudes Survey.

Ben Crum is Professor of Political Science at the Vrije Universiteit Amsterdam and co-director of ACCESS EUROPE, the Amsterdam Centre for Contemporary European Studies. A political theorist by training, Crum's research focuses on the way contemporary processes of internationalization, European integration in particular, affect established practices and understandings of democracy and solidarity.

Keith Dowding is Professor of Political Science in the School of Politics and International Relations, Research School of Social Science, Australian National University. He has published eight books (most recently *The Philosophy and Methods of Political Science*, 2016, Palgrave), edited twelve books, and published around 150 articles on subjects in political theory, urban politics, public policy and administration, and comparative politics. He was editor of the *Journal of Theoretical Politics* (1996–2013).

Selen A. Ercan is Senior Research Fellow in the Institute for Governance and Policy Analysis at the University of Canberra, Australia. Her research interests include theory and practice of deliberative democracy, social movements, and interpretivist approaches to policy analysis.

Steven Griggs is Professor of Public Policy at De Montfort University, UK. His research interests are in political discourse theory and its contribution to the understanding of policy-making. He has recently published *The Politics of Airport Expansion in the UK* (with David Howarth) and the edited collection, *Practices of Freedom* (with Aletta J. Norval and Hendrik Wagenaar).

Joop J.M. van Holsteyn is Associate Professor and supernumerary Professor in Electoral Research at the Department of Political Science, Leiden University, the Netherlands. His research focuses on voting behavior, public opinion and opinion polling, and party membership in the Netherlands. He has published articles (in English) in, for example, *Acta Politica, Electoral Studies, International Journal of Public Opinion Research, Party Politics, Public Opinion Quarterly* and *West European Politics*.

Laura Horn is Associate Professor in the Department of Social Sciences and Business, Roskilde University. Her main research area is the critical political economy of Europe. Her publications include *Regulating Corporate Governance in the EU* (Palgrave, 2011), *Contradictions and Limits of Neoliberal European Governance* (Palgrave, 2008) and articles published in, for example, *Global Labour Journal, Globalizations* and *New Political Economy*.

David Howarth is Professor in Social and Political Theory at the University of Essex, UK. His research examines poststructuralist theories of society, politics and policy-making. His publications include *Discourse, Logics of Critical Explanation in Social and Political Theory* (with Jason Glynos) and *The Politics of Airport Expansion in the UK* (with Steven

Griggs). He recently published the monograph, *Poststructuralism and After*.

Galen A. Irwin is Emeritus Professor of Political Behaviour and Research Methods at Leiden University, the Netherlands. He studied political science at the universities of Kansas and Florida State. His research interests include voting studies and public opinion. He is co-author of *Governance and Politics of the Netherlands* (Basingstoke and New York: Palgrave Macmillan, 2014, 4th edition).

Richard S. Katz is Professor of Political Science at The Johns Hopkins University in Baltimore. He was co-editor of the *European Journal of Political Research* (2006–2012). His books include *A Theory of Parties and Electoral Systems* (Johns Hopkins, 1980, 2006), *Democracy and Elections* (Oxford, 1997), *Handbook of Party Politics*, edited with William Crotty (Sage, 2006) and *The Challenges of Intra-Party Democracy*, edited with William P. Cross (Oxford, 2013). He is a member of the Executive Committee of the European Consortium for Political Research.

Hans Keman is Emeritus Professor of Comparative Political Science at the Vrije Universiteit (VU) Amsterdam. He has published widely on comparative politics, methods in political science and on democracy, the welfare state, party politics and institutional analysis. Keman has been editor of the *European Journal of Political Research* and *Acta Politica*. In 2012 he published with Ian Budge, Michael McDonald and Paul Pennings *Organizing Democratic Choice* (Oxford University Press).

Kees van Kersbergen is Professor of Comparative Politics at the Department of Political Science of Aarhus University, Aarhus, Denmark. He has published widely in the areas of welfare state studies, public policy and political parties in major journals. His latest book is *Comparative Welfare State Politics* (2014, Cambridge University Press, with Barbara Vis).

Bert Klandermans is Professor in Applied Social Psychology at the Vrije Universiteit, Amsterdam, the Netherlands. He has published extensively on the social psychology of protest. In 2013 he received the Harold Lasswell Award of the International Society of Political Psychology for his lifelong contribution to political psychology. In 2014 he received the John D. McCarthy Award from Notre Dame University for his contribution to the study of social movements and collective action.

Jan Kleinnijenhuis (PhD Vrije Universiteit Amsterdam, 1990) is Professor of Communication Science at the Vrije Universiteit Amsterdam, the Netherlands. His research addresses the nature of political and economic communication, especially agenda building, news effects, and methods for automated and semi-automated content analysis.

Staffan Kumlin is Associate Professor of Political Science at the University of Oslo. His research concerns comparative political behavior in European welfare states. He authored *The Personal and the Political: How Personal Welfare State Experiences Affect Political Trust and Ideology* (Palgrave Macmillan, 2004) and is co-editor of *How Welfare States Shape the Democratic Public: Policy Feedback, Participation, Voting, and Attitudes* (Edward Elgar, 2014).

Jan-Erik Lane has taught politics and economics at many universities around the world. He has been a member of several editorial boards of political and social science journals. He has been a Full Professor in three universities and is now a Fellow with the Public Policy Institute in Belgrade. Among his publications are *Comparative Political Economy*, *The New Institutional Politics* (both with Svante Ersson) and *Culture and Politics* (with Uwe Wagschal).

David Marsh is Professor of Public Policy in the Institute for Governance and Policy Analysis at the University of Canberra. He is the author or editor of nine books and has published over 120 articles. For his sins, he is a Bristol Rovers supporter.

Michael D. McDonald is Professor of Political Science and Director of the Center on Democratic Performance at Binghamton University (SUNY). His research focuses on questions about democratic representation and electoral procedures. His articles have been published in journals such as the *American Political Science Review*, *Journal of Politics*, *Political Analysis*, *European Journal of Political Research*, and *Comparative Political Studies*. His books have been published by Oxford University Press.

Ferdinand Müller-Rommel is Professor of Comparative Politics and Director of the Center for the Study of Democracy at Leuphana University Lüneburg, Germany. He has published numerous books and journal articles on political executives, party government, party systems and political parties in Western, Central and Eastern Europe.

Andreas Nölke is Professor of Political Science with a particular focus on international relations and international political economy at Goethe University (Frankfurt am Main). He also is associated with the Amsterdam Research Centre for International Political Economy (ARCIPE). Before joining Goethe University, he taught at the universities of Konstanz, Leipzig, Amsterdam and Utrecht.

Edward C. Page has a BA in German and Politics (Council for National Academic Awards, 1976); MSc in Politics (Strathclyde, 1977) and PhD in Politics (Strathclyde, 1982). He was a Lecturer at the University of Strathclyde from 1978 to 1981 and a Professor at the University of Hull from 1981 to 2001. Since 2001 he has been working as a Professor for the London School of Economics. Research interests include British and comparative public policy and administration, law-making and bureaucracy. Recent books include *Policy Without Politicians* (Oxford University Press, 2012), *Changing Government Relations in Europe: From Localism to Intergovernmentalism* (edited with M. Goldsmith, Routledge, 2010), *Policy Bureaucracy: Government With a Cast of Thousands* (with the late Bill Jenkins, Oxford University Press, 2005).

Paul Pennings is Associate Professor at the Vrije Universiteit Amsterdam. He has published widely on parties and party systems, consensus democracies, the welfare state and comparative methodology. Currently his research focuses on explaining the variation in the satisfaction with governmental and democratic performance over time, cross-nationally and between societal groups.

B. Guy Peters is Maurice Falk Professor of American Government at the Department of Political Science of the University of Pittsburgh, USA and Distinguished Professor of Comparative Governance at the Department of Public Management and Governance of the Zeppelin University, Germany. His areas of expertise are comparative public policy and administration, and American public administration.

Benoît Rihoux is Full Professor in Political Science at the Université catholique de Louvain. His substantive research interests include political parties, social movements, organizational studies and policy processes. He is involved in the development of comparative research designs, comparative methods and qualitative comparative analysis (QCA) and has published extensively in that field. He is joint academic convenor of the ECPR Methods School.

Arjan H. Schakel is Assistant Professor in Research Methods at Maastricht University. He is author (with Liesbet Hooghe, Gary Marks, Sandra Chapman-Osterkatz, Sara Niedzwiecki and Sarah Shair-Rosenfield) of the book *Measuring Regional Authority* (Oxford University Press, 2016) and editor (with Régis Dandoy) of the book *Regional and National Elections in Western Europe* (Palgrave Macmillan, 2013).

Manfred G. Schmidt is Professor in Political Science at the University of Heidelberg. His major research interests are political institutions and public policy in the Federal Republic of Germany, comparative public policy and democratic theory. Manfred Schmidt is the winner of the Stein Rokkan Prize in Comparative Social Research in 1981. In 1995 he was awarded the Leibniz Preis of the German Research Foundation. His numerous book publications include *Political Institutions in the Federal Republic of Germany* (2003), *Demokratietheorien* (*Theories of Democracy*, 2010, 5th edition), *The Rise and Fall of a Socialist Welfare State* (co-authored with Gerhard A. Ritter, 2013) and *Das politische System Deutschlands: Institutionen, Willensbildung und Politikfelder* (*Germany's Political System: Institutions, Political Process and Public Policies*, 2016, 3rd revised edition).

Philippe C. Schmitter is currently Professor Emeritus at the European University Institute (EUI). He was a member of its Department of Political and Social Sciences from 1996 to 2004, after ten years at Stanford University. He received his PhD from the University of California, Berkeley. Currently, he has been a recurrent Visiting Professor at the Central European University in Budapest, at the Istituto delle Scienze Humanistiche in Florence and the University of Siena.

Esther Seha is Postdoctoral Researcher in Comparative Politics at the Center for the Study of Democracy at Leuphana University Lüneburg, Germany. Her research lies at the intersection of political institutions and democratization research with a focus on the reform of political institutions in defective democracies.

Isabelle Stadelmann-Steffen is Associate Professor in Comparative Politics with the University of Bern. Her main research interests concern comparative welfare state research and political behavior and attitudes. Current research projects aim at linking these two areas by considering potential policy feedback effects, mainly in the field of family and energy policy.

Barbara Vis is Professor of Political Decision Making at the Department of Political Science and Public Administration of the Vrije Universiteit Amsterdam, the Netherlands. She published on the politics of welfare state reform, political parties' behavior and political methodology in journals such as, *American Journal of Political Science*, *European Journal of Political Research* and *Sociological Methods and Research*. Her latest book is *Comparative Welfare State Politics* (2014, Cambridge University, with Kees van Kersbergen).

Uwe Wagschal received his MA in political science (1992), his Diploma in economics (1993) and his PhD in political science (1996) from the University of Heidelberg. He taught as a lecturer at several universities (Heidelberg,

Bremen, Zurich, Vienna and Sankt Gallen). In 2003 he became Professor for Public Policy and Empirical Methods at the University of Munich and in 2005 at the University of Heidelberg. Since 2009 he has been Professor for Comparative Politics at the University of Freiburg. He has published *Public Finances, Direct Democracy* and *Public Policy*.

Sally Widdop is a Research Manager at Ipsos MORI, UK. She is based in the Research Methods Centre and advises on questionnaire design, cognitive interview techniques and random probability sample design for international surveys. Prior to joining Ipsos MORI, Sally spent over eight years working at City, University of London and had a leading role in the design, coordination, and implementation of the European Social Survey.

Angela Wigger is Associate Professor Global Political Economy at the Radboud University, the Netherlands. Her research focuses on responses to the economic crisis and power configurations with respect to resistance. Her publications include *The Politics of European Competition Regulation. A Critical Political Economy Perspective* (Routledge, 2011), as well as publications in, for example, *New Political Economy, Review of International Political Economy* and *Journal of Common Market Studies*.

Lizzy Winstone is a Researcher in the Centre for Comparative Social Surveys at City, University of London. Lizzy has been part of the Core Scientific Team for the European Social Survey (ESS) since 2011, and is also involved in a wide range of activities related to the ESS, including survey design, pre-testing questions and monitoring fieldwork in a number of countries.

Jaap J. Woldendorp is Assistant Professor at the Department of Political Science and Public Administration of the Vrije Universiteit Amsterdam, the Netherlands, and has published in Dutch and internationally on the Dutch welfare state and on corporatism, party government, and institutions and macroeconomic performance from a comparative perspective. His publications include articles in *European Political Science Review, European Journal of Political Research, Acta Politica, Economic and Industrial Democracy* and *Journal of Public Policy*.

Sherry Zaks is a PhD candidate at the University of California, Berkeley. Her substantive research examines the conditions under which rebel groups are able to transition into political parties in the aftermath of civil wars. Her methodological interests lie in developing and refining tools for conducting rigorous qualitative research.

Acknowledgements

Developing and organizing a *Handbook* is a complex but rewarding venture. We are grateful to all the contributors. In particular, the way they responded positively to the (double blind) reviews by fellow experts, who – together with the editors – have critically but constructively evaluated all chapters in order to enhance their quality. Although it goes almost without saying that the editors remain responsible for the final version of the contributions, we feel that this procedure has indeed paid off.

We thank the reviewers, who have been helpful in raising the quality of the contributions: Bart Bes (Vrije Universiteit Amsterdam, the Netherlands), Ian Budge (University of Essex, UK), Kris Deschouwer (Vrije Universiteit Brussels, Belgium), Jan van Deth (University of Mannheim, Germany), Dietmar Braun (University of Lausanne, Switzerland), Roland Czada (University of Osnabrück, Germany), Christoffer Green-Pedersen (University of Aarhus, Denmark), Colin Hay (Sheffield University, UK and Sciences Po, France), Detlev Jahn (University of Greifswald, Germany), Wolfgang Müller (University of Vienna, Austria), Henk Overbeek (Vrije Universiteit Amsterdam, the Netherlands), Paul Pennings (Vrije Universiteit Amsterdam, the Netherlands), Barbara Vis (Vrije Universiteit Amsterdam, the Netherlands), Paul Whiteley (University of Essex, UK), and Reimut Zohlnhöfer (University of Heidelberg, Germany).

Producing a manuscript and keeping track of the various chapter versions is an arduous task, not only for editors who can only perform this enterprise thanks to the indispensable secretarial support and assistance. The editors are therefore grateful to Aniek IJbema, Margriet Lambert and Deborah Bakker for their efforts during the production of the chapters and the *Handbook* as a whole. Finally, Anne-Carine Verhage has been helpful in developing the cover of the book

Hans Keman and Jaap J. Woldendorp
Vrije Universiteit Amsterdam
The Netherlands
March 2016

Introduction
Hans Keman and Jaap J. Woldendorp

Political science – as many of the social science disciplines – is a multifarious discipline in terms of types of theoretical approaches and related diversity of methods. Political science analysis is therefore characterized by its variety and is often contested across the discipline. This is largely owing to the nature and radius of its core substance, that is, the role of politics in society and its systemic properties. Political processes involve individuals (the political actors, such as political leaders, Members of Parliament, electors, victims, party members and citizens), organizations (for example, parties, governments, movements, trade unions and businesses) and institutions (be they formal or informal rules, conventions, traditions or temporary measures; see, for example, Keman 1998; Lijphart 2012). Hence, analytical tools are discussed in terms of units and their occurrence at different levels and of analysis.

Originally nation-states were considered to be the main organizing tenet of political processes, but this is no longer the case. States were often organized as multi-layered entities of governing bodies, but we notice increasingly the emergence of transnational and international regimes (such as international governmental organizations – IGOs). Hence, political processes cannot and should not be studied by focusing on the nation-state per se. Instead the focus ought to be on a 'systemic multi-level' meta-approach to understanding the dynamics of politics in the contemporary world (Braun and Magetti 2015). That is, we need to consider the political world as a more or less organized system that is characterized by systemic (or within-system) features that can be discerned at various levels or layers (Hooghe and Marks 2009). In the real world this may involve a federation and its constituent parts or sub-national units within a centralized state (for example, municipalities), or the members of an international governing body, such as the United Nations Organization (UNO) or the European Union (EU). Hence, both theory and method in political science are characterized by complex interactions between political actors (likeminded parties or organized interests) operating at different levels of the polity, which vary in space and time and are in need of different methods and approaches to capture the political process both descriptively and analytically (for example, Pennings et al. 2006).

If this contention holds, then it follows that researching political processes and their ramifications is a challenging and complex assignment for any political scientist. In this handbook we deliver an overview of the basic principles of political science research based on a *systemic* view organizing a *meta*-theoretical 'approach' to introduce and discuss the various aspects of epistemology in relation to methodology as used throughout the discipline. It should be made clear immediately that our 'systemic' view is not to be considered as a 'paradigm' nor as a 'unique selling point'. Rather we consider this view to be a useful heuristic device to show how and when different approaches, methods and related applications can be best used to analyze political activities at different systemic levels of a polity (whether local, regional, federalized or united national, supra-national or transnational).

As in most disciplines, we proceed from a basic point of departure and related assumptions (as is explained in Chapter 1). First, political actors and institutions are the starting point of any research. Their interactions and relations are essential to understand any type of political system, be it a democracy, an autocracy or a dictatorship. Political processes and their outcomes (like elections, policy-making, conflict management or regime change) should therefore be analyzed within their relevant systemic framework. Hence, before we start collecting data and information, let alone analyzing them, it is paramount to elaborate the underlying or guiding theory and formulate a clear and meaningful set of research questions (or hypotheses). These preliminary activities define the type of research design, the analytical tools and the empirical information needed (qualitative or quantitative), not the other way around (Brady and Collier 2004).

Secondly, studying processes implies that both change and continuity have to be taken into account as well as the patterned variation in terms of space and time (for example, Bartolini 2000). This means that the approach to politics implies that *inter alia* the comparative method and its logic is seen as a central asset to political analysis. However, we do not claim that this is the only way to go (although we do consider it to be the 'royal' way; Keman 1993). We can make a valid distinction between 'implicit' and 'explicit' modes of comparison (Mair 1996). Implicit comparison is almost always used intuitively by researchers in the social sciences when assessing situations, developments and outcomes. For example, 'benchmarks' are quite often used to observe and judge events. Conversely, explicit comparisons are often used intentionally by academic researchers to explain horizontal political processes (such as, relations between parties and government) and vertical political processes (such as, a state vis-à-vis its citizens) controlling for their systemic differences over time and space (for example, Flora et al. 1999; Pierson 2000; Budge et al. 2012).

Thirdly, different approaches exist which are (sometimes strongly) contested, and this also applies to the mode of analysis and related types of empirical information. Our point of departure is that any type of political research should be open to replication, reliable in terms of the sources and data used, and valid as regards measurements (in relation to the concepts used; see Chapters 2 and 4). This statement appears to be almost superfluous, but it is not. A major divide within social sciences and political science in particular concerns qualitative versus quantitative types of data and analysis. Yet, as Brady and Collier (2004) put forward, it is not whether or not the method and related techniques are more or less superior but, rather, whether or not the academic-cum-scientific standards to be used are honored. We share this view and maintain that empirical information must be solid and responsibly reported. This applies to the historical approach and method as well as to constructivist types of research or quantitative data analysis (King et al. 1994; Pennings et al. 2006).

In sum, this handbook assumes that political processes can be studied and analyzed by using a systemic and multi-layered approach as a heuristic and organizing device, and postulates that politics is manifested at various levels of governance and by various societal activities. Political actors and institutions are central to any type of 'politics' and ought to be studied in spatial terms and across time (depending on the research question). This means that, in our view, both implicit and explicit types of comparison underlie most types of political research and that analytical inferences should be based on empirical information, be it qualitative or quantitative. Hence, the idea is that the standards of empirical-analytical social science are shared and applied. These ideas guide and structure this handbook. The contents of this book have been organized around five themes that make the 'story line'.

Part I, 'Political science: range, scope and contested methodologies', occupies the broad theme of how political science not only developed over time and in multifarious ways, but also what it has in common as a discipline with the social sciences in general (Chapter 1). Apart from the obvious commonality that all social sciences study human interactions in relation to their contexts, the range and scope of explanation is an essential and contested topic. Therefore two chapters are devoted to the underlying logics (causality and argumentation) inherent in social science as well as the various ontologies and epistemology that are discussed (and often contested) among political scientists (Chapters 2 and 3). Other chapters concern comprehensive dimensions that are prevalent in any type of political scientific research; that is, the meaning and importance of conceptualization and measurement (Chapter 4), and the role of time (change) and spatial dimensions (areas or specific systemic features) are introduced in Chapter 5. Finally, Chapter 6 concludes this part by elaborating the seminal attempt to develop a universal and comprehensive theory of political processes by means of Easton's systems theory, which represents the origins of the systemic multi-level approach that governs this handbook.

Part II, 'Approaches: exploring political interactions', consists of critical overviews of prevalent approaches within contemporary political science. As Verba (1996) once stated, the development of political science can be characterized as having basically the same menu, however, it is consumed at different tables. This becomes visible in Part II (and extends Chapter 1). On the one hand, broad overviews are presented that deal with the study of horizontal and vertical interdependencies such as multi-level governance (Chapter 7), political regimes (Chapter 8), the pros and cons of institutional analysis (Chapter 9) and of international and transnational politics (Chapter 12). On the other hand, the role and position of (horizontal) political action is treated by focusing on political parties, party government, interest groups and social movements, in Chapters 10 and 11. The remaining chapters of Part II introduce two important branches of political science: political economy as a problem-solving approach of politics and public policy performance (Chapter 13), and the relationship between political theory and normative methods to discuss 'real-world' problems (Chapter 14). The chapters of this part show both the dilemmas and the related conundrums in respect of developing theory and method that allow for solving 'puzzles'.

Part III, 'Analyzing politics: data–concepts–techniques', is the 'hands-on' part of this handbook, presenting and discussing the dos and don'ts of various ways of collecting empirical information and how to organize different types of data (Chapter 15). This basic information is further developed by chapters on institutional analysis (Chapter 16), analyzing voting behavior (Chapter 17) and survey techniques (Chapter 18). Chapters 20 and 22 introduce the reader to advanced types of data analysis: modelling political processes and the secrets of multi-level regression analysis linking micro-data to macro-variation. Finally, two chapters are devoted to the specific features of quantitative (Chapter 19) and qualitative approaches (Chapter 21) illustrating that the so-called qualitative–quantitative division is less deep than often is suggested; both approaches can be fruitfully employed especially within the context of systemic multi-level analysis.

In Part IV, 'Research tools: quantitative and qualitative applications', the micro-level and macro-level division and how to bridge it is discussed and elaborated in more detail (Chapter 23). Chapter 24 introduces the political science student to the mainstream quantitative technique, regression analysis, widely used in political science. Chapter 25 introduces configurational comparative methods, such as qualitative comparative analysis (QCA) and fuzzy-sets, and Chapter 26 discusses different types of discourse analysis, illustrated by various concrete examples. We continue this part with diverse types of research tools that are often ignored or badly understood. Chapter 27 focuses on case studies, while Chapter 28 shows the uses and misuses of cluster analysis. Finally, Chapter 29 introduces a recent form of policy analysis using process tracing. This part is intended to make the student of political science familiar with often-used techniques and to show when and how to apply these – doing research yourself.

Finally, Part V, 'Evaluation and relevance of research output', consists of elements in academia that are often not discussed and simply discarded. For example, in Chapter 30 the question of the political relevance of political science research is raised. The same issue, differently directed, is discussed in Chapter 31, namely, how to assess the actual performance of existing types of policy research. In another way Chapter 32 deals with the comparable problem of evaluating by replication to what extent existing and accepted findings hold up in view of new data or techniques. The final chapter (Chapter 33) is a service to advanced researchers, namely, how to publish your results depending on the readership (for example, academics, non-academics, policy-makers, opinion makers or the general public). Different publics require different types of publication strategy.

To conclude, this handbook covers a wide range of topics, issues, approaches and techniques that have in common that they are not only discussed but also used in political science analysis. We contend that you cannot operate as a political scientist without taking into account the wide and diverse spectrum of political science theory – be it encompassing, middle range or specific. Likewise, we are convinced that any type of theorizing cannot ignore the ontological and epistemological issues that are prevalent in social sciences as a whole. Furthermore, we believe that empirical political science needs to elaborate its theoretical development in close conjunction with the available techniques of data analysis, whether qualitative or quantitative. This handbook intends, therefore, to be a helpful tool for the political scientist to explore the relationship between theory, method and data, and to develop a proper research design that comes up with a valid and reliable answer to the research question under scrutiny. If the handbook serves this purpose, it will, in our view, contribute positively to the status of political science as a useful and advanced discipline within the social sciences and beyond.

REFERENCES

Bartolini, S. (2000), *The Class Cleavage: The Electoral Mobilization of the European Left 1880–1980*, Cambridge, MA: Cambridge University Press.
Brady, H.D. and D. Collier (2004), *Rethinking Social Enquiry: Diverse Tools, Shared Standards*, Lanham, MD: Rowman and Littlefield.
Braun, D. and M. Maggetti (eds) (2015), *Comparative Politics: Theoretical and Methodological Challenges*, Cheltenham, UK and Northampton, MA, USA: Edward Elgar.
Budge, I., H. Keman, M.D. McDonald and P. Pennings (2012), *Organizing Democratic Choice. Party Representation over Time*, Oxford: Oxford University Press.
Flora, P., S. Kuhnle and D. Urwin (1999), *State Formation, Nation-Building and Mass Politics in Europe: The Theory of Stein Rokkan*, Oxford: Oxford University Press.
Hooghe, L. and G. Marks (2009), 'A postfunctionalist theory of European integration: from permissive consensus to constraining dissensus', *British Journal of Political Science*, **39** (1), 1–23.
Keman, H. (1993), *Comparative Politics: New Directions in Theory and Method*, Amsterdam: VU Press.
Keman, H. (1998), *Institutions and Political Choice: On the Limits of Rationality*, Amsterdam: VU-University Press
King, G., R.O. Keohane and S. Verba (1994), *Designing Social Inquiry: Scientific Inference in Qualitative Research*, Princeton, NJ: Princeton University Press.
Lijphart, A. (2012), *Patterns of Democracy: Government Forms and Performance in Thirty-Six Countries*, 2nd edn, New Haven, CT and London: Yale University Press.
Mair, P. (1996), 'Comparative politics: an overview', in R.E. Goodin and H.-D. Klingemann (eds), *A New Handbook of Political Science*, Oxford: Oxford University Press, pp. 309–35.
Pennings, P., H. Keman and J. Kleinnijenhuis (2006), *Doing Research in Political Science: An Introduction to Comparative Methods and Statistics*, London: Sage.
Pierson, P. (2000), 'Increasing returns, path dependence, and the study of politics', *American Political Science Review*, **94** (2), 251–67.
Verba, S. (1996), 'The citizen as respondent: sample surveys and American democracy presidential address', *American Political Science Review*, **90** (1), 1–7.

PART I

POLITICAL SCIENCE: RANGE, SCOPE AND CONTESTED METHODOLOGIES

1 Political science: researching a multifaceted topic in essentially contested ways*
Philippe C. Schmitter

1 INTRODUCTION

Political science has its distinctive subject matter – the exercise of power and its consequences for society – and its distinctive set of assumptions, concepts, theories and methods.[1] These shape the way in which its practitioners identify topics and transform them into subjects worthy of being taught, researched and published. In a 'normal' physical or social science, such foundational elements are virtually invisible since they are regarded as givens and accepted without controversy. Political science has only rarely been a 'normal' science in this sense.[2] The scholars who been practicing it since Plato and Aristotle have frequently disagreed on what these are – even though all of them ultimately draw on the same accumulated wisdom of their predecessors. They engage in endless disputes about basic assumptions and core concepts; they draw both of these from contending, if not contradictory, theories and they apply a wide range of methods – both empirical and normative, quantitative and qualitative.

The core of their problem rests with the changing nature of the discipline's subject matter: *power*. Its exercise can be omnipresent but elusive; obvious when it involves force or coercion, but invisible when it focuses on manipulating preferences or invoking conformity to norms. Actors often pretend that they are not acting politically – while doing so – and virtually everyone has an incentive not to admit what his or her true objectives are. Maddeningly, the most powerful actors often have to do nothing since subordinates have already been programmed to obey or are convinced that it is in their best interest to do so. The consequences produced by the exercise of power are always risky, but usually calculable when circumscribed by established rules and practices; however, during periods of rapid change, they are fundamentally uncertain and, hence, incalculable. They are usually bundled together with allegedly 'natural' social, cultural or economic phenomena from which they are exceedingly difficult to disentangle. Of decisive importance as the discipline has become more self-proclaimed 'scientific' is the fact that power is not only difficult to define, but singularly difficult to measure, especially quantitatively. Experimentation, controlling for existing conditions and measuring precisely for the effect of deliberately introduced conditions, is usually not possible and even when it has been used the results can be misleading. One of the most salient features of politics involves so-called 'fallacies of composition'. What is true or workable at one level of aggregation produces very different results when practiced on a larger – or smaller – scale. Democratic individuals do not necessarily produce democratic regimes, and the inverse can be the case for autocratic individuals. If, as Aristotle noted, a science should only 'look for precision in each class of things just so far as the nature of the subject admits', then, political scientists face a more daunting task of being precise than any of the other social scientists.[3]

Their science rests on seven foundational components, all of which can be and have been 'essentially' disputed: (1) agents; (2) units; (3) motives; (4) mechanisms; (5) regimes; (6) methods; and (7) theories.

2   AGENTS

This is the most distinctive feature of a human science as opposed to a natural or physical science. It begins with the assumption that the objects of research are also its subjects. In the case of politics, this means that agents can make relevant choices that are not completely determined by the conditions in which they find themselves. If this were not the case, if as contemporary politicians have so often proclaimed, 'There Is No Alternative' were really the case, there would be no politics and, hence, no political science. Binding collective decisions would be made by the experts who know what that only alternative is and how to apply it.

Agency also implies that the subjects have the capacity for reflexivity. They are historical in the sense that their present actions are influenced by reflections ('memories') from the past, and, hence, by learning they may alter their responses ('lessons') when faced with analogous situations in the present. Inversely, agents may find themselves anchored in habits of obedience ('standard operating procedures'; for example, March and Olsen 1989) that can be difficult to break when new opportunities appear. Moreover, the very process of researching the power relations among actors – past or present – can produce changes in the behavior or expectations of those who are being studied ('anticipated reactions').

The vast majority of political science researchers presume that these agents are *individual and autonomous human beings* faced with and capable of making choices between alternative and consequential actions. They may agree that these actors are uniquely capable of exerting political agency, but they differ considerably over the properties that humans are capable of bringing to bear on their choices. Recently, thanks to the wholesale importation of assumptions from neo-liberal economics, these individuals are supposed to have pre-established and relatively fixed preferences, are able to rank these preferences consistently, possess adequate information about alternative courses of action and theories about their effects, and will predictably choose the course that they think best realizes those preferences, and still have the same preferences once the consequences of their choice have been experienced. This generic conception also reflects the much deeper ideological commitment of modern social and political thought to liberal individualism and rational progress. Shifting to a different micro-foundation would seem to declare that politics is a 'passionate' activity rooted in raw emotion, blind faith, mindless imitation, instinctual tradition, collective stupidity and/or random events – and, hence, incapable of collectively improving the world that we live it.

Without going so far, there are two grounds for calling this time-worn foundation into question. The first has to do with the sheer complexity and contingency that surrounds the contemporary individual. He or she cannot possibly know what are the 'real' (or, even less, all of the available) alternatives and what all of their eventual consequences will be – which means that he or she must rely on the *surrounding social milieu* in order to make these choices. Moreover, this individual is very likely to discover upon reflection that he or she has many conflicting interests or passions – especially over different time horizons – and, hence, cannot rank them consistently. Also, if those reasons were not enough, he or she is typically acting within a multilayered and polycentric set of institutions capable of making binding collective decisions affecting him or her – some public and some private. All of which implies that agent preferences cannot be fixed, but are always contingent on which policies are being proposed and by whom, and they will probably change during the course of political exchange between the various layers and centers of power.

The second reason for resetting the micro-foundations of political science is even more subversive of the prevailing orthodoxy. What if most of the significant actors were *permanent organizations*, not individual persons? Granted that these organizations are composed of individuals and some of them may depend very closely on the contributions and allegiance of these persons, but many do not and have developed elaborate rules and sources of support that cannot be reduced to such individual actions. They embody collective choices made long ago and have acquired a reputation and legitimacy of their own. Also, not infrequently, these political parties, interest associations, social movements, non-governmental organizations, business firms, government agencies and private foundations are in the business of teaching individuals what their preferences should be and committing them to obeying policies made in their name.

If we switch to organizations as the principal actors, the political scientist's task is greatly facilitated. By their very nature, these organized actors have internal processes for dealing with the diverse motives of their members and followers – and for coming up with a mediated expression of their interests, convictions and passions that is publicly justifiable and normatively appropriate. Granted, there is plenty of room for dissimulation, strategic action and outright hypocrisy on their part, but revealing these will be facilitated by the more abundant and public nature of the information that organizations are compelled to provide.

3   UNITS

Ever since Aristotle collected the constitutions of 158 Greek city-states, the privileged unit in political science for both observation and analysis was supposed to have a relatively autonomous economy, a self-governing polity and a distinctive collective identity – all institutionalized and coinciding with one another in a given territory. Eventually, thanks to the evolution of European polities and their overseas empires, almost everywhere this unit became the *sovereign national state*. It is usually presumed that only within the sovereign national state are agents capable of making choices and implementing them effectively, individuals or organizations capable of calculating their interests and passions, mechanisms of competition and cooperation capable of operating, and most regimes capable of developing stable and complementary institutions. Nothing is more firmly rooted in the foundations of political science than this assumption.

However, what if this unit of analysis can no longer be taken for granted? What if that presumed coincidence between autonomy, capacity, identity and territory has been disrupted beyond repair? In the contemporary world, no political unit can realistically connect cause and effect and produce intended results without regard for the actions of agents beyond their borders. Virtually all of these political units have persons and organizations within their borders that have identities, loyalties and interests that overlap with persons and organizations in other polities. Nor can one be assured that polities with the same formal political status or level of aggregation will have the same capacity for agency. Depending on their insertion into multilayered systems of production, distribution and governance, their capacity to act or react independently to any specific opportunity or challenge can vary enormously. This is most obviously the case for those units that are subordinate parts of *empires*; it also is the case for national states that have entered into *supra-national arrangements*, such as the European Union (EU), or signed *binding international treaties*, such as those of the International Monetary Fund (IMF) or the World Trade Organization (WTO). Not only do they occasionally find themselves publicly shamed or found guilty by such organizations, but also they regularly anticipate such constraints and alter their behavior accordingly.

If that were not enough, many national polities have granted or recently been forced to concede extensive powers to their *sub-national units* and, in some cases, these provinces, cantons, or *départements* have even entered into cooperative arrangements with equivalent units in neighboring national states. Political scientists need to dedicate much more thought to the units they choose and the properties these units supposedly share with regard to the specific agent, motive, mechanism or regime that they are examining. There still remains a great deal of variation that can be explained only by conditions prevailing at the national level, but exorcising or ignoring the increasingly complex external and internal settings in which these allegedly sovereign national units are embedded can result in a serious analytical distortion (Hooghe et al. 2014).

4   MOTIVES

Establishing who the agents are does not tell us what is driving their political actions. Again, contemporary political science has its orthodox response: *self-interest* (sometimes tempered by the caveat, 'rightly understood'). Presumptively, the individual political agent can invariably be relied upon to maximize, that is, choose the alternative that best satisfies his or her own and highest ranked preference at the lowest cost and without reference to anyone outside the immediate family. Needless to say, for this motive to dominate, the agent must have a comprehensive knowledge of what these alternatives are and a reliable understanding of what consequences they may produce – not to mention, the time to make such a calculation. There is a simpler solution which, nevertheless, is still rooted in self-interest. He, she or it can choose to minimize, that is, to choose the alternative that seems to avoid the worst possible outcome in terms of either cost or ranking. In between the two lies the reasonable possibility of 'satisficing', that is, mini-maxing his or her or its course of action somewhere between the two extremes (Keman 1998).

The scenario changes when the presumed motive is other-regarding rather than strictly self-regarding. In this case, actors have *convictions* about what is at stake in any given political transaction. Historically, analysts of politics tended to stress such motives as family honor, ethical responsibility, personal glory, religious belief, conformity to tradition or, even, justice and fairness. The emergence and eventual dominance of capitalism demonstrated the enormous advantage to the individual in pursuing his or her own interest in economic advantage without regard for others; but why should this always be the case in politics where the response of others (strategic or not) is a crucial condition for success and may not always be rooted in purely material terms?

Human beings can also have *passions* that cannot be reduced either to self-interest or conviction. They care about expressing themselves emotionally, about participating with each other in collective actions, about fulfilling their potential, even about caring for the welfare of the whole society or political unit in which they live. Without some degree of irrational passion, it would be impossible to understand why individuals choose to participate in 'lost causes', to devote such energy and resources to 'utopian ideals' or, even, to vote in 'elections with obvious winners' where, objectively, their contribution to success or failure is irrelevant or meaningless.

Finally, the most banal (and probably most frequent) motive of all is *habit*. Established regimes – whether democratic or not – cultivate a wide range of routinized behaviors that are simply expected of their subjects or citizens. Granted, some of these are 'shadowed' by the prospect that non-conformity may result in a coercive response by authorities; however, most of them are apparently voluntary – but do not involve any of the motives mentioned above.

5   MECHANISMS

The mantra of the discipline (especially where it is practiced in 'real-existing' democracies) is *competition*. Agents exercise their relative power by competing with each other in order to better satisfy their respective interests, convictions or passions. This usually presumes the existence of a pre-established institutional context, that is, a regime, in which conflicting motives are channeled by mutually respected rules into a process that limits the use of power resources and the range of possible outcomes, that is, by the existence of a government and state. The American science of politics was literally built upon the presumption these rules would be constitutional in form and democratic in process. Elsewhere – in continental Europe, Latin America, Africa and Asia – this should not be taken for granted (Lijphart 1977). Only recently and only in some units has the exercise of power been domesticated in this fashion to the mutual benefit of the agents involved.

The major distortion within the discipline comes when political scientists assume that electoral competition is the major expression of this process. The fact that political parties compete with each other for the representation of territorial constituencies and the right to form governments – even when these elections are freely and fairly conducted, and their outcomes uncertain – does not exhaust the mechanisms whereby political agents compete with each other. Not surprisingly, these other mechanisms are populated less with individuals than with organizations: competition between interest associations to influence public policy; demonstrations by social movements to set the public agenda or to block the implementation of policies. All of these are important (and often highly institutionalized) features of competition in modern polities that deserve at least as much attention as the more sporadic and routinized conduct of elections.

If these rules defining the mechanisms of competition do not exist or are strongly contested, political agents are likely to engage in unruly *conflict* not bound by such *de jure* or *de facto* constraints and to exercise their power primarily by threatening or exercising coercion to impose their respective interests, passions or convictions. Here the assumption is that all political units are plagued with multiple social cleavages whose interests, passions and convictions cannot be simultaneously satisfied or managed. Classes, sectors, professions, genders, generations, religions, regions, clans and clienteles – not to mention, the growing number of cleavages rooted in lifestyle preferences – want different treatment from public authorities. Not all of these can be domesticated according to mutually acceptable rules. What is crucial for understanding the outcome of these power conflicts is whether they are distributed cumulatively so that they reinforce each other or they are cross-cutting ('pluralistic') such that they tend to produce momentary coalitions and different sets of winners and losers over time and across issues.

The intra-disciplinary line separating the study of domestic politics from international relations has long depended on this distinction in which the former supposedly involved orderly competition and the latter rested on a presumed 'anarchy' of conflict without binding rules. More recently, this line has become less plausible as a barrier within the discipline of political science, since conflict has become at least as significant within states (especially failed ones) as between them and since a large number of interstate units – regional and functional – have emerged to regulate competition across national borders.

Another mechanism also deserves a more prominent place in the foundations of political science, namely, *cooperation*. If competition is not to degenerate into conflict, political agents have first to cooperate by agreeing upon the rules – formal or informal – that limit and channel their use of power. Many of these are habits or strictures inherited from previous generations ('path dependence'), but they are continuously subject to challenges as power relations and the identity of agents change and therefore require re-affirmation by contemporary agents. Moreover, politicians also cooperate in order to ally with each other, both to modify the pre-existing rules of engagement and to affect present policy outcomes. While it is understandable that political science should privilege competition – if only because its presence is much more visible and consequential – cooperation deserves more status and attention than it usually receives. So does its perverse form, *collusion*, that is, when inside agents act in agreement to prevent outsiders from competing through the usual mechanisms (Katz and Mair 1995).

The third mechanism is *conformity*. This is the mechanism that is the least obvious and the most difficult to explain. Most of political science presumes the manifest presence of its subject matter (not to mention its importance to human beings). How, then, do we observe and explain its opposite, namely, seemingly apolitical behavior – actors doing nothing in situations where they might, even should, have acted for one motive or another? The temptation is to explain this as a matter of habit or of having no interest, passion or conviction concerning what is at stake, but this would be to ignore two very important and omnipresent mechanisms of political life. *Fear* is the most obvious of these. Actors conform because they fear the effect that their actions may have upon their rulers. The more desirable of the two is *legitimacy*. Actors conform – even when it violates or offends one or another of their motives – because they regard their rulers as entitled to exercise authority for any one of many reasons (for example, Weber 1922 [1972]): genealogical inheritance, divine providence, victory in war, protection from predation, technical expertise, charismatic leadership or, as has become increasingly common, selection by winning a competitive election.

The fourth mechanism is *rebellion*. We might regard this as simply an exaggerated form of conflict, but it involves more than that. Through this mechanism, actors do not just use force (or the threat of it) to obtain concessions or subordinate opponents. Rebels seek to apply violent means to eliminate their opponents from the political game, to change its rules unilaterally and, in some cases, to change the very boundaries of the unit itself. In its most exaggerated version, *revolution*, they do not limit their efforts to changing the strictly political regime, but go beyond this to alter (presumably, irrevocably) the rules and routines surrounding other, social and economic, regimes.

6 REGIMES

Most students of contemporary politics assume that the unit they are analyzing has a relatively stable configuration of institutions that are complementary with each other, that is, it has a regime, presumably as the result of a prior historical experience of searching among alternatives and eliminating incompatible ones through competition or conflict. The actions produced by its agents, motives and mechanisms are somehow – functionally, ideationally, intentionally or constitutionally – related to each other at a higher level, such that their nature or importance cannot just be assessed alone. They are embedded in an institutionalized whole that conditions what roles can be played by individuals or organizations, self-or other-regarding interests, passions or convictions, competitive, conflictual or cooperative mechanisms, and so on. These regimes are given labels and it is presumed that those in the same generic category will share many foundational elements. At one time, there were three such labels: *democratic*, *totalitarian* and *authoritarian* or *autocratic*. More recently, 'totalitarian' has dropped out, thanks to the collapse of the Soviet Union and the transformation of China, and been replaced with '*hybrid*' or some other diminutive version of democracy or aug-mentative version of autocracy. Each of these can be broken down further by the analyst into sub-types when exploring the performance of more specific agents, motives or mechanisms. The recognition of such diversity means giving up the quest for universalistic 'covering laws' that can be applied to any agent, motive or mechanism. Individuals or organizations do not behave the same way in democracies and autocra-cies; the 'reasonableness' and 'appropriateness' of interests, passions or convictions depend on the institutions to which they are addressed; and mechanisms such as competitive elections or cooperative multiparty alliances can take on different meanings depending on their complimen-tary relationship with other arrangements for competition/conflict or cooperation/collusion.

7 METHODS

The study of politics has been 'multi-methodological' since its beginning – and seems to be becoming more so with time. Plato and Aristotle could not have used more different methods for drawing their respec-tive inferences. Ever since then, new methods have been introduced and very few have been eliminated. For most purposes, political science has been precluded from applying the most powerful of scientific methods, namely, the use of controlled experiments. The consequences of exercising power – not to mention the controversies surrounding it – are simply too great to permit the student to introduce some treatment and hold all other potential sources of variation constant.[4] Politics is a continuous activity that is embedded in a multiplicity of contingencies that cannot be halted or controlled at the will of the researcher. Granted that small-scale laboratory-like experiments have increasingly been attempted by political scientists, but they face very serious problems of inference when shifted to another level of aggregation (or when conducted with groups recruited on a different basis). 'Quasi-experiments' in which real world data over time are subjected to some specific policy treatment and the subsequent results are monitored have been more successful, but they also suffer from serious problems of inference because they cannot control for simultaneous treatments in related domains.

This leaves most of political science dependent upon data generated by the political process itself: descriptive accounts by journalists, memoires by participants, documents from official and unofficial sources, statistical reports from government agencies, and so on. The simplest and most comprehensible method has always been to tell a plausible story (usually a chronological one) using explicitly defined variables and identifying (usually inductively) the relationships between them – something that has been more recently and elegantly termed 'process-tracing'. This is usually based on qualitative observations, but can also include quantitative observations. More complicated is the statistical manipulation of exclusively quantitative data for the variables postulated as relevant and testing for the magnitude, direction and significance of their interrelationships. This has the distinct advantage of appearing more scientific (and less subject to observer bias), but is contingent upon whether the data are valid indicators of what they claim to be. The fact that we can put a number on virtually anything is less important than whether that number is meaningful in terms of the variable being measured.

One method that is widely regarded as distinctive of political science is the measurement of public opinion through surveys of randomly selected, representative samples of the population. Leaving aside that the method was transplanted from social psychology, data from this source has become an important original contribution to the understanding of politics for mass publics, but also for elite groups and individual politicians. At one moment in the evolution of the discipline, it was even claimed that this 'behavioral' data was sufficient for understanding all of politics (at least in liberal democratic regimes). Since then, the claims for this method have become less ambitious. Today, there remains a persistent competition among political scientists as to which method should best be applied to which subject, but most would agree that no single method would suffice for all subjects.

8 THEORIES

A theory is some combination of the elements outlined above, expressed by means of a specific set of concepts, their relationships (sometimes expressed in terms of explicit hypotheses) and their putative outcomes. Needless to say, given the variety of agents, units, motives, mechanisms and regimes, the combinations and permutations would seem to be virtually unlimited, although at any one moment in time within the discipline only a few are likely to be regarded as plausible.

In Table 1.1, you will find a spatially schematized and temporally compressed representation of the genealogical roots, trunks and branches that have evolved into contemporary and empirical discipline of political science. Its deepest root lies in *sociological constitutionalism* as invented by Aristotle and subsequently nourished until 1900 by Polybius, Machiavelli, Montesquieu, Alexis de Tocqueville, Karl Marx, Moisei Ostrogorski, Max Weber, Emile Durkheim, Roberto Michels, Gaetano Mosca, and Vilfredo Pareto. Through various extensions and permutations this has become the branch subsequently labeled as *historical political sociology*.

Table 1.1   Family tree or genealogy of political science over time

COLLECTIVISM INSTITUTIONALISM ◄------------► INDIVIDUALISM					
Multi-level and regional governance	Political development	Democratization and transition	Electoral behavior	Public policy and public choice	
International relations	Area studies	State formation	Interest politics and party politics	Public administration	Political economy
Law	Anthropology		Social psychology	Economics	

HISTORICAL POLITICAL SOCIOLOGY: around 1900	POLITICAL INSTITUTIONS: around 1900
e.g, *De Tocqueville, Marx, Durkheim, Weber, Michels, Ostrogorski, Mosca, Pareto*	e.g. *Montesquieu, Mills, Bryce, Bodin, Burdeau, Lowell, Duguit, Wilson*
Social constitutionalism	Normative (and legal) constitutionalism
Patriarchs: *Machiavelli and Aristotele*	Patriarchs: *Plato and Polybios*

Source: Adapted from Schmitter (2009, 2013).

The other deep root lies in '*normative speculation*' practiced by Plato and later to be converted into *legal constitutionalism* fertilized around the turn of the twentieth century by distinguished Anglo-French jurists such as Léon Duguit, Georges Burdeau, James Bryce, A. Lawrence Lowell and Woodrow Wilson.

Political science became a voracious consumer of conceptual and methodological innovations from other, increasingly professionalized, social science disciplines – first, from *social psychology* with the so-called 'behaviorist movement' and later (and somewhat more surreptitiously) from *anthropology* with the 'structural-functionalist approach'. Political scientists have always borrowed ideas and concepts from *economics*, especially from such early political economists as Adam Smith, Karl Marx, John Stuart Mill, David Ricardo, Jeremy Bentham, Friedrich List and Adolf Wagner, but the real novelty of the past few decades has been the transfer of neo-liberal root assumptions, deductive thinking and mathematical modeling techniques from *economics* into the study of political institutions.

Currently, the genealogical matrix of theory in political science is more or less a 'fuzzy set', it is not a neat and structured development. It is certainly not single, tapered with an elegant peak. Its most curious aspect, however, is the number of practitioners who are settled there and who seem content with sharing the same generic label: *institutionalists*. Closer inspection reveals that this matrix of theory contains an extraordinary variety of issues. All they seem to agree upon is that 'institutions matter'. They differ widely on what institutions are, how they come about, why is it that they matter and which ones matter more than others. Moreover, some of those settled there will even admit that other things also matter: collective identities, citizen attitudes, cultural values, popular memories, external pressures, economic dependencies, even instinctive habits and informal practices – not to mention the old favorites of Machiavelli, *fortuna* and *virtù* – when it comes to explaining, and especially to understanding, political outcomes. Strangely, if the genealogy illustrated in Table 1.1 is at all valid, almost all of those now nested in the canopy seem preoccupied with explaining why 'their' specific type of institutionalism is more important than the others and how 'their' institutions have a greater impact on individual behavior and unit performance. The twin trunks in Table 1.1 suggest that they should be at least as concerned with explaining how some combination of social forces and cultural conditions or of legal framing and economic calculus created them in the first place and is still supporting such a variety of institutions.[5]

How do we choose the right theoretical mix to apply when studying politics? The potential combinations are virtually unlimited, especially if we add to the seven foundations all of the sub-components of each. Granted, at any one moment in time not all of them will be regarded as plausible. Aristotle probably had the best idea: the mix should depend on the *objective* characteristics of the subject matter you have chosen to explain. Plato would probably have replied, no, it ought to depend on the *normative* purpose you are trying to fulfil. A more historically minded researcher might be guided by the *subjective* perception of the agents involved – their 'discourse' when trying to explain what they are doing. A more career-minded political scientist would probably respond by picking what is currently *fashionable* in the discipline. None of these 'shortcuts' through the maze of foundational elements is a guarantee of success, but each of them definitely points the researcher in a different direction and, worse, may lead to quite different conclusions about power, its uses and its consequences.

9   CONCLUSION

Aristotle famously argued that political science was the 'master science' since all of the other human sciences depended upon the order or disorder produced by politics. Ironically, this assertion of its superiority has also been a source of weakness. Political science is bound to be an 'open science'. It reaches into and affects crucial aspects of other realms of human behavior and is, therefore, bound to be penetrated by assumptions and concepts coming from them. Law, philosophy, sociology, psychology and, especially, economics have all claimed to be more closed and, therefore, self-referential sciences. Each of them has attempted to penetrate the deepest foundations of political science. At times, this has threatened to deprive the discipline of its distinctive focus on the use of power and its conversion (sometimes) into legitimate authority to resolve conflicts and achieve collective purposes. In recent decades, attempts have been made to reduce the study of politics to the voluntary exchange of information, the joint product of individual opinions, the rational search for optimal institutions or the deliberative discourse between consenting persons or organizations. This may have served to illuminate some of its peripheral aspects and to expand its scope of inquiry, but they have all floundered when trying to explain situations in which 'the preferences, desires or intentions of one or more actors bring about conforming actions, or predispositions to act, of one or more other actors' (Dahl 1982, p. 16). When some person (and, even more, when some established public or private organization) can alter the distribution of information, manipulate the attitudes of individuals, restrict the range of 'acceptable' solutions or distort the course of deliberations, the outcome becomes different – often radically different – than that envisaged by any of these models. If political scientists were to narrow their research agenda to situations where these conditions were not present, not only would they be depriving their discipline of the cornerstone of its foundations, but they would also become incapable of providing useful knowledge to the politicians, representatives, citizens and subjects who have to cope with the very real existence of power and its consequences.

NOTES

*   This is a substantially combined, revised and expanded version of two previously published articles: Schmitter (2009) and Schmitter (2013). By permission of Oxford University Press.
1.   Machiavelli thought there should be two political sciences: one masculine, the other feminine. In the former, power was channeled by 'dikes and dams' so that its exercise was relatively institutionalized and its consequences were more predictable. In the latter, power flowed erratically in accordance with the whims of *fortuna*. He lamented being condemned to living in female times and, therefore, having to invent a 'new science of politics'. Almost all contemporary political scientists assume (implicitly) that they are living in male times and this will be (explicitly) presumed in this chapter.
2.   There have been moments when political scientists seemed to be in agreement on these fundamentals, for example, constitutionalism at the beginning of the twentieth century; behaviourism with its exclusive reliance on individual attitudes in the 1950s and 1960s; structural-functionalism with its attention to the performance of core tasks necessary for the survival of the political system in the 1970s and 1980s; and rational choice with its assumption that actors seek to maximize their (imputed) preferences at the margin in each successive transaction in the 1990s and early twenty-first century. However, even during these periods of the relative hegemony of a paradigm, there were always detractors within the discipline and, eventually, all of them ended up being discredited or pushed to the periphery. The comparison with economics is striking where the orthodoxy of neo-liberalism installed itself and managed to drive out all practitioners of competing paradigms.
3.   Aristotle, *Nicomachean Ethics*, bk 1, ch. 3, pp. 2–3.
4.   Which is also why, with few exceptions, political scientists are banned from using the method of participant observation.
5.   A major exception to this generalization is the burgeoning literature on democratization which might even be characterized as 'obsessed' with both the social and cultural origins and the legal and economic aspects of institutions that may emerge in the aftermath of autocracy.

FURTHER READING

Introduction to Thinking about Politics

Aristotle, *Politics*.
Machiavelli, N., *The Prince*.
Tocqueville, A. de, *Democracy in America*.

Methods and Design of Research

Brady, H.E. and D. Collier (eds) (2010), *Rethinking Social Inquiry: Diverse Tools, Shared Standards*, Lanham, MD: Rowman & Littlefield.
Della Porta, D. and M. Keating (eds) (2008), *Approaches and Methodologies in the Social Sciences*, Cambridge: Cambridge University Press.
King, G., R.O. Keohane and S. Verba (1994), *Designing Social Inquiry: Scientific Inference in Qualitative Research*, Princeton, NJ: Princeton University Press.

REFERENCES

Aristotle, *Nicomachean Ethics*, Book 1.
Dahl, R.A. (1982), *Dilemmas of Pluralist Democracy: Autonomy vs. Control*, New Haven, CT: Yale University Press.
Hooghe, L., A.H. Schakel and M. Marks (2014), 'Multilevel governance and the state', in S. Leibfried, E. Huber, and J. Stephens (eds), *Oxford Handbook on Transformations of the State*, Oxford: Oxford University Press.
Katz, R.S. and P. Mair (1995), 'Changing models of party organization and party democracy: the emergence of the Cartel Party', *Party Politics*, **1** (January), 5–28.
Keman, H. (1998), 'Political institutions and public governance', in R. Czada, A. Hëritier and H. Keman (eds), *Institutions and Political Choice: On the limits of Rationality*, Amsterdam: VU-University Press, pp. 109–33.
Lijphart, A. (1977), *Democracy in Plural Societies*, New Haven, CT: Yale University Press.
March, J. and J. Olsen (1989), *Rediscovering Institutions: The Organizational Basis of Politics: A Comparative Exploration*, New York: Free Press.
Schmitter, P.C. (2009), 'The nature and future of comparative politics', *European Political Science Review*, **1** (1), 33–61.
Schmitter, P.C. (2013), 'Political science', in J. Krieger, C.N. Murphy and M.E. Crahan (eds), *Oxford Companion to Comparative Politics*, vol. 2, New York and Oxford: Oxford University Press, pp. 248–57.
Weber, M. (1922), *Wirtschaft und Gesellschaft* (*Economy and Society*), vol. 5, reprinted 1972, Tübingen: Mohr.

2 Epistemology and approaches: logic, causation and explanation*
Dirk Berg-Schlosser

1 INTRODUCTION

In a very basic sense, it is important to distinguish three fundamental notions (and fields of inquiry):

1. *Ontology* (the 'study of being') is concerned with the question of what exists?[1] This is the realm of general philosophy, diverse world views (*Weltanschauungen*) and ideologies, each claiming some absolute truths or justifications. Here, at this level of argumentation, we only can agree to disagree (see further, Chapter 3).
2. *Epistemology* (literally the study of knowledge, that is, the theory of science) addresses the question, what can we know? What are the foundations of scientific knowledge? What evidence do we have? Scientific explanations in this sense are based on logical reasoning and empirical observations. Again, there are many controversies, but within certain 'schools of thought' and the respective scientific disciplines some agreements can be found.
3. *Methodology* (the reflection about and the knowledge of procedures and tools in science) answers the question, how do we acquire scientific knowledge? How reliable and valid are our tools and techniques? How can we be sure of the evidence? How can these insights be inter-subjectively (that is, among scientists in a particular field) transmitted and accepted? Also, which *standards* are to be maintained in the social sciences in order to achieve a certain degree of accepted knowledge?

The *social* sciences (dealing with human beings and their interactions) cover a particular area which is distinguished from the natural sciences (dealing with inanimate objects and nature) in a number of important respects. These concern the multi-dimensionality of their subject matter, the 'malleability' of their objects changing over time, and the fact, that we as human beings and investigators are ourselves to some extent part of the subject matter which, again, poses special epistemological problems of interacting with our object of investigation.

In this chapter, first, the basic epistemological foundations of the social sciences will be briefly presented. Then different approaches to causality are discussed. Here, we focus on practical aspects of social science research methods and their applications leaving aside broader ontological concerns in the philosophy of science (see also Chapter 3 in this volume). Finally, some conclusions are drawn from the ongoing epistemological and methodological controversies between more quantitatively (King et al. 1994) or more qualitatively oriented researchers (Brady and Collier 2010) and statistical or set-theoretical perspectives (Goertz and Mahoney 2012, and Chapters 19 and 21 in this volume).

Most of the discussions in this chapter refer to the empirically oriented social sciences in general. *Political* science refers to a specific substance matter (see the introduction in Badie et al., 2011, and Chapter 1 in this volume), but its sub-disciplines also have specific methodological emphases. So, for example, 'comparative politics' mostly deals with research questions at the macro-level of analysis, that is, states or larger political units with, necessarily, a limited number of cases in the real world. By contrast, 'political sociology' is mostly concerned with the micro-level and a large N, as in electoral studies, or the meso-level of organized groups with a large, but nevertheless limited number of cases. International relations again deal with a limited number of actors, states and their representatives, but also international organizations and non-governmental organizations (NGOs). Accordingly, the methodological tool kits most applicable to these disciplines and the causal implications to be drawn from them vary and will be elaborated in the remainder of this chapter.

2   THE EPISTEMOLOGICAL FOUNDATIONS OF THE SOCIAL SCIENCES

Multi-dimensionality: the social sciences deal, more or less implicitly or explicitly, with three distinct *dimensions*:

- an *objective* dimension, some tangible objects as in the natural sciences;
- a *subjective* dimension of human perceptions and consciousness; and
- a *normative* dimension of human values and judgments.

In the social sciences, different approaches emphasize one of these dimensions. For example, historical-materialist (Marxist) approaches take the *object* dimension, the modes of production) as their starting point. Behavioralists emphasize *subjective* perceptions and related human

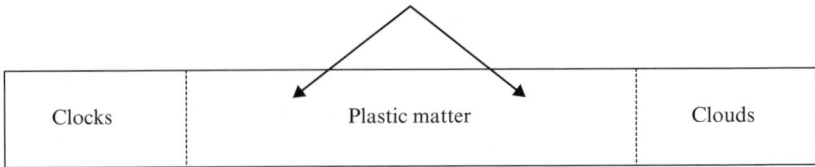

Figure 2.1   Degree of determination of theories

actions. *Normative*-ontological approaches (such as Plato) discuss basic values of a 'good' political order.

The malleability of the substance matter: in Karl Popper's (1972) view the 'degree of determination of theories' is located on a continuum between, at the extremes, 'clocks' and 'clouds'. Clocks are highly deterministic, mechanical systems which allow for great precision in predicting or retrodicting (as in astronomy). By contrast, clouds are almost intangible, have no clear structures or patterns and remain unpredictable. In between is a more malleable 'plastic' substance where Almond and Genco (1977) place the social sciences (see Figure 2.1).

The distinction between naturalist theories, which take the 'real' world as given, and constructivist theories, which consider the world to be merely constructed by our concepts and perceptions, are worlds apart. Realist theories take an intermediate position accepting a real world as perceived by our senses, but constructing and interpreting it through our concepts and theories (Moses and Knutsen 2012). Naturalist theories are located to the left of the continuum in Figure 2.1, constructivist theories to the right. In between is the area of medium-range theories, bounded in time and space. Carl Hempel's (1965) 'covering laws' at best refer to the 'clocks' on the left. Statistical methods (and restrictions) apply to the 'probabilistic' realm, still more to the left, with possibilities, based on large numbers, of 'statistical inference'.

In the social sciences with a small number of cases often only conditions of occurrence, more in the middle, can be established. In fact, there is not a single absolute 'law' in the social sciences. Even Duverger's laws (1951) about the impact of electoral systems on party systems or Anthony Downs's median voter theorem (1957) are highly contextualized and are not applicable in all situations. Systematic comparative methods like qualitative comparative analysis (QCA; see Chapter 25 in this volume) can establish some covering conditions in these respects. Further to the right, qualitative studies of even fewer cases can be found; these can be deeper and more complex, but even less generalizable.

2.1 Self-Referential Aspects

All these things are further complicated by the fact that we ourselves are part of this substance matter (Luhmann 1984). This creates *self-referential* situations and poses specific problems of perception or objectivity, and can create interactions with the objects we study, as, for example, self-fulfilling or self-defeating prophecies in electoral studies or in the stock or currency markets. However, it also opens up specific possibilities of understanding and concurrent interpretations ('*Verstehen*' in Max Weber's, 1904 [1949], sense) and more sensitive interpretations of others and the world we live in. Constructivist approaches can dig deeper into this subjectivity and the possible plurality of meanings in Foucault's (1970) sense (see also Chapter 26 in this volume). This is another *differentia specifica* of the social sciences as compared to the natural sciences. From all this follows a high-level of responsibility regarding the societal relevance of what we are doing in a normative sense (as is elaborated in Chapter 30 in this volume).

2.2 Linking Levels of Analysis

In the social sciences several *levels of analysis* have to be distinguished, each referring to different types of entities to be observed:

- a *macro*-level referring to large social entities like entire societies, economies, states;
- a *micro*-level of individual persons living and acting in these entities; and
- a *meso*-level of more or less organized groups of persons and associations in between.

The links between these levels and their interactions can be illustrated with James Coleman's (1990) 'bathtub' (see Figure 2.2).

An explanation of social events starts at the macro-level on the upper left-hand side (the conditions of occurrence). These then shape the possible perceptions and actions of individuals at the micro-level. In order to become effective in a larger sense, these actions often have to be aggregated by organizations at the meso-level on the right-hand side (for example, social movements, interest groups and political parties). These then shape the final outcome at the macro-level on the right-hand side (the explanandum).

In this way the major emphases of important theoretical approaches also can be illustrated: macro-(for example, historical-materialist) theories can be located at the upper left-hand corner drawing direct

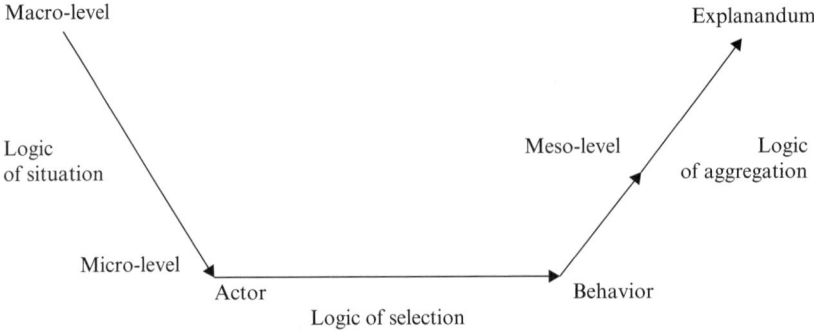

Source: Adapted from Coleman (1990) and Esser (1993).

Figure 2.2   Linking levels of analysis

conclusions as to the explanandum on the upper right-hand side. By contrast, methodological individualists start at the micro-level, often based on heroic assumptions as to the rational behavior of actors, for example about a '*homo oeconomicus*' in economic theory maximizing his or her material benefits or voters making their (rational) choice accordingly.

Such assumptions can be extended to include a more comprehensive situation of individual actors as restricted, resourceful, evaluating, expecting, maximizing men (or women) in Hartmut Esser's (1993) sense. Other aspects concern various social identities (family ties, group membership, ethnic, religious communities, and so on) and more tendencies to individualism in modern societies. Bounded rationality finally takes into account some restrictions at the macro-level (such as institutional conditions or available opportunities; see Elster 1989; Czada et al. 1998).

The meso-level on the right-hand side of Figure 2.2 poses specific problems of aggregation, for example, for collective actions with the possibility of free-riding by those who are not part of a particular organization but nevertheless share the benefits (for example, of union activities; see Olson 1968). Similarly, assumptions of rationality or individual preferences at the micro-level cannot be aggregated so easily and collective rationality may differ from individual ones (Simon 1996, ch. 2).

This whole pattern can also be sequenced showing dynamic interactions and sometimes be analyzed in terms of path dependency over time (that is, former choices restrict opportunities; see also Chapter 5 in this volume). In sum, we all live in a multi-dimensional, ever-changing world of which we are all part in our specific ways and with which we have to deal with different methods and approaches. This makes our efforts to come to understand it all the more complex and difficult, but also more challenging and worthwhile.

3 THINKING ABOUT CAUSALITY

In the empirical social sciences different approaches to establish *causality* can be distinguished depending on a realist, critical or rational epistemological perspective and the level and type of observations (evidence).

3.1 Hume's Regularity Model

The most basic approach has been developed concerning the object dimension in the natural sciences derived from a highly deterministic (clock-like) perspective. David Hume (1748) summarized this *regularity model* of causation by listing three conditions to be necessary to speak of a strict (and testable) causality (or X → Y):

- Contiguity: the cause and effect must be discernable in time and space;
- Succession: the cause must be prior to the effect;
- Constant conjunction: there must be a *constant* relation between the cause and the effect.

In this way many causes and effects in (Newtonian) physics or non-organic chemistry, for example, can be explained. John Stuart Mill (1843 [1862]), who shared this view, elaborated this by setting up a list of rules (canons) for strictly controlled research designs.

The first is the method of agreement: one factor in common, same outcome. In his own words:

> If two or more instances of the phenomenon under investigation have only one circumstance in common, the circumstance in which alone all the instances agree is the cause (or effect) of the given phenomenon. (Mill, vol. 1, p. 428)

The second is the method of difference: absence of one factor, different outcome.

> If an instance in which the phenomenon under investigation occurs, and an instance in which it does not occur, have every circumstance in common save one, that one occurring only in the former; the circumstance in which alone the two instances differ, is the effect, or the cause, or an indispensable part of the cause, of the phenomenon. (Mill, vol. 1, p. 429)

The third, the indirect method of difference, applies the method of agreement once before and once after an event (for example, an external stimulus or an additional substance). This single additional factor is then seen as responsible for the changed outcome.

Altogether, Mill's methods are based on mechanical and deterministic relationships. This method presupposes a testable model or theory and is not purely inductive. Nevertheless, they are useful for identifying more general conditions of occurrence of a phenomenon (Cohen and Nagel 1934) at the macro-level (upper left-hand side in Coleman's bathtub, Figure 2.2).

In the social sciences we often find a plurality of causes and probabilistic relationships. Such causes can be multiple or conjunctural in Mill's sense, which means that several combinations of factors may lead to the same outcome (*equifinality*).

Hume's regularity model can be specified further by identifying necessary and sufficient conditions. Necessary conditions are always present for a certain outcome, that is, in set-theoretical terms the outcome is a subset of the condition. Sufficient conditions explain the outcome by themselves, and there can be several, but they may not be necessary (that is, the condition is a subset of the outcome). For example, to hold regular elections can be considered to be a necessary condition for modern democracies. By themselves, however, these are not sufficient to define a democracy because other elements have to be present as well. We may also distinguish different types of democracy (for example, presidential or parliamentary systems which exhibit a different combination of factors; see Badie et al. 2011; also Chapter 8 in this volume).

3.2 Statistical Models

When we move from the deterministic clock-like world more towards a *probabilistic* world, causal relationships can no longer be ascertained with such certainty. Instead, they are at best based on a very large number of observations as a proportion of the total (occurring almost always) or probability calculations of random samples drawn from a large universe of cases assuming a normal distribution (Gauss 1809). Here, usually a linear additive model of causation is assumed as expressed in a standard ordinary least squares (OLS) regression model, the workhorse of quantitative analysis in the social sciences (see, for example, Blalock 1979; also Chapter 24 in this volume). Applying OLS regression has been useful for many purposes, but it is important to note that only the overall average values across all cases analyzed are taken into account.[2]

Random selection of cases can also be used in 'controlled group experiments' where two sub-groups of a larger population are drawn at random and can, therefore, be assumed to be largely identical on major demographic and other characteristics. If an external stimulus is introduced to one group and not the other, such as a medical treatment, and the outcome in that group changes (for example, the disease is cured), then the change in outcome can be attributed to this stimulus. This resembles Mill's method of difference, but is now based on probability calculations and allowing for an error term. Such procedures have become common practice in some fields and are considered the gold standard of quasi-experimental research.

In the social sciences, the experimental situation is often artificial. For example, in behavioral economics or political science one randomly selected group of persons (often college students) may be given a certain incentive (often cash rewards) to induce a certain behavior which is not offered to another randomly selected group. Then the different outcome is observed and, if there is a difference, attributed to the effect of the stimulus. This can be done in closely controlled laboratory situations testing the assumptions of a specific model in economics or political science. Some actual field experiments may also be possible, for example, assessing the effects of different forms of political campaigning by randomly selecting different target groups exposing one to a particular form of campaigning (like door-to-door canvassing) and not the other (Green and Gerber 2008). These can be consciously designed, but they may also occur naturally, for example, when one community is exposed to a particular event and not another very similar event leading to a different outcome. This can be treated as if a random selection of the two groups had occurred. A similar situation arises, when attitudes of the same group of persons are assessed before or after a major economic crisis or political event (for example, the attacks on the World Trade Center in New York on 11 September 2001) leading to a change in outcome. This can be measured at the micro-level by survey research, but changes at the macro- (political system-) level may also be attributed to major crises such the Great Depression in the interwar period (for a detailed assessment see, for example, Berg-Schlosser and Mitchell 2002). This, once again, resembles, Mill's indirect method of difference.

Strictly speaking, such randomly selected groups are never completely identical. The same individual cannot be a member of the group receiving the treatment and of the control group at the same time. Here we speak of *counterfactual* reasoning about phenomena that did not occur. In a broader ontological sense this means we are speaking of a different counterfactual world (Lewis 1986). Statistically, this problem of impossible-to-observe causal effects is addressed by replacing them with average causal effects over a population of units. In practice this has not been applied much so far (see Goertz and Mahoney 2012).

3.3   Small and Medium N Analyses

When we deal with even smaller numbers, such as comparing entire countries, societies, economies at the macro-level where no random samples can be drawn, other more recently developed techniques can be used. One technique is a derivation and further advancement of Mill's canons, again in a set-theoretical sense. *Case selection* then must be determined by other criteria (see also Chapter 27 in this volume):

- meaningful selection of cases based on theoretical and substantive concerns; cases must be drawn from a sufficiently *homogenous* (*ceteris paribus*) universe in order to be comparable;
- within that universe maximum *heterogeneity* should be achieved to allow for the greatest possible variance and range of explanations.

Most similar and most different systems designs (Przeworski and Teune 1970) are then possible. Complexity can then be reduced by identifying factors related to the respective outcome: most similar systems – different outcome (MSDO) and most different systems – same outcome (MDSO) research designs (De Meur and Berg-Schlosser 1996; Keman, 2011). This principle is illustrated in Figure 2.3 for three cases (represented by the circles). Only in the shaded areas can possible causes for the respective outcome be looked for. All the white zones can be excluded and are controlled in this way.

This procedure pre-supposes, however, that most similar and most dif-

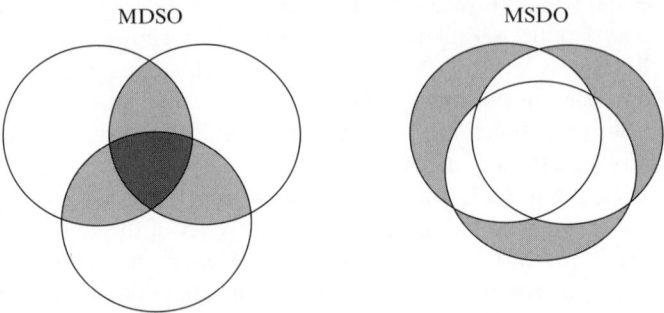

Figure 2.3   Matching and contrasting of cases, MDSO and MSDO designs

ferent cases can actually be identified. This has to be based on extensive historical and contemporary case knowledge and has to be operationalized in a systematic manner in order to be inter-subjectively transparent. One such operationalization has been provided by De Meur and Berg-Schlosser (1996) based on Boolean distances (that is, values of 1 or 0) on a large number of variables in a comprehensive systems framework. In this way, the focus of attention can be narrowed down considerably (as with a microscope in biology) and the actual factors leading to the respective outcome may be identified. It must be kept in mind, however, that this procedure is just a specific technique and will only lead to meaningful results if, as for Mill's canons, the true factors have actually been included in the analysis. Thus, spurious relationships, as with statistical correlations, may also occur. It is, therefore, essential, that such findings are confronted with intensive case knowledge and can be confirmed or refuted by the respective country experts in a constant dialogue between theory and data (Ragin 1987). Such results remain limited to the actual cases and period examined (internal validity). They can be further validated by examining other constellations of cases in time and space (see Chapter 5 in this volume). In the longer run, empirical theory of the respective field of investigation can be strengthened in this way (enhancing its external validity).[3]

In a similar small and medium N situation operates, to the largest part, QCA in its different crisp-set, multi-value, and fuzzy set variants based on set theory and Boolean algebra as developed by Charles Ragin (1987) and his collaborators (Rihoux and Ragin 2009; see also Chapter 25 in this volume). Here, the initial complexity of cases is reduced by placing them and the conditions leading supposedly to a particular outcome in a truth table. At this stage, often already important contradictions (cases with identical conditions having different outcomes) become apparent. These have to be eliminated as much as possible, for example by testing other hypotheses and improved theory (see Chapter 32 in this volume). The most important rule in QCA is therefore: if two Boolean expressions differ in only one causal condition yet produce the same outcome, then the causal condition that distinguishes the two expressions can be considered irrelevant and can be removed to create a simpler, combined expression (Ragin 1987, p. 93). However, the same caveats as for the MSDO/MDSO procedures apply; this procedure, strictly speaking, only establishes an *internal validity* of findings and the results may be spurious and have to be confronted with intensive case knowledge. It is also important to note that such procedures with different outcomes often reveal *asymmetric* relationships which means that a theoretical explanation for a positive outcome need not be the reverse for a negative outcome. This is also in contrast to many of the large N statistical procedures (Goertz and Mahoney 2012, ch. 5).

3.4   Case Studies and Process Tracing

Large N (statistical), controlled experimental and smaller N comparative studies can show strong relationships between certain variables or combinations of factors, but the precise *causal mechanisms* at work remain in a black box. These can be ascertained by detailed causal process observations (CPOs) and process tracing *within* individual cases. As in a detective story, the true culprit and the precise sequence of events must be found. Here, however, the research interest does not consist of explaining a single event (the outbreak of a war, a revolution, a political assassination, and so on) in an 'idiographic' manner, but to come up with a theoretical explanation which is valid for many similar circumstances (Beach 2012; see also Chapter 29 in this volume).

Another approach in this context is a 'Bayesian' approach which builds upon previous experiences and in this way increases confidence in particular findings. As Derek Beach puts it: 'New empirical evidence updates our belief in the validity of the hypothesis, contingent upon: 1) our prior confidence based on existing research, 2) the probative value of the evidence in relation to the hypothesis, and 3) the amount of trust we can place in the evidences' (Beach 2012, p. 12).

In actual practice, however, stronger theories based on case studies have remained relatively rare and their actual scope (range in time and space) has to be determined. One such possibility consists in combining the findings of intensive within-case process tracing with broader comparative small N or even large N statistical studies to establish the external validity of results in *multi-method* research (Bergman 2008; Berg-Schlosser 2012).

4   CONCLUSIONS

The attempts of the social sciences to arrive at general and valid theoretical findings have to be seen in their specific epistemological situation: the reality they deal with is highly complex (multi-dimensional), changing over time in many ways, and, to some extent, influenced by the researchers themselves (that is, subject–object relationship). Nevertheless, as has been briefly discussed here, there are different approaches and ways to deal with this. These are treated here from a realist empirical perspective and depending on the number of (possible) cases to be observed. Large N, small N and single case studies all have their respective strengths and weaknesses leading to different approaches (quantitative versus qualitative, statistical versus set-theoretical). These do not necessarily exclude each other and often can be supplementary in mixed-method research. This can work both ways, for example, testing a strong causal mechanism found by process tracing in a single case by systematically comparing it across a greater number of cases as in QCA. Similarly, strong relationships discovered in a large N statistical analysis can be validated by looking more intensively into individual cases identifying closer causal links (see Chapter 19 in this volume).

Altogether, macro- and micro-levels of analysis can also be brought into a closer relationship. Some causes at the macro-level are more remote, identifying more general conditions of occurrence. Against this background more specific proximate assumptions as, for instance, regarding the rational behavior of actors or concrete social and political attitudes and behavior as reported by survey research (see Chapter 18 in this volume) or in experimental studies, come into play. In this way, the historical and geographical range of observations and their causal analysis can be delineated more closely as 'middle range' theories.

Many controversies and discussions are still underway (see Chapter 3 in this volume). In fact, in spite of the often soft image of the social sciences, they often are much harder in terms of the complexities and situations they have to cope with. Nevertheless, since Hume's and Mill's methods, significant progress has been made and important insights of theoretical and practical relevance have been gained.

NOTES

* For the preparation of this chapter discussions during the IPSA summer schools on concepts and methods in political science with colleagues at various locations have been extremely helpful. The resulting eclectic text (and its limitations) are, of course, my own.
1. Examples of ontological reasoning are, for instance, René Descartes putting forward '*je pense donc je suis*' (I think and thus I exist) or Karl Marx who stated '*Der Mensch ist was er isst*' (what man consumes shows his becoming). The former example is typical for 'idealism', whereas the latter is typical for 'materialism'. Both ontologies are considered as universal truths for how to view and interpret reality.
2. Often specific outliers are ignored. Similarly, problems of multicollinearity (interactions among the independent variables) or endogeneity (interaction with the error term) may occur. See Chapters 19m section 3.3 and 24, section 4.
3. Internal validity means that the result is meaningful for the cases included, whereas external validity implies that the outcomes can be generalized.

REFERENCES

Almond, G.A. and S. Genco (1977), 'Clouds, clocks, and the study of politics', *World Politics*, **29** (4), 489–522.

Badie, B., D. Berg-Schlosser and L. Morlino (eds) (2011), *International Encyclopedia of Political Science*, vol. 8, Thousand Oaks, CA: Sage.

Beach, D. (2012), *Process Tracing Methods: Foundations and Guidelines*, Ann Arbor, MI: University of Michigan Press.

Berg-Schlosser, D. (2012), *Mixed Methods in Comparative Politics: Principles and Applications*, Basingstoke, UK: Palgrave Macmillan.

Berg-Schlosser, D. and J. Mitchell (eds) (2002), *Authoritarianism and Democracy in Europe, 1919–39: Comparative Analyses*, Basingstoke, UK: Palgrave Macmillan.

Bergman, M.M. (ed.) (2008), *Advances in Mixed Methods Research: Theories and Applications*, London: Sage.

Blalock, H.M. (1979), *Social Statistics*, 2nd revised edn, Auckland, CA: McGraw-Hill International Book Co.

Brady, H.E. and D. Collier (2010), *Rethinking Social Inquiry: Diverse Tools, Shared Standards*, 2nd edn, Lanham, MD: Rowman & Littlefield.

Cohen, M.R. and E. Nagel (1934), *An Introduction to Logic and Scientific Method*, New York: Harcourt.

Coleman, J.S. (1990), *Foundations of Social Theory*, Cambridge, MA: Harvard University Press.

Czada, R.M., A. Héritier and H. Keman (1998), *Institutions and Political Choice: On the Limits of Rationality*, Amsterdam: VU-University Press.

De Meur, G. and D. Berg-Schlosser (1996), 'Conditions of authoritarianism, fascism and democracy in inter-war Europe: systematic matching and contrasting of cases for "small-N" analysis', *Comparative Political Studies*, **29** (4), 423–68.

Downs, A. (1957), *An Economic Theory of Democracy*, New York: Harper.

Duverger, M. (1951), *Les Partis Politiques* (*Political Parties*), Paris: Colin.

Elster, J. (1989), *Nuts and Bolts for the Social Sciences*, Cambridge: Cambridge University Press.

Esser, H. (1993), *Soziologie: Allgemeine Grundlagen* (*Sociology: General Basics*), Frankfurt am Main: Campus.

Foucault, M. (1970), *The Order of Things*, London: Routledge.

Gauss, C.F. (1809), *Theoria Motus Corporum Coelestium in Sectionibus Conicis Solem Ambientium*, Hamburg: Sumtibus F. Perthes and I.H. Besser.

Goertz, G. and J. Mahoney (2012), *A Tale of Two Cultures: Qualitative and Quantitative Research in the Social Sciences*, Princeton, NJ: Princeton University Press.

Green, D.P. and A.S. Gerber (2008), *Get Out the Vote: How to Increase Voter Turnout*, 2nd edn, Washington, DC: Brookings Institution Press.

Hempel, C.G. (1965), *Aspects of Scientific Explanation and other Essays in the Philosophy of Science*, New York: Free Press.

Hume, D. (1748), *Philosophical Essays concerning Human Understanding: By the Author of the Essays Moral and Political*, London: A. Millar.

Keman, H. (2011), 'Comparative methods', in D. Caramani (ed.), *Comparative Politics*, Oxford: Oxford University Press, pp. 47–59.

King, G., R.O. Keohane and S. Verba (1994), *Designing Social Inquiry*, Princeton, NJ: Princeton University Press.

Lewis, D.K. (1986), *Counterfactuals*, Oxford: Blackwell.

Luhmann, N. (1984), *Soziale Systeme* (*Social Systems*), Frankfurt am Main: Suhrkamp.

Mill, J.S. (1843), *A System of Logic*, 2 vols, 5th edn 1862, London: Savill and Edwards.

Moses, J.W. and T.L. Knutsen (2012), *Ways of Knowing: Competing Methodologies and Methods in Social and Political Research*, 2nd edn, London: Palgrave Macmillan.

Olson, M. (1968), *The Logic of Collective Action: Public Goods and the Theory of Groups*, New York: Schocken Books.

Popper, K. (1972), *The Logic of Scientific Discovery*, London: Routledge.
Przeworski, A. and H. Teune (1970), *The Logic of Comparative Social Inquiry*, New York: Wiley-Interscience.
Ragin, C.C. (1987), *The Comparative Method: Moving Beyond Qualitative and Quantitative Strategies*, Berkeley, CA: University of California Press.
Rihoux, B. and C.C. Ragin (eds) (2009), *Configurational Comparative Methods*, London: Sage.
Simon, H. (1996), *The Sciences of the Artificial*, 3rd edn, Cambridge, MA: MIT Press.
Weber, M. (1904), 'Objectivity in social science and social policy', reprinted 1949 in M. Weber, *The Methodology of the Social Sciences*, trans. and eds E. Shils and H. Finch, Glencoe, IL: Free Press, pp. 49–112.

3 Taking critical ontology seriously: implications for political science methodology
Angela Wigger and Laura Horn

1 INTRODUCTION

To be 'critical' has become fashionable among social scientists in various disciplines. Only a few decades ago, the prefix 'critical' was almost automatically associated with Western Marxism and in particular the Frankfurt School. Today, the term critical is no longer limited to a single theoretical approach, but pertains to a vast range of approaches, including feminist, reflexive, postcolonial, postmodern or poststructuralist studies, and studies committed to a post-positivist epistemology more generally. But what does critical social science actually mean? Which implications does critical research have for fundamental questions of *ontology* (the central premises on the constitutive elements that underpin social reality), *epistemology* (the assumptions about how knowledge about this reality can be produced) and *methodology* (how this knowledge is gathered and ordered)?

This chapter offers a primer on a few core dimensions of critical social science and its central premises. It discusses first what critical social science is not, and clarifies key differences between what is commonly referred to as 'mainstream' and 'critical' social science perspectives. It addresses the role of normative claims and identifies the emancipatory commitment inherent in critical approaches as a distinguishing feature. Drawing on critical realism as an illustration of a philosophy of science and as a critical ontology, the chapter then engages with meta-theoretical questions about why critical perspectives privilege ontology over epistemology – that is, why we need to accept that social reality is constituted by complex power relations that evolve from a constant dialectical interplay of structure and agency over time, and that these power relations are revealed in both ideational and material dimensions. To illustrate what a critical 'way of knowing' looks like, critical feminist perspectives in political science are highlighted as concrete examples. In the concluding part, we emphasize the core arguments for indeed taking critical ontology seriously, and outline avenues for further engagement and debate.

2 THE 'CRITICAL' IN CRITICAL SOCIAL SCIENCE

Critical social sciences are united by a commitment to a more just and egalitarian society. This section discusses how critical perspectives differ from other traditions, which might arguably also claim to be committed to human progress but without accepting such a commitment as fundamental starting point for the study of social reality. In the following, we discuss what it means to be 'critical' in social science.

The prefix 'critical' is a self-assigned label that is often used, and sometimes abused, without explaining what it means to be critical. It has a strongly positive connotation and suggests deep and comprehensive thinking that questions the scientific orthodoxies and taken-for-granted assumptions of so-called 'mainstream' research – a label that is used to demarcate critical research vis-à-vis established theories, forms of inquiry and methods conducted by a perceived majority of scholars. 'Critical' scholars often refer to 'mainstream' research in a pejorative sense as if it was intellectually inferior. The juxtaposition critical versus mainstream also implies that critical research is almost by definition located at the margins of social sciences, and thus can never become the prevailing approach. To challenge dominant theories and established common-sense knowledge, to pose new questions and to reopen established intellectual terrains is an academic virtue. Who would not want to be critical within social sciences? There is a risk that references to the term critical are merely a rhetorical assertion and that inflationary tendencies surface with increasing usage of the term. Prior to outlining what it means to be critical, it is thus important first to understand what it is not.

First, a 'critical' perspective tends to be conflated with disagreements and repudiations of existing theories and (mainstream) approaches, normative beliefs, ideas or ideologies. However, if to be critical merely implied to refute existing academic ideas and approaches, and to unravel taken-for-granted assumptions, it would be a redundant prefix. Throughout history, scholars from different political persuasions have continuously challenged existing academic ideas, dominant knowledge claims and practices informed by such knowledge. As Karl Marx, one of the key exponents of critical scholarship, famously stated: *de omnibus dubitandum* – we should always have doubts about everything, and to leave error unrefuted is to encourage intellectual immorality. Knowledge and ideas are always fallible, contested and thus disputable, which is why academics should continuously challenge and *re*-search their answers (cf. Kuhn 1962 on paradigm shifts). Particularly, academics should always remain self-reflective and critical towards their own perspective. In academic contexts, the term *critique* seems more accurate than *criticism*: whereas criticism can be understood as passing a negative judgment, scientific critique can be understood as an inquiry into how truth claims are reached and legitimized as a naturalized state of affairs, as well as how such truth claims authoritatively inform social practices. It follows that the prefix critical should be more than a just a posh synonym for criticizing (see Sayer 2009, p. 768). Moreover, because scientific critique is inherent to social sciences in general, critical research should thus go beyond scientific critique. Scientific critique is certainly an important first step in challenging 'scientific discoveries' by means of deconstruction, demystification, de-legitimization of truth claims, but does not in itself imply a critical perspective on social reality.

Approaches to critical social science differ significantly within the broad field of political science. For instance, neo-Gramscian (Cox 1981; Gill 1993) and transnational historical materialist perspectives (Cafruny and Ryner 2003; Overbeek 2004; Van Apeldoorn 2004; Van der Pijl 2004) criticize the capitalist social relations of production and the particular power configurations and conflicts emanating from these relations. The goal of research is to produce knowledge that allows for social emancipation and, more or less implicitly or explicitly, overcoming capitalism. Critical feminist research, as we will elaborate in a later section, rather than accepting the class dimension as primary ontological focus, problematizes and challenges different forms of coercive and asymmetrical social power relations alongside race, gender or people with different sexual orientations. In the field of international relations, the critical project is also devoted to opening up space for discussions in academia. The so-called Third Debate, for example, sought to broaden the epistemology to post-positivist approaches (see Linklater 1992; Booth et al. 1996). In particular, postmodern and poststructuralist approaches sought to deconstruct, demystify and de-legitimize the pursuit of universally valid laws and truth claims in academic knowledge production (Ashley 1981).

Second, to be critical is sometimes misconstrued as being primarily, or even exclusively concerned with the promotion of normative commitments in scientific work. Critical scholars are often rebutted as normative or biased, or accused of lacking the necessary objectivity and scholarly distance to the research object. These charges are rooted in the belief that researchers can effectively distinguish between facts and values. There is a widespread misconception that perceives positivist epistemologies as synonymous with 'science' or what is sometimes somewhat presumptuously referred to as 'normal' science (see Kurki and Wight 2007). As will be argued below, conflating 'critical' with 'normative' obscures the essential fact that any ontology is normative in its point of departure in social reality.

   Critical scholarship rejects the claim to value neutrality and the possibility of a radical subject–object separation according to which the researcher can take a clear distance from what she or he is observing. The rejection of some sort of Archimedean point of reference, according to which researchers can objectively perceive the subject of inquiry, however, does not imply that critical scholars are more normative than their ostensibly value-neutral mainstream colleagues, nor are normative claims sufficient for being a critical scholar. Critical scholars rather state underpinning values and norms that inform their research more explicitly and more openly. By positioning their ontological starting point within a critical spectrum, critical scholars render the underlying commitments of their research intelligible. The 'critical' hence does not per se precede the ontological, but is rather inextricably and dialectically linked to assumptions about social reality. As Cox (1986, p. 207) has famously stated, 'theory is always for someone and or some purpose'. Theories are like a filter that selects, eliminates and highlights certain aspects of social reality, and thereby theories inevitably create and distort this reality. Theories that do not question existing unequal social relations of power, implicitly or explicitly legitimize, reproduce and reaffirm the position of predominant forces (Linklater 2001, p. 26). It follows that there can be no objective or neutral theory, nor research for that matter. Theories are always political. Scholars need to be aware of the value-bound nature of any theory, including their own, and seek to disclose the relation between knowledge production and power. This is illustrated well in feminist contributions to philosophy of science, distinguishing between androcentric social science, which has long produced knowledge about men, for men, and feminist perspectives, which rely on 'situated knowledge' and the acceptance of knowledge production as inherently gendered (Harding 1991). As the next section demonstrates, the defining feature of critical social science is that it seeks to be explicitly political by enabling emancipatory action on the basis of explanatory scientific critique, a critique that shows the gap between contemporary social reality and the aspired ideal of a just, egalitarian and free society.

3   EMANCIPATION AND SOCIAL CHANGE IN CRITICAL PERSPECTIVES

Analyzing and critiquing existing structures of social inequality imply putting the existing social order into question rather than accepting it as a given. The identification of constraints placed on agents and their demands, uncovering and questioning the workings of social structures and prevailing ideas prepares the ground for political alternatives that improve the conditions of social life. Thus, critical research essentially seeks to explore and elucidate the theme of human emancipation through raising awareness about alternative futures. This is based on the fundamental belief, as Adorno (1951 [2001], p. 34) emphatically put it, of being 'capable of perceiving that things could be different and better'.

At the same time, there is also a recognition that social structures cannot be changed easily and immediately in the foreseeable future, which is why critical theory is characterized by a certain pessimism or melancholy. However, in line with Antonio Gramsci's famous maxim 'pessimism of the intellect, optimism of the will', critical research may start off with a negative ontology but also engages with positive utopias imagining different societies and political institutions. Thus in addition to offering a particular way of understanding the world, critical research can be a guide of strategic action. As Cox (1996, p. 90) argued, an integral part of critical scholarship is not only to explain and criticize structures in the existing social order, but also to formulate coherent visions of alternatives that allow transcending this order. Critical scholars seek to actively promote, invigorate and convoke alternative futures and contribute actively to the politicization and the resilience of social struggles and transformative praxis. Philosophy and praxis hence are very much interlinked. In Habermas's (somewhat dichotomous) categories (1971), while the goal of empiric-analytical sciences is prediction, and hence control, critical-historical/hermeneutic sciences are geared towards self-reflective knowledge, aimed at emancipation. As Tickner points out (2005, p. 4) most feminist knowledge-building is much closer to the second category, with feminist scholars being active in promoting gender equality, legal and political actions to end violence against women, and/or addressing systematic gender oppression in patriarchal/capitalist societies.

To work towards alternatives that transcend the current order and to induce social change implies leaving the ivory towers of academia that safely distance scholars from political struggles. This is also entailed in Marx's (1845 [1969], ch. 1) rallying cry in the 'Theses on Feuerbach': 'The philosophers have only interpreted the world, in various ways; the point is to change it' (ibid., p. 667). The unification of theory and praxis is centerpiece of critical theory, or as Wright (2010, p. 26) put it: 'diagnosis and critique of society tells us why we want to leave the world in which we live; the theory of alternatives tells us where we want to go; and the theory of transformation tells us . . . how to make viable alternatives achievable'. Critical theory does not prescribe a fixed pathway towards such an alternative order. Critical theory rather entails 'a plurality of forms of the philosophy of praxis' (Gill 2012, p. 519). As a consequence, 'critical thought can neither be singular, nor imprisoned by practices of theoretical closure' (ibid.).

It is because of this explicit emancipatory commitment that critical research is often accused of being normative or even 'unscientific'. Such accusations are, however, often overly concerned with the conditions for the production of knowledge and methodological issues rather than 'the being', thereby privileging epistemology over ontology (see Bhaskar 1975; Wight 2006). The next section discusses why ontological questions should receive primacy, and what the implications are for political science research.

4   META-THEORETICAL COMMITMENTS OF CRITICAL SOCIAL SCIENCE

To be critical goes hand in hand with a whole range of ontological and epistemological assumptions. This section offers an overview, if all too brief, of the main meta-theoretical dimensions and commitment underpinning critical social science. Critical realism is discussed as one possible critical ontology.

Many political science traditions frequently ignore questions of ontology, or ontology is declared metaphysical and thus unscientific to deal with. This is problematic as scholars associated with empiricism and/or positivism, often depart from a particular (epistemological) conception of what social science ought to be, and then (often implicitly) make the social ontology fit that conception (see Buch-Hansen and Wigger 2011, p. 11). For example, if scholars depart from the epistemological understanding that empirical observations can validate or, in a Popperian sense, falsify hypothesized, and thus assumed, law-like generalizations deducted from theories (see Popper 1963), primacy is given to mere theory testing over analyzing and explaining social reality, or what is sometimes also referred to as 'theoreticism'. One of the pitfalls of theoreticism is that analyses and propositions are developed to make them fit the theoretical assumptions. That is, theories determine what the researcher observes or believes observe, namely, a repetition of socioeconomic patterns and outcomes. Critical research seeks to break with such epistemological fallacies by giving primacy to ontology over epistemology. As Cox (1996, p. 144) has noted, '[o]ntology lies at the beginning of any enquiry'. As is elucidated further below, departing from ontology provides an avenue in which 'no epistemological or methodological divides need to be accepted, defended or bridged' (Wight 2006, p. 1).

Critical realism is both a philosophy of science and also an ontology that underpins a wide range of critical perspectives. It offers a dialectical understanding of structure and agency, the material and the ideational dimension of social reality. History and social phenomena are considered the open-ended and contingent outcomes of a dynamic interplay between material structures, discourses and agents. Social phenomena thus reflect the interrelated and interdependent relation among all these dimensions, which cannot be reduced to another. Critical realism thereby rules out theoretical reductionism from the outset. Both material and ideational structures underpin social power relations and, albeit not directly visible or accessible, have causal powers, as do agents that constitute these power relations. Only through understanding how agency and structure, the ideational and the material dimension interact can political phenomena be explained and ways to change political outcomes be explored.

Genuine importance is assigned to agency as embedded within the reality of social structures, which can have ideational, material and institutional dimensions. Ontologically, structures pre-exist agency. Structures are always the outcome of human activities undertaken in the past and agents are confronted with pre-existing structures that either facilitate or constrain their social activities. This, however, does not imply a deterministic understanding of structure and agency. Agents can reproduce social structures through their practices, but they can also deviate from such structures and transform them. As Cox (1981, p. 217) put it: 'Structures do not determine people's actions in any mechanical sense but constitute the context of habits, pressures, expectations, and constraints within which action takes place'. Or as Marx (1852 [2008], p. 398) famously stated in *The Eighteenth Brumaire of Louis Bonaparte*: 'Men [sic] make their own history, but they do not make it as they please; they do not make it under self-selected circumstances, but under circumstances existing already, given and transmitted from the past'.

Agency thus needs to be understood within a pre-structured, historically contingent context. Structures underlie the reality we see and enable some people to act while constraining the actions of others, but they do not define the action of agents. Agents are not puppets on a string whose moves are determined by some puppet master's decisions. Although co-constituted by structure, agents are not programmed to reproduce the same structural features. At the same time, agents cannot be omnipotent puppet masters that pull all the strings. Structure makes agency possible and, at the same time, structures are the outcome of agency. Agency should not be seen as a single event, but as cumulative actions 'that have as consequences either the maintenance or the transformation of structures' (Cox 2001, p. 56). If we understand agents as 'causally powerful elements'

(Patomäki and Wight 2000, p. 230), this implies by definition an evolutionary rather than a deterministic approach to social science.

Within critical theory and research more generally, the causal power of agency is thus crucial, and departs from the notion that we deal 'with a continuing process of historical change' (Cox 1986, p. 209). Institutions, social and power relations and influential structures should not be understood as a given, but as part of a constantly changing reality, which is why critical theory is always a theory of history. Critical theory rejects the idea that the world order as we know it is static, or that social phenomena can be explained on the basis of generally valid or universal laws about social regularities. Instead, critical research acknowledges the 'openness, contingency and contextually variable character of social change' (Sayer 2000, p. 3). Critical theory generally takes agency seriously by perceiving the social reality, and thus also the future, as open-ended. Social phenomena are never predetermined before they happen, or as Jessop (2005, p. 53) put it: 'the future remains pregnant with a surplus of possibilities'.

In a rationalist-positivist scientific outlook, social reality is limited to what a theory or a hypothesis is about. This systematically ignores certain problems, people and situations, while giving disproportionate attention to others. Such a starting point neglects that there might be other aspects of reality that matter in the search for explanations, which is why a positivist epistemology suffers from anti-realism (see also, Patomäki and Wight 2000, p. 216). It is this fallacy and the consequential impoverished ontology of rationalism – among other issues – that is critiqued by critical realism (Patomäki and Wight 2000, p. 215). Within positivism, only what is observable is believed to exist, and everything that can be observed is perceived as knowledge. Ontology and epistemology thereby become one, or rather the ontological definition of what exists is reduced to the epistemological definition of what can be observed, and how. In consequence, a positivist epistemology often entails a preoccupation with methods; yet without reflection on the underlying methodological dimension. Methods are the means through which positivists believe scientists are able to identify the regularities in the world and discover universal truths. Critical research, in contrast, is not driven by methods but by questions about an observed social phenomenon.

From a critical realist vantage point, social science is not a deductive process that attempts to seek out event conjunctions but rather 'aims at identifying and illuminating the structures, powers, and tendencies that structure the course of events' (Patomäki and Wight 2000, p. 223). The process to uncover underlying structures is called *retroduction*. Rather than departing from a general law about the nature of social reality and its causal mechanisms (*deduction*), or collecting a wide range of empirical observations aimed at revealing such a general law (*induction*), retro-duction starts out from the level of the identified social phenomenon and moves to a different 'deeper' level in order to explain the phenom-enon, to identify a causal mechanism responsible (Lawson 1999, p. 10). Epistemologically speaking, knowledge is produced through a continuing process of confrontation between theoretical presumptions and '*evidential statements* generated in and through transitive enquiry' (Jessop 2005, p. 43, original emphasis).

Critical realists distinguish between the real, the actual and the empiri-cal. The real entails all structures and mechanisms that have causal powers, while the events that follow within special initial conditions are referred to as the actual, and observations of these actual events are referred to the empirical (Jessop 2005, p. 41). A key assumption is that reality exists also outside of our observational reach and that there is an intransitive and a transitive dimension of knowledge about this reality. The intransitive dimension refers to the real structure or mechanism that exists independently of people's knowledge about it, while the transitive dimension refers to the knowledge acquired through empirical analysis (Bhaskar 1975, p. 6). Critical realism leaves sufficient room for the inter-subjective aspect of reality that we experience, however, as Sayer (2000, p. 12) writes: 'Observability may make us more confident about what we think exists, but existence itself is not dependent on it.' Knowledge pro-duction is always subject to historical conditions and, as it is impossible to achieve complete and absolute knowledge, social constructs and knowl-edge, is always fallible and variable.

5   METHODOLOGICAL IMPLICATIONS AND CRITICAL RESEARCH IN POLITICAL SCIENCE

After this *tour d'horizon* through the ontological and meta-theoretical commitments of critical research in social science, this section deals with its epistemological and methodological implications. As Hay (2002, p. 63) reminds us, the relationship between ontology, epistemology and meth-odology is irreducible and directional; thus, the sequence of ontology–epistemology–methodology should in itself be coherent and consistent.

Critical perspectives, as we have argued above, contradict the assump-tion that there is a 'world out there' characterized by patterns and regu-larities that can be experienced through systematic observations, and that these observations can correlate with each other. The same scientific methods cannot be applied to natural and social science; there is no 'unity of science'. As Horkheimer (1937 [1989], p. 200) argued, 'the facts which our senses present to us are socially pre-formed in two ways: through the historical character of the object perceived and through the historical character of the perceiving organ'. In this vein, critical theory rejects the belief that observed correlations contribute to the growth of knowledge when accumulated over time, and that the ultimate purpose of science is to uncover observed regularities, restated as natural laws.

Theory provides an auxiliary instrument that provides essentially uncertain images for the researcher to assess the real. It allows for moving from the scale and detail of the empirics to the condensed, focused space and to move from pure description of the social phenomenon to the abstraction of possible causes. This is generally referred to as the *method of abstraction*, which offers a methodological pathway and which allows for an iterative and dialectical engagement between the abstract and the concrete, between philosophy of science and the empirical realm without giving into empiricism. The term 'method' here refers to a fundamental analytical strategy, rather than concrete research methods and techniques. As Marx insisted in the *Grundrisse* (1857 [1973], p. 101), 'the method of rising from the abstract to the concrete is the only way in which thought appropriates the concrete, reproduces it as the concrete in the mind. But this is by no means the process by which the concrete itself comes into being.' Moving from abstract concepts to concrete events or social phenomena renders it possible to grasp the specific meaning of abstract concepts in a given spatio-temporal conjunction. Abstraction here thus does not imply universality or generalized rules, but rather a re-concretization of theory or theoretical concepts. Abstract theory is thus important but not all-determining. The changing nature of political orders means that theoretical concepts are in constant need of adjustment (Cox 1986, p. 209). Theories may be the result of previous academic research and offer analogies, but they need to be evaluated in the light of a changing social reality and the specificity of the phenomenon under investigation (the explanandum). Theories never entail universal or general knowledge. Thus, as opposed to testing hypotheses derived from a theory with the assigned status of an iron law in the positivist deductive-hypothetical model, the key issue in a critical realist approach is 'what the real world must be like for a specific explanandum to be actualized' (Jessop 2005, p. 43).

Only when this methodological dimension is clear can the actual choice *of methods* for how to go about the concrete process of gathering empirical data be made. In all this, critical perspectives are explicitly pluralist with regard to methods; 'critical' research does not require a specific method or analytical strategy, provided that there are good reasons for the chosen method and that it corresponds to the commitments outlined above. Having outlined what 'critical' research is and how it is consistent

Table 3.1   Core dimensions of social science paradigms

	Rationalism	Critical social science
Ontology	Atomistic, rational actors (voluntarism), or objective rationality of a structure or a system (structural determinism); reductionism	Dialectical interplay between agency/structure/ideational/material
	Timeless law-like regularities	Context-dependent hierarchies and processes
	Linear or cyclical assumptions about history	History as open-ended and contingent, focus on social change
Epistemology	Positivist, subject–object distinction, truth claims through universally valid knowledge	Post-positivist; reflectivist; understanding of 'reality' mediated through abstraction (knowledge as social/historical product)
Theory	Parsimony, theoreticism	Complexity, iteration
Analytical strategies	Causal inference, falsification of hypotheses	Retroduction, conceptualization, ladder of abstraction, dialectics
Research objectives	Value-free, objective, predictive	Emancipatory, science as social practice

in its core commitments, Table 3.1 presents the core dimensions of critical social science vis-à-vis the rationalist paradigm. The question now is, what does such a critical approach look like, as a coherent and positive research program in practice?

6   FEMINIST PERSPECTIVES AS CRITICAL RESEARCH

Feminist perspectives constitute an important example of critical research. This section illustrates how a critical feminist approach puts forward a fundamental critique of ontological and epistemological assumptions about core concepts in political science, for instance, the concept of 'the state', the relationship between structure and agency, and the way knowledge is assumed to be neutral of power alongside gender dimensions. Feminist approaches embody the core commitments of critical social science, focusing on critique, critical knowledge, as well as social change.

It is important to point out, however, that while there is a wide range of feminist approaches that focus on 'women' in political science, not all of these are necessarily *critical* perspectives. For instance, there is a large body of literature of positivist scholarship in the field of gender and international relations, focusing on terrorism, interstate wars, human rights and public opinion (Reiter 2014). Engagements between these positivist scholars and post-positivist researchers can be fruitful and result in important complementary findings. However, their point of departure in terms of ontological, epistemological and methodological dimensions differ fundamentally. For this section, it is instructive to focus on these differences to grasp the meaning of 'critical' research.

Critical, or 'standpoint' feminist perspectives, have 'an explicitly critical understanding of the state as a set of patriarchal practices that support, yet silence, the structural disadvantages that women face' (Hansen 2010, p. 21). Unlike many other political science approaches, feminist scholars do not take the separation between 'public' and 'private', between political spaces and the household for granted. Rather, it is through exposing and questioning these binaries that feminists for example highlight the household as crucial site of unequal social power relations. The state as social category is not seen as an abstract, ahistorical concept. Rather than departing from an ontology that would see states as autonomous, individualistic actors in an anarchic international state system (such as is the case in realism as one of the dominant theories in international relations), feminist ontologies are 'based on social relations that are constituted by historically unequal political, economic and social structures' (Tickner 2005, p. 6). Structure and agency are linked dialectically through understanding core concepts such as 'gender' and 'women' as social constructs in the form of intersubjective norms, roles, frames and discourses, rather than biological sex and external attributes. How this matters is illustrated well in the difference between liberal and critical feminist approaches (see Fraser 2013; Pruegl 2014). While liberal feminism tends to focus primarily on 'women actors' (and their absences) in organizations and institutions, that is, arguing for equality between men and women in terms of representation, critical feminism questions the actual structures in which these actors are constituted in the first place. Hence, rather than working within a given institutional and legal setting, such as the government, parliament or corporate board rooms, a critical approach seeks to analyze how they came about, what the key mechanisms of power are, and how they can be changed. By taking the structural power of patriarchal social relations into consideration, critical feminist perspectives can indeed show how the agency of women is engendered, limited and constituted through these broader social-cultural and economic structures. Crucially, this complex and open-ended understanding of social power relations renders it possible for critical feminist perspectives to engage with multiple dimensions of inequality, not just on the basis of gender but also race, ethnicity or class (Walby 2011). This openness and plurality have been highlighted in discussions between critical feminist and other critical perspectives, whose ontological primacy is often more limited and does not transcend class as a fundamental social category. The 'troubled engagement' between critical feminist economists and historical materialists on possibilities for gendered analyses of globalization is rather instructive here (Waylen 2006).

In line with critical commitments to emancipatory epistemology and praxis, feminist perspectives use critical inquiry and reflection on social injustice to transform, and not simply explain the social order. Critical feminist approaches emerge from a deep skepticism about 'universal' knowledge claims, where knowledge has been created by men, for men. This epistemological commitment encourages opening new lines of inquiry versus simply 'filling in gaps' in already established disciplinary terrains (Ackerly and True 2010, p. 2). In this vein, women are both subject matter and creators of knowledge (Tickner 2005, p. 7). It is worth noting here that just as there is no specific or unique method for 'critical' research in general, there is no unique feminist research method (Tickner 2005, p. 3). Critical feminists employ a wide range of research tools such as those outlined in this volume, but also ethnographic methods such as thick description or open interviews. In line with the reflective engagement of critical social science, feminist scholars are highly attentive to their own positioning as researchers.

More importantly, where knowledge is seen as power and a potential tool for emancipation, it is not possible to separate thought from action, and knowledge from practice. It is here that critical feminist perspectives anchor their commitment to social change in addressing the political, economic and cultural inequalities women are facing. As Tickner (2005, p. 4) stresses:

> [M]uch of feminist scholarship is both transdisciplinary and avowedly political; with the goal of bringing about change, it has explored and sought to understand the unequal gender hierarchies, as well as other hierarchies of power, which exist in all societies, to varying degrees, and their effects on the subordination of women and other disempowered people.

7   CONCLUDING REFLECTIONS

Critical perspectives constitute an important part of the ongoing debates within the broader field of political science, such as this handbook seeks to provide. As has been argued above, critical perspectives are not merely concerned with a critique of existing approaches but, rather, contribute to a more comprehensive understanding of, and fundamental, change in social power relations. In this endeavor, critical approaches are never static but need to be continuously revisited, questioned and developed further. The firm rejection of any form of determinism renders critical perspectives constructive tools to discuss possibilities for social change and alternatives, without having to compromise on academic integrity and a thorough and methodological engagement with social reality. The concrete crystallization of a critical perspective into actual research practice is dependent on the (inter)disciplinary, contextual and personal objectives for any given research. As this chapter has shown, there are many different pathways for critical research in political science. Rather than advocate one specific approach, we have highlighted the critical dimension in a philosophy of science such as critical realism, and the critical epistemology and emancipatory commitment in many feminist research traditions. Most importantly, we have discussed the notion of 'critical' not as a badge of honor or as a label that researchers can choose to take on or off as they please. Rather, in touching upon the outlines of some of the core contemporary and emerging critical perspectives in political science, our aim was to show the possibilities and potential of critical research.

Critical perspectives are characterized by their open and pluralist positioning within the social sciences; it is through dialogue, reflection and critique that they engage with other perspectives. As this chapter has shown, critical perspectives can make important contributions to the collective endeavor of understanding and explaining social reality that constitutes the social sciences. Through their commitment to social change, they can also help us create a more just and egalitarian world.

FURTHER READING

Introduction

Sayer, A. (2009), 'Who's afraid of critical social science?', *Current Sociology*, **57** (6), 767–86.

Application

Jaeger, J. and E. Springler (eds) (2015), *Asymmetric Crisis in Europe And Possible Futures: Critical Political Economy and Post-Keynesian Perspectives*, London and New York: Routledge.

Advanced

Fraser, N. (2013), *Fortunes of Feminism*, London and New York: Verso.

REFERENCES

Ackerly, B. and J. True (2010), *Doing Feminist Research in Political and Social Science*, Basingstoke, UK: Palgrave Macmillan.
Adorno, T.W. (1951), *Minima Moralia: Reflections from a Damaged Life*, reprinted 2001, London: Verso.
Ashley, R. (1981), 'Political realism and human interests', *International Studies Quarterly*, **25** (2), 204–36.
Bhaskar, R. (1975), *A Realist Theory of Science*, Leeds: Leeds Books.
Booth, K., S. Smith and M. Zalewski (eds) (1996), *International Theory: Positivism and Beyond*, Cambridge: Cambridge University Press.
Buch-Hansen, H. and A. Wigger (2011), *The Politics of European Competition Regulation: A Critical Political Economy Perspective*, London: Routledge.
Cafruny, A.W. and M. Ryner (eds) (2003), *A Ruined Fortress? Neoliberal Hegemony and Transformation in Europe*, Lanham, MD: Rowman & Littlefield.
Cox, R.W. (1981), 'Social forces, states and world orders: beyond international relations theory', *Millennium*, **10** (2), 126–55.
Cox, R.W. (1986), 'Social forces, states and world orders', in R.O. Keohane (ed.), *Neorealism and its Critics*, New York: Columbia University Press, pp. 204–45.
Cox, R.W. (1996), *Approaches to World Order*, Cambridge: Cambridge University Press.
Cox, R.W. (2001), 'The way ahead: towards a new ontology of world order', in R.W. Jones (ed.), *Critical Theory and World Politics*, Boulder, CO: Lynne Rienner, pp. 45–60.
Fraser, N. (2013), *Fortunes of Feminism: From State-Managed Capitalism to Neoliberal Crisis*, London and New York: Verso.
Gill, S. (1993), *Gramsci, Historical Materialism and International Relations*, Cambridge: Cambridge University Press.
Gill, S. (2012), 'Towards a radical concept of praxis. Imperial "common sense" versus the postmodern prince', *Millennium*, **40** (3), 505–24.
Habermas, J. (1971), *Knowledge and the Human Interest*, Boston, MA: Beacon Press.
Hansen, L. (2010), 'Ontologies, epistemologies, methodologies', in L. Shepherd (ed.), *Gender Matters in Global Politics*, New York: Routledge, pp. 17–27.
Harding, S. (1991), *Whose Science? Whose Knowledge? Thinking from Women's Lives*, Ithaca, NY: Cornell University Press.
Hay, C. (2002), *Political Analysis. A Critical Analysis*, Basingstoke, UK: Routledge.
Horkheimer, M. (1937), *Traditional and Critical Theory in Critical Theory: Selected Essays*, reprinted 1989, New York: Continuum.
Jessop, B. (2005), 'Critical realism and the strategic-relational approach', *New Formations*, **56** (Autumn), 40–53.
Kuhn, T.S. (1962), *The Structure of Scientific Revolutions*, Chicago, IL: University of Chicago Press.
Kurki, M. and C. Wight (2007), 'International relations and social science', in T. Dunne, M. Kurki and S. Smith (eds), *International Relations Theories: Discipline and Diversity*, Oxford: Oxford University Press, pp. 14–35.
Lawson, T. (1999), 'Developments in economic as realist social theory', in S. Fleetwood (ed.), *Critical Realism in Economics-Development and Debate*, New York: Routledge.
Linklater, A. (1992), 'The question of the next stage in international relations theory: a critical-theoretical point of view', *Millennium*, **21** (1), 77–98.

Linklater, A. (2001), 'The changing contours of critical international relations theory', in J.R. Wyn (ed.), *Critical Theory and World Politics*, Boulder, CO: Lynne Rienner.

Marx, K. (1845), 'Theses on Feuerbach', reprinted 1969 in *The German Ideology*, Moscow: Progress, ch. 1.

Marx, K. (1852), *The Eighteenth Brumaire of Louis Bonaparte*, reprinted 2008, Moscow: Progress.

Marx, K. (1857), *Grundrisse. Introduction to the Critique of Political Economy*, reprinted 1973, New York: Random House.

Overbeek, H. (2004), 'Transnational class formation and concepts of control: towards a genealogy of the Amsterdam Project in international political economy', *Journal of International Relations and Development*, **7** (2), 113–41.

Patomäki, H. and C. Wight (2000), 'After postpositivism? The promises of critical realism', *International Studies Quarterly*, **44** (2), 213–37.

Popper, K.R. (1963), *Conjectures and Refutations*, London: Routledge.

Pruegl, E. (2014), 'Neoliberalising feminism', *New Political Economy*, **20** (4), 614–31.

Reiter, D. (2014), 'The positivist study of gender and international relations', *Journal of Conflict Resolution*, **59** (7), 1301–26.

Sayer, A. (2000), *Realism and Social Science*, London: Sage Publications.

Sayer, A. (2009), 'Who's afraid of critical social science?', *Current Sociology*, **57** (6), 767–86.

Tickner, A. (2005), 'What is your research program? Some feminist answers to international relations methodological questions', *International Studies Quarterly*, **49** (1), 1–22.

Van Apeldoorn, B. (2004), 'Theorizing the transnational: a historical materialist approach', *Journal of International Relations and Development*, **7** (2), 142–76.

Van der Pijl, K. (2004), 'Two faces of the transnational cadre under neo-liberalism', *Journal of International Relations and Development*, **7** (2), 177–207.

Walby, S. (2011), 'Globalization and multiple inequalities', in E.N.-L. Chow, M.T. Segal and T. Lin (eds), *Analyzing Gender, Intersectionality and Multiple Inequalities: Global, Transnational and Local Contexts*, Bingley: Emerald Books, pp. 17–34.

Waylen, G. (2006), 'You still don't understand: why troubled engagements continue between feminists and (critical) IPE', *Review of International Studies*, **32** (1), 145–64.

Wight, C. (2006), *Agents, Structures and International Relations. Politics as Ontology*, Cambridge: Cambridge University Press.

Wright, E.O. (2010), *Envisioning Real Utopias*, New York: Verso.

4 Relating theory and concepts to measurements: bridging the gap
Paul Pennings

1 INTRODUCTION

Developing concepts is a crucial step in every type of research in political science. Conceptualization is the process of developing concepts which are abstract notions in our theories or hypotheses. They have to be specified as precisely as possible in order to get a common understanding about their meaning and application. Since all concepts are complex and abstract, they must be broken down into components that are measurable. This is difficult because many concepts are not directly observable. The main object of this chapter is to indicate the tension between the concept as an object of analysis and the concept as a means to accomplish empirical-analytical analysis of political phenomena. The examples given will relate to one of most central and contested concepts in political science: democracy.

2 THE BASICS OF CONCEPTUALIZATION

A good concept should be able to bridge the gap between theory and data. Most concepts are multidimensional, but the complexity (that is, the number of levels) differs (Goertz 2005). The basic level entails a general abstract notion like democracy, interest groups, welfare state, institutions and so on, that is used in theories. The secondary level divides the basic concepts into constitutive dimensions. In case of democracy these are, for example, participation and competition (see Box 4.1). However, these examples cannot be taken for granted as multiple approaches to conceptualizing and measuring democracy exist in the literature. They can be broadly divided into either minimalist (quantitative) or maximalist (substantialist or inclusive) conceptualizations, each having strengths and weaknesses. A minimalist will opt for a few indicators like universal suffrage, regular elections and basic civil rights (for example, Vanhanen 2003; Freedom House 2015). Some, for example Przeworski et al. (2000), use only one indicator, namely, whether key government offices are filled through contested elections or not. A maximalist will strive for an in-depth

---

BOX 4.1   FROM CONCEPT TO MEASUREMENT: THE MINIMALIST DEFINITION OF DEMOCRACY

From Concept to Measurement: The Minimalist Definition of Democracy

If democracy is conceptualized according to the minimalist definition (participation and contestation), its real world components might be identified as:

Participatory capacity: the ability of citizens to participate in the selection and workings of their government
Contestability of political office: the capacity of any citizen to obtain office.

---

analysis taking into account many factors that contribute to the functioning of democracies, such as political equality in actual practice. An example of the latter is V-Dem that seeks to capture seven different conceptions of democracy (namely, participatory, consensual, majoritarian, deliberative, egalitarian, electoral and liberal democracy) in all countries since 1900 using 329 specific indicators (Coppedge et al. 2014). The third level is the operationalization level. This level is most detailed in order to enable data gathering on indicators. In case of participation, for example, one may use indicators like turnout and party membership.

In order to adequately bridge the gap between theory and data, a number of requirements should be met. It is not sufficient to list a (large) number of dimensions of a concept. It is also important to relate the dimensions to each other in causal terms by means of hypotheses. To bridge that gap, the requirements must refer directly to real-world phenomena while remaining conceptually related to your theory. They must clearly specify a causal relationship between those real-world phenomena in a way that logically follows from your theory. They must also clearly establish the temporal and spatial dimensions by being applicable to certain places, actors, time periods, and so on. For example, a theory on democracy should not only describe what democracy is, but also indicate under what conditions it will be stronger or weaker. There are several types of such causal propositions. They can be conditional (if presence/absence of X, then presence/absence of Y), mathematical (increase of 1 unit X = decrease of 1 unit Y), continuous (the greater X, the greater Y) or differencing (if high X, then low Y) (King et al. 1994; Singleton and Straits 2009). Often more than one X is relevant. If these causal factors are not equally important, their weight must be specified. For example, are cultural, political or economic factors more decisive for the rise and endurance of democracies? (Lipset 1959).

BOX 4.2   LEVELS OF MEASUREMENT: DIFFERENT SCALES
OF DEMOCRACY

Levels of Measurement: Different Scales of Democracy

Nominal: categorization and numerical assignment for mutual exclusive, but not ordered, categories. Hence there is no assumption of ranking. For example: 0 = presidential democracy, 1 = parliamentary democracy.

Ordinal: categorization and numerical assignment for comparison using a mathematical rank ordering of outcomes (higher/lower). The order matters but not the difference between values. For example: 1 = undemocratic, 2 = quasi-democratic, 3 = fully democratic.

Interval: intervals between measures represent equal distance across the entire scale. For example: On a 1 to 10 scale of 'democracy' the difference between 1 and 2 is the same as the difference between 9 and 10.

Ratio: has all the properties of an interval variable plus an absolute reference point. For example, voter turnout rate can be zero, meaning non-voting.

The underlying theory should specify how the basic concepts can be measured. Goertz (2005) has distinguished between three issues that need to be taken into account: aggregation, types of scales and equivalence. Aggregation is about how the individual parts are defined and weighted. If we conceptualize democracy, for example, do we seek to combine data on countries, elections or (groups of) citizens? (Coppedge and Gerring 2011). These choices have consequences for the type of causal inferences that can be made.

The type of scale refers to how the units are scored (see Box 4.2). An important choice in the operational definition is the level of measurement. We may opt for nominal, ordinal, interval or ratio levels of measurements. This choice has consequences for the type of analysis that can be done with the data (see Chapter 19 in this volume). The scale can be qualitatively oriented (nominal) or aiming at quantitative analysis (ordinal or interval or ratio). Moving to a higher scale of measurement broadens the range of appropriate statistical techniques (Pennings et al. 2006). Whether this is feasible depends on the conceptualization of democracy: is it conceived as dichotomous (democracy versus non-democracy) or as continuous (varying degrees of democracy across time and space) (Seawright and Collier 2014).

Equivalence denotes the problem whether the same value can be assigned to cases that are not truly identical. This might be especially problematic in the grey zone and/or if units score zero on several indicators. In case of the concept of democracy, many researchers have made different choices in these respects and therefore also reach at different operationalizations and conclusions. The debate on Lijphart's conceptualization of democracy is an example of how different researchers may differ on categorizing countries into the same category (see, for an overview of this debate, Bormann 2010).

3 TRANSFORMING CONCEPTS INTO UNITS OF MEASUREMENT

Concepts are often abstract so that it is hard to apply them on a diversity of cases. How to solve this problem? One solution that is not recommended is 'concept stretching' by making a concept even broader so that it applies to more cases. This process is illustrated by Sartori (1970) by means of the 'ladder of generality', that is, enhancing a wider use of a theoretical concept by extension (of its initial meaning) or by means of intension (limiting observations to specified categories) (Keman 2014). Extension leads to under-specification. In that case the broadened concept is related to such a large number of diverse cases that the concept becomes meaningless. Intension, on the other hand, can lead to over-specification. We could try to solve this by means of introducing a hierarchy of attributes belonging to the initial concept. We may define two core features of democracy (for example, competition and participation), and list a number of attributes that make up the optimal mode of democratization. By requiring that the core attributes must be available (opposition and participation) we can develop a categorization of democratic systems in which more or fewer of the other (additional) features are available. The more generally the basic requirements are defined, the more cases can be included (Collier and Levitsky 1997). Creating new analytic categories can be especially useful for the in-between cases with a mixed character. To make the definition more precise can thus usefully serve both to introduce finer differentiation and to avoid conceptual stretching, but it also modifies the definition of democracy itself (Collier and Levitsky 1997).

In sum, the main problem in the quantifying approaches is how to increase the units of observations (or cases) without losing the original meaning or definitions of the core concept. In order to achieve this we need a proper operational definition of a concept that prescribes which measurements are appropriate to measure it. As such, the operational definition of a concept bridges the gap between the general definition of a concept and the available data. Operationalization is defined as the process to obtain an adequate operational definition, which renders a valid transformation that can be reliably measured. In the democracy example, we could decide to define opposition and participation as the core attributes of democracy and operationalize these by distinguishing between a number of related indicators. Dahl (1973) opted for these indicators: freedom to form and join organizations, freedom of expression, right to vote, eligibility for public office, right of political leaders to compete for support, alternative sources of information, and free and fair elections, Institutions for making government policies depend on votes. Potential problems are that these indicators are diverse in terms of measurement and also controversial in the sense that one can make a valid argument in favor of another set of indicators which could lead to different results (Coppedge and Gerring 2011). Usually, various data and, as a consequence, various operational definitions can be imagined to measure a theoretical concept. In the case of democracy we should bear in mind that states have a strong interest in being recognized as democratic so that measuring democracy solely by means of formal characteristics, such as 'elections' and 'freedom to speech', may lead to an incorrect assessment.

A different approach to operationalization stems from the case-based (qualitative) approaches. They have in common that they search for detailed case evidence. Sometimes this means that the number of cases is limited, but this is not necessarily so. For example, in the case of democracy several studies use a variety of primary sources to give a detailed account of different episodes of democratization using in-depth country knowledge. The results may lead to a rejection of the conclusions that were based on quantitative indicators (Seawright and Collier 2014). Hence, bridging the gap between concepts and measurement using a qualitative approach may lead to different conclusions compared with those using quantitative approaches.

4   VALIDITY: CRITERIA TO EVALUATE THE QUALITY OF OPERATIONALIZATION AND MEASUREMENTS

The main criteria to judge the quality of measurements are validity and reliability. Internal validity is the extent to which the measurement of a concept corresponds accurately to the real-world phenomena that we seek to measure. In that case operationalization fits the concept (which is often only partly true). External validity (or reliability) indicates the degree to which the measure is consistent, that is, repeated measurements would give the same result. By correlating an indicator with comparable indicators we can assess whether reliability poses a problem. Alternatively, by looking at the empirical distribution of cases we can assess whether this is in line with common expectations. We discuss each of these forms of validity.

The validity of measurements, often referred to as *construct validity*, is defined as the degree to which inferences can be made from operationalization to the theoretical constructs on which they were based, and refers to the closeness of the correspondence between the measurements and the concept being measured. One way to assess construct validity is to do a pilot study in which the researcher obtains results for different groups of countries. This test will show to what extent the countries are grouped as expected. If some countries are grouped erroneously, the measurements should be adapted. This approach is similar to *face validity* in which we ask whether 'on its face' measurement results are a good translation of the construct. Assessments of face validity are often based on the agreement of measurement results with common-sense expectations, regardless of the precise definitions of the concept. Alternatively, we can look at *content validity* by checking operationalization against a detailed description of the content domain (if available). In the case of democracy such detailed descriptions do exist, so that we should be able to argue which indicators are (or are not) included in the operationalization and with what effects. In general it is a good idea to (try to) test the construct validity before the main research starts, by means of pilot studies in order to establish the validity of the research.

Correlational validity (or '*internal validity*') is obtained by using a traditional, but imprecise, measurement device as a yardstick to verify the correspondence between the measurements and the concept being measured. We judge correlational validity by correlating the measures we are evaluating with alternative measures, or with measures of other but related variables. Newer measurement devices should be able to reproduce the measurements of the older devices, albeit with greater precision. The refined results should, however, correlate highly with the old results unless significant errors are prevalent in the old ones. In the case of democracy, several indicators are available that are often used as yard stick, such as those of Freedom House (2015) and Vanhanen (2003).

The *predictive validity* (or '*external validity*') of measurements refers to their usefulness in making correct predictions about real-world phenomena. A judgment with respect to external validity presupposes a causal theory with the concept being measured as an independent variable. Our measure should be able to correctly predict phenomena that we theoretically think it should be able to predict. In the case of democracy, the indicator should be able to predict the degree of corruption, civil war, violence and so on. For democracies these numbers should be low compared with non-democracies. Predictive validity is an important hallmark of validity, since it relates the usefulness of the obtained measurements to the context of prevailing theories.

Since concepts and measurement are closely related, the word 'validity' is not only used in the context of the validity of measurements, but also in the context of the validity of theories. A theory is said to be 'internally valid' when it holds for the cases being investigated. A theory is said to be 'externally valid' when the theory also holds for the cases to which the theory applies which were not included in the data analysis. External validity (or 'reliability') of research findings is a synonym of generalizability of research findings.

A measure is highly reliable if it produces similar results under consistent conditions. Reliability, however, cannot compensate for low validity. The reliability of measurements is related to the validity of measurement in the same way as a standard deviation from the mean is related to the mean. Measurements are not reliable when separate measurements have a large variance, that is, when the precise measurement results for a given unit of measurement at a given time are unclear. It should be noted that a negligible variance of separate measurements does not imply that the measurements are valid: they may all be far from the truth collectively.

Often there is a trade-off between validity and reliability. This is also the case with the minimalist and maximalist conceptualizations of democracy. The former are often strongest in terms of their reliability, while the latter commonly are better in terms of their measurement validity. This makes the concept and the measurement of democracy contested, since it invokes much debate in the literature on the criteria that should be regarded as more important. Quantitative researchers often prefer the parsimony of replication, while qualitative approaches usually prioritize comprehensive measures that are less easily replicated.

5   FROM OPERATIONALIZATION TO DATA

Each measurement fills in a slot in a data matrix, with units (of measurements) in the rows, and variables (indicators of concepts) in the columns. For each combination of a unit of measurement and an indicator we would like to obtain a value. This value may result from aggregation. In that case the value of a democracy indicator such as turnout (which unit of analysis is per country per election year) is actually an aggregation of the voting behavior of individual voters (unit of measurement in the first stage). If we ignore this aggregation, this may result in an 'ecological fallacy', which occurs when aggregated data on a country is used to conclude information about individuals (such as voters) or the other way around. We could argue, for example, that in countries with a low turnout, the voters are dissatisfied with democracy, but this statement is wrong if in reality there are significant differences in the degree of satisfaction of individual voters that are independent from whether they voted or not.

Measurements do often not lead to a completely filled rectangular data matrix as many data are simply not available. There are a number of strategies to cope with this problem and all have pros and cons. List-wise deletion (complete-case analysis) removes all data for a case that has one or more missing values. It means that all units of measurement with a missing value on one or more of the variables relevant for an analysis are excluded from the analysis. This is only advisable when the excluded units are not important for arriving at a reliable answer. When the number of units of measurement is large compared with the number of missing values, this solution is often preferred.

Pairwise deletion (available-case analysis) is an alternative to list-wise deletion. For example, in case of a correlation matrix, for each pair of variables for which data is available, the correlation coefficient will take that data into account. In this way, pairwise deletion attempts to minimize the loss of data that occurs in list-wise deletion. The advantage is that fewer units of measurement will be discarded. The disadvantage is that the units of analysis (n) differ in each analysis. As a consequence, it is not always easy to reconstruct which units of measurement bear a special weight for the outcomes of data analysis.

A third possibility is to substitute the missing values by approximations. This is possible by interpolation or extrapolation or by cross-sectional mean substitution. These techniques will predict the value of the dependent variable for an independent variable that is among our data (interpolation) or outside the range of our data (extrapolation). In the case of extrapolation it is assumed that our observed trend continues for values of x outside the range we used to form our model. Of the two methods, interpolation is mostly preferred because we have a greater likelihood of obtaining a valid estimate. Interpolation and extrapolation are often used to fill in the gaps in time series. Both may result in erroneous estimates of the statistical properties of time series models. In addition they may overlook important sudden changes. The literature on democracy has shown many examples of changes in the process of democratization that, if missing in the data, should not be overwritten by one of these techniques. Instead, a more in-depth analysis is necessary in order to obtain data on the missing cases.

6   CONCLUSION

This chapter discussed the basics of bridging the gap between concept and measurement. This gap is inevitable since the former is abstract and the latter is specific. As many concepts are not directly observable, we must find a way to operationalize them by means of an operational definition. In the case of a contested concept, such as power and democracy, there are several competing ways to arrive at this goal. In the case of democracy, operationalization clearly depends on whether it adheres to a minimalist or a maximalist definition.

Validity and reliability provide important criteria for the quality assessment of an operationalization. A measurement tool is reliable if it yields stable and consistent results when repeated over time. It is valid to the extent that we are measuring what we hope to measure. Both quality criteria should be met as much as possible, although there is a trade-off between them.

FURTHER READING

Goertz, G. (2005), *Social Science Concepts: A User's Guide*, Princeton, NJ: Princeton University Press, available at: http://press.princeton.edu/titles/8089.html.
An in-depth discussion of the construction and analysis of concepts and their role in social research.
Singleton, R.A. Jr and B.C. Straits (2009), *Approaches to Social Research*, 5th edn, New York: Oxford University Press.
An overview of the main research designs and methods of data collection.

REFERENCES

Bormann, N.-C. (2010), 'Patterns of democracy and its critics', *Living Reviews in Democracy*, **2** (3), 1–14.
Collier, D. and S. Levitsky (1997), 'Democracy with adjectives: conceptual innovation in comparative research', *World Politics*, **49** (3), 430–51.
Coppedge, M. and J. Gerring (2011), 'Conceptualizing and measuring democracy: a new approach', *Perspectives on Politics*, **9** (2), 247–67.
Coppedge, M., J. Gerring, S.I. Lindberg and J. Teorell (2014), 'Varieties of democracy (V-Dem): dataset', accessed 25 January 2016 at http://kellogg.nd.edu/projects/vdem/.
Dahl, R. (1973), *Polyarchy: Participation and Opposition*, Newhaven, CT: Yale University Press.
Freedom House (2015), *Freedom in the World 2015*, accessed 25 January 2016 at https://www.freedomhouse.org.
Goertz, G. (2005), *Social Science Concepts: A User's Guide*, Princeton: Princeton University Press.
Keman, H. (2014), 'Comparative research methods', in D. Caramani (ed.), *Comparative Politics*, Oxford: Oxford University Press, pp. 47–59.

King, G., R.O. Keohane and S. Verba (1994), *Designing Social Inquiry: Scientific Inference in Qualitative Research*, Princeton, NJ: Princeton University Press.

Lipset, S.M. (1959), 'Some social requisites of democracy: economic development and political legitimacy', *American Political Science Review*, **53** (1), 69–105.

Pennings, P., H. Keman and J. Kleinnijenhuis (2006), *Doing Research in Political Science. An Introduction to Comparative Methods and Statistics*, London: Sage.

Przeworski, A. (2000), *Democracy and Development: Political Regimes and Economic Well-Being in the World, 1950–1990*, vol. 3, New York: Cambridge University Press.

Sartori, G. (1970), 'Concept misformation in comparative politics', *American Political Science Review*, **64** (4), 1033–53.

Seawright, J. and D. Collier (2014), 'Rival strategies of validation. tools for evaluating measures of democracy', *Comparative Political Studies*, **47** (1), 111–38.

Singleton, R.A. Jr and B.C. Straits (2009), *Approaches to Social Research*, 5th edn, New York: Oxford University Press.

Vanhanen, T. (2003), *Democratization: A Comparative Analysis of 170 Countries*, London and New York: Routledge.

5 On time and space: the historical dimension in political science*
Hans Keman

1 INTRODUCTION

The 'art' of history is considered by many as a close companion to political science. As the British historian Sir John Seeley wrote: 'History without political science has no fruit, political science without history has no root'. Hence there appears to be a natural relationship between the disciplines. Historical accounts and analyses offer rich information and empirical evidence on our 'past'. This can be and is used by political scientists to validate their research and to develop their theories. Conversely many historians have also made good use of concepts and ideas developed within the social sciences and political science in particular.

The development of the relationship between historical analysis and social science theory and methods started to develop in a more systematic and goal-oriented fashion in the second half of the nineteenth century. For example, Karl Marx, Max Weber and Gaetano Mosca made use of historical information but also explicitly framed this within their theories of social and economic *change and development* (Hofstadter and Lipset 1968). In this chapter I subsequently discuss: theory, method and meta-choices; the mutual character of politics and history; understanding change – time and space. I conclude by means of some reflections on ontologies, methodology and a few caveats to be aware of using the historical dimension in political science research.

2 THEORY, METHOD AND META-CHOICES

The British historian E.H. Carr wrote a book titled *What is History*. He emphasized that *historiography* (see Table 5.1) was the key to understanding historical developments. In fact, he urged, that 'facts' in history could always be contested for two reasons: they are constructs as interpreted by the observer, and thus, are at best relatively true. In addition, Carr considered history to be a part of the social sciences and therefore should employ an approach that enabled the student to give meaning to history.

Table 5.1   Terms used by historians and adopted by political scientists using historical analysis

Terms in use	Explanation
Historiography	Comparable to methodology in the social sciences: it concerns the critical assessment of the validity and reliability of the evidence and sources reported and the interpretation of the events analyzed and conclusions drawn. The latter aspect is often defined as a 'school' or approach. See Schneider and Woolf (2011) for further information
Primary or secondary sources	Primary evidence is all types of first-hand unaltered observations by the researcher (for example, original documents, materials and diaries). Second-hand (or hear-say) evidence is derived from publications, memoirs or statistics and so on, that are developed later. Social scientists tend to rely on this type of information
Counterfactual history	Also called 'what-if' history aiming at explaining the impact of a new development (for example, the abolition of slavery; Fogel and Engerman 1988). Mostly used by economic historians, but also by political historians (for example, what would have happened if the nuclear bomb had not been operational at the end of the Second World War?)
Critical juncture	An event or series of (more or less simultaneous) events that is seen as a fundamental change in society and thereby shifting the historical context and related interpretations. An example is Romein (1971) arguing that between 1890 and the Great War, society changed in all respects (culturally, politically and socially)
Diachronic analysis	Two-dimensional analysis: time and space. This is relevant if we undertake comparative case analysis, for the conditions and context are often different from one case to another. Therefore we must decide how time and space are critical for comparison. See Pierson (2003)
Sequencing	Ordering of events and relevant developments along two trains of thought: (1) chronically (using time series: ordering data in fixed intervals) (Floud 1973); and (2) logically meaning that certain events can only have taken place in a certain order regardless of time (Mahoney and Rueschemeyer 2003, ch. 1). This ordering may for example explain diffusion processes like democratization
Path dependency	Events or decisions made in the past define and often limit the room for manoeuver in the future. There is no point of return to the former situation or to make a drastic change (for example, explaining 'policy inertia'). For instance, once railways were introduced they defined the infrastructure to be(come) and became an almost exclusive alternative to extant means of transportation (see Pierson 2000).

For Carr the central focus was 'progress' (Carr 1961 [1990], pp. 181–2). Yet, however important (and contested) Carr's book has been, it must be understood as an approach to history as social science, and not as a theory of history.

Conversely the work of Karl Marx, Max Weber, Jan Romein and Fernand Braudel can be seen as examples of theories of history. Why? All these historians departed from the idea that historical analysis serves the purpose of explaining change and development. Marx and Braudel are representatives of this theoretical approach. Marx wished to explain the past, present and future of socio-economic order: the development from feudalism to stages of capitalism toward a communist society. Braudel, the leader of the so-called 'Annals School' in France, maintained that long-term cycles (climate, demography and technology) are determining how and to what extent politics and economics develop. Contrary to Marxist interpretations of change due to economic systems and concurrent power distribution, the Annals School stressed the role of infrastructural needs within a society and the variations in political authority over time. It was not the 'classes' that made history, but the existing structural conditions in which individuals lived and had to cope (see, for example, Braudel 1973). Yet, both Marx and Braudel shared the belief that neither events nor persons could or would fundamentally change society. They also had a common understanding of the structural conditions of development and how these interacted with politics (the state) and economics (capitalism). In short, both Marx and Braudel (1982) argued it was 'structure' rather than 'agency' that could explain change (Giddens 1971).

According to Max Weber and Jan Romein (a Dutch historian), explaining the past in view of the present means regarding man's actions as being contingent upon 'culture' in the wider sense of the word (that is, the interplay between man and environment that shape social and economic relations over time). For Max Weber this led to, for example, his 'ideal-typical' constructions to demonstrate change and how this may affect future developments (one of the famous ideal type is the patterned change in political authority; Weber 1922 [1972], pp. 106–10). In fact, his theory is that through larger scales of social activity by individuals organizational pressure shall lead to secularization, formalization and rationalization of developments that change the economy and politics of a society. Romein developed a similar approach focusing on culturally driven patterns of behavior (Romein 1971). Hence, 'agency' determines how and to what extent society changes, albeit contingent upon factors like capitalism, religion and traditions.

In summary: although it is often thought by social scientists that there is hardly any theory in history, this view is incorrect. The same goes for

Table 5.2   Meta theoretical differences in theories of history

	Structure versus agency	
Deterministic and evolutionary	Karl Marx	Jan Romein
Interactive and contextual	Fernand Braudel	Max Weber

Source: Keman (2013).

methods (see sections 4 and 5). All four historians can be considered as innovators in their own right and as being close to social scientists. This also implies that their approaches can be discerned in terms of meta-theory: structure versus agency and determination versus interaction (see Table 5.2 and Hay 2002).

Whether or not this division is wholly correct, the relevance is to see that – as in the social sciences – there are different 'models' to study historical patterns of societal change to explain the developments between past and present. These patterns, be they long or short term, global or area bound, interactions or contingencies, have laid (fertile) ground for the relationship between the social sciences and history. However, one difference remains between the analytical content and set-up of historical analysis and political analysis – the latter being comparative and seeking generalization, whereas the former is more directed towards singularity, less inclined to generalization. In sum, whereas historians tend to tell a specific 'story' over time, social scientists set out to analyze across cases (spatial) using temporal variation as a variable (Bartolini 1993).

3   POLITICAL SCIENCE AND HISTORICAL ANALYSIS

In contrast to political science in the US, historical analyses never completely disappeared from the research agenda in Europe after the Second World War. Much political science remained more or less descriptive or ideographic. It took until the 1970s for historical analysis to be reintroduced (and accepted) as an approach in the social sciences (see Mahoney and Rueschemeyer 2003; Tilly 2012). The 'return' of historical analysis is, then, a two-pronged development: on the one hand, a more intensive use of historical (and reliable) information provided by the historian (that is, secondary sources) and, on the other hand, the trend to do our own historical analysis (primary sources; see Table 5.1 for the difference). However, as Mahoney and Rueschemeyer rightly assert, both have the ambition to develop new insights. They define this as, 'comparative historical analysis aims at the explanation of substantively important outcomes by describing processes over time using systematic and contextualized comparisons' (Mahoney and Rueschemeyer 2003, p. 6). Note the term 'comparative'. This may be confusing; it can signify comparing over time as well as across cases. If we compare sequences across cases, it is called a *diachronic* analysis, and if over time, it concerns a *synchronic* type of analysis (see Table 5.1). The second element in the above definition concerns 'important outcomes'. This is an ambiguous notion. Why is an outcome important or not? In retrospect we only know that an outcome is seen by many as important. However, is it important? For example, with the help of hindsight the outcome of First World War was perhaps important because it meant a watershed in Europe in terms of democratization (Therborn 1977), and is also considered as a cause of Second World War (Hobsbawm 1994). Hence, important outcomes of a historical process, also labelled 'critical junctures' (see Table 5.1), need to be formulated carefully by means of research questions to explain puzzles over time and must be specified spatially (that is, the same phenomena can occur in different places) to compare these properly regarding their temporal variation (Pierson 2000).

Short and tall: comparative historical analysis is an important asset in relating political science to history as an approach to explain and describe change in society. As Charles Tilly puts it: 'Every significant political phenomenon lives in history, and requires historically grounded analysis for its explanation' (2007, p. 536). By identifying causal configurations the researcher is capable of developing theory that is conducive to explaining outcomes (Keman 2013). Secondly, by unfolding the temporal structure of events a systematic comparison becomes meaningful (Flora and Alber 1981). Thirdly, by choosing deliberately comparable cases, for example, 'most similar' or 'contrasting cases', enables the researcher to control contextual variation. A caveat is in place, however; not all types of historical information are always relevant nor is any type of historical analysis suited for understanding change and development. On the contrary, this depends on the research question asked and the arguments developed to answer it.

4   ANALYZING POLITICS OVER TIME AND SPACE

Historical research has often concerned itself with 'big questions', such as the causes of revolution (Skocpol 1998), the breakdown of democracies (Barrington Moore 1966) or the emergence of the (national) state (Tilly 1990). However, it does not signify that political historical analysis only seeks to develop comprehensive explanations. As will be discussed below

Table 5.3   Schematic overview of modes of comparative historical analysis

Type of analysis	Explaining outcomes	Analysing diversity	Showing patterned variations
	CAUSALITIES:	*CONFIGURATIONS:*	*CONDITIONS:*
Use of historical method	Temporal structuring and sequencing of events	Contextual examination of most likely causes	Systemic variables of conditions over time
Political science topics	Institutional development of welfare statism	Emergence of the modern state and democratization	Continuity or breakdown of democracy
	EXPLAINING	DEVELOPING	CONFIRMING
Type of theory and method	by critical junctures and path dependencies	theory by conceptual and descriptive inference	hypotheses using QCA or contrasting case analysis
Examples by:	Chris Pierson, Paul Pierson, Flora and Alber	North and Thomas, Rokkan and Urwin	Barrington Moore, Berg-Schlosser and Mitchell

Source: Keman (2013).

(see also Table 5.3), most historical research is topic driven, where patterned variations across cases and diversity over time are central.

This overview can be seen as an elaboration of how historical analysis is used in political science. It serves to showing the variation in theory and methods. Some suggest that the historical approach tends to be 'eclectic' or singular (cf. Mahoney and Rueschemeyer 2003, p. 12). However the selection of topics presented and methods used in Table 5.3 are not random: the examples have all to do with the developments of democracy and the changing role of the state. In this way theoretical approaches such as institutionalism or democratization, as well as explaining outcomes of state intervention (for example, policy performance over time), can be researched.

4.1   Institutional Developments and Welfare Statism

It goes almost beyond saying that institutions are at the core of analyzing macro-scopical units (or systems) such as democracy and the welfare state (Pierson 2009). In general, institutions are considered as the 'rules' of the political game that define the room to maneuver of political actors (see Chapters 9 and 16 in this volume). Although the institutions of democratic decision-making change only slowly over time, a cross-time analysis can reveal how the origins and temporal variation of welfare states is influenced by the sequencing of social policies. For instance, Flora and Heidenheimer (1981) show that the origins of, and measures taken in, European polities vary considerably over time across those countries explaining differences in types of welfare statism. At the same time, however, a convergent tendency can be observed in the long run and can be explained to some extent by certain critical junctures (for example, the First World War, the Depression and the Second World War). Only after 1945 do we witness the establishment of the welfare state across a large part the Organisation for Economic Co-operation and Development (OECD) world, but still with ample variation in state expenditures, generosity and universal coverage (Schmidt 2012).

How can we account for this comparative variation over time and yet a 'similar' outcome after the Second World War? For Paul Pierson (2003) it has to do with path dependencies (see Table 5.1) that are caused by institutional differences between European polities. Secondly, the critical junctures mentioned earlier implied a shift from incomplete to full democratization. In the views of Pierson and Schmidt, the origins, emergence and growth of European welfare states is the result of 'slow moving' causes and the interplay between institutionalizing the democratic state and shifts in the power distribution within the polities as regards policy formation. Hence, it appears to be the temporal sequence that structures the order of events in each polity towards the welfare state. This process explains the eventual outcomes in terms of the type of welfare state that has developed over time (cf. Flora and Alber 1981). Using the historical dimension contributes to the appreciation of extant welfare state research; it nuances universal explanations such as modernization and secularization, on the one hand, and pure political or economic explanations, on the other (Keman 2013). In short, introducing explicitly the historical dimension has brought us more detailed evidence and has helped to decipher the puzzling relationship between democracy and welfare by discerning multiple causal factors by means of historical analysis.

4.2   The Modern State and Democratization

In 1968 Nettl wrote an intriguing essay on the 'stateness' of societies. His idea was that public authority became increasingly 'politicized' owing to changing societal demands, on the one hand, and because industrialization and infrastructural development required a more active state, on the other. From this perspective it is easy to understand that both state and modernizing society in conjunction with the process of democratization would be considered as a multifarious phenomenon emerging over time as a changing configuration of functions, institutions and roles. Max Weber, for instance, developed the idea that rational-legal authority was the form of the modern state. In this conception – derived from his ideal type of political authority and change over time – there is little room for variation. His '*Herrschaftstypologie*' is a hypothesis; sooner or later all forms of political authority will converge to rational-legal authority. However, although this convergent tendency may have developed, at the same time it is also obvious that the variation in design and activities of states remain considerable. Why would that be?

First, the differences between states have to do with contextual differences that require different types of state functions or roles for performance (for example, in terms of sovereignty, facilitating economic transactions, and developing the infrastructure). Secondly, the process of democratization changes dramatically the relationship between state organization and civil society. Whereas the state was the prime coercive force that could and would regulate society and conduct war at will (cf. Tilly 1990), it could not continue this way after democratization. That is, the institutionalization of (autocratic forms of) state power by democratization changed the role and public functions of the state: (1) the rule of law constrains public powers; (2) it makes government accountable; and (3) it reduces open coercion. All this, however, hardly emerged simultaneously, producing varied configurations of state intervention across time and space (see Box 5.1).

In summary, by means of comparative historical analysis the rather abstract political science theories of the state have been developed towards

---

BOX 5.1   EMERGENCE OF THE EARLY-MODERN STATE AND ITS ROLE IN ECONOMIC DEVELOPMENT

The role and influence of the emerging bourgeoisie is tellingly elaborated by Douglass North. This Nobel Prize-winning economist explained the growing involvement of public authority to be the result of the need for regulating economic behavior that drives path dependent developments of state intervention (see Table 5.1). By comparing Spain, England and the Dutch Republics in the seventeenth and eighteenth centuries, North and Thomas found that the more autocratic the ruling elite in Spain, the less efficient and effective trading could be. Conversely, where the rules (regulating behavior) were effectively applied and the state supported and protected commerce instead of religion or the nobility, greater wealth was generated. This type of state intervention led to considerable comparative advantages over other countries. That is, public authority with checks and balances is conducive to internal peace and is mutually beneficial for state and economic development of capitalism (see North and Thomas 1988).

a more heuristic and descriptive account regarding state-formation (Tilly 1990), state intervention (North and Thomas 1988) and developing state autonomy (Weber 1972). Hence, historical analysis not only puts flesh on the theory, but also makes clear that political theories often need refinement and contextualization (Anderson 1975) in terms of sequencing using time and space together (see Table 5.1).

4.3   Socio-Cultural Features and the Development of the Nation-State

Stein Rokkan (see Flora et al. 1999) sees the historical process of state formation and nation building as fundamental to understand the era of mass politics. Hence, state formation is also part of the democratization in the second half of the nineteenth century that is closely intertwined with the development toward nation and state as the political authority within 'closed territories' (Rokkan and Urwin 1983, p. 135). As a comparativist *pur sang*, Rokkan seeks to develop a 'model of Europe' where three types of variables allow for a European wide historical analysis (pre-condition or structures, interventions or events and a set of outcomes; Rokkan and Urwin 1983, p. 138). In addition, the slow converging patterns of democracy and state formation in the first half of the twentieth century must also be seen as a consequence of the Napoleonic wars, establishing a common platform for nationalism and constitutional developments across Europe. The eventual result is, according to Flora et al. (1999), that the timing of developing contemporary democracy and related forms of mass politics during the nineteenth and twentieth centuries can be understood as a history-driven configuration with the eventual establishment of representative government as an outcome. In short, Rokkan drew conceptual and analytical 'maps' of Europe and not only showed that historical analysis is required to answer 'big' questions, but also that without a theoretical and systematic agenda, historical evidence will fall short to develop a configuration that brings order to the huge diversity in the relationship between state and society.

4.4   Democracy and the Modern State: A Complex and Vulnerable Relationship

Both Barrington Moore (1996) and Berg-Schlosser and Mitchell (2002) have produced intensive comparative historical analyses of the relations between state and democracy. These studies illustrate not only how comparative analysis can contribute to the development of further insights, but also how to do this by using different methodological approaches. Whereas Barrington Moore uses a 'contrasting cases' type of analysis, Berg-Schlosser and Mitchell use the qualitative case analysis (QCA) approach (see Chapters 25 and 27 in this volume) to account for underlying commonalities and to dispel conclusions based on 'singular' hypotheses.

Although Barrington Moore is criticized for biased case selection, ignoring the laboring and poor classes as well as the international context, both his idea of modelling societal progress (change) and the role of violent disruptions (junctures) has certainly contributed to our thinking about regime change and state intervention (see Box 5.2).

In the 1990s, Dirk Berg-Schlosser formed an international research group to study the inter-war period (that is, 1919–39). The group included political historians who were expert for a country and experts in comparative democratic theory. Two things make this project interesting: (1) it deliberately combines political science and history expertise; and (2) theory and method are a central concern to analyze this specific era. The theoretical starting-point was to scrutinize (more or less) accepted views on democratic consolidation (for younger democracies) and the

---

BOX 5.2   CONTINUITY OF BREAKDOWN OF DEMOCRACY IN THE TWENTIETH CENTURY

Barrington Moore's analysis includes nine countries of which two (China and Russia) never democratized, in two (Germany and Italy) the democratic polity broke down between the two World Wars, in two cases democratization, Mexico and Japan, only occurred after 1945 and in the other cases (Britain, France, and the US), democracy remained the 'only game in town'. The research question entertained is 'To what extent has the social stratification and economic development been conducive to how the polity was shaped over time?' and explains the subsequent process of democratization. In fact, Barrington Moore's model of explaining successful versus failed democratization is by comparing different 'routes to modernization' (Barrington Moore 1966, p.417ff). He discerned three different 'routes' towards consolidated democracy, interrupted democratization and no democracy at all. Hence, by means of historical analysis using secondary sources (see Table 5.1) three different 'routes' were developed explaining the outcome: democracy or autocracy. Secondly, he showed that in all cases war played a role as a 'critical juncture' that sooner or later triggered events which were always embedded in socio-economic and political institutional conditions at that time. Barrington Moore not only demonstrates that comparative historical analysis provides a suitable approach to analyze this type of 'big' question, but also by comparing clusters shows that the (eventual) outcomes are 'most different': continued democracy, breakdown to fascism and emerging communism. Hence, the three different routes can be explained by three similar variables: economic development (capitalism or not), societal structuration ('no bourgeoisie, no democracy') and the existing type of state (autocracy or not).

stability (of established democracies) in Europe. The shared point of departure was 'polyarchy' (cf. Dahl 1984) as the 'only game in town' by applying QCA (see Chapter 25 in this volume) in order to establish the relationship between theory and method. A methodological innovation was to distinguish between sufficient and necessary conditions (for change): the former can be seen as causalities explaining the diversity, and the latter as conditions promoting convergence.

The Berg-Schlosser research design was based in great detail on historical information, but this information was 'filtered' by means of variables representing multiple causes of change across similar or different cases (see also, Bartolini 1993). This type of historical comparative analysis allows us to conclude what factors make regime change (or not) more or less likely (see Berg-Schlosser and Mitchell 2002, pp. 267–9). As with Barrington Moore, it is obvious that the historical approach is required to study democratization and democratic performance, but is also in need of theoretical guidance. To quote Berg-Schlosser and Mitchell (2002, p. 269): 'in this way, political science and history can be brought into a mutually fruitful symbiotic relationship'.

5   ONTOLOGIES, METHODOLOGY AND A FEW CAVEATS

A common problem in both history and the social sciences has always been the so-called subject–object relationship. That is, the researcher is part of what is analyzed; his or her ontology defines how knowledge (facts, evidence and the human reality as such) is generated and must be interpreted. This perennial problematic has led to controversies and debates in both academic disciplines (Mahoney and Rueschemeyer 2003; see also Chapters 3 and 26 in this volume). Examples are, for instance, 'Historismus' and 'Positivism' representing the development towards a more scientific approach to establish both as academic disciplines during the late nineteenth and early twentieth centuries (see also, Carr 1990). These epistemological debates were conducive to the idea of separating subject from object by means of empiricism and the tendency towards 'value free' science (for example, Max Weber). It also led to alternative views on methodology. The historians and political scientists who were introduced earlier in this chapter are examples of this. Differences still remain between the two disciplines. Historians tend to depart from a broad view of human development (recall Romein and Weber) and how to interpret past and present (if not future, like Marx). Political scientists still focus more on specific theoretical questions using the historical dimension and its methods to answer questions rather than telling a 'history'. In sum, ontological shifts and methodological changes led to a lasting debate on 'structure' versus 'agency' (Hay 2002) that is characterized by various ontologies and methodological choices. That is, both disciplines have transformed themselves into academic disciplines where theory and method are closely intertwined and aim at explaining eventual outcomes of societal and political change. Secondly, there is an increasing tendency to 'borrow' methods from each other: for example the use of quantitative history (Floud 1973) and the application of counterfactual analysis (Fogel and Engerman 1988). Counterfactual analysis or 'iffy-history' aims at explaining historical outcomes by means of hypothesizing alternatives. To some extent this type of analysis is concurrent with the study of path dependencies and the impact of critical junctures (Pierson 2000). Conversely, the return of the historical dimension in social science can also be seen as the re-invention of history as an explanatory device. Hence, in terms of methods and the tendency to focus on theory guided research questions both disciplines appear to converge in theory, ontology and method. In addition, the collection of evidence (primary or secondary sources – see Table 5.1) is scrutinized in terms of validity (to check if concepts are equivalent over time and across the cases under review; Bartolini 1993) and reliability (to check if the evidence is uncontested). Finally, does the presentation of the evidence collected and presented allow for convincing conjectures regarding the theory-driven research question?

To conclude this section: the relationship between ontology and methodology is relevant to understand the variations in methods of historical analysis and political science, and social scientists ought to be aware of this in order to make full use of historical analysis.

6   CONCLUSION

Both disciplines have more in common than differences that separate them. This should not surprise the reader, since human beings are the prime object of historical and social research. Hence, the focus of explanation is on how mankind interacts with the environment and how that shapes its actions and related outcomes. Further, both in political science and in history, change and development are crucial topics to understand the past and the present. Finally, both time and space are constitutive for the study and generation of knowledge on political man and society.

However, this is not all. The overall object and goal of both disciplines remains different: singular and specific reconstruction and interpretation are considered important for historians (that is, historiography; see Table 5.1), whereas analyzing outcomes by conditions and context seem to be crucial for the political science (causalities and conjunctures). Secondly, in much social science research it appears that the appreciation of the historical dimension tends to be instrumental: it contributes to finding explanations or confirming theory (recall, for example, Barrington Moore). Thirdly, where historians tend to emphasize diversity and uniqueness, political scientists rather seek to identify convergence and linearity by means of comparisons. There is nothing wrong with that, but the caveat is that the research aims and methods for each discipline remain different regarding the use of time, space and evidence.

Nevertheless, interactions between history and political science are fruitful and beneficial, and can be further developed and more systematically elaborated. In contemporary terminology it concerns a 'win-win' situation, which has been stimulated by (comparative) political science and is welcomed by historians. Alternatively, social and political scientists have not only made (good) use of historians' labor, but have also increasingly applied the historical method to develop new insights to enrich existing theories, if not to solve analytical puzzles.

NOTE

*   This chapter is a revised and shortened version of a chapter published in A. Zimmer (ed.) (2013), *Civil Societies Compared: Germany and the Netherlands*, Baden-Baden: Nomos.

FURTHER READING

Carr, E.H. (1961), *What is History?*, 2nd edn 1990, London: Penguin.
Mahoney, J. and D. Rueschemeyer (eds) (2003), *Comparative Historical Analysis in the Social Sciences*, Cambridge: Cambridge University Press.
Tilly, C. (2009), 'Why and how history matters', in R.E. Goodin and C. Tilly (eds), *The Oxford Handbook of Contextual Political Analysis*, Oxford: Oxford University Press. pp. 417–37.

REFERENCES

Anderson, P. (1975), *Lineages of the Absolutist State*, London: Taylor & Francis.
Barrington Moore, G. Jr (1966), *Social Origins of Dictatorship and Democracy: Lord and Peasant in the Making of the Modern World*, London: Penguin.

Bartolini, S. (1993), 'On time and comparative research', *Journal of Theoretical Politics*, **5** (2), 131–67.

Berg-Schlosser, D. and J. Mitchell (eds) (2002), *Authoritarianism and Democracy in Europe, 1919–1939: Comparative Analyses*, London: Palgrave.

Braudel, F. (1973), *Capitalism and Material Life*, New York: Harper & Row.

Braudel, F. (1982), *On History*, Chicago, IL: University of Chicago Press.

Carr, E.H. (1961), *What is History?*, 2nd edn 1990, London: Penguin.

Dahl, R. (1984), 'Polyarchy, pluralism and scale', *Scandinavian Political Studies*, **7** (4), 225–40.

Fogel, R. and S. Engerman (1988), *Time on the Cross: The Economics of American Negro Slavery*, Lexington, MA: D.C. Heath.

Flora, P. and J. Alber (1981), *Modernization, Democratization and the Development of Welfare States in Western Europe: The Development of Welfare States in Europe and America*, Piscataway, NJ: Transaction Books.

Flora, P. and A.J. Heidenheimer (eds) (1981), *The Development of Welfare States in Europe and America*, London: Routledge.

Flora, P., S. Kuhnle and D. Urwin (1999), *State Formation, Nation-Building and Mass Politics in Europe: The Theory of Stein Rokkan*, Oxford: Oxford University Press.

Floud, R. (1973), *An Introduction to Quantitative Methods for Historians*, London: Taylor & Francis.

Giddens, A. (1971), *Capitalism and Modern Social Theory: An Analysis of the Writings of Marx, Durkheim and Max Weber*, Cambridge: Cambridge University Press.

Hay, C. (2002), *Political Analysis: a Critical Introduction*, London: Palgrave.

Hobsbawm, E. (1994), *The Age of Extremes: The Short Twentieth Century, 1914–1991*, New York: Vintage Books.

Hofstadter, L. and S.M. Lipset (1968), *Sociology and History: Methods*, New York: Basic Books.

Keman, H. (2013), 'History and social science: symbiosis or synthesis?', in A. Zimmer (ed.), *Civil Societies Compared: Germany and the Netherlands*, Baden-Baden: Nomos.

Mahoney, J. and D. Rueschemeyer (eds) (2003), *Comparative Historical Analysis in the Social Sciences*, Cambridge: Cambridge University Press.

Nettl, J.P. (1968), 'The state as a conceptual variable', *World Politics*, **20** (4), 559–92.

North, D.C. and R.P. Thomas (1988), *The Rise of the Western World: A New Economic History*, Cambridge: Cambridge University Press.

Pierson, C. (2009), *Beyond the Welfare State: The New Political Economy of Welfare*, Cambridge: Polity Press.

Pierson, P. (2000), 'Increasing returns, path dependence, and the study of politics', *American Political Science Review*, **94** (2), 251–67.

Pierson, P. (2003), 'Big, slow-moving and . . . invisible: macrosocial process in the study of comparative politics', in J. Mahoney and D. Rueschemeyer (eds), *Comparative Historical Analysis in the Social Sciences*, Cambridge: Cambridge University Press, pp. 177–207.

Rokkan, S. and D. Urwin (1983), *Economy, Territory, Identity: Politics of West European Peripheries*, London: Sage.

Romein, J. (1971), *Historische Lijnen en Patronen*, Leiden: Querido.

Schmidt, M.G. (2012), *Der deutsche Sozialstaat. Geschichte und Gegenwart* (*The German Welfare State. Past and Present*), Munich: C.H. Beck.

Schneider, A. and D. Woolf (eds) (2011), *The Oxford History of Historical Writing*, vol. 5, Oxford: Oxford University Press.

Skocpol, T. (ed.) (1998), *Democracy, Revolution, History*, Ithaca, NY: Cornell University Press.

Therborn, G. (1977), 'Capital and suffrage', *New Left Review*, **103** (1), 3–42.

Tilly, C. (1990), *Coercion, Capital and European States AD 990–1990*, Cambridge, MA: Harvard University Press.

Tilly, C. (2007), 'Why and how history matters', in R.E. Goodwin (ed.), *The Oxford Handbook of Political Science*, Oxford: Oxford University Press, ch. 26.

Weber, M. (1922), *Wirtschaft und Gesellschaft* (*Economy and Society*), reprinted 1972, Tübingen: Mohr.

6 Systems theory: the search for a general theory of politics
Hans Keman

1 INTRODUCTION

Systems theory as an approach in political science emerged in the 1950s attempting to develop a general theory of politics by linking behavioralism to structural-functionalism (Charlesworth 1968). Although David Easton (1917–2014) is the most well-known protagonist, there are many other political scientists who have not only attempted to develop this approach for the social sciences, but have also applied it for research of political processes (for example, Karl Deutsch, Gabriel Almond and Bingham Powell). Until the 1980s, systems theory was often considered as a model to relate policy-making to (democratic) politics as part of the 'policy turn in political science' (Torgerson 1995, p. 228). This has been conducive to debates regarding the question 'Does politics matter?' in democracies (for example, Castles 1982; Bingham Powell 2007) or how to understand 'political development' (see Przeworski et al. 2000; Almond et al. 2008).

In this chapter I first discuss the introduction of systems theory in political science after World War II as an approach that could lead to a universal theory of politics (if not a paradigm). Second, an outline of this approach is discussed in terms of its main features and how it is seen to explain political process in general and policy formation in particular. Third, I deal with the pros and cons of systems theory as a 'theory' and with its feasibility as an empirical tool for political analysis. Next I present an example of empirical analysis based on systems theory. Finally, the contemporary state of the art is discussed as regards its use and standing as a political science approach.

2 THE INTRODUCTION OF SYSTEMS THEORY IN POLITICAL SCIENCE

The first generation of postwar political scientists (many of them served in this war) were convinced that traditional political science leaned too much on ideas and principles emanating from the humanities. They were looking for a more 'scientific' approach to analyze and explain politics, democratic politics in particular. Instead of focusing only on ideas, principles, institutions and norms of behavior, politics needed to be studied with more rigor based on empirical footing (Easton 1965). In particular during the 1950s and 1960s, literature focusing on systems theory, functionalism and quantitative methods was booming.[1]

This movement towards a more 'scientific' approach is known as the 'behavioral revolution' where human interaction and its consequences for the working of the polity stood central. For example electoral studies and studies of party systems and democratic action became strongly 'positivist' or empirically founded. Yet, this development was considered by its critics at the time as merely analyzing fragments of the political process as a whole and could not lead to a general theory of politics. Whereas the partial approaches within behavioralism were mostly derived from psychology to analyze and understand human interaction (see, for an overview, Barker and Hansen 2005) or applied ideas from economics to explain politics (such as Schumpeter and Downs), systems theory claimed to analyze the political process from beginning to end as embedded in its social, economic and cultural environment.

Another influence to 'modernize' political science was the urgent need to develop theories that could cope with the question to what extent democratic governance could be proven to be superior to other regimes (see also Chapter 8 in this volume) and therefore being functional to govern society in a stable fashion without resorting to oppression and violence (Dahl 2000). Originally structural functionalism, a holistic approach, was seen by many as a proper point of departure. Functional action (for example, party behavior) was considered in this approach as part of a structure (for example, democratic society) and could explain political actions by means of comparing societies focusing on their economic and cultural differences (Almond et al. 2008, pp. 45–51). However, although Robert Merton (1957) defined this approach as a 'middle range' theory instead of claiming universal validity, structural functionalism lacked a feasible link to empirical application and was considered to be teleological if not tautological and static.

Systems theory, *inter alia* known from the natural sciences, can therefore be considered as an attempt to bridge structural functionalism and the empirical (behavioral) generation of knowledge (Farr et al. 1995). Furthermore, systems theory claimed to be able to detect and understand why a dynamic system can stay generally stable under changing conditions and pressures. This claim is based on 'cybernetics' or 'autopoiesis' (that is, the self-regulating or steering capacity of a system and its survival). Easton and others such as Karl Deutsch in his book on the *Nerves of Government* (1963) followed this trajectory to 'translate' general systems theory for use in political science. Next I present the elaboration and potential application of systems theory in terms of cybernetics.

3 SYSTEMS THEORY AND THE STUDY OF POLITICS

Although systems theory in political science is almost always identified with the work of David Easton, this idea was shared by others as well (see Young 1968, pp. 14–19). Other than in holistic approaches such as structural functionalism, systems theory assumes continual movement and change. General systems theory therefore assumes that – given the patterned interactions between the system's components – information exchange (material and immaterial) is common to all systems and thus the key to understanding how a system works and is more or less stable.[2] Hence, knowing one part of a system enables us to know something about another part. The information content of a 'piece of information' is proportional to the amount of information that can be inferred from that piece and allows for coordination (Kuhn 1974).

According to Kuhn (1974) systems can be either controlled (cybernetic) or uncontrolled (chaotic). In the former information is recognized, and changes are responses to the information (like the central heating system; see endnote 2). Kuhn refers to this as the *detector*, *selector* and *effector* functions of the system. The detector is concerned with the communication of information between components within the system. The selector is defined by the rules (or institutions) that exist and are in use to make decisions, and the effector is the means by which transactions influence the eventual development of the system. Communication and transactions are central to the working of the system as they define intersystem interactions. Communication is the exchange of information (such as political contestation), while transaction involves the exchange of matter-energy (for example, public policy). All organizational and social interactions always involve communication and transaction. Kuhn's approach stresses that the role of decision is to move a system towards an equilibrium. Communication and transaction provide the vehicles (detector and selector) for a system to achieve equilibrium through the selector. '*Culture* is communicated, learned patterns and *society* is a collectively of people having a common body and process of culture' (Kuhn 1974, p. 154, original emphases). When society is viewed as a system, culture is seen as defining the patterns of interactions in the system. Social analysis is therefore the study of 'communicated, learned patterns common to relatively large groups (of people)' (ibid., p. 157).

The systems' analysis can follow two lines of enquiry. A cross-sectional approach deals with the interaction between two systems (for example, politics and economics), while a *developmental* approach deals with the changes in a system over time (see also Chapter 5 in this volume). Finally, it ought to be stressed that systems cannot be seen as operating in a vacuum, but are affected by its environment (that is, economic development and societal and cultural change having an impact on the political system within any society; Merkel 2014). How does this translate into a viable model for political science? As an example, Easton developed a simple diagram showing the basic principles of a political process (Easton 1957, p. 384).

As can immediately be seen from Figure 6.1, the *input–output* relation is crucial and becomes dynamic by means of the feedback loop. This implies that systems theory as applied to 'politics' assumes that the underlying process is circular and reiterated. Secondly, inputs (from society) can vary from being positive to negative (that is, support and demands) as regards the relative stability of the political system due to the nature of the feedbacks resulting from the eventual output (decisions or policies). Hence, the more adequate (or functional) the input–output relationship the political system appears to perform considering the environment (society and related sub-systems like the economy or the prevalent

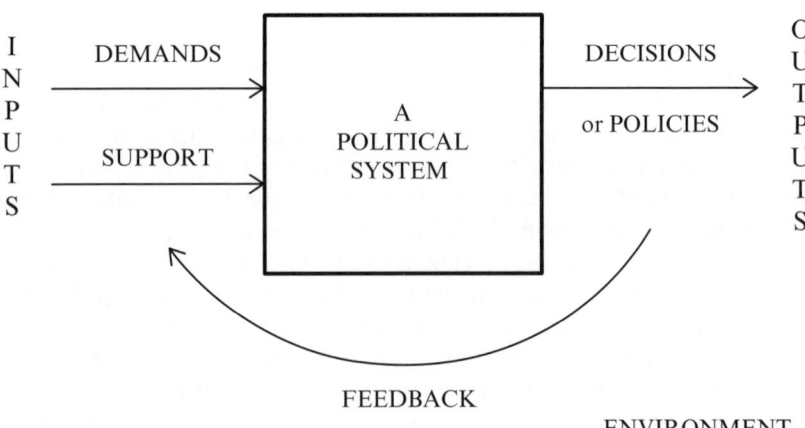

Source: Easton (1957, p. 384).

Figure 6.1   Inputs – political system or processes – outputs

culture), the closer a system will remain to produce optimal outcomes or an equilibrium.[3]

However simple or obvious this application to understanding political processes seems to be, it requires an elaboration of what the units of analysis are and how they are interconnected. In addition essential to understanding processes in systems theory is to know how information flows work within the system as well as between systems, and what type of transactions are fulfilled that characterize the input–output relationship. Both requirements indicate the feasibility of the circular process as well the eventual system perseverance. This idea is *inter alia* developed by a Deutsch (1963, p. 124ff.) and adopted by Nikolas Luhmann (1995). They asserted that information and related patterns of exchange defined the working of a system by means of coordination and its self-regulating or steering capacities (that is, autopoiesis). However, these ideas either did not travel very far or became obsolete in political science. Most developments in systems theory in political science at present still depart from the Easton's ideas.

The core problem in system theory concerns the operationalization of what a system vis-à-vis its environment is, how the components are interrelated and, finally, how to develop a model that could indeed explain its dynamic equilibrium (or optimal outcomes). A system can be defined by its parts that make up the whole or by its specific quality as a whole. The former is the reductionist approach whereas the latter is a functional view: what part does, for example, a political system play within overall system or environment? As Robert Jervis (1997, p. 6) proposes, it is a combination of both that distinguishes a political system from its environment when (1) the system's units are interconnected in such a way that change in one unit is conducive to change in others; (2) a system produces behavior and actions by its parts that is different from that of single elements; (3) exogenous pressures affect intra-system elements according to 1 and 2 and endogenous changes affect the environment. A political system can be recognized by its intra-system process that is different from others (for example, the economic, social or international system) and by its external effects that cannot be produced by another type of system.

The next question begging for an answer is how to apply systems theory to the dynamics of a political system. Again, as with many core concepts within political science (such as 'power' or the 'state') the definition of what politics entails is contested. Easton's definition is widely known: '*those interactions through which material and immaterial values are authoritatively allocated for a society*, and are (or can be made) *binding for society*' (Easton 1965, p. 21, emphasis added).

This abstract definition allows for inclusion of many aspects we find in other definitions, such as (re)distributive politics, (state) authority, public versus private, power and influence, regulating society, decision-making and so on. However, many critics have pointed out that the concept of a 'value' – whether material or not – is ambiguous and dependent on cultural and historical variations (such as religion, prevalent norms and mode of production; see for example, Weber 1922 [1972]). Yet, that does not imply that allocating values by an authority (for example, governmental policy-making) on this level of abstraction is flawed. It is up to the researcher to develop this concept (value) considering time and space in relation to systemic specifics (see Almond et al. 2008; Chapter 5 in this volume). What is essential here is whether or not Easton's definition of the 'political' indeed delineates boundaries of the political system.

A political system is evidently part of a larger system which can be labelled 'society'. Whereas, for instance, the concept of the 'state' is central to the study of international relations, a political system is always embedded in society at large or its 'environment' (see Figure 6.1). Contrary to others, systems theory defines its boundaries in view of its own characteristics as the 'political' sphere vis-à-vis the non-political. The delineations have produced the same type of debates as with the concept of 'politics'. Yet, there is some common ground: the powers vested in a regime that is capable of directing society by regulating social and economic issues and developments, if and when this is manifested in effective collective action. This requires political governance that is acceptable to most (that is, legitimacy; see Merkel 2014) and is conducive to a system's perseverance or maintenance (that is, equilibrium). If not, a political system either disappears (for example, a failed state) or is transformed (that is, by revolution). Hence, the conclusion must be that boundaries of a political system are fluid and dependent on environmental pressures.

This conception understandably is one of the critical issues in systems theory and it has led to – among other criticisms – much debate on how to analyze and understand political stability and change. Criticisms of systems theory are manifold: one category is ontological, that is, criticizing its 'conservative' perspective regarding stability which prejudices the present state over change. This seems incorrect: the present defines merely the state of affairs rather than an ideological judgment.[4] A second category of criticism concerns the assumed idea of a biological parallel: politics would be equi-functional to a human being (or any living creature). This may be a valid argument. However, it does not mean that the approach is deemed to be inadequate. A third objection is that it overlooks the empirical variety of and within existing political systems, and ignores the specific relationship between, for example, state and society in the past and present by underspecifying what the 'throughput' or conversion process implies for system stability. Finally, as already mentioned, systems theory seems to be inadequate as an explanatory approach. In its claim to be universal or general this criticism is correct, but as a heuristic and descriptive tool systems theory can be useful to develop proto-theories of political change and related consequences for a society.

In this section I have elaborated the relationship between general systems theory and its application for use in political science I have followed the 'translation' of David Easton and presented some of the issues of debate regarding this translation. The main critiques regard the level of abstraction that is reducing its application to empirical analysis. This is a rightful criticism and has often led to a partial use of systems theory (for example, focusing on input mechanisms, such as the voter–party linkage only or on outputs such as policy-making without including the effects of policy performance). This partial use of systems theory has indeed weakened the claim of universal use for political analysis. Yet, in comparative politics systems theory is regularly used as a heuristic device to develop descriptive analyses claiming the potential benefits of understanding if not explaining political processes (Lijphart 2008). In the next section the specifics of the workings of a political system is presented.

4 HOW A POLITICAL SYSTEM CAN BE ANALYZED: PARLIAMENTARY REGIMES

David Easton claims

> That there is a need for general theory in the study of political life is apparent. The only question is how best to proceed . . . At this stage it appears that system theory, with its sensitivity to the input-output exchange between a system and its setting offers a fruitful approach. (Easton 1957, p. 400)

In this section an example of how we can develop a research design by following and elaborating systems theory is elaborated. This example will allow us to discuss some of the main criticisms of the use of systems theory in political science: the model is too abstract for specific analysis; equilibrium as a point of reference is *post hoc* observation; the conversion part of the model is a 'black box'; and measuring change is insufficient for analyzing system dynamics.

The example, parliamentary regime analysis, is chosen because it

BOX 6.1   INPUTS – GATEKEEPERS – CONVERSION – OUTPUTS – FEEDBACKS – SYSTEM SURVIVAL

- *Flows of external influence*. Influences and pressures emanating from other systems, such as international, ecological, cultural, economic and demographic, as well as from society as a whole affect the working of any political system all the time. There are political issues and societal problems that arise from these systems and require political action, if and when it concerns the public space (for example, pollution) or affects society at large (for example, an economic or a refugee crisis).
- *Inputs: demands and support*. Inputs are necessary for any system to operate in a viable and effective fashion. Without inputs the system receives no information and the political process becomes superfluous or obsolete. Demands are inputs requesting for (desired) political action. Not all demands are recognized but those that are put forward by 'gatekeepers' (for example, parties or organized interests, and movements) are, and often manifest themselves as policy issues. Support is an input that is either recognized by (silent) permissive behavior and compliance within society (diffuse support) or by explicit and specific consent (like electoral participation).
- *Gatekeepers and decision-making*. Institutions and procedures define the role of political actors regarding decision-making, and their role as 'selectors' for action. Political actors are filtering various demands, both external and internal, in order to convert these by choice and decision in terms of public policy formation. Political actors also enhance support for the extant regime by means of responsive and responsible behavior in relation to outputs produced.
- *Outputs: allocation and (re)distribution*. Central to systems theory in politics is the extent to which political actors are capable to 'convert' demands into policy choices. Without the development of public policies by means of authoritative allocation of (material and immaterial) measures and a fair (re)distribution of resources that are (or can be made) binding for society, negative feedback effects will occur.
- *Positive and negative feedbacks*. A 'feedback loop' is the system's capacity to generate support. It connects the effects of the outputs (the binding allocation of values and resources) with incoming demands and supports. Hence, there is a circulatory relationship between inputs and outputs. It completes the political circuit through its input–conversion–output– feedback process. Two types of feedback loops can be discerned: (1) negative feedback relates to the (mis)information regarding the system and the (non-)regulation of errors; and (2) goal-transforming feedback is concerned with the purposeful redirection of the system. Feedback often suffers from misdirection owing to inaccuracy, lacking responsiveness, path dependency and time lags. Overload of demands or missing information and inadequate conversion can result in tendencies towards a disequilibrium or at least forms of political instability.
- *System survival*. A political systems is maintained if and when there is a positive relationship (correlation) between inputs and outputs. A necessary condition is the signalling of incoming influences, demands and support

and the related selection and conversion by political actors (gatekeepers) within the institutional framework of the system (regime), and adequate policy-making (government). The structure-induced equilibrium between input and output explains over time (dynamics) a system's survival.

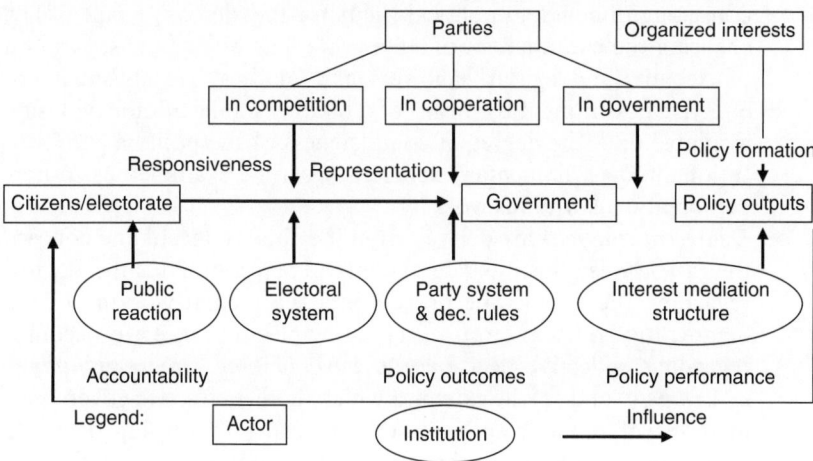

Source: Pennings et al. (2006, p. 184).

Figure 6.2 Chain of democratic control and command: performance as a sequential system

allows for a more specific political science elaboration of systems theory (that is, not universal in terms of 'global', but general with respect to representative government). The presentation departs from the research question, to what extent are democratic deficits and political instability of parliamentary democracies a result of system overload, inefficient decision-making and inadequate policy formation? This question has been posed by many political scientists (such as Crozier et al. 1975; Lijphart 2008), but is in the view of Wolfgang Merkel (2004, 2014), Ian Budge et al. (2002, 2012) and Keman (2004, 2014) insufficiently answered in a coherent and encompassing fashion. Therefore systems theory has been applied under the label of 'complex democracy' (cf. Schmidt 2008, p. 273). Figure 6.2 represents a democratic system seen as complex democracy, including stages of participation, representation and governance. This model is sequential and cyclical: from input via throughput to output feeding back to input which can be analyzed dynamically for each election and government.

The central concepts of 'complex democracy' captured in Figure 6.2 are elaborated below. They also are indicators of more specific hypotheses for empirical research.

- *Democracy* can be defined as an integrated system (the 'polity') consisting of civil and political rights for the 'demos', a rule of law ensuring the containment of state powers as well as the separation of executive and legislative powers, and finally, the establishment of effective government by means of a binding public authority. Using available data the degree of completeness of the polity as an institutionalized parliamentary democracy can be examined as to how democratic institutions work.

- *Democratic deficits* are derived from the above concept and concern the gap between (justified) demands (and perceptions) of the 'demos' regarding the democratic process and the factual working of the democratic polity in terms of: (1) principles that direct procedures regarding collective decisions on *participation – representation – government*; and (2) the extent to which there is effective governance in terms of input (responsiveness of parties of turning demands into policy options) – throughput (accountable conversion by government of policy choices) – output (material and immaterial outcomes, that is, policy performance). This sequence represents what democratic performance is or should be. However, the lower the trust in political institutions and actors and their behavior in the process of conversion, the less the eu-functionality of participation (for example, in elections), representation (for example, by parties and organized interests) and governance (policy-making), the wider the 'gap' between politics and society may be (come) and the more defective a democracy will be (Keman 2004).

- *Institutions and actors* are the cornerstones of the system: institutions are defined as formal and informal (convention) rules that direct the political process. Actors are the players involved and are constrained by the rules that also allow for opportunities (cf. Scharpf 1997). That is, actors are to a large extent dependent on the institutional design of the polity, whereas institutions have interdependent qualities and often explain path-dependent developments (as policy legacies do; Bardach 2009). Adverse interactions of institutions and actors can signify Democratic Deficits if and when the rules or conventions are considered as outdated, insufficient or inefficient. If so, then it can be expected that an optimal structure induced equilibrium (cf. Shepsle 1995) cannot be achieved by actors. In summary, the interplay and impact of institutions and actors is part of the conversion process and will influence the type of feedbacks (in terms of support and demand) as a result of political decision-making.

- *Political instability* occurs if and when support is minimal and demand overload or external influences make public authority actions (policies) be perceived as weak or even incapable often leading to reluctant compliance of citizens or abstaining from voting; Keman 2014). In addition, in situations where 'stalemates' exist between parties, organized interests or large groups of citizens this will impair the emergence of 'structural induced equilibria' and political instability. This may lead to institutional adaptation (for example, the federalization of Belgium), the replacement of actors (for example, Italy in the early 1990s) or the emergence of an alternative government (for example, Greece in 2015).

- *Political parties* are characterized by a triplet of goal-oriented behavior: vote-seeking, office-seeking and policy-seeking behavior (Katz and Crotty 2006). Parties have policy preferences (ideology) and recruitment procedures, and appear to be crucial and indispensable political actors within parliamentary systems. However, parties are often mistrusted and tend to forgo their role as gatekeepers. This effect becomes particularly visible in examining the congruence between citizens' demands and party choices (degree of responsiveness) and the congruence between party policy preferences (policy agenda) and the eventual authoritative allocation of values by governmental actions (Keman 2006; Bingham Powell 2007).

- *Organized interests* also represent societal demands and issues. They can collude with certain parties, but can also remain 'independent' like popular movements. Depending on the institutional structure of the polity organized interests are more or less involved in representation and governance. This defines their role as gatekeeper and potential influence in pressurizing specific demands (for example, Euroscepticism). Organized interests may well contribute to democratic deficits, if institutionalized in a non-transparent system of interest intermediation. The question is to what extent these actors influence binding policy-making or the eventual type and direction of feedback.

- *Party government:* democratic governments are dependent on their composition and rate of survival to convert input into output as intended in terms of goal transformation. Governments steer the 'ship of state' by directing other bodies of the political system.

Representative government is considered here as the central agency of any democratic system. Party governance is the core mechanism – transforming the inputs of a system into outputs – allowing us to understand the variations in democratic procedures bureaucracies and concomitant levels of policy performance. This depends on the institutional configuration of the system which determines the chances to develop a more structure-induced equilibrium. Hence, the issue is whether or not party government has sufficient room to manoeuver to develop and carry out policies producing sufficient positive feedback and thereby generating support in terms of popular trust in parties and government (Budge et al. 2012).

- *Exogenous factors:* a political system that is defined to represent the 'national' state and society cannot be considered a 'closed' system. Every country has an international environment and interacts with other countries economically (for example, openness to the world market), politically (for example, membership of international organizations) and socially (such as tourism, sports and media). These factors do have an impact on domestic politics and society that varies for each country in terms of sensitivity (for example, changes on the world market) or vulnerability (coping with external changes). The question is to what extent these exogenous factors will be relevant for understanding the level of democratic performance in terms of system stability to avoid democratic deficits, that is, low levels of support or even legitimacy?

The above presentation is an illustration of how to apply the ideas of systems theory to a more specific research question. It demonstrates that it is possible to develop a research design regarding the implications of complex democracy in relation to system perseverance by asking to what extent democratic deficits impair the working of parliamentary democracy (as intended). An example of this type of research are Merkel (2014) by means of a comparative analysis whether or not we should think of representative democracy developing into a crisis and what systemic variables may explain this. Another example is Scholten (1968) who has developed a case study with regard to the Dutch political system, investigating to what extent 'consociationalism' (collaboration by elected political elites) is less an exception to the rule but rather a type of democracy that is intra-system driven. A final example is Budge et al. (2002, 2012), who analyze both intra- and extra-system pressures in view of a system's stability by means of comparative analysis of the Organisation for Economic Co-operation and Development (OECD) world. These examples can serve as an illustration of Easton's expectation that: 'It (that is, systems theory analysis) is an economical way of organizing presently disconnected political data and promises interesting dividends' (Easton 1957, p. 400).

5 CONCLUSION: SYSTEM THEORY AND EXTANT APPLICATIONS

Systems theory in contemporary political science is often used. Initially it was considered a promising route towards a general theory of politics. However, as it proved difficult to 'ground' the theory by means of empirical analysis, it lost much of its appeal. This coincided with the demise of 'behavioralism' in 1970s and it was David Easton who acknowledged this in his address as president of the American Political Science Association (APSA) in 1981 (discussing the post-behavioral revolution). Nevertheless, many political scientists still use systems theory as a descriptive tool or for partial analysis of political processes. Hence this approach remains a valuable asset in political science although many researchers tend to overlook the deeper meaning of systems theory, especially as regards the topic of a 'dynamic equilibrium' and the question of system perseverance in view of *intrasystem* instability or *extrasystem* disturbances.

As stated earlier, from the 1980s onwards there was a turn to public policy (or: outputs and outcomes) as a central topic in political science. Many of these practitioners indirectly used elements of systems theory (for example, Torgerson 1995; Bardach 2009, p. 936ff.). In comparative politics, systems theory became popular among those who advocated, for example, the analysis of the comparative development of politics (Almond et al. 2008) and polities (Lijphart 2008), or the 'Does politics matter' thesis (Keman 2002), or researched the development of the welfare state (Schmidt 2002). The conclusion must be, therefore, that systems theory has played an important part in postwar political science, and is still widely used, albeit not as a paradigm or dominant approach that Easton, Deutsch or Luhmann thought it would be(come).

NOTES

1. Publications on or applying systems theory to cases were paramount in the 1950s and 1960s (for example, Scholten 1968). Still it is widely used in political science jargon either descriptively or as a research design (for example, Google Scholar produces over 36 000 citations), however, after 1990 the number decreases.
2. A simple illustration may serve here: a central heating system works adequately if and when the information given (input) is correctly recognized and transformed into

adequate action, here changing the temperature (throughput), resulting in the desired and stable climate (output).

3. Equilibrium is not an absolute point defining stability *per se*, but is rather a reference point to what is labelled the 'optimum' being the Euclidean point of gravity within a system or, as Shepsle (1995) formulates, a structure-induced equilibrium, meaning that no better outcome can be achieved without disturbances within the system. Discussions regarding 'stability' have long been raging in political science. We will not repeat this debate and stick to the concept of an optimum or equilibrium that makes a system persevere.

4. In addition, there have been overall rejections of systems theory pointing to its inherent 'status quo' bias as well as its (underlying) meaning of manipulating society by political elites. I consider this as politicized criticisms that can neither be rejected nor confirmed.

FURTHER READING

Bingham Powell, G., R. Dalton, K. Strøm and G.A. Verba (2014), *Comparative Politics Today: A World View*, 14th edn, New York: Pearson.

Keman, H. (2002), 'Policy-making capacities of European party government', in K.R. Luther and F. Müller-Rommel (eds), *Political Parties in New Europe: Political And Analytical Challenges*, Oxford: Oxford University Press, pp. 32–61.

Young, O. (1968), *Systems of Political Science*, Englewood Cliffs, NJ: Prentice Hall.

REFERENCES

Almond, G.A., G. Bingham Powell, R. Dalton and K. Strøm (2008), *Comparative Politics Today: A Theoretical Framework*, 5th edn, New York: Pearson Longman.

Bardach, E. (2009), 'Policy dynamics', in B. Goodin (ed.), *The Oxford Handbook of Political Science*, Oxford: Oxford University Press, pp. 934–64.

Barker, D. and S. Hansen (2005), 'All things considered: systematic cognitive processing and electoral decision-making', *Journal of Politics*, **67** (2), 319–44.

Bingham Powell, G. (2007), 'Aggregating and representing political preferences', in C. Boix and S.C. Stokes (eds), *The Oxford Handbook of Comparative Politics*, Oxford: Oxford University Press, ch. 27.

Budge, I., H. Keman, M. McDonald and P. Pennings (2002), 'Comparative government and democracy', in H. Keman (ed.), *Comparative Democratic Politics: A Guide to Contemporary Theory and Research*, London: Sage, pp. 65–97.

Budge, I., H. Keman, M. McDonald and P. Pennings (2012), *Organizing Democratic Choice*, Oxford: Oxford University Press.

Castles, F.G. (1982), *The Impact of Parties: Politics and Policies in Democratic Capitalist States*, London and Beverly Hills, CA: Sage.

Charlesworth, J.C. (1968), *Contemporary Political Analysis*, New York: Free Press.

Crozier, M., S.P. Huntington and J. Watanuki (1975), *The Crisis of Democracy*, New York: New York University Press.

Dahl, R.A. (2000), *On Democracy*, New Haven, CT and London: Yale University Press.

Deutsch, K.W. (1963), *The Nerves of Government: Models of Political Communication and Control*, New York: Free Press.

Easton, D. (1957), 'An approach to the analysis of political systems', *World Politics*, **9** (3), 383–400.

Easton, D. (1965), *A Systems Analysis of Political Life*, New York: Wiley.

Farr, J., J. Dryzek and S. Leonard (1995), *Political Science in History: Research Programs and Political Traditions*, Cambridge: Cambridge University Press.

Jervis, R. (1997), 'Complexity and the analysis of political and social life', *Political Science Quarterly*, **112** (4), 569–93.

Katz, R. and W.J. Crotty (eds) (2006), *Handbook of Party Politics*, London: Sage.

Keman, H. (2002), 'Policy-making capacities of European party government', in K.R. Luther and F. Müller-Rommel (eds), *Political Parties in the New Europe. Political and Analytical Challenges*, Oxford: Oxford University Press, pp. 32–61.

Keman, H. (2004), 'Polyarchy & defected democracy around the world', *Acta Politica*, **39** (3), 102–20.

Keman, H. (2006), 'Party government formation and policy preferences: an encompassing approach?', in J. Bara and A. Weale (eds), *Democratic Politics and Party Competition*, London: Routledge, pp. 33–55.

Keman, H. (2014), 'Democratic performance of parties and legitimacy in Europe', *West European Politics*, **37** (2), 309–30.

Kuhn, A. (1974), *The Logic of Social Systems*, San Francisco, CA: Jossey-Bass.

Lijphart, A. (2008), *Thinking about Democracy: Power Sharing and Majority Rule in Theory and Practice*, London: Sage.

Luhmann, N. (1995), *Social Systems*, Stanford, CA: Stanford University Press.

Merkel, W. (2004), 'Embedded and defective democracies', in A. Croissant and W. Merkel (eds), *Democratization: Consolidated or Defective Democracy?* Special issue of *Problems of Regime Change*, **11** (5), 33–58.

Merkel, W. (ed.) (2014), *Demokratie und Krise: Zum schwierigen Verhältnis von Theorie und Empirie* (*Democracy and Crisis: On the Complex Relationship between Democracy and Crisis*), Wiesbaden: Springer VS.

Merton, R. (1957), *Social Theory and Social Structure*, London: Free Press of Glencoe.

Przeworski, A., M. Alvarez, J.A. Cheibub and F. Limongi (2000), *Democracy and Development. Political Institutions and Well-Being in the World, 1950–1990*, Cambridge: Cambridge University Press.

Pennings, P., H. Keman and J. Kleinnijenhuis (2006), *Doing Research in Political Science*, London: Sage.

Scharpf, F.W. (1997), *Games Real Actors Play*, Boulder, CO: Westview Press.

Schmidt, M.G. (2002), 'The impact of political parties, constitutional structures and veto players', in H. Keman (ed.), *Comparative Democratic Politics: A Guide to Contemporary Theory and Research*, London: Sage, pp. 166–84.

Schmidt, M.G. (2008), *Demokratietheorien* (*Theories of Democracy*), 5th edn, Opladen: Leske und Budrich.

Scholten, G.H. (1968), 'Easton's Systems Analysis en het Nederlandse politieke systeem', in *Acta Politica*, **3** (3), 214–38.

Shepsle, K.A. (1995), 'Studying institutions: some lessons from the rational choice approach', in J. Farr, J. Dryzek and S. Leonard (eds), *Political Science in History: Research Programs and Political Traditions*, Cambridge: Cambridge University Press, pp. 279–95.

Torgerson, D. (1995), 'Policy analysis and public life: the restoration of phronesis?', in J. Farr, J. Dryzek and S. Leonard (1995), *Political Science in History: Research Programs and Political Traditions*, Cambridge: Cambridge University Press, pp. 225–51.

Weber, M. (1922), *Wirtschaft und Gesellschaft* (*Economy and Society*), vol. 5, reprinted 1972, Tübingen: Mohr.

Young, O. (1968), *Systems of Political Science*, Englewood Cliffs, NJ: Prentice Hall.

PART II

APPROACHES: EXPLORING POLITICAL INTERACTIONS

7 Applying multilevel governance*
Arjan H. Schakel

1 INTRODUCTION

Multilevel governance (MLG) is perhaps one of the most widely used concepts in political science and public policy. When you perform a Google Scholar search with the words 'multilevel governance' you will be overwhelmed by the number of 'hits', which total up to no less than 14 399.[1] Starting with four results in 1993, steadily climbing to 111 for 2000 and then exponentially increasing to 1320 in 2010 and to 2100 in 2014. Zürn et al. (2010, p. 1) found that MLG has been a central topic in 15–20 academic journal articles published per year for the period 2000 to 2009. The 'hits' reveal that MLG has been applied to a wide variety of MLG systems ranging from global institutions, regional organizations, such as the European Union (EU), national governments and subnational governments. There are probably as many definitions as scholars who apply MLG, but what appears to be one common denominator is that MLG is used to describe processes of reallocation of authority away from central states (Hooghe and Marks 2003; Bache and Flinders 2004; Enderlein et al. 2010).

The burst of publications on MLG led to a paradoxical situation. When so many scholars are employing the concept of MLG, surely it must be a very fruitful concept to analyze MLG systems. However, as Piattoni (2009, p. 163) notes, when a concept is widely applied to a vast number of disparate phenomena they may run into the danger of 'over-stretching' (Sartori 1970). That is, 'distortions' may occur when the concept does not fit a new set of cases (Collier and Mahon 1993). What kind of 'authority' is transferred? What is the 'direction' of the transfer of authority and to 'whom'? What is a 'level' and which upward and downward 'levels' are included in the study? Given the wide application of MLG we may raise the questions of what it helps to study and what it actually helps to explain? (Smith 2002; Piattoni 2009).

This aim of this chapter is to identify the main strengths and weaknesses of applying MLG. The objective is not to provide a comprehensive literature review (for recent excellent overviews see, for example, Eising (2015), Piattoni (2009, 2010) and Stephenson (2013)). Rather the goal is to explore the analytical leverage of the concept of MLG.

The next section discusses the origin and subsequent development of MLG and the section after that will illustrate how MLG has been applied to study policy-making within the European Union. Then I proceed to explore how far MLG provides insights into the development of a multi-level Europe. The penultimate section will explore the link between MLG and methodological nationalism and the final section summarizes and concludes.

2   THE DEVELOPMENT OF THE CONCEPT OF MULTILEVEL GOVERNANCE

The introduction of the concept of MLG can be traced back to two seminal book chapters by Gary Marks published in the early 1990s. Marks was interested in the reforms of the European Community's (EC's) structural funds policy which came along with the Maastricht Treaty. There was a considerable growth in the budget available for structural policy and there had been fundamental innovations in the administration of the structural funds. To explain the growth of funding for structural policy Marks (1992) adopted a state-centric perspective whereby member states were conceived as the ultimate arbiters of the pace and direction of European integration. However, in order to get a better understanding of the reforms of the structural funds, Marks relied on a 'more open-textured, multilevel perspective in which EC institutions are seen as independent political actors, and member states appear as complex political institutions in contested national and regional political arenas' (Marks 1992, p. 192). By focusing on a policy that went beyond the areas that are 'transparently dominated by member states [such as] financial decisions, major pieces of legislation, and the treaties' Marks found that the Commission had played a vital role and that subnational governments had become increasingly important for policy-making (Marks 1993, p. 392).

The observed difference in decision-making processes between policy areas was important because it directly confronted the main theories on institutional reform within the European Union. The debate in the litera-ture was dominated by two strands of thought. On the one hand, there were (neo)functionalists who conceived that the process of institutional change was driven by supranational institutions which could further integration by shaping institutional competencies, resources and decision-making rules (Haas 1958). Supranational institutions were able to enhance integration as soon as member states provided them with some author-ity. On the other hand, there were intergovernmentalists who argued that decision-making – including treaties and the institutional set-up of supranational institutions – was dominated by the member states and their executives (Moravcsik 1998). Marks (1993) claimed that both views did not adequately capture daily policy-making within the EU and that existing theory did not acknowledge the important role that subnational levels play.

Multilevel governance posed in particular a challenge to liberal intergovernmentalism. The central government is conceived by liberal intergovernmentalists as representing a sovereign state which has high boundary and relational integrity and controls decision-making internally vis-à-vis subnational actors and societal groups and externally vis-à-vis other sovereign states and international organizations (Bartolini 2005). The authority exercised by European institutions is pooled or delegated by the member states to make commitments more credible (Keohane and Hoffmann 1991, p. 277). Intergovernmentalists link national preference formation to strategic bargaining between states in a two-level game. National interests are framed in domestic political conflict and, once formulated, are bargained in intergovernmental fora (Moravcsik 1998). In this view, European policy-making is largely determined by central governments or their representatives and non-state interests can influence European policy only through the central government which acts as a 'gate-keeper'. Multilevel governance posed a different and opposing picture. In the case of EU structural funding Gary Marks observed that subnational governments 'have developed vertical linkages with the Commission that bypass member states and challenge their traditional role as sole intermediary between subnational and supranational levels of government' (Marks 1993, p. 402).

Looking at the conceptual origins of MLG we can concur with Piattoni's (2009, p. 165) observation that the original argument by Marks (1992, 1993) 'was stronger in its "destructive part" (*pars destruens*) than its "constructive part" (*pars construens*)'. Multilevel governance was introduced to provide for a better account of a particular decision-making process and thereby empirically challenged existing views about European policy-making, but the theoretical merits beyond that were not yet clear. Some scholars went even further and criticized MLG because it 'lacks a causal motor of integration or a set of hypotheses' (Jordan 2001, p. 201). Multilevel governance is indeed not a 'standard theory', but that does not mean that expectations can be derived as will be discussed in the next section.

3   MULTILEVEL GOVERNANCE IN THE EUROPEAN UNION

Multilevel governance may not have predictive power with regard to the question of how governance arrangements within the European Union have come to be, but it can illuminate how policies are produced within the EU (Stephenson 2013, p. 818). Multilevel governance generates hypotheses with regard to the question of whether the EU represents a system of MLG rather than one dominated by national governments (George 2004, pp. 116–17). Marks et al. (1996) offer two alternative models of the European Union. A state-centric model posits that state executives are the ultimate decision-makers for European policy-making and, when supranational institutions are set up, they serve the interests of state executives. Because state executive decision-making is done on the basis of unanimity, decisions are likely to reflect the lowest common denominator across state positions. In the state-centric model, state executives are also unitary actors and their negotiation positions can only be influenced in a discrete domestic political arena. Non-governmental and subnational groups can constrain state executives within the domestic political arena where state executives developed their preferences, but the final position and bargaining at the European level is within the full remit of member state governments (Marks et al. 1996, p. 345).

From an MLG perspective, decision-making is shared by actors at different levels rather than under the full control of state executives. Supranational institutions such as the European Commission, the European Court of Justice and the European Parliament do not act on behalf of state executives and independently influence policy-making. States do incur gains and losses arising from decision-making at the European level and lowest common-denominator policy outcomes mainly concern decisions with regard to the scope of integration. Member states do not function as 'gatekeepers' of interests of subnational groups and domestic actors operate in both national and supranational arenas (Marks et al. 1996, p. 346).

The two contrasting models present testable propositions with regard to the question of who decides in European policy-making. On the basis of secondary sources, Marks et al. (1996) explored the validity of the two models across four phases of the policy-making process (Table 7.1). The findings do not unequivocally provide support for either of the models but they do pose a significant challenge to the state-centric model. The authors conclude that MLG does not reject that state governments are important but rather that European policy-making 'is characterized by mutual dependence, complementary functions and overlapping competencies' (Marks et al. 1996, p. 372).

Table 7.1   *Multilevel governance in the European Union according to policy stage*

Policy stage	Multilevel governance
Policy initiation	Agenda-setting is shared between the Commission, Council and European Parliament. Interests groups and subnational actors strive to influence the process
Decision-making	The Council is the senior actor in the decision-making stage but the European Parliament and the European Commission are indispensable partners through the co-decision and conciliation procedures
Implementation	The European Commission is directly involved in day-to-day implementation in a number of policy areas. Subnational authorities and interests groups participate in implementation through comitology
Adjudication	With the help of the European Commission and national courts, the European Court of Justice has transformed the legal order in a supranational direction

Note: The table summarizes the main findings of Marks et al. (1996, pp. 356–71).

The academic debate about whether a state-centric or MLG model provides a better description of European policy-making is ongoing, but the example indicates that MLG can generate testable hypotheses to guide empirical research. The study by Marks et al. (1996) illustrates that MLG is not a theory in the traditional sense. That is, from MLG we cannot derive precise hypotheses when and how decision-making powers will be dispersed from central government. However, when MLG is applied to a multilevel political system we can explore how far authority is monopolized by central governments or whether powers are shared among subnational and supranational institutions and non-state interests.

In addition to understanding the 'nature of the beast' scholarly interest was also devoted to understanding the workings of EU's jurisdictional architecture. Drawing on his prior analysis of German politics, Scharpf (1988) introduced the 'joint decision making trap' to show how divergent national interests under EU membership prevented national governments from making policy while blocking the EU from taking joint decisions. Scharpf's analysis underscored the expectation that MLG could hamper effective policy-making in the EU since it introduces institutional complexity, multiple veto-players and various supranational and subnational actors vying for influence. However, Scharpf's article was published at the same time as the EU was entering into a phase of major institutional innovations, starting with the Single European Act in 1986 (Eising 2015, p. 173). These developments induced Arthur Benz to take up the puzzle of how the EU was able to escape from the joint decision-making trap. Benz (2010, p. 220) describes the EU as a loosely coupled structure of MLG which uses a 'flexible combination of cooperation, competition and control' to avoid clashes between member states. Policy solutions are found by seeking consensus even under majoritarian rules, by allowing derogations to treaty commitments, and by legislating by directive that binds in goals but not means.

Eising (2015, p. 174) observes that the important theoretical contributions by Scharpf and Benz to the study of EU multilevel governance 'draw on established theoretical frameworks (such as neo-institutionalism, rational choice, systems and negotiation theories), integrate interaction mechanisms and mid-range theorems into these theories (hierarchy, joint decision-making, loose and tight coupling of levels, etc.) and *link them to the institutional configuration of multilevel settings*' (emphasis added). This observation underlines the criticisms by Jordan (2001, p. 201) who notes that MLG 'needs to be fleshed out with causal accounts drawn from other theoretical traditions'. From MLG one can derive expectations for what kind of system the EU is, but in order to increase understanding of the functioning of MLG within the EU, scholars have to rely on other theories.

4   MULTILEVEL GOVERNANCE BELOW AND ABOVE THE CENTRAL STATE

Multilevel governance has contributed to our understanding of the functioning of the EU but has MLG something to offer in understanding developments in governance *within* the state? Institutional reform at the European level has coincided with decentralization within the state (Loughlin 2004). Writing at about the same time as Marks (1992, 1993) introduced the concept of MLG, Mény and Wright (1985) and Page (1991) noticed that regionalization processes took off in various countries in the 1970s and 1980s. Sharpe (1993) observed a rise of what he labeled 'meso-government' since the 1970s. The twinning processes of regionalization and Europeanization spurred a literature on 'new' regionalism (Keating and Loughlin 1997) which suggested that regionalism was stimulated by European integration through structural policy and the reinforcement of the principles of subsidiarity and partnership by the Maastricht Treaty in 1992. The early 1990s also witnessed the introduction of the notion of 'Europe of the Regions' which refers to a federal Europe in which the constituent units would be regions and not nation-states (Loughlin 1996).

Enthusiasm for a European federation of regions have by now toned down. The Committee of the Regions, a consultative assembly of subnational leaders across the EU, has issued a Charter for Multilevel Governance which sets out principles and methods for involving regions in national and European decision-making. The goal is 'Europe *with* the regions' not 'Europe *of* the regions' (Schakel et al. 2015, p. 277, original emphases). Multivariate analysis suggests that the effect of European integration on subnational authority is muted (Schakel 2009; Tatham 2012). The simultaneous processes of downward and upward reallocation of authority have inspired MLG scholarship to study the restructuring of polities.

Hooghe and Marks (2003) distinguished between two ideal types of governance which they simply labelled type I and type II. Type I MLG is drawn from federalism whereby authority is allocated across general-purpose, non-intersecting jurisdictions which are responsible for providing a number of policies. One may find type I jurisdictions at few levels from the local to the global and the institutional framework tends to be system-wide and durable (Hooghe and Marks 2003, pp. 236–7). In contrast, type II MLG consists of a set of special-purpose jurisdictions that carry out specific tasks. Type II jurisdictions may overlap (that is, they are not 'nested'), they can operate at various territorial scales and they tend to be flexible (ibid., pp. 237–9). Subnational dispersion of authority follows the logic of type I whereas type II arrangements can be found at the national/international frontier where functionally differentiated type II arrangements are set up by type I general-purpose jurisdictions (Hooghe and Marks 2010). The concept of MLG was originally employed in the analysis of *policies* and the two ideal types of MLG allow for exploring the territorial restructuring of *polities* (Eising 2015; Piattoni 2010).

To what extent has authority been reallocated downwards and upwards from central states? Hooghe et al. (2010) track decentralization to regions – defined as intermediate tiers between national and local government with an average population of more than 150 000 – in 42 countries for 1950 until 2006. Regional authority is estimated along two domains: self-rule (the authority exercised by regional government over those who live in the region) and shared rule (the authority exercised by a regional government or its representatives in the country as a whole). The authors find that out of 27 EU countries in 2006, 21 have become more regionalized. Twenty additional levels of government have been established and not one disestablished. The biggest drivers of the growth of regional authority have been the proliferation of elected institutions at the regional level (from eight to 20 assemblies), and the accumulation of the functions of government held by those institutions.

Börzel (2005) has charted the evolution of formal rules concerning national/EU decision-making across 18 policy areas from the Rome

Treaty (1957) to the Constitutional Treaty (2005). Formal decision-making is estimated according to scope (the extent to which the EU plays a role in policy) and depth (the supranational or intergovernmental character of the decision rules). In 1957, the EU had only significant competences in agriculture, but with various treaty reforms the number of policies allocated to the EU has gradually increased. The EU has now extensive competencies for economic external relations, environment and consumer protection, occupational health and safety standards, economic freedoms, energy and transport, territorial, economic and social cohesion, and monetary policy. There is not one policy which has shifted back from the European to the national level.

Börzel (2005) and Hooghe et al. (2010) show that regionalization and Europeanization are coherent processes of change and both studies give credence to the claim that the jurisdictional architecture of Europe has become multilevel. How can we explain the rise in MLG within the EU? Here Jordan's criticism of MLG comes to the fore again: MLG 'lacks a causal motor' and 'it does not explain the creation of MLG' (Jordan 2001, p. 201). However, we can gain insight into the causes of MLG by drawing on literature which theorizes the structure of government.

According to a public goods perspective, the structure of government will reflect the efficient production of public goods given their economies of scale and externalities (Oates 1972; Alesina and Spolaore 2003). Multilevel governance should be very common since the externalities and scale effects of most policies provided by government – for example, health, education, economic development, spatial planning, environment and welfare services – encompass a variety of territorial scales so we would expect some policies to be decentralized and others to be provided by central or supranational government. The process of regionalization parallels the growth of government responsibility for welfare, environmental, education, health, and transport (Sharpe 1993). The territorial scope of externalities and scale effects of these policies are diverse and, as a result, are most efficiently delivered at the local, regional and national levels (Ter-Minassian 1997; Osterkamp and Eller 2003). European integration largely follows a functional logic (for example, international trade, transport, energy, competition, environment, research, and immigration), however, other policies (for example, regional and cohesion policy and agricultural subsidies) became European competences because they were political side-payments (Alesina et al. 2005). In addition, not all policies with collective functional benefits are fully Europeanized, such as national security, defense and foreign policy. These policies are often considered to touch upon the core of national sovereignty and these exceptions draw our attention to a second approach for understanding the structure of government.

Identity may function as a powerful 'magnet' and attract decision-making authority to lower jurisdictional scales. Territorial-based and distinct groups may demand self-rule so that they can decide policy according to their own preferences. The presence of ethnic or territorial minorities and their effects on the jurisdictional design within the state has been widely acknowledged in the literature (Amoretti and Bermeo 2004; Brancati 2008). Research has also shown that national identities may impact heavily on preferences with regard to the level European integration (Carey 2002; Hooghe and Marks 2005). Also, jurisdictional design above and below the state have become politicized. The growth of regional parties leads to an increased and intensified demand for self-rule (Massetti and Schakel 2013) and a deepening and widening Europe went alongside with a growing number and increasing electoral strength of Eurosceptic parties in the member states (Szczerbiak and Taggart 2008).

5 MULTILEVEL GOVERNANCE AND METHODOLOGICAL NATIONALISM

Multilevel governance concerns the analysis of upwards, downwards and sideways transfers of decision-making authority away from the central government to other (non-)governmental actors. Multilevel governance may pose three challenges to the sovereign state (Piattoni 2009, p. 173). First, states have pooled authority in international organizations and have become increasingly subject to international coordination and regulation. Second, unitary states devolve powers to subnational units to the point of federal arrangements whereby authority is divided over government tiers. Third, public power is also increasingly shared with non-governmental and private interest groups.[2] These three challenges nicely tie into a criticism posed by methodological nationalism.

Methodological nationalism refers to the tendency within social science to focus on the nation-state as the main unit of analysis in studying social and political life, and, in consequence, to neglect actors below and above the state as a unit for political analysis (Jeffery and Wincott 2010). According to Ulrich Beck 'it is a nation-state outlook on society and politics, law, justice and history' that has governed the social science imagination (Beck 2002, p. 52). Social science scholars often conceive the nation-state to be the most important scale at which social and political life is organized and often distinguish between different nation-states so that comparative analysis at that scale can be carried out. The critique of methodological nationalism does not imply that work based on nation-states as a unit of analysis is not useful. Rather, the critique of methodological nationalism points out a potential risk. That is, taking nation-states as a unit of analysis may import an unreflected assumption that everything else is subordinate to national politics; it underscores the uncritical methodological assumption that the national scale of politics is the only one of 'real' importance. As a consequence, phenomena not manifest or not perceived to be significant at the scale of the nation-state can remain 'hidden from view' (Wimmer and Glick Schiller 2002, p. 302).

At the subnational level, MLG opened up a whole world which was, conceptually speaking, inhabited only by unitary and federal states. Many countries created or reformed subnational tiers of government but very few countries moved between the unitary and the federal categories. The scale of change becomes apparent only when we escape methodological nationalism. Multilevel governance within the state poses a significant challenge for future research. Building the datasets around regional units of analysis that will enable a more nuanced appreciation of the regional dimensions of multilevel statehood is difficult, for the simple reason that there are many more regions than there are states (Jeffery and Schakel 2013).

Instead of seeing state executives as the main drivers of European integration and the prime producers of European policy, MLG draws scholarly attention towards the influence exercised by supranational and subnational actors. Multilevel governance broadens the scope of relevant units of analysis and thereby reveals that, in day-to-day European policy-making, authority is shared among a variety of actors and institutions. Multilevel governance has succeeded in challenging the view present in much of EU scholarship that nation-states are dominant and thereby MLG has proven to be a powerful corrective for methodological nationalism in EU studies.

6   CONCLUSION

This chapter set out to explore the analytical leverage of applying the concept of MLG. The introduction of MLG served to provide a precise description of day-to-day policy-making in the EU and thereby posed a weighty challenge to theory. Central states do not monopolize decision-making in the EU; rather, authority is shared with supranational institutions and subnational actors which mobilize at the European level. Multilevel governance has been criticized because it is not a theory. However, MLG allows for deriving hypotheses with regard to the functioning of multilevel systems. The criticism has merit in that scholars need to rely on well-established theoretical frameworks to illuminate the operating logic of multilevel institutions and to provide insight into the causes of reallocation of authority. Multilevel governance enhances scientific inquiry by challenging methodological nationalism. The central state is not the only or the most important unit of analysis for understanding decision-making in multilevel political systems. Scholars should also take account of a variety of supranational and subnational institutions and actors who also exercise significant authority. To summarize:

- Multilevel governance refers to the vertical and horizontal dispersion of authority away from central states.
- The main criticism with regard to the concept of multilevel governance is that it is not a theory but just a mere concept useful for descriptive purposes.
- From multilevel governance we can generate hypotheses with regard to the functioning of multilevel political systems.
- Scholars need to rely on other theories to understand the working mechanisms of multilevel governance systems and to identify causes for the reallocation of authority away from central states.
- Applying multilevel governance enhances scientific inquiry by enlarging the scope of relevant units of analysis from central states to supranational and subnational governments and actors.

NOTES

*   This chapter was written while I was a Fellow at the Hanse-Wissenschaftskolleg in Delmenhorst, Germany. I would like to thank Michaël Tatham and an anonymous reviewer for comments.
1. The Google Scholar search was done on 6 February 2015 with the words 'multilevel governance' in the search field and citations are not included. The number of 'hits' are underestimated since the hyphenated variant ('multi-level governance') was not used for the search.
2. This chapter primarily discusses examples of MLG within the EU and its member states. For examples of MLG applied to global governance and non-governmental actors see respectively Zürn (2012) and Eising (2015).

ESSENTIAL READING

Bache, I. (2008), *Europeanization and Multilevel Governance: Cohesion Policy in the European Union and Britain*, Lanham, MD: Rowman & Littlefield.
Bache, I. and M. Flinders (eds) (2004), *Multi-Level Governance*, Oxford: Oxford University Press.
Enderlein, H., M. Zürn, and S. Wälti (eds) (2010), *Handbook on Multi-Level Governance*, Cheltenham, UK and Northampton, MA, USA: Edward Elgar.

Hooghe, L. and G. Marks (2001), *Multi-Level Governance and European Integration*, Lanham, MD: Rowman & Littlefield.
Piattoni, S. (2010), *The Theory of Multi-Level Governance: Conceptual, Empirical, and Normative Challenges*, Oxford: Oxford University Press.
Stephenson, P. (2013), 'Twenty years of multi-level governance: "Where does it come from? What is it? Where is it going?"', *Journal of European Public Policy*, **20** (6), 817–37.

REFERENCES

Alesina, A. and E. Spolaore (2003), *The Size of Nations*, Cambridge, MA: MIT Press.
Alesina, A., I. Angeloni, and L. Schuknecht (2005), 'What does the European Union do?', *Public Choice*, **123** (3–4), 275–319.
Amoretti, U.M. and N. Bermeo (eds) (2004), *Federalism and Territorial Cleavages*, Baltimore, MD: Johns Hopkins University Press.
Bache, I. and M. Flinders (eds) (2004), *Multi-Level Governance*, Oxford: Oxford University Press.
Bartolini, S. (2005), *Restructuring Europe: Center Formation, System Building and Political Structuring between the Nation-State and the European Union*, New York: Oxford University Press.
Beck, U. (2002), 'The terrorist threat: world risk society revisited', *Theory, Culture and Society*, **19** (4), 39–55.
Benz, A. (2010), 'The European Union as a loosely coupled multi-level system', in H. Enderlein, S. Wälti, and M. Zürn (eds), *Handbook on Multilevel Governance*, Cheltenham, UK and Northampton, MA, USA: Edward Elgar, pp. 214–27.
Börzel, T.A. (2005), 'Mind the gap! European integration between level and scope', *Journal of European Public Policy*, **12** (2), 217–36.
Brancati, D. (2008), 'The origins and strengths of regional parties', *British Journal of Political Science*, **38** (1), 135–59.
Carey, S. (2002), 'Undivided loyalties: is national identity an obstacle to European integration?', *European Union Politics*, **3** (4), 387–413.
Collier, D. and J.E. Mahon Jr (1993), 'Conceptual "stretching" revisited: adapting categories in comparative analysis', *American Political Science Review*, **87** (4), 845–55.
Eising, R. (2015), 'Multilevel governance in Europe', in J.M. Magone (ed.), *Routledge Handbook of European Politics*, London: Routledge, pp. 165–83.
Enderlein, H., M. Zürn, and S. Wälti (eds) (2010), *Handbook on Multi-Level Governance*, Cheltenham, UK and Northampton, MA, USA: Edward Elgar.
George, S. (2004), 'Multi-level governance and the European Union', in I. Bache and M. Flinders (eds), *Multi-Level Governance*, Oxford: Oxford University Press, pp. 307–26.
Haas, E.B. (1958), *The Uniting of Europe: Political, Social and Economic Forces, 1950–57*, Stanford, CA: Stanford University Press.
Hooghe, L. and G. Marks (2003), 'Unraveling the central state but how? Types of multi-level governance', *American Political Science Review*, **97** (2), 233–43.
Hooghe, L. and G. Marks (2005), 'Calculation, community, and cues: public opinion on European integration', *European Union Politics*, **6** (4), 421–45.
Hooghe, L. and G. Marks (2010), 'Types of multi-level governance', in H. Enderlein, S. Wälti, and M. Zürn (eds), *Handbook on Multilevel Governance*, Cheltenham, UK and Northampton, MA, USA: Edward Elgar, pp. 17–31.
Hooghe, L., G. Marks, and A.H. Schakel (2010), *The Rise of Regional Authority: A Comparative Study of 42 Democracies*, London: Routledge.
Jeffery C. and D. Wincott (2010), 'The challenge of territorial politics: beyond methodological nationalism', in C. Hay (ed.), *New Directions in Political Science*, Basingstoke, UK: Palgrave Macmillan, pp. 167–88.

Jeffery, C. and A.H. Schakel (2013), 'Insights: methods and data beyond methodological nationalism', *Regional Studies*, **47** (3), 402–4.

Jordan, A. (2001), 'The European Union: an evolving system of multi-level governance . . . or government?', *Policy & Politics*, **29** (2), 193–208.

Keating, M. and J. Loughlin (eds) (1997), *The Political Economy of Regionalism*, London: Frank Cass.

Keohane, R.O. and S. Hoffmann (1991), *The New European Community: Decision Making and Institutional Change*, Boulder, CO: Westview.

Loughlin, J. (1996), '"Europe of the regions" and the federalization of Europe', *Publius*, **26** (4), 141–62.

Loughlin, J. (2004), *Subnational Democracy in the European Union*, Oxford: Oxford University Press.

Marks, G. (1992), 'Structural policy in the European Community', in A.M. Sbragia (ed.), *Europolitics: Institutions and Policymaking in the 'New' European Community*, Washington, DC: Brookings Institute, pp. 191–225.

Marks, G. (1993), 'Structural policy and multi-level governance in the EC', in A.W. Cafruny and G.G. Rosenthal (eds), *The State of the European Community: The Maastricht Debate and Beyond*, Boulder, CO: Lynne Rienner, pp. 391–411.

Marks, G., L. Hooghe, and K. Blank (1996), 'European integration from the 1980s: state-centric v. multi-level governance', *Journal of Common Market Studies*, **34** (3), 341–78.

Massetti, E. and A.H. Schakel (2013), 'Ideology matters: why decentralisation has a differentiated effect on regionalist parties' fortunes in Western democracies', *European Journal of Political Research*, **52** (6), 797–821.

Mény, Y. and V. Wright (eds) (1985), *Centre-Periphery Relations in Western Europe*, London: George Allen & Unwin.

Moravcsik, A. (1998), *The Choice for Europe. Social Purpose and State Power from Messina to Maastricht*, Ithaca, NY: Cornell University Press.

Oates, W.E. (1972), *Fiscal Federalism*, New York: Harcourt Brace Jovanovich.

Osterkamp, R. and M. Eller (2003), 'How decentralized is government activity?', Cesifo DICE Report No. 1/2003, 32–5.

Page, E.C. (1991), *Localism and Regionalism in Europe*, Oxford: Oxford University Press.

Piattoni, S. (2009), 'Multilevel governance: a historical and conceptual analysis', *Journal of European Integration*, **31** (2), 163–80.

Piattoni, S. (2010), *The Theory of Multi-Level Governance: Conceptual, Empirical, and Normative Challenges*, Oxford: Oxford University Press.

Sartori, G. (1970), 'Concept misformation in comparative politics', *American Political Science Review*, **64** (4), 1033–53.

Schakel, A.H. (2009), 'A postfunctionalist theory of regional government: An inquiry into regional authority and regional policy provision', dissertation, Vrije Universiteit Amsterdam.

Schakel, A.H., L. Hooghe, and G. Marks (2015), 'Multilevel governance and the state', in S. Leibfried, E. Huber, M. Lange, J.D. Levy, and J.D. Stephens (eds), *The Oxford Handbook of Transformations of the State*, Oxford: Oxford University Press, pp. 266–82.

Scharpf, F.W. (1988), 'The joint-decision trap: lessons from German federalism and European integration', *Public Administration*, **66** (3), 239–78.

Sharpe, L.J. (1993), The European meso: an appraisal, in L.J. Sharpe (ed.), *The Rise of Meso Government in Europe*, London: Sage, pp. 1–39.

Smith, A. (2002), 'Studying multi-level governance. Examples from French translations of the structural funds', *Comparative and International Administration*, **75** (4), 711–29.

Stephenson, P. (2013), 'Twenty years of multi-level governance: "Where does it come from? What is it? Where is it going?"', *Journal of European Public Policy*, **20** (6), 817–37.

Szczerbiak, A. and P. Taggart (eds) (2008), *Opposing Europe? The Comparative Party Politics of Euroscepticism*, Oxford: Oxford University Press.

Tatham, M. (2012), 'You do what you have to do? Salience and territorial interest represen-tation in EU environmental affairs', *European Union Politics*, **13** (3), 434–50.
Ter-Minassian, T. (1997), 'Intergovernmental fiscal relations in a macroeconomic perspective: an overview', in T. Ter-Minassian (ed.), *Fiscal Federalism in Theory and Practice*, Washington: International Monetary Fund, pp. 3–24.
Wimmer, A. and N. Glick Schiller (2002), 'Methodological nationalism and beyond: nation-state building, migration and the social sciences', *Global Networks*, **2** (4), 301–34.
Zürn, M. (2012), 'Global governance as multi-level governance', in D. Levi-Faur (ed.), *The Oxford Handbook of Governance*, Oxford: Oxford University Press, pp. 730–44.
Zürn, M., S. Wälti, and H. Enderlein (2010), 'Introduction', in H. Enderlein, S. Wälti, and M. Zürn (eds), *Handbook on Multi-Level Governance*, Cheltenham, UK and Northampton, MA, USA: Edward Elgar, pp. 1–13.

8 Regime types: measuring democracy and autocracy
Manfred G. Schmidt

1 INTRODUCTION

Regime types such as democracy and autocracy are mutually exclusive and opposite from each other. Many classifications and typologies have been put forward in political science with respect to regime types. Although there is agreement on the major features demonstrating what makes these types differ from each other, there is much less agreement on how to measure them and, in particular, as regards the within-differences (see Collier et al. 2008). Yet it is important to define and measure the variation within and between democratic and autocratic regimes because it enables the researcher to analyse relationships between regimes and, for example, economic development, political participation and opposition, transitions as well as regression from the one type to the other (Geddes 2009). This chapter portrays major measures of democracy and autocracy ranging from R.A. Dahl's path-breaking *Polyarchy* (1971) and the Polity IV Project to the Freedom House political rights and civil liberties ratings and more recent indices such as the Status Index of the Bertelsmann Transformation Index, the Effective Democracy Index and the Combined Index of Democracy.

2 TOWARDS MEASURING DEMOCRACIES AND AUTOCRACIES

It is not a simple undertaking to come up with precise measurements for democracies and their non-democratic counterparts, autocracies. For a long time, Aristotle's definition of the different systems of government with their varying number of rulers and the quality of their rule was considered the standard by which regimes were measured. Aristotle categorized democracy as an egocentric version of rule by the many, in contrast to rule of the demos in favour of the common good and in further contrast to rule by the few, such as in aristocracies or oligarchies, and to rule by one, as in the case of a monarchy or a tyranny (Everson 1996). Later, indicators at a higher level of measurement were put into play to classify systems of government such as the percentage of the adult population which participated in national elections (Nohlen and Stöver 2010).

The universal franchise and the participation of the citizenry in elections to vote the political leadership in and out of office constitute only one dimension of democracy, though; democracy also includes opportunities for unimpeded public contestation in interest articulation, interest aggregation and decision-making. Robert Dahl measured both of these dimensions – participation and contestation or opposition – for 114 countries in his ground-breaking work *Polyarchy* (Dahl 1971). He defined participation as 'eligibility to participate in elections', which he measured by the 'percent of adult citizens eligible to vote', using a three-part scale: less than 20 percent, 20–90 percent and over 90 percent (Dahl 1971, pp. 232–4). It was a more complex undertaking, though, to measure the second dimension, the 'degree of opportunity for public contestation or political opposition' (ibid., p. 235). In order to accomplish this, a long list of variables were selected from the *Cross-Polity Survey* (Banks and Textor 1971) as indicators of the most important conditions for public contestation: the right to freely form organizations, freedom of expression and of the press, access to independent sources of information, free and fair elections, and institutions that guarantee responsive government policies (Dahl 1971, pp. 235–7). Using these criteria, Dahl identified 26 democracies in the late 1960s, defining democracies as 'fully inclusive polyarchies' (ibid., p. 248), by which he meant developed but not perfectly democratic regimes. To this he added three countries with more electoral restrictions – Chile, Switzerland and the USA – and six 'near-polyarchies', including Turkey and Venezuela.

Dahl's *Polyarchy* is a major contribution to the measurement of democracy (and indirectly to the measurement of autocracies). Since then, a wealth of studies have continued to further develop the measurement of democratic and autocratic regimes. Examples of these studies include the contributions in Inkeles (1991) and Vanhanen (2003), who, following Dahl's *Polyarchy*, developed an index of democratization for 170 states from the nineteenth to the early twenty-first century. Vanhanen, though, reduced the dimension of 'participation' to the percentage of active voters in a population. Moreover, he used a single indicator for Dahl's complex dimension of contestation, which he measured by subtracting from 100 the percentage of votes received or seats held by the strongest party in a national parliamentary election (Vanhanen 2003, pp. 59–67; see also Table 8.1).

Of the various measurements of democracy, only those that are especially productive for the comparative analysis of systems of democratic

Table 8.1   Measurements of democracy and autocracy for selected sovereign states from the twentieth to the twenty-first century

1 State	2 Democracy minus autocracy ('Polity') 1950	3 Democracy minus autocracy ('Polity') 2013	4 Vanhanen's index of democratization 2001	5 Political Rights rating 2013	6 Civil Liberties rating 2013	7 Extended Status Index (Bertelsmann Stiftung 2014) 2013	8 Combined Index of Democracy (KID3D) 1996–2010
China	−8	−7	0.0	7	6	5	0.00
Germany	10	10	35.5	1	1	0	9.74
France	10	9	27.7	1	1	0	9.22
Great Britain and Northern Ireland	10	10	33.5	1	1	0	9.75
India	9	9	17.1	2	3	1	7.48
Netherlands	10	10	38.4	1	1	0	9.81
North Korea	−7	−10	0.0	7	7	5	0.00
Russian Federation	−9	4	28.0	6	5	4	3.26
Saudi Arabia	−10	−10	0.0	7	7	5	0.00
Sweden	10	10	37.7	1	1	0	9.93
Tunisia			1.6	3	3	3	2.16
USA	10	10	34.4	1	1	0	9.59

Table 8.1 (continued)

Notes:

Russian Federation: values for 1950 refer to the Soviet Union.

Columns 2 and 3: 'Polity' indicators from Polity IV (Marshall et al. 2014). 10: fully developed democracy; 6–9: democracy; 1–5: open anocracy; −5 to 0: closed anocracy; −10 to −6: autocracy.

Column 4: Democratization index (Vanhanen 2003, p. 141ff.). Maximum: 100 (fully developed democracy), minimum: 0 (full autocracy).

Columns 5 and 6: Freedom House Index of Political Rights (2013) and Index of Civil Liberties (2013) (Puddington 2014, pp. 82–3).

Column 7: Status Index, as augmented by the author, based on Bertelsmann Stiftung (2014, p. 25). Ordinal scale measurements of the established democracies were added (by which is meant states with values of 1 or 2 on the Freedom House political rights and civil liberties ratings, provided that these states have not been classified as defective democracies on the Status Index). The newly added states have received a status of 'democracy' and receive a rating of 0. A rating of 1 means 'democracy in the process of consolidation'; 2 means 'defective democracy'; 3 stands for 'strongly defective democracy'; 4 for 'moderate autocracy'; and 5 for 'hardline autocracy'.

Column 8: The Combined Index of Democracy (KID3D Index) is calculated by taking the third root of the product of the World Bank rule of law indicator, the Polity IV democracy indicator and the sum of the Freedom House political rights and civil liberties ratings. 0–4.99: autocracy; 5–6.99: defective democracy; 7–10: non-defective democracy (Lauth 2013). The simple KID Index is the square root of the product of KID3D and the World Bank political instability index (Lauth 2013).

and autocratic government – according to the criteria of validity, reliability, differentiation, availability of cross-sectional and longitudinal data, and applicability to measuring democracy and autocracy – will be given a more thorough introduction in this chapter (Schmidt 2010, pp. 370–98).[1]

3 DEMOCRACY AND AUTOCRACY MEASURES FOR THE NINETEENTH, TWENTIETH AND TWENTY-FIRST CENTURY

Most of the measurements of democracy that have been developed since the 1970s record more precisely than their predecessors the extent to which political institutions control the executive by means of separation of powers, checks and balances, and fundamental rights that are not subject to political negotiation (Freedom House 2014). Consequently, these measurements of democracy are more sensitive to one of the central pillars of modern constitutional democracies: the institutional limitations on the executive's power to shape political decision-making processes. One example is the Polity IV Project's scales of democracy and autocracy, which record democratic and non-democratic regime types around the world from the early nineteenth to the twenty-first century (Marshall et al. 2014). According to Polity IV, democracy is characterized by three key items: (1) institutions and processes that allow citizens to effectively express their political preferences and to combine these preferences into a package of alternatives from which they can choose, (2) institutional constraints on the executive and (3) guaranteed civil rights and liberties for all citizens of the state. If all of these conditions are met, the regime in question is classified as an institutionalized democracy (Marshall et al. 2014, p. 14). When the degree of democracy of a regime type is being measured, though, only the first and second key items are included; the third key item, civil rights and liberties, is not used.

The Polity IV Project measures systems of government in three steps. In the first step, an indicator of democracy ('Democracy') comes into play; this is followed by an indicator of autocracy in the second step ('Autocracy'). In the third step, both indicators are combined to give an aggregate value ('Polity'). The indicators of democracy and autocracy are each based on an 11-point scale that ranges from 0 (no democracy or no autocracy) to 10 (maximal democracy or maximal autocracy). Democracy is measured by means of four indicators that are weighted and added together: (1) the degree of competitiveness of political participation (coded using a three-point scale that ranges from competitive to non-competitive); (2) the openness of recruiting office-holders; (3) the degree of competitiveness of executive recruitment (where the difference between electing the office-holder and authoritarian selection is decisive); and (4) limitations on the executive (using a scale that ranges from powerful institutional constraints on executive power – which Polity IV ascribes to the USA and Germany – to the executive being allowed a great deal of flexibility – as in the case of France during the presidency of Charles de Gaulle).

When autocracy is being measured, a fifth indicator, the regulation of political participation (differentiated according to whether fragmented or restricted), is added to the four democracy indicators. According to Polity IV, autocracies are largely characterized by non-competitive, repressively regulated political participation, by undemocratic, non-competitive recruitment of the political leadership and by an executive with a great deal of leeway for action. Polity IV measures the degree of democracy and degree of autocracy separately and combines the two measurements into one indicator, 'Polity', that is supposed to represent the regime type in all its democratic and non-democratic facets.

'Polity' is calculated by subtracting the autocracy score from the democracy score. The final score can therefore range from -10 to $+10$. Minus 10 indicates a regime that does not have a single democratic quality but has a top score on the autocracy scale, such as North Korea. Plus 10, on the other hand, is used to characterize a regime that has no autocratic qualities but has the highest score on the democracy scale ('full democracy'), such as most of the Western European and North American countries. Values between $+6$ and $+9$ signify (simple) democracy. Autocracies are characterized by scores between -6 and -10, for example, Qatar and Saudi Arabia. The remaining values indicate open or closed 'anocracies', that is, incoherent autocratic–democratic mixes, for example, currently the Russian Federation.

In 2013, Polity IV counted 35 'full democracies' and 59 further simple democracies (that is, having a 'Polity' score between $+6$ and $+9$). Thus, 57 percent of all countries were more or less democratic in 2013. That is comparatively many, as a historical comparison shows. In 1875, only 8 countries were democratic (that is, having a 'Polity' score of at least $+6$): Belgium, Costa Rica, France, Greece, Columbia, New Zealand, Switzerland and the USA. In 1950, the number was up to 24, or 30 percent of all countries, and in 1989, on the eve of the fall of the Iron Curtain, there were 36 democracies. All the other states were either pure autocracies – in 2013, for instance, they numbered 20 – or intermediate forms with incoherent scores of democracy and autocracy, the so-called 'open anocracies' or 'closed anocracies' (in 2013, there were 50 in all).

Judging by the numbers and relative frequencies, democracy has gained in importance, yet years of democratic expansion were followed by phases of stagnation and contraction. Examples of the latter include the triumphal march of fascism across Italy in the 1920s and the collapse of democracy in Germany, Austria and Spain in the 1930s. In addition, a number of European democracies were occupied by the German army during the Second World War. Even after the end of the war, democracy suffered several setbacks; Poland, Hungary, Czechoslovakia and East Germany fell under the Soviet sphere of influence. Furthermore, a number of democracies collapsed during the 1950s and 1960s, especially in the Third World. Even during the third wave of democratization (Huntington 1991) starting in the early 1970s, there were some democracies that collapsed, such as Argentina (1976–82), Chile (1973–87) and Lebanon (since 1975; see: Marshall et al. 2014).

The designers of the democracy and autocracy scales did pioneer work with their measures that reach all the way back to the early nineteenth century. They smoothed the way for comparative research on regime structures, their prerequisites and their consequences. This is a notable accomplishment worthy of praise. However, the Polity IV measurements of democracy and autocracy are not without their problems. The indicators deal with the constitutional reality only in part and with the existence and realization of civil rights and liberties not at all. The basic idea of measuring the constraints on the executive needs to have a more complex measurement added, for instance, a measurement on the model of the index of counter-majoritarian institutions (Schmidt 2010, p. 332, table 8) or on the model of the veto player theory (Tsebelis 2002). In addition, the Polity IV Project's measurements of democracy and autocracy are rather executive-heavy. For one thing, the difference between suffrage for the few and suffrage for all adult citizens is not taken fully into consideration in these measurements. This is also true of the treatment of the relative sizes of electorates and of the voters' ability to have a say in voting the political leadership in and out of office. This has resulted in serious errors. Here is one example: according to Polity IV, the USA has been a respectable institutionalized democracy since 1810. However, that is a historical misrepresentation, since in the early nineteenth century only a small proportion of adults in the United States were eligible to vote. Also, in the early 1830s, when Alexis de Tocqueville visited America, which he described in *De la Démocracie en Amérique* (1830 and 1835 [1981]), America was still miles away from being a non-defective democracy. For example, slaves were barred from political participation until the abolition of slavery. Even after the introduction of the universal franchise, though, political participation rights, particularly those of African Americans, were cut back on a large scale.

4   POLITICAL RIGHTS AND CIVIL LIBERTIES: THE FREEDOM HOUSE RATINGS

The reports published by Freedom House, a non-profit organization in Washington, DC, contain useful measurements of democracy and autocracy. Freedom House has provided yearly measurements since 1971 on the state of political rights and civil liberties in every contemporary sovereign state. The political rights rating and the civil liberties rating are used to chronicle this information. A state is said to grant its citizens political rights if it allows them to form political parties that have significantly different agendas and whose leaders compete to acquire or maintain positions of political leadership in open, competitive and organized elections. Civil liberties are said to exist in a country if it respects and promotes citizens' civil rights and liberties, their right of free association and their property rights.

The political rights and civil liberties ratings each range from 1 to 7. The value 1 represents full rights or fully developed civil liberties, and 7 represents the complete absence of political rights or civil liberties. The two scores are then combined to give a freedom rating. This rating ranges from 2 to 14, where 2 indicates secure, comprehensive political rights and comprehensive civil liberties. This value (or a neighbouring value) signals lively political participation and highly developed civil liberties in the sense of the constitutional liberal democracies of Europe and North America. The value of 14, on the other hand, signals the complete absence of these rights and opportunities for participation; examples include Saudi Arabia and North Korea.

Freedom House groups its observations into 'free', 'partly free' and 'not free' states, according to whether the average of the political rights and civil liberties scores lies between 1.0 and 2.5 ('free'), between 3.0 and 5.0 ('partly free') or between 5.5 and 7.0 ('not free'). In 2013, for instance, Freedom House ranked 88 countries as 'free'. This represents 45 percent of all countries and 40 percent of the global population. In contrast, 59 countries, or approximately 30 percent of all countries, were rated that year as 'partly free', and 48 countries (25 percent) as 'not free'.

The political rights and the civil liberties ratings measure the right of association and civil rights and liberties. They can also be taken as proxies for constitutional democracies and indirectly as proxies for autocracies. Here, democracy is taken to mean a political system in which the people freely select leaders to make decisions on their behalf from among competing groups and individuals who have not been put forward by the government. This is a close borrowing of Joseph Schumpeter's definition of democracy (Schumpeter 1942 [1996]). However, in contrast to

Schumpeter, Freedom House combines competition for political leadership positions and participation with the civil rights and liberties of a liberal democracy.

Freedom House uses extensive questionnaires to measure political rights and civil liberties. The types of questions used and their wording have changed over time, for the better. Critics have failed to properly take this into account, though, as in the case of the work by Munck and Verkuilen (2002), who criticize the Freedom House ratings for their shortcomings. Today, the political rights rating is based on ten questions. Three questions aim to assess the procedural quality of elections, four questions quantify the extent of political pluralism and the chances of participation for various groups – the population as a whole, the opposition and minorities – and the final three questions are directed at the functioning of government, with special consideration paid to transparency, leadership ability and susceptibility to corruption. The civil liberties rating, on the other hand, is based on 15 questions. The aim of these is to assess the extent of (1) freedom of expression and belief, (2) associational and organizational rights, (3) rule of law, including the independence of the judiciary, and (4) guarantees of personal autonomy and individual rights (such as freedom of movement, property rights and legal protections against exploitation).

Freedom House also differentiates between 'electoral democracies' and 'liberal democracies' in its reports. Although liberal democracies are characterized by participation, independent decision-making and the ability of the people or their representatives to vote the political leadership in or out of office, their hallmark is extensively developed, untrammeled civil liberties, which electoral democracies lack. This form of democracy limits itself to the features of participation, reasonably independent decision-making, and regular elections, including the population voting its rulers into or (less frequently) out of office.

The freedom index published by Freedom House, which results from the addition, or alternatively the average, of the political rights and civil liberties ratings, is reflective of a concept of democracy that overlaps a great deal with the idea of the constitutional state. For this reason, this freedom index traces the contours of constitutional democracies more precisely than many other indices of democracy. A low score on the freedom index indicates that a democracy has strong constitutional underpinnings, while a relatively high score signals that democracy is under only weak constitutional constraints, indicating that it is a structurally defective democracy (for more on this, see section 5.1).

Despite their strengths, the Freedom House ratings require revision in some places. The categorization of the countries surveyed is often based on reliable data, but sometimes it rests on intuitive observation and judgment. The USA has received mild ratings despite Guantanamo and targetted killings on the orders of the government. Israel, too, receives remarkably mild civil liberties scores, despite its familiarity with state-sanctioned killings and its actions as an occupying force in Palestinian areas. In addition, the concepts used in the political rights and civil liberties checklists have not always been clearly operationalized. Moreover, the calculations and weighting of the observed results are not always clearly laid out. This has raised doubts as to the reliability of the Freedom House ratings. On the other hand, specific questions about the construction of the political rights and civil liberties ratings have led to major improvements in the quality of the measurements. The depth of the Freedom House dataset deserves more recognition than its critics have given it credit for; only Polity IV and Vanhanen (2003) provide a more comprehensive set of cross-sectional and longitudinal data for the comparison of democracies and autocracies.

5   'STATUS OF DEMOCRACY' AND GOVERNANCE-BASED INDICES OF DEMOCRATIC AND AUTOCRATIC REGIMES

5.1   Democracy and Autocracy in the Bertelsmann Transformation Index

The measurements of democracy introduced so far have opened up new areas of research. Nevertheless, there are still gaps. For example, their indicators have a blind spot where 'domain democracies' are concerned. These are the defective democracies (Croissant and Merkel 2004; Keman 2004) in which large sectors of society are controlled by groups whose power has not been democratically legitimized, such as the military or guerrilla movements. Other types of defective democracies are the 'exclusive', the 'illiberal' and the 'delegative' democracies. 'Exclusive' democracies exclude a substantial portion of adult citizens from voting; illiberal democracies are plagued by serious civil rights shortcomings, and 'delegative democracies' are characterized by highly concentrated, supermajoritarian varieties of presidential government (Merkel 2013, p. 223).

Defective democracies are by no means rare. Today, they make up over 50 percent of all democracies, on average, but with major regional differences. The majority of them are to be found in the post-Soviet countries that arose from the break-up of the Soviet Union, in the Middle East and in North Africa, as well as in francophone Africa. Also, while the percentage of defective democracies in anglophone Africa and Latin

America is high, the percentage in continental, central and southeastern Europe is extremely low (Croissant and Merkel 2004; also Keman 2004).

Defective democracies are also an object of study of the Bertelsmann Transformation Index (BTI), which has been published every two years since 2003 and which deals with the transitions to democracy and a market economy (Bertelsmann Stiftung 2014). One part of the BTI, in particular, is suitable for the measurement of democracies and autocracies: the Status Index. This index of the status of democracy is based on five components that are measured using data acquired from expert surveys: stateness, political participation, rule of law, stability and legitimacy of democratic institutions, and political and social integration.

The indicators of stateness are used to evaluate whether the national structures of the state are intact and whether there is a division between church and state. In the case of political participation, the main questions address whether citizens determine their political leadership through free elections and the extent to which they have other political rights, such as freedom of expression and freedom of association. The criteria for rule of law indicate the extent to which the state authorities place checks and balances on each other and the extent to which civil rights and liberties are guaranteed. The stability and legitimacy of democratic institutions are measured using questions about their effectiveness and efficiency and about their acceptability. The last component, political and social integration, is measured using questions about four thematic areas: first, stability, social entrenchment and the party system's ability to articulate its interests; second, the existence of an effective system of interest groups acting as intermediaries; third, the degree of conformance to democratic norms; and fourth, the status of civic self-organization and the creation of social capital (Bertelsmann Stiftung 2014, pp. 8–9, 126–7).

According to BTI data from 2013, the most successful transitions are taking place in Uruguay, Estonia, Taiwan, the Czech Republic and Poland, as well as in 15 other states. All of the other democracies surveyed in the BTI (which do not include the established constitutional democracies, such as Britain, France and Germany) are either simple defective democracies – 41 of them, including the Ukraine – or highly defective, totalling 14 and including Tunisia. In addition to democracies, the BTI data cover autocracies. According to the BTI published in 2014, 21 states were labelled as 'moderate autocracies' (including Singapore and the Russian Federation) and 33 states were categorized as 'hard-line autocracies', including China, Saudi Arabia and North Korea.

In contrast to the other measurements of democracy, the Bertelsmann Transformation Index excludes the established democracies in Europe and America. This shortcoming could easily be rectified: the Status Index could be transformed into an ordinal scale and supplemented with measurements for the established democracies that are already on an ordinal scale (see Table 8.1).

5.2   New Measures of Democracy: Democratic Rights, Rule of Law and Quality of Governance

Some of the newer measurements of democracy include part of the governance data from the World Bank (Kaufmann et al. 2013) and multiply them (or part of them) with the Freedom House political rights and civil liberties ratings. This multiplication is used to establish conditionality: only when political rights and civil liberties as well as high-quality governance are present can a country be considered a full democracy. This is the foundation for the construction of varying types of indices of effective democracy. One version links democratic rights with indicators of rule of law and a corruption index (Alexander et al. 2012). This index of effective democracy (EDI) is calculated by multiplying the Freedom House freedom rating with the average of the World Bank rule of law index and its control of corruption index (Alexander et al. 2012, pp. 45–6). The index resulting from these calculations is described by its authors as 'the most reliable and valid index of democracy that is currently available' (ibid., p. 41).

Another index, the Combined Index of Democracy (KID), is based on a combination of democratic rights, rule of law and political stability (Lauth 2013). This index includes freedom and equality, as well as political and legal controls, and rests on the assumption, that the monopoly of power on the part of the state is a prerequisite of democracy. The exact measurement of the combined index of democracy is based on the Polity IV democracy and autocracy scales, the Freedom House freedom index and the World Bank rule of law and political stability indicators. The measured values are combined into a scale from 0 to 10, in which 0 indicates complete autocracy and 10 fully developed democracy. Values from 0 to 4.99 reflect various degrees of autocracy, values from 5 to 6.99 stand for defective democracies, and the range from 7 to 10 represents non-defective democracies (see Table 8.1).

6   ADVANTAGES AND LIMITATIONS OF THE MEASUREMENTS OF DEMOCRACY AND AUTOCRACY

The comparative measures of democracy and autocracy are statistically highly correlated. That is also true of the indicators of democracy and autocracy in the early twenty-first century, which are compiled in Table 8.1; the correlation coefficient ranges from +/−0.7 to +/−0.9 (calculated using the Spearman's rank correlation coefficient formula). There is a large degree of correspondence between the measurements of the western European and North American constitutional states. Most of the indicators characterize them as a homogenous core group of the world's leading democracies. The one exception is Vanhanen's index of democratization, which is especially responsive to party-system fragmentation and to voter turnout, both of which vary from one country to another.

Despite correlating significantly, the measurements of the degree of democracy and autocracy for individual countries diverge to a sometimes considerable extent. This mainly applies to the hybrid – partly autocratic, partly democratic – regimes. The Russian Federation, for example, received Freedom House ratings of 6 and 5 in 2013 and is therefore classified as highly autocratic. Polity IV, on the other hand, gave Russia a score that year of 4 on a scale ranging from +10 to −10, while the Status Index classified Russia as moderately autocratic. If Vanhanen's index is brought into the mix, the findings become even more heterogeneous. According to this index, the Russian Federation, at least in 2001, clearly outstripped members of the European Union, such as Romania, with a democratization score of 28.0 versus 20.5.

The indicators of democracy and autocracy described above have opened new vistas for research. This deserves acknowledgment, even if these indicators have some weaknesses. While they are able to record the differences in the degree of democracy and of autocracy, other criteria are necessary in order to identify specific types of democracy and autocracy. Good candidates for this include, for example, Lijphart's (2012) differentiation between majoritarian and consensus democracies, and the typologies of autocracy by Cheibub et al. (2010) and Hadenius et al. (2012). Cheibub et al. (2010) distinguish primarily between royal, military and civilian dictatorships. Hadenius et al. (2012), on the other hand, differentiates six types of autocracy: monarchy, military regime, one-party regime, multi-party autocracy and no-party autocracy, plus a category 'other'.

One of the weaknesses of a number of measurements of democracy and autocracy is *pseudo*-exactness. The interval scaled indicators of democracy and the indices of democracy that make use of the World Bank governance indicators, in particular, are plagued by a particularly large problem of *pseudo*-exactness. Consider these examples: is Denmark, with a democratization index of 44.2, according to Vanhanen (2003), really 8.7 points more democratic than Germany? Would not a simpler scale level such as that of the Freedom House ratings be more acceptable where both countries are ranked equal? Also, can China's rule of law score of

4.55 (as measured by the World Bank rule of law index for the years from 1996 to 2012) really be exactly 0.87 points higher than the Ecuador's rule of law score (3.68) (Lauth 2013)?

The ratings of democracy discussed up to this point do not actually capture the quality of participation, but rather its quantity. But even that occurs in an incomplete way because most of these ratings except Vanhanen (2003) disregard direct democratic arrangements or opportunities for participation at the sub-national level. In addition to the properties of the democracy and autocracy ratings that are in need of correction, there are two other problems: up to now, they have shown absolutely no response to the democratic deficits that result from delegating rights of sovereignty to international or transnational organizations, as in the case of the European Union's structural democratic deficit (Schmidt 2010, pp. 399–411). Moreover, the measurements of rule of law did not respond to the threats to fundamental rights that have arisen as a result of the excessive use of security-motivated, computer-based data-gathering and surveillance, even in established democracies.

Despite their weaknesses, though, the more recently introduced measurements of democracy and autocracy have provided some illuminating insights. They record the degree of democracy and autocracy in different regime types more thoroughly and more systematically than the older indicators. The precise measurement of a regime type also serves as a safeguard against illusions about the prevalence of democracy. A reading of most of the ratings of democracy in Table 8.1 shows that, both before and after the historical turning point of the years 1989–90, only a minority of the world's population has lived or does live in developed and entrenched democracies.

NOTE

1. More datasets on democracies or autocracies alone, for instance, the Democracy Barometer (Bühlmann et al. 2012), on the one hand, and Cheibub et al. (2010) and Hadenius et al. (2012), on the other, are not included.

FURTHER READING

Hague, R. and M. Harrop (2013), *Comparative Government and Politics: An Introduction*, 9th edn, Basingstoke, UK and New York: Palgrave Macmillan.
Mesquita, B.B. de and A. Smith (2011), *The Dictator's Handbook: Why Bad Behavior is Almost Always Good Politics*, New York: Public Affairs.
Schmidt, M.G. (2014), 'Public policy in autocracies and democracies', in A. Croissant,

S. Kailitz, P. Koellner and S. Wurster (eds), *Comparing Autocracies in the Early Twenty-First Century: The Performance and Persistence of Autocracies*, vol. 2, London and New York: Routledge, pp. 39–56.

REFERENCES

Alexander, A.C., R. Inglehart and C. Welzel (2012), 'Measuring effective democracy: a defense', *International Political Science Review*, **33** (1), 41–62.

Banks, A.R. and R.B. Textor (1971), *Cross-Polity Survey*, Cambridge, MA: MIT Press.

Bertelsmann Stiftung (ed.) (2014), *Transformation Index BTI 2014: Political Management in International Comparison*, Gütersloh: Bertelsmann Stiftung.

Bühlmann, M., W. Merkel, L. Müller, H. Giebler and B. Wessels (2012), 'Ein neues Instrument zur Messung von Demokratiequalität' ('A new instrument for measuring the quality of democracy'), in G. Pickel and S. Pickel (eds), *Zeitschrift für Vergleichende Politikwissenschaft*, vol. 2, Wiesbaden: VS Verlag für Sozialwissenschaften, pp. 115–59.

Cheibub, J.A., J. Gandhi and J.R. Vreeland (2010), 'Democracy and dictatorship revisited', *Public Choice*, **14** (1), 67–101.

Collier, D., J. LaPorte and J. Seawright (2008), 'Typologies: forming concepts and creating categorical variables', in J. Box-Steffensmeir, H. Brady and D. Collier (eds), *The Oxford Handbook of Comparative Politics*, Oxford: Oxford University Press, pp. 152–232.

Croissant, A. and W. Merkel (ed.) (2004), 'Special issue: consolidated or defective democracy? Problems of regime change', *Democratization*, **11** (5), special issue.

Dahl, R.A. (1971), *Polyarchy: Participation and Opposition*, New Haven, CT and London: Yale University Press.

De Tocqueville, A. (1830 and 1835), *De la Démocracie en Amérique*, reprinted 1981, Paris: Flammarion.

Everson, S. (1996), *Aristotle: The Politics and the Constitution of Athens*, Cambridge: Cambridge University Press.

Freedom House (2014), *Freedom in the World 2014 Methodology*, Washington, DC: Freedom House.

Geddes, B. (2009), 'What causes democratization?', in C. Boix and S.C. Stokes (eds), *The Oxford Handbook of Comparative Politics*, Oxford: Oxford University Press, pp. 317–39.

Hadenius, A., J. Teorell and M. Wahman (2012), *Authoritarian Regimes Data Set. Version 5.0.*

Huntington, S.P. (1991), 'Democracy's third wave', *Journal of Democracy*, **2** (2), 12–34.

Inkeles, A. (ed.) (1991), *On Measuring Democracy: its Consequences and Concomitants*, New Brunswick, NJ and London: Transaction.

Kaufmann, D., A. Kraay and M. Mastruzzi (2013), *The Worldwide Governance Indicators, 2013 Update, Aggregate Indicators of Governance 1996–2012*, Washington, DC: World Bank, accessed 6 June 2014 at http://www.govindicators.org.

Keman, H. (2004), 'Polyarchy & defected democracy around the world: a research note', *Acta Politica*, **39** (3), 102–20.

Lauth, H. (2013), *Datensatz, Kombinierter Index der Demokratie (KID), 1996–2012*, Würzburg: Institut für Politikwissenschaft und Soziologie.

Lijphart, A. (2012), *Patterns of Democracy. Government Forms and Performance in Thirty-Six Countries*, 2nd edn, New Haven, CT and London: Yale University Press, Routledge.

Marshall, M.G., T.R. Gurr and K. Jaggers (2014), *POLITY™ IV PROJECT, Political Regime Characteristics and Transitions: 1800–2012, Dataset Users' Manual*, Colorado State University, Fort Collins, CO.

Merkel, W. (2013), 'Vergleich politischer Systeme: Demokratie und Autokratien' ('Comparing political systems: democracy and autocracy'), in M.G. Schmidt, F. Wolf and S. Wurster (eds), *Studienbuch Politikwissenschaft*, Wiesbaden: Springer VS, pp. 207–36.

Munck, G.L. and J. Verkuilen (2002), 'Conceptualizing and measuring democracy: evaluating alternative indices', *Comparative Political Studies*, **35** (1), 5–34.

Nohlen, D. and P. Stöver (eds) (2010), *Elections in Europe: A Data Handbook*, Baden-Baden: Nomos.

Puddington, A. (2014), 'The Freedom House Survey for 2013: the democratic leadership gap', *Journal of Democracy*, **25** (2), 77–92.

Schmidt, M.G. (2010), *Demokratietheorien: Eine Einführung* (*Theories of Democracy. An Introduction*), Wiesbaden: VS Verlag für Sozialwissenschaften.

Schumpeter, J.A. (1942), *Capitalism, Socialism and Democracy*, reprinted 1996, London and New York: Routledge.

Tsebelis, G. (2002), *Vetoplayer Theory: How Political Institutions Work*, Princeton, NJ: Princeton University Press.

Vanhanen, T. (2003), *Democratization: A Comparative Analysis of 170 Countries*, London and New York: Routledge.

9 Institutional analysis: progress and problems
B. Guy Peters

1 INTRODUCTION: THE TRADITION OF INSTITUTIONAL ANALYSIS

Institutions and institutional analysis was at the core of political science from the time of Aristotle until the middle of the twentieth century. In this long-standing tradition of analysis, the formal structures of the public sector were assumed to dominate governing. Further, there was an assumption embedded in this approach that institutions could be designed and if they were designed properly then governments would be effective, if not necessarily beneficent. Therefore, all we really needed to know about the public sector was what the constitution, or analogous rules forming the institutions of government, said. In this tradition of comparative politics, analysis was dominated by legal discussions of constitutions with the assumption that what those documents said actually happened as designed by their framers or at least provided an (idealist) measure to judge the 'best practices' (Rhodes 2008).

This formal-legalism in comparative analysis was largely unchallenged until the beginning of the twentieth century. Then, beginning with scholars such as Arthur Bentley (1908), the dominance of institutions was challenged, especially within the context of democratic political systems. That challenge to the dominance of institutional analysis was expanded in the 'behavioral revolution' in political science that shifted the focus for analysis away from formal structures toward the individuals who inhabit those structures, and who vote for the political leaders who inhabited the formal structures. That individualistic foundation for political analysis was, albeit differently argued, reinforced in the 1980s through the development of rational choice theory (Hindmoor 2015), which also was characterized by methodological individualism (March and Olsen 1989). In both cases, however, the preferences of the individuals involved in the institutions were exogenous to those institutions, with the institution merely being an arena for their actions (Keman 1998).

The remainder of this chapter addresses four major dimensions within the 'new' institutionalism. The first is contemporary institutional theory in political science, discussing the varieties now in use. The second section discusses the consequences of institutional choices for making public policy and the management of conflict. This discussion is followed by a section on the challenges to institutions and institutional theory, and finally there is a brief conclusion emphasizing the principal points of the analysis.

2   NEO-INSTITUTIONALISM AND THE REVIVAL OF INSTITUTIONAL ANALYSIS

The dominance of behavioral and rational choice approaches within political science led scholars, predominantly in the US, to advocate other approaches that could serve as alternative paradigms for political science. In particular, James March and Johan Olsen (1989) argued for a return to the organizational and institutional foundations of political science. Their discussion was particularly targeted at rational choice approaches, arguing that a logic of appropriateness developed within an institution could be contrasted to the logic of consequentiality that served as the foundation of rational choice approaches. Hence, in this approach to institutions – normative institutionalism – the preferences of members are endogenous to the institution and are learned through organizational socialization. Likewise, decisions are made by appeals to the values, myths, symbols and routines of the institution, rather than to more 'rational' criteria. This perspective on institutions depends on the capacity of institutions to create commitment on the part of their members to the goals and values of the institution. Rather than being shaped by legal norms or by personal desires for maximization, behavior within the institution is shaped by understandings of what is the right thing to do given the values of the institution.

The assertion of the importance of institutions by March and Olsen opened the 'new institutionalism' in political science (see Peters 2010). The normative institutionalism was followed rather quickly by historical institutionalism, stressing the role of path dependency in defining the persistence of institutions and their policies (Thelen et al. 1992). Further, rational choice theory, albeit operating with very different assumptions than the other versions of institutionalism, continued to develop important perspectives on institutions stressing the use of rules (Ostrom 1990; Scharpf 1997) and the constraints imposed by formal structures (Czada et al.1998; Tsebelis 2000).

These various approaches contained in the 'new institutionalism' had some features in common with the old institutionalism, notably the recognition that structure does matter for behavior and that individuals may not be quite as atomistic in their political behaviors as assumed by some theorists. But these approaches also departed significantly from the mold of the old institutionalism (Radaelli et al. 2012). One of most important deviations is the explicit concern with theory, and the integration of a variety of theoretical approaches into the more general concern with institutions.

For example, the normative theory has a very strong foundation in organizational sociology, especially the work of scholars such as Philip Selznick, W.W. Powell, and Berger and Luckman. In the work of all these scholars institutions are defined, often in large part, by the values held by their members and propagate by the institution. Likewise, rational choice institutionalism brings in a number of standard economic arguments about organizations and institutions, such as principal–agent theory and transaction cost analysis (see Peters 2010), as well as the more general question of solving collective action problems. Also a relative newcomer to the literature – discursive institutional theory (Schmidt 2010) – integrates discourse theory and to some extent constructivism into the analysis (see also Rhodes 2008, p. 92ff.).

The above integration of social science theory into institutional analysis alters substantially the formalism that characterized the old institutionalism in the discipline, but that is not the only change of importance. Another is the recognition that there are important informal elements in institutions, much as in organizations and traditions. Again, this involves importing ideas from organizational sociology into the study of political institutions, but in political science these informal relationships are also crucially with social actors. Rather than being largely autonomous and legalistic, institutions have come to be theoretically considered closely connected to political actors of all sorts and their interactions.

In addition to understanding the interactions of public sector institutions with actors in their environment, the concern with informal institutions in institutional theory has also considered the manner in which formal and informal institutions interact to produce governance. For example, Helmke and Levitsky (2004) analyzed the possible combination of formal and informal action in producing governance. These interactions were analyzed in terms of the effectiveness of the institutions and the extent to which their goals are compatible. For example, if their goals are compatible, informal institutions can substitute for ineffective formal institutions, whereas if their goals are divergent they function in a competitive relationship.

Finally, the new institutionalism also began to raise questions about measurement, attempting to make institutionalism more compatible with other components of the social sciences. Rather than an institution simply existing as a formal structure, the more social scientific approach raises questions such as the extent to which it is an institution–institutionalization (Thornton et al. 2012) and the likelihood of the institution surviving in what can be a competitive environment with a limited number of niches for institutions and organizations. And indeed the approach raises questions about the difference between an organization and an institution.[1] Finally, the approach has become more concerned with the consequences of institutional choices made in the past (Pierson 2000) in relation to processes of political decision-making and public policy performance (Schmidt 2002).

Whereas much of the formal approach to institutions focused on the internal processing of those institutions, the new institutionalism tends to focus more on the effects that institutional choices have on political behavior and on the outcomes of political process. These consequences may result from constitutional choices (Sartori 1997) and they may also result from lower-level design choices. Elinor Ostrom's work on institutional analysis and design (Ostrom and Basutro 2011) demonstrates the linkage among these levels of choice and the differential consequences that institutional choices of different types may have for public policies.

The emphasis on the consequences of institutional choices extends to some aspects of the institutions themselves, as well as to the public policies produced by those institutions. Unlike older versions of institutionalism, however, the analysis driven by New Institutionalism is directed more at social scientific questions and is carried out using the theories and methods of the contemporary social sciences (Vis et al. 2007). The normative institutionalism, for example, focuses on the capacity of institutions to create predictability of behaviors through creating an internal normative structure (see Wildavsky 1987).

One of the more important of the issues for designing institutions is the desire to create equilibrium within institutions that might otherwise be incapable of producing stable patterns of decision-making. The logic of institutional capacities to general equilibrium was initially advanced by William Riker and then developed further by Kenneth Shepsle (2008). For example, although there may be multiple opinions of a special policy issue, voting rules within institutions limit the political to make policy and to maintain political stability (Scharpf 1997). Although institutional equilibrium is desirable, it also may lead to excessive rigidity.

3 CREATING INSTITUTIONAL DIFFERENCE AND ITS CONSEQUENCES

As well as creating stability and making political equilibria possible, political institutions also produce differences in political behaviors and public policy. The differences that emerge may reflect underlying political, social and economic differences, but differences in institutions permit those forces to have varying levels of impact on the decisions made by the public sector. Further, political institutions may shape the capacity of the public sector to govern effectively, as well political stability (Weaver and Rockman 1993; Keman 1998)

3.1 Parliamentary versus Presidential versus Semi-Presidential

One of the most commonly cited differences among institutions is the difference between presidential and parliamentary government (Colomer and Negretto 2005). The familiar argument is that the fusion of powers in a parliamentary government, with the executive dependent upon a majority in the legislature, provides for greater governance capacity. On the other hand, that separation of powers provides a constraint on excessive action by any institution, and enhances the capacity for, or necessity of, consensus over policy (Lijphart 2008).

As well as those familiar statements about the differences between presidential and parliamentary systems, there has been a continuing debate on the 'perils of presidentialism'. Especially for less-developed political systems, Juan Linz (1994) has argued that presidential systems are more unstable than parliamentary systems. The inability to change the political executive legally between elections, it is argued, tends to generate extra-legal changes. Other scholars (see Carreras 2014) have argued that presidential systems have tended to be more open to 'outsider' presidents and tend to be less effective in governance.

The competing advantages and disadvantages of both presidential and parliamentary forms of government led to the development of semi-presidentialism in France, a pattern that was then copied in a number of other countries (see Elgie 2011). However, even that trichotomy of formats for relationships between the legislature and the executive does not take into account the variety of institutional designs attempting to balance the powers of legislative and executive actors in governing (Tavits 2009). Thus, institutional analysis can move beyond the rather simple analyses of the past and develop more precise measurements of institutional patterns (see below; see also Colomer 2001; Woldendorp and Keman 2010).

3.2 Federal versus Unitary

The distinction between federal and unitary states is another of the classic dichotomies in comparative politics that emphasizes differences among political institutions, and the capacity of those institutions to reflect and manage difference. The foundations of federal or unitary government are constitutional, with some division of the tasks of government and a sharing of sovereignty generally enshrined in basic legal documents. Further, there are marked differences within each of these formal categories, with some unitary systems permitting their subnational governments substantially greater freedom than some federal governments.

The dichotomy between federal and unitary structures is increasingly being supplanted by a more general institutional conception of 'multi-level governance' (Bache and Flinders 2004). Originally developed to describe patterns of governance in the European Union, the concept has become generalized as a means of understanding the complexities of political interactions among levels of government within virtually all governments. Further, the varieties of these interactions are increasingly being conceptualized and the structural implications further explored as means of analyzing how governance functions territorially (Hooghe et al. 2010).

Whether expressed in structural constitutional forms or in more dynamic political forms, the manner in which governance occurs in space is an important institutional feature of any political system. It shapes not only opportunities for political participation but also the policy choices made by the governments involved. Further, it can be important for nation-building by either creating uniformity of services or allowing for differences that reflect the wishes of various segments of the population (Castles 2007).

3.3 Electoral Laws

Although it has been understood for some time that electoral laws can influence the outcome of elections, this understanding has been elaborated and the linkages made more explicit. First, this analysis emphasizes the extent to which law is an institution, and electoral laws in particular are crucial for shaping electoral outcomes and party systems (Taagepera and Shugart 1989). Those electoral outcomes will in turn influence the possible coalitions in government and the policies that will be adopted by those governments. For example, most two-party systems would be difficult to maintain without the single-member district and a plurality voting system.

Further, the consequences of electoral laws for outcomes of elections demonstrates the extent to which institutions exist in an environment composed of other institutions. At a more macro-level electoral laws can also determine to some extent the possibilities for coalitions within the parliament, and therefore the types of governments and policies that will be selected. There will, of course be other influences on those outcomes, but electoral laws represent the beginning point for the creation of governing coalitions.

4 INSTITUTIONS FOR MANAGING DIFFERENCE

As well as creating differences among types of political systems, political institutions have also developed in ways that can manage and minimize social and economic conflicts. Politics is about difference – whether that difference is based on more or less objective characteristics of individuals and groups or whether it is based on ideas. Those differences are inevitable but if they are unmanaged or are allowed to become too intense then breakdown of political systems becomes possible if not probable. Therefore, just as institutional rules in potentially unstable legislatures, so too can rules manage instability in society taken at large (Lijphart 2008).

Although any number of such institutional arrangements for creating stability have been developed, two have been of particular relevance – one for dealing with social differences and the other for coping more with economic differences. Consociationalism has been conceived as a means of coping with deeply divided societies, whether those divisions are based on religion, language or ethnicity (Lijphart 2008; but see Selway and Templeman 2012).

The basic idea of consociationalism is to create relative peace among social groups by creating integration and trust among each of the social groups (for example, the pillarization in the Netherlands), and then cooperation among the elites of each group. That cooperation among the elites depends heavily on conducting many of their interactions in private (secrecy). Without this the elites would not be able to bargain successfully and to, in effect, give away some of the interests of the mass supporters they represent.[2]

More recently social pacts have been utilized in post-conflict societies as mechanisms for creating and maintaining peace among ethnic groups. The instruments used to achieve that end are not dissimilar to those used within consociationalism (Higley and Gunther 1992). Just as was true for consociationalism, the success of these agreements tended to be the separation of the elites from their ethnic supporters. Also, similar to consociationalism, the success of these arrangements has been variable, with some producing enduring peace and other breaking down with new ethnic or religious conflict (for example, Lebanon).

While consociationalism and social pacts are institutions designed to manage social conflicts, corporatism in its several variants is designed to manage economic conflicts, or at least to involve economic actors in making policy decisions (Molina and Rhodes 2002). Just as different social groups are represented by their elites in consociational processes, so too are economic groups – especially business and labor – represented in making economic policies that will affect them. Their role in policymaking is institutionalized and legitimized, so that the concerns of major interests in society will not be ignored (Woldendorp 2005).

In both consociational and corporatist solutions to social difference, the development of effective institutions is crucial. While these institutions are less formalized than legislatures and bureaucracies, these are patterns of institutionalized behaviors designed for resolving conflicts. Further these patterns of interaction evolve and persist, and have been able to adapt to changing social and economic conditions. They have not, however, been able to be exported to all countries that have these internal conflicts but which lack other apparent preconditions, such as organized socio-cultural parties of centralized trade unions, for successful conflict resolution.

5   CHALLENGES TO INSTITUTIONAL ANALYSIS

Although institutional analysis has made a number of contributions to the study of contemporary politics and government, there are several important challenges that remain for this approach, especially if it is to function as a paradigm for political and policy analysis. These challenges are especially important if institutionalism is to be understood as an alternative paradigm to rational choice and behavioralism in political science. While it is easy to say that institutions do matter (Weaver and Rockman 1993), it is more difficult to move beyond rather impressionistic arguments about the importance of structures and institutions in political life.

5.1   Measurement

The first vexing question about institutions is a measurement question – when does an institution become an institution? The literature often tends to treat institutions as dichotomies, with the institution existing or not or the one or the other type (see section 3). If, however, we think of these structures more as variables, then the degree of institutionalization of the structure will vary. Some structures may be strongly institutionalized, and some only weakly institutionalized. Likewise, institutions may vary across time – consociationalism or corporatism differs in degree or simply faded away as an institutional arrangement or as a political modus (Lijphart 2012).

The above argument, however, begs the question because it depends upon a workable definition of institutionalization and with that a clear definition of what constitutes an institution. For example, Selznick (1957) discusses institutionalization as infusing a structure with values and that definition would appear to work well for normative institutionalism in political science. For historical institutionalism the extent to which the established 'path' is being followed appears to be a viable measure of institutionalization, but that in turn requires a rather precise definition and measurement of the path dependency (Pierson 2000). Huntington (1965, p. 364) argues that four variables – adaptability, complexity, autonomy and coherence – can be employed to measure the level of institutionalization of a structure. An institutionalized structure will need to be able to adapt to its environment and at the same time find means of maintaining some autonomy from that environment (see Chapter 6 in this volume). For instance, public bureaucracies must maintain autonomy in order to regulate society, but must also understand society they rule.

While Huntington's measures are defined in terms of institutionalization and the stability of structures, they might also be employed as a more general means of gauging the nature of public sector institutions (Ragsdale and Theis 1997). For example, the variable of autonomy has become important in understanding the behavior of organizations in the public bureaucracy (see Laegreid et al. 2008) and theoretical approaches to complexity in the public sector also have come to occupy an increasingly important position in public policy and administration (Duit and Galaz 2008). More recently various data collections have been developed to measure (often comparatively) the degree of institutionalization and differences.

5.2   Change

Change represents a second significant challenge for institutional theory. The strength of institutionalism is that it can describe and explain stability. While stability can be an important attribute for structures in the public sector, it can also be a problem for structures that must adapt to changing environments and demands. Therefore, a major theoretical challenge is to identify ways to accommodate change in theories that emphasize permanence, while the practical challenge is how to design institutions that can provide stability while at the same time being capable of effective adaptation to a changing environment (Scharpf 1997).

The challenge of accommodating change is especially pressing for the historical institutionalism. As already noted, the fundamental logic of this version of institutional theory has been that patterns of policy or of structures in the public sector will persist unless there is some significant intervention. The original emphasis on punctuated equilibria as the mechanism for change appeared to deny the possibility of more incremental change that typifies most policy and organizational change in the public sector (Pierson 2000).

Scholars working in this tradition have argued that a least four types of more adaptive change occur within institutions – displacement, layering, drift and conversion (see Mahoney and Thelen 2010). These mechanisms for change maintain much of the existing programs but are also characterized by some forms of transformation of these programs. The identification of these forms of change helps in the theoretical interpretation of change, but they may be more descriptive than explanatory. Further, the relationship between these forms of change and more dramatic formats of change that was central to the original versions of historical institutionalism is still an issue for debate.

The major theoretical question that remains for change is providing explanations for the adoption of change, and explanations for resistance of change. In historical institutionalism resistance is central to the approach and may be based on positive returns of the participants in the institution, on perceived costs of change, or simply on habit. Change, however, can be brought about if there is a viable alternative to the status quo that can be used to motivate alterations in the existing patterns (Peters et al. 2005). Given the ideational and behavioral foundations of the sociological and discursive versions of institutionalism, the motivation for change will also involve having some set of ideas or values that can be considered superior to the status quo (Rhodes 2008). The superiority of those values and practices, however, may be assessed on pragmatic grounds as well as on more abstract criteria.[3]

5.3   Individuals and Institutions

This relationship is to some extent a version of the classic structure and agency question in the social sciences. More exactly, however, this is a question of the extent to which individuals can shape the institutions of which they are members, and in turn the extent to which they are shaped by those institutional memberships. Paradoxically, institutions are human inventions but then we allow our behaviors and our beliefs to be shaped by those institutions and to resist change in those structures (see also Keman 1998).

The several versions of institutional theory provide different answers to this basic question about the linkages of individuals and institutions. The argument that preferences of individuals are endogenous – shaped by their membership in the institution – is central to the logic of normative versions of institutionalism. This can be contrasted with the logic of exogenous preferences in rational choice versions, where individuals maintain their basic utility maximization values during their membership in the institution. Although perhaps less clearly stated, historical institutionalism also assumes that individuals will to some extent be shaped by their involvement with an institution, if only to create a set of habits that they will follow and that assist in the maintenance of path dependency (Sarigil 2009).

Institutions are also shaped and adapted by their members. This shaping of institutions may occur through conscious actions taken by the leaders and designers of institutions. Some scholars, especially those coming from the rational choice perspective, argue that institutions can develop due to incentives and disincentives for behaviors (Hall and Soskice 2001). For the normative version (for example, Rothstein 1998), as well as for constructivist institutionalism (see Hay 2008), individuals within the institution bring with them ideas, values and behaviors that may, over time, alter the institution (March and Olsen 1989). If, for example, the individuals joining an institution at one point in time are markedly different from those in previous periods, the institution may have to adapt to the importation of new members, or perhaps fail. For constructive versions of institutionalism the coordinative discourses within the structures will continue to shape the nature and change of the institution.

6   CONCLUSION: THE PROMISE OF INSTITUTIONAL ANALYSIS

Institutions and institutional analysis have been central to political science since its inception, and this mode of analysis remains crucial. Institutional analysis has been able to move away from its formal and legal foundations to utilize a range of theoretical perspectives and to contribute to theoretical developments in the field. With those developments institutional analysis is not only capable of describing the institutions central to governance but can make more analytically interesting statements about the dynamics of institutions, and about the dynamics of institutional fields that shape governance.

Institutional analysis deals with both theoretical discourses and abstract analyses, as well as with more descriptive analyses of the effects of particular institutional arrangements on systemic political processes and policy formation. These both are important for understanding the ways in which structure influences the outcome of political processes. Although they are both important elements of institutional approaches they are sometimes difficult to link effectively. However, both versions of institutionalism contribute to the understanding of politics and governance.

Although institutional theory has made a number of contributions to political science, a number of significant questions and challenges remain. As noted, an approach largely premised on explaining persistence does encounter some difficulties when attempting to cope with change. Also, an approach that has been developed in contemporary political science as an alternative to atomistic approaches may find integrating individual action into structural explanations a challenge. Perhaps most fundamentally, identifying an institution and measuring the extent of institutionalization remains crucial for including institutional analysis in contemporary political science.

NOTES

1. One standard answer to this question is given by Douglass North (1990) with institutions being the rules of the game, and organizations being the teams playing the game.
2. This method of managing social difference was successful in the Netherlands but enjoyed variable success in other cases such as Malaysia, Belgium, Canada and Colombia.
3. That is, do the new values work better for the institution, enabling it to reach its goals more effectively than the values and practices that are being replaced?

FURTHER READING

March, J.G. and J.P. Olsen (1989), *Rediscovering Institutions: The Organizational Basis of Politics*, New York: Free Press.
North, D.C. (1990), *Institutions, Institutional Change and Economic Performance*, Cambridge: Cambridge University Press.
Ostrom, E. (1990), *Governing the Commons: The Evolution of Institutions of Collective Action*, Cambridge: Cambridge University Press.
Peters, B.G. (2010), *Institutional Theory in Political Science; The New Institutionalism*, 3rd edn, London: Continuum.
Shepsle, K.A. (1986), 'Institutional equilibrium and equilibrium institutions', in H. Weisberg (ed.), *Political Science: The Science of Politics*, New York: Agathon.
Weaver, R.K. and B.A. Rockman (1993), *Do Institutions Matter? Government Capabilities in the United States and Abroad*, Washington, DC: Brookings Institution.

REFERENCES

Bache, I. and M. Flinders (2004), *Multi-Level Governance*, Oxford: Oxford University Press.
Bentley, A.F. (1908), *The Process of Government: A Study of Social Pressures*, Chicago, IL: University of Chicago Press.

Carreras, M. (2014), 'Outsider presidents, institutional performance, and governability in Latin America', dissertation, University of Pittsburgh, Pittsburgh, PA.

Castles, F.G. (ed.) (2007), *The Disappearing State? Retrenchment Realities in an Age of Globalisation*, Cheltenham, UK and Northampton, MA, USA: Edward Elgar.

Colomer, J.M. (2001), *Political Institutions: Democracy and Social Choice*, Oxford: Oxford University Press.

Colomer, J.M. and G.L. Negretto (2005), 'Can presidentialism work like parliamentarism?', *Government and Opposition*, **40** (1), 60–89.

Czada, R., A. Héritier and H. Keman (eds) (1998), *Institutions and Political Choice: On the Limits of Rationality*, Amsterdam: VU-University Press.

Duit, A. and V. Galaz (2008), 'Governance and complexity – new issues in governance theory', *Governance*, **21** (4), 311–35.

Elgie, R. (2011), *Semi-Presidentialism: Sub-Types and Democratic Performance*, Oxford: Oxford University Press.

Hall, P.A. and D. Soskice (2001), 'An introduction to varieties of capitalism', in *Varieties of Capitalism: The Institutional Foundations of Comparative Advantage*, Oxford: Oxford University Press, pp. 50–51.

Hay, C. (2008), 'Constructivist institutionalism', in R. Rhodes, S.A. Binder and B. Rockman (eds), *The Oxford Handbook of Political Institutions*, Oxford: Oxford University Press, pp. 56–74.

Helmke, G. and S. Levitsky (2004), 'Informal institutions and comparative politics: a research agenda', *Perspectives on Politics*, **2** (4), 725–40.

Higley, J. and R. Gunther (1992), *Elites and Democratic Consolidation in Latin America and Southern Europe*, Cambridge: Cambridge University Press.

Hindmoor, A. (2015), *Rational Choice*, vol. 2, Basingstoke, UK: Palgrave.

Hooghe, L. and G. Marks (2003), 'Unraveling the central state, but how? Types of multi-level governance', *American Political Science Review*, **103** (1), 233–43.

Hooghe, L., G. Marks and A.H. Schakel (2010), *The Rise of Regional Authority: A Comparative Study of 42 Countries*, London: Routledge.

Huntington, S.P. (1965), *Political Order in Changing Societies*, New Haven, CT: Yale University Press.

Keman, H. (1998), 'Political institutions and public governance', in R. Czada, A. Héritier and H. Keman (eds), *Institutions and Political Choice: On the Limits of Rationality*, Amsterdam: VU University Press, pp. 109–33.

Laegreid, P., K. Verhoest and W. Jann (2008), 'The governance, autonomy and coordination of public sector organizations', *Public Organization Review*, **8** (1), 93–6.

Lijphart, A. (2008), *Thinking about Democracy: Power Sharing and Majority Rule in Theory and Practice*, London: Sage.

Lijphart, A. (2012), *Patterns of Democracy: Government Forms and Performance in Thirty-Six Countries*, vol. 2, New Haven, CT and London: Yale University Press.

Linz, J.J. (1994), *The Failure of Presidential Government*, Baltimore, MD: Johns Hopkins University Press.

Mahoney, J. and K. Thelen (2010), *Explaining Institutional Change: Ambiguity, Agency and Power*, Cambridge: Cambridge University Press.

March, J.G. and J.P. Olsen (1989), *Rediscovering Institutions: The Organizational Basis of Politics*, New York: Free Press.

Molina, O. and M. Rhodes (2002), 'Corporatism: the past, present and future of a concept', *Annual Review of Political Science*, **7** (June), 305–31.

North, D.C. (1990), *Institutions, Institutional Change and Economic Performance*, Cambridge: Cambridge University Press.

Ostrom, E. (1990), *Governing the Commons: The Evolution of Institutions of Collective Action*, Cambridge: Cambridge University Press.

Ostrom, E. and X. Basutro (2011), 'Crafting analytical tools to study institutional change', *Journal of Institutional Economics*, **7** (3), 317–43.

Peters, B.G. (2010), *Institutional Theory in Political Science: The New Institutionalism*, vol. 3, London: Continuum.

Peters, B.G., J. Pierre and D.S. King (2005), 'The politics of path dependency: political conflict in historical institutionalism', *Journal of Politics*, **67** (4), 1275–300.

Pierson, P. (2000), 'Increasing returns, path dependence and the study of politics', *American Political Science Review*, **94** (1), 261–7.

Radaelli, C., B. Dente and S. Dossi (2012), 'Recasting institutionalism: institutional analysis and public policy', *European Political Science*, **11** (3), 537–50.

Ragsdale, L. and J.J. Theis (1997), 'The institutionalization of the American presidency, 1924–92', *American Journal of Political Science*, **41** (6), 1280–318.

Rhodes, W. (2008), 'Old institutionalisms', in R. Rhodes, S.A. Binder and B. Rockman (eds), *The Oxford Handbook of Political Institutions*, Oxford: Oxford University Press, pp. 90–208.

Rothstein, B. (1998), *Just Institutions Matter: The Moral and Political Logic of the Universal Welfare State*, Cambridge: Cambridge University Press.

Sarigil, Z. (2009), 'Paths are what actors make of them', *Critical Policy Studies*, **3** (1), 121–40.

Sartori, G. (1997), *Comparative Constitutional Engineering: An Inquiry into Structures, Incentives and Outcomes*, New York: New York University Press.

Scharpf, F.W. (1997), *Games Real Actors Play*, Boulder, CO: Westview Press.

Schmidt, M.G. (2002), 'The impact of political parties, constitutional structures and veto players', in H. Keman (ed.), *Comparative Democratic Politics: Guide to Temporary Theory and Research*, London: Sage, pp. 166–85.

Schmidt, V.A. (2010), 'Taking ideas and discourse seriously: explaining change through discursive institutionalism as the fourth new institutionalism', *European Political Science Review*, **2** (1), 1–25.

Selway, J. and K. Templeman (2012), 'The myth of consociationalism: conflict reduction in divided societies', *Comparative Political Studies*, **45** (12), 1542–71.

Selznick, P. (1957), *Leadership in Organizations: A Sociological Interpretation*, Berkeley, CA: University of California Press.

Shepsle, K. (2008), 'Rational choice institutionalism', in R. Rhodes, S.A. Binder and B. Rockman (eds), *The Oxford Handbook of Political Institutions*, Oxford: Oxford University Press, pp. 23–37.

Taagepera, R. and M.S. Shugart (1989), *Seats and Votes: The Effects and Determinants of Electoral Systems*, New Haven, CT: Yale University Press.

Tavits, M. (2009), *Presidents with Prime Ministers*, Oxford: Oxford University Press.

Thelen, K.A., S. Stenmo and F. Longstreth (1992), *Structuring Politics: Historical Institutionalism in Comparative Analysis*, Cambridge: Cambridge University Press.

Thornton, P.H., W. Ocasio and M. Lounsbury (2012), *The Institutional Logics Perspective*, Oxford: Oxford University Press.

Tsebelis, G. (2000), *Veto Players: How Political Institutions Work*, Princeton, NJ: Princeton University Press.

Vis, B., J. Woldendorp and H. Keman (2007), 'Do miracles exist? Analyzing economic performance comparatively', *Journal of Business Research*, **60** (5), 531–8.

Weaver, R.K. and B.A. Rockman (1993), *Do Institutions Matter? Government Capabilities in the United States and Abroad*, Washington, DC: Brookings Institution.

Wildavsky, A. (1987), 'Choosing preferences by constructing institutions: a cultural theory of preference formation', *American Political Science Review*, **81** (1), 3–22.

Woldendorp, J. (2005), *The Polder Model: From Disease to Miracle? Dutch Neo-Corporatism 1965–2000*, Amsterdam: Thela Thesis.

Woldendorp, J. and H. Keman (2010), 'Dynamic institutional analysis: measuring corporatist intermediation', *Quality and Quantity*, **44** (2), 259–75.

10 Political actors: parties–interest groups–government
Nicole Bolleyer

1 INTRODUCTION

This chapter discusses the changing roles of political organizations in contemporary democracies, particularly *political parties* but also *interest groups*. While providing platforms for citizens to engage in the political process, they try to exercise political influence during distinct phases of the political decision-making process: parties recruit candidates for political office, run elections, with the ultimate goal to implement policies when taking over government. Interest groups represent their members' interests by lobbying political decision-makers, thereby aiming to influence public policy. This chapter argues that despite their very different functions in the political process, their relationship to society and to the state has undergone changes that are characterized by basic parallels linked to the growing individualization of Western societies. See Table 10.1 for the core themes.

In the context of this chapter, *political organizations* are defined as self-governing, membership-based, voluntary organizations (Salamon and Anheier 1998, p. 216). Members are individual citizens (rather than other organizations) who can express their (long-term oriented) affiliation through various means (for example, fee paying, organizational work and/or participation in events). Voluntary implies the constant right of (and from the organizational perspective threat of) individual exit of those members (Hirschman 1970). This is important since it puts organizations under pressure to keep members happy. Furthermore, it creates tensions between internal demands of members and the attempts of organizational elites to achieve broader goals: think about a party's difficult attempts to run elections with a broad and inclusive program targeting wide parts of the electorate (beyond its traditional 'core constituencies') without giving up policy commitments crucial to party activists which would trigger internal protest.

The question of how citizens link to democratic politics has gained considerable salience over the past few decades. Attachments to organizations, such as political parties, unions or churches, have weakened

Table 10.1   Core themes discussed

Core themes discussed	Open research questions	Examples for data to use
Changing party–society/ interest group–society relations	Do parties/interest groups decline or simply change? Do they still care about their members? What does being a member mean in advanced democracies?	Membership figures Survey data capturing citizens' and party/interest group members' attitudes Organizational statutes Interview data (for example, organizational elites)
Changing party–state relations	Are parties and interest groups really increasingly dependent on state resources rather than on membership fees? Are they increasingly regulated/controlled by the state?	Budget composition of parties and interest groups Change of legislation (for example, eligibility criteria to receive state subsidies and attached reporting criteria)

and the creation of long-lasting organizational ties to citizens and with it stable support by citizens has become a major challenge for not only political but social organizations in general (Biezen et al. 2011). The notion that parties as representatives of citizens' preferences are forced to operate in increasingly individualized societies are in decline and risk – in their linkage and representative functions – being replaced by more issue-specific or participatory organizations gained considerable prominence (Lawson and Merkl 1988). Discussions and debates about 'party failure' – declaring political parties as outdated channels for political participation in modern polities – led some to look to interest groups and movements as foci for civil engagement in politics. More issue-specific and less conventional forms of political participation as implemented by social movements (defined as organizations trying to challenge the political system – see also Chapter 11 in this volume) but also interest groups (defined as organizations trying to change particular policies through conventional channels) were expected to replace and compensate for the declining capacity of parties to fulfil their representative functions. However, this initial optimism has died down. Interest groups were found to often be devoid of internal democracy or participation, and movement organizations have tended to transform into something difficult to distinguish from conventional interest groups (for example, Jordan and Maloney 1997). Simultaneously, many parties have attempted to democratize their procedures by involving members in the selection of party leaders or introducing primaries for the selection of party candidates (Cross and Katz 2013). The claim of widespread party decline might have been premature. Instead, an assessment of how parties, but also interest groups, have adapted and transformed might be more fruitful to understand their role in modern democracy. In the context of this debate, this chapter now looks at parties' and interest groups' changing relationship with society and government, two developments many scholars consider to be closely intertwined.

2 POLITICAL PARTIES AND INTEREST GROUPS BETWEEN SOCIETY AND THE STATE

The debate around the decline of political parties centered on their role in society, their growing disengagement with their membership and their increasing dependency from state resources. More specifically, the importance of sustaining a traditional membership organization has been questioned, a membership organization composed of a nation-wide network of local branches that allows ordinary citizens' bottom-up involvement in the party's operation across the country. The same goes for a party's close ties to specific groups in the electorate defining the party's core supporters whose interests the party represents in the political process. Naturally, if societies individualize and group affiliations weaken, investments in local infrastructures and ties to clearly demarcated societal groups might increasingly be outdated. Kirchheimer pointed out as early as the 1960s that the transformation of parties (for example, their increasing dependence on state funding) is triggered by 'present conditions of spreading secular and mass consumer-goods orientation, with shifting and less obtrusive class lines' putting 'parties under pressure to become catch-all people's parties' (1966, p. 190). Such parties are less strongly rooted in particular groups in society and deliberately diversify and broaden their support base. This, inevitably, has implications for the relationships they have with their members.

Reflecting this argument, research nowadays points to the decreasing incentives and increasing costs for party leaders in modern democracies of recruiting and retaining members (for example, Mair 1997). In many democracies party membership has declined (Biezen et al. 2011). At the same time, parties are increasingly dependent on state resources to finance costly campaigns, in turn, devaluing the contributions of ordinary members (Katz and Mair 1995; Biezen and Kopecký 2008). Meanwhile, aspiring to win elections, party elites increasingly rely on professional advisors and value maneuverability in terms of policy which tends to be unpopular with members (Dalton and Wattenberg 2000; Webb et al. 2002; Farrell 2006). However, even if extra-parliamentary party building is less central in modern democracies owing to fundamental changes in societal structures and increasing availability of alternative funding sources, such as direct state subsidies, having a loyal membership is still important to parties. This is the case even though the notions of membership increasingly diversify by parties offering different types of membership roles (for example, a formal supporter status next to full membership) that impose fewer obligations on those members and might be more short term (Scarrow 2014; Gauja 2015).

Interestingly, claims around the fundamental change of parties and new forms of organization could be – at first – nicely illustrated by colorful examples such as the former Forza Italia (FI) formed by Silvio Berlusconi (in 2009 it merged into the Popolo della Libertà) which was considered the prototype of a 'virtual party' or 'business model of party organization' (McCarthy 1996; Hopkin and Paolucci 1999). When the party started out, it had little grassroots presence and was heavily reliant on its leader, Berlusconi, and the resources provided by his corporation, Fininvest. At that time, Fininvest formed FI's organizational core and was indistinguishable from the party itself. However, later on, the party built up a traditional membership organization including hundred thousands of members and several thousand ambitious office-holders. Simply put, after having suffered various electoral defeats at the subnational level, it felt the need to establish itself as an 'organized' and 'entrenched' party (Pasquino 2003, p. 207). This reorientation is particularly noticeable because it happened despite the party's strong position in the Italian party system, its superior financial resources and media access, privileges hardly any organizationally new party ever enjoys in advanced democracies. Even for a party with plenty of resources, organization seems to provide something money cannot buy, despite campaigns becoming increasingly professionalized and costly and despite the impact of short-term advertising on voting behavior is growing (for example, Dalton and Wattenberg 2000; Webb et al 2002; Dalton 2003; Farrell 2006). Such case studies of parties investing in building up a membership organization were echoed by comparative cross-national studies pointing to the connection between organization-building and party electoral success as well as party survival (Bolleyer 2013).

However, what about interest groups or associations more broadly – organizations that do not run elections but try to represent their members' interests in the democratic process? Membership organizations as suitable vehicles to pursue collective goals in individualized societies have been questioned in party and interest group research and research on voluntary organizations generally. Looking at American democracy, Skocpol notes that decades ago organizations were 'association-builders' that brought together groups of individuals that met regularly and jointly engaged in representative governance. 'Leaders who desired to speak on behalf of masses of Americans found it natural to proceed by recruiting self-renewing mass memberships' (Skocpol 2001, n.p.). Instead, in increasingly individualized societies, a 'new' more efficient associative logic has come to the forefront:

> Even a group aiming to speak for large numbers of Americans does not absolutely need members. And if mass adherents are recruited through the mail, why hold meetings? From a managerial point of view, interactions with groups of members may be downright inefficient . . . direct mail members can be more appealing because . . . 'they contribute without "meddling"' and 'do not take part in leadership selection or policy discussions.' This does not mean the new advocacy groups are malevolent; they are just responding rationally to the environment in which they find themselves. (Skocpol 2001, n.p.)

Similarly, the increasing dependency of parties on state resources and their increasing regulations by the state seem not to be unique to parties but increasingly apply to interest groups as well. Also here we find a shift in organizations' relationship with society that is associated with more intense relationships with, or dependency on, the state. Interest group experts observe the transformation of environmental advocacy groups into 'protest businesses' that increasingly compete for state resources to sustain their finances and, as a consequence, are driven less by their activist base (Jordan and Maloney 1997, 2007). Even more, public policy scholars, welfare state experts and civil society scholars discuss the transformation of voluntary associations driven by volunteers into 'voluntary agencies' driven by professional staff oriented towards service provision on behalf of the state (DiMaggio and Anheier 1990; Billis 2010). As a growing number of countries have adopted party laws, more and more countries establish (either compulsory or voluntary) lobby registers trying to regulate the access of interest groups to political decision-makers, sometimes imposing constraints that restrict access, sometimes attempting to assure transparency of who talks to whom. Of 19 advanced democracies, ten have by now regulated lobby access through statutory law or parliamentary proceedings, with the UK, Austria, Netherlands, Ireland and France having adopted their first regulations only in the past few years (for example, Holman and Luneburg 2012). Furthermore, state subsidies have become an increasingly important income source for those groups that try to sustain themselves not solely through lobbying but through provision of services, yet again impacting on their relationship with their membership. In a recent study, Smith (2011, pp. 203–4) indicated that associations in the US are increasingly dependent on, and compete for, government contracts and with it become subject to government regulation and monitoring in relation to standards of service provision and eligibility requirements. As the elites of different parties are considered to become indistinguishable and to distance themselves from their members, '[v]oluntary agencies with government contracts tend to adopt similar internal practices' (Smith 2011, p. 212) as well. The conflicts resulting from these developments, which are accompanied by the increased influence of paid staff at the cost of members, parallel those identified in the party literature, for example, conflicts between professional staff and ideologically committed volunteers mirroring the simultaneous accountability of the organization to its members and the state as provider of funding (Smith 2011, pp. 212–14). When conflicts occur, the legal accountability to the state creates stronger pressure, particularly in large organizations, since the withdrawal of state funding has a stronger impact on the organization's operations than member exit, as long as the latter does not occur on a mass scale (Lansley 1996, pp. 225–6; 235). Or, as Cornforth and Spear (2010, p. 75) put it, there has been a trend in voluntary associations involved in welfare provision to 'commoditize' membership and see it primarily as a source of funding rather than a mechanism for accountability, an observation that parallels observations made by party scholars. Both literatures at the same time indicate that membership fees become a less important income source, with state subsidies becoming more important (Davies 2011).[1] This is also the case in environmental interest groups, initially hailed as a providing a new, less hierarchical and more participatory form of political involvement for citizens. Struggling with high membership turnover, to assure their survival, long-lived environmental organizations started to rely less on membership subscriptions and more on more reliable sources of income such as public subsidies and support by foundations (Jordan and Maloney 1997, 2007; Bosso 2003).

Returning to the question of how parties and interest groups operate in contemporary democracies, the crucial difference between them lies in the way they seek political influence and what they need 'organization' for: influencing political decision-making and (sometimes) providing services to their constituents (interest groups), and running elections to make policy decisions in parliament and government (parties). Given this difference, the need to operate *within* public institutions in a (reasonably) cohesive manner concerns parties alone, which brings us to another debate – around the viability of party government and party democracy (Mair 2006). That said, while interest groups in any setting can try to develop close ties to political parties as a channel of influence, in the context of corporatist settings especially, employer organizations and unions work closely with government, making and sometimes implementing economic policy. This provides direct access to political decision-making and puts them under similar pressures. The role of parties in and relationship of interest groups with government are discussed in turn.

3 PARTIES, INTEREST GROUPS AND GOVERNMENT

Even if parties do care less about their membership organization and their societal ties than in the past, this development does not mean that parties become less relevant to government or to governing. The debate has so far mainly focused on parties' weakening representative functions and the consequences for the viability of party government (Mair 2006, 2007). This is because despite the recent turn towards studying party–state (rather than predominantly party–society) relations, party research still adheres to the traditional perspective on parties: it conceptualizes parties as vehicles for citizen representation rather than decision-making organizations, which explains why empirical studies analyzing parties as governmental actors are still rare (Blondel 1995, pp. 128–9; Cansino 1995, p. 124; Strøm et al. 2003; Keman 2006). A notable exception is the literature on government coalitions, dealing with their durability and the governance arrangements through which interdependencies between ministries allocated to different parties are managed (for example, Budge and Keman 1993; Lupia and Strøm 2008). One important question raised in this literature is the tension between the policy compromises necessary to make a coalition work and the individual mandate given to each party by their followers to implement the party's particular (individual) program. These debates provide important insights into the working of party government. Yet again, assessing to what extent parties implement the programs they run elections with once in government, ultimately starts out from the notion of *political parties' as citizen representatives*. This, in turn, suggests that coalition governments tend to lack a clear mandate and fall short of meeting the normative standards of 'party government' realized ideal – typically by single-party majority cabinets (Katz 1987).

Moving away from the question of whether parties realize the policies they were elected to implement, as the yardstick for whether democratic government works, we can alternatively ask how *parties as organizations* contribute to governing functionally. This alternative perspective becomes evident when starting with Rose (1984, p. 14) who argued that 'Those who step aboard the ship of state find that they are subject to powerful currents, and are not taking command of a passive or easily maneuvered vessel'. If governing is difficult in functional terms, the question is not only whether parties are responsive or responsible and choose to make policies reflecting their manifestos once in power (including all the complications of coalition government already referred to), but also how to run government. Hence, we also need to ask how parties as organizations and collective actors handle the basic challenges to govern in the first place and why they might handle these challenges better than the available alternatives, such as a depoliticized expert government.

When it comes to policy-making, the core of 'governing' which is thought to keep parties increasingly busy, some leading scholars consider parties as replaceable by specialized agencies and experts (Mair 2006; Sartori 2005, pp. 27–8). A party is depicted as 'as an agency which plans and carries out a policy at the governmental level' (Sartori 2005, p. 24). Administrative and policy studies, however, stress that 'carrying out a policy' is much less the point than coping with the increasing need to deal with interdependencies and spillover effects across policy issues and areas (for example, Verhoest et al. 2007; see Chapter 31 in this volume). Intensified by the growing scope of government activities, parties face the need to simultaneously handle a variety of interdependent policies within an internally differentiated government apparatus composed of functionally specific as well as generalist jurisdictions. Thus, we need to conceptualize a party's role not only in the light of citizen expectations but also considering the functional pressures generated by public office to capture the requirements of party government – defined as the capacity of parties to translate the possession of the highest formal offices of a political regime into operational control of government (Rose 1969, p. 413).

Irrespective of whether parties assure policy-making in line with citizen preferences (the core of their representative function), party linkages facilitate communication and coordination among the different decision-making arenas of the government apparatus. Different from expert government or candidate-centered politics, party government helps public office-holders to cope with intensifying coordination pressures. Parties counteract fragmentation and reduce complexity. They integrate government processes irrespective of functional divides generated by increasing specialization and functional differentiation. This is often overlooked, although Sjöblom (1987, p. 176) has emphasized that the capacity to counteract specialization by coordinating across policies is a main function of parties. More specifically, party linkages capture a shared organizational affiliation between office-holders, connections rooted in office-holders' belonging to and common socialization within a membership organization that also operates outside public institutions and thereby creates connections between its office-holding members that cut across functional divides. Being forced to run elections across a wider range of issues, party politicians need to adopt a generalist outlook, which in itself, once occupying government posts, facilitates communication and coordination between decision-making arenas. A shared organizational affiliation is expected to support these processes, even at times when actors' opinions differ on the specific policies at stake (Bolleyer 2011).

While party linkages might increase coordination efficiency in the face of interdependent policy issues and areas which is an issue that needs more exploration in future research, this observation is unrelated to whether policy-making follows a clear mandate which is linked to a separate normative standard derived from parties' role as representatives. The latter presupposes the capacity of a party to implement those policies promised in its manifesto and thereby to effectively represent citizen preferences, which is usually considered as the accountability of party government (Katz 1987; Budge et al. 2012). As indicated earlier, this depends on whether a party governs alone and whether it has majority support in parliament. Owing to the constant need for inter-party compromises the match between individual party programs and government action is likely to be limited in systems run by coalition governments which are prevalent in advanced democracies. The integration of policy across ministries, sectors and issues – which a party as organization might assure between the ministries it occupies (all ministries in a single-party cabinet, only some in a coalition) – is unrelated to this evaluation. But it is still an important dimension of the functioning of contemporary (party) democracy (Keman and Müller-Rommel 2012).

However, where do interest groups come in? The relationship between parties and interest groups is often described as an exchange relationship in which interest groups aim at winning favors for their membership or constituencies by supporting a party with votes, supplying campaign volunteers or contributing funds (Mueller and Murrell 1986). While multiple factors play a role in whether individual interest groups can successfully lobby parties inside or outside government, two partially intertwined aspects are particularly crucial: what kind of interest group we look at (and whether and, if so, to which parties it might have close ties) and which type of system of interest representation a group operates in. Starting with the latter, the distinction between corporatism and pluralist systems of interest representation is crucial for the type of relationship (specific) interest groups – notably employer organizations and unions – have with the government. In a pluralist system of interest representation, such as the United States, politics is considered as a marketplace in which individuals, political parties and interest groups compete for influence on government policy. Importantly, especially early pluralists assumed access to policy-making to be equally distributed, an assumption often criticized as disregarding obvious inequalities between groups in financial or other resources as well as the bias in the mobilization of interests able to enter the political process to start with (Schattschneider 1960). In corporatist or neo-corporatist systems access to (especially socio-economic) policy-making is thought to be much more restricted. Here we find institutionalized processes of negotiations between the government and a few (hierarchically organized) peak institutions representing business and labor, jointly maintaining (and monopolizing) stable procedures of developing and implementing policies. While some interest groups might focus their support on the party in government and thus shift affiliation, others develop close and lasting ties to specific parties that share the same ideology (McMenamin 2013), such as the historically grown and often highly institutionalized relationship between unions and social democratic parties. Bringing the type of interest group and the type of system together, shifting alliances seem to feature more strongly in pluralist settings, while corporatist systems, such as the Netherlands, Norway or Austria, incentivize close alignments between interest groups and the parties of government (Katzenstein 1984; Strøm and Svåsand 1997; Woldendorp 2005). Which system of interest representation allows more influence on interest groups on government is hard to judge per se. It crucially depends on what type of interest group we look at (whether a group has established an 'insider status' with regard to government or not) and what type of channels of influence it tries to cultivate (for example, targeting government or the media) when operating within a particular opportunity structure. This is why measuring interest groups' actual influence in policy-making has remained a major challenge in interest groups research (Baumgartner and Leech 1998; Baumgartner et al. 2009).

4   CONCLUSIONS

Future research on parties and on interest groups will have to explore in greater detail how changing relationships of organizations to the state feed back to the way they relate to members and supporters, and thus to representing society. The type of democracy – a majoritarian democracy characterized by one-party majority governments or a consensus democracy typically governed by coalitions – or the type of system of interest representation (pluralism versus corporatism) are bound to have a crucial impact on how parties and interest groups operate respectively. We saw that the existing literature on parties and interest groups suggests that state subsidies, regulation and monitoring might reinforce (in large membership organizations possibly 'natural') tendencies towards centralization and professionalization and decrease organizations' interest in cultivating a loyal and active membership. This, in turn, might support processes of citizen alienation from parties and interest group alike and reduce their representative potential in modern democracies. To conceptualize and assess in detail how democratic states (through legislation or court rulings) might influence the evolution of parties and interest groups will remain an important theme, especially in an age of 'anti-politics' (Flinders 2010). At the same time, future work on party government and the assessment of the challenges parties are confronted with in advanced democracies needs to go beyond parties' political role as citizen representatives and the 'mandate theory' underpinning it. Party functions linked to representing citizens and to governing need to be analytically distinguished since they refer to different perspectives on parties, to parties as vehicles for citizen demands as opposed to decision-making actors. When operating in complex environments and addressing multiple functions simultaneously, these two roles of parties might conflict and the conditions helping a party to meet the demands of the former role, might weaken its capacity to meet the latter. While conflicts have been highlighted between strategies through which parties pursue their various political goals, such as maximizing votes and accessing government (Müller and Strøm 1999), they have received less attention between political and merely 'functional' roles. The latter deserve more attention not only because parties' ties to society weaken as stressed in the literature. If citizens do increasingly oppose partisan and politicized government, they ought to care more about effective governing rather than the realization of ideological convictions. To fully recognize parties' contribution to governing might not necessarily compensate for their declining representative capacity in terms of legitimacy. Citizens might not be satisfied with a 'functional underpinning' of party government alone, but we still need to know to what extent contemporary party government can be justified in functional terms.

ACKNOWLEDGEMENTS

This research has received funding from the European Research Council under the European Union's Seventh Framework Programme (FP7/2007-2013)/ERC grant agreement no. 335890 STATORG. The support is gratefully acknowledged.

NOTE

1. Note that organizations in the voluntary or third sector do not necessarily have individual members, although many do, especially those that were formed bottom-up and grew out of citizen initiatives.

FURTHER READING

Jordan, G. and W. Maloney (2007), *Democracy and Interest Groups: Enhancing Participation?* London: Palgrave Macmillan.
Müller, W.C. and H.M. Narud (2013), *Party Governance and Party Democracy*, New York: Springer.
Scarrow, S. (2014), *Beyond Party Members: Changing Approaches to Partisan Mobilization*, Oxford: Oxford University Press.

REFERENCES

Baumgartner, F. and B.L. Leech (1998), *Basic Interests: The Importance of Groups in Politics and Political Science*, Princeton, NJ: Princeton University Press.
Baumgartner, F.R., J.M. Berry, M. Hojnacki, D.C. Kimball and B.L. Leech (2009), *Lobbying and Policy Change: Who Wins, Who Loses, and Why*, Chicago: The University of Chicago Press.
Biezen, I. van and P. Kopecký (2008), 'The state and the parties: public funding, public regulation and rent-seeking in contemporary democracies', *Party Politics*, **13** (2), 235–54.
Biezen, I. van, P. Mair and T. Poguntke (2011), 'Going, going . . . gone? The decline of party membership in contemporary Europe', *European Journal of Political Research*, **51** (1), 24–56.
Billis, D. (ed.) (2010), *Hybrid Organizations and the Third Sector: Challenges for Practice, Theory and Policy*, Basingstoke, UK: Palgrave.
Blondel, J. (1995), 'Towards a systemic analysis of government–party relationships', *International Political Science Review*, **16** (2), 127–43.
Bolleyer, N. (2011), 'The influence of political parties on policy coordination', *Governance*, **3** (24), 467–92.
Bolleyer, N. (2013), *New Parties in Old Party Systems: Persistence and Decline in 17 Democracies*, Oxford: Oxford University Press.
Bosso, C.J. (2003), 'Rethinking the concept of membership in nature advocacy coalitions', *Policy Studies Journal*, **31** (3), 397–411.
Budge, I. and H. Keman (1993), *Parties and Democracy: Coalition Formation and Government Functioning in Twenty States*, Oxford: Oxford University Press.
Budge, I., H. Keman, M. McDonald and P. Pennings (2012), *Organizing Democratic Choice*, Oxford: Oxford University Press.
Cansino, C. (1995), 'Party government: in search for a theory: introduction', *International Political Science Review*, **16** (2), 123–6.
Cornforth, C. and R. Spear (2010), 'The governance of hybrid organisations', in D. Billis (ed.), *Hybrid Organizations and the Third Sector: Challenges for Practice, Theory and Policy*, Basingstoke, UK: Palgrave, pp. 70–80.
Cross, B. and R.S. Katz (eds) (2013), *The Challenges of Intra-Party Democracy*, Oxford: Oxford University Press.

Dalton, R.J. (2003), *Democratic Challenges, Democratic Choices: The Erosion of Political Support in Advanced Industrial Democracies*, Oxford: Oxford University Press.

Dalton, R.J. and M. Wattenberg (eds) (2000), *Parties without Partisans: Political Change in Advanced Industrial Democracies*, Oxford: Oxford University Press.

Davies, S. (2011), 'Outsourcing and the voluntary sector: a review of the evolving policy landscape', in I. Cunningham and P. James (eds), *Voluntary Organisations and Public Service Delivery*, London: Routledge, pp. 15–36.

DiMaggio, P.J. and H.K. Anheier (1990), 'The sociology of nonprofit organizations and sectors', *Annual Review of Sociology*, **16**, 137–59.

Farrell, D.M. (2006), 'Political parties in a changing campaign environment', in R.S. Katz and W. Crotty (eds), *Handbook of Party Politics*, Oxford: Oxford University Press and London: Sage, pp. 122–33.

Flinders, M. (2010), 'In defence of politics', *Political Quarterly*, **81** (3), 309–26.

Gauja, A. (2015), 'The construction of party membership', *European Journal of Political Research*, **54** (2), 232–48.

Halpin, D. (2014), *The Organization of Political Interest Groups*, London: Routledge.

Hirschman, A.O. (1970), *Exit, Voice and Loyalty: Responses to the Decline in Firms, Organizations and States*, Cambridge: Harvard University Press.

Holman, C. and W. Luneburg (2012), 'Lobbying and transparency: a comparative analysis of regulatory reform', *Interest Groups & Advocacy*, **1** (1), 75–104.

Hopkin, J. and C. Paolucci (1999), 'The business firm model of party organisation: cases from Spain and Italy', *European Journal of Political Research*, **35** (5), 307–39.

Jordan, G. and W. Maloney (1997), *The Protest Business: Mobilizing Campaign Groups*, Manchester: Manchester University Press.

Jordan, G. and W. Maloney (2007), *Democracy and Interest Groups: Enhancing Participation?* London: Palgrave Macmillan.

Katz, R.S. (1987), 'Party government and its alternatives', in R.S. Katz (ed.), *Party Governments: European and American Experiences*, Berlin and New York: Walter de Gruyter, pp. 1–26.

Katz, R.S. and P. Mair (1995), 'Changing models of party organization and party democracy: the emergence of the cartel party', *Party Politics*, **1** (1), 5–28.

Katzenstein, P. (1984), *Corporatism and Change: Austria, Switzerland, and the Politics of Industry*, Ithaca, NY: Cornell University Press.

Keman, H. (2006), 'Party government formation and policy preferences: an encompassing approach?', in J. Bara and A. Weale (eds), *Democratic Politics and Party Competition*, London: Routledge, pp. 33–55.

Keman, H. and F. Müller-Rommel (2012), *Party Government in the 'New Europe': Trends and Developments*, London: Routledge.

Kirchheimer, O. (1966), 'The transformation of the Western European party system', in J. LaPalombara and M. Weiner (eds), *Political Parties and Political Development*, Princeton, NJ: Princeton University Press, pp. 177–200.

Lansley, J. (1996), 'Membership participation and ideology in large voluntary organisations: the case of the National Trust', *Voluntas*, **7** (3), 221–40.

Lawson, K. and P. Merkl (eds) (1988), *When Parties Fail*, Princeton, NJ: Princeton University Press.

Lupia, A. and K. Strøm (2008), 'Coalition theory and cabinet governance: an introduction', in W.C. Müller, T. Bergman and K. Strøm (eds), *Cabinets and Coalition Bargaining: The Democratic Life Cycle in Western Europe*, Oxford: Oxford University Press, pp. 51–83.

Mair, P. (1997), *Party System Change: Approaches and Interpretations*, Oxford: Clarendon Press.

Mair, P. (2006), 'Ruling the void? The hollowing of western democracy', *New Left Review*, **42** (November–December), 25–51.

Mair, P. (2007), *The Challenge to Party Government*, EUI Working Paper SPS 2007/09, European University Institute, Department of Political and Social Sciences, Fiesole, Italy.

McCarthy, P. (1996), 'The overwhelming success and the consequent problems of a virtual party', in R. Katz and P. Ignazi (eds), *Italian Politics: A Review*, Oxford: Westview Press, pp. 31–55.

McMenamin, I. (2013), *If Money Talks, What Does it Say? Corruption and Business Financing of Political Parties*, Oxford: Oxford University Press.

Mueller, D.C. and P. Murrell (1986), 'Interest groups and the size of government', *Public Choice*, **48** (2), 125–45.

Müller, W.C. and K. Strøm (eds) (1999), *Policy, Office, or Votes? Howe Political Parties in Western Democracies Make Hard Choices*, Oxford: Oxford University Press.

Pasquino, G. (2003), 'A tale of two parties: Forza Italia and the Left Democrats', *Journal of Modern Italian Studies*, **8** (2), 197–215.

Rose, R. (1969), 'The variability of party government: a theoretical and empirical critique', *Political Studies*, **17** (4), 413–45.

Rose, R. (1984), *Do Parties Make A Difference?* London: Macmillan.

Salamon, L.M. and H.K. Anheier (1998), 'Social origins of civil society: explaining the non-profit sector cross-nationally', *Voluntas*, **9** (3), 213–48.

Sartori, G. (2005), 'Party types, organisation and functions', *West European Politics*, **28** (1), 5–32.

Scarrow, S. (2014), *Beyond Party Members: Changing Approaches to Partisan Mobilization*, Oxford: Oxford University Press.

Schattschneider, E.E. (1960), *The Semisovereign People: A Realist's View of Democracy in America*, New York: Holt, Rinehart and Winston.

Sjöblom, G. (1987), 'The role of political parties in Denmark and Sweden, 1970–1984', in R.S. Katz (ed.), *Party Governments: European and American Experiences*, Berlin and New York: Walter de Gruyter, pp. 155–201.

Skocpol, T. (2001), 'Associations without members', *American Prospect*, accessed 27 August 2015 at http://prospect.org/article/associations-without-members.

Smith, S.R. (2011), 'Contracting with voluntary service agencies in the USA: implications for employment and professionalisation', in I. Cunningham and P. James (eds), *Voluntary Organisations and Public Service Delivery*, London: Routledge, pp. 202–24.

Strøm, K. and L. Svåsand (eds) (1997), *Challenges to Political Parties: The Case of Norway*, Ann Arbor, MI: Michigan University Press.

Strøm, K., W.C. Müller and T. Bergman (eds) (2003), *Delegation and Accountability in Parliamentary Democracies*, Oxford: Oxford University Press.

Verhoest, K., G. Bouckaert and B.G. Peters (2007), 'Janus-faced reorganization: specialization and coordination in four OECD countries in the period 1980–2005', *International Review of Administrative Sciences*, **73** (3), 325–48.

Webb, P., D. Farrell and I. Holliday (eds) (2002), *Political Parties in Advanced Industrial Democracies*, Oxford: Oxford University Press.

Woldendorp, J. (2005), *The Polder Model: From Disease to Miracle? Dutch Neo-Corporatism 1965–2000*, Amsterdam: Thela Thesis.

11 Social movements and political action
Bert Klandermans

1 INTRODUCTION

Protests in 'new' democracies about 'stolen elections', street demonstrations in 'old' democracies against austerity measures, revolts in the Arab world for more democracy, occupied squares all over the world against inequality and for better governance, contentious tweets, Facebook pages and YouTube films – almost daily our media reports on how people engage in politics in contentious manners, but not all attempts to influence politics are contentious. Citizens who aim to influence politics can also engage in party politics and enter the electoral arena. Indeed, so-called 'losers of globalization' rally behind radical right populist parties expressing their discontent in the electoral arena, while parties that fail to deal successfully with the financial crisis are voted out of office. It has been argued that contentious politics have become more important, while traditional political parties lose support. Is that so and, if so, why would that be? Related to that, why is it that some individuals engage actively in politics while others remain apathetic? Rational choice theorists have argued that rational citizens would not take part in any political action, thereby evoking the *paradox of politics*. That is, it might be rational to refrain from participation; but the fact remains that many people do take part in politics, movement politics and party politics alike.

McAdam and Tarrow (2010), reflecting on the study of contentious politics, observe that scholars of social movements have largely neglected to pay attention to elections, while election researchers have failed to include social movements in their designs. However, social movements pursue their struggle in the socio-political realm, which makes sociology and political science the disciplines par excellence to study these struggles. Yet, while they became a central object of study in sociology, political scientists have paid comparatively little attention to social movements (Burstein and Linton 2002; McAdam and Su 2002). Sociologists – by contrast – have long been interested in informal or emergent social and political processes (McAdam and Su 2002). From the outset, it has virtually been a truism among sociologists that policy is affected by political action (Burstein and Linton 2002), whereas 'political scientists have tended to view social movements as ineffectual, stressing instead the role of elections and public opinion as the main popular mechanisms mediating policy shifts' (McAdam and Su 2002, p. 697). The literature on political participation is inconclusive (Hutter 2014). Some argue that party politics and movement politics reinforce each other – people who engage in party politics are more likely to engage in movement politics, and vice versa (in statistical terms a positive correlation). Others reason that the two alternate – that is, people who participate in the one activity are less likely to participate in the other (a negative correlation). Hutter (2014) proposed a third option, namely, the two follow their own logic (no correlation). I hold that any arrangement between movements and parties is conceivable. They may compete, complement each other or collaborate (Goldstone 2003, 2004; Johnston 2011).

In the following, I develop a framework for the analysis of political participation – both movement and party politics. The framework connects the micro, meso and macro levels, and separates demand, supply and mobilization as factors influencing the dynamics of political participation. Understanding political participation requires research that focuses on *individual citizens* – what are their fears, hopes and concerns? What are the issues they care for? What are the motives they have? What opportunities do they perceive? Moving beyond the current state-of-the-art, I elaborate on participation in party politics and movement politics within a single conceptual, theoretical and methodologically comparative framework accounting for the choices individual citizens make. Research of political participation tends to neglect that even in identical circumstances individuals diverge widely in the ways they act politically. A proper understanding of that variation requires a framework that integrates the micro, meso and macro levels of analysis. Such integration is frequently asked for but sparsely done. Figure 11.1 depicts such a framework. The agents at the micro level are citizens who attempt to promote or protect their interest or principles (demand of politics). Their counterparts at the meso level are movement organizations and political parties that offer opportunities to participate (supply of politics). Mobilization campaigns connect demand and supply. The better the fit of demand and supply and the more persuasive the mobilization campaigns, the more likely that citizens will seize the opportunities offered. Citizens, political parties, and movement organizations are embedded in multi-organizational fields that further shape the demand and supply of politics. Regimes, institutions and social cleavages define the opportunities and constraints imposed by the socio-economic and political context. Research with a comparative design is needed comparing political participation by individual citizens over time and place to test the framework. Throughout the chapter I provide examples of such research, stemming from a large comparative study among participants in street demonstrations.[1]

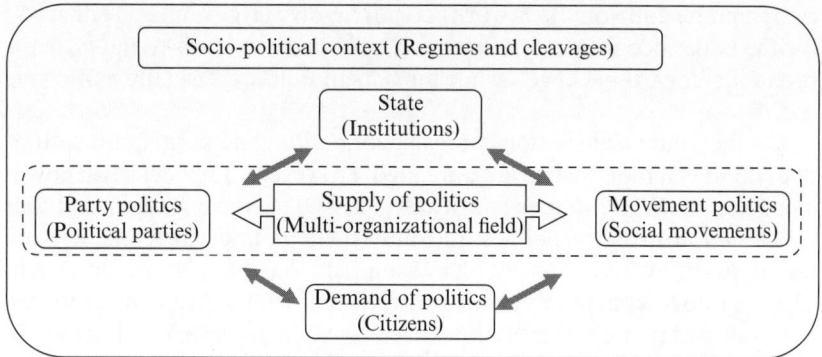

Figure 11.1   Routes to political influence

2   PARTICIPATION IN MOVEMENT POLITICS AND PARTY POLITICS

I define political participation as 'action by ordinary citizens directed toward influencing some political outcomes' (Brady, cited in Teorell et al. 2007, p. 336). Movements and parties are two forms politics might take in democratic systems. I believe it was Charles Tilly who once said that social movements is politics with other means. Movement politics centers on activities such as signing petitions, mass demonstrations, occupations of public sites, boycotts, strikes, violence against property and people to mention the most common examples. Party politics involves activities such as voting, contacting, campaigning, donating money, party membership and running for office. Recently, virtual forms of action were added to the repertoire. Comparative studies reveal that countries differ widely in terms of the level of political activity of their citizens (Teorell et al. 2007; Dalton et al. 2009; Weldon and Dalton 2011) both quantitatively (number of activities) and qualitatively (types of activities). Activities in the two arenas differ significantly. Party politics is far more institutionalized than movement politics; elections are held at regular intervals, at predefined local, national or supranational levels, passing along according preset rules. Movement politics, on the other hand, is far less predictable. Movement politics can always take place as there is no institutionalized rhythm prescribing when and how protest events should occur. It is also less clear who takes part in movement politics, in what roles and with what impact. Usually, only small percentages of a population take part in movement politics, while much larger proportions take part in elections (Teorell et al. 2007, although other forms of party politics (membership, campaigning and voluntary work) do not involve large numbers either. As for the issues people are mobilized for, party politics tends to mobilize for broad ideological packages, while movement politics is usually more issue specific.

The fact that participation in movement politics and party politics differ does not mean that the two are unrelated. However, the evidence on how is inconclusive. While Barnes and Kaase's (1979) classical study found that participation in party politics and movement politics correlate, a more recent study by Teorell et al. (2007) suggests that the two are unrelated. These authors report low or statistically insignificant correlations between electoral and non-electoral political activities. In any event, neither study suggests that political activities are crowding each other out, as the correlations between diverging political activities are not negative but insignificant or positive.

Several authors observe that movement politics has become more frequent over the past 30 years (see Dodson 2011; but see McCarthy et al. 2013 for diverging figures on the USA). Others argued that social movements became a regular phenomenon in democratic societies (Goldstone 2004). At the same time, a decline of participation in party politics is reported (Dalton and Wattenberg 2000). Some labeled this trend 'movementization of politics' (Neidhardt and Rucht 1993), while others coined the term 'movement society' (Meyer and Tarrow 1998). Goldstone (2004) emphasizes that we must study movements in the context of 'external relational fields' – a concept akin to multi-organizational fields – including other movements, countermovements, political and economic institutions, state authorities and actors, various elites and various publics. McAdam and Tarrow (2010) theorize about the various ways in which movement politics influences election campaigns. Movements can introduce new forms of collective action in the campaign; they can join electoral coalitions or even become a party; they can engage in electoral mobilization, and they can polarize parties internally (Heaney and Rojas 2007; Hutter 2014).

The suggestion that social movements have become commonplace concerns the relative significance attributed to social movement organizations and political parties as intermediaries between citizens and the state. Thus conceived, an increased importance of one of these players necessarily implies a change in the significance of the other (Jenkins and Klandermans 1995). Giugni et al. (1999) reason that if party politics fails, movement politics takes over and, compared to working our way through political institutions, contentious collective actions can be remarkably effective provided that the right ingredients are in place, as convincingly demonstrated by the 'Colored Revolutions' and the events in the Arab world.

Some 20 years ago I estimated on the basis of various literature reviews that approximately one-third of the instances of collective political action had some degree of success (Klandermans 1989).

Since Barnes and Kaase's classic study, the socio-political world has changed profoundly. Think of the various waves of democratization or the emergence of the Internet to mention a few changes. The handful of studies of movement and party politics within a single framework published since Barnes and Kaase's classic work (1979) all come with limitations. They rarely take the individual as their unit of analysis, or issues people care for as their point of departure. They include a small number of countries (Teorell et al. 2007; Hutter 2014), only Western democracies (Hutter 2014), or a limited set of independent variables (Teorell et al. 2007; Van der Meer et al. 2009; Norris 2011).

3 DYNAMICS OF POLITICAL PARTICIPATION: THEORETICAL FRAMEWORK

Generally, citizens have four options when it comes to influencing politics: refrain from any influence attempt, engage in party politics only, engage in movement politics only, and engage in both party and movement politics. I maintain that each citizen has issues he or she cares so much for that he or she would engage in politics. That raises the questions of: 'which issues, what action would they take, and why?' I seek the answer in the integration of dynamics at the micro, meso, and macro levels. What are the motives people have? To what extent do parties and movement organizations appeal to these motives, and what are the opportunities and constraints regimes impose?

4 PEOPLE AND THEIR MOTIVES: DYNAMICS OF DEMAND

Dynamics of demand refer to the factors determining people's propensity to take part in political action. Such propensity can be studied with regard to party and movement politics. Reviewing studies of *electoral* participation, Pennings (2002) distinguishes three theoretical approaches: (1) The *sociological approach* focusing on group-related variables such as class, religion or, more recently, groups demarcated by matters such as immigration or the environment. The sociological approach holds that people vote for parties that support the social group they identify with. (2) The *psychological approach* puts an emphasis on long-term psychological dispositions, such as values and ideology. Old values such as religious versus secular and Left versus Right and new values such as materialism versus post-materialism appear to correlate significantly with party choice (Knutsen 1995; see also Pennings 2002). (3) The economic approach building on the assumption that voters are rational and make voting decisions in a calculating manner by choosing the party that provides more benefits than any other.

Coming from political science as well, Dalton et al. (2009) distinguish grievances, resources and political values as determinants of protest participation. Grievances the authors operationalize as relative deprivation and political dissatisfaction; resources as group membership and education; and political values as left–right self-placement and post-material values. On the basis of an analysis of World Value Survey (wave 3 and 4) data of 78 countries, the authors conclude that protest participation is not related to grievances, but is related to people's resources and values. These findings corroborate a basic tenet of the sociological resource mobilization theory that resources rather than grievances make people protest. In the social psychological literature on political protest, three fundamental motives of protest participation are distinguished: identification, instrumentality and ideology (Van Stekelenburg and Klandermans 2007). 'Identification' refers to protest participation as a mark of identification with a group, 'instrumentality' to protest participation under the assumption that circumstances can be changed by collective political action at affordable costs, and 'ideology' refers to protest participation as an expression of one's principles. Each motive contributes uniquely to the readiness to participate in collective political action. To these motives 'emotions' such as anger and fear must be added. Anger functions as amplifier and accelerator; fear as attenuator and inhibitor (Van Stekelenburg and Klandermans 2007; Van Zomeren et al. 2008). Readiness to participation does not relate 'one-to-one' to actual participation. Studies that monitor both intended and actual participation reveal at best moderate correlations (see Klandermans and Oegema 1987).

I have combined the various frameworks into a single model which aims to account for participation in both movement and party politics, comprising identification, motivation and emotions. Figure 11.2 displays the hypothesized relationships between these factors and readiness to participate. The model departs from the assumption that the issues people care for can be interests or principles and that some level of group identification is needed for an issue to be perceived as shared. The more people identify with the group whose interests or principles are violated, the stronger their motivation to undertake political action on behalf of the group. When people's interests are violated I expect them to be primarily

BOX 11.1   PARADERS VERSUS PROTESTORS

Some demonstrations are ritual parades such as May Day parades or gay prides, others are protest events. A ritual parade is an event recurring at fixed intervals and sometimes at fixed dates, while the occurrence of a demonstration is unforeseeable. Demonstrations have moments of spontaneity which are less likely in ritual parades. A demonstration is by definition politicized; a parade not necessarily. However, circumstances may politicize a parade, when the claims, slogans, goals relate to current political controversies. Parades are a goal in themselves. They are not aiming to achieve some external goal. They are expressive rather than instrumental. Yet, parades are not purely symbolic. They provide benefits such as a sense of belonging, emotional energy and collective effervescence. In terms of the motivation to participate, we expected the paraders in the CCC-project to be more ideologically and less instrumentally motivated, unlike the protestors who we expected to be instrumentally motivated rather than ideologically. This is indeed what we found: on standardized scales paraders scored −.26 on the instrumentality scale versus −.10 on the ideology scale, as compared to .11 and .00, respectively, for the protestors.

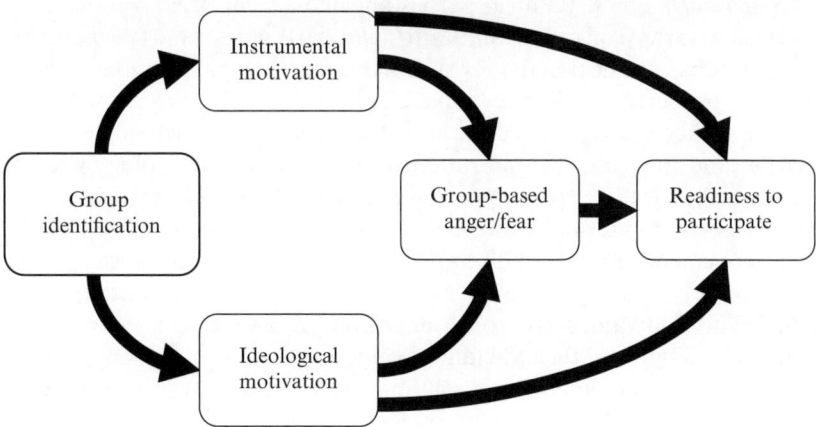

Figure 11.2   Dynamics of demand

instrumentally motivated; when their principles are at stake ideologically. Efficacy is assumed to be of crucial significance in people's motivation to participate. Corcoran et al. (2011) demonstrate the significance of efficacy in a study on protest participation across 48 countries. Feelings of efficacy also seem to play a role in the arousal of emotions (Klandermans et al. 2008). When people feel inefficacious they are more likely to experience fear; when they feel efficacious they display anger.

5   ORGANIZATIONS AND THEIR APPEALS: DYNAMICS OF SUPPLY AND MOBILIZATION

The stronger people's readiness to take part in political action, the more susceptible they are to appeals by political actors, be it parties or movements. The choice they end up making depends on the supply of politics they encounter. This brings us to the meso level, which plays a crucial role in the dynamics of political participation. Here the questions to study are: What are the multi-organizational fields citizens, parties and movement organizations are embedded in? How do citizens assess the supply of activities parties and movements offer? What is their ideological profile, the issues they 'own' and their effectiveness? Which communication channels are employed? Are people connected to the mobilizing structures that movements and parties have assembled? Are they embedded in formal, informal and virtual social networks, and do they talk politics in those networks? No matter how strong a demand of politics there is in a society, it will not get very far without appealing supply and effective communication channels.

Supply of politics. Political parties and movement organizations offer citizens a variety of opportunities to take part in politics, ranging from conventional political activities such as voting or petitioning to violence against property or people. Some of those activities are attractive to people, other are not. In addition to the variety of activities they offer, parties and movement organizations differ in terms of ideology and the issues they 'own'. Next to types of activities, the supply of politics can be categorized in terms of ideology and issues. Usually, the issues parties and movement organizations emphasize fit into their ideological profile. Therefore, we may hypothesize that a decision to become politically active implies not only a decision to act but also a fit between a movement's or party's ideology and the individual's values.

The most common ideological dimensions employed in studies of party politics and movement politics are left–right and materialism–post-materialism (Pennings 2002; Dalton et al. 2009; Van der Meer et al. 2009), more recently in the European context supplemented by a radical populism dimension (Hutter 2014). Comparing 20 Western democracies, van de Meer et al. (2009) conclude that left-wing citizens are more likely to contact officials, campaign, persuade others, cooperate, and protest, while right-wing citizens are more likely to vote. Hutter (2014) reports similar findings – left-wingers are more likely to choose movement participation if they want to influence politics, while right-wingers are more likely to invest in party politics. Comparing citizens from 78 countries across the globe Dalton et al. (2009) report that left-wing citizens and people

BOX 11.2   DEMONSTRATORS ARE LEANING TO THE LEFT

In a study conducted by Swen Hutter (2014) participants in street demonstrations appear to lean toward the political left. We included the classical left/right
self-placement scale in our CCC-questionnaire. On the scale from 0 = 'left' to
10 = 'right' respondents could indicate their ideological leaning. Almost 90 percent
of the demonstrators self-classify at the left halve of the scale. A comparison of
our demonstrators with the general population in their country clearly corroborates
Hutter's finding (Table 11.1). Whereas the mean of the general population hovers
around the midpoint of the scale, the CCC-sample in each country unmistakable
positions itself at the left end of the scale.

Table 11.1   Left–right self-placement (means on a scale 0–10)

	General population	CCC-demonstrators
Belgium	5.0	3.2
Czech Republic	4.8	3.5
Italy	4.7	1.4
Netherlands	5.3	3.3
Spain	4.7	2.0
Sweden	5.5	2.1
Switzerland	5.1	2.3
United Kingdom	5.0	2.9

who adhere to post-materialist values are more likely to participate in
protest than right-wing citizens. Comparing participants in more than 20
demonstrations in Belgium, Verhulst (2011) finds that traditional leftist
ideology is linked with participation in 'old' issues and post-materialism
with participation in 'new' issues. Similarly, 'old' parties such as the Social
Democrats or the Christian Democrats are more characterized by the
left–right distinction, while 'new' parties such as 'Greens' are better por-
trayed as post-materialists (Jansen 2011). Election research suggests that
voters will choose the party which is closest to their own position on the
left–right dimension – the so-called proximity hypothesis (Pennings 2002).
Theories on issue voting, however, argue that rather than enduring ideological preferences, short-term issues currently direct voters' preferences
more and more.

Multi-organizational fields. Movement organizations and political
parties are embedded in multi-organizational fields (Klandermans 1992).
Multi-organizational fields can be defined as the total possible number of
organizations with which a political party or a movement organization

might establish specific links, and these links can be supportive or antagonistic. The boundaries between supporters and antagonists remain fluid and may change in the course of events. Organizations that were indifferent may choose, or be forced, to take sides; coalitions may fall apart and allies may become opponents. The composition of organizational fields is not random, but relates to the social cleavages in a society, be it class, religion, ethnicity, left-right affiliation, or environmental issues, and so on (Verhulst 2011). Multi-organizational fields require a new way of looking at mobilization (Goldstone 2004). Individuals are objects of persuasive communication not only from the movement organization or party they sympathize with, but also from competing organizations, opponents, countermovement organization, and so on (Born et al. 2013). This can be offline and online.

Mobilization. Demand and supply remain potentials, if not mobilization would bring the two together. Mobilization can be broken down into *consensus mobilization* (the dissemination of the views of the political actor), and *action mobilization* (the transformation of sympathizers into participants; Klandermans 1984).The more successful consensus mobilization has been, the larger the pool of sympathizers a mobilizing organization can draw from. Action mobilization can be broken down into four separate steps (Klandermans and Oegema 1987): people (1) need to sympathize with the cause, (2) need to know about the upcoming event, (3) must want to participate, and (4) and must be able to participate. Each step brings the supply and demand closer together until an individual takes the final step and participates.

Social embeddedness. In the mobilization process social embeddedness is thought to play a pivotal role. First, individuals do not make their decisions to take part in politics in isolation. Social networks function as communities, wherein discursive processes take place to form consensus. Klandermans et al. (2008) provide evidence for such mechanisms: immigrants are more likely to participate in protest provided that they are embedded in social networks which offer an opportunity to discuss politics. This is where people talk about politics and are mobilized for political activities (Gamson 1992). Second, people who are integrated in a social network are more likely targeted by a mobilizing message and informed of upcoming events, and – equally important – are kept to their promises to participate (Klandermans and Oegema 1987). Walgrave and Klandermans (2010) demonstrated how open and closed communication channels and weak and strong ties weave a web that influences how easy or difficult it is to reach and mobilize potential participants. In the digital era social media have become an integral part of social embeddedness (Earl and Kimport 2011).

BOX 11.3   SOCIAL EMBEDDEDNESS

People are more or less embedded in the networks of the organizers of a demonstration. Forty-five percent of the demonstrators in the CCC-study were members of one of the organizations that staged the demonstration. Verba et al. (1995) once succinctly reasoned that people take part in politics because they 'want', because they 'can' and because 'somebody asked'. The latter obviously concerns mechanisms of mobilization. We could imagine that people who are affiliated to the organizers are more likely being asked by co-members of that organization. In that sense we could expect networks to be important conduits of recruitment. The figures in Table 11.2 convincingly confirm these assumptions.

Table 11.2   *Conduits of recruitment: percentages*

	Not asked by co-members	Asked by co-members	
Not embedded	88.3	11.7	100
Embedded	56.3	43.7	100

People who are embedded in networks of the organizers are far more often asked by co-members of an organization to take part in the demonstration than people who are not embedded.

6   CODA

Movements and parties are major intermediaries between citizens and the state. Citizens who want to influence politics can engage in movement politics, party politics, or both. Sociology and political science seem to have divided labor such that social movements are studied by the former and political parties by the latter. I have argued in favor of studying participation in movement and party politics with a single theoretical framework, as choices individuals have. Such a framework comprises dynamics of demand, dynamics of supply and mobilization. Whether and how mobilization attempts reach individual citizens depends on how they are embedded in the multi-organizational field in society. The more organizers succeed in appealing to the motives that drive participants, the more people will be prepared to engage in politics. Identity, instrumentality and ideology all spur individuals onto the streets. More so if emotions amplify people's motivation.

NOTE

1. Caught in the Act of Protest: Contextualizing Contestation (CCC) is a comparative study of street demonstrations in 8 European countries (Belgium, Czech Republic, Italy, the Netherlands, Spain, Sweden, Switzerland and the UK). The data presented in this chapter are based on the 71 demonstrations we covered between November 2009 and summer 2013. In total 14 455 participants returned questionnaires distributed during the demonstrations. All questionnaires and procedures are standardized. Identical questions and indicators are employed in each country and for each demonstration. Obviously, these so-called protest surveys are not the only 'game in town'. I refer to Chapters 15 and 18 in this volume for a discussion of other methods.

FURTHER READING

Deth, J. van, J.R. Montero and A. Westholm (eds) (2007), *Citizenship and Involvement in European Democracies: A Comparative Analysis*, London: Routledge.

Hutter, S. (2014), *Protesting Culture and Economics in Western Europe: New Cleavages in Left and Right Politics*, Minneapolis, MN: University of Minnesota Press.

Klandermans, B. and C. Roggeband (eds) (2007), *The Handbook of Social Movements across Disciplines*, New York: Springer.

McVeigh, R. (2009), *The Rise of the Ku Klux Klan: Right-Wing Movements and National Politics*, Minneapolis, MN: University of Minnesota Press.

Snow, D.A. and S.A. Soule (2010), *A Primer on Social Movements*, New York: W.W. Norton.

Stekelenburg, J. van, C. Roggeband and B. Klandermans (eds) (2013), *The Future of Social Movement Research: Dynamics, Mechanisms and Processes*, Minneapolis, MN: University of Minnesota Press.

REFERENCES

Barnes, S.H. and M. Kaase (1979), *Political Action: Mass Participation in Five Western Democracies*, London: Sage.

Born, M.J., A. Akkerman and R. Torenvlied (2013), 'Trust your boss or listen to the unions? Information, social identification, trust and strike participation', *Mobilization*, **18**(2), 161–78.

Burstein, P. and A. Linton (2002), 'The impact of political parties, interest groups, and social movement organizations on public policy: some recent evidence and theoretical concerns', *Social Forces*, **81** (2), 380–440.

Corcoran, K.E., D. Pettinicchio and J.T.N. Young (2011), 'The context of control: a cross-national investigation of the link between political institutions, efficacy, and collective action', *British Journal of Social Psychology*, **50** (4), 575–605.

Dalton, R.J. and M.P. Wattenberg (2000), *Parties without Partisans*, Oxford: Oxford University Press.

Dalton, R.J., A. van Sickle and S. Weldon (2009), 'The individual–institutional nexus of protest behaviour', *British Journal of Political Sociology*, **40** (1), 51–73.

Dodson, K. (2011), 'The movement society in comparative perspective', *Mobilization*, **16** (4), 475–94.

Earl, J. and K. Kimport (2011), *Activism in the Internet Age*, Cambridge, MA: MIT Press.

Gamson, W.A. (1992), *Talking Politics*, Cambridge: University of Cambridge Press.

Giugni, M., D. McAdam and C. Tilly (1999), *How Social Movements Matter*, Minneapolis, MN: University of Minnesota Press.

Goldstone, J.A. (2003), *States, Parties and Social Movements*, Cambridge: Cambridge University Press.

Goldstone, J.A. (2004), 'More social movements or fewer? Beyond political opportunity structures to relational fields', *Theory and Society*, **33** (3), 333–65.

Heaney, M. and F. Rojas (2007), 'Partisans, nonpartisans, and the antiwar movement in the United States', *American Politics Research*, **35** (4), 431–64.

Hutter, S. (2014), *Protesting Culture and Economics in Western Europe: New Cleavages in Left and Right Politics*, Minneapolis, MN: University of Minnesota Press.

Jansen, G. (2011), 'Social cleavages and political choices: large-scale comparisons of social class, religion and voting behaviour in western democracies', dissertation, Radboud University, Nijmegen.

Jenkins, C.C. and B. Klandermans (eds) (1995), *The Politics of Social Protest: Comparative Perspectives of States and Social Movements*, Minneapolis, MN: University of Minnesota Press.

Johnston, H. (2011), *States and Social Movements*, Cambridge: Polity.

Klandermans, B. (1984), 'Mobilization and participation: social psychological expansions of resource mobilization theory', *American Sociological Review*, **49** (5), 583–600.

Klandermans, B. (1989), 'Organizational effectiveness', in B. Klandermans (ed.), *Organizing for Change: Social Movement Organizations In Europe and the United States, International Social Movement Research*, vol. 2, Greenwich, CT: JAI Press, pp. 383–94.

Klandermans, B. (1992), 'The social construction of protest and multi-organizational fields', in A. Morris and C. Mueller (eds), *Frontiers in Social Movement Theory*, New Haven, CT: Yale University Press, pp. 77–103.

Klandermans, B. and D. Oegema (1987), 'Potentials, networks, motivations and barriers: steps toward participation in social movements', *American Sociological Review*, **52** (4), 519–31.

Klandermans, B., J. van der Toorn and J. van Stekelenburg (2008), 'Embeddedness and identity: how immigrants turn grievances into action', *American Sociological Review*, **73**, 992–1012.

Knutsen, O. (1995), 'Party choice', in J.W. van Deth and E. Scarborough (eds), *The Impact of Values*, Oxford: Oxford University Press, pp. 500–536.

McAdam, D. and Y. Su (2002), 'The war at home: antiwar protests and congressional voting, 1965 to1973', *American Sociological Review*, **67** (5), 696–721.

McAdam, D. and S. Tarrow (2010), 'Ballots and barricades: on the reciprocal relationship between elections and social movements', *Reflections*, **8**, 529–42.

McCarthy, J.D., P. Rafail and A. Gromis (2013), 'Recent trends in public protest in the U.S.A.: the Social Movement Society thesis revisited', in J. van Stekelenburg, C. Roggeband and B. Klandermans (eds), *The Changing Dynamics of Contention*, Minneapolis, MN: University of Minnesota Press.

Meyer, D. and S. Tarrow (1998), *The Social Movement Society: Contentious Politics for a New Century*, Boulder, CO: Rowman & Littlefield.

Neidhardt, F. and D. Rucht (1993), 'Auf dem Weg in die Bewegungsgesellschaft? Über die Stabilisierbarkeit sozialer Bewegungen', *Sozialer Welt*, **44**, 305–26.

Norris, P. (2011), *Democratic Deficits*, Cambridge: Cambridge University Press.

Pennings, P. (2002), 'Voters, elections and ideology in European democracies', in H. Keman (ed.), *Comparative Democratic Politics*, London: Sage, pp. 99–121.

Teorell, J., M. Torcal and J.R. Montero (2007), 'Political participation, mapping the terrain', in J. van Deth, J.R. Montero and A.Westholm (eds), *Citizenship and Involvement in European Democracies*, London, Routledge, pp. 334–57.

Van der Meer, T.W.G., J. van Deth and P.L.H. Scheepers (2009), 'The politicized participant. Ideology and political action in 20 democracies', *Comparative Political Studies*, **42**, 1426–57.

Van Stekelenburg, J. and B. Klandermans (2007), 'Individuals in movements: a social psychology of contention', in B. Klandermans and C. Roggeband (eds), *The Handbook Social Movements across Disciplines*, Kluwer, pp. 157–204.

Van Zomeren, M., T. Postmes and R. Spears (2008), 'Toward an integrative social identity model of collective action: a quantitative research synthesis of three socio-psychological perspectives', *Psychological Bulletin*, **134**, 504–35.

Verba, S., K.L. Schlozman and H.E. Brady (1995), *Voice and Equality: Civic Voluntarism in American Politics*, Cambridge: Harvard University Press.

Verhulst, J. (2011), 'Mobilizing issues and the unity and diversity of protest events', dissertation, University of Antwerp.

Walgrave, S. and B. Klandermans (2010), 'Open and closed mobilization patterns. The role of channels and ties', in S. Walgrave and D. Rucht (eds), *The World Says No to War: Demonstrations against the War in Iraq*, Minneapolis, MN: University of Minnesota Press, pp. 169–93.

Weldon, S. and R.J. Dalton (2011), 'Democratic structures and democratic participation: the limits of consensualism theory', unpublished paper, Simon Fraser University, Vancouver.

12 International relations and transnational politics

Andreas Nölke

1 FOREWORD

For a long time the sub-field of international relations has been studied by approaches where nation states were the focus (for example, neo-realism and neo-liberal institutionalism). However, increasingly not only inter-state (more specifically, intergovernmental) relations but also transnational relations have come to the fore. In particular the role of non-governmental organizations (NGOs) (such as Greenpeace and Amnesty International), autonomously acting international agencies (such as the World Bank) and various transnational interest associations (such as the European Roundtable of Industrialists) have become the subject of analysis in international relations. Theories such as neo-realism and neo-liberal institutionalism, however, are unable to analyze transnational politics, given their government-centric categories. These developments require fresh approaches to analyze the different patterns of transnational versus intergovernmental policies and to identify the conditions for their relative salience.

The chapter uses policy network analysis as an approach for distinguishing between intergovernmental and transnational relations, and illustrates its application in various settings. It starts with highlighting the basic distinction between transnational and inter-state politics, as well as its importance (section 2). Next, it operationalizes this distinction by juxtaposing intergovernmental co-operation and transnational policy networks. Policy network analysis as a method in order to distinguish these two types is described in section 3 and the pros and cons of alternative approaches are discussed in the same section. Section 4 develops framework conditions for the relative salience of both types of policy-making and illustrates the transnational–inter-state distinction, as well as the role of selected framework conditions based on applications involving international agencies, NGOs and subnational administrative actors. The final section concludes with the main findings, normative implications and further research requirements.

2   INTRODUCTION: TRANSNATIONAL VERSUS INTER-STATE POLITICS

Since the 1970s, the question of whether global politics should be characterized as inter-state politics or as transnational politics has become a central puzzle in international relations scholarship (Risse 2013). How shall we characterize global politics – as the plain interaction between the 'billiard balls' of inter-state politics, or as the more complex 'cobwebs' of transnational politics (Rochester 2002)? Traditionally, international relations have been studied as inter-state politics. Since the early 1970s, however, this traditional picture has increasingly been cast into doubt by the increasing importance of a number of transnational actors (see Box 12.1). Since 11 September 2001 (9/11) at the latest, the importance of transnational actors such as terrorist networks has become familiar to the wider public (Schneckener 2006). Before this recent burst of attention for transnational actors, multinational companies were the most widely known cases of the latter (Keohane and Nye 1974, 1981). Other well-known cases of transnational politics include the European Union (EU) multi-level governance system (Marks et al. 1996), but also the activities of transnational organized crime (Galeotti 2001) or of transnational private security providers (Coker 2001).

For the analysis of whether we should classify global politics as

---

BOX 12.1   ALTERNATIVE UNDERSTANDINGS OF TRANSNATIONAL POLITICS

As with other popular concepts in political science, there are competing understandings of the term 'transnational'. The dominant and most widely quoted utilization of the term 'transnational politics' or 'transnational politics' in international relations follows the understanding outlined above (Keohane and Nye 1981; Risse-Kappen 1995a). Still, in order to clarify the options available, two alternative understandings need to be mentioned. On the one side, an important alternative utilization is the concept of transnational (private) governance (Djelic and Sahlin-Andersson 2006; Graz and Nölke 2008; Hale and Held 2011). Here, the focus is not on developing research methods in order to distinguish inter-state and transnational politics, but to analyze an alternative form of governing, where non-state actors play a strong or even exclusive role, in contrast to traditional inter-governmental organizations. On the other side, an important alternative utilization is the concept of transnational historical materialism (Cox 1987; Gill 1991; Van der Pijl 1998; Overbeek 2000; Van Apeldoorn 2002). Here, again, the focus is not on developing research methods in order to distinguish inter-state and transnational politics, but on developing an alternative substantial theory of international relations, based on class-theoretical works of authors such as Karl Marx and Antonio Gramsci.

inter-state or as transnational politics, the concept of policy networks has become increasingly dominant (Nölke 2000, 2004). Since the 1990s, policy networks have gained quite some currency within international relations. While the concept has inspired research in diverse types of transnational networks, such as epistemic communities (Haas 1992), transnational advocacy networks (Keck and Sikkink 1998), transnational knowledge networks (Stone 2004) and transgovernmental networks (Slaughter 2004), its most congruent equivalent is the concept of global public policy networks as developed by Wolfgang Reinicke and associates (Reinicke 1998, 1999; Reinicke et al. 2000; Witte et al. 2000). Here, transnational (or global) policy networks are recently proposed to be a key instrument of global governance. According to this perspective, networks do not only lead to more flexible and efficient policies (Reinicke 1998, p. 89ff.), but also to a democratization of international politics, owing to their ability to involve major stakeholders in a more transparent and broad-based dialogue (Witte et al. 2000, p. 178, 180ff.; see also Dingwerth 2003, pp. 73–6).

If we combine the resource dependency framework, the most widely established policy network theory (see Börzel 1997), with the concept of transnational politics (as conceptualized by Risse-Kappen 1995b, p. 3), we can define transnational policy networks as a group of public and/or private organizations where at least one organization does not operate on behalf of a national government or an intergovernmental entity. These organizations are connected by a significant level of interactions (at least partially) across national boundaries and participate in policy-making and implementation through an exchange of resources. Typical resources to be exchanged in transnational policy networks include finance, information, legitimacy and the offer of participation in policy design. Actors within transnational policy networks include all types of public and private organizations, including interest groups, subnational governments, state agencies and international secretariats. Networks generally are grouped for a certain issue area, but may vary in their saliency during different phases of the policy process. Actors within these networks are to a varying degree dependent on resources which other actors control. Thus, the European Commission, for example, allows an interest group a role in policy design or in the allocation of funds during implementation, while at the same time the interest group provides the Commission with information and legitimacy. Whereas the interest group may largely rely on the Commission for political influence, the Commission may choose among a number of competing interests.

Based on this definition, we can now clearly distinguish transnational policy networks from intergovernmental cooperation. First, both forms of international politics differ very much regarding their core actors. Whereas

Table 12.1   Transnational policy networks versus intergovernmental cooperation

	Transnational network	Intergovernmental cooperation
Actors	Organizations	Governments
Dynamic	Inter-organizational resource dependencies	Government preferences
Focus	Sectoral policies	Sectoral and cross-sectoral policies

intergovernmental cooperation (see Table 12.1) is based on governments acting as unitary and only important actors, transnational policy networks are based on a multitude of organizational actors. The latter include different types of non-state actors, but also different government agencies acting on their own, in the absence of clear guidance by governments as a whole. Second, the basic dynamic underlying both types of international politics is very different. Whereas transnational policy networks are kept together by inter-organizational resource dependencies, international organizations and regimes are based on the preferences of the participating governments (theories of international relations differ, however, very much regarding their interpretation of these preferences as being based on interest, power or norms; see Hasenclever et al. 1997). Finally, the scope of both forms of institutions can be different: Whereas (transnational) policy networks are always focused on sectoral (or subsectoral) issues, intergovernmental cooperation can take on a much broader scope, as in case of international organizations such as the EU or the United Nations (international regimes usually are also limited to one sector).

Both transnational policy networks and intergovernmental cooperation as described above are stylized; in reality there is frequently a combination of both. Even more so, transnational policy networks very much benefit from the existence of intergovernmental cooperation, as international institutions contribute a great deal to the viability of these networks (see below). Transnational policy networks can also contribute to the evolution of intergovernmental cooperation, insofar as the preparatory work for new international regimes or organizations may be done within transnational policy networks.

To summarize, the concept of policy networks is able to aid our understanding of the distinction between transnational politics and intergovernmental cooperation. Transnational politics differ from intergovernmental cooperation as regards the actors involved, the basic dynamics and the scope of the issues involved.

3 POLICY NETWORK ANALYSIS AS A METHOD FOR DISTINGUISHING TRANSNATIONAL POLITICS AND INTERNATIONAL RELATIONS

How can we find out whether cross-border politics can best be studied as transnational politics or international or, more precisely, intergovernmental relations? Based on the traction the network concept has gained in the study of transnational politics, the most widely used method is to apply policy network analysis. Policy networks assume that policies are not being created and implemented by a central authority (government or parliament), but by resource exchanges between a number of public and private organizations, predominantly at the sector level (Mayntz 1993, p. 40). The affinity between the concepts of policy networks and transnational actors becomes obvious at once – both cast the traditional picture of politics into doubt, especially the central role of governments as unitary actors therein. Both concepts highlight the important role of organized societal actors as well as the independent role of fractions of the state apparatus. Both concepts deal with empirical issues which neither follow the typical logic of domestic politics in Western societies (party competition and the hierarchy of the state), nor the typical logic of international relations (anarchy). Thus, transnational policy networks stand at the focus of a double dynamic with both national and international roots: 'Just as much policy making is now transnational . . . , involving both international and domestic players, . . . policy making is also both public and private at one and the same time' (Forsythe 2000, p. 176).

Given the popularity of the policy network concept within public policy, it is no surprise that there are different, competing 'network schools'. The most sophisticated treatment of policy networks within domestic settings is based on categories of (inter-)organizational sociology, which assume that political decision-making and implementation is mainly based on the exchange of material and immaterial resources between mutually – but frequently asymmetrically – dependent organizations. Sociological inter-organization theories are based on an organization-environment perspective, where the most important feature of this environment are other organizations (see Jansen and Schubert 1995a). The focus is on the relationships between the organizations involved and on the consequences of these interactions for the policy outcome (Jansen and Schubert 1995b, p. 7). The most important competing policy network school is the 'governance model'. The latter is more interested in a normative comparison between networks, markets and hierarchies as alternative types of social coordination (Börzel 1997). However, it has a strong normative focus and thus is less well suited for the analytical study of global politics as either transnational or inter-governmental.

The state of the art of the study of inter-organizational policy network analysis can be summarized as follows. The *actors* within transnational policy networks are organizations. The spectrum of organizations may be rather wide; it can include business (associations), labor unions, NGOs, research institutes and think tanks. Typical members of transnational policy networks also involve ministries, sub-state governments and other state agencies that are acting on their own (not on behalf of a national government). Of particular importance are international organizations, that is, the staff of international organizations who have the ability to act autonomously. Here we have to distinguish between (parts of) international organizations that serve as an arena for inter-governmental cooperation (such as the UN Security Council, or the Council of Ministers in the EU) and the staff units of international organizations with autonomous capacity (such as the European Commission or the World Bank). Many international organizations, such as the Organisation for Economic Co-operation and Development (OECD) and the World Health Organization (WHO) combine the features of arena and autonomous bureaucracy, thereby making a fine-grained analysis necessary for distinguishing between the two. *Interactions* within transnational policy networks may take different forms, for example, conferences, telephone calls or letters between representatives of organizations. Interactions within transnational policy networks serve specific purposes, such as to get access to political arenas, gather political information, mobilize political support or execute political influence (Jansen and Schubert 1995c, p. 12).

Policy networks are based on the exchange of *resources*. Typical resources involve finance, analytical resources, legitimacy and the provision of political influence (political resources).[1] Political resources are mainly based on legal responsibilities and involve the ability to let other organizations participate in the design of political decisions. Financial resources involve the competence to decide about the allocation of money (for example, economic assistance and investment). Analytical resources include not only the provision of information in the narrow sense of the word, but also expertise, strategies or implementation plans, frequently based on the quality and quantity of staff. Legitimacy as a resource involves acceptance by political opinion and the mobilizations of political support (votes, political loyalty and so on).

A typical resource *exchange* involves an interaction during which one (governmental) organization allows another organization to participate in the design of a political decision while at the same time receiving information, finance or legitimacy from this organization. Transnational policy networks, however, also involve the pooling of resources from several organizations in order to exchange this resource pool against political resources of a governmental organization. The substantial content of a political decision may thus be explained by the resource allocation within a transnational policy network. Exchange within inter-organizational networks is necessary if single organizations need resources that they cannot produce on their own and other organizations can provide these organizations and themselves need resources that the first organization can provide. Thus, the resource dependency model departs from a relative independence of organizations – formally these are autonomous, but de facto they are dependent on resources controlled by other organizations. Common to all organizations is the desire to maximize their influence over political decisions and to avoid dependencies on other organizations (Rhodes et al. 1996, p. 368). Influence over political decisions is meant both to maximize (or at least stabilize) an organizational resource base and to further the specialist perspective of an organization, for example, as an environmental NGO, ministry of finance or labor union. In order to exchange resources, interactions have to have a certain durability; a single inter-organizational contact mostly is not sufficient for the membership within a transnational policy network.

Not all organizations of a *network* are connected with all other organizations; networks mostly have some 'holes' in their structure. Membership of a network, therefore, is less based on interaction density, but rather on the participation within policy design. Not all network interactions within a transnational policy network are strictly transnational, but one of the transnational interactions has to have a meaningful influence on policy design. Network structures become particularly important, if single organizations are able to derive a particular influence based on their central position in the network, for example, as a 'linking pin organization'. The focus of a transnational policy network normally is a policy field. Policy fields are based on a specific content, as based on the competence of a specific ministry, international organization or regime. Decisions within policy fields are made by political actors, that is, actors with the ability to make generally binding regulations.[2] Policy networks are not limited to decisions in the narrow sense, but also include the implementation of these decisions. Whether a political decision will become the focus of a transnational policy networks also depends on the decision of a transnational actor, for example, whether a transnational NGO decides to attempt to influence domestic policy-making in a given country.

While some of the behavioral assumptions of the policy network concept may simply be transferred from the national to the transnational level, others have to be developed anew. This is most particularly true for the different foci of transnational policy networks. At the national level, the focus of the concept is clear, since generally binding decisions are mostly taken by government and/or parliament. Policy networks therefore study the political decision-making process leading to laws and other public decisions. There is far more diversity at the transnational level. Basically, we can distinguish four different constellations in which transnational policy networks do evolve (Nölke 2000, 2004):

- The political transnationalization of a border region is a case of a transnational policy network at the *sub-national* (or micro-regional) level, for example, in an Euregio. Here, local and regional authorities, but also social groups from both sides of the border coordinate their activities or form coalitions to jointly influence an (inter) governmental authority (for example, Blatter 2000).
- Even more prominent are transnational policy networks at the (macro-)*regional* level, within regional integration schemes. The most prominent case is the multi-level governance system of the EU, where a multitude of networks have been studied (for example, Kohler-Koch and Eising 1999; Peterson and Bomberg 1999), for instance, between the European Commission and local/regional authorities in the field of regional development policy (Marks et al. 1996).
- Given the independent decision making capacity of some *international organizations* such as the World Bank or the International Monetary Fund, transnational actors form networks in order to influence the decisions made by these organizations (for example, Reinalda and Verbeek 1998; Slaughter 2004).
- Both the negotiation and the implementation of *international regimes*, for example, in the framework of the United Nations, may also be transnationalized. Here, transnational actors such as businesses, NGOs, labor unions or academic think tanks lobby for an adequate representation of their particular interests (for example, Keck and Sikkink 1998).

In conclusion, policy network analysis assists us in deciding whether a specific case of cross-border politics should be studied as transnational politics or intergovernmental relations. Based on the resource dependency school in organizational sociology, this analysis can be applied in very different settings and looks at the actors involved, the resources exchanged, the network structure and the network focus.

4   FRAMEWORK CONDITIONS FOR THE SALIENCE OF TRANSNATIONAL POLICY NETWORKS AND EMPIRICAL APPLICATION

Under which conditions are transnational policy networks relevant? The basic idea is that transnational policy networks are not ubiquitous, but only relevant under certain conditions. Dealing with these conditions allows us to focus on the crucial differences between intergovernmental cooperation and transnational policy networks. Owing to the open character of the policy network concept it has to be combined with other theories in order to answer this question. Most important is the combination with theories dealing with the structural and institutional context of a policy sector, given the strong actor focus of the policy network concept (see Lenschow 1995, p. 33). Again, we may depart from studies of policy networks at the domestic level for some more precise hints about the relationship between network context and the relevance of transnational policy networks. Here, the resource dependency approach already contains a basic assumption:

> [P]olicy networks are not useful tools for analyzing all political systems. The approach assumes a degree of pluralism, the relative separation of public and private actors, and complex policies needing many resources, which are not concentrated in the state. For example, if resources are concentrated in a strong national gatekeeper, policy networks are less likely to emerge and, where they do exist, will be less important for explaining policy outcomes. (Rhodes et al. 1996, p. 382)

Thus, we may assume that the relevance of transnational policy networks depends on the institutional configuration of the state(s) involved. If state structures are centralized, there is little need for state actors to exchange resources with other state actors or with private actors. In contrast, if state structures are very much fragmented and resources are dispersed between different organizations, horizontally (for example, between different ministries and agencies) or vertically (between different levels of government, for example, in a federal system), the relevance of policy networks increases. This does not only add to the importance of resource exchanges between domestic actors, but also between domestic and transnational actors. In the context of local/regional cross-border cooperation, for example, we may thus expect a higher relevance of transnational policy networks at the border between two federal states than between two unitarian states.

The relevance of policy networks, however, does not only depend on the dispersion of resources among state actors, but also on the ability of societal actors to mobilize an attractive resource volume as a basis for exchange with state actors. Societal interests, however, differ in their ability to organize themselves in a way that allows them to mobilize a significant volume of resources. Based on Olson's (1965) theory of collective goods, we may assume that rather *homogeneous interests* are easier to be organized than heterogeneous interests and may therefore better be able to mobilize the resources which are necessary for the participation in policy networks. This assumption also has repercussions on the relevance of transnational networks, because the latter may be impeded by the absence of transnational societal actors with substantial resources. Thus, we may expect a higher relevance of transnational policy networks in a sector which is marked by a powerful role of a few big multinational enterprises than in a sector where societal interests are rather diffuse, for example, dominated by a high number of small- and medium-scale enterprises.

Taking a more institutionalist perspective, the absence of resourceful transnational actors may also be caused by important societal groups choosing national rather than transnational channels for interest representation. This decision may be caused by a long tradition of relying on the nation state to further a particular societal interest as in case of labor unions (see Streeck 1998, p. 177). Examples for different degrees of the national institutionalization of societal interests again are provided by the European Union, where some groups form powerful Euro-associations in order to lobby the Commission or the European Parliament, whereas others rather prefer to go through their national governments and the Council of Ministers. The latter of course implies a more limited relevance of transnational policy networks.

Turning to the international context, transnational policy networks may also become relevant because of the activities of an international secretariat. If a secretariat such as the European Commission or the World Bank strives for (or has already been allocated) a prominent role in a given policy sector, it frequently is dependent on information and legitimacy resources provided by other (public and private) organizations. In a more general perspective, a high degree of international institutionalization can also take the form of an important role of international norms within a particular issue area (see Risse-Kappen 1995b, pp. 28–32). In this case, transnational actors may use these norms in order to justify their demands (that is, increase their legitimacy resources) or may need the negotiation of a new norm to mobilize at a transnational level at all.

A further group of assumptions does not depart from characteristics of the public and private actors involved, but rather from aspects of the specific problem at hand. Here, research on domestic politics has already pointed towards the role of different policy types (Lowi 1972) for the relevance of policy networks. In this case, redistributive policies are far less probable to be dealt with by these networks, because of their high degree of politicization. Thus, their design will hardly be decided by inter-organizational resource exchanges, but rather by public debate between fractions of government and parliament. Distributive policies, instead, incur heavy resource dependencies between donor and recipient organizations – the former need information (frequently also legitimacy) provided by the latter in order to allocate their financial resources effectively. The same mechanism may be assumed for the case for transnational policy networks where redistributive policies are supposed to lead to intergovernmental patterns of decision-making, whereas distributive policies are more conducive to transnational patterns.

5   SUMMARY AND EVALUATION

The utilization of the policy network concept in various empirical settings allows us to identify a number of framework conditions that indicate whether transnational politics can be assumed to be of high salience. All these conditions (Table 12.2) can in principle be combined with each other. Thus, the highest relevance for transnational policy networks is to be expected in a situation characterized by high international institutionalization, distributive policies, strong and homogenous societal interests without a strong institutionalization at the national level and a high institutional fragmentation of state structures. A typical case for a high salience of transnational politics thus would be in the system of EU multi-level governance, in a policy field such as regional development and involving actors from Germany (Marks et al. 1996) – or in global development policy based on the interaction of the Bretton Woods Institutions with transnational environmental NGOs (Nölke 2003).

Policy network analysis thus can be understood as a useful technique for identifying and analyzing circumstances where global politics should be understood as transnational and not as intergovernmental politics. Its

Table 12.2   Framework conditions for a high salience of transnational politics

International institutionalization	High
Policy type	Distributive
Homogeneity of transnational societal interest	High
National institutionalization of societal interest	Low
Institutional fragmentation of state structures	High

main advantage is its ability to provide analytical categories that can be applied in very different settings. However, it has two main shortcomings and thus needs to be complemented by other analytical concepts for a comprehensive study of global politics. First, the inter-organizational resource dependency policy network concept is an analytical concept and thus does not include a meaningful measure for the normative evaluation of transnational politics. Thus it needs to be combined with concepts from, for example, normative political theory, democracy studies or political economy in order to determine whether transnational policy networks really can deliver on the hopes articulated by their proponents. Second, policy network analysis has been developed for the study of peaceful policy-making. Some of the most important cases of transnational politics, however, are based on rather violent means and we need to develop alternative approaches in order to systematically study the salience of transnational politics as favored by terrorist networks and organized crime.

These issues have been raised:

- Distinction between transnational and intergovernmental politics.
- Policy network analysis as a method for distinguishing between transnational and intergovernmental politics.
- Framework conditions for a high salience of transnational politics.
- Advantages and shortcomings of policy network analysis for the study of cross-border politics.

NOTES

1. For different descriptions of the resources to be exchanged in policy networks see Jansen and Schubert (1995c, p. 12) and Rhodes et al. (1996, p. 368). In a transgovernmental perspective, Keohane and Nye (1974, p. 49ff.) list funds, prestige, information, consent and legitimacy.
2. In agreement with the general discussion on policy networks, the focus is on decisions which bind a plurality of actors. Thus, for example, it may be less suitable to study decisions regarding individual actors, for example, regarding the terms of an investment of one multinational enterprise and its host country.

FURTHER READING

Introduction to Subject

Josselin, D. and W. Wallace (eds) (2001), *Non-State Actors in World Politics*, Houndmills: Palgrave.

Application

Haynes, J. (2012), *Religious Transnational Actors and Soft Power*, Farnham, UK: Ashgate.

Advanced Text

Reinalda, B. (ed.) (2011), *The Ashgate Research Companion to Non-State Actors*, Farnham, UK: Ashgate.

ESSENTIAL READING

Keohane, R.O. and J.S. Nye (eds) (1981), *Transnational Relations and World Politics*, 3rd edn, Cambridge: Cambridge University Press.
Risse, T. (2013), 'Transnational actors and world politics', in W. Carlsnaes, T. Risse-Kappen and B.A. Simmons (eds), *Handbook of International Relations*, 2nd edn, London: Sage, pp. 426–52.
Risse-Kappen, T. (ed.) (1995), *Bringing Transnational Relations Back in Non-State Actors, Domestic Structures and International Institutions*, Cambridge: Cambridge University Press.

REFERENCES

Blatter, J. (2000), *Entgrenzung der Staatenwelt? Politische Institutionenbildung in grenzüber-schreitenden Regionen in Europa und Nordamerika* (*Dissolution of the World of States? The Formation of Institutions in Cross-Border Regions in Europe and North America*), Baden-Baden: Nomos Verlag.
Börzel, T.A. (1997), *Policy Networks: A New Paradigm for European Governance?*, vol. 19, Florence: European University Institute.
Coker, C. (2001), 'Outsourcing war', in D. Josselin, and W. Wallace (eds), *Non-State Actors in World Politics*, Basingstoke, UK: Palgrave, pp. 189–202.
Cox, R. (1987), *Production, Power and World Order*, New York: Columbia University Press.
Dingwerth, K. (2003), 'Globale Politiknetzwerke und ihre demokratische Legitimation. Eine Analyse der Weltstaudammkommission' ('Global policy networks and their democratic legitimacy: an analysis of the World Commission on Dams'), *Zeitschrift für Internationale Beziehungen*, **10** (1), 69–109.
Djelic, M.-L. and K. Sahlin-Andersson (2006), *Transnational Governance: Institutional Dynamics of Regulation*, Cambridge: Cambridge University Press.
Forsythe, D.P. (2000), *Human Rights in International Relations*, Cambridge: University Press.
Galeotti, M. (2001), 'Underworld and upperworld: transnational organized crime and global society', in D. Josselin, and W. Wallace (eds), *Non-State Actors in World Politics*, Basingstoke, UK: Palgrave, pp. 203–17.
Gill, S. (1991), *American Hegemony and the Trilateral Commission*, Cambridge: Cambridge University Press.
Graz, J.-C. and A. Nölke (eds) (2008), *Transnational Private Governance and its Limits*, London: Routledge.
Haas, P.M. (1992), 'Introduction: epistemic communities and international policy coordination', *International Organization*, **46** (1), 1–35.

Hale, T. and D. Held (eds) (2011), *The Handbook of Transnational Governance: Institutions and Innovations*, Cambridge: Polity Press.

Hasenclever, A., P. Mayer and V. Rittberger (1997), *Theories of International Regimes*, Cambridge: Cambridge University Press.

Jansen, D. and K. Schubert (eds) (1995a), *Netzwerke und Politikproduktion: Konzepte, Methoden Perspektiven*, (*Networks and the Production of Policies: Concepts, Methods, Perspectives*), Marburg: Schüren.

Jansen, D. and K. Schubert (1995b), 'Vorwort' ('Preface'), in D. Jansen and K. Schubert (ed.), *Netzwerke und Politikproduktion: Konzepte, Methoden, Perspektiven* (*Networks and the Production of Policies: Concepts, Methods, Perspectives*), Marburg: Schüren, pp. 7–8.

Jansen, D. and K. Schubert (1995c), 'Netzwerkanalyse, Netzwerkforschung und Politikproduktion. Ansätze zur "cross-fertilization"' ('Network analysis, network research and the production of policies: attempts for "cross-fertilization"'), in D. Jansen and K. Schubert (eds), *Netzwerke und Politikproduktion: Konzepte, Methoden, Perspektiven* (*Networks and the Production of Policies: Concepts, Methods, Perspectives*), Marburg: Schüren, pp. 9–23.

Keck, M. and K. Sikkink (1998), *Activists Beyond Borders: Advocacy Networks in International Politics*, Ithaca, New York: Cornell University Press.

Keohane, R.O. and J.S. Nye (1974), 'Transgovernmental relations and international organizations', *World Politics*, **27** (1), 39–62.

Keohane, R.O. and J.S. Nye (eds) (1981), *Transnational Relations and World Politics*, 3rd edn, Cambridge: Cambridge University Press.

Kohler-Koch, B. and R. Eising (eds) (1999), *The Transformation of Governance in the European Union*, London: Routledge.

Lenschow, A. (1995), 'Environmental policy making in the European Community: learning in a complex organization', paper presented at the Convention of the International Studies Association, Chicago, 21–25 February.

Lowi, T.J. (1972), 'Four systems of policy: politics and choice', *Public Administration Review*, **32** (4), 298–310.

Marks, G., L. Hooghe and K. Blank (1996), 'European integration from the 1980s: state-centric versus multi-level governance', *Journal of Common Market Studies*, **34** (3), 341–78.

Mayntz, R. (1993), 'Policy-Netzwerke und die Logik von Verhandlungssystemen' ('Policy networks and the logic of negotiation systems'), in A. Héritier (ed.), *Policy-Analyse: Kritik und Neuorientierung*, Opladen: Westdeutscher Verlag, pp. 39–56.

Nölke, A. (2000), 'Regieren in transnationalen Politiknetzwerken? Kritik postnationaler Governance-Konzepte aus der Perspektive einer transnationalen (Inter-) Organisationssoziologie' ('Governing in transnational policy networks? Critique of post-national concepts of governance from the perspective of a transnational sociology of (inter-) organizational relations'), *Zeitschrift für Internationale Beziehungen*, **7** (2), 331–58.

Nölke, A. (2003), 'The relevance of transnational policy networks: some examples from the European Commission and the World Bank', *Journal of International Relations and Development*, **6** (3), 277–99.

Nölke, A. (2004), 'Transnationale Politiknetzwerke: Eine Analyse grenzüberschreitender politischer Prozesse jenseits des regierungszentrischen Modells' ('Transnational policy networks: an analysis of cross-border political processes beyond the government-centric model'), habilitation thesis, University of Leipzig, Leipzig.

Olson, M. Jr (1965), *The Logic of Collective Action*, Cambridge, MA: Harvard University Press.

Overbeek, H. (2000), 'Transnational historical materialism: theories of transnational class formation and world order', in R. Palan (ed.), *Global Political Economy: Contemporary Theories*, London: Routledge, pp. 168–83.

Peterson, J. and E. Bomberg (1999), *Decision-Making in the European Union*, New York: St Martin's Press.

Reinalda, B. and B. Verbeek (eds) (1998), *Autonomous Policy Making by International Organizations*, London: Routledge.

Reinicke, W.H. (1998), *Global Public Policy. Governing without Government?* Washington, DC: Brookings Institution Press.

Reinicke, W.H. (1999), 'Trilateral networks of governments, business, and civil society: the role of international organizations in global public policy', paper presented for the Pre-UNCTAD X Seminar on the Role of Competition Policy for Development in Globalizing World Markets, Geneva, 14–15 June.

Reinicke, W.H., F.M. Deng, J.M. Witte, T. Benner, B. Whitaker and J. Gershman (2000), *Critical Choices: The United Nations, Networks and the Future of Global Governance*, Ottawa: International Development Research Centre.

Rhodes, R.A.W., I. Bache and S. George (1996), 'Policy networks and policy-making in the European Union: a critical appraisal', in L. Hooghe (ed.), *Cohesion Policy and European Integration*, Oxford: Oxford University Press, pp. 367–87.

Risse, T. (2013), 'Transnational actors and world politics', in W. Carlsnaes, T. Risse-Kappen and B.A. Simmons (eds), *Handbook of International Relations*, 2nd edn, London: Sage, pp. 426–52.

Risse-Kappen, T. (ed.) (1995a), *Bringing Transnational Relations Back in Non-State Actors, Domestic Structures and International Institutions*, Cambridge: Cambridge University Press.

Risse-Kappen, T. (1995b), 'Introduction', in T. Risse-Kappen, *Bringing Transnational Relations Back in Non-State Actors, Domestic Structures and International Institutions*, Cambridge: Cambridge University Press, pp. 3–36.

Rochester, J.M. (2002), *Between Two Epochs: What's Ahead for America, the World, and Global Politics in the Twenty-First Century?* Upper Saddle River, NJ: Prentice Hall.

Schneckener, U. (2006), *Transnationaler Terrorismus. Charakter und Hintergründe des 'neuen' Terrorismus* (*Transnational Terrorism: Character and Background of the 'New' Terrorism*), Frankfurt am Main: Suhrkamp.

Slaughter, A.-M. (2004), *A New World Order*, Princeton, NJ and Oxford: Princeton University Press.

Stone, D. (2004), 'Knowledge networks and global policy', paper presented at the Fifth Pan-European International Relations Conference, The Hague, September.

Streeck, W. (1998), 'Industrielle Beziehungen in einer internationalisierten Wirtschaft' ('Industrial relations in an internationalized economy'), in U. Beck (ed.), *Politik der Globalisierung*, Frankfurt am Main: Suhrkamp, pp. 169–202.

Van Apeldoorn, B. (2002), *Transnational Capitalism and the Struggle over European Integration*, London: Routledge.

Van der Pijl, K. (1998), *Transnational Classes and International Relations*, London: Routledge.

Witte, J.M., W. Reinicke and T. Benner (2000), 'Beyond multilateralism: global public policy networks', *Internationale Politik und Gesellschaft*, **3** (2), 176–88.

13 Political economy: economic miracles and socio-economic performance
Barbara Vis, Jaap J. Woldendorp and Kees van Kersbergen

1 INTRODUCTION

Political economy is a sub-field in political science that examines the interaction between the democratic political context and the capitalist market economy. Scholars in this field are particularly interested in identifying under which conditions and to what extent political institutions, say the type of democracy (majoritarian or consensus, for example, Lijphart 2012), promote or impair countries' socio-economic or welfare state development and performance. Political economists try to explain different types of performance (that is, dependent variables), ranging from economic growth, income inequality, unemployment, human capital formation and poverty to the generosity of welfare state arrangements, the coverage of social risks like old age and sickness, and redistribution (for example, Wilensky 2006; Lijphart 2012; Van Kersbergen and Vis 2014; Lupu and Pontusson 2011). The explanatory, independent variables political economists focus on also cover a wide variety, ranging from the type of welfare state (liberal, conservative or social-democratic; Van Kersbergen and Vis 2014; Esping-Andersen 1990)[1] to the type of democracy (for example, consensus or majoritarian, Lijphart 2012), and from the type of interest group representation (corporatism or pluralism, for example, Lijphart 2012; Jahn 2014) to institutional variables such as central bank independence (for example, Iversen and Soskice 2006) or openness of the economy (for example, Calderón and Fuentes 2006). Political economists typically employ comparative research designs to explain the variation in policy output and/or performance between (groups of) countries. Research methods employed include qualitative techniques, such as small-n comparative case studies, quantitative techniques, such as various forms of descriptive and inferential statistics, and techniques in between qualitative and quantitative approaches, such as (fuzzy-set) qualitative comparative analysis ((fs)QCA) (see Rihoux and Ragin 2009; Schneider and Wagemann 2012; Chapter 25 in this volume).

While there is agreement on some issues in the political economy literature, for instance, on which countries qualify as corporatist and which do not, the findings of both qualitative and quantitative studies with regard to the variation in policy performance remain inconclusive. In this chapter, we argue that these inconclusive findings derive from substantive problems relating particularly to the dependent variables' conceptualization and operationalization.[2] This holds for instance for two streams of political economy literature on socio-economic performance: the 'miracle' literature and the quantitative literature on socio-economic performance. These are the two bodies of work that we focus on here. We propose that these studies would benefit from a common, theoretically founded, conceptualization and operationalization of their dependent variable. The reason is that this would help to select those independent variables (political context and institutional) that are theoretically relevant and to empirically test their impact. This chapter thus does not discuss the entire field of political economy; a field that comprises many different sub-fields, including the 'miracle' literature and the quantitative literature on socio-economic performance. To indicate the breath of the political economy literature, Box 13.1 provides some key references for the different sub-fields of political economy.

2 INSTITUTIONS, 'MIRACLES' AND SOCIO-ECONOMIC PERFORMANCE

As indicated, we focus on two streams of political economy literature that examine socio-economic performance. The first is the 'miracle' literature that typically draws on single case studies or small-n comparisons and tends to select cases on the dependent variable (that is, cases that perform 'miraculously'). The second body of literature is the typically quantitative literature that examines the variation in different types of socio-economic performance across countries and over time. In these literatures, the dependent variables used generally lack substantive grounding. Even though both streams of literature have offered many useful insights, their findings are also often contradictory. The latter seems to result from a too broad assortment of different conceptualizations and empirical indicators, many of which are typically not well-founded theoretically.

Figure 13.1 displays a stylized overview of political economy research into the relationships between institutions, policy outputs and policy outcomes. This figure shows that in the political economy literature, various institutions (such as the type of democracy or the type of welfare state) are hypothesized to explain both (different) policy

BOX 13.1   KEY REFERENCES FOR THE DIFFERENT SUB-FIELDS OF POLITICAL ECONOMY

Overview

- Weingast, B.R. and D.A. Wittman (eds) (2008), *The Oxford Handbook of Political Economy*, Oxford: Oxford University Press.

Welfare State Development and Welfare State Change

- Castles, F.G. (2004), *The Future of the Welfare State*, Oxford: Oxford University Press.
- Castles, F.G., S. Leibfried, J. Lewis, H. Obinger and C. Pierson (eds) (2010), *The Oxford Handbook of the Welfare State*, Oxford: Oxford University Press.
- Clasen, J. and N.A. Siegel (eds) (2007), *Investigating Welfare State Change. The 'Dependent Variable Problem' in Comparative Analysis*, Cheltenham, UK and Northampton, MA, USA: Edward Elgar.
- Green-Pedersen, C. (2004), 'The dependent variable problem within the study of welfare state retrenchment: defining the problem and looking for solutions', *Journal of Comparative Policy Analysis: Research and Practice*, **6** (1), 3–14.
- Huber, E. and J.D. Stephens (2001), 'Welfare states and productive regimes in the era of retrenchment', in P. Pierson (ed.), *The New Politics of the Welfare State*, Oxford: Oxford University Press, pp. 107–46.
- Korpi, W. (2010), 'Class and gender inequalities in different types of welfare states: the Social Citizenship Indicator Program (SCIP)', *International Journal of Social Welfare*, **19** (supplement s1), 14–24.
- Pierson, P. (2011), 'The welfare state over the very long run', ZeS-Working Paper No. 02/2011, University of Bremen, Centre for Social Policy Research (ZeS), Bremen, accessed 3 November 2015 at http://hdl.handle.net/10419/46215.
- Scruggs, L.A. and J.P. Allan (2008), 'Social stratification and welfare regimes for the twenty-first century: revisiting the three worlds of welfare capitalism', *World Politics*, **60** (4), 642–64.
- Scruggs, L.A., D. Jahn and K. Kuitto (2014), 'Comparative Welfare Entitlements Dataset 2 (Version 2014-03)', University of Connecticut, Storrs, CT and University of Greifswald, Griefswald, Germany.
- Swank, D. (2002), *Global Capital, Political Institutions, and Policy Change in Developed Welfare States*, Cambridge: Cambridge University Press.
- Van Kersbergen, K. and B. Vis (2014), *Comparative Welfare State Politics: Development, Opportunities, and Reform*, Cambridge: Cambridge University Press.

Varieties of Capitalism

- Becker, U. (2009), *Open Varieties of Capitalism: Continuity, Change and Performance*, London: Palgrave Macmillan.

- Becker, U. (ed.) (2011), *The Changing Political Economies of Small West European Countries*, Amsterdam: Amsterdam University Press.
- Hall, P.A. and D.W. Gingerich (2009), 'Varieties of capitalism and institutional complementarities in the political economy: an empirical analysis', *British Journal of Political Science*, **39** (3), 449–82.
- Hall, P.A. and D. Soskice (eds) (2001), *Varieties of Capitalism. The Institutional Foundations of Comparative Advantage*, Oxford: Oxford University Press.
- Hancké, B., M. Rhodes and M. Thatcher (eds) (2007), *Beyond Varieties of Capitalism. Conflict, Contradictions, and Complementarities in the European Economy*, Oxford: Oxford University Press.
- Thelen, K. (2011), 'Varieties of capitalism: trajectories of liberalization and the new politics of solidarity', *Annual Review of Political Science*, **15** (1), 137–59.

Corporatism and Pluralism

- Alvarez, R.M., G. Garrett and P. Lange (1991), 'Government partisanship, labor organisation, and macroeconomic performance', *American Political Science Review*, **85** (2), 539–56.
- Calmfors, L. and J. Driffill (1988), 'Bargaining structure, corporatism and macroeconomic performance', *Economic Policy*, **3** (6), 13–61.
- Crépaz, M.M.L. (1992), 'Corporatism in Decline? An empirical analysis of the impact of corporatism on macroeconomic performance and industrial disputes in 19 industrialized democracies', *Comparative Political Studies*, **25** (2), 139–68.
- Flanagan, R.J. (1999), 'Macro-economic performance and collective bargaining', *Journal of Economic Literature*, **37** (3), 1150–75.
- Hassel, A. (2006), *Wage Setting, Social Pacts and the Euro: A New Role for The State*, Amsterdam: Amsterdam University Press.
- Jahn, D. (2016), 'Changing of the guard: trends in corporatist arrangements in 42 highly industrialized societies from 1960–2010', *Socio-Economic Review*, **14** (1), 47–71.
- Lijphart, A. (2012), *Patterns of Democracy: Government Forms and Performance in Thirty-Six Countries*, 2nd edn, New Haven, CT and London: Yale University Press.
- Molina, O. and M. Rhodes (2002), 'Corporatism: the past, present, and future of a concept', *Annual Review of Political Science*, **5** (June), 305–31.
- Wilensky, H.L. (2006), 'Trade-offs in public spending finance: comparing the well-being of big spenders and lean spenders', *International Political Science Review*, **27** (4), 333–58.

Types of Democracy

- Anderson, L. (2001), 'The implications of institutional design for macroeconomic performance: reassessing the claims of consensus democracy', *Comparative Political Studies*, **34** (4), 429–52.

- Armingeon, K.A. (2002), 'The effects of negotiation democracy: a comparative analysis', *European Journal of Political Research*, **41** (1), 81–105.
- Crépaz, M.M.L. (1996), 'Consensus versus majoritarian democracy. Political institutions and their impact on macroeconomic performance and industrial disputes', *Comparative Political Studies*, **29** (1), 4–26.
- Franzese, J.R. Jr (2002), *Macroeconomic Policies of Developed Democracies*, Cambridge: Cambridge University Press.
- Lijphart, A. (2012), *Patterns of Democracy: Government Forms and Performance in Thirty-Six Countries*, 2nd edn, New Haven, CT and London: Yale University Press.
- Lijphart, A. and M.M.L. Crépaz (1991), 'Corporatism and consensus democracy in eighteen countries: conceptual and empirical linkages', *British Journal of Political Science*, **21** (2), 235–46.
- Przeworski, A., M.E. Alvarez, J.A. Cheibub and F. Limongi (2000), *Democracy and Development: Political Institutions and Well-Being in the World, 1950–1990*, Cambridge: Cambridge University Press.
- Roller, E. (2005), *The Performance of Democracies*, Oxford: Oxford University Press.

Performance and Outcomes

- Kenworthy, L. (2006), 'Institutional coherence and macroeconomic performance', *Socio-Economic Review*, **4** (1), 69–91.
- Lane, J.-E. and S.O. Ersson (2000), *The New Institutional Politics: Performance and Outcomes*, London: Routledge.

Partisanship

- Garrett, G. (1998), *Partisan Politics in the Global Economy*, New York: Cambridge University Press.
- Hibbs, D.A. (1977), 'Political parties and macroeconomic policy', *American Political Science Review*, **71** (4), 1467–87.
- Schmidt, M.G. (1996), 'When parties matter: a review of the possibilities and limits of partisanship influence on public policy', *European Journal of Political Research*, **30** (2), 155–83.

'Miracle' Literature

- Becker, U. and H. Schwarz (eds) (2005a), *Employment 'Miracles': A Critical Comparison of Dutch, Scandinavian, Swiss, Australian and Irish Cases versus Germany and the US*, Amsterdam: Amsterdam University Press.
- Delsen, L. (2002), *Exit Polder Model? Socioeconomic changes in the Netherlands*, Westport, CT: Praeger.
- Visser, J. and A. Hemerijck (1997), *A Dutch Miracle: Job Growth, Welfare Reform, and Corporatism in the Netherlands*, Amsterdam: Amsterdam University Press.

Central Bank Independence

- Alesina, A. and L.H. Summers (1993), 'Central bank independence and macroeconomic performance: some comparative evidence', *Journal of Money, Credit and Banking*, **25** (2), 151–62.
- International Monetary Fund (IMF) (2009), *World Economic Outlook. Sustaining the Recovery*, ch. 3, accessed October 2009, www.imf.org.
- Iversen, T. (1998), 'Wage bargaining, central bank independence, and the real effects of money', *International Organization*, **52** (3), 469–504.
- Iversen, T. (1999), *Contested Economic Institutions: The Politics of Macroeconomics and Wage Bargaining in Advanced Democracies*, Cambridge: Cambridge University Press.
- Iversen, T. and D. Soskice (2006), 'New macroeconomics and political science', *Annual Review of Political Science*, **9**, 425–53.
- Iversen, T., J. Pontusson and D. Soskice (eds) (2000), *Unions, Employers and Central Banks: Wage Bargaining and Macroeconomic Policy in an Integrating Europe*, Cambridge: Cambridge University Press.

Openness of the Economy

- Calderón, C. and R. Fuentes (2006), 'Complementarities between institutions and openness in economic development: evidence for a panel of countries', *Cuadernos de Economia*, **43** (127), 49–80.
- Edwards, S. (1998), 'Openness, productivity and growth: what do we really know?', *Economic Journal*, **108** (447), 383–98.
- Frankel, J.A. and D. Romer (1999), 'Does trade cause growth?', *American Economic Review*, **89** (3), 379–99.
- Sachs, J.D. and A. Warner (1995), 'Economic reform and the process of global integration', *Brookings Papers on Economic Activity*, **26** (1), 1–118.

outputs and (different) policy outcomes. This leads us to the following observations:

- Policy outputs and policy outcomes may become conflated in the research design; and in quite a number of studies, they indeed are.
- Disentangling possible direct effects of institutions on policy outcomes from the indirect effects through policy outputs is difficult theoretically and empirically.
- In empirical reality, concrete cases (typically countries) and institutions (the independent, explanatory variables) often tend to go together (see also Table 13.1, p. 197). These relationships make it difficult, theoretically as well as empirically, to determine what actually has which effect on policy outcomes.

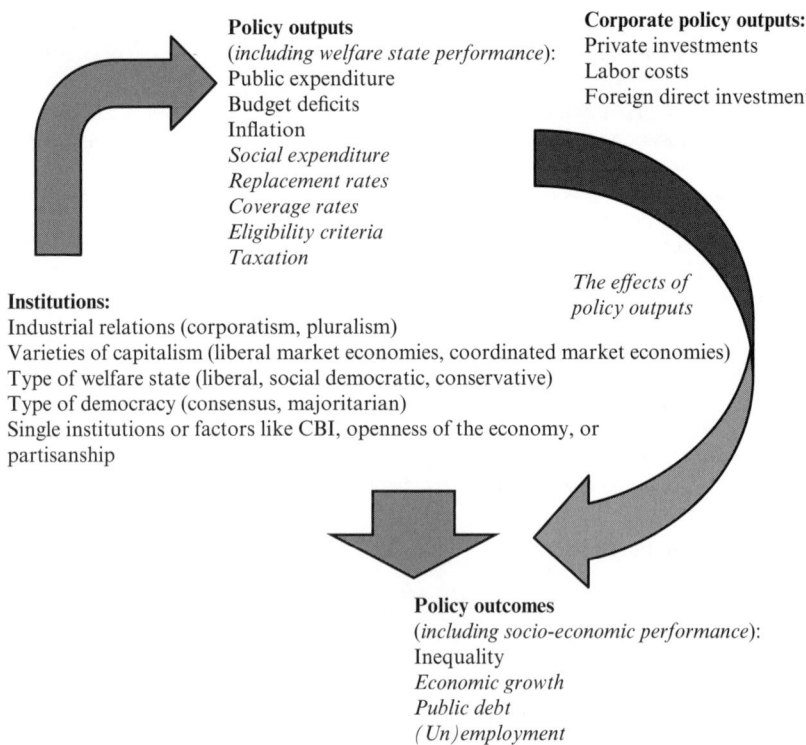

Policy outputs
(*including welfare state performance*):
Public expenditure
Budget deficits
Inflation
Social expenditure
Replacement rates
Coverage rates
Eligibility criteria
Taxation

Corporate policy outputs:
Private investments
Labor costs
Foreign direct investments

*The effects of
policy outputs*

Institutions:
Industrial relations (corporatism, pluralism)
Varieties of capitalism (liberal market economies, coordinated market economies)
Type of welfare state (liberal, social democratic, conservative)
Type of democracy (consensus, majoritarian)
Single institutions or factors like CBI, openness of the economy, or
partisanship

Policy outcomes
(*including socio-economic performance*):
Inequality
Economic growth
Public debt
(Un)employment

Note: This stylized overview of possible relationships between institutions, outputs
and outcomes does not claim to be exhaustive. Rather, it provides an illustration of the
argument we make in this chapter. See also Jahn and Kuitto (2011, p. 722) for a different
conceptualization of institutions, outputs and outcomes.

*Figure 13.1   Institutions, welfare state performance and socio-economic
performance*

These observations underlie our argument on the importance of paying
more attention to the dependent variable(s) in political economy research.
To further exemplify our argument and to propose how to move forward,
we now discuss the literature on 'miracles' and the quantitative literature
on socio-economic performance.

3   MIRACLES

The political economy literature speaks of an economic 'miracle' when a country's socio-economic performance (significantly) exceeds expectations. How does one explain the occurrence of such (economic) miracles? This is the central question of a substantial body of political economy research, usually single case studies or small-n analyses (for example, Visser and Hemerijck 1997; Delsen 2002; Becker and Schwartz 2005a; Becker 2011). These studies employ a more or less implicit comparative perspective in that the miraculous performance of the country under investigation represents a puzzle in comparison to other, less well-performing countries or to the same country at an earlier point in time. In this sense, miracle case studies enhance our understanding of the countries investigated (a good example is Visser and Hemerijck's 1997 seminal study of the Dutch miracle). However, such studies often fail to offer a framework for comparative analysis beyond the single case. Because of the lack of this broader comparative perspective, the 'miracle' research is characterized by the absence of a common conceptualization and operationalization of what constitutes an (economic) miracle. Theoretical conceptualizations of a miracle vary from very elaborate: 'a combination of welfare reform (whilst maintaining overall social security), fiscal conservatism, job creation and economic growth' (Visser and Hemerijck 1997), to very succinct: 'high employment' (Green-Pedersen and Lindbom 2005) (cited from Vis et al. 2007, p. 532). If the 'miracle' investigated is defined by contrasting it to earlier bad performance in the same country, then what is miraculous derives from disastrous past performance. This practice is visible in the empirical operationalizations used. Some researchers 'try to use as many indicators as possible . . . (especially Visser and Hemerijck 1997; Merrien and Becker 2005)' (Vis et al. 2007, p. 532) and this makes generalization of the findings difficult. The same applies to the regular mixing up of different types of performance measures, including outputs such as public expenditure, social expenditure and the budget deficit, but also outcomes such as economic growth, (un)employment and inequality; see Figure 13.1).

Because the conceptualization and operationalization of the miracles usually span a wide variety of phenomena, the explanation of the miracles also ranges from (a combination of) government policies to world market developments, and from changes in corporatism to changes in the economy, such as the shift from industry to services, or simply luck (for example, Visser and Hemerijck 1997; Becker and Schwartz 2005b).

Summing up, the (economic) miracle research would benefit from a more explicit and genuine comparative (case study) approach (Lijphart

1975). First, what makes the socio-economic performance of a country miraculous has to be specified both historically (in terms of a within country comparison over time) and cross-nationally (in terms of a systematic comparison with the performance of other countries that in principle could have performed similarly as the miracle country). Second, output and outcome indicators should be clearly distinguished in the development of a common standard of what can be considered to be an economic miracle. A sharper specification and operationalization of the dependent variable 'miracle' would certainly help the field to generate stronger theory about the causes of (economic) miracles.

4   QUANTITATIVE STUDIES ON (THE VARIATION IN) SOCIO-ECONOMIC PERFORMANCE

Quantitative large-n studies in political economy research are more explicitly comparative in design than are the 'miracle' studies. The former's aim is to explain differences in socio-economic performance across (groups of) countries and over time. Studies in this tradition usually also provide a better theoretical underpinning of the conceptualization and operationalization of the independent variables that are considered to have an effect on (good) socio-economic performance. In fact, there are extensive discussions on this, usually yielding a variety of definitions and operationalizations of the (often institutional) independent variables (see Figure 13.1). Interestingly, despite these discussions, there is ample agreement on the classification of countries. Corporatism is an example here. Even though there is much conceptual discussion (for example, Crépaz 1992; Siaroff 1999; Molina and Rhodes 2002; Wilensky 2006; Jahn 2016), there is still broad agreement on the classification of countries as corporatist or not. Likewise, despite discussion on the federal-unitary dimension of Lijphart's (2012) types of democracy (consensus versus majoritarian, for example, Lane and Ersson 2000), scholars agree on how to place countries in the categories of the two types of democracy. The same applies for research using the varieties of capitalism approach (for example, Kenworthy 2006; Soskice 2007; Hall and Gingerich 2009) or the type of welfare state (for example, Esping-Andersen 1990; Van Kersbergen and Vis 2014; but see Castles 2004 and Chapter 29 in this volume). So, despite big theoretical debates on big institutional variables such as corporatism, type of democracy or the type of welfare state, there is actually broad agreement on its relevance and on which countries belong to which category of institutional arrangement.

There are also extensive theoretical and empirical discussions on other possible explanatory factors for socio-economic performance, either as separate explanations or in combination. In these discussions four factors are considered to be particularly relevant: partisanship (for example, Hibbs 1977; Alvarez et al. 1991; Schmidt 1996); the degree of central bank independence (for example, Iversen and Soskice 2006); the degree of openness of the economy (for example, Calderón and Fuentes 2006); and the extent of corporatism (see above).

Despite these extensive discussions, however, much less substantive attention has been paid to the fact that for a majority of countries these institutional (independent and explanatory) variables hang together (see Figure 13.1 and Table 13.1 below). Liberal welfare states tend to be majoritarian democracies with a pluralist political economy and low(er) central bank independence and economic openness, whereas both conservative and social democratic welfare states tend to be consensus democracies with corporatist political economies and high(er) central bank independence and economic openness. Substantively, this makes it difficult to establish which independent variable actually does what (and why) to these countries' performance – the dependent variable. Theoretically, this remains a puzzle to be solved. Although there is broad agreement on concepts, measurement and classifications, there remains broad disagreement on which factors offer the best explanation for the variation in socio-economic performance. Likewise, researchers disagree on the effects of the institutional variables such as corporatism and the type of democracy or welfare state. Empirical research tends to offer inconclusive or contradictory evidence on the impact of all these explanatory factors on different types of performance (for example, Hall and Gingerich 2009; Kenworthy 2006; Wilensky 2006; Becker 2009).

What might be the reason for these puzzling findings? One answer is that, as in the miracle discussion, too little substantive attention has been paid to the dependent variable: socio-economic performance. As in the miracle discussion, a substantively grounded common standard of performance is lacking. Instead, quantitative large-n studies use a wide variety of performance conceptualizations and, hence, a wide variety of empirical indicators of that performance that usually lack substantive grounding, except perhaps that using more indicators is better (for example, Lijphart 2012, p. 263).

In addition, also in quantitative large-n studies, various types of indicators are lumped together: economic performance (for example, economic growth); policy performance (for example, budget deficit and social expenditure); corporate policy performance (for example, private investment and labor costs); and indicators of which it is unclear what kind of performance they actually measure (for example, strike activity, change of money supply or openness of the economy) (see, for example, Hicks and Kenworthy 1998; Traxler 2004). Improving the substantive and theoretical foundation for the conceptualization and operationalization of the dependent variable (socio-economic or welfare state performance) will help researchers to reach more conclusive and less contradictory empirical and theoretical conclusions on the impact of the various independent variables on the different types of performance.

5   CONCEPTUALIZATION OF THE DEPENDENT VARIABLE

How to overcome this state of affairs? We propose that the political economy literature, both qualitative and quantitative, should devote more attention to the dependent variable problem, that is, how to conceptualize and operationalize the dependent variable. The welfare state literature can serve as an example here (see Box 13.2). Regarding socio-economic performance: In what types of performance are we theoretically interested? How and why do we think that our independent variable(s) may influence that type of performance? This means that if we are interested in economic

---

BOX 13.2   THE DEPENDENT VARIABLE PROBLEM IN WELFARE STATE RESEARCH

In the comparative literature on welfare states, the so-called 'dependent variable problem', that is, the problem of how to conceptualize and measure welfare state performance, change and reform, has been acknowledged since the early 1990s (Esping-Andersen 1990; Green-Pedersen 2004; Clasen and Siegel 2007). What we can take from the discussion, is that there should be a one-on-one correspondence between a researcher's theoretical definition of a concept and its empirical operationalization. For instance, Esping-Andersen's (1990) theoretical re-definition of welfare state regimes in terms of social rights granted demanded an operationalization that actually measured such social rights: replacement rates of benefits, duration of benefits, contribution period, and so on. The theory made the, until then, typically used measure of welfare state generosity – social expenditures as a percentage of gross domestic product (GDP) – entirely inappropriate: social expenditure does not exclusively measure rights, but to a large extent also measures 'need', for instance, how many people are receiving unemployment benefit. If social expenditures were used, we would come to the confusing conclusion that the countries that are bad at fighting unemployment are the best-performing welfare states. If a researcher is interested in the share of public expenditures going to programs of the welfare state per se, and hence has a different theoretical interest in the welfare state, using social spending as a percentage of GDP as a measure is appropriate.

performance, we should have a substantive argument that explains why one or more particular indicators are indeed indicators of economic performance, and not of something else (for instance, welfare state performance or some other form of policy performance – that is, policy output – such as corporate policy performance).

Let us use overall economic performance as an example. How to define such performance substantively? Even though the 'miracle' literature has not offered a consistent concept of socio-economic performance, it has offered a number of suggestions (for example, Visser and Hemerijck 1997; Delsen 2002; Becker and Schwarz 2005b). In this literature, and in the quantitative literature on the variation in socio-economic performance, three types of indicators are most commonly used for economic performance: measures of (un)employment, economic growth, and budget deficits or public debt (see Vis et al. 2007, 2012, 2013). Economic performance, particularly excellent economic performance (that is, a miracle), should be considered to be relatively independent of short-term government policies. If economic performance, let alone overall economic performance, would be simply a matter of governments doing the 'right' thing, countries would not go through economic cycles and all countries would experience a continuous economic miracle. In our view, economic growth, total employment and public debt are very difficult for governments to influence positively or manipulate simultaneously. If a country scores well on all three indicators at the same time, this constitutes excellent overall economic performance, as opposed to policy performance (including welfare state performance), corporate performance or some other, undefined category of performance. Also to count as an economic miracle, a country should do better than other countries on all counts at the same time.

The next step is to establish how countries perform on different types of economic performance, including 'miraculous' performance and 'disastrous' performance. For this, we can assess simultaneously countries' performance on all three indicators (economic growth, total employment and public debt). An interesting, relatively new, technique to do this is fuzzy-set ideal type analysis (for example, Vis et al. 2007; for a more elaborate overview of fuzzy-set fsQCA, see Chapter 25 in this volume). This technique combines ideal type analysis and fuzzy sets, whereby a fuzzy-set is a 'a fine-grained, [pseudo] continuous measure that has been carefully calibrated using substantive and theoretical knowledge relevant to set membership' (Ragin 2000, p. 7). With three indicators, there are eight ideal types of performance (2^3). The two extremes are the miracle ideal type (a positive score on all three indicators simultaneously) and the disaster ideal type (no positive score on any of the three indicators simultaneously). There are also six intermediate performance types to which countries may belong, but which are theoretically less interesting.[3] The fuzzy-set ideal type analysis scores all countries on each ideal type, per time period, thus providing a rank order of overall economic performance across countries and over time, while also giving substantive information on the nature of that performance. Table 13.1 presents the results of the fuzzy-set ideal type analysis for the miracle ideal type and the disaster ideal type for four time periods (1975–79, 1985–89, 1995–99 and 2001–05). The results, for instance, show that Austria had membership to the miracle ideal type in the 1970s, but not after that. Australia, conversely, performed 'miraculously' from the 1970s until the 2000s. As a final example, Norway moved from having membership to the miracle ideal type in the 1970s to non-membership in the 1980s, but moved back to membership in the 1990s. Table 13.1 also reveals that there are more 'miracles' than there are 'disasters'. Belgium and Italy are the most 'disastrous' cases, having membership to the disaster ideal type in the 1990s and 2000s.

How then to use this dependent variable to tackle the puzzling inconclusive findings of quantitative larger-n studies? A first step is to use institutional variables such as corporatism, type of democracy or type of welfare state to find out if there is a relation between these institutions and the substantively grounded measure of overall economic performance. In this case, the industrial relations system (corporatist or pluralist), type of democracy (consensus or majoritarian) (see Vis et al. 2012), and the type of welfare state (liberal, conservative or social-democratic) display no relationship (see Table 13.1); both corporatist and pluralist countries can perform 'miraculously' or 'disastrously', as can both consensus democracies and majoritarian ones, or liberal, social-democratic or conservative welfare states. Neither is there evidence to suggest alternative relationships such as, for instance, a hump-shaped relationship with highly centralized (corporatist) or highly decentralized (pluralist) industrial relation systems doing better than the in-between cases (for example, Calmfors and Driffill 1988; Hall and Gingerich 2009; Kenworthy 2006). For the type of industrial system (corporatism or pluralism), type of democracy (consensus or majoritarian) and type of welfare state (liberal, conservative or social-democratic) there is divergence of overall economic performance over time, which suggests that country-specific factors may be more relevant for overall economic performance than the institutional set-up of a country. Note that, as we discussed above, and in the analysis presented in Table 13.1, we can see an interrelationship between the independent variables, or more exactly, the absence of a relationship: there are no countries that are both corporatist and majoritarian (this also holds if we add the in-between ideal types). Corporatist consensus democracies, however, may be either social-democratic or conservative welfare states, whereas

Table 13.1   Miracle and disaster ideal types, industrial relations system, type of democracy and type of welfare state (1975–2005)

Economic performance model	1975–79	1985–89	1995–99	2001–05
A positive score on all three indicators				
Miracle ideal type				
Corp. + cons. + socdem.	Denmark; Norway	Finland; Sweden	Norway	–
Corp. + cons. + conserv.	Austria; Germany	–	–	–
Plural. + cons. + conserv.	–	Portugal	Portugal	–
Plural. + cons. + liberal	–	–	–	Ireland; New Zealand (NZ)
Corp. + major. + ?	–	–	–	–
Plural. + major. + lib.	Australia	Australia; UK; US	Australia; *NZ*; UK	Australia; *US*
Plural. + major. + conserv.	France	–	–	–
A positive score on none of the indicators				
Disaster ideal type				
Corp. + cons. + conserv.	–	–	Belgium	Belgium
Plural. + cons. + conserv.	–	–	Italy	Italy
Corp. + major. + ?	–	–	–	–
Plural. + major. + conserv.	–	–	–	France
Plural. + major. + lib.	–	NZ	–	–

Notes: Corp. means corporatism; cons. means consensus; socdem. means social democratic welfare state; conserv. means conservative welfare state; lib. means liberal welfare state; plural. means pluralist (that is, non-corporatist); major. means majoritarian. We report only the miracle ideal type and the disaster ideal type here, not the in-between ideal types in which countries perform well on two or one indicator (see Vis et al. 2012 for these results). Countries displayed in italics score 50/50 in two ideal types (the other of which is an in-between ideal type that is not reported here). Finally, New Zealand changed from being a majoritarian country in the 1970s and 1980s to a consensus democracy in the 2000s.

Source: Vis et al. (2012, pp. 86, 88), welfare state type added.

pluralist majoritarian democracies may be either liberal or conservative welfare states.

The absence of a relationship between the institutional set-up of a country and that country's overall economic performance over time spills over in the research findings of a second step of a political economic enquiry into the relationship of other (combinations of) explanatory factors (or conditions) on overall economic performance. In this analysis, we examine whether there are necessary and/or sufficient (combinations of) conditions for strong overall economic performance of countries over time. Fuzzy-set qualitative comparative analysis (for example, Rihoux and Ragin 2009; Schneider and Wagemann 2012; and Chapter 25 in this volume) is an approach that is particularly apt for such a question. The fsQCA analysis finds no consistent relationships of necessity or sufficiency (nor both) among the conditions leftist partisanship, high central bank independence, high openness of the economy and corporatism and strong overall economic performance. Instead, there are different combinations of factors (conditions) for different countries in different periods and no combinations at all in most countries or periods. As with the fuzzy-set ideal type analysis, the evidence of the fsQCA analysis suggests that country-specific factors may be more relevant for the relative success or failure of a country's overall economic performance over time. The results of both investigations corroborate some of the existing analyses (for example, Becker and Schwarz 2005b; Kenworthy 2006; Wilensky 2006; Becker 2009, ch. 6).

The absence of a (causal) relationship between the independent institutional variables and the example of a substantively grounded dependent variable of (overall) economic performance elucidates why other large-n statistical analyses yielded puzzling, inconclusive evidence (see Vis et al. 2012). Depending on the performance indicators used and the time frame researched, some (combinations of) factors or conditions indeed have some impact in some countries in some periods, but there also is no combination of factors that always has a consistent impact in all countries.

6   EVALUATION

'Miracle' studies have greatly improved our understanding of particular countries, whereas the quantitative studies on socio-economic performance have elucidated how institutional variables may influence such performance. Both strands of political economy literature, however, lacked a substantive grounding of the dependent variable of interest: socio-economic performance. This has impaired the generalizability of the findings and has led to contradictory findings. Consequently, theorizing the causes of miraculous performance or socio-economic performance more generally has remained haphazard. The comparative research that is based on the substantively grounded variable of overall economic performance discussed in this chapter suggests that there is no (causal) relationship between the institutional variables and economic performance. It is most likely country-specific factors that are more relevant for explaining economic performance over time. That is, there seems to be no master causal variable (or combination of causal factors) that can explain economic performance in all countries over time.

What lessons should we draw for comparative political economy research into the socio-economic performance of nations? First and foremost, the researcher has to establish in what type of performance he or she is interested and why. This is a substantive, theory-driven exercise that up until now is too often neglected in qualitative and quantitative research alike. Secondly, the issue of the independent variables that are used and that hang together should also be theoretically tackled so as to be able to establish, substantively and empirically, which independent variable actually does what to what type of performance. Only when both the independent and dependent variables have been substantively conceptualized and operationalized would it be possible to conduct cross-national or case study comparative research that will fruitfully contribute to theory development.

We conclude by stating that we do not claim that using fuzzy-set techniques for political economy research is the only, or even the best, way forward. Rather, the use of these techniques and the substantively grounded variable of economic performance as an outcome and not an output have illustrated the limitations of the 'miracle' literature as well as the inconclusive or contradictory evidence generated by the larger-n research into socio-economic performance. It has also pointed towards the possible direction for future research: case-(that is, country-) based research but from a truly comparative perspective (for example, Lijphart 1975), that is, using a substantively grounded definition and operationalization of the dependent variable and theoretically disentangling the various independent institutional variables that may explain the dependent variable.

NOTES

1. There are also other ways of clustering welfare states in different types (for example, Castles 2004, see also Chapter 29 in this volume), but here we use Esping-Andersen's well-known typology as an illustration. For an in-depth re-assessment of Esping-Andersen's typology see Scruggs and Allan (2008).
2. We argue that the dependent variable problem is the most urgent problem to be

addressed (see Box 13.2), but we will also show that there is a substantive problem with the independent institutional variables that are most commonly used, since these usually tend to go together. For instance, corporatism is a feature of social-democratic and conservative welfare states but not of liberal welfare states that are pluralist (see Table 13.1).
3.   Three models in which countries score positive on two of the three indicators simultaneously (three different combinations) and three models in which countries score positively on only one of the three indicators (three different possibilities).

REFERENCES

Alvarez, R.M., G. Garrett and P. Lange (1991), 'Government partisanship, labor organisation, and macroeconomic performance', *American Political Science Review*, **85** (2), 539–56.
Becker, U. (2009), *Open Varieties of Capitalism: Continuity, Change and Performance*, London: Palgrave Macmillan.
Becker, U. (ed.) (2011), *The Changing Political Economies of Small West European Countries*, Amsterdam: Amsterdam University Press.
Becker, U. and H. Schwarz (eds) (2005a), *Employment 'Miracles'. A Critical Comparison of Dutch, Scandinavian, Swiss, Australian and Irish Cases versus Germany and the US*, Amsterdam: Amsterdam University Press.
Becker, U. and H. Schwartz (2005b), 'Conclusion: the importance of lucky circumstances, and still the liberal-social democratic divide', in U. Becker and H. Schwarz (eds), *Employment Miracles*, Amsterdam: Amsterdam University Press, pp. 231–49.
Calderón, C. and R. Fuentes (2006), 'Complementarities between Institutions and openness in economic development: evidence for a panel of countries', *Cuadernos de Economia*, **43** (127), 49–80.
Calmfors, L. and J. Driffill (1988), 'Bargaining structure, corporatism and macroeconomic performance', *Economic Policy*, **3** (6), 13–61.
Castles, F.G. (2004), *The Future of the Welfare State*, Oxford: Oxford University Press.
Clasen, J. and N.A. Siegel (eds) (2007), *Investigating Welfare State Change. The 'Dependent Variable Problem' in Comparative Analysis*, Cheltenham, UK and Northampton, MA, USA: Edward Elgar.
Crépaz, M.M.L. (1992), 'Corporatism in decline? An empirical analysis of the impact of corporatism on macroeconomic performance and industrial disputes in 19 industrialized democracies', *Comparative Political Studies*, **25** (2), 139–68.
Delsen, L. (2002), *Exit Polder Model? Socioeconomic Changes in the Netherlands*, Westport, CT: Praeger.
Esping-Andersen, G. (1990), *The Three Worlds of Welfare Capitalism*, Princeton, NJ: Princeton University Press.
Green-Pedersen, C. (2004), 'The dependent variable problem within the study of welfare state retrenchment: defining the problem and looking for solutions', *Journal of Comparative Policy Analysis: Research and Practice*, **6** (1), 3–14.
Green-Pedersen, C. and A. Lindbom (2005), 'Employment and unemployment in Denmark and Sweden: success or failure for the universal welfare model?', in U. Becker and H. Schwarz (eds), *Employment Miracles*, Amsterdam: Amsterdam University Press, pp. 65–87.
Hall, P.A. and D.W. Gingerich (2009), 'Varieties of capitalism and institutional complementarities in the political economy: an empirical analysis', *British Journal of Political Science*, **39** (3), 449–82.
Hibbs, D.A. (1977), 'Political parties and macroeconomic policy', *American Political Science Review*, **71** (4), 1467–87.
Hicks, A. and L. Kenworthy (1998), 'Cooperation and political economic performance in affluent democratic capitalism', *American Journal of Sociology*, **103** (6), 1631–72.

Iversen, T. and D. Soskice (2006), 'New macroeconomics and political science', *Annual Review of Political Science*, **9**, 425–53.

Jahn, D. (2014), 'Changing of the guard: trends in corporatist arrangements in 42 highly industrialized societies from 1960–2010', *Socio-Economic Review*, **14** (1), 47–71.

Jahn, D. and K. Kuitto (2011), 'Taking stock of policy performance in Central and Eastern Europe: policy outcomes between policy reform, transitional pressure and international influence', *European Journal of Political Research*, **50** (7–8), 719–48.

Kenworthy, L. (2006), 'Institutional coherence and macroeconomic performance', *Socio-Economic Review*, **4** (1), 69–91.

Lane, J.-E. and S.O. Ersson (2000), *The New Institutional Politics: Performance and Outcomes*, London: Routledge.

Lijphart, A. (1975), 'The comparable case strategy in comparative research', *Comparative Political Studies*, **8** (2), 158–77.

Lijphart, A. (2012), *Patterns of Democracy: Government Forms and Performance in Thirty-Six Countries*, 2nd edn, New Haven, CT and London: Yale University Press.

Lupu, N. and J. Pontusson (2011), 'The structure of inequality and the politics of redistribution', *American Political Science Review*, **105** (2), 316–36.

Merrien, F.X. and U. Becker (2005), 'The Swiss miracle: low growth and high employment', in U. Becker and H. Schwarz (eds), *Employment Miracles*, Amsterdam: Amsterdam University Press, pp. 111–33.

Molina, O. and M. Rhodes (2002), 'Corporatism: the past, present, and future of a concept', *Annual Review of Political Science*, **5**, 305–31.

Ragin, C.C. (2000), *Fuzzy-Set Social Science*, Chicago, IL and London: University of Chicago Press.

Rihoux, B. and C.C. Ragin (eds) (2009), *Configurational Comparative Methods: Qualitative Comparative Analysis (QCA) and Related Techniques*, Los Angeles, CA: Sage.

Schmidt, M.G. (1996), 'When parties matter: a review of the possibilities and limits of partisanship influence on public policy', *European Journal of Political Research*, **30** (2), 155–83.

Schneider, C.Q. and C. Wagemann (2012), *Set-Theoretic Methods for the Social Sciences: A Guide to Qualitative Comparative Analysis*, Cambridge: Cambridge University Press.

Scruggs, L.A. and J.P. Allan (2008), 'Social stratification and welfare regimes for the twenty-first century: revisiting the three worlds of welfare capitalism', *World Politics*, **60** (4), 642–64.

Siaroff, A. (1999), 'Corporatism in 24 industrial democracies: meaning and measurement', *European Journal of Political Research*, **36** (2), 175–205.

Soskice, D. (2007), 'Macroeconomics and varieties of capitalism', in B. Hancké, M. Rhodes and M. Thatcher (eds), *Beyond Varieties of Capitalism: Conflict, Contradictions, and Complementarities in the European Economy*, Oxford: Oxford University Press.

Traxler, F. (2004), 'The metamorphoses of corporatism: from classical to lean patterns', *European Journal of Political Research*, **43** (4), 571–98.

Van Kersbergen, K. and B. Vis (2014), *Comparative Welfare State Politics: Development, Opportunities, and Reform*, Cambridge: Cambridge University Press.

Vis, B., J. Woldendorp and H. Keman (2007), 'Do miracles exist? Analyzing economic performance comparatively', *Journal of Business Research*, **60** (5), 531–8.

Vis, B., J. Woldendorp and H. Keman (2012), 'Economic performance and institutions: capturing the dependent variable', *European Political Science Review*, **4** (1), 73–96.

Vis, B., J. Woldendorp and H. Keman (2013), 'Examining variation in economic performance using fuzzy-sets', *Quality and Quantity*, **47** (4), 1971–89.

Visser, J. and A. Hemerijck (1997), *A Dutch Miracle: Job Growth, Welfare Reform, and Corporatism in the Netherlands*, Amsterdam: Amsterdam University Press.

Wilensky, H.L. (2006), 'Trade-offs in public spending finance: comparing the well-being of big spenders and lean spenders', *International Political Science Review*, **27** (4), 333–58.

14 Political theory and its normative methods
Keith Dowding

1 INTRODUCTION

There are many different types of normative political theory (or political philosophy); I restrict myself to discussing 'analytic' political theory and will not cover so-called 'continental' political theories, such as 'hermeneutics', 'post-structuralism', post-modernism, discourse analysis, or various ways of examining ideology, and other forms of pragmatic ethics. Some of these approaches are covered in other chapters or – although considered eligible in general for cognitivist political moral theory – are less directly relevant with respect to doing analytic normative political theory, including conceptual analysis, the use of intuitions and reasoned argument in the development of normative principles and grand theories within a largely Rawlsian agenda (Rawls 1971). I therefore concentrate upon certain methodological techniques: conceptual analysis; the use of intuitions and thought experiments; issues around reasonable (dis)agreement; and substantial approaches developing specific political theories, namely contract and ideal observer theory.

Normative political theory is largely shielded from theoretical advances in political science except by the most unsystematic osmosis, despite Rawls's professed desideratum that it should be conducted in the knowledge of the facts of human psychology and institutions. In part that is because the very nature of those facts is often challenged, and challenged methodologically. The boundary between moral and political philosophy is less sharp than that between political science and normative theory; indeed, much work on the nature of social justice and the form that political societies should take stands equally within each. The feminist slogan that the personal is political also explicitly maintains that no such distinction can be made (Hanisch 1969). Political philosophy is Socratic, in that arguments continue and those which prevail at any given moment depend simply on which side in the dialogue is currently dominating the floor.

I first look at the role of normative political theory. I then consider, in turn, conceptual analysis, the nature of evidence in normative theorizing and constitutional theory – that is, how we come to accept the legitimacy of our political institutions and the character of theories of social justice; for the latter, how we come to accept the moral and political principles that underlie the social order. Finally, I consider the main way in which normative theory is conducted: the Socratic dialogue.

2   WHAT IS THE ROLE OF NORMATIVE POLITICAL THEORY?

John Rawls's *A Theory of Justice* was published in 1971. That same year saw the first issue of *Philosophy and Public Affairs* (*PPA*). Together they can be said to set the agenda for modern normative political theory. Rawls ushered in a phase of studying grand theorizing about what the constitution of society should be, given sets of basic values. Political philosophy is now dominated by rival such theories, often based upon different primary sets of values. Debate concerns why some values – say freedom, or rights or equality – should be the primary values in a normative political constitution. In contrast (though it also covers issues of social justice), *PPA* set the agenda for using the tools of normative enquiry to examine basic moral and political problems such as abortion, the nature of just wars, the relative roles of the state and parents in educational policy, and so on.

Methods used in the first area include the nature and role of contract theory, reasonable agreements and conceptual analysis of the basic values used in theory construction. The second area likewise involves conceptual analysis, but also the use of moral intuitions or considered judgments in case-studies. Conceptual analysis is at the heart of both, and it is to that I turn first.

3   CONCEPTUAL ANALYSIS

We cannot do political theory without using basic moral and political concepts. Even when they are not explicitly defined, we rely upon some understanding of political and moral terms. Concepts are not usually thought to take on truth-values: any given definition of 'freedom' or 'respect' is not true or false; but it might be more or less useful, or more or less in keeping with standard usage. Words take on their own conventional meaning, and their meaning changes with usage. We can map ideological change within a society by these shifts in meaning. Often the major writers of the past gain their importance because their use of concepts can be seen, at least in retrospect, as a crucial shift in extension and/or normative connotation (Skinner 2002). Thus, even when terms are not explicitly defined, conceptual usage and hence analysis becomes important. Explicit conceptual analysis, however, is a key method of political analysis. There are three important principles or constraints of conceptual analysis: the semantic, the normative and the methodological (Dowding and Van Hees 2007).

The first constraint suggests that concepts should accord with everyday usage as far as possible. There can be technical justifications for defining terms otherwise, including the demands of precision, of consistency and coherence with other concepts, and of theoretical extension. So we might restrict the use of the term 'exploitation' to make it more precise, we might set its boundaries so it fits nicely with our definitions of 'freedom' and 'rights'; while the idea of what constitutes 'exploitation' might expand as our notion of what is socially unjust enlarges. Through justifying our normative claims in what Barry (1990) calls 'political argument', we might thereby change the meaning, both normative connotation and/or extension of terms. We might create new terms. If a society had no concept of 'rape', then conveying sexual abuse would be more problematic and the lack of such a term would affect our moral attitudes to certain sorts of behavior, so words might need to be co-opted as part of an argument. As words must take on new extensions, so their normative force extends; or their normative force might alter along with a concept's extension. These two elements form important parts of both the logic and rhetoric of political argument. Nevertheless, the semantic constraint suggests all such extensions ought to be conducted within the scope of extending ordinary usage lest the philosophical vocabulary become a technical account requiring translation into ordinary language usage.

The normative criterion involves the idea that changing the extension of concepts should not overly change their normative force. We might apply the idea of 'exploitation' to new forms of behavior and this might entail that the normative meaning alters slightly. For example, we might find it necessary to distinguish 'justified' and 'unjustified' exploitation, or consider exploitation to be part of a broader set of actions warranting moral opprobrium. However, if we were to extend the term so much that its negative moral connotations disappear or become a minor element, then this would break the normative constraints of conceptual analysis. Sometimes the normative connotation of terms alters, not because their extension as such alters, but because terms' empirical implications change. Terms can even, over time, reverse their normative force. 'Democracy' was once seen as dangerous because it was associated with the chaos that would inevitably ensue (so it was assumed) from a popular franchise. Such chaos is no longer associated with the term, allowing it to take on almost universal acceptance as normatively positive. (Of course, instability in a democracy does lead political elites to justify running a country undemocratically.)

The methodological constraint is merely to acknowledge that terms such as 'freedom' and 'equality' might take on rather different meanings in different contexts and the relationship between those meanings might be complex. We might distinguish between legal and moral rights, for example; thus we need to be contextually sensitive when defining moral and political concepts.

Other criteria for good conceptual analysis suggest that concepts should be as parsimonious as possible – that is, that they cannot be further analyzed – meaning that even as theories change, their basic concepts will not alter. That would be the ideal for theory development, but is unattainable in political theorizing; the grand theories and principles are too closely entwined with their basic concepts. However, concepts should not be defined to fit with theoretical desiderata; rather, theories should be designed to promote the desiderata derived from their basic concepts. For that reason concepts should be as non-normative as possible. Concepts should fit naturally into normative desiderata and not be 'gerrymandered'. Just as electoral districts should be defined by features such as equal size, physical geography, demography, and not created to fix electoral out-comes, concepts should be developed on the basis of natural desiderata rather than in order to promote specific conclusions. This principle leads to the view that concepts should be as value-free as possible. To define coercion as 'non-justified interference', rather than as 'interference of a particular character', is to further moralize coercion from the normative connotations it naturally enjoys. 'Coercion' suggests being forced against one's will and that already carries a negative connotation. Nevertheless, we might still justify coercion in certain circumstances. Hence to define coercion as 'non-justified interference' rather than as 'interference of a certain kind' is to gerrymander the concept, perhaps to use it to suggest that certain political principles, even when they force people against their will, are non-coercive.

In theory we should make concepts as simple as possible and as inde-pendent of each other as possible. The way we analyze freedom will affect the way we analyze coercion, but as far as possible those concepts should be identified independently, so that developing one concept will have as little effect on others as possible. Quine's (1960) famous account of holism in theory suggests that conceptual change will reverberate throughout the entire semantic universe: changing one concept will change all others. However, we might think of this as an earthquake. In one region of the world it may have mighty effects; elsewhere sensitive instruments might register it, but in practical terms it will have no noticeable impact. We can accept Quine's logical argument that concept change will affect all other concepts relevant to the theory, without believing it has any concrete impact on those other concepts. By defining terms as independently as possible, we can encourage that supposition by not explicitly creating inter-linkages, while acknowledging that closely related concepts will be affected by concept change in their neighbors.

Concepts are an important part of theory building, and they take on some of their meaning from the theory of which they are a part. Concepts do not, however, take on a truth-value; they have no propositional content. Rather, they fix a term by extension and take on further meaning by the implications of that extension given our theoretical understanding of the world. Theories and principles, even if moral and political, do have propositional content and to that extent take on truth-values. A theory of justice can be false to the extent that if it were applied it would not entail the outcomes that are supposed by its proponents. Feasibility constraints are an important part of normative political theorizing even if, as Cohen (2008, ch. 6) maintains, moral principles might rely upon no facts.

Many normative theorists use the distinction between concepts and conceptions (Rawls 1971, p. 5), where a conception is a less abstract and more specified version of a concept. In this sense a 'concept' is a set made up of members that are 'conceptions'. In the terms I use here, both are concepts; it is simply that what Rawls terms 'conceptions' have a more restricted domain of application.

4   EVIDENCE IN NORMATIVE THEORY

Empirical evidence can affect normative theory just as it affects positive theory – for example, empirical evidence about the introduction of universal enfranchisement. The normative criterion suggests that our basic moral values or intuitions need to be taken into consideration when evaluating concepts and theories. The use of imaginary cases (or 'intuition pumps'; Dennett 2013) to test the implications of normative theories is a major method in moral and political philosophy. Such stories are used to test theories' implications. Does the theory get the right answer to the problem posed? Famous intuition pumps such as 'Trolley' (should we divert a tram from its course, saving five people but causing the death of another?) and its variants (what difference does it make if we save the five by pushing someone in front of the tram to stop it?) (Foot 1968; Thomson 1985; Otsuka 2008) are used to examine our views on consequentialism (what we do should be determined by evaluating the likely outcomes), deontological theories (those based on assigning rights), and so on. An important issue is the nature of that evidence.

If we take our immediate apprehension of what we should do in Trolley or similar cases to be a baseline empirical test that theories need to pass, then we need to examine such evidence systematically. Experimental psychologists have done so (Haidt 2012; Greene 2013), and find that people tend to agree roughly in proportion of 65–85 percent on one course of action – a course that can vary with the specific details of the study. They demonstrate, moreover, that the conditions under which such imaginary cases are presented can affect the results. Work using functional magnetic resonance imaging (fMRI) scans demonstrate that different parts of the brain are involved according to whether one takes a deontological or consequentialist line. Very roughly, emotional processes tend to lead to personalized deontology and calculative processes to more consequentialist conclusions.

What are we to make of this evidence with regard to normative theory? Normative theory is supposed to guide action, not merely describe what we think. Greene (2013) concludes that we need to discount our 'emotional' reactions and become utilitarians. Most normative theorists seem to think that their intuitive reaction needs to guide further theory development. Part of the issue concerns how we regard the evidence. For Greene, the evidence tells us something about ourselves and not about what constitutes good action-guiding moral theory. After all, moral theory is supposed to tell us what we should do, not what we would do (Williamson 2007, ch. 7). For most normative writers, the evidence of their intuitions is telling them something constitutive about moral theory. By contrast, empirical evidence in positive theories is an epistemic check upon the theory: does the theory provide correct predictions? We might consider evidence for normative theory to be ontological: does the theory constitute morality?

Rawls (1951 [2001], 1971, pp. 48–51) elucidates the concept of reflective equilibrium as a process by which we can take evidence to theories and theories to evidence, modifying each in turn to reach a reasoned judgment in reflective equilibrium. We do not accept intuitions as they strike us, but consider them in the light of our theory, and then reconsider our theory in the light of those reconsidered judgments. We reflect both upon the theory and our immediate apprehensions in the light of the theory in order to reach reflective equilibrium. Rawls's idea is to reject foundational moral theories (such as utilitarianism) that sometimes conflict with some of our basic moral intuitions. However, allowing such intuitions too much credence will make normative theory highly conservative (Singer 2005). A wide interpretation of reflective equilibrium that allows any intuitions to be revised to fit with radical theories (Daniels 1996) will not overcome the problem that Rawls first designed reflective equilibrium to overcome. Normative theories could radically diverge from our extant moral views.

A bigger problem not discussed in the normative literature concerns uniqueness. Any reflection upon rival grand theories and various intuitions we might have about imaginary (or real) cases could lead to multiple equilibriums. After all, in many imaginary cases everyone agrees upon the right outcome but disagrees about what this tells us about theory. In 'Surgeon' we are asked if a surgeon who has five patients soon to die without organ transplants (two need a lung each, two a kidney each and one a heart) should remove the organs of a healthy patient newly arrived for his annual check-up who luckily is a perfect genetic match for all five (Thomson 1985). It is universally agreed that the surgeon should not. The example, often used against consequentialist utilitarian thinking, does not cause utilitarians much angst, since they can explain why the healthy patient can feel safe from the surgeon's knife on rule-utilitarian grounds (for example, Braybrooke 2004; Hayry 2013).

Reflective equilibrium can enable both deontological and utilitarian theories to agree over easy cases, but on different grounds. They reach different reflective equilibriums. We can also have utilitarians disagreeing with other utilitarians, and deontologists disagreeing with each other over the specifics of theories and judgments in imaginary cases. Again, these mark different equilibriums following reasoned reflection. We need an equilibrium selection process, but none so far has been attempted. The methodological problem is that it is not clear where we should start, since the nature of the evidence, and the nature of the theory with regard to that evidence, is not clear.

One such criterion might be parsimony. Certainly the justification of not coercively removing the organs from someone is more parsimoniously explained by giving people rights simply on the basis of their common humanity rather than showing it is consistent with maximizing welfare based upon the likely consequences of following rules that would lead people to fear going to hospital lest their organs be removed. So deontology seems more parsimonious in this example. But then deontological explanations can be less parsimonious when it comes to explaining why we should come to others' assistance in times of need. Parsimony does not provide a straightforward equilibrium selection device for moral theories.

Perhaps there is not much more to say. Reflective equilibrium is an inductive not a deductive process. We induce from our intuitions reflections on our theory that then lead to further reflection on those intuitions. Despite several hundred years of discussion, Hume's problem of induction has never been satisfactorily solved (Howson 2000). Induction cannot be rationally justified (that is, perhaps, that induction is not deduction). Perhaps the methods of political philosophy in the form of reflective equilibrium also cannot be rationally justified, but as with induction we cannot help but use them. Also, (Karl Popper 1989 notwithstanding) we cannot do science without induction, and cannot normatively theorize without using intuitions. Nevertheless, this suggests that reflective equilibrium is too open-ended for us to conceive of a satisfactory end state to moral theory.

5   CONSTITUTIONAL THEORY

The plurality of values and the possibility of disagreement over grand value systems have led political philosophy to consider constitutional means to people's living together harmoniously. While people need not agree in their first-order moral views, they might be able to reach second-order agreement over how we manage first-order conflict (Barry 1995); or, in Rawls's (1993) terms, theories of justice are political not metaphysical or comprehensive. To that end contract theory has been the major tool in modern political philosophy. This is the method of examining under ideal conditions what moral or political obligations would people agree to in order to form the society in which they live. The chief issue here is what to put into the assumptions. Theories that assume contracts are for mutual advantage will either allow the strong to exploit the weak (Barry 1989) or require constraints. Harsanyi (1955, 1977), Rawls (1971) and Buchanan (1991) all constrain by their own particular versions of the veil of ignorance. That, together with some differences in assumptions about the rational decision procedures that would be adopted by contractors, leads to different recommendations for the just constitutional order.

Similarly, how we view the way constitutions will be treated by people with full knowledge of their situation in society will affect how we think constitutions should be initially specified. Conservatives follow Hume in thinking we should consider all to be knaves, others take it that we should assume some mix of knaves and knights (Le Grand 2003), yet others still that we should construct our ideal theory assuming that the conditions specified will be respected by those to whom they apply (Cohen 2008). In part these disagreements about assumptions are about the purpose of normative theorizing. Ideal theorists believe that normative theory is about what should be, even in the absence of what can be. Realists consider normative theory has to include what can be within its purview (Williams 2005), though even then there can be considerable debate over the modal and methodological status of 'can be'.

The assumptions of what goes into traditional contract theory have been more radically critiqued. Pateman (1988) argues that traditional contract theory with its emphasis on the constitutional political order rather than social relations more generally leads to a male-centered analysis. Mills (1997) suggests that the contractual tradition has been blind to ethnicity and grand white male theorizing leads to specific types of constitutional order. Mills and Pateman take different lines on what this entails for contractualism. Pateman thinks contractualism itself is biased, Mills that we need to ensure the assumptions are correct to specify the conditions of justice (see their debate in Pateman and Mills 2007).

Other versions of contract theory remove it from its veil of ignorance conditions and into the setting of bargaining with extant societies (Buchanan 1991; Binmore 1994, 1998; Barry 1995; Scanlon 1998). Barry and Scanlon operate with the idea of 'reasonable rejection'. Contracts between peoples with different value systems need to agree upon principles of stable and peaceful social order. The sorts of appeal made in arguments to justify one of set of principles over another must be applicable to all contractors. If one contractor appeals to revelation, then she must accept the contrary revelation of another. Less dramatically, if our intuitions or considered judgments vary over a moral dilemma, we must agree on a principle to determine how those intuitions are to count – such as a majoritarian decision mechanism that counts those considered judgments equally. Binmore's game-theoretic account examines the game of life as a repeated set of contracts that develop with the changing circumstances of people – though his Whiggish principles entail that it too appeals to culture-bound forms of reasonableness.

All of these contractual grand theories are open to the criticisms above on the relevant interpretations of evidence and its relationship to the theory – though to no greater extent than any other rival theory. Sen (2009) has critiqued what he calls 'transcendental theories', but his own preferred method (Adam Smith's ideal observer) is no less vulnerable to similar critique. All grand theories suffer from trying to square the circle of plural values and inconsistent intuitions, and all are too abstract to straightforwardly apply to legislative advice to deal with real-life political and social problems.

6   SOCRATIC DIALOGUE

The central role of Socrates in the dialogues of Plato and Xenophon gave rise to the term Socratic dialogue, a method of normative analysis rarely used explicitly in essay-writing today. The writer develops a narrative in which protagonists discuss moral and philosophical issues. Usually, of course, one protagonist is given the central role and their arguments prevail. However, in some ways Socratic dialogue is the primary method of normative theorizing. While essays are not written as narratives with characters, writers debate with each other, and the author's own voice is that of the central character, given the best lines. Real dialogue levels the playing field and must remain the major method of normative theorizing. By pointing out contradiction, unclear reasoning, muddles or problems in the views of others, we can make them improve their thought, remove contradiction by shifting their ground and sharpen their claims to make them clearer. We cannot assume that such dialogue will bring agreement, certainly not at the fundamental level, but we can hope that the endless normative theorizing leads to an ever tightening in the helix of the positions as they circle around each other.

Normative theorizing requires consistency but can never fully attain it, since there is too much that is contrary in our basic moral intuitions as they are applied to an ever-changing society. There are multiple reflective moral equilibriums and we have little idea of even where to start examining how to choose between them. None of that implies, however, that we cannot have criteria that make some principles preferable to others, and some theories more plausible than others. Which are more plausible at any given time depends on the stage in the spiral of argument we have attained and the current conditions of our society.

FURTHER READING

Introductory

Swift, A. (2001), *Political Philosophy: A Beginner's Guide for Students and Politicians*, Cambridge: Polity.

Application

Temkin, L.S. (2012), *Rethinking the Good: Moral Ideals and the Nature of Practical Reasoning*, Oxford: Oxford University Press.

Advanced

Blau, A. (ed.) (2016), *Methods in Political Theory*, Cambridge: Cambridge University Press.

REFERENCES

Barry, B. (1989), *Theories of Justice: A Treatise on Social Justice*, vol. 1, London: Harvester Wheatsheaf.

Barry, B. (1990), *Political Argument: A Reissue with a New Introduction*, New York: Harvester Wheatsheaf.

Barry, B. (1995), *Justice as Impartiality: A Treatise on Social Justice*, vol. 2, Oxford: Oxford University Press.

Binmore, K. (1994), *Game Theory and the Social Contract, I: Playing Fair*, Cambridge, MA: MIT Press.

Binmore, K. (1998), *Game Theory and the Social Contract, II: Just Playing*, Cambridge, MA: MIT Press.

Braybrooke, D. (2004), *Utilitarianism: Restorations; Repairs; Renovations*, Toronto: Toronto University Press.

Buchanan, J.M. (1991), *The Economics and Ethics of Constitutional Order*, Ann Arbor, MI: University of Michigan Press.

Cohen, G.A. (2008), *Rescuing Justice and Equality*, Cambridge, MA: Harvard University Press.

Daniels, N. (1996), *Justice and Justification: Reflective Equilibrium Theory in Practice*, New York: Cambridge University Press.

Dennett, D.C. (2013), *Intuition Pumps and Other Tools for Thinking*, London: Allen Lane.

Dowding, K. and M. Van Hees (2007), 'Counterfactual success and negative freedom', *Economics and Philosophy*, **23** (2), 141–62.

Foot, P. (1968), 'The problem of abortion and the doctrine of double effect', in P. Foot, *Virtues and Vices and Other Essays in Moral Philosophy*, Oxford: Basil Blackwell, pp. 19–32.

Greene, J.D. (2013), *Moral Tribes: Emotion, Reason and the Gap between Us and Them*, New York: Penguin.

Haidt, J. (2012), *The Righteous Mind: Why Good People are Divided by Politics and Religion*, Harmondsworth: Penguin.

Hanisch, C. (1969), 'The personal is the political', *Notes from the Second Year: Women's Liberation*, pp. 76–9, accessed 1 June 2016 at http://www.carolhanisch.org/CHwritings/PersonalisPol.pdf.

Harsanyi, J.C. (1955), 'Cardinal welfare, individualistic ethics, and interpersonal comparisons of utility', *Journal of Political Economy*, **63** (2), 309–21.

Harsanyi, J.C. (1977), *Rational Behavior and Bargaining Equilibrium in Games and Social Situations*, Cambridge: Cambridge University Press.

Hayry, M. (2013), *Liberal Utilitarianism and Applied Ethics*, London; Routledge.

Howson, C. (2000), *Hume's Problem: Induction and the Justification of Belief*, Oxford: Oxford University Press.

Le Grand, J. (2003), *Motivation, Agency and Public Policy: Of Knights and Knaves, Pawns and Queens*, Oxford: Oxford University Press.

Mills, C.W. (1997), *The Racial Contract*, Ithaca, NY: Cornell University Press.

Otsuka, M. (2008), 'Double effect, triple effect and the trolley problem: squaring the circle in looping cases', *Utilitas*, **20** (1), 92–110.

Pateman, C. (1988), *The Sexual Contract*, Oxford: Polity Press.

Pateman, C. and C.W. Mills (2007), *Contract and Domination*, Oxford: Polity Press.

Popper, K.R. (1989), *Conjectures and Refutations: The Growth of Scientific Knowledge*, revised and corrected edn, London: Routledge.

Quine, W.V.O. (1960), *Word and Object*, Cambridge, MA: MIT Press.

Rawls, J. (1951), 'Outline of a decision procedure for ethics', reprinted in J. Rawls (2001), *Collected Papers*, Cambridge, MA: Harvard University Press, pp. 1–19.

Rawls, J. (1971), *A Theory of Justice*, Oxford: Oxford University Press.

Rawls, J. (1993), *Political Liberalism*, New York: Columbia University Press.

Scanlon, T. (1998), *What We Owe to Each Other*, Cambridge, MA: Harvard University Press.

Sen, A. (2009), *The Idea of Justice*, Cambridge, MA: Harvard University Press.

Singer, P. (2005), 'Ethics and intuitions', *Journal of Ethics*, **9** (4), 331–52.

Skinner, Q. (2002), *Vision of Politics, Vol. 1: Regarding Method*, Cambridge, Cambridge University Press.

Thomson, J.V. (1985), 'The trolley problem', *Yale Law Journal*, **94** (6), 1395–415.
Williams, B. (2005), *In the Beginning Was the Deed: Realism and Moralism in Political Argument*, Princeton, NJ: Princeton University Press.
Williamson, T. (2007), *The Philosophy of Philosophy*, Oxford: Blackwell.

PART III

ANALYZING POLITICS: DATA–CONCEPTS–TECHNIQUES

15 Organizing and developing data sets: exemplified by the Party Government Data Set
Jaap J. Woldendorp

1 INTRODUCTION

This chapter argues that there are three issues with collecting and compiling data sets for political science research (cf. Woldendorp 2012). The first issue regards the tension between developing a research question and design based on specific theoretical considerations that require particular data and possibly compiling a relevant data set for a broader array of theoretical approaches and research questions. The second issue is how to include (institutional) change or incorporate data suited for new approaches that often require different levels of measurement in existing data sets. The final issue is how to improve the validity (do concepts travel across time and space?) and the reliability of the information generated (are the data correctly organized and sufficiently replicable by other researchers?).[1]

How to tackle these issues? Disaggregation, in my view, is the key. The more disaggregated the data collected, the more useful a data set is for a greater variety of research as the individual researcher can transform the information to his or her own needs. The more disaggregated the data set, the easier it is to incorporate institutional change over time or new data. Disaggregation also improves validity as the concepts remain relatively straightforward and it also allows for cross-referencing with other data sets to improve reliability.

The case for disaggregation is argued using the Party Government Data Set (Woldendorp et al. 2000, 2011) as an example. In the first section the Party Government Data Set (PGD) is introduced. In the second section the case for more data on a lower level of aggregation is argued. In the third section some specific areas of data collection and their match to relevant government data are briefly discussed. The fourth section deals with the institutional (constitutional) context. The fifth and final section concludes. The chapter also provides overviews of digital and other data sets for further use in comparative politics.[2]

BOX 15.1   RECOMMENDED READING

Websites Giving Overviews of Data Sets

Inter-university Consortium for Political and Social Research (ICPSR): https://www.icpsr.umich.edu/icpsrweb/ICPSR/.
European Representative Democracy Data Archive (ERDDA): http://www.erdda.se/.
European Legislative Politics Research Group (ELPRG): http://www.elprg.eu/data.htm.
Gesellschaft Sozialwissenschaftlicher Infrastruktureinrichtungen (GESIS) Data for Comparative Research: http://www.gesis.org/das-institut/kompetenzzentren/european-data-laboratory/data-resources/data-for-comparative-research/.
Guide to Political Science Information Resources: http://guides.lib.purdue.edu/content.php?pid=129089&sid=1108493.
Macro Data Guide, an International Social Science Resource: http://www.nsd.uib.no/macrodataguide/index.html.

General Political Data Sets

Africa Research Program Political Data: http://africa.gov.harvard.edu/data/politic.htm.
CIA Factbook: https://www.cia.gov/library/publications/the-world-factbook/.
Comparative Political Datasets Armingeon et al.: http://www.ipw.unibe.ch/content/team/klaus_armingeon/comparative_political_data_sets/index_ger.html.
Cross-national Time-series Data Archive: http://www.databanksinternational.com/32.html (commercial data base).
Finer, S.E. (1997), *The History of Government from the Earliest Times*, vol. 3, Oxford: Oxford University Press.
Lane, J.-E., D. McKay and K. Newton (1997), *Political Data Handbook. OECD Countries*, 2nd edn, Oxford: Oxford University Press.
Lijphart, A. (2012), *Patterns of Democracy. Government Forms and Performance in Thirty-Six Countries*, New Haven, CT and London: Yale University Press: http://polisci.ucsd.edu/faculty/lijphart.html.
Parties, Governments and Legislatures: http://www.wzb.eu/en/persons/thomas-r-cusack?s=5662.
Political Database of the Americas: http://pdba.georgetown.edu/history.html.
Political Handbook of the World, annual handbook since 1928, from 1975 edited by Arthur Banks et al. Issue 2008, published by CQ, Oxford and Washington, DC: Sage.
Political Resources on the Net, Parties, Government and Media: www.politicalresources.net.
Polity IV Project. Political Regime Characteristics and Transitions, 1800–2013: http://www.systemicpeace.org/polity/polity4.htm.

2   THE PARTY GOVERNMENT DATA SET

The PGD is used as an example but the set is not considered to be the only one or the most complete (see Woldendorp 2012). A major advantage of the data set is that it captures a part of the full life cycle of party government as depicted in Figure 15.1.

Figure 15.1 shows the full life cycle of party government in parliamentary democracies and is based on research by Budge and Keman (1990). This research assumes there is a strong link between office-seeking and policy-seeking behavior of political parties: parties not in office cannot implement policies or at best only amend them (McDonald and Budge 2005; Strøm et al. 2008). In order to get into office, parties need votes. The outcome of parliamentary elections, the type of democracy, the party system and the related systems of interest intermediation (corporatism or pluralism) shape the (institutional) room to maneuver for the parties. Within the process of democratic governance, the PGD focuses on party government specifically. The core data collected are based on a 'theory guided' set up and include:

- the duration of government,
- the reasons for termination of government,
- the type of government,

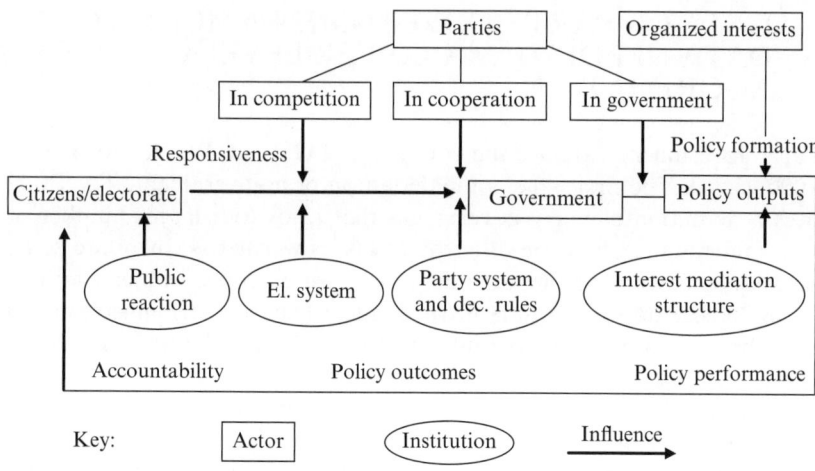

Source: Pennings et al. (2006, p. 184).

Figure 15.1   *Chain of democratic control and command: performance as a sequential system*

- the parties in or supporting government and their seats in the lower house of parliament,
- the total number of seats in the lower house of parliament,
- the ideological complexion of government and parliament (CPG),
- the number of cabinet ministers,
- the prime minister and party affiliation, and
- the number of reshuffles, that is the simultaneous movement or replacement of two or more cabinet ministers in the life time of a government.

These data are relevant for the explanation of not only party government formation, but also of its policy and macroeconomic performance and of electoral feedbacks in parliamentary democracies.

In addition, but only in Woldendorp et al. (2000), the PGD provides the identification of ministries and competencies (portfolios or policy areas) and the name and sex of the ministers in charge and their party affiliation at the start of each government, as well as a short outline of the institutional framework of the countries included as of 1998–2000. I return to the institutional context of party government later after dealing with the core data collected in the PGD and discussing other areas of the full life cycle of party government where data collection could be improved.

3   DATA ON PARTY GOVERNMENT: MORE DATA NEEDED ON A LOWER LEVEL OF AGGREGATION

Party government data are the core of the PGD (see Woldendorp et al. 2000, ch. 1). The first issue is the definition of a government. The PGD uses a definition of party government that leads to a larger number of governments than in some other data sets. Nevertheless, there are some data sets that also use the same definition (for example, Müller-Rommel et al. 2008; ParlGov; Comparative Political Datasets Armingeon et al.) and this enhances validity, and reliability of the information as data can be cross-checked. Next, the PGD and most other data sets focus on cabinet ministers only and do not collect information on junior ministers. Also, the PGD only provides data on individual cabinet ministers until 1998. In this area there is definite room and need for improvement of data collection. Then, the PGD lists the starting date of a government and its duration in days as days are the lowest level of aggregation that allows researchers to construct their own measures of duration (for example, survival). This enhances the validity of the data. Furthermore, the PGD

BOX 15.2   CABINET DATA

Cabinet Data

Berglund, S., J. Ekman and F.H. Aarebrot (eds) (2004), *The Handbook of Political Change in Eastern Europe*, 2nd edn, Cheltenham, UK and Northampton, MA, USA: Edward Elgar.

Blondel, J. and F. Müller-Rommel (eds) (1997), *Cabinets in Western Europe*, 2nd revised edn, London: Palgrave Macmillan.

Blondel, J., F. Müller-Rommel and D. Malová (2006), *Governing New European Democracies*, London: Palgrave Macmillan.

Budge, I. and H. Keman (1990), *Parties and Democracy. Coalition Formation and Government Functioning in Twenty States*, Oxford: Oxford University Press.

Chiefs of State and Cabinet Members of Foreign Governments (CIA): https://www.cia.gov/library/publications/world-leaders-1/index.html.

Comparative Parliamentary Democracy Data Archive (CPDA): http://www.erdda.se/.

Comparative Politics Greifswald: http://comparativepolitics.uni-greifswald.de/data.html.

De Winter, L. (2002), 'Parties and government formation, portfolio allocation, and policy definition', in K.R. Luther and F. Müller-Rommel (eds), *Political Parties in the New Europe. Political and Analytical Challenges*, Oxford: Oxford University Press, pp.171–207.

De Winter, L. and P. Dumont (2006), 'Parties into government', in R.S. Katz and W.J. Crotty (eds), *Handbook of Party Politics*, London: Sage, pp.175–88.

Druckman, J.N. and A. Roberts (2007), 'Communist successor parties and coalition formation in Eastern Europe', *Legislative Studies Quarterly*, **32** (1), 5–31.

European Representative Democracy Data Archive (ERDDA): http://www.erdda.se/.

Governments Data (McDonald): http://www.binghamton.edu/political-science/research/.

Governments in Europe Data Archive (GEDA): http://www.erdda.se/.

Ismayr, W. (ed.) (2010), *Die Politische Systeme Osteuropas*, 3rd edn, Wiesbaden: VS-Verlag.

Keesing's World News Archive (commercial database): https://www.jcsonlineresources.org/catalogue/keesings-world-news-archive.

Müller-Rommel, F., K. Fettelschoss and P. Harst (2004), 'Party government in Central Eastern European democracies: a data collection', *European Journal of Political Research*, **43** (6), 869–93.

Müller-Rommel, F., H. Schultze, P. Harfst and K. Fettelschoss (2008), 'Parteienregierungen in Mittel- und Ost-Europa: Empirische Befunde im Ländervergleich 1990 bis 2008', *Zeitschrift für Parlamentsfragen*, **39** (4), 810–31.

Parliament and Government Composition Database (ParlGov) (Döring and Manow): http://www.parlgov.org/.

Political Data Yearbook (1992–) *European Journal of Political Research*.

Ryals, C. and C.S.N. Golder (2010), 'Measuring government duration and stability in Central Eastern European democracies', *European Journal of Political Research*, **49** (1), 119–50.

Strøm, K., W.C. Müller and T. Bergman (eds) (2003), *Delegation and Accountability in Parliamentary Democracies*, Oxford: Oxford University Press.

Strøm, K., W.C. Müller and T. Bergman (eds) (2008), *Cabinets and Coalition Bargaining. The Democratic Life Cycle in Western Europe*, Oxford: Oxford University Press.

Timmermans, A.I. (2003), *High Politics in the Low Countries. An Empirical Study of Coalition Agreements in Belgium and The Netherlands*, Aldershot, UK and Burlington, VT: Ashgate.

Tsebelis Veto Players: http://sitemaker.umich.edu/tsebelis/veto_players_data.

Woldendorp, J., H. Keman and I. Budge (2000), *Party Government in 48 Democracies (1945–1998). Composition–Duration–Personnel*, Dordrecht: Kluwer Academic.

Woldendorp J., H. Keman and I. Budge (2011), *Party Government in 40 Democracies (1945–1998). Composition–Duration–Personnel*: http://fsw.vu.nl/nl/wetenschappelijke-afdelingen/bestuurswetenschap-en-politicologie/medewerkers/woldendorp/party-government-data-set/index.asp.

Continuous update of the information in Woldendorp et al. (2011): http://web.missouri.edu/~williamslaro/data.html

uses seven reasons for termination, based on the classification of von Beyme (1985). This type of information is conceptually meaningful but depends on the information available in other sources such as Keesing's World News Archive or the *European Journal of Political Research*'s (*EJPR*'s) *Political Data Yearbooks*.[3] Therefore, the reliability of the data remains problematic. Other data sets use different reasons for termination and can be used for validation. Also in this area there is definite room and need for improvement of comparable data collection. Next, the PGD lists six types of government, including governments that have a caretaker function, as do some other data sets (for example, Comparative Political Data Sets (CPDS); Müller-Rommel et al. 2008), which again enhances validity and reliability as data can be cross-checked. Then, the PGD lists the ideological CPG. This is in itself a useful measure to investigate, for example, policy performance of different governments (Keman 2002; Schmidt 2002) or party system dynamics (McDonald and Budge 2005). It is also an additive index of Left–Right composition of governments and parliaments showing variation in time. Nevertheless, there is room and need for improvement of data collection concerning disaggregated data on the left–center–right position of political parties which would allow individual researchers to construct their own substantively grounded indices. The CPDS also shows the measure CPG; this allows at least for increased reliability. Finally, the PGD lists the number of cabinet ministers, the name and sex of the prime minister and party affiliation, and the number of reshuffles for each government. In the Woldendorp et al. (2000)

version, the PGD also lists the name, sex, party affiliation and competencies (portfolios) of all cabinet ministers at the start of each government. This is definitely also an area in which development and updating is possible and needed.

To improve the PGD set additional data would need to be collected and existing data would need to be disaggregated. For instance, additional data on the organizational changes of ministries and competencies over time (for example, Strøm et al. 2008) and on aspects of the bargaining process leading up to government formation, such as the introduction of junior ministers into the division of portfolios between parties (for example, De Winter and Dumont 2006) would greatly enhance its usability for comparative research. An important issue here is which data do we need (theory) and are these data at all collectable cross-nationally and over time. At present they are usually available as single case studies (for example, Strøm et al. 2003, 2008) or as an annual update in the *EJPR*'s *Political Data Yearbook*.

Next, it would be a great improvement if data on the careers of individual cabinet and junior ministers during the lifetimes of governments could be included, instead of merely listing the number of reshuffles, as would be the disaggregation of ministerial competencies from a priori defined aggregated ministries such as Foreign Affairs or Social Affairs (as is at present the case in Woldendorp et al. 2000). Not to mention the disaggregation of the competencies that could not be distributed to these ministries and that are now lumped together under 'Other'. Collecting this type of data at the lowest possible level of aggregation would encourage and enable much more detailed research into the distribution of portfolios over parties and of the policy-making capacities of governments than is at present possible. This disaggregation would also allow a link to research and data sets that focus on political elites (for example, Cotta and Best 2007 – see Box 15.3) and would open up additional possibilities of comparative research that at the moment are mostly explored in the form of qualitative – 'thick description' – research of single or a few cases.

The PGD set is focused on party government, however, the full life cycle of party government comprises of a sequence of events, actors and institutions on which data are collected (see Figure 15.1). Using this analytical set-up the next section discusses some specific areas of data collection and how best to match these data with the relevant government data in the PGD set.

BOX 15.3   POLITICAL ELITES

Political Elites

Best, H. and M. Cotta (eds) (2000), *Parliamentary Representatives in Europe 1848–2000: Legislative Recruitment and Careers in Eleven European Countries*, Oxford: Oxford University Press.
Blondel, J. and J.-L. Thiebault (eds) (1991), *The Profession of Government Minister in Western Europe*, London: Macmillan.
Chiefs of State and Cabinet Members of Foreign Governments (CIA): https://www.cia.gov/library/publications/world-leaders-1/index.html.
Cotta, M. and H. Best (eds) (2007), *Democratic Representation in Europe. Diversity, Change, and Convergence*, Oxford: Oxford University Press.
Dowding, K. and P. Dumont (eds) (2009), *The Selection of Ministers in Europe: Hiring and Firing*, Abingdon, UK: Routledge.
Dowding, K. and P. Dumont (eds) (2014), *The Selection of Ministers Around the World*, London: Routledge.
People in Power (commercial data base): www.peopleinpower.com/.
Pilet, J.-B. and W.P. Cross (eds) (2014), *The Selection of Political Party Leaders in Contemporary Democracies. A Comparative Study*, London: Routledge.
Political Leaders (Arhigos): http://www.rochester.edu/college/faculty/hgoemans/data.htm.
Semenova, E., M. Erdinger and H. Best (eds) (2013), *Parliamentary Elites in Central and Eastern Europe. Recruitment and Representation*, London: Routledge.
World Statesmen: http://www.worldstatesmen.org/.

---

4   DATA ON THE LIFE CYCLE OF PARTY GOVERNMENT

Citizens: in systems of representative government the citizen is considered as the 'principal', in particular in parliamentary systems. Comparative data over time on citizen's opinions on policies and values and on political and civil liberties is now available in quite a number of data sets (see Chapter 18 in this volume). However, it would be helpful to systematically collect this data in either a separate, cumulative data set or to better connect the data available to the information on party government as presented in the PGD or other sets.

Political parties: data on political parties (for example, policy dimensions, electoral manifestos, party families, Left–Centre–Right) is widely available in different data sets. But data collection in some areas remains underdeveloped. In particular with regard to comparative data on internal party organization, party rules, party finance, factions, historical development (origins, mergers, splits and new party formation)

BOX 15.4   CITIZENS, DEMOCRACY, ELECTIONS

Citizens

Democracy: A Citizen Perspective. An Interdisciplinary Centre of Excellence (Lauri Karvonen): www.dce.abo.fi/index.html.
Democratic Accountability and Linkages Project: https://web.duke.edu/democracy/index.html.
Eurobarometer: http://ec.europa.eu/public_opinion/index_en.htm.
European Social Survey (ESS): http://www.europeansocialsurvey.org/.
European Values Study: http://www.europeanvaluesstudy.eu.

Democracy

Boix, C., M. Miller and S. Rosato (2013), 'A complete data set of political regimes', *Comparative Political Studies*, **46** (12), 1523–45: http://cps.sagepub.com/content/46/12/1523.full.pdf+html.
Democratic Accountability and Linkages Project: https://web.duke.edu/democracy/index.html.
European Representative Democracy Data Archive (ERDDA): http://www.erdda.se/
Freedom House http://www.freedomhouse.org.
Polity IV Project, *Political Regime Characteristics and Transitions, 1800–2013*: http://www.systemicpeace.org/polity/polity4.htm.
Sustainable Governance Indicators (SGI): www.sgi-network.org/ (Bertelsmann Stiftung).
Vanhanen, T. (1997), *Prospects of Democracy: A Study of 172 Countries*, London: Routledge.
Vanhanen, T. (2000), 'A new data set for measuring democracy 1810–1998', *Journal of Peace Research*, **37** (2), 251–65.

Elections

Adam Carr's Election Archive (ACEA): http://psephos.adam-carr.net/.
Comparative Study of Electoral Systems (CSES): http://cses.org/.
European Election Database: http://www.nsd.uib.no/european_election_database.
European Election Study: http://www.tcd.ie/Political_Science/staff/michael_marsh/ees_trend_file.php.
International Institute for Democracy and Electoral Assistance (IDEA): http://www.idea.int/esd/world.cfm.
Keesing's World News Archive(commercial database): https://www.jcsonlineresources.org/catalogue/keesings-world-news-archive.
Mackie, T.T. and R. Rose (1990), *The International Almanac of Electoral History*, 3rd revised edn, Houndmills: Macmillan (until 1981): https://www.icpsr.umich.edu/icpsrweb/ICPSR/studies/8247?keyword=international+politics&permit%5B0%5D=AVAILABLE.

Median Voter (McDonald): http://www.binghamton.edu/political-science/research/
National Election Surveys in individual countries.
Nolen, D. and P. Stöver (eds) (2010), *Elections in Europe: A Data Handbook*,
Baden-Baden: Nomos Verlagsgesellschaft.
Parliament and Government Composition Database (ParlGov) (Döring and
Manow): http://www.parlgov.org/.
Parties and Elections in Europe: http://www.parties-and-elections.eu/.
Political Data Yearbook (1992–), *European Journal of Political Research*.
Siaroff, A. (2000), *Comparative European Party Systems: An Analysis of
Parliamentary Elections Since 1945*, New York: Garland.
The Institutions and Elections Project: http://www.binghamton.edu/political-
science/institutions-and-elections-project.html.
Voter Turnout Database (IDEA): http://www.idea.int/vt/viewdata.cfm.

and their division in Left–Centre–Right (for example, Heidar and Koole 2000).

Party system: although comparative data on the party systems is well covered by a variety of data sets, there is a lack of comparative and comparable data on features like the centrality and dominance of parties, that is, the pivotness of a party in its party system (for example, Keman 2010) that can be connected to other party government data.

Government formation: except for data on votes of investiture and of (constructive) no confidence or policy dimensions, this is an area where comparative data is quite scarce. The data available on the actual process of government formation are (single) case studies (for example, Dowding and Dumont 2014). To be able to collect additional data on the lowest level of aggregation possible, it is necessary to determine which data are needed (theory) and whether it is possible to collect and compare them (De Winter and Dumont 2006).

Type of democracy: comparative data on the type of democracy is extensively available, including institutional (constitutional) constraints or veto points (see below). However, most of these data are available as rather static indices that cover a few points in time or even whole periods, or as information on the institutional (constitutional) set-up of a country at the current point in time. The data therefore cannot account for changes over time. To be able to present the information available on the lowest possible level of aggregation in order to allow researcher to construct their own indices two issues need to be resolved. First, how to account for potential changes over time to be able to connect the data with corresponding governments. Second, how to incorporate new theoretical ideas like veto points or veto players and determine in which direction the impact goes (see the Comparative Politics website of the University of Greifswald for

BOX 15.5   PARTIES AND PARTY POLICY POSITIONS

Parties

Beyme, K. von (1985), *Political Parties in Western Democracies*, Aldershot, UK: Gower.

Castles, F.G. (1982), *The Impact of Parties. Politics and Policies in Democratic Capitalist States*, London: Sage.

Comparative Parties Data Set Swank: http://www.marquette.edu/polisci/faculty_swank.shtml.

Comparative Politics Greifswald: http://comparativepolitics.uni-greifswald.de/data.html.

Democratic Accountability and Linkages Project: https://web.duke.edu/democracy/index.html.

Heidar, K. and R. Koole (eds) (2000), *Parliamentary Party Groups in European Democracies: Political Parties Behind Closed Doors*, London: Routledge.

Katz, R.S. and W.J. Crotty (eds) (2006), *Handbook of Party Politics*, London: Sage.

Luther, K.R. and F. Müller-Rommel (eds), *Political Parties in the New Europe. Political and Analytical Challenges*, Oxford: Oxford University Press.

Parties in Parliaments and Governments (McDonald): http://www.binghamton.edu/political-science/research/.

Pilet, J.-B. and W.P. Cross (eds) (2014), *The Selection of Political Party Leaders in Contemporary Democracies: A Comparative Study*, London: Routledge.

Party Policy Positions

Benoit, K. and M. Laver (2006), *Party Policy in Modern Democracies*, London and New York, Routledge: http://www.tcd.ie/Political_Science/ppmd/.

Budge, I., H.-D. Klingemann, A. Volkens, J. Bara and E. Tanenbaum (eds) (2001), *Mapping Policy Preferences. Estimates for Parties, Electors, and Governments, 1945–1998*, Oxford: Oxford University Press.

Comparative Politics Greifswald: http://comparativepolitics.uni-greifswald.de/data.html.

Electoral Studies (2007), *Special Issue on Comparing Measures of Party Positioning: Expert, Manifesto, Survey*, **26** (1), 1–234.

Klingemann, H.-D., A. Volkens, J. Bara, I. Budge and M. McDonald (2006), *Mapping Policy Preferences II. Estimates for Parties, Electors, and Governments in Eastern Europe, European Union, and OECD 1990–2003*, Oxford: Oxford University Press.

Manifesto Project Database: https://manifesto-project.wzb.eu/.

Moury, C. (2012), *Coalition Government and Party Mandate. How Coalition Agreements Constrain Ministerial Action*, London: Routledge.

Timmermans, A.I. (2003), *High Politics in the Low Countries. An Empirical Study of Coalition Agreements in Belgium and The Netherlands*, Aldershot, UK and Burlington, VT: Ashgate.

examples). For instance, is European Union (EU) membership a veto point limiting or expanding the room to maneuver of national governments?

Organized interests and type of interest intermediation: the comparative data on organized interests largely covers the type of interest intermediation, that is, pluralism or corporatism. Akin to the data on the type of democracy, these data are also presented as static indices or yes/no variables. More dynamic scales of corporatism either give slightly different scores for countries in different periods (for example, Siaroff 1999) or only include the level of wage-setting coordination between social partners (see the Comparative Politics website of the University of Greifswald for an example). Therefore, the first point for the collection of this kind of data is again to develop theoretical guidance to provide the available data on the lowest level of aggregation that allows researcher to construct their own indices. The next point is to account for change over time (if there is any). Finally, to connect these data to the relevant governments and to establish in which direction the impact goes.

Policy outputs and macroeconomic performance: Figure 15.1 shows the feedback loop of accountability with regard to policy outputs and macroeconomic performance. This type of data is usually based on data collected by the Organisation for Economic Co-operation and Development

---

BOX 15.6   INTEREST INTERMEDIATION

Interest Intermediation

Comparative Politics Greifswald: http://comparativepolitics.uni-greifswald.de/data.html.
Comparative Political Dataset (CPDS) (Siaroff 1999: 1970, 1980, 1990, 1995): http://www.ipw.unibe.ch/content/team/klaus_armingeon/comparative_political_data_sets/index_ger.html.
Golden, M., P. Lange and M. Wallerstein (2009),Union Centralization among Advanced Industrial Societies: An Empirical Study (1950–2000)', 7 July: http://hdl.handle.net/1902.1/10193.
ICTWSS, database on Institutional Characteristics of Trade Unions, Wage Setting, State Intervention and Social Pacts in 34 countries between 1960 and 2012: http://www.uva-aias.net/208.
International Labour Organisation (ILO): www.ilo.org.
Kenworthy, L. (2003), 'Quantitative indicators of corporatism', *International Journal of Sociology*, **33** (3), 10–44 (until 2000).
Manifesto Project: Election Manifestos Political Parties (corporatism = per 405): https://manifesto-project.wzb.eu/.
Siaroff , A. (1999), 'Corporatism in 24 industrial democracies: meaning and measurement', *European Journal of Political Research*, **36** (2), 175–205.

BOX 15.7 GOVERNANCE INDICATORS AND MACROECONOMIC DATA

Governance Indicators

Sustainable Governance Indicators (SGI) (Bertelsmann Stiftung): www.sgi-network.org/.
World Bank: http://info.worldbank.org/governance/wgi/index.asp.

Macroeconomic Data (Policy Performance and Macroeconomic Performance)

Allan, J.P. and L. Scruggs (2004), 'Political partisanship and welfare state reform in advanced industrial societies', *American Journal of Political Science*, **48** (3), 496–512.
Becker, U. and H. Schwartz (eds) (2005), *Employment 'Miracles': A Critical Comparison of the Dutch, Scandinavian, Swiss, Australian and Irish Cases versus Germany and the US*, Amsterdam: Amsterdam University Press.
Castles, F.G. (ed.) (2007), *The Disappearing State? Retrenchment Realities in an Age of Globalisation*, Cheltenham, UK and Northampton, MA, USA: Edward Elgar.
European Commission Annual Macro-Economic Database: www.ec.europa.eu/economy_finance/db_indicators8648_en.htm.
European Statistics (EUROSTAT): http://epp.eurostat.ec.europa.eu/portal/page/portal/eurostat/home/.
Huber, E. and J.D. Stephens (eds) (2001), *Development and Crisis of the Welfare State: Parties and Policies in Global Markets*, Chicago, IL and London: University of Chicago Press.
International Monetary Fund (IMF): www.imf.org.
Kersbergen, K. van and B. Vis (2014), *Comparative Welfare State Politics. Development, Opportunities, and Reform*, Cambridge: Cambridge University Press.
Korpi, W. and J. Palme (2008), *The Social Citizenship Indicator Program (SCIP)*, Stockholm: Swedish Institute for Social Research, Stockholm University: https://dspace.it.su.se/dspace/handle/10102/7.
Organisation for Economic Co-operation and Development (OECD): www.oecd.org.
Scruggs, L., D. Jahn and K. Kuitto (2014), *Comparative Welfare Entitlements Dataset 2* (Version 2014-03), University of Connecticut and University of Greifswald: http://cwed2.org/publications.php & http://comparativepolitics.uni-greifswald.de/data.html.
Vliet, O. van, and K. Caminada (2012), 'Unemployment replacement rates dataset among 34 welfare states 1971–2009, an update, extension and modification of the scruggs welfare state entitlements data set', NEUJOBS Special Report No. 2. Leiden, Leiden University: http://www.neujobs.eu/.
World Bank: www.worldbank.org.

(OECD), EUROSTAT or the International Monetary Fund (IMF). The main (theoretical) issues regarding this domain is, first, to differentiate between policy performance (for example, budget deficit or (in)equality) and macroeconomic performance (for example, (un)employment or economic growth) (see Vis et al. 2012) and, secondly, how to connect these data to the relevant governments.

5   THE INSTITUTIONAL CONTEXT

Using the formal constitutional set-up of the countries as of 1998–2000, the PGD provides data on their institutional features (only in Woldendorp et al. 2000). The data concern:

- the head of state and their formal powers over government,
- the state format: federal versus unitary, centralized versus decentralized, and veto powers (additive index of referendum, strong bicameralism, domination of government over parliament, and rigid constitution),
- the structure of parliament: number and size of chambers,
- the electoral system: maximum period between elections, electoral formula, introduction of universal suffrage,
- the relationship between the executive and the legislative: vote of investiture or of (no) confidence, the powers of parliament, government and head of state over each other,
- the decision rule in parliament: amending the constitution (quorum and type of majority decision), referendum and the right to initiate it, the number of referendums, and
- the organizational features of government: the role of the prime minister, the relation between ministers and parliament (Member of Parliament or not), the rules of cabinet decision-making (collective or otherwise),
- The rule of law: the role of the judiciary, constitutional review or not, and constitutional flexibility.

The main issue with the usability of these data is that they represent additive indices that provide a single snapshot of a specific period (1998–2000). That is also the case with most institutional variables provided in other data sets (see above). They are additive indices that provide a single snapshot covering one or a few points in time or even an entire period (but see the Comparative Politics website of the University of Greifswald).

To widen the scope for the use of these comparative data, the data

---

BOX 15.8   CONSTITUTIONS, PARLIAMENTS, POLITICAL INSTITUTIONS

Constitutions

Comparative Constitutions Project: http://comparativeconstitutionsproject.org/.
Constitution Finder: http://confinder.richmond.edu/.
Constitutions, Treaties and Declarations: www.psr.keele.ac.uk/const.htm.
Inter-Parliamentary Union (IPU): www.ipu.org.
International Constitutional Law: http://www.servat.unibe.ch/icl/.
The Institutions and Elections Project: http://www.binghamton.edu/political-science/institutions-and-elections-project.html.

Parliaments

Comparative Parliamentary Democracy Data Archive (CPDA): http://www.erdda.se/.
European Representative Democracy Data Archive (ERDDA): http://www.erdda.se/.
Inter-Parliamentary Union (IPU): www.ipu.org.

Political Institutions

Mobilising Institutions: http://www.ucd.ie/civicact/mobilisinginstitutionscodebook.pdf.
Hooghe, L., G. Marks and A. Schakel (eds) (2008), 'Regional authority in 42 countries, 1950–2006: a measure and five hypotheses', *Regional and Federal Studies*, **18** (2 and 3), special issue, 111–302.
The Institutions and Elections Project: http://www.binghamton.edu/political-science/institutions-and-elections-project.html.
Inter-Parliamentary Union (IPU): www.ipu.org.

---

should be presented at the lowest possible level of aggregation and allow for change over time. That would allow researchers to construct their own, substantively driven indices as well as the inclusion of other (new) institutional features such as EU membership or national scrutiny of EU decisions that feature in some other data sets but suffer from the same lack of variation. However, this is easier said than done and only shows how difficult it can be to provide truly comparative data over time that suit the broadest possible array of theoretical approaches.

6   CONCLUSION

This chapter on organizing and developing data sets has argued that disaggregation of data is the best way to meet the three important issues with collecting and compiling data sets for comparative political science research this chapter has identified. The first issue is the tension between compiling particular data for a particular research question and design and possibly compiling relevant data for a broader array of theoretical approaches and research questions. The second issue is to include (institutional or other) change over time or incorporate data suited for new approaches. The final issue is how to improve the validity and the reliability of the information generated. Disaggregation allows researchers to construct their own aggregated indices. Disaggregation also enhances validity and reliability. The less elaborated and aggregated the data collected or constructed are, the more likely they will travel conceptually and the easier it is to cross-check the data with other data sets. Reliability of the data will always give rise to disputes as different sources will contradict each other and mistakes will be made. Open access to existing data sets and communication between their compilers will help to remedy these imperfections up to a point, and it will certainly further the analysis of the life cycle of democratic governance and of its viability as a political system.

NOTES

1. For a discussion on the use of expert surveys see Mair (2001) and on the relative merits of content analysis, expert surveys and opinion polls see Keman (2007). See also Chapter 4 in this volume on the relation of theory and concepts to measurements.
2. These overviews are comprehensive but cannot claim to be exhaustive and not all data sets are available digitally. See also Chapter 8 in this volume for a discussion of the Polity IV and Freedom House data sets and Chapter 18 in this volume on surveys.
3. If no information is available, the PGD notes an x.

REFERENCES

Beyme, K. von (1985), *Political Parties in Western Democracies*, Aldershot, UK: Gower.
Budge, I. and H. Keman (1990), *Parties and Democracy: Coalition Formation and Government Functioning in Twenty States*, Oxford: Oxford University Press.
Comparative Political Datasets Armingeon et al. (CPDS), http://www.ipw.unibe.ch/content/team/klaus_armingeon/comparative_political_data_sets/index_ger.html.
Cotta, M. and H. Best (eds) (2007), *Democratic Representation in Europe. Diversity, Change, and Convergence*, Oxford: Oxford University Press.
De Winter, L. and P. Dumont (2006), 'Parties into government', in R.S. Katz and W.J. Crotty (eds), *Handbook of Party Politics*, London: Sage, pp. 175–88.

Dowding, K. and P. Dumont (eds) (2014), *The Selection of Ministers Around the World*, London: Routledge.

European Journal of Political Research (EJPR) (1992–present), *Political Data Yearbook*.

Heidar, K. and R. Koole (eds) (2000), *Parliamentary Party Groups in European Democracies: Political Parties Behind Closed Doors*, London: Routledge.

Keesing's World News Archive (commercial database): https://www.jcsonlineresources.org/catalogue/keesings-world-news-archive.

Keman, H. (2002), *Comparative Democratic Politics: A Guide to Contemporary Theory and Research*, London: Sage.

Keman, H. (2007), 'Experts and manifestos: different sources – same results for comparative research?', *Electoral Studies*, **26** (1), special issue, 1–14.

Keman, H. (2010), 'Strategy development and variations of party government', in J. Raschke and R. Tils (eds), *Strategie in der Politikwissenschaft – Konturen eines neuen Forschungs felds* (*Strategy in Political Science – Outline(s) of a New Field of Research*), Wiesbaden: VS Verlag, pp. 183–210.

Mair, P. (2001), 'Searching for the position of political actors: a review of approaches and a critical evaluation of expert surveys', in M. Laver (ed.), *Estimating the Policy Position of Political Actors*, London: Routledge, pp. 10–30.

McDonald, M. and I. Budge (2005), *Elections, Parties, Democracy: Conferring the Mandate*, Oxford: Oxford University Press.

Müller-Rommel, F., H. Schultze, P. Harfst and K. Fettelschoss (2008), 'Parteienregierungen in Mittel- und Ost-Europa: Empirische Befunde im Ländervergleich 1990 bis 2008' ('Party government in Central and Eastern Europe: empirical data from a cross-country comparison 1990 to 2008'), *Zeitschrift für Parlamentsfragen*, **39** (4), 810–31.

Parliament and Government Composition Database (ParlGov), http://www.parlgov.org/.

Pennings, P., H. Keman and J. Kleinnijenhuis (2006), *Doing Research in Political Science*, 2nd edn, London: Sage.

Schmidt, M.G. (2002), 'The impact of political parties, constitutional structures and veto players', in H. Keman (ed.), *Comparative Democratic Politics. A Guide to Temporary Theory and Research*, London: Sage, pp. 166–85.

Siaroff, A. (1999), 'Corporatism in 24 industrial democracies: meaning and measurement', *European Journal of Political Research*, **36** (2), 175–205.

Strøm, K., W.C. Müller and T. Bergman (eds) (2003), *Delegation and Accountability in Parliamentary Democracies*, Oxford: Oxford University Press.

Strøm, K., W.C. Müller and T. Bergman (eds) (2008), *Cabinets and Coalition Bargaining: The Democratic Life Cycle in Western Europe*, Oxford: Oxford University Press.

Vis, B., J. Woldendorp and H. Keman (2012), 'Economic performance and institutions: capturing the dependent variable', *European Political Science Review*, **4** (1), 73–96.

Woldendorp, J. (2012), 'Enhancing and improving data on party government', in H. Keman and F. Müller-Rommel (eds), *Party Government in the New Europe*, London and New York: Routledge, pp. 185–214.

Woldendorp, J., H. Keman and I. Budge (2000), *Party Government in 48 Democracies 1945–1998: Composition – Duration – Personnel*, Dordrecht: Kluwer Academic.

Woldendorp, J., H. Keman and I. Budge (2011), 'Party government in 40 democracies 1945–2008: composition – duration – personnel', accessed 8 August 2016 at http://fsw.vu.nl/nl/wetenschappelijke-afdelingen/bestuurswetenschap-en-politicologie/medewerkers/woldendorp/party-government-data-set/index.asp.

16 Political institutions*

Klaus Armingeon

1 INTRODUCTION

In a narrow understanding, political institutions denote established official organizations having an important role in the life of a country, such as a legislature. For a long time, political science scholars studied institutions in such a narrow sense. The main focus centered on either the national parliament, executive or judiciary bodies of government. Only formal organizations with a political role were considered to be a political institution. The goal of political science was to understand such institutions by providing general descriptive knowledge. After reading such descriptions, it was clear how these formal organizations were structured, but it was absolutely not clear to what extent these descriptions of institutions could help in explaining policies and politics. In contrast to this view, institutions in the present academic debate in the social sciences denote routines, norms, procedures and rules. A larger number of hypotheses and theories are based on this broader understanding of institutions. In this chapter, I discuss the modern use of institutions in political science and some of the theoretical approaches utilizing institutions as either the dependent or independent variable (section 2). Section 3 deals with the operationalization of institutions and data sources. Finally, I critically evaluate the different conceptions of institutions. While the bulk of the new institutional analysis implicitly assumes that institutions have the same effect in different circumstances in democratic nations, I argue that these effects are highly context-dependent. In addition, institutions can be stretched, bent or violated. The power of the institution is frequently overstated.

2 WHAT ARE POLITICAL INSTITUTIONS AND WHAT ARE THEY FOR?

It was only in the past four decades that political science adopted a definition of institutions that was much broader and took over important insights from the sociological research. This new institutionalism defined institutions not only as formal organizations and rules, but also as 'formal or informal procedures, routines, norms and conventions embedded in the organizational structure of the polity or political economy' (Hall and Taylor 1996, p.938). According to this definition, any institution which has a political role – that is, the authoritative allocation of material and non-material values in a given society – is a political institution.

One insight on which this definition is based is the sociological idea of the general functions of institutions. Institutions structure society by increasing the predictability of individual behavior. An example from sociology is the institution of marriage. It creates rights and duties and expected behavior: partners have material and immaterial responsibilities to each other and to their children. There is a set of expected behavioral patterns. Individuals may violate these norms of marriage. They may commit adultery and not care for their children. However, in these cases they have to cope with formal and informal sanctions. The role of institutions in the political system becomes immediately clear if we consider the case of a political system without institutions in a thought experiment: there would be no rules on how to select political actors, such as candidate nominations within parties or electoral laws. Likewise politicians would not undergo the training over the span of a political career that teaches leaders fundamental skills, such as the 'dos and don'ts' in political organizations. Moreover, there would be no rules on how authoritative decisions are taken – such as rules on legislation – neither would there be laws or any organizations and rules on implementing policies. From this thought experiment it is obvious that a working political system without institutions is unthinkable.

A second insight from the sociological tradition concerns informal institutions. In addition to the parliament, executive and judicial bodies, there are many institutions which have a lesser extent of formality: political groups, parties, party systems, interest groups, systems of interest groups and cooperation patterns between interest groups and the state, norms of adequate behavior of political actors, standard procedures of policy development and standard procedure of policy implementation, including informal cooperation patterns, types of social security provided by public policies and private actors (interest groups or families and so on). We only see parts of the political life if we narrow the definition of institutions to formal institutions.

How do institutions structure politics and policy-making? The literature lists at least three important contributions of institutions:

1. They constrain political actors by sanctioning deviations from the institutionally prescribed behavior and by rewarding appropriate behavior. Consider the case of a consensus democracy. Those who violate the unwritten rules of the game – such as actively seeking a

compromise – will be ignored or opposed by their fellow politicians. Those playing by the rules will have a higher likelihood of reaching compromises that are in their own interest.

2.   They solve collective action dilemmas. Politics is replete with situations where actors have strong incentives to deviate from an optimal solution, which is in the common interest of all parties. This is the well-known prisoner's dilemma. For example, all governments are interested in a worldwide reduction of CO_2, but for each actor the best situation is to not adhere to environmental norms, while their counterparts do. Institutions provide a solution to overcoming this common problem by including enforceable sanctions that deter nations from not complying with the norms agreed upon by all governments.

3.   They create meaning and identity. A very good example is 'constitutional patriotism' (Sternberger 1990). In nations that have no common culture – for example, the US or Switzerland – or have a history on which it is hard to build a positive identification – for example, Germany after Hitler – citizens have to identify themselves as belonging to one nation by the shared and positively evaluated institutions such as the constitutions. For example in multicultural Switzerland there is no common culture, language or history, but a very strong identification based on the idea that the Swiss belong together and are distinguishable from other nations by combining neutrality, strong federalism and direct democracy.

One major implication of this conceptualization of institutions is their 'stickiness'. If institutions reinforce the predictability of individual or collective behavior, then this requires that they are relatively stable and do not change immediately if circumstances change. This is exactly their function: to make political life foreseeable even if we do not know the precise circumstances. For instance, even if we do not know the domestic and international developments at the time of the next national election, political parties know much about their competitive position and success rates given the electoral laws and this allows them to develop long-term strategies. A second major implication is that institutions make a significant difference. Although there may be the same pressing needs and requirements of the economy or the same political power distributions in a number of countries, policies and policy outcomes are different owing to the institutions that mediate between functional requirements or political conflicts and policy outcomes. Hence in its pure forms, functionalist or conflict-theoretical explanations are not compatible with an institutionalist explanation.

The neo-institutionalist turn in political science is marked by important theoretical contributions. Examples of this perspective include: a book by March and Olsen, *Rediscovering Institutions, The Organizational Basis of Politics* (March and Olsen 1989) and Tsebelis's monograph on veto players (Tsebelis 2002). Other landmark studies had an important influence on the development of the scientific debate. Peter Katzenstein analyzed the institution of corporatism in small countries that are exposed to the world market (Katzenstein 1985). Fritz Scharpf showed how social democratic governments were constrained or enabled in their economic policies by different national institutions of economic policy-making (Scharpf 1991). Scharpf and Renate Mayntz coined the term of 'action-centered institutionalism' (Mayntz and Scharpf 1995). It denotes an analytical approach that sees actors as strategically behaving in a given context of institutions. Arguably this approach has influenced much of the recent research in comparative political economy on which I will focus for the remainder of this chapter.

This research has created a number of hypotheses on the effect of institutions for which considerable empirical evidence could be mobilized. Let us mention some examples of such hypotheses:

- Corporatist institutions – that is, the regular cooperation of state and interest group in commonly designing and implementing public and private policies – lower unemployment, strike activity and increase the capacity to cope flexibly with external challenges (Cameron 1984; Katzenstein 1985).
- Consociational institutions – that is, formal and informal oversized coalitions with the aim of including as many actors as possible and to find consensus between these actors – leading to kinder and gentler democracies (Lijphart 2012).
- Welfare state institutions – such as the type, structure and combination of public social insurances – have specific redistributive effects (Esping-Andersen 1990).
- The higher the number of veto -players, that is, actors whose consent to a policy change is indispensable, the lower the reform activity in a country (Tsebelis 2002).
- Federalism constrains big government (Obinger et al. 2005).
- Direct democracy constrains big government (cf. Vatter 2014, pp. 358–71).
- Strong independent national banks limit the fiscal room of maneuver for central governments (Scharpf 1991).
- Institutions are a major reason for path dependence of public policy. Path dependence denotes the incremental character of policy change. It is argued that policies are institutionally embedded. For

---

BOX 16.1   INSTITUTIONS

Institutions are 'formal or informal procedures, routines, norms and conventions embedded in the organizational structure of the polity or political economy' (Hall and Taylor 1996, p.938). They are 'sticky' since they react not immediately to any change in their environment. Otherwise they could not contribute to the predictability of individual and collective behavior even if the context is not known. Institutions constrain political actors by sanctioning deviations from the institutionally prescribed behavior and by rewarding appropriate behavior. They solve collective action dilemmas and create meaning and identity.

---

example, if a pension system is based on a large public pension administration, pension reforms are the more likely the more they are compatible with the present organization (Pierson 2000).

3   HOW TO OPERATIONALIZE INSTITUTIONS AND WHERE DO WE FIND THE DATA?

There is no limited set of indicators for the large number of different political institutions with different relevance for different policy fields. Any attempt at operationalizing one of these endless numbers of institutions has to start from the underlying theoretical concept and the causal assumptions of the given institutions and its assumed effects.

Some indicators are simple, at least at first glance. If we are interested in the question of an independent central bank limiting the fiscal options of a central government, a simple dummy question will help. The same goes for electoral laws supporting stable majorities in parliament – usually first-past-the-post rules – as compared to rules aimed at proportional representation of citizens in parliament. However, then more difficult questions will arise: with regard to which criteria is a central bank coded as being independent from government? How shall we deal with electoral laws that are neither pure majoritarian nor pure proportional representation rules? The answer comes from our theories and analytical perspectives, which define the relevant aspects of an institution. We may, for example, define federalism differently, if we are interested in federalism as a regionalized system of political participation or as an impediment of power of central government.

Even more problematic are indicators, which measure complex institutional configurations. How do scholars measure the type of welfare state, the extent of consensus democracy or the variant of a type of capitalism?

For some frequent research questions – such as the limitation of the power of central government in social and economic policy-making – indicators are established. For example Manfred Schmidt developed an index of institutional constraints of central state governments (Schmidt 1996) which ranges from 0 to 6. High values indicate powerful constraints. It is an additive index of six dummy variables with '1' indicating constraints: (1) is the country a European Union (EU) member? In this case national government is constraint by EU rules. (2) Is the political system federal? If yes, central governments have to coordinate with regional governments. (3) Is it difficult to amend the constitution? This being the case, policy change may be prevented by constitutional rigidity. (4) Has the parliament a strong second chamber? If there are two important chambers, a government needs to have a majority in both houses. (5) Is the central bank autonomous? In such a case governmental fiscal policies can be counteracted by the strategies of the central bank. (6) Are there frequently referenda? In countries with a strong direct democracy government decisions can be vetoed by popular vote.

Although this proved to be a very useful indicator in comparative political analyses, it is a very coarse measure. In some policy fields, monetary policy is highly irrelevant. If we ask whether a government is constrained in its reforms of abortion rules, it does not matter whether the bank is independent. Arguably much more important is the role and power of the Catholic Church. In addition, it is not only the selection of an indicator but also the weighting of the elements comprising such indicator. A simple additive index assumes that EU membership is equally important as the difficulty in amending institutions. This is just an assumption, though. With equally good reasons we could assign the EU membership a weight of '2' and the strength of the second chamber a weight of '0.5'. Finally, the easy availability of such indicators in comparative data sets (for example in Armingeon et al. 2016) frequently lure researchers in putting such variables in their regressions models without carefully considering whether this indicator is really a valid measure of what the researchers want to analyze.

BOX 16.2 OPERATIONALIZATION INSTITUTIONS

As any operationalization, the measurement of institutions has to be theory driven. It requires careful conceptual work. When applying published and easily available indices of institutions, researches have to think whether every element of the composite index may produce the hypothesized outcome.

4   WHAT DIFFERENCE DO INSTITUTIONS MAKE?

Institutions have become an important topic of comparative research. In particular, in the comparative welfare state and political economy scholarship, they are major explanatory variables. In one of the most influential contributions on the relationship between economic and political systems, Hall and Soskice identified different types of capitalism ranging from liberal to coordinated market economies. Institutions and their complementarity are the distinguishing elements of these 'varieties of capitalism' (VoC) (Hall and Soskice 2001). In a similar vein, the current problems of the eurozone are traced backed to institutional differences between member countries (Hall 2014).

The institutionalist perspective tends to overstress the importance of institutions at least due to two implicit assumptions. The first assumption could be called the assumption of a constant logic and effect. Basically, it is assumed that the underlying logic and the effect of a given institution do not change across countries and over time. The second assumption is the assumption of the rigidity of an institution, which hardly can be changed by actors or circumstances. Both assumptions are heroic, though.

4.1   A Constant Logic and Effect?

The shortcomings of the assumption of a constant logic or effects of institutions can be illustrated by three important institutions (see also Baccaro and Howell 2011; Culpepper 2016): consociationalism, welfare states and industrial relations.

In its original conceptualization, consociationalism denotes an institutional set-up in segmented societies which cannot risk the neglect of the interest of one of the major societal segments, otherwise civil war or secession may occur. The famous examples are the Dutch society in the late nineteenth and early twentieth centuries, when the cultural-religious camps had different interests (Lijphart 1968) or the Swiss society with regional constituent units (Lehmbruch 1967). These societal segments

---

BOX 16.3   CONSOCIATIONALISM

Historically, consociationalism is a standard operating procedure of elites in segmented societies, which consists of negotiations and compromise between representatives of the various societal segments. Examples are the elite behavior in post-war Austria, Belgium, the Netherlands or Switzerland.

were homogeneous and individuals had strong contacts within their segment but hardly contacts across segments. These isolated pillars were represented by elites. They were the legitimate spokesmen of their respective segments and could make binding decisions on behalf of their constituencies, which they bargained between each other across segments. The standard operating procedure was hence bargains between elites. It is obviously difficult to measure this exactly. It can be approximated by measuring institutions which are correlated, such as grand coalitions or electoral laws creating proportional representation. Starting from such data sets (Lijphart 1989, 2012), we see considerable institutional inertia – the democracies of the 2000s are not considerably less consensual as compared to the democracies after World War II. However, beneath this institutional surface considerable change of causal structure occurred. The social segments disintegrated. The links between segments and elites became much weaker. Citizens no longer trust the elites in their society without much reservation. Elites can no longer take for granted that their constituencies will accept decisions taken in inter-elite bargaining. While the institution of consensus democracy remained stable, the underlying logic has changed considerably.

Another example is that of welfare states (WFS). Following the path-breaking work by Esping-Andersen (1990) we distinguish between three types of WFS: a generous and redistributive Scandinavian type, which aims at equality; a relatively generous but non-redistributive continental type, which aims at saving the hierarchical structure of society and the paramount role of the family, and a parsimonious, non-redistributive Anglo-Saxon type which is oriented towards poverty prevention. These three types of WFS should have an effect both on expenditure levels and on benefits and eligibilities. Figure 16.1 depicts an indicator of WFS generosity in terms of benefits and rights. It is based on a data set by Lyle Scruggs and co-authors who collected data on coverage of pension, sickness and unemployment insurances and the wage replacement rate of these schemes. This is a coarse indicator, which adds up and averages coverages and eligibility, usually ranging from 0 to 1 (maximum generosity).[1]

Figure 16.2 shows the extent of social security expenditures in the three types of WFS. It is based on social security transfer spending, for which comparable data are available since the 1960s (Armingeon et al. 2016).

Both figures demonstrate that liberal WFS are considerably less generous than conservative or social democratic WFS. The theoretically expected difference between conservative and social democratic WFS is less clear, though. More important, however, is the change in the level of generosity by WFS type. By 2010, liberal WFS offered a level of generosity which was typical of social democratic WFS in the 1970s or 1960s. Seen

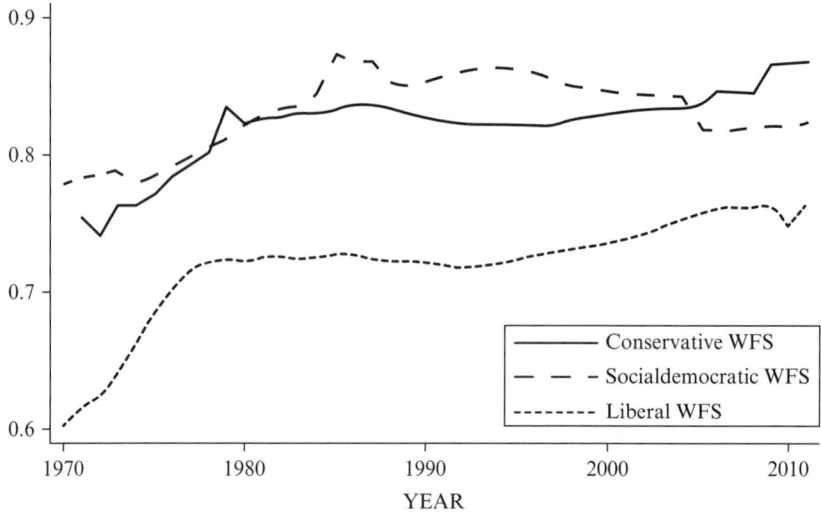

Figure 16.1   Welfare state generosity by type of welfare state (coarse additive indicator of coverage and eligibility)

BOX 16.4   WELFARE STATE

The welfare state has been created as a reaction to the change from rural to indus-trial society. Its historical core is composed of major insurances or public provisions against the costs of sickness and the incomes losses owing to invalidity, unemploy-ment and retirement. This historical core has been expanded in terms of benefits, services and coverage of risks. Today the welfare state of mature democracies consumes on average a quarter of the national product.

---

through the lenses of the 1970s, today all WFS are Socialdemocratic, and seen through the lenses of 2010, the WFS of the 1970s in Scandinavia and on the continent had a level of generosity, which is today typical of liberal WFS. Although institutional set-ups remained unchanged, the effects of these institutions have changed tremendously.

A similar example comes from industrial relations and the relationship between state, trade unions and employers. Baccaro and Howell analyzed industrial relation systems. They found that there is a little institutional change over time and across countries. However, although these differ-ent institutions remained in place, their outcomes converged towards a 'neo-liberal pattern' (Baccaro and Howell 2011). A similar finding can be

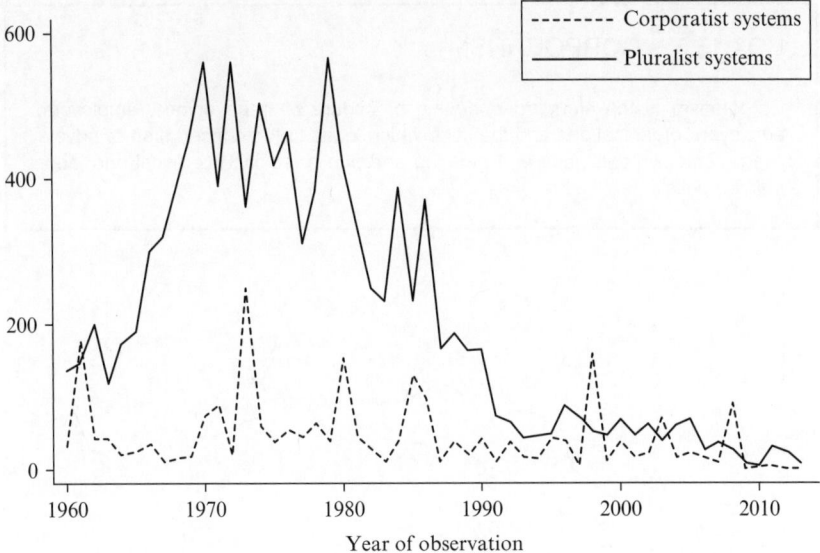

Figure 16.2 Welfare state expenditures by type of welfare state (social security transfers percentage gross domestic product)

reached if strike activity is compared between different systems of interest intermediation. The literature usually distinguishes between countries with strong traditions of negotiation between the industry and the state ('social partnership') and pluralist systems with a much higher level of conflict (Cameron 1984). Figure 16.3 shows the average level of strike activity (working days lost by 1000 workers) in pluralist and corporatist systems of industrial relations (source: Armingeon et al. (2016).[2]

Even if we assume that the institutions did not change dramatically, the institutional outcomes lead to a decline in strike activity in all systems of industrial relations since the turn of the century. Hence, and in contrast to much of the claims of the institutionalist accounts of comparative political economy, we know very little about institutional effects and outcomes even though we know a great deal about the institutional differences.

4.2 Reforming, Bending or Violating Institutions

Political institutions need to be stable and resistant to short-term changes in their economic, social and political environment. Otherwise they could not deliver predictability of behavior, being their functional *raison d'être*. Alternatively, at least in the medium to long run they have to adapt to

BOX 16.5   CORPORATISM

Corporatism is the standard operating procedure of trade unions, employers, employers' organizations and the state which leads to the concertation of private (wage, employment, price and product) and public (social, tax, fiscal and labor market) policies.

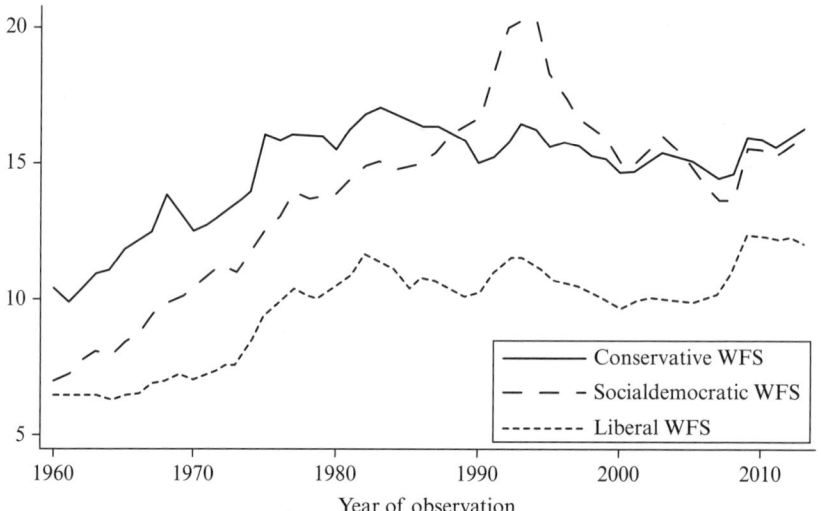

Source: Armingeon et al. (2016).

Figure 16.3   *Average level of strike activity in pluralist and corporatist systems of industrial relations*

the basic changes of environmental structures of their environment. Most of the comparative literature on political institutions has pointed to path dependency, institutional rigidity and the absence of major institutional changes. It was assumed that institutions only change in extraordinary circumstances, so called critical junctures (Krasner 1988), such as revolutions, major crises or breakdown of regimes.

Although there is strong evidence for considerable institutional rigidity, this perspective overlooks two important aspects of institutional change. One concerns incremental reform. The other aspect is that actors may have primacy over institutions. They may bend or ignore institutions at will because of their power.

The argument about incremental but substantial reform has been convincingly summarized by Wolfgang Streeck and Kathleen Thelen (2005). (1) Institutions may be displaced successively by other institutions. (2) They may become very differently from the past by a process of layering: to the existing institutional core new elements are added, which produce very different outcomes. (3) Institutions may experience drift, if they are not maintained and adapted to environmental changes. A good example is the Bismarckian welfare state that does not cover new socials risks of modern society. (4) Institutions may also be converted. Policymakers can assign new tasks to institutions. Although they stay in place, they serve new functions. (5) Finally, institutions can be exhausted. The regime of early retirement in Germany worked for a long time to solve problems on the labor market; once circumstances changed the institution no longer worked.

However, institutions are not only in constant and incremental flux. They can be bent or ignored by powerful actors. This situation is often ignored by institutionalist perspectives, such as the actor-centered institutionalism of Scharpf and Mayntz. In this vein of research, actors pursue strategies and have options that are institutionally feasible. They operate in an institutionally defined corridor of political options. However, there are also instances, when actors stretch the walls of this corridor or just ignore these institutional limitations. The recent history of the monetary union of the EU is replete with such strategies of stretching or violating. One major example of bending the rules are the cases of Germany and France from the sanctions of the Stability and Growth Pact of the European Monetary Union (EMU). Although both countries were in excess of deficits in the early 2000s, the sheer political power of Germany and its Chancellor Schröder avoided sanctions, which should have been collected according to the pact (Spiegel 2012, pp. 32–4). Moreover, in the recent Great Recession, the European governments clearly violated the spirit of the rules of the treaty by bailing out countries such as Greece. This is just one example, when once there are pressing needs or strong interests, actors can gain primacy over institutions. This example suggests that institutional analyses have to consider whether powerful actors are in accordance with the institutions. Actor's political power may break institutions. Arguably extant institutional research has overemphasized the role of institutions and underemphasized the role of political power.

BOX 16.6   INSTITUTIONALIST PERSPECTIVE

The institutionalist perspective tends to overstress the importance of institutions. The underlying logic and the effect of a given institution may change across countries and over time. Institutions are much less rigid, than frequently assumed. Actors or circumstances may change institutions or their effects.

NOTES

*   This article has been written while the author was fellow at the Collegio Carlo Alberto, Moncalieri.
1. Following the standard classification in works using the Esping-Andersen typology, I classify Denmark, Finland, Norway and Sweden as Social Democratic welfare states, Austria, Belgium, France, Germany, Italy, Netherlands and Switzerland as conservative welfare states and Australia, Canada, Ireland, Japan, New Zealand, the UK and the USA as liberal welfare states.
2. Denmark, Sweden, Norway, Austria, Belgium, Germany, Netherlands, and Switzerland were classified as corporatist systems; Canada, the UK, the USA and New Zealand were considered to be pluralist systems of industrial relations.

FURTHER READING

Introduction

Mahoney, J. and D. Rueschemeyer (eds) (2003), *Comparative Historical Analysis in the Social Sciences*, Cambridge: Cambridge University Press.

Advanced and Applications

Lijphart, A. (2012), *Patterns of Democracy: Government Form and Performance in Thirty-Six Countries*, 2nd edn, New Haven, CT: Yale University Press.
Streeck, W. and K. Thelen (eds) (2005), *Beyond Continuity. Institutional Change in Advanced Political Economies*, Oxford: Oxford University Press.

REFERENCES

Armingeon, K., C. Isler, L. Knöpfel, D. Weisstanner and S. Engler (2016), *Comparative Political Data Set I 1960–2014*, Berne: Institute of Political Science, University of Berne.
Baccaro, L. and C. Howell (2011), 'A common neoliberal trajectory', *Politics & Society*, **39** (4), 521–63.
Cameron, D.R. (1984), 'Social democracy, corporatism, labour quiescene, and the representation of economic interest in advanced capitalist society', in J.H. Goldthorpe (ed.), *Order and Conflict in Contemporary Capitalism*, Oxford: Clarendon Press, pp. 143–78.

Culpepper, P.D. (2016), 'Capitalism, institutions, and power in the study of business', in O. Fioretos, T.A. Falleti and A. Sheingate (eds), *Oxford Handbook of Historical Institutionalism*, Oxford: Oxford University Press, in press.

Esping-Andersen, G. (1990), *The Three Worlds of Welfare Capitalism*, Princeton, NJ: Princeton University Press.

Hall, P.A. (2014), 'Varieties of capitalism and the euro crisis', *West European Politics*, **37** (6), 1223–43.

Hall, P.A. and D. Soskice (eds) (2001), *Varieties of Capitalism: The Institutional Foundations of Comparative Advantage*, Oxford: Oxford University Press.

Hall, P.A. and R.C.R. Taylor (1996), 'Political science and the three new institutionalisms', *Political Studies*, **44** (5), 936–57.

Katzenstein, P.J. (1985), *Small States in World Markets: Industrial Policy in Europe*, Ithaca, NY and London: Cornell University Press.

Krasner, S.D. (1988), 'Sovereignty: an institutional perspective', *Comparative Political Studies*, **21** (1), 66–94.

Lehmbruch, G. (1967), *Proporzdemokratie: Politisches System und politische Kultur in der Schweiz und Österreich* (*Democracy-based Proportional Representation of Regional or Socio-cultural Groups: Political System and Political Culture in Switzerland and Austria*), Tübingen: Mohr (Siebeck).

Lijphart, A. (1968), *The Politics of Accommodation. Pluralism and Democracy in the Netherlands*, Berkeley and Los Angeles, CA: University of California Press.

Lijphart, A. (1989), 'From the politics of accommodation to adversarial politics in the Netherlands: a reassessment', *West European Politics*, **12** (1), 139–53.

Lijphart, A. (2012), *Patterns of Democracy: Government Form and Performance in Thirty-Six Countries*, 2nd edn, New Haven, CT: Yale University Press.

March, J.G. and J.P. Olsen. (1989), *Rediscovering Institutions. The Organizational Basis of Politics*, New York: Free Press and London: Macmillan.

Mayntz, R. and F.W. Scharpf (1995), 'Der Ansatz des akteurszentrierten Institutionalismus' ('The approach of actor-centered institutionalism'), in R. Mayntz and F.W. Scharpf (eds), *Gesellschaftliche Selbstregelung und politische Steuerung* (*Societal Self-Regulation and Political Steering*), Frankfurt am Main and New York: Campus, pp. 39–72.

Obinger, H., S. Leibfried and F.G. Castles (eds) (2005), *Federalism and the Welfare State: New World and European Experiences*, Cambridge: Cambridge University Press.

Pierson, P. (2000), 'Increasing returns, path dependence, and the study of politics', *American Political Science Review*, **94** (2), 251–67.

Scharpf, F.W. (1991), *Crisis and Choice in European Social Democracy*, Ithaca, NY: Cornell University Press.

Schmidt, M.G. (1996), 'When parties matter: a review of the possibilities and limits of partisan influence on public policy', *European Journal of Political Research*, **30** (2), 155–83.

Spiegel (2012), 'Finanzpolitik', *Der Spiegel*, no. 29, 16 July, accessed 23 August 2016 at http://www.spiegel.de/spiegel/print/d-87347210.html.

Sternberger, D. (1990), 'Verfassungspatriotismus' ('Constitutional patriotism'), in D. Sternberger (ed.), V*erfassungspatriotismus* (*Constitutional Patriotism*), Frankfurt am Main: Insel, pp. 13–16.

Streeck, W. and K. Thelen (2005), 'Introduction: institutional change in advanced political economies', in W. Streeck and K. Thelen (eds), *Beyond Continuity. Institutional Change in Advanced Political Economies*, Oxford: Oxford University Press, pp. 1–39.

Tsebelis, G. (2002), *Veto Players: How Political Institutions Work*, Princeton, NJ: Princeton University Press.

Vatter, A. (2014), *Das politische System der Schweiz: Grundlagen, Institutionen und Vergleich* (*The Political System of Switzerland: Foundations, Institutions, and Comparison*), Baden-Baden: Nomos (UTB).

17 Studying voting behavior
Joop J.M. van Holsteyn and Galen A. Irwin

1 INTRODUCTION

Elections are everywhere. Even autocratic rulers feel that general elections provide them with a modicum of legitimacy and for representative democracies 'the electoral connection . . . still [is] the primary basis of citizen influence' (Dalton 1988, p. 127). As elections are omnipresent, it is not surprising that they have attracted the interest of political scientists. Here the focus is on the behavior of ordinary citizens in the electoral process. The discussion is divided into three sections: (1) the goals of electoral research; (2) the methods employed to answer research questions; and (3) the main theoretical approaches.

2 THE GOALS OF ELECTORAL RESEARCH

Two major questions define the research area. The first asks why citizens participate in elections. It is clear that in cost–benefit terms it is irrational to vote (for example, Downs 1957) – but many people do. As puzzling as this question is, here we focus upon the second question: why do voters choose the party or candidate they decide to support? The goal of electoral research can be either to predict the outcome of an election or to explain how voters come to their decisions.

3 METHODS: PREDICTION

The year 1824 in the United States looms large in the quest to predict elections: it is perhaps the first election that involved mass citizen participation and 'straw polls' were held in an effort to gauge public leanings (Smith 1990). In the 1880s, the *Boston Globe* began to develop a system based on key-precincts, 'whose voting behaviors were consistently most typical of the others' (Littlewood 1998, p. 12) and, towards the end of the nineteenth century, newspapers began to conduct surveys of voters. The most famous of these polls was carried out by the *Literary Digest* when it sent millions of postcards, which were to be mailed back, in 1936. The incorrect prediction that Landon would beat Roosevelt eventually helped lead to the demise of the magazine (Squire 1988).

3.1 Commercial Polls

The failure of the *Literary Digest* poll coincided with the rise of commercial polling at the 1936 US presidential election. Archibald Crossley, Elmo Roper and George Gallup employed principles of scientific methods for polling and their success has led to the establishment of public opinion firms around the world. Branch organization European Society for Marketing and Opinion Research (ESOMAR) boasts 4900 members in 130 countries.[1] Many of these carry out election polling. Most pollsters, however, shy away from claiming that their results are predictions; they often only claim to provide snapshots of public opinion. In recent years, in several countries a 'poll of polls' has been introduced: analysts compile the results of various polling companies and thus, hopefully, obtain more accurate results.

3.2 Exit Polls

In the mid-1960s, with the aim of predicting the election outcome quickly, exit polls were introduced (Van Dam and Beishuizen 1967; Levy 1983; Mitofsky 1991). Exit polling involves choosing polling stations either according to the principle of key-precincts or at random, where researchers approach voters to fill in a short questionnaire including how they have just voted. These 'votes' are tabulated so that a news medium can call the results before the real votes have been counted. Various countries (for example, the USA, Great Britain and the Netherlands) have a tradition of exit polls, and elsewhere, such as the former USSR and the Balkans, it has been claimed that exit polls may provide a validity check on the official election results (see, for example, Fisher et al. 2010).

3.3 Prediction Markets

In 1988 researchers at the University of Iowa introduced the Iowa Electronic Market. In the case of an election prediction market, buyers can buy and sell candidate futures. Prediction markets are not based on principles of random sampling, but on the informed expectations of buyers and sellers. There remains controversy concerning the accuracy of markets versus 'regular' polls (for example, Berg et al. 2008; Erikson and Wlezien 2008; Rothschild 2009); such markets have nevertheless been introduced around the world.

3.4   Economic Models

At the end of the 1970s and early 1980s, forecasts based upon economic indicators began to appear. These models are grounded in the theory of retrospective voting (Fiorina 1981), that if times are bad, voters will 'throw the rascals out' (for example, Miller and Wattenberg 1985). Various economic measures have been used in such models. For the 2012 US elections, ten models were developed for forecasting the presidential election (Campbell 2012); economic models have also been applied in, for instance, Australia, Canada, Great Britain and France. Assessing the accuracy of such forecasts depends upon what criteria are used and what expectations one has concerning the degree of accuracy (Leigh and Wolfers 2006; Campbell 2009), but in general the results are mixed (see also the special symposium 'Electoral forecasting' in *Electoral Studies* (2010), **30** (2), 247–87).

4   METHODS: EXPLANATION

Most political scientists do not aspire to predict election outcomes and set themselves the goal of understanding and explaining individual behavior. The greatest amount of scientific work on electoral behavior has been in attempting to explain why individuals have voted as they have. In this research, a number of methods have been employed.

4.1   Election Statistics

Virtually every entity that holds elections will collect the results by geographical unit. Combined with ecological data, these statistics can be used to analyze voting behavior by producing maps and graphs to show the distribution of support across a geographical area or by adding contextual data to explain individual behavior. Election statistics have the advantage that they are available for elections for which no other data are available. This approach, however, is more generally applicable, not only for historical but also for contemporary analyses. Since the first issue (1982) of *Electoral Studies*, that is, the journal 'covering all aspects of voting', almost half of all original election papers are at least partly based on various kinds of aggregate data and official election results.[2]

In ecological analyses, electoral statistics are combined with other measures on the aggregate level to make inferences concerning individual behavior, or results from two elections may be used to estimate voter transition probabilities or floating voters (for example, Russo 2013).

Use of such statistics runs the risk of committing the ecological fallacy, which amounts to drawing incorrect explanatory decisions concerning the behavior of individual voters (see, however, for example, King 1998; King et al. 2004).

4.2 Surveys

In the 1930s US pollsters began to conduct surveys based upon 'modern' principles of statistical sampling. Ideally a sample of between roughly 1000 and 2000 respondents is drawn at random from a sampling frame that covers the population for which parameter estimates are to be made.

Respondents can be approached in a variety of ways. One of the earliest and most popular is to conduct a personal interview. Such face-to-face interviews have the advantage of producing higher response rates than other methods, but they are very expensive. A less expensive method involves sending questionnaires to respondents by mail. However, response rates are generally (far) lower than for face-to-face interviews. A contemporary version of this technique is sending out questionnaires or a link to questionnaires by email (see, for example, Callegaro et al. 2014; see also Chapter 18 in this volume). A major and as yet unsolved problem for these methods is how to obtain an adequate sampling frame and draw a random sample. Self-selection bias is a major problem in such Internet or online surveys (Couper 2008; Vehovar et al. 2008; Bethlehem 2010; Bethlehem and Biffignandi 2012). Moreover, there are strong indications that data from such self-selection online panels result in both less accurate estimates of proportions and different relations between relevant variables that cannot be corrected by weighing (Brüggen et al. forthcoming).[3]

As access to telephones increased, telephone interviews became popular. The costs are less than for face-to-face interviews, and as computer assisted interviewing became available, the data could be compiled quickly. A disadvantage is that the length of the interview must be limited, whereas longer interviews can be held face-to-face. This problem increased with the introduction of cell phones, which also has made it very difficult to randomly sample for telephone interviews.

4.3 Experiments

Unless a so-called panel design is employed, surveys are most often conducted at a single point in time. If the time dimension between cause and effect cannot be established, the research is *ex post facto*. Experiments can do a better job of establishing causality as a result of control and randomization; quasi-experimental methods are also available (Campbell and

Stanley 1963). After the pioneering work of Eldersfeld (1956), the use of experiments in electoral research has risen since the 1970s (Morton and Williams 2008; Druckman et al. 2011). An influential example is the work by Ansolabehere and Iyengar (1995) on turnout; research on candidate evaluation has been carried out by, for example, Lodge and Steenbergen (1995) and Lau and Redlawsk (2006). Media effects are another area that has been investigated using experimental techniques.[4]

4.4   Focus Groups

Some scholars argue that surveys yield superficial results and they desire 'to get behind the numbers'. This can be done with focus groups, which typically consist of between six and 12 participants, who may have been selected at random or to represent a specific group (for example, Krueger and Casey 2009). A moderator attempts to stimulate discussion and gain reactions in the form of opinions or attitudes concerning the central topic presented. Focus group research seems to have been introduced into American presidential election campaigns in 1972 (Jacobs and Shapiro 1995) and is now firmly entrenched in market research and election campaigns around the world. Their use in the study of individual voting behavior, however, is still limited.[5]

5   THREE MAIN APPROACHES OF VOTING BEHAVIOR

In order to understand voting behavior, a research must have a theoretical starting point or framework. Three approaches – the sociological, social-psychological and economic – have been dominant in the field of electoral research.

5.1   Sociological Approach

Although classic studies by Rice (1928) and Gosnell (1930) preceded it, the dawn of modern electoral research can likely be found in the survey of voting carried out by Paul Lazarsfeld and associates at the 1940 US presidential election (Lazarsfeld et al. 1944). The view of the voter upon which their study was based was that of a rational independent consumer. The design of the study reflected this vision, incorporating media content analysis and a seven-wave panel of interviews. The study, however, was – given its goal – a disaster: there were no media effects and voters did not shift their preference during the campaign. What saved the study was the inclusion of socio-demographic variables (for example, social-economic status and religion) that were found to be related to vote choice.[6] So this study and the follow-up (Berelson et al. 1954) founded the sociological approach or Columbia School of voting behavior. The key notion is captured in a famous quote: 'a person thinks, politically, as he is, socially. Social characteristics determine political preference' (Lazarsfeld et al. 1944, p. 27).

Even though there has been much discussion concerning the decline of religious and class voting, such socio-structured voting has been and continues to be a major focus of voting behavior. The continued relevancy of the approach is reflected in *Electoral Studies*; although the relative number of papers in which this perspective is dominant was greater in the first 15 years, the perspective has been employed ever since.

5.2 Social-Psychological Approach

Instead of viewing social characteristics as direct determinants of vote choice, researchers at the University of Michigan placed them at the beginning of a 'funnel of causality' together with social status and parental characteristics. These were funneled through the social-psychological concept party identification, that is, 'a psychological identification, which can persist without legal recognition or evidence of formal membership and even without a consistent record of party support' (Campbell et al. 1960, p. 121). Party identification directly impacted on party choice as well as served as a filter that influenced candidate and issue perceptions, and other factors in the funnel closer to the ultimate vote choice.

The founders of the so-called Michigan School carried out national election studies in 1952 and 1956, the data from which were analyzed in *The American Voter* (Campbell et al. 1960). This study has inspired so many scientific pieces that it is impossible to begin to discuss or even mention them (see, however, Nie et al. 1976; Miller and Shanks 1996; Lewis-Beck 2008; see also the special issue of *Electoral Studies*, **28** (4) in 2009).

In exporting the Michigan model to Europe (and elsewhere), major challenges were raised concerning the key concept of party identification. First, it was difficult to translate the particular survey question into local languages. Moreover, voters were more likely to use ideological identifiers than the names of specific parties. Also, scholars demonstrated that party choice was more stable than party identification (for example, Budge et al. 1976; Thomassen 1976; LeDuc 1981), which violated the concept (see however, for example, Cain and Ferejohn 1981; Johnston 1992). The concept of party identification has also been challenged within the United States, for example by Fiorina (1981), who conceives of party identification as a running tally of our perceptions of the parties through-out our lifetime. Nevertheless, despite the domestic and international critiques, the concept of party identification continues to inspire research and plays a central role in theories of political socialization, the concept of the normal vote, and theories of dealignment and realignment.

5.3   Economic Approach

As influential as the Columbia and Michigan schools have been, by the 1980s they had been surpassed in number of citations in leading journals (Wattenberg 1991, p. 19) by the seminal work of Anthony Downs (1957) in the third classic approach: the economic approach. Downs's approach is known as the economic approach, because he adapted principles from economic theory to examine politics. Downs developed a deductive theory of democracy; he made assumptions about the behavior of political actors and deduced what could be expected to occur. Primary among his assumptions was that both voters and parties are rational actors and behave as 'utility maximizers'. For voters this implies that they attempt to maximize the benefits they will receive from their votes. Rational choice models also assume that voters base their decision on political goals, rather than other possibilities. Thirdly, voters need and gather (costly and often imperfect) information in order to make their vote decisions.

Downs introduced the influential concept of spatial relationships into electoral research. He posited a single ideological dimension along which voters could be positioned and showed that this should lead to a two-party system with the parties located close to the center of the distribution. This has inspired studies of the dimensionality of party systems and to the establishment of proximity or smallest distance models in which the individual voter chooses the party closest in the party space. An amendment to the proximity model is the directional model; Rabinowitz and Macdonald argue that voters choose the party that most strongly represents their opinion and choose a direction first and subsequently select the party that, within a region of acceptability, most strongly supports that opinion (for example, Rabinowitz 1978; Rabinowitz and Macdonald 1989; Macdonald et al. 1991). Combinations of proximity and directional models in a unified theory of voting are suggested as well (for example, Merrill III and Grofman 1999).

6   OTHER APPROACHES

The aforementioned approaches have structured research on voting behavior for over half of a century, but there are other ideas that have been employed to examine voting behavior.

6.1   Economic Voting

Whereas Downs assumed that voters looked to past performance as a means to prospectively judge expected benefits, Key (1966) argued that they looked to performance to reward or punish incumbents. The primary area of concern was performance of the economy. If the economy was performing well, the incumbent government would be rewarded; if it was going badly, the incumbent would be punished (for general overviews, see, for example, the special issues of *Electoral Studies* (2000), **19** (2–3), (2013), **32** (3); Lewis-Beck and Stegmaier 2007).[7]

As regards economic voting, two questions are crucial (for a sophisticated perspective on economic voting, see Van der Brug et al. 2007). One relates to the distinction between prospective and retrospective voting. The second major question concerns what is being evaluated. Many people assume that voters are looking at how government performance affects their own pocketbook. This pocketbook or egotropic voting can be contrasted with sociotropic voting, which is based upon an evaluation of how governmental performance has affected the general economy. Despite the general notion that egotropic voting dominates, more empirical research has found support for sociotropic voting (for example, Lewis-Beck and Paldam 2000).

6.2   Strategic Voting

The orthodox view (Catt 1996) is that the voter will vote for the party that he or she favors most: the sincere vote model. Using whichever of the characteristics are deemed relevant, the voter evaluates the parties/ candidates and determines which fits most closely to an ideal and casts a vote for it. However, already in 1869 Henry Droop formulated the wasted vote hypothesis; supporting a most favored candidate who has no chance of winning is a 'wasted vote' and we would do better to choose between candidates who stand a chance of winning (Riker 1982). Numerous studies have examined the wasted vote from the perspective of tactical or strategic voting and extended it to various electoral systems (for example, Cox 1997).

Strategic voting is a form of non-sincere voting, that is, voting for a party other than the most preferred. Proportional representation (PR) was supposed to be an antidote to the wasted vote, since seats are allocated proportionally. Nevertheless, voters in PR systems do employ strategic considerations; for example, they may attempt to influence the composition of the government coalition. Other considerations are investigated as well, such as choosing a party that will take a more extreme position in coalition negotiations. This latter is related to the theory of compensatory vote, arguing that voters are interested in policy and that their calculus is more extensive and policy oriented than has been imagined (for example, Kedar 2005, 2009).

6.3   Emotions and Personality

The above-mentioned approaches essentially rely on cognitive models of voter choice; to some degree they all assume a rational independent voter. However, in the 1980s political scientists began to conclude that emotions could not be excluded from electoral research (for example, Marcus 2000) and a number of emotions have been examined, for example, fear and anxiety, anger and enthusiasm. Also, new methods have been employed, such as testing saliva samples of voters to evaluate their cortisol levels as evidence of stress. Westen *cum suis* have used magnetic resonance imaging (MRI) brain scans to examine motivated reasoning based on the assumption that when reason and emotion collide, emotion wins (Westen et al. 2006; Westen 2007). Marcus and associates have put forward the theory of affective intelligence, which argues that anxiety leads voters to seek information and rely less upon other cues, whereas enthusiasm and anger increase the likelihood that the voter will have less attention for the political environment and fall back on partisanship (for example, Marcus et al. 2000).

Emotions have been studied in various contexts, for example, with respect to the impact on the evaluation of political candidates and within the more general context of the processes of political personalization and presidentialization of politics. It has been argued that the role of candidates and their individual characteristics is increasing in electoral importance, and emotional evaluations in particular, and both the personality and personality traits of candidates and voters are assumed to play a role in the contemporary electoral calculus (for example, Poguntke and Webb 2005; Karvonen 2010; Aarts et al. 2011; Bittner 2011; Lobo and Curtice 2014).

7 CONCLUDING REMARK

For contemporary electoral researchers and their future colleagues, the increased volatility and heterogeneity of the electorate in advanced representative democracies is a given (for example, Weßels et al. 2014). The fact that so many methodological approaches and various methods of data collection and analysis are available should be considered an advantage. The same holds as regards the existence of a variety of validated theoretical notions and substantive approaches of the voters of the twenty-first century and their individual electoral calculus. Elections are everywhere – and hopefully they are there to stay, as well as scholars who study electoral behavior and who face the challenging task of describing, explaining and predicting the important individual behavior of citizens in democratic political systems in performing the not so simple act of voting (cf. Dalton and Wattenberg 1993; Kelley and Mirer 1974).

NOTES

1. www.esomar.org (accessed 3 August 2016).
2. http://www.journals.elsevier.com/electoral-studies (accessed 3 August 2016).
3. See also Chapter 18 in this volume for a discussion on panels.
4. In the first five years of its existence *Electoral Studies* did not contain a single paper primarily based on an experimental approach; in the most recent decade about 5 percent of all original articles used such an approach. Note also that in 2014 the first issue of the *Journal of Experimental Political Science* was published.
5. During a period of over 30 years no original election papers have been found in *Electoral Studies* that were based exclusively upon focus group research.
6. It remains intriguing why Lazarsfeld would have adopted the calculating voter model and not have included sociological characteristics of voters in the original design. In his native Austria, and most of Europe, there were mass parties that drew their support primarily from specific social groups. Had studies of voting behavior originated in Europe, these social groups would have been the focus of electoral research and a sociological approach would have been the obvious choice.
7. At least in the first 15 years of the twenty-first century, a very substantial number of papers in *Electoral Studies* employ the perspective of economic voting.

FURTHER READING

Introductory

Eijk, C. van der and M.N. Franklin (2009), *Elections and Voters*, Basingstoke, UK: Palgrave Macmillan.

Example

Brug, W. van der, C. van der Eijk and M.N. Franklin (2007), *The Economy and the Vote: Economic Conditions and Elections in Fifteen Countries*, Cambridge: Cambridge University Press.

Advanced

Bittner, A. (2011), *Platform or Personality? The Role of Party Leaders in Elections*, Oxford: Oxford University Press.
Weßels, B., H. Rattinger, S. Rossteutscher and R. Schmitt-Beck (eds) (2014), *Voters on the Move or on the Run?*, Oxford: Oxford University Press.

REFERENCES

Aarts, K., A. Blais and H. Schmitt (eds) (2011), *Political Leaders and Democratic Elections*, Oxford: Oxford University Press.
Ansolabehere, S.S. and S. Iyengar (1995), *Going Negative: How Political Advertising Divides and Shrinks the American Electorate*, New York: Free Press.
Berelson, B.R., P.F. Lazarsfeld and W.N. McPhee (1954), *Voting*, Chicago, IL: University of Chicago Press.
Berg, J., R. Forsythe, F. Nelson and T. Rietz (2008), Results from a Dozen Years of Election Futures Market Research, in C.R. Plott and V.L. Smith (eds), *Handbook of Experimental Economic Result*, Amsterdam: Elsevier, pp. 742–51.
Bethlehem, J. and S. Biffignandi (2012), *Handbook of Web Surveys*, Hoboken, NJ: Wiley.
Bethlehem, J.G. (2010), 'Selection bias in web surveys', *International Statistics Review*, **78** (2), 161–88.
Bittner, A. (2011), *Platform or Personality? The Role of Party Leaders in Elections*, Oxford: Oxford University Press.
Brüggen, E., J. van den Braken and J.A. Krosnick, 'Establishing the accuracy on online panels for survey research', forthcoming paper.
Budge, I., I. Crewe and D. Farlie (eds) (1976), *Party Identification and Beyond: Representations of Voting and Party Competition*, London and New York: Wiley.
Cain, B. and J. Ferejohn (1981), 'Party identification in the United States and Great Britain', *Comparative Political Studies*, **14** (1), 31–47.
Callegaro, M., R.P. Baker, J. Bethlehem, A.S. Göritz, J.A. Krosnick and P.J. Lavrakas (eds) (2014), *Online Panel Research: A Data Quality Perspective*, Chichester, UK: John Wiley & Sons.
Campbell, A., P.E. Converse, W.E. Miller and D.E. Stokes (1960), *The American Voter*, Chicago, IL: University of Chicago Press.
Campbell, D.T. and J.C. Stanley (1963), *Experimental and Quasi-Experimental Designs for Research*, Chicago, IL: Rand McNally.
Campbell, J.E. (2009), 'Forecast recap', *PS: Political Science and Politics*, **42** (1), 19–25.
Campbell, J.E. (2012), 'Forecasting the 2012 American national elections', *PS: Political Science and Politics*, **45** (4), 610–12.
Catt, H. (1996), *Voting Behaviour: A Radical Critique*, London and New York: Leicester University Press.
Couper, M.P. (2008), *Designing Effective Web Surveys*, Cambridge: Cambridge University Press.
Cox, G.W. (1997), *Making Votes Count. Strategic Coordination in the World's Electoral Systems*, Cambridge: Cambridge University Press.

Dalton, R.J. (1988), *Citizen Politics in Western Democracies*, Chatham, NJ: Chatham House.

Dalton, R.J. and M.P. Wattenberg (1993), 'The not so simple act of voting', in A.W. Finifter (ed.), *Political Science: The State of the Discipline II*, Washington: American Political Science Association, pp. 193–218.

Downs, A. (1957), *An Economic Theory of Democracy*, New York: Harper & Row.

Druckman, J.N., D.P. Green, J.H. Kuklinski and A. Lupia (eds) (2011), *Cambridge Handbook of Experimental Political Science*, Cambridge: Cambridge University Press.

Eldersfeld, S.J. (1956), 'Experimental propaganda techniques and voting behavior', *American Political Science Review*, **50** (1), 154–65.

Erikson R.S. and C. Wlezien (2008), 'Are political markets really superior to polls as election predictions?', *Public Opinion Quarterly*, **72** (2), 190–215.

Fiorina, M.P. (1981), *Retrospective Voting in American National Elections*, New Haven, CT: Yale University Press.

Fisher, S.D., J. Kuha and C. Payne (2010), 'Editorial: getting it right on the night, again – the 2010 UK general election exit poll', *Journal of the Royal Statistical Society*, **173** (4), 699–701.

Gosnell, H.F. (1930), *Why Europe Votes*, Chicago, IL: University of Chicago Press.

Jacobs, L.R. and R.Y. Shapiro (1995), 'The rise of presidential polling: the Nixon White House in historical perspective', *Public Opinion Quarterly*, **59** (2), 163–95.

Johnston, R. (1992), 'Party identification measures in the Anglo-American democracies: a national survey experiment', *American Journal of Political Science*, **36** (2), 542–59.

Karvonen, L. (2010), *The Personalisation of Politics: A Study of Parliamentary Democracies*, Colchester: ECPR Press.

Kedar, O. (2005), 'When moderate voters prefer extreme parties: policy balancing in parliamentary elections', *American Political Science Review*, **99** (1), 185–99.

Kedar, O. (2009), *Voting for Policy, not Parties: How Voters Compensate for Power Sharing*, Cambridge: Cambridge University Press.

Kelley, S. and T.W. Mirer (1974), 'The simple act of voting', *American Political Science Review*, **68** (2), 572–91.

Key, V.O. (1966), *The Responsible Electorate: Rationality in Presidential Voting 1936–60*, New York: Vintage Books.

King, G. (1998), *A Solution to the Ecological Inference Problem*, Princeton, NJ: Princeton University Press.

King, G., O. Rosen and M. Tanner (eds) (2004), *Ecological Inference: New Methodological Strategies*, Cambridge: Cambridge University Press.

Krueger, R.A. and M.A. Casey (2009), *Focus Groups: A Practical Guide for Applied Research*, 4th edn, Thousand Oaks, CA: Sage.

Lau, R.R. and D.P. Redlawsk (2006), *How Voters Decide: Information Processing during Election Campaigns*, New York: Cambridge University Press.

Lazarsfeld, P.F., B.R. Berelson and H. Gaudet (1944), *The People's Choice: How the Voter Makes Up His Mind in a Presidential Campaign*, New York: Columbia University Press.

LeDuc, L. (1981), 'The dynamic properties of party identification: a four nation comparison', *European Journal of Political Science*, **9** (3), 257–68.

Leigh, A. and J. Wolfers (2006), 'Competing approaches to forecasting elections: economic models, opinion polling and prediction markets', *Economic Record*, **82** (258), 325–40.

Levy, M.R. (1983), 'The methodology and performance of election day polls', *Public Opinion Quarterly*, **47** (1), 47–54.

Lewis-Beck, M.S. (2008), *The American Voter Revisited*, Ann Arbor, MI: University of Michigan Press.

Lewis-Beck, M. and M. Paldam (2000), 'Economic voting: an introduction', *Electoral Studies*, **19** (2–3), 113–21.

Lewis-Beck, M. and M. Stegmaier (2007), 'Economic models of voting', in R.J. Dalton and H.-D. Klingemann (eds), *The Oxford Handbook of Political Behavior*, Oxford: Oxford University Press, pp. 518–37.

Littlewood, T.B. (1998), *Calling Elections: The History of Horse-Race Journalism*, Notre Dame, IN: University of Notre Dame Press.

Lobo, M.C. and J. Curtice (eds) (2014), *Personality Politics? The Role of Leader Evaluations in Democratic Elections*, Oxford: Oxford University Press.

Lodge, M. and M. Steenbergen (1995), 'The responsive voter: campaign information and the dynamics of candidate evaluation', *American Political Science Review*, **89** (2), 309–36.

Macdonald, S., O. Listaug and G. Rabinowitz (1991), 'Issues and support in multiparty systems', *American Political Science Review*, **85** (4), 1107–31.

Marcus, G.E. (2000), 'Emotions and politics', *Annual Review of Political Science*, **3**, 221–50.

Marcus, G.E., W.R. Neuman and M. MacKuen (2000), *Affective Intelligence and Political Judgement*, Chicago, IL: University of Chicago Press.

Merrill III, S. and B. Grofman (1999), *A Unified Theory of Voting: Directional and Proximity Spatial Models*, Cambridge: Cambridge University Press.

Miller, A.H. and M.P. Wattenberg (1985), 'Throwing the rascals out: policy and performance evaluations of presidential candidates, 1952–1980', *American Political Science Review*, **79** (2), 359–72.

Miller, W.E. and M. Shanks (1996), *The New American Voter*, Cambridge, MA: Harvard University Press.

Mitofsky, W.J. (1991), 'A short history of exit polls', in P.J. Lavrakas and J.K. Holley (eds), *Polling and the Presidential Election Coverage*, Newbury Park, CA: Sage, pp. 83–99.

Morton, R.B. and K.C. Williams (2008), 'Experimentation in political science', in J.M. Box-Steffensmeier, H.E. Brady and D. Collier (eds), *The Oxford Handbook of Political Methodology*, Oxford: Oxford University Press, pp. 339–56.

Nie, N., J. Petrocik and S. Verba (1976), *The Changing American Voter*, Cambridge, MA: Harvard University Press.

Poguntke, T. and P. Webb (eds) (2005), *The Presidentialization of Politics: A Comparative Study of Modern Democracies*, Oxford: Oxford University Press.

Rabinowitz, G. (1978), 'On the nature of political issues: insights from spatial analysis', *American Journal of Political Science*, **22** (4), 793–817.

Rabinowitz, G. and S.E. Macdonald (1989), 'A directional theory of issue voting', *American Political Science Review*, **83** (1), 93–121.

Rice, S. (1928), *Quantitative Methods in Politics*, New York: Alfred A. Knopf.

Riker, W.H. (1982), 'The two-party system and Duverger's Law: an essay on the history of political science', *American Political Science Review*, **76** (4), 753–66.

Rothschild, D. (2009), 'Forecasting elections: comparing prediction markets, polls, and their biases', *Public Opinion Quarterly*, **73** (5), 895–916.

Russo, L. (2013), 'Estimating floating voters: a comparison between the ecological inference and the survey methods', *Quantity and Quality*, **48** (3), 1667–83.

Smith, T. (1990), 'The first straw poll: a study of the origins of election polls', *Public Opinion Quarterly*, **54** (1), 21–36.

Squire, P. (1988), 'Why the 1936 Literary Digest poll failed', *Public Opinion Quarterly*, **52** (1), 125–33.

Thomassen, J.J.A. (1976), 'Party identification as a cross-national concept: its meaning in the Netherlands', in I. Budge, I. Crewe and D. Farlie (eds), *Party Identification and Beyond*, London: Wiley, pp. 63–79.

Van Dam, M.P.A. and J. Beishuizen (1967), *Kijk op de kiezer: Feiten, cijfers en perspectieven op basis van het Utrechtse kiezersonderzoek van 15 februari 1967 (A Perspective on the Voter: Facts, Figures and Perspectives from an Electoral Study in the City of Utrecht, 15 February 1967)*, Amsterdam: Het Parool.

Van der Brug, W., C. van der Eijk and M. Franklin (2007), *The Economy and the Vote: Economic Conditions and Elections in Fifteen Countries*, Cambridge: Cambridge University Press.

Vehovar, V., K. Manfreda and G. Koren (2008), 'Internet surveys', in W. Donsbach and M.W. Traugott (eds), *The SAGE Handbook of Public Opinion Research*, Los Angeles, CA: Sage Publications, pp. 272–83.

Wattenberg, M.P. (1991), *The Rise of Candidate-Centered Politics: Presidential Elections of the 1980s*, Cambridge, MA: Harvard University Press.

Weßels, B., H. Rattinger, S. Rossteutscher and R. Schmitt-Beck (eds) (2014), *Voters on the Move or on the Run?*, Oxford: Oxford University Press.

Westen, D. (2007), *The Political Brain*, New York: Public Affairs.

Westen, D., P.S. Blagov, K. Harenski, C. Kilts and S. Hamann (2006), 'Neural bases of motivated reasoning: an fMRI study of emotional constraints on partisan political judgment in the 2004 U.S. presidential election', *Journal of Cognitive Neuroscience*, **18** (11), 1947–58.

18 The role of high-quality surveys in political science research
Sarah Butt, Sally Widdop and Lizzy Winstone

1 INTRODUCTION

Surveys have become one of the most commonly used methods of quantitative data collection in the social sciences. They provide researchers with the means to collect systematic micro-data on the attitudes, beliefs and behaviors of a range of individual actors including (but not limited to) the general public, voters, political activists and elected officials. The scope to collect comparable data in different settings makes them a particularly valuable tool for studying differences in attitudes and behavior across time and across countries. Surveys have provided empirical data and contributed to theory building across a range of topics in political science including: political culture (Almond and Verba 1963) and values (Inglehart 1977), electoral choice (Butler and Stokes 1969), political engagement (Verba and Nie 1972), social and political trust (Putnam 2000), and democratization (Evans and Whitefield 1995).

The primary means by which to capture 'the ebb and flow of public opinion' (Brady 2000, p. 47), survey evidence is also widely used by political actors besides academic researchers. Political polling is a ubiquitous feature of campaigns for public office at all levels, while policy-makers use surveys to explore possible drivers of behavior and monitor public attitudes towards key issues. Surveys are also a major source of political information for journalists and the general public. They provide a crucial link between citizens and government and as such may help to shape the political landscape and to ensure the openness and transparency of governments. Atkeson (2010, p. 10) argues that 'without survey research methods it would be nearly impossible to understand the public and its role and value in democratic governing'.

Since the introduction of surveys to the social sciences in the 1930s (see Heath et al. 2005 for more on the history of surveys), their availability has continued to spread. Surveys now have global reach, covering nearly every country in the world. There are a growing number of established surveys available as well as increased opportunities for researchers to collect their own data. The potential for using survey data to understand political attitudes, behavior and dynamics increases as survey methodology, data collection techniques and the statistical tools available for analysis evolve. Researchers are increasingly able to overcome one of the limitations of survey research – a reliance on correlational studies – and determine causality through the use of statistical techniques such as propensity matching and panel studies which allow for the use of quasi-experimental designs (Atkeson 2010). The practice of embedding experiments in social surveys is also becoming more common, enabling researchers to study the causal effect of different stimuli on political decision-making (Druckman et al. 2006). Growing opportunities for data linkage, combining survey data with contextual data from other sources, provide scope to explore societal influences on individual attitudes and behavior (Groves 2011).

As with any data collection tool, however, the quality of the inferences to be drawn from survey data are only as good as the data collection methodology employed. Good survey design should seek to minimize potential sources of error (bias) that can occur in all stages of data collection. The proliferation of academic, commercial and user-generated surveys available to political scientists – and the growing availability of alternative forms of data – makes it important to be able to distinguish the good from the bad. This is the case for those designing their own survey, for researchers making use of existing survey data for secondary analysis and for researchers wishing to use surveys as a vehicle for conducting experiments.

In this chapter we first define what a survey is and identify the essential features of survey data. We discuss what makes a good survey, taking the European Social Survey as a case study. We provide examples of other surveys likely to be of interest to political scientists and consider how survey data can be enhanced by combining it with other forms of data. We conclude by arguing that surveys remain critical to the study of political science, with other forms of data complementing, but not replacing, high-quality surveys.

2 WHAT IS A SURVEY?

Surveys can be distinguished by three main features, established by pollster George Gallup in the 1930s and broadly present ever since (Heath et al. 2005): targeting random samples of a defined population; use of standardized 'closed' questions to measure the attitudes and characteristics of respondents; and generation of quantitative data for statistical analysis.

Within this basic formulation there is wide scope for surveys to use different designs to address questions relevant to political science and other social science disciplines. Examples of different types of surveys available and their potential uses are shown in Box 18.1.

Researchers have the option of conducting secondary analysis of existing data sets, many of which are freely available to download, or of conducting a bespoke survey. Collecting your own data makes it possible to tailor the survey design to your research questions. Survey data

---

BOX 18.1   TYPES OF SURVEYS

Cross-national surveys   Carried out in multiple countries to understand how attitudes and behavior vary according to differences in culture, institutions or economic conditions.
Examples: World Values Survey; European Social Survey; European Values Study.
National time series   General social surveys conducted in a specific country often contain variables likely to be of interest to political scientists. Data are available over time, allowing analysis of trends.
Examples: US General Social Survey (since 1973);[1] German General Social Survey – ALLBUS (since 1980);[2] British Social Attitudes Survey (since 1983).[3]
Election surveys   Conducted around the time of national elections in many countries, these seek to explain election outcomes and voter behavior by collecting information on vote choice and participation, attitudes towards election issues and government performance.
Examples: American National Election Studies (since 1952);[4] Swedish National Election Studies (since 1956);[5] British Election Study (since 1964).[6]
Surveys of political subgroups   Further our understanding of the dynamics of political representation and the interplay between political elites, activists and the public.
Examples: Surveys of political party members/activists (Seyd and Whiteley 2004) and candidates for political office and elected officials (Walczack and Van der Brug 2013).
Panel studies   Collect data from the same individual at multiple time points to explore changes in attitudes and behavior. Can focus on the effect of particular events, for example, election campaigns or track respondents over many years to study political socialization.
Examples: Belgian Political Panel Study 2006-2011;[7] European Election Study Panel 2014.[8]

Notes:
1.   http://gss.norc.org/.
2.   http://www.gesis.org/en/allbus.
3.   http://www.natcen.ac.uk/our-research/research/british-social-attitudes/.
4.   http://www.electionstudies.org/studypages/download/datacenter_all_NoData.php.
5.   http://www.valforskning.pol.gu.se/english/.
6.   http://discover.ukdataservice.ac.uk/series/?sn=200003.
7.   http://www.kekidatabank.be/opac/index.php?lvl5notice_display&id5836.
8.   http://eeshomepage.net/panel-study-2014/.

can now be collected quickly and relatively cheaply via Internet survey tools such as SurveyMonkey[1] while online panels such as the LISS panel in the Netherlands[2] and the GESIS panel in Germany[3] allow researchers to include their own questions on established surveys. However, there are potential limitations to online surveys, for example, participants may not be fully representative of the population, as well as challenges associated with designing your own questionnaire (see later in this chapter). Using data from a pre-existing survey may provide the best option for accessing high-quality data.

3   WHAT MAKES A GOOD SURVEY?

Regardless of the type of survey being conducted or the research question(s) it is intended to address, a good survey aims to achieve:

- representativeness – data are representative of the population of interest allowing researchers to use it to draw robust conclusions about the entire population;
- reliability – any differences observed in data collected across different respondents reflect genuine differences in attitudes or behavior rather than being the result of the way the data are collected; and
- validity – the survey accurately measures what it is intended to measure.

This depends on minimizing the various sources of error that can occur at all stages of data collection including errors associated with population coverage, sampling, non-response and measurement (Biemer and Lyberg 2003; Groves et al. 2009).

We discuss below how survey design can influence the level of survey error and the extent to which survey data can be considered representative, reliable and valid. We illustrate the discussion with examples of survey best practice taken from the European Social Survey (ESS).[4] Established in 2001, the ESS is a biennial cross-national survey of public attitudes and opinions. Data are collected from a representative sample of adults aged 15 and over in between 20 and 30 countries each round. Consisting of a core questionnaire that remains the same in every round alongside round-specific rotating modules, the face-to-face survey covers many topics of interest to political scientists, including: satisfaction with democracy, political trust, citizen engagement and attitudes towards immigration. The ESS aspires to the highest standards and is widely regarding as having raised the bar in terms of methodological rigor and transparency in cross-national research (Groves et al. 2008).

The ESS is not the only example of a good survey. Details of other high-quality international surveys which may be of interest to political scientists are given in Appendix Table 18A.1. We focus on cross-sectional, cross-national studies with some time-series availability since these provide breadth of coverage and rich data for comparative research.

3.1   Sampling

One way to ensure that survey data are representative is to conduct a census of the population. However, for reasons of practicality and cost, it is much more common to survey a sample of the population.

Probability sampling is the most robust approach to minimize errors associated with sampling. Respondents are sampled at random from the population of interest and cannot be substituted, that is, if the target respondent is unavailable or unwilling to participate, they cannot be replaced with someone else. This ensures that each member of the survey population has a known non-zero chance of being selected to participate and enables data users to estimate sampling error and assess the accuracy of survey estimates. The ESS requires that a random sample of all adults aged 15 and over and resident in private households is drawn in each country. To avoid coverage error that is, to ensure everyone in the population has a chance of being selected, where possible the sample is drawn using an accurate and complete sampling frame such as a population register or comprehensive list of all postal delivery points. In the absence of a suitable frame, carefully specified procedures are used to ensure representativeness (see Häder and Lynn 2007 for more on ESS sampling procedures).

Quota sampling is a commonly used, quicker and cheaper alternative to probability sampling. Unlike under probability sampling, interviewers have some flexibility in recruitment; provided that they interview the right mix of people to meet a set of pre-determined quotas – based for example on gender, age or employment status – they are free to select respondents (Smith 2008). They do not need to spend time persuading reluctant respondents or making multiple calls at an address to contact a specific individual; they can simply conduct the interview with individuals who are willing and available. The achieved sample is seemingly representative because it is similar in composition to that of the population with respect to the quota characteristics (ibid.). However, the fact that interviewers are free to select the most willing and available respondents – who are likely to have different characteristics from individuals who are harder to reach – increases sampling error and the risk that the data collected are biased.

3.2   Response Rates

For survey data to be representative of the underlying population, it is important to minimize any errors or bias that may occur as a result of survey non-response. In recent years it has become more difficult to contact and to persuade people to participate in surveys (Stoop et al. 2010). Although not necessarily the case, lower response rates make it more likely that participants have different characteristics compared with non-participants and hence that the characteristics of those who actually participate in the survey (the achieved sample) no longer accurately reflect those of the underlying population. Bias can result if the characteristics under-/over-represented among actual respondents are related to the attitudes and behaviors the survey is designed to measure. The ESS exerts a lot of effort to minimize non-response error. Countries are set a demanding response rate target of 70 percent and, although this may not be achieved, are expected to get as close to this as possible. Countries are also asked, where possible, to monitor respondent characteristics during fieldwork and target particular hard-to-reach groups to try and ensure that the final sample achieved is as balanced as possible.

3.3   Questionnaire Design

The reliability and validity of survey instruments can be improved, and measurement error reduced, by good questionnaire design. There are a number of different approaches to question design available to researchers looking to measure complex concepts effectively via surveys. Survey questions can be used to ask about behavior or facts; about knowledge and about attitudes (Bradburn et al. 2004). Survey questions may be open or closed. Closed questions that require respondents to choose from a pre-determined set of response options are more frequently used in survey research. Open questions, where respondents answer in their own words, are more costly to administer and analyze but can provide more flexibility.

Whatever the type of question being asked, there are some general principles that good questionnaire designers should observe in order to avoid bias (see Box 18.2).

Using questions previously developed and tested by other researchers can be a good way of ensuring valid and reliable measurement. Questionnaires developed for social surveys are generally an open resource and researchers are free to replicate the measures they contain.

**BOX 18.2   PRINCIPLES OF QUESTIONNAIRE DESIGN –
KROSNICK AND PRESSER (2010, P. 264)**

Use simple, familiar words (avoid technical terms, jargon and slang).
Use simple syntax.
Avoid words with ambiguous meanings, i.e. aim for wording that all respondents
will interpret in the same way.
Use wording that is specific and concrete (as opposed to general and abstract).
Make response options exhaustive and mutually exclusive.
Avoid leading or loaded questions that push respondents toward an answer.
Ask about one thing at a time (avoid double-barreled questions).
Avoid questions with single or double negations.

It is, however, important to bear in mind that items shown to work in one context (country and time period) may not be transferable to other contexts. There are question banks available that can be searched to find suitable items on different topics previously fielded in other surveys.[5] All questionnaires fielded as part of the ESS (translated into all relevant languages) are available to download from the ESS website, alongside detailed information about their development.

3.4   Pre-Testing

One way to enhance the quality of questions and minimize measurement error is to test draft questions. Pre-testing can establish whether a question is likely to be understood by respondents, whether it is understood consistently across different respondents, that is, is reliable, and is understood as intended, that is, is valid (Presser et al. 2004). The ESS conducts several types of qualitative and quantitative pre-testing. Expert review – where specialists in both survey methodology and the relevant substantive topic critique a draft question – is used throughout the design process. Cognitive interviewing is also used, whereby respondents are asked a question as if they were in a real survey interview and then either verbalize their thought process or are probed on their understanding and how they selected an answer (see Willis 2005). Quantitative pre-testing is carried out by including draft questions on omnibus surveys that is, buying questionnaire space on a commercial quota survey for testing purposes, and by running a pilot survey. The data generated is used to identify items with high item non-response – which may suggest a question is too difficult or sensitive for respondents to answer – or skewed distributions, which might indicate a lack of variation in opinion on a topic. Quantitative pre-tests also provide scope for more detailed statistical analysis allowing the relationships between variables to be explored and providing insight into whether the draft questions are measuring the desired concepts.

Pre-testing is particularly important in a cross-national context where the risk of introducing measurement error is increased owing to differences in language and culture across countries. The ESS pre-testing takes place in several countries, allowing differences in translation and culture to be taken into account. National coordinators who manage implementation of the survey in each country also review how well questions might work in their country (Prestage and Humphreys 2013).

3.5   Achieving Equivalence

To make valid and reliable comparisons between data collected across different groups of respondents and minimize measurement error, it is critical that all survey respondents receive the same stimulus and interpret the meaning of questions in the same way. This is known as the principle of equivalence (Jowell 1998). Simply presenting all respondents with an identical question may not be sufficient to achieve equivalence given that different respondents may understand the same question in different ways. Equivalence can be an issue for any survey owing to the inevitable heterogeneity of respondents in terms of vocabulary or levels of education. However, it is often a particular concern for cross-national surveys and surveys repeated over time, as the meaning of questions can vary from one country or time point to another.

A question may be understood differently in different countries for several reasons. A concept's relevance may vary depending on the institutional, policy or cultural context. For example, a question measuring attitudes toward direct democracy may be less readily understood by respondents in countries where referendums rarely take place compared with those in which they are common (Winstone et al. 2016). Researchers often face a choice between trying to formulate questions which are sufficiently general to apply in all countries and providing country-specific adaptations. The latter may improve measurement at the national level but preclude direct cross-national comparisons (Smith 2004). A question may also be understood differently due to the way it is translated. It might be that the 'translated word or phrase has acted as a slightly different stimulus from the one intended' (Jowell 1998, p. 4). The ESS adopts rigorous procedures to try to ensure translations use functionally equivalent words and phrases. A parallel 'ask the same question' approach – where all countries translate the same questions taken from a central source questionnaire – is used in combination with a committee based approach to translation, following translation, review, adjudication, pre-testing and documentation (TRAPD) procedures (Harkness 2007).

3.6   Mode

Choice of mode – whether the survey is self-administered via mail or the Web or administered by interviewers face to face or over the telephone – can introduce survey error, and hence affect the representativeness, reliability and validity of the data collected in a number of ways (Roberts 2007).

Face-to-face surveys such as the ESS are considered to be the gold standard for achieving a representative sample of the population. Modes reliant on technology, particularly online surveys, risk introducing coverage error if not everyone in the population of interest has access to the technology in question. There may also be a greater risk of sampling error with self-administered surveys; in the absence of an interviewer present to monitor who actually completes the questionnaire, postal or online surveys may simply be completed by the most willing or first-available individuals rather than a truly representative cross-section of the population. Finally, response rates are generally lower for self-administered surveys compared with face-to-face surveys.

Self-administered modes may, however, help to reduce measurement error and improve the reliability and validity of the data. Particularly with questions that are sensitive, in the presence of an interviewer respondents may adjust their responses to avoid embarrassment, to present a positive image of themselves or to give an answer they feel the interviewer wants to hear, for example, falsely claiming to have voted in the last election to appear as a better citizen. Relying on interviewers also carries a risk of introducing interviewer effects into the data (De Leeuw 2008). If one interviewer asks a question differently to another, this could affect the reliability and validity of the data collected. Fielding questions prone to social desirability bias or interviewer effects via self-administered modes may help to improve measurement. Where interviewers are used, as on the ESS, interviewer training and briefing is crucial to ensure standardized interviewing and minimize interviewer effects.

3.7   Availability

Designing a high-quality survey can be complex, costly and time-consuming. It is therefore worth taking advantage of the wealth of existing surveys whose data are often freely available for secondary analysis. Data from national surveys can often be accessed via national data archives.

Similarly, data from large-scale cross-national or international projects are often readily available. The ESS makes all its data available via its website.[6]

However, free data does not necessarily mean good data. The best data sources also provide access to documentation about the survey undertaken. This might include the questionnaire and other materials used by the interviewer plus information about sample design, response rates, mode, when fieldwork was conducted and by whom. Surveys such as the ESS go one step further and publish known deviations about the data following the premise that imperfections should not be concealed from potential users (Jowell et al. 2007). Data users should be provided with a full picture of how a survey was conducted and be able to make an assessment of the quality of a survey as a source of data.

4   COMBINING SURVEY DATA WITH INFORMATION FROM OTHER SOURCES

Researchers' understanding of individual attitudes and behaviors can greatly be enhanced by combining survey data with information from other sources. Such data linkage can, for example, provide valuable information about the context in which individuals operate and help to explain variation across space and time.

There is a wide range of pre-existing contextual information available which can be matched to survey data at national or sub-national level including data on political institutions, regime performance, electoral outcomes and economic indicators. Chapter 15 in this volume discusses such data and provides examples of readily available data sources.

Increasingly, established surveys provide users with data sets in which the survey data are already linked to a variety of contextual data. The ESS, for example, makes a variety of demographic, economic and political information available. This can be linked to the survey data at different levels of geography using the nomenclature of territorial units for statistics (NUTS) classification devised by Eurostat for producing European Union (EU) regional statistics (Rydland et al. 2007). One potentially important source of contextual information for political scientists is information on the content of media coverage. The amount and tone of media coverage of particular events, including (but not limited to) election campaigns, has the potential to influence individual attitudes and behavior, and differences in media coverage may help to explain differences in outcomes across countries or across time (see, for example, Vliegenthart et al. 2008). To enable researchers to study and control for such media effects, the ESS makes information on the topics and tone of media coverage available alongside the main survey data.

5   THE FUTURE: DO WE STILL NEED SURVEYS?

The contribution that surveys have made to political science – and social science more generally – over the past 80 years is undeniable. Demand for the types of insight surveys can provide is higher than ever. In many respects, there has never been a better time to use surveys given the number of high-quality data sets available and the continued development of new statistical techniques allowing more sophisticated analysis of these data.

However, surveys also face uncertainty as they try to adapt to a changing society and the emergence of new technology (Couper 2013). The cost of delivering high quality surveys is rising whilst participation rates are falling (Groves 2011). The Internet has made it possible to collect large amounts of data quickly and cheaply. However, there are concerns that opt-in web panels cannot provide data of comparable quality to other surveys (Callegaro et al. 2014).

The challenges facing survey research, together with the growing availability of data from other sources, raises the question of whether there is a continued need for surveys. 'Big data' automatically generated as a result of government administration, commercial transactions and social media now swamp the availability of survey data (Mayer-Schönberger and Cukler 2013). Savage and Burrows (2007, p. 891) contend that 'where data on whole populations are routinely gathered as a by-product of institutional transactions, the sample survey seems a very poor instrument'.

However, while the growth in what Groves (2011) terms 'organic data' undoubtedly offers opportunities to researchers, such data also face a number of limitations which means they cannot compete with 'designed' survey data on the key attributes of representativeness, reliability, validity or availability. Some of the main limitations associated with organic data include: incomplete coverage, that is, unrepresentativeness given that certain types of people are more likely to use Twitter or store loyalty cards; possible measurement bias in data originally intended for a different purpose (for example, do people tell the truth on Facebook?); lack of consistency in the way data are generated, especially a lack of continuity over time as technology changes; and the proprietary nature of data which may be available to researchers only at high cost, if at all (Couper 2013). User-generated organic data are a useful addition to, rather than a replacement for, survey data. Specifically designed sample surveys will continue to provide insights into the thoughts, aspirations and behaviors of large populations in ways that data tracking naturally occurring behaviors are unlikely ever to capture (Groves 2011).

The amount and types of data available – from surveys and other sources – will continue to expand. It is essential that those involved in survey data collection adhere to the principles of good survey design, thereby ensuring that sources of error are minimized and the key strengths of surveys as a source of valid and reliable data representative of the population of interest are maintained. They must also fully document the process and, wherever possible, make the data and documentation freely available to other researchers so as to maximize their value. At the same time, there is an obligation on data users to think critically about their choice of data and select the data source that is most suitable for answering their research questions. We hope that the issues and examples highlighted in this chapter will help with this task.

NOTES

1. www.surveymonkey.com.
2. www.lissdata.nl.
3. http://www.gesis.org/en/services/data-collection/gesis-panel/.
4. www.europeansocialsurvey.org.
5. http://ukdataservice.ac.uk/get-data/other-providers/question-banks.aspx.
6. www.europeansocialsurvey.org.

FURTHER REFERENCES

De Leeuw, E., J. Hox and D. Dillman (2008), *International Handbook of Survey Methodology*, New York: Taylor and Francis.
De Vaus, D. (2013), *Surveys in Social Research*, 6th edn, London: Routledge.
ESOMAR/WAPOR guide to opinion polls and published surveys:http://wapor.org/esomarwapor-guide-to-opinion-polls/.
Groves, R., F.J. Fowler, M. Couper, J. Lepkowski, E. Singer and R. Tourangeau (2009), *Survey Methodology*, 2nd edn, New York: Wiley.
Jowell, R., C. Roberts, R. Fitzgerald and G. Eva (2007), *Measuring Attitudes Cross-Nationally: Lessons from the ESS*, London: Sage.

REFERENCES

Almond, G. and S. Verba (1963), *The Civic Culture: Political Attitudes and Democracy in Five Nations*, Newbury Park, CA: Sage.
Atkeson, L. (2010), 'The state of survey research as a research tool in American politics', in J.E. Leighley (ed.), *The Oxford Handbook of American Elections and Political Behaviour*, Oxford: Oxford University Press.

Biemer, P. and L. Lyberg (2003), *Introduction to Survey Quality*, New York: Wiley.
Brady, H.E. (2000), 'Contributions of survey research to political science', *Journal of Political Science and Politics*, **33** (1), 47–57.
Bradburn, N., S. Sudman and B. Wansink (2004), *Asking Questions: The Definitive Guide to Questionnaire Design – for Market Research, Political Polls and Social and Health Questionnaires*, San Francisco, CA: John Wiley and Sons.
Butler, D. and D. Stokes (1969), *Political Change in Britain: Forces Shaping Electoral Choice*, New York: St Martin's Press.
Callegaro, M., R. Baker, J. Bethlehem, A. Goritz, J.A. Krosnick and P. Lavrakas (eds) (2014), *Online Panel Research: A Data Quality Perspective*, Chichester, UK: John Wiley and Sons.
Couper, M. (2013), 'Is the sky falling? New technology, changing media and the future of surveys', *Survey Research Methods*, **7** (3), 145–56.
De Leeuw, E. (2008), 'Self-administered questionnaires and standardized interviews', *The Sage Handbook of Social Research Methods*, London: Sage, pp. 235–313.
Druckman, J.N., D.P. Green, J.H. Kuklinski and A. Lupia (2006), 'The growth and development of experimental research in political science', *American Political Science Review*, **100** (4), 627–35.
Evans, G. and S. Whitefield (1995), 'The politics and economics of democratic commitment: support for democracy in transition societies', *British Journal of Political Science*, **25** (4), 485–514.
Groves, R.M. (2011), 'Three eras of survey research', *Public Opinion Quarterly*, **75** (5), 861–71.
Groves, R.M., J. Bethlehem, J. Diez Medrando, P. Gundelach and P. Norris (2008), *Report of the Review Panel for the European Social Survey*, Strasbourg: European Science Foundation.
Groves, R.M., F.J. Fowler, M. Couper, J. Lepkowski, E. Singer and R. Tourangeau (2009), *Survey Methodology*, 2nd edn, New York: Wiley.
Häder, S. and P. Lynn (2007), 'How representative can a multi-nation survey be?', in R. Jowell, C. Roberts, R. Fitzgerald and G. Eva (eds), *Measuring Attitudes Cross-Nationally: Lessons from the European Social Survey*, London: Sage, pp. 33–52.
Harkness, J. (2007), 'Improving the quality of translations', in R. Jowell, C. Roberts, R. Fitzgerald and G. Eva (eds), *Measuring Attitudes Cross-Nationally: Lessons from the European Social Survey*, London: Sage, pp. 79–93.
Heath, A., S. Fisher and S. Smith (2005), 'The globalisation of public opinion research', *Annual Review of Political Science*, **8**, 297–333.
Inglehart, R. (1977), *The Silent Revolution: Changing Values and Political Styles Among Western Publics*, Princeton, NJ: Princeton University Press.
Jowell, R. (1998), 'How comparative is comparative research?' Economics and Social Research Council, Centre for Research into Elections and Social Trends, Working Paper No. 66, September.
Jowell, R., R. Fitzgerald, C. Roberts and G. Eva (2007), *Measuring Attitudes Cross Nationally*, London: Sage.
Krosnick, J.A. and S. Presser (2010), 'Question and questionnaire design', in J.D. Wright and P.V. Marsden (eds), *Handbook of Survey Research*, 2nd edn, Bingley: Emerald Group, pp. 263–313.
Mayer-Schönberger, V. and K. Cukier (2013), *Big Data: A Revolution that Will Transform How We Live, Work, and Think*, London: Houghton Mifflin Harcourt.
Presser, S., J. Rothgeb, M.P. Couper, J.T. Lessler, E. Martin, J. Martin and E. Singer (eds), (2004), *Methods for Testing and Evaluating Survey Questionnaires*, Hoboken, NJ: Wiley.
Prestage, Y. and A. Humphreys (2013), *SAGE Research Methods Cases: The European Social Survey*, London: Sage.
Putnam, R. (2000), *Bowling Alone: The Collapse and Revival of American Community*, New York: Simon and Schuster.
Roberts, C. (2007), 'Mixing modes of data collection: a methodological review', Economic

and Social Research Council (ESRC) National Centre for Research Methods Briefing Paper NCRM/008, ESRC, Southampton.

Rydland, L.T., S. Arnesen and A.G. Østensen (2007), 'Contextual data for the European Social Survey: an overview and assessment of extant sources', Norwegian Social Science Data Services, Bergen.

Savage, M. and R. Burrows (2007), 'The coming crisis of empirical sociology', *Sociology*, **41** (5), 885–99.

Seyd, P. and P. Whiteley (2004), 'British party members: an overview', *Party Politics*, **10** (4), 355–66.

Smith, T. (2004), 'Developing and evaluating cross-national survey instruments', in S. Presser, J.M. Rothgeb, M.P. Couper, J.T. Lessler, E. Martin, J. Martin and E. Singer (eds), *Methods for Testing and Evaluating Survey Questionnaires*, New York: Wiley, pp. 431–52.

Smith, P. (2008), 'Is random probability sampling really much better than quota sampling?', Ipsos MORI internal research paper, unpublished.

Stoop, I., J. Billiet, A. Kock and R. Fitzgerald (2010), *Improving Survey Response Lessons Learned from the European Social Survey*, Chichester, UK: John Wiley and Sons.

Verba, S. and N. Nie (1972), *Participation in America: Political Democracy and Social Equality*, New York: Harper and Row.

Vliegenthart, R., A.R. Schuck, H.G. Boomgaarden and C.H. de Vreese (2008), 'News coverage and support for European integration, 1990–2006', *International Journal of Public Opinion Research*, **20** (4), 415–39.

Walczak, A. and W. van der Brug (2013), 'Representation in the European Parliament: factors affecting the attitude congruence of voters and candidates in the EP elections', *European Union Politics*, **14** (1), 3–22.

Willis, G.B. (2005), *Cognitive Interviewing: A Tool for Improving Questionnaire Design*, Thousand Oaks, CA: Sage.

Winstone, L., S. Widdop and R. Fitzgerald (2016), 'Constructing the questionnaire: the challenges of measuring attitudes towards democracy across Europe', in M. Ferrin and H. Kriesi (eds), *How Europeans View and Evaluate Democracy*, Oxford: Oxford University Press, pp. 21–39.

APPENDIX

Table 18A.1 Cross-national surveys available for secondary analysis

Survey	Coverage	Mode	Topics of interest	Data available (at September 2016)	Websites (at September 2016)
Global					
World Values Survey	>180 countries	Face to face or telephone (in remote areas); internet and mail (in exceptional circumstances)	Examples from 2010–14: priorities for country; desired characteristics for society and democracy; interest in politics; political action; voting – local and national elections; perceptions of corruption in elections	1981–84; 1990–94; 1995–98; 1999–2004; 2005–09; 2010–14	Information and Data: http://www. worldvaluessurvey.org/ wvs.jsp
Comparative Study of Electoral systems	>50 countries	Face to face, telephone or self-completion; also combination of telephone and self-completion or face to face and self-completion	Vote choice; evaluations of candidate, party, current and retrospective economic performance and of the electoral system itself. District level data for each respondent. System level data on aggregate electoral returns, electoral rules and formulas, and regime characteristics	1996–2001; 2001–06; 2006–11; 2011–16	Information: http://www.cses.org/ Data registration: http:// www.cses.org/verify. htm

Survey	Countries	Mode	Content	Frequency	Information and data
International Social Survey Programme (ISSP)	c. 50 countries	Face to face or self-completion	Specific modules on citizenship (2004, 2014) and role of government (1985, 1990, 1996, 2006)	Annual survey: 1985–2014	Information: http://www.issp.org/index.php Data: http://www.gesis.org/en/issp/search-and-data-access/
European European Values Study	47 countries	Face to face	Political interest; willingness to join in political actions; left–right placement; post-materialism; support for democracy	1981; 1990; 1999; 2008	Information and data: http://www.gesis.org/en/services/data-analysis/survey-data/rdc-international-survey-programs/european-values-study/
European Quality of Life Survey	>34 countries	Face to face	Unpaid voluntary work in political party/trade union; participation in political activities; trust in institutions; political trust; quality of public services	2003; 2007; 2011–12	Information: http://www.eurofound.europa.eu/surveys/eqls/index.htm Data: http://www.eurofound.europa.eu/surveys/availability/index.htm
European Social Survey	>30 countries	Face to face	Every survey: political interest; trust; efficacy; political participation; party allegiance and socio-political orientations; (2002–03) 43 questions on citizenship, involvement	Biennial: 2002–03; 2004–05; 2006–07; 2008–09; 2010–11; 2012–13; 2014-15	Information: www.europeansocialsurvey.org Data: http://www.europeansocialsurvey.org/data/round-index.html

Table 18A.1 (continued)

Survey	Coverage	Mode	Topics of interest	Data available (at September 2016)	Websites (at September 2016)
European Social Survey			and democracy; (2012–13) 45 questions on understandings and evaluations of democracy		
European Barometers					
Standard Eurobarometer	>30 countries	Face to face; telephone interviewing (in some countries)	Examples from 2013: political attitudes and behaviors – including life in the European Union; the Europeans and the financial crisis; EU 2020 objectives; EU citizenship and media use in the EU	Several times a year: 1974–2015	Information: http://ec.europa.eu/COMMFrontOffice/PublicOpinion/ Data: http://www.gesis.org/eurobarometer-data-service/survey-series/standard-special-eb/
Central and Eastern Eurobarometer	>20 Eastern European countries	Face to face	Economic and political trends; evaluation of economic and democratic reforms; perception of Europe & the European Union and its role in Eastern Europe	Annually: 1990–97	Information and data: http://www.gesis.org/eurobarometer-data-service/survey-series/central-eastern-eb/

	Countries	Method	Topics	Years	Information and data
Candidate countries – Eurobarometer	13 countries (all applied for 2001 EU membership)	Face to face	Political participation and trust in institutions; attitudes towards & information about the EU; European Parliament elections; attitudes towards and knowledge about the enlargement process; the future of Europe etc.	Yearly: 2000; 2001; 2004 and Several times a year: 2002 and 2003	Information and data: http://www.gesis.org/eurobarometer-data-service/survey-series/candidate-countries-eb/

Global Barometers

	Countries	Method	Topics	Years	Information and data
Americas Barometer	26 countries – North, Central and South America and Caribbean	Face to face in all countries except Canada and the US who use an online panel	Left-right and liberal-conservative scales; community participation; political action; pride in political systems in country; political trust; democracy; social and political tolerance; corruption	Biennial: 2004, 2006, 2008, 2010, 2012	Information: http://www.vanderbilt.edu/lapop/index.php Data: http://www.vanderbilt.edu/lapop/request-datasets.php
Afrobarometer	> 35 countries	Face to face	Public opinions on democracy, governance; social capital; political participation; national identity	1999–2001; 2002–03; 2005–06; 2008–10; 2011–13; 2014–15	Information: http://www.afrobarometer.org/index.php Data: http://www.afrobarometer.org/data
Asian Barometer	13 countries (3 rounds); 8 countries (1 round)	Face to face	Trust in institutions; social capital; political participation; electoral	2001–03; 2005–08; 2010–12; 2013–16	Information: http://www.asianbarometer.org/

Table 18A.1 (continued)

Survey	Coverage	Mode	Topics of interest	Data available (at September 2016)	Websites (at September 2016)
Asian Barometer			mobilization; citizen involvement and partisanship; regime legitimacy and citizen preferences for democracy; efficacy; citizen empowerment; system responsiveness; democratic vs. authoritarian values		intro/program-overview Application form for data files: http://www.asianbarometer.org/survey/data-release
Global Barometers					
(South) Caucasus Barometer	3 countries – Armenia, Azerbaijan and Georgia	Face to face	Socio-economic issues and political attitudes – including participation in political activities; perception of domestic politics; political trust in 17 different groups; issues facing the country; fair treatment by the government; freedom of speech; role of government; protest actions; voting	Annually 2008–15	Information: http://caucasusbarometer.org/en/about/ Data: http://caucasusbarometer.org/en/datasets/

19 Quantitative data analysis in political science
Paul Pennings

1 INTRODUCTION

Three important issues in doing social science research are the causality problem (how to theorize), the classification problem (how to conceptualize) and the scalability problem (how to operationalize). These issues are equally important for both quantitative and qualitative research. In this chapter the focus is on quantitative techniques, in particular the various ways in which numerical data can be analyzed in order to generate meaningful pattern and results. These techniques are often used in studies on elections, political participation, economic trends, government expenditures and so on (Pennings et al. 2006).

Two types of quantitative data analysis are available. The first type is explorative and confirmative analysis using statistical techniques such as scalability analysis, factor analysis and cluster analysis (see also Chapters 24 and 29 in this volume). These techniques help to conceptualize and operationalize by determining the degree to which variables are (dis)similar. If variables are very similar they might as well be merged into a single category or dimension.

The second type is multivariate causal analysis. The main methods for causal data analysis are cross-table elaboration, analysis of variance and (most importantly) regression analysis. These techniques help to explore the interrelationships between multiple (dependent and independent) variables (see, for a detailed overview and description, Tufte 1974; Pennings et al. 2006; Chapters 22 and 24 in this volume).

In this chapter these techniques are introduced and applied to the party manifestos database (MARPOR, see Box 19.1) (Volkens et al. 2013). These applications serve as examples of how the techniques can be used and the type of results and conclusions that can be derived from them (all based on a selection of 20 advanced democracies for the years 1960–2013).

BOX 19.1   THE MANIFESTO PROJECT: MARPOR

The general purpose of the Manifesto Project for the past 30 years has been to measure political preferences of parties across time and space. The project is based on quantitative content analyses of parties' election programs from more than 50 countries covering all free, democratic elections since 1945. (https://manifestoproject.wzb.eu/).

---

2 DISCUSSION AND APPLICATIONS OF EXPLORATIVE AND CONFIRMATIVE ANALYSIS

A number of explorative and confirmative analyses are frequently used in political science. Among them are scalability analysis and factor analysis. These techniques focus on the (dis)similarity of variables: to which extent do they fit together in a scale or dimension?

2.1   Scalability Analysis

Often a variety of related indicators of a concept can be imagined. Which of them measure the concept in a valid way? We may solve this theoretically or empirically. In party manifesto research, for example, references to 'law and order', negative references to 'welfare state expansion' and references to 'free enterprise' may be considered as signs of a rightist party ideology. This is an interpretative way of deciding on the 'best' indicators.

However, often it is quite likely that there is a considerable mismatch between what we theoretically expects and what the empirical data show us. In the previous example, it is possible that also right-wing parties refer positively to 'welfare state expansion' because they want to please voters and because they are (like all parties) part of mixed economies in which welfare policies are basically accepted by all parties, irrespective of their color. In order to argue that items form a scale (that is, belong together) we will often need empirical proof, not just expectations.

Scalability analysis tests whether multiple indicators build up to a scale (see Box 19.2). The aim of scalability analysis is to test whether indicators really 'add up'. We should not expect perfect scales from party manifesto data since a party may pick up only one issue from a set of related issues in a given campaign.

As an example we will use the indicators for Laver and Budge's concept of 'state intervention' (Laver and Budge 1992, pp. 23–5). Five of the 54 categories used in the content analysis project are assumed to measure

---

BOX 19.2   SCALABILITY ANALYSIS

Scalability analysis measures the extent to which items measure the same underlying concept.

Scale: a measurement instrument composed of a collection of items that combine into a total score to reveal the level of a latent variable.

Likert scale: presents respondents with statements and asks to what degree they agree or disagree with the statements.

Cronbach's alpha: a common statistical method for measuring reliability by analyzing how responses to each item in a scale relate to each other.

Error: the lack of accuracy in a scale by taking the difference between a perfectly accurate scale (1) and a scale's reliability (that is, Cronbach's alpha), which ranges from 0 to 1.

---

state intervention, that is, the percentages of programs devoted to 'regulation of capitalism', 'economic planning', 'protectionism: positive', 'controlled economy' and 'nationalization'. The percentages devoted to these categories are simply added to measure 'state intervention'. Laver and Budge assume on the basis of face validity that these indicators measure the same underlying concept.

Scalability analysis can help to remove non-scalable items which are identical, parallel or 'repeated' measurements of one concept. The resulting Likert scale is a summative scale that cancels out the errors in the separate indicators. This scale discerns the units of analysis more precisely than the separate indicators because there are less measurement errors (Pennings et al. 2006).

Cronbach's alpha is used to test whether summing separate indicators adds to the discriminating power of the theoretical concept. The value of Cronbach's alpha tends to increase when the number of indicators increases, since errors are cancelled more easily when the number of indicators increases. As a rule-of-thumb test, psychologists and survey sociologists use a minimum value for alpha of roughly $+0.67$. Within the context of the Manifesto content analysis of party programs, less stringent criteria should be applied, since authors of party programs, as opposed to respondents in survey research, feel free to address only one theme from a set of more or less related themes.

Since Laver and Budge added their five indicators of 'state interventionism' without giving them weights, a test of their scale using Cronbach's will show whether they all measure the same underlying concept. Table 19.1 presents the results for the percentage indicators of state interventionism plus the dichotomized indicators of this concept. Cronbach's alpha is positive ($+0.59$), although too low by the standards for Likert attitude

Table 19.1   Scalability analysis: Cronbach's alpha for five items of 'state intervention'

	Percentage indicators α = +0.29 (column below: α with indicator excluded*)	Dichotomized indicators α = +0.59 (column below: α with indicator excluded)
Market regulation (403)	0.27	0.54
Economic planning (404)	0.24	0.50
Protectionism: positive (406)	0.28	0.58
Controlled economy (412)	0.12	0.51
Nationalization (413)	0.16	0.51

Note: * The percentage refers to Cronbach's alpha after the item has been excluded: if alpha is lower than 0.29 (left-hand column) or 0.59 (right-hand column) the item should not be removed.

scales. The moderate value of alpha suggests that parties tend to address issues from the same issue group of 'state intervention' but that they will often focus on one or a few of them. If we take into account that parties were not forced in any way to address the themes that were put forward by the Manifesto researchers, the alpha-score of +0.59 is sufficiently high to warrant unweighted addition of the issues.

To test whether all the indicators indeed belong to the same scale, values for Cronbach's alpha are also computed when specific items are removed from the scale. If Cronbach's alpha increases when a specific indicator is removed from the scale, then that indicator apparently did not belong to the scale. The alpha values in both the left and the right columns show that the deletion of protectionism would hardly affect the scale; it is redundant.

The discussion of scalability analysis has shown that a scale or index should not be taken for granted. It is wise to test the internal consistency of the scale. Not only scalability analysis but also factor analysis can be used for that goal.

2.2   Factor Analysis

'Factor analysis' summarizes the variability among observed, correlated variables by means of a potentially lower number of unobserved variables called factors (see Box 19.3). It differs in one important aspect from scalability analysis. It often does not depart from a theoretical concept but indicates which indicators measure the same underlying concept which is unknown when the analysis starts. Factor analysis has many variants.

BOX 19.3   TERMINOLOGY OF FACTOR ANALYSIS

Factor analysis summarizes the variability among observed, correlated variables by means of a potentially lower number of unobserved variables called factors.
Factor: the extracted dimension.
Factor scores: the scores of the units of analysis on the factors.
Communality: the explained variance in an indicator by the factor. When there are as many principal components as variables, then the communality for all variables is 1.
Eigenvalue: the degree to which one factor explains the variance in the selected items.

Table 19.2   Factor analysis: results of a principal component analysis

Variable	Communality	Factor	Eigenvalue	Pct of Var.	Cum. Pct
Regulation (403)	0.36	1.00	1.927	38.5	38.5
Economic planning (404)	0.46				
Protectionism: positive (406)	0.23				
Controlled economy (412)	0.44				
Nationalisation (413)	0.44				

Principal components analysis is the simplest type, and is based on the same principle as Cronbach's alpha. The weighted scale should discern the units of analysis more succinctly than the separate indicators, since measurement errors in the latter hamper their discerning power. The factor scores – weights for the separate indicators – are ascertained in such a way that the discriminatory power (variance) of the underlying concept is maximized.

Table 19.2 shows the results from the principal components analysis on the five indicators for 'state intervention' (see Box 19.3 for an explanation of the terminology). The largest eigenvalue is 1.927 which indicates that the power of the resulting scale of 'state interventionism' to distinguish between the various party programs under investigation is 1.9 times as high as the power of separate indicators to do so. Since five items were included in the component, this amounts to an explained variance in the values of the indicators by the ultimate values on the concept of 'state interventionism' of 1.927 / 5 = 0.385, or 38.5 per cent. Since 100 – 38.5 per cent of unique variation in the indicators remains, it is safe to conclude that the concept 'state interventionism' is not able to capture the larger part of the variation in the attention of parties for each of the separate five indicators of 'state interventionism'.

The disadvantage of factor analysis is that it provides no information on the meaning or correct interpretation of the extracted dimension(s). Since interpretation plays an important role in its usage, one should be careful with this technique.

Taken together the techniques discussed above offer different ways to analyze the (dis)similarity of variables. They present valuable techniques to bridge the gap between concept and measurement since the results are indicative for the degree of internal and/or external validity.

3   DISCUSSION AND APPLICATIONS OF MULTIVARIATE CAUSAL ANALYSIS

A limitation of the previously discussed techniques is that they are rather descriptive. In order to explain one needs to utilize different techniques such as cross tables, analysis of variance and regression.

3.1   Cross-Table Elaboration

The method of analyzing multivariate relationships with cross tables is called cross-table elaboration. A cross table offers a way to categorize units into groups that are defined by the researcher. Here we will illustrate the method for three variables. The general idea is that the relationship between the two variables of primary interest, x and y – in our example, the relationship between left–right ideology and state interventionism – should be split up for each category of the remaining nominal variable z – in our example, for each state of the economy and the electoral system. Thus, the relationship between state interventionism, the electoral system and economic tide is shown in partial tables for each value of z. In the jargon of cross-table elaboration, they are held constant.

When the variable being controlled for is either an intervening variable or an exogenous variable responsible for spurious correlation, the associations in the partial tables will be small compared with the bivariate association (see Box 19.4). The column percentages in corresponding cells of the partial tables will be equal to each other. When the variable being controlled for is an interacting variable the association should be strong in some partial tables but low in others.

Table 19.3 shows how left-right relates to state interventionism which is dichotomized at the median (which value is 4). Nearly 60 percent of the left parties is interventionist and 41.5 percent is non-interventionist.

BOX 19.4 SPURIOUS RELATIONSHIP

A statistical relationship in which two variables that have no direct causal connection are wrongly inferred that they do, owing to the presence of a certain third,
unseen factor (confounding variable). By introducing this third variable and by
testing whether it affects the correlation between the two main variables that one
is interested in we can make this problem observable.

Table 19.3 Cross-table between right–left ideology and the degree of state
interventionism (row percentages)

	Interventionist	Non-interventionist	Total (n)
Left	58.5	41.5	1000
Right	23.8	76.2	923
Total	41.9	58.1	1923

Note: Phi = 0.35, p = .000.

Of the right parties 76.2 percent is non-interventionist and 23.8 percent
is interventionist. The overall correlation between right–left ideology and
state interventionism is 0.35 which is remarkably low. This means that
there is not a one-to-one relationship between party ideology and state
interventionism. One important reason may be that the selected countries
are all advanced mixed economies in which both state and market play an
important role in public policy-making.

This is also indicated by the correlations between state interventionism,
economic tide and electoral systems (Table 19.4).

The weak correlations indicate that the economic tide and type of electoral system hardly matter for the degree of state interventionism, although
such correlations are suggested in the literature. We should control for a
third variable if there is a strong theoretical reason to do so and/or if the
impact of such a variable has been shown in the literature. In our example
the absence of such a third factor implies that party ideologies are quite
rigid and do not vary a lot between time periods and electoral systems.

3.2 Analysis of Variance

Models for the analysis of variance (ANOVA) have a dependent variable
with an interval level of measurement (see Box 19.5). In ANOVA models
may include multiple independent nominal variables, interactions between

Table 19.4   Correlations between state interventionism, economic tide and electoral systems

	Economic tide		Electoral systems	
	Low	High	Proportional representation	Majoritarian
State interventionism	0.36	0.31	0.36	0.34
n	1329	594	1387	536

Note: Economic tide is based on the time periods 1960–85 (low), 2000–2014 (low), 1985–2000 (high).

BOX 19.5   TERMINOLOGY OF ANALYSIS OF VARIANCE

ANOVA provides a statistical test of whether or not the means of several groups are equal.

Sum of squares (*SS*): the squared distance between each data point (*Yi*) and the sample mean, summed for all *N* data points.

Degrees of freedom (*Df*): the numbers of pieces of information about the 'noise' from which an investigator wishes to extract the 'signal'. This is one less than the samples or levels of the explanatory variable ($a - 1$), (for example, four nations, giving three degrees of freedom for the effect).

The mean-square (*MS*): the average sum of squares, in other words the sum of squared deviations from the mean *X* divided by the appropriate degrees of freedom.

F-ratio: reveals the significance of the hypothesis that *Y* depends on *X*. It comprises the ratio of two mean-squares: within groups and between groups. A large proportion indicates a significant effect of *X*.

Significance: the probability of mistakenly rejecting a null hypothesis that is actually true. Normally it should be lower than 0,05.

Interaction effect: the degree to which a combination of two independent variables affect the dependent variable.

---

the various nominal independent variables and covariates – variables with a higher level of measurement – as additional independent variables to explain the value of the independent interval variable. Many other specifications, such as repeated measurements or varying contrast groups, can also be handled by ANOVA models.

The printed output of the analysis of variance deals primarily with the statistical significance of nominal variables and their interactions. Thus, if we are interested in general questions, such as whether nominal variables or their interactions have an effect on the dependent variable at all, ANOVA output should be requested. If we are interested in the

Table 19.5   Analysis of variance on the degree of state interventionism

Source	Type III sum of squares	df	F-ratio	Sig.
Model	48 358.442	6	425.244	.000
rightleft	3 433.134	1	181.138	.000
elsys	389.748	1	20.564	.000
tide	716.190	1	37.787	.000
rightleft * elsys	11.464	1	.605	.437
rightleft * tide	235.892	1	12.446	.000
Error	36 333.269	1917		
Total	84 691.710	1923		

Note: * Means interaction effect. See Box 19.7 for the terminology.

precise effects of specific conditions, the regression approach is to be preferred.

Table 19.5 shows the degree to which state interventionism differs per right–left ideology, electoral system and economic tide: these are the variables that have been explored previously by means of cross-table elaboration (see Box 19.5 for the terminology used in the table). The difference is that we can now detect the relative impact (indicated by the *F*-ratio) of these nominal variables plus the interaction effects. Table 19.5 confirms the patterns that were previously indicated by the cross table. Right–left ideology is the most important discriminating factor and variations in economic tide are slightly more important than variations in electoral systems. There is only one significant interaction effects between right–left and tide (meaning that left parties become slightly more interventionist than right parties when the economic tide is high). Since this effect is small, the results mean that the preferences of right and left parties for more or less state interventionism are context independent. Parties are characterized by ideological rigidity and will not easily change or adapt their ideological profile because this might alienate voters and hence cost votes (Budge et al. 2012).

3.3   Regression Analysis

Regression analysis is probably the most frequently used technique for data analysis in political science (see, for the assumptions, Chapters 22 and 24 in this volume). Regression analysis is the appropriate technique whenever dependent and independent variables have an interval level of measurement (see Box 19.6).

Regression itself cannot indicate the degree of causality since this is a

---

BOX 19.6   TERMINOLOGY OF REGRESSION

Regressions are used to measure and describe the relationship between two variables, X and Y (bivariate regression).

The linear model for regression is: $Y_i = \beta_0 + \beta_1 X_i + \varepsilon_i$ for a population.

The 'Y' variable: the dependent variable or response variable (vertical axis).

The 'X' variable: the independent variable or predictor variable (horizontal axis). If there is more than one predictor the analysis is called a multiple regression.

The β_0 value: the value of Y at the point where the line crosses the Y axis. This value is called the intercept.

The β_1 value: the slope that gives the change in Y per unit of X. It determines the incline or angle of the regression line.

The values ε_i (error term): the deviations of the observations from the regression line.

The t statistic: the beta coefficient divided by its standard error. The higher a coefficient compared to its standard error, the higher will be the t-value.

---

theoretical and a methodological problem. From a methodological angle causal statements rest on a comparison in time, in space or in both. If particular combinations of values on two separate variables occur more frequently than expected on the basis of the frequency distributions of the separate variables, then these variables are related to each other in a statistical sense (see also Boxes 19.4 and 19.7).

A causal relationship assumes not merely a statistical relationship, but also a time dimension and a direction. A causal effect of a variable x on a variable y implies that changing the value of x will produce another value of y after a (short or long) while. The concept of causality implies the concept of an *independent* variable and a *dependent* variable. A causal relationship is a unidirectional relationship ($x \rightarrow y$). Reciprocal causal relationships ($x \leftarrow\rightarrow y$) can be understood as two separate causal unidirectional relationships. A variable x is said to have an effect on a nominal variable y when changing x's value will, after a while, increase

---

BOX 19.7   CORRELATION COEFFICIENT

The Pearson product-moment correlation coefficient, also known as r, R, or Pearson's r, is a measure of the strength and direction of the linear relationship between two variables (interval measurement) without any causal claim or proof.

It should be distinguished from the so-called Rank correlation that is used for rankings of different variables (ordinal measurement) or different rankings of the same variable.

the chance that variable y will show a particular value. In the case of an ordinal, interval or ratio dependent variable y, causality means that changing x's value increases the chance that y will increase (or decrease) after a while. A linear causal relationship exists when the ratio of the resulting change in the dependent variable to the preceding change in the independent variable is a given constant, regardless of the starting values of the dependent and the independent variable, or the precise history of the causal process.

Regression offers a number of ways to study causal relationships (see for some examples on politics and policy, Tufte 1974). We can determine the relative weight of the causal factors; the absence of a causal impact can be measured; the total weight of all factors (R^2) shows whether important factors have been omitted; the impact of the factors per country can be studied by means of analysis of the residuals; the combined causal impact of variables can be studied (interactions); the indirect effects can be studied. We will demonstrate some of these features in our application of regression that seeks to explain policy preferences in favor of free market, economic planning, welfare statism and international peace by two competing variables: right–left party ideology and the right–left median voter position. These two independent variables represent the main theoretical positions in the debate on party responsiveness (Budge at al. 2012):

- the Downsian model: $Y = a + (b \times \text{median voter position}) + e$;
- the salience model: $Y = a + (b \times \text{ideology}) + e$;
- the combined model: $Y = a + (b \times \text{ideology}) + (b \times \text{median voter position}) + e$.

The Downsian model predicts that party policy positions reflect the median voter position. The salience model predicts that parties are rigid and will stick to their own ideological profile. The combined model integrates these two models by predicting that the emphasis on a policy area is a function of both ideology and public opinion. Table 19.6 shows the results of a regression analysis on the combined models for four policy areas (see Box 19.6 for an explanation of the terminology). The results on the basis of these computations do provide more support for the saliency model than for the Downsian model. Parties are to a large extent ideologically driven and are less inclined to adapt their policy profiles to shifting voter preferences.

The explained variance (Adj. R^2) is rather low. This is interesting as it means that both right and left parties are likely to put some emphasis on these policy domains. Often it is illuminating to have not only a look the relationship s between variables (as in Table 19.6), but also at the

Table 19.6   *A regression analysis of policy output on party ideology and*
             median voter positions

	Market		Planning		Welfare		International peace	
	Beta	*t*	Beta	*t*	Beta	*t*	Beta	*t*
Right-left	0.62	30.4	−0.42	−18.4	−0.45	−20.4	−0.38	−16.3
Median voter	−.14	−6.9	−.05	−2.2	−0.04	−2.0	0.03	1.1
Adj. R^2		0.34		0.19		0.22		0.14

Note: See Box 19.7 for the terminology.

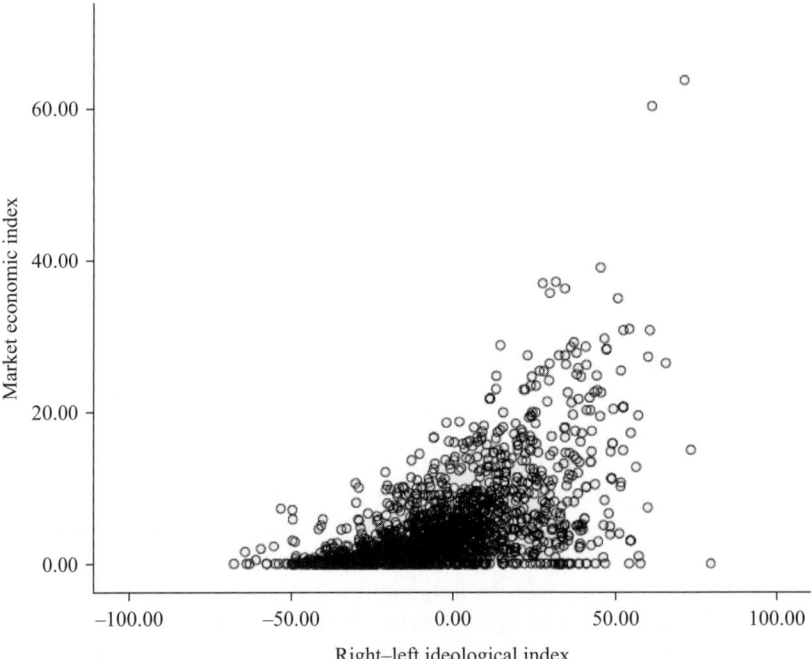

Figure 19.1   *Scatter plot of the right–left scale (X) and the market*
               positions (Y)

distribution of the cases by means of a scatter plot. Figure 19.1 shows
such a plot between the right–left scale (X) and the market positions (Y).
Scores below 0 can be considered as left as higher than 0 as right. The plot
confirms that many left parties score positive on pro-market economy, but

right parties have on average relatively higher scores. The plot shows that many right and left parties have comparable scores on market economy. This can be explained by the fact that all included countries are capitalist democracies in which markets play an important role in both the private and the public economy. The plot also indicates that this issue is more salient in some countries than in others given the many low scores on market economy which indicate low saliency.

Regression is a powerful technique to assess the strength of (assumed) causal relationships. Similar to most quantitative techniques, it allows for both a variable-oriented and a case-oriented analysis of causality. Often the combination of both types is most fruitful. The regression in our example shows that the causal impact of right–left ideology is much stronger than the effect of the right–left median voter position. This, again, underlines the rigid ideological right–left positions that more or less drive the policy positions on market, planning, welfare and international peace. Similar results are also found in case of cross-table elaboration and ANOVA which also show the relative strong impact of ideology.

4   CONCLUSION

This chapter discussed the basics of the main types of quantitative data analysis and applied them to text analysis of party manifestos. The results show that these forms of analysis provide great tools to reveal patterned variations in data, provided that no assumptions are violated (see Chapters 22 and 24 in this volume) and concepts are measured adequately. The chapter shows that all the methods produce more or less the same outcomes. Therefore the choice of the 'proper' technique to analyze data is, to some extent, a matter of taste.

The explorative techniques help to bridge the gap between concepts and measurement. They are important tools to assess the internal and/ or external validity of measurements. The explanatory techniques help to validate a causal relationship that is often the most central component of theories. Although these techniques are helpful, their outcomes are strongly dependent on the case selection, the operationalization and the non-violation of assumptions.

FURTHER READING

Discussion of the basics of doing social science research from a quantifying (positivist) perspective:

King, G., R. Keohane and S. Verba (1994), *Designing Social Inquiry*, Princeton, NJ: Princeton University Press, pp. 99–114.
A general introduction to multivariate statistics and applications in political science:
Pennings, P., H. Keman and J. Kleinnijenhuis (2006), *Doing Research in Political Science. An Introduction to Comparative Methods and Statistics*, London: Sage.
A practical guide for doing statistical analysis using software:
Field, A. (2013), *Discovering Statistics using IBM SPSS Statistics*, London: Sage (also available for R and SAS, see: http://www.statisticshell.com/).

REFERENCES

Budge, I., H. Keman, M. McDonald and P. Pennings (2012), *Organizing Democratic Choice: Party Representation Over Time*, Oxford: Oxford University Press.
Laver, M. and I. Budge (1992), *Party Policy and Government Coalitions*, Houndmills: Macmillan.
Pennings, P., H. Keman, J. Kleinnijenhuis (2006), *Doing Research in Political Science: An Introduction to Comparative Methods and Statistics*, London: Sage.
Tufte, E.R. (1974), *Data Analysis for Politics and Policy*, Englewood Cliffs, NJ: Prentice-Hall.
Volkens, A., J. Bara, I. Budge, M.D. McDonald and H. Klingemann (eds) (2013), *Mapping Policy Preferences from Texts. Statistical Solutions for Manifesto Analysts*, Oxford: Oxford University Press.

20 Models in political science: forms and purposes
Robin E. Best and Michael D. McDonald

1 MODELS IN POLITICAL SCIENCE: FORMS AND PURPOSES

Models in political science are knowledge tools. At a minimum they provide simplified depictions of a state of the political world; at their best they provide a means for understanding transitions from one state to another. Models give organization to our thinking by focusing on the essential elements of a political phenomenon under investigation. To do so they hold to one side an enormous variety of details associated with a phenomenon that, until we know more, is liable to clutter our thinking and muddle our understanding. Thus, it is imprudent to think of models as knowledge itself; models are spurs to knowledge.

Building models is a common exercise; most of us engage in it on a daily basis. Giving an example or using analogies, metaphors or similes in everyday conversation are forms of models – 'I feel like a fish out of water'. A model is designed to compare an easily understood situation with a state of the world that is more difficult to understand without a recognizable reference point. Unlike everyday comparisons, however, political science models do not leave to chance whether the easily understood referent is easily understood; rather, the key elements in a political science model are fully exposed. In this entry we first introduce five types of models commonly used in political science and use an everyday example to explain why it is essential to describe their elements fully and explicitly. We follow on with examples of each type and offer thoughts about its virtues and shortcomings.

2 BASIC FEATURES OF MODELS

Political science models take a variety of forms. Five common types include: (1) verbal, (2) descriptive statistical, (3) causal statistical, (4) mathematical and (5) computational. Regardless of the type, the essential first task of a political scientist is to expose fully the key elements of a situation or process. An example with reference to everyday life makes it easy to understand why.

Take as the example the banter among a group of seven friends deciding what to do about dinner. The driver of the one available car says 'I'll pick up Thai food', to which a member of the group replies 'Let's make the decision in a democratic way'. What, then, are they going to do as democrats? Are they going to discuss all the options? Is the agenda – that is, the possible options – totally open? Must everyone cast a vote? We do not know, but for this next moment let's say the answer to those questions is yes. In the end the vote divides one for Thai, two for Greek, three for Italian and one for Mexican. Is selecting the highest voted option, Italian, a violation of the 'model' of democracy, reflecting as it does the plurality but not necessarily the majority choice? The answer to this, as to the earlier questions, is that we do not know, because the core concepts of the model of democracy were not fully exposed.

In fewer words, models as knowledge tools are of little use when the answer to whether the observed situation comports with the model is that 'we don't know'. The point of modeling for the purpose of gaining knowledge is, of course, to know something after making the comparison between what the model indicates is expected to exist or occur and what actually exists or occurs. Therefore, regardless of the model form, its elements have to be so fully exposed that no doubt remains about the fit between the model and the observed reality.

3 VERBAL MODELS

The Westminster model of parliamentary government is a frequently referenced verbal model. An especially simple version of it has these five elements:[1] (1) unitary and centralized government – that is, all sub-national governments are creatures of the central government and dependent on grants of authority from it; (2) asymmetric bicameralism – that is, one of two legislative chambers holds most of the lawmaking power; (3) a predominantly two-party system – that is, all or nearly all parliamentary seats are occupied by members of two major parties; (4) one-party cabinets – that is, government ministers come from one political party; and (5) elections in single-member districts using plurality rule – that is, members of parliament are elected from districts with one winner decided by the highest vote total, regardless of whether that total constitutes a majority.

One way to use the model is to compare the current situation in the UK to the key elements. The reasonable conclusion is that UK politics and government are drifting away from the Westminster model's place of origin. Power has been devolved to Scotland, Wales and Northern Ireland. The role and composition of the House of Lords have been frequently debated and augmented since the 1990s. In 2014, the House of Commons had not two parties but a dozen, and the third largest party (Liberal Democrats) after the turn into the twenty-first century has occupied as many as 8 percent of seats in the Commons. The non-predominance of the two major parties following the 2010 elections required a government formation with both Liberal Democrats and Conservative Party members occupying cabinet positions. While elections to the Commons still use the single-member district plurality form – with a proposal to alter that form defeated in a 2011 referendum – proportional representation forms are used to elect the UK's members to the European Parliament and to elect members of the Northern Irish and Scottish assemblies. All of this drifting, all of these changes, spur us to ask what stands behind them and where along the path away from the Westminster model is the present-day UK government (*the* government of Westminster) likely to end up?

The spur to knowledge from verbal models comes, most especially, from generating questions. What is causing the government of Westminster to drift away from the Westminster model? Why does the Dutch government with its unitary, centralized and asymmetric bicameralism so noticeably differ on the other three features? Can the model be pushed to a deeper conceptual level to describe the Westminster model as a consequence of a preference for majoritarian decision making in contrast to a preference for consensus decision making (see, for example, Lijphart 2012)? The verbal model's shortcoming is that it is usually too static. We learn that one political situation more or less comports with the verbal description, but we seldom learn why unless and until we turn to one of the other model forms to get greater purchase on cause and effect.

4   DESCRIPTIVE STATISTICAL MODELS

Descriptive statistics are often used for comparing worldly events to a distribution of events that could occur naturally. One descriptive statistics example, rich with implications, comes from a time (1870–1910) when statistics was just beginning to cohere as the discipline it is today. One of the catalytic figures in its development was Francis Edgeworth, a British philosopher and political economist. In 1898, in one of his many illustrations of what can be understood by thinking about how the world comports with a descriptive statistical model, Edgeworth used the normal distribution as a benchmark abstraction to explain why a political system with two parties contesting elections in single-member districts, as in

Britain around that time, is prone to rewarding the majority party with a disproportionately large share of seats. For instance, the 1885 UK election had the Liberal Party winning 56 percent of the British seats (not including Irish seats) with 52 percent of the two-party British vote. A year later the general election saw the Conservative Party win over two-thirds of the British seats with only about 53 percent of the British vote.

What stands behind these disproportionate seat bonuses for a majority party? Edgeworth proposed modeling the situation as a natural consequence of the fact that the constituency vote percentages take shape in a form similar to a normal distribution. One example of such a distribution of constituency vote percentages is shown in Figure 20.1. To illustrate how and why a party with the vote majority gains its disproportionate seat bonus, we give a slight vote majority to Party A by setting the center

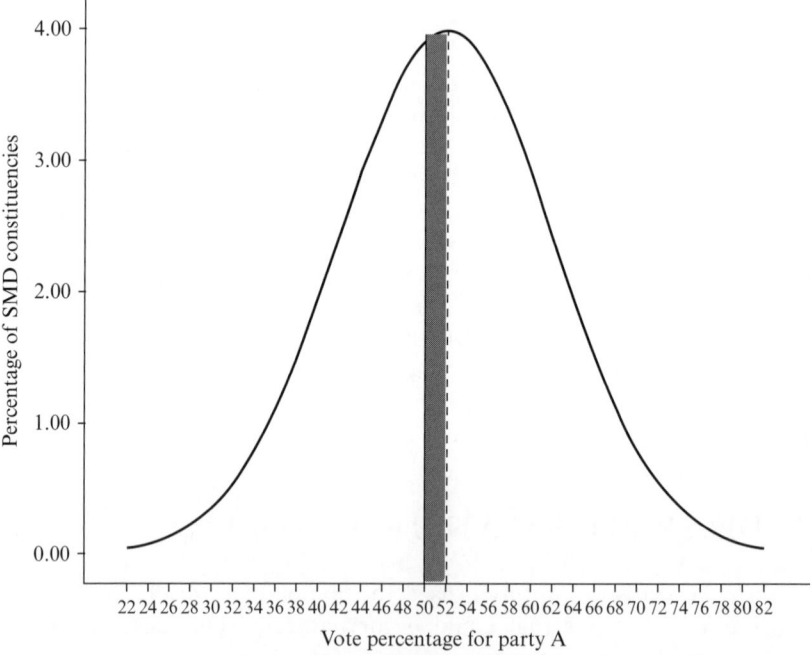

Note: The graph illustrates that when a constituency vote percentage distribution forms a normal distribution (bell-shaped curve) with a standard deviation of ten, a two-point vote swing above 50:50 favoring party A (from 50 to 52 percent), produces constituency wins for party A in 58 percent of the constituencies. Thus, party A wins 8 percent of the seats above 50 for a two-point vote swing above 50.

Figure 20.1   Hypothetical constituency vote percentage distribution among single-member districts for a two-party system

of the distribution at 52 percent. In this illustration we set the standard deviation of constituency vote percentages at ten; this tells us that just over two-thirds of the districts have vote percentages in the 42 to 62 range (that is, ±10 points around the mean of 52). Since the normal distribution is symmetric about its mean, half the constituencies have votes greater than 52 percent and half have vote percentages less than 52. At issue is what percentage of the seats resides in the interval between 50 and 52. In this depiction, 8 percent of the area, which means 8 percent of the constituencies and therefore seats won, fall in the 50 to 52 interval. By moving the normal distribution from a mean of 50, where both parties would win half the seats, to just two points higher, 52 percent, the majority party can expect to pick up a disproportionately large 8 percent of the seats (58 percent in all) in response to a shift of just 2 percent of the vote.

Not all such distributions of vote percentages in a two-party system have standard deviations of ten. That is not a problem for the model; indeed it is a benefit in the sense that it expands our understanding. Between 1920 and 1970 the standard deviation of the constituency vote percentages in Britain was in the region of 13.5, which meant, according to the model as well as in reality, the seat bonus declined to something on the order of 3 to 1, 3 percent of the seats won by the majority party for each vote percentage point in excess of 50. In the United States, from 1950 onward, the standard deviation was even larger – in the range of 18 to 29. This reduces the majority bonus in the US to something typically less than 2 to 1. This spurs the question, why does the standard deviation change over time or differ across countries (see, for example, Tufte 1973; King and Gelman 1991; Johnston et al. 2001)?

Pitfalls when applying descriptive statistical models, even one as rich as Edgeworth's, occur not from variations on the theme within the model's parameters themselves. Those often have something important to tell us. Rather, when the assumed circumstances of the world do not actually fit, there is no way that something useful can be learned. For instance, the fundamental assumption of the Edgeworth normal distribution model is that the political system has exclusively (or nearly so) two parties. When a significant third party enters the electoral competition, as in Britain after 1970 and especially in Britain from the mid-1980s onward, application of the model was disrupted in a most serious way, so much so that it was no longer useful except to say that we are on the wrong modeling track.

5   CAUSAL STATISTICAL MODELS

Causal statistical analysis focuses on how some outcome of interest responds to one or more features of the political system – for example, winning a large percentage of seats responds to (is caused by) winning a large percentage of votes. The form of model takes a verbal statement and restates it in a statistical formulation, often as a linear equation:

$$Y_i = a + bX_i + e_i. \tag{20.1}$$

The Y_i term is the outcome of interest – such as party seat percentages – for some individual unit (for example, country). The X_i is a condition of that unit – such as party vote percentages. The idea is that Y rises and falls in response to the condition of X being high or low. The a term is a fixed number that records the level of the outcome, Y, when X is absent (X = 0), and the b term is a fixed number that records how much Y responds to a unit shift in X – for example, under proportional representation rules, party seats (Y) respond, in theory, by a one percentage point increase for each one percentage point increase in votes (X). Finally, and critically, the e_i term is added to represent all unknown and unaccounted for contributions to Y that are implicitly, but very definitely, assumed to contribute in idiosyncratic ways. Put differently, for purposes of the model, the e_i additions are assumed to be just so much random noise.

As one illustration of a causal statistical model we can extend our interest in large-party seat bonuses to political systems that use proportional representation rules. By rule, proportional rules award seat percentages to parties in response to the vote percentages each party wins: 0 votes yields 0 percent of seats; 5 percent of the vote yields 5 percent of the seats; 40 percent of the vote yields 40 percent of the seats. Is it so? The causal statistical model allows us to check, with the caveat that we first need to think about possible random variation. We do have to expect some degree of randomness if only to accommodate what, by rule, would be fractional seats. Thirty-seven percent of the vote is expected to yield 55.5 of the seats for a parliament of 150, so maybe the system rounds up sometimes and rounds down at other times. In a statistical formula, the causal connection between seats and votes under proportional representation rules is this:

$$S\% = 0 + 1.0 \ V\% + e_i. \tag{20.2}$$

We can examine whether this is an accurate reflection of reality in a variety of different ways in regard to a variety of different types of parties. Here, our focus is on whether there is a seat bonus for large parties.

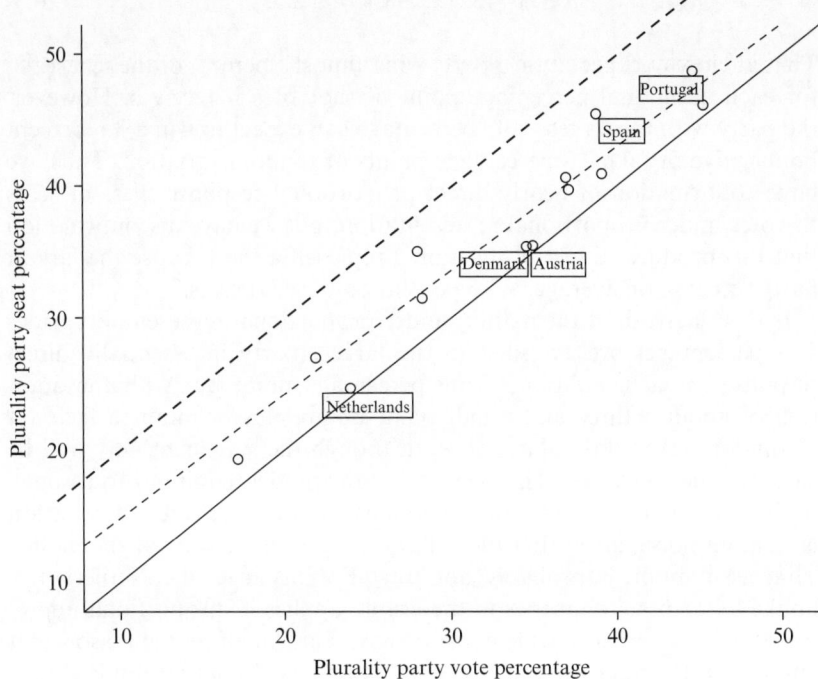

Note: The graph displays the seat–vote percentage relationship for the plurality party in 13 nations using proportional representational rules, and illustrates that the party with the most votes typically receives a seat percentage bonus – a seat percentage above its vote percentage – of 3.6 percentage points.

Figure 20.2   Relationship between party seat and vote percentages of the party with the highest votes in 13 European democracies

Figure 20.2 shows the seat–vote relation for the parties that won the largest vote percentage in an election of 13 European countries using proportional representation rules. The line diagonally bisecting the graph is the expectation representing the one-to-one seat–vote expectation. Clearly, each and every country awards seats to its largest vote-winning party in a manner that is slightly above that expectation. Roughly, a party with 20 percent of the vote wins about 23 percent of the seats; a party with 30 percent of the vote wins about 33 percent of the seats; and a party with 40 percent of the vote wins about 43 percent of the seats.

According to the statistical model calculations, the best fitting line (shown as a dashed line in the graph) is

$$S\% = 3.6 + .98 \ V\% \pm 2.3. \qquad (20.3)$$

That is, close to expectation a party wins almost 1 percent or the seats (.98) for each additional percentage point of the votes it receives. However, the party with the largest vote percentage can expect to win a 3.6 percent bonus, give or take 2.3 percentage points of random variation. Thus, we have confirmation of nearly direct proportional responsiveness of seats to votes under proportional representation, but we have disconfirmation that this produces direct proportional representation because the largest party receives, on average, a 3.6 percent point seat bonus.

Is this the truth of the matter: under proportional representation rules seat percentages are awarded to the largest party in essentially direct response to each additional vote percentage point but with the addition of about a three and a half point bonus plus or minus a little bit of random error? Probably not, even though the statement may well be close to true. Why not? The elements of the model require us to assume, until checked later, that all the deviations from the statistical description is random noise, given that the e_i term is an essential part of the model. That assumption is probably not true. For instance, the Netherlands, unlike all 12 other countries in the graph, applies its proportional representation to one nationwide constituency. This might be the reason that among the 13 countries, the Netherlands seat–vote relationship is closest to directly proportional. Also, on the two sides of the statistical line we have Denmark and Austria, which applies a decision rule to take account of would-be fractional seats that is systematically less favorable to larger parties than, say, the decision rule for would-be fractional seats in Spain and Portugal. That is, the assumption that 'all other forces are random' is almost certainly not true and thus the model is, perhaps, something approximating the true state of political affairs, but it is not truth itself.

Is this assumption of 'all other forces are random' a serious shortcoming for this sort of model? It can be, but it need not be. It is a problem when the results of the analysis are taken as confirmation. If we were to say that we can see from the analysis in Figure 20.2 that the single casual force that produces seats percentages for the party with the largest vote is proportional with a 3.6 percent seat bonus, because the results are consistent with that statement, then there is a serious problem. If, however, we recognize that the consistency between the evidence with the proposition also includes the usually unstated implication that nothing else matters but idiosyncratic random forces, the serious problem can be turned into a virtue. Why and how? The causal descriptive model is amenable to extension and reconsideration by adding terms to the model to check whether their contribution can be deemed idiosyncratic and random or whether we need to include them expressly because they make systematic and meaningful contributions to the outcomes.

6 MATHEMATICAL MODELS

Mathematical models begin with a set of a priori assumptions about the political world. The implications of these assumptions for political phenomena are then derived through the meticulous application of logic, which is formalized using numbers and symbols. Deductive in approach, mathematical models are known for putting all their pieces on display: every assumption is made explicit and every logical step made between assumption and implication is clearly presented. Requiring such clarity and consistency means that mathematical models usually present an especially simplified representation of political phenomena. The simplicity keeps the application tractable and makes the implications generalizable.

Mathematical models can take different forms depending on the question at hand. Game theoretic models examine the interactions of more than one individual and are commonly employed to gain traction on questions of whether there is an equilibrium result jointly made, usually through uncoordinated strategic decisions. Spatial models are often used to investigate the equilibrium positions of political actors in a one-or multi-dimensional political space. Social choice models aim to shed light on the equilibrium behavior of groups of rational individuals.

Since mathematical models rely on logical consistency, when their implications are put to the test by comparison with observations, it is the assumptions of the model that are being examined. If the assumptions hold, then the implications derived from these assumptions necessarily follow. Although this type of model can begin from virtually any assumption (the most useful models begin with plausible assumptions, of course), all mathematical models of politics employ two basic assumptions characteristic of rational choice theory. One is methodological individualism, which takes the individual as the unit of analysis; the other is rational, goal-oriented behavior. The predicted outcomes come in the form of stable equilibria. If the actors in a mathematical model find themselves in an equilibrium situation, then no actor has an incentive to change her or his behavior unilaterally. Equilibria are the predictions of mathematical models in the sense that (1) if the actors find themselves in equilibrium, this situation is expected to remain stable, and (2) if the actors are not in equilibrium (and there is one), the actors' behavior moves them toward that situation.

One of the most familiar, if often criticized, mathematical models of political behavior is the theory of the calculus of deciding whether to vote. An individual's decision to turnout – R – is seen as a function of a cost–benefit calculation (see, for example, Downs 1957; Tullock 1968; Riker and Ordeshook 1968). The benefit (B) comes from seeing one's preferred party or candidate win multiplied by the probability (P) that the individual's vote decides the outcome. The costs (C) include gathering information about parties and candidates and the time and expense of going to the polls. In equation form, the calculus of voting is $R = PB - C$.

The implication of this model implies that rational citizens should rarely, if ever, turn out to vote in an election. That is because voting involves some nonzero cost while the probability that a single vote decides an election should be judged by a reasoned person to be essentially zero. It is in this sense that the significant numbers of voters we observe turning out to vote in an election is often described as a 'paradox'. The discovery of this paradox tells us that at least one of the model's assumptions must be flawed. Because we can be reasonably sure that the probability of casting the decisive vote is zero and the costs are surely nonzero, the flaw must reside with how voters think about the benefits of voting.

Another prominent example is William Riker's (1962) theory of minimum-winning government coalitions, which assumes office-seeking parties. Since office-seeking parties prefer to hold closely as much of the spoils of office as they can, we expect parties that have to form coalitions to form cabinet governments will choose coalition partners that amount to the barest possible majority. Axelrod's (1970) treatment of minimum-winning connected coalitions amended Riker's size principle by allowing political parties to give weight to policy considerations – that is, to care about the ideological position of their coalition partners rather than caring exclusively about the spoils of office. So, the idea of a minimum-winning connected coalition added a spatial component to the model of government formation.

As is clear from the examples, some of the advantages of mathematical models of politics stem from the clarity of their assumptions and their rigorous logic. The formalization can be an advantage in itself, since – if executed properly – it guarantees that the model is logically consistent. Perhaps a more noteworthy advantage of mathematical models is the relative ease with which properly constructed models can be falsified. If a mathematical model does not line up well with what we observe occurring in the world, this tells us that we have made at least one faulty assumption. In this sense, mathematical models may do the best job of telling us exactly where we went wrong in our thinking. In the calculus of voting, for example, voters must clearly derive benefits from voting that do not depend on the decisiveness of their vote. Thus, by signaling precisely the area of the model that requires improvement, mathematical models can propel research into new, fruitful areas of inquiry.

The simplicity and highly abstracted nature of mathematical models make their assumptions relatively easy to evaluate, but the cost of this level of abstraction is to put too much to the side for the sake of simplicity. Individuals are often assumed to have the same or similar set of motivations, complicating factors are ignored, and only a very limited number of influences on individual behavior are included in any particular model. As a consequence, mathematical models rarely present a picture of the political world that closely matches reality. Furthermore, the reliance upon methodological individualism is in itself a limiting factor, and groups or organizations such as political parties, interest groups, governments and, even, states have been assumed to act as rational individuals. Finally, the static nature of many mathematical models may also be problematic, as they may fail to account for changes in relationships that occur across time.

7 COMPUTATIONAL MODELS

Currently, most applications of computational models are formed as simulations – also referred to as agent-based models. Their aim is to gain insight into patterns of interaction that occur in complex, often dynamically complex, political environments. From them we hope to gain traction on the complexity of political behavior by first defining the terms of the behavior of political actors and their environment, and then by examining the large-scale effects of their repeated interactions. Similar to mathematical models, simulation models begin with a set of a priori assumptions about political actors, their goals and their environment. Thereafter, the two types diverge. While mathematical models assume optimizing individuals and look for stable equilibria, the actors – often called 'agents' – adjust their behavior in response to what has and has not been shown to improve their situation in the past. Such models are dynamic by nature, as the actors are in a system of perpetual motion and constant adaptation (Laver 2005, p. 263). The systems of constant change and complexity of political interaction generated by simulation models are often preferred to mathematical formulations for their ability to represent the complexity of political phenomena that do not seem easily, or sometimes ever, to reach equilibrium.

Although simulation models are used less frequently than some of the other model types described above, their popularity and use has increased in recent years, in part as a result of more powerful and sophisticated computing capabilities. Robert Axelrod's (1984, 1997) use of simulations to explore the possibility of observing cooperation in an iterated prisoner's dilemma is perhaps the most well-known application of simulation models, where he evaluates the outcomes and implications for actors who approach the game with different strategies. His work provided insight into the potential for actors to engage in cooperation that has broad applicability both inside and outside of political science. In research on party competition, simulation models have been used to gain insight into party strategies under varying electoral conditions (Kollman et al. 1998; Laver 2005; Laver and Sergenti 2012). These models begin with the observation that political parties rarely, if ever, reach and remain in the equilibrium predicted by mathematical models of party positioning. Party position-taking is then modeled as a dynamic and ongoing process where actors (typically, party leaders) respond and react to their previous attempts at electoral success.

Simulation models have an advantage in modeling the dynamics of complex political processes, since this is precisely what they set out to do. Thus, researchers unsatisfied with the typically static nature of mathematical models and their predicted equilibria may turn to simulation models in order to more accurately represent dynamic processes. Simulation models can also both allow and account for a higher degree of complexity than other modelling techniques, as highly complex patterns of interaction may prove intractable using formalized logic. However, their complexity can also be their disadvantage. Although simulation models begin with a relatively simplified view of the world, the patterns of interaction produced from the simulation can be so complex as to prevent us from drawing general conclusions that can then be applied to other situations. In short, by modeling more of the complexity of political behavior, simulation models can make it more difficult to extract the most important relationships and explanations of political phenomena.

8   CONCLUSION

We make progress toward enlightened understanding in everyday conversation by using examples, analogies, metaphors and similes. Political science makes progress in understanding the political world using a similar sort of tool, models. A political science model makes explicit the key elements of a situation and the assumptions required to make a comparison applicable.

Different tools are needed for different projects, and so it is when choosing a useful model to arrive at an improved understanding of politics. Verbal models are good for exploratory projects where we want to get a firm grip on something less familiar by comparing it to something quite familiar. Descriptive statistical models are useful when we are thinking about the distribution of a variety of outcomes and wondering whether it comports with a well-known statistical distribution. Causal statistical models are good for comparing claims that political outcomes are responses to one or more political, social or economic forces. Mathematical models are adept at tracing out the necessary implications of choices made by goal-oriented, rational decision-makers. Simulations are especially helpful for thinking in the abstract about complex and adaptive actions and reactions among continuously interacting individuals and groups.

Can any of these models tell us definitely why the political world is as it is and about what is liable to come next? No, that is asking too much. They can and do, importantly, enhance our current understanding and point us in the direction of useful questions to ask next.

NOTE

1. For a more through description of the Westminster model, see Lijphart (1984, pp. 4–20).

FURTHER READING

Introduction

Clark, K.A. and D.M. Primo (2012), *A Model Discipline: Political Science and the Logic of Representations*, Oxford, UK: Oxford University Press.

Application

Laver, M. and E. Sergenti (2012), *Party Competition: An Agent-Based Model*, Princeton, NJ: Princeton University Press.

Advanced Text

Riker, W.H. and P. Ordeshook (1973), *An Introduction to Positive Political Theory*, Englewood Cliffs, NJ: Prentice-Hall.

Other Advanced Text

Morton, R.B. (2004), *Methods and Models: A Guide to the Empirical Analysis of Formal Models in Political Science*, New York: Cambridge University Press.

REFERENCES

Axelrod, R. (1970), *Conflict of Interest: A Theory of Divergent Goals with Applications to Politics*, Chicago, IL: Markham.

Axelrod, R. (1984), *The Evolution of Cooperation*, New York: Basic Books.

Axelrod, R. (1997), *The Complexity of Cooperation*, Princeton, NJ: Princeton University Press.

Downs, A. (1957), *An Economic Theory of Democracy*, New York: Harpur.

Edgeworth, F.Y. (1898), 'Miscellaneous applications of the calculus of probabilities', *Journal of the Royal Statistical Society*, **51**, 534–44.

Johnston, R., C. Pattie, D. Dorling and D. Rossiter (2001), *From Seats to Votes: The Operation of the UK Electoral System Since 1945*, Manchester: Manchester University Press.

King, G. and A. Gelman (1991), 'Systematic consequences of incumbency advantage in U.S. House elections', *American Journal of Political Science*, **35** (1), 110–38.

Kollman, K., J.H. Miller and S.E. Page (1998), 'Political parties and electoral landscapes', *British Journal of Political Science*, **28** (1), 139–58.

Laver, M. (2005), 'Policy and the dynamics of political competition', *American Political Science Review*, **99** (2), 263–81.

Laver, M. and E. Sergenti (2012), *Party Competition: An Agent-Based Model*, Princeton, NJ: Princeton University Press.

Lijphart, A. (1984), *Democracies: Patterns of Majoritarian and Consensus Government in Twenty-One Countries*, New Haven, CT: Yale University Press.

Lijphart, A. (2012), *Patterns of Democracy: Government Forms and Performance in Thirty-Six Countries*, 2nd edn, New Haven, CT: Yale University Press.

Riker, W.H. (1962), *The Theory of Political Coalitions*, New Haven, CT: Yale University Press.

Riker, W.H. and P.C. Ordeshook (1968), 'A theory of the calculus of voting', *American Political Science Review*, **63** (1), 25–43.

Tufte, E.R. (1973), 'The relationship between seats and votes in two-party systems', *American Political Science Review*, **67** (2), 540–54.

Tullock, G. (1968), *Toward a Mathematics of Politics*, Ann Arbor, MI: University of Michigan Press.

21 Qualitative methods in political science
Selen A. Ercan and David Marsh

1 INTRODUCTION

Qualitative methods focus on understanding the meaning underlying an intention, action, object or phenomenon. In other words, researchers adopting qualitative methods aim to develop an understanding, an interpretation, of the way in which those they study understand their actions and the context in which they act. In political science research, qualitative methods are usually contrasted with quantitative methods, which typically deal with large amounts of data, using surveys and statistical methods, with the aim of establishing causal relationships between social phenomena. As such, qualitative methods are usually underpinned by an interpretivist epistemological position, while quantitative methods are underpinned by positivism. Given these differences, qualitative and quantitative methods have often been seen as mutually exclusive modes of generating and analyzing data (Bryman 1988). In this chapter, we take issue with that position, without denying that there is a clear link between ontology, epistemology and methodology.

This chapter is divided into four sections. In the first section, we briefly outline the two major epistemology approaches in political science, while recognizing their links to ontological positions. Some of these issues were raised in Chapters 2 in this volume, which mainly discusses the positivist position, and Chapter 3 in this volume, which explores critical realism, a third position not considered here given space constraints. We focus mainly upon the role that qualitative research plays within these approaches and, as such, pay rather more attention to interpretivism than do Chapters 2 and 3, because it is the position most associated with the use of qualitative methods. However, we also emphasize that positivists or critical realists can, and do, draw on qualitative methods, albeit for different purposes.

In the second section, we discuss three qualitative methods for generating data; ethnography, interviews and focus groups and photo-elicitation. In the third section, we consider three approaches for analyzing qualitative data; content analysis, discourse analysis and frame analysis. There are various other methods of generating and analyzing data qualitatively. We focus here only on selected examples, because our purpose is not to offer a comprehensive list of qualitative methods, but rather to show that there are specific principles and techniques associated with such methods. These should not be considered as second best to statistical methods, or equated with an 'anything goes' approach. Those who intend to use qualitative methods should be aware of the principles that underpin a qualitative methodology, the different methods utilized within this methodological position and the limitations involved in this approach in order to use them effectively.

Finally, in the fourth section, we identify and respond to major criticisms often levelled, usually by positivists, against the use of qualitative research methods. Overall, we argue that, while the distinction between quantitative and qualitative methods is useful heuristically, it is not as big as is usually assumed (for a similar argument, see Kritzer 1996). However, how researchers use these methods, and combine them, depends on their ontological and epistemological positions (Moses and Knutsen 2007).

2 THE ROLE OF QUALITATIVE METHODS IN POLITICAL SCIENCE RESEARCH

We contend, like Furlong and Marsh (2010), that the ontological and epistemological positions adopted by researchers underpin what they study, how they study it and, crucially, what they think they can claim on the basis of what they find; so, for us, ontology underpins, epistemology, which in turn underpins methodology (for a discussion of these issues, see Furlong and Marsh 2010). Here, we look at how positivists and interpretivists approach these issues.

In broad terms, a positivist operates with a realist ontology, arguing that there is a 'real' world 'out there', independent of our interpretation of it. In epistemological terms, they argue that, if we use the right methods in the right way, then we can establish 'objective', causal relationships between social phenomena. To do so, they need to collect data about a population[1] (for example, all people between 18 and 25 in Australia) or a representative sample of that population (either randomly selected or matched to the population in terms of demographic characteristics). Once the data is collected, then it is analyzed with the aim of establishing causal patterns, perhaps between age and various types of political participation (voting, party or group membership, participation in demonstrations and so on), invariably using statistical analysis. For a positivist, theory serves to generate hypotheses which can then be tested and falsified (or not).

The aim of positivist research is to establish causal links between the variables studied. So, if we studied how the relationship between age and political participation is affected by education, we might find a positive relationship between participation and age that increases as people grow older (or we might not). On this basis we might claim that both increased age and increased education lead to greater levels of political participation, but that education has more effect than age on that participation. These are the type of conclusions a positivist wishes to draw and to do so he or she needs largely quantitative data, linked to statistical analysis (see also Part VI in this book).

None of this means that positivists do not utilize qualitative data but, we would argue, it plays a different role for them than it does for the interpretivist. Positivists tend to use qualitative research for two reasons; to generate ideas which can subsequently be tested quantitatively and to investigate in more detail results found in quantitative research.

So, we might undertake qualitative research to develop the questions to be used in a subsequent quantitative analysis. For example, before Pattie et al. (2004) undertook their quantitative study of political participation in the UK, they conducted a series of semi-structured interviews and, on the basis of these, they developed indicators of 'political' participation which had not previously been used in the literature. We might also use qualitative methods to further investigate the findings of the quantitative study. Again, Pattie et al. (2004) provide an example, because they interviewed a non-representative sub-sample (all respondents who agreed to be interviewed) after initially analyzing their data, to add depth to their understanding of their respondents' responses. While positivists can use qualitative methods then, they *tend* to use them as an ancillary to their main concern, which is to develop a generalizable causal explanation.

All this means that, for a positivist, ontology is prior to, and underpins, epistemology, and this epistemological position underpins the methodology and methods used. So, the link between a realist ontology, a positivist epistemology and a quantitative methodology is strong.

In contrast, an interpretivist researcher's concern is with understanding, rather than explanation. To an interpretivist, there is no world independent of our understanding or interpretation of it. So, no matter what methods we use, or how we use them, we cannot establish causal relationship between social phenomena. For interpretivists, the *double hermeneutic* is axiomatic; research involves establishing their understanding (as researchers), one level of the hermeneutic, of their respondents' understanding of their actions, the second level of the hermeneutic (Ball 1987).

As such, interpretivists would focus upon young people's understanding of politics and how that understanding affects the way they act and the meaning they attach to that action both in the formal political arena and in areas that many positivists would possibly regard as non-political. This approach directs the interpretivist to the use of qualitative methods which allow her to tease out her respondents' understandings of their actions. On this basis, an interpretivist would critique the idea that the researcher can be objective, focusing instead on the need for the researcher to be reflexive, considering how her interpretations of the actions of others is affected by her own values and experience.

Consequently, reflexivity is crucial in the interpretivist tradition. An interpretivist acknowledges that value judgments cannot be avoided; indeed, values are intrinsic to interpretive analysis. On this account, 'meaning' does not simply exist out in the social world to be picked up by a detached researcher, instead, meaning is something that a researcher reconstructs in a dialogue with the subjects of analysis (Wagenaar 2011, p. 9). So, rather than attempting to control the effects of bias in empirical research, qualitative researchers within an interpretivist research tradition explicitly acknowledge it in the process of generating their empirical findings.

For an interpretivist, theory, if we choose to call it that, plays a very different role than for a positivist. Theories, and propositions derived from them, cannot be falsified, because there is no world independent of our interpretation of it which can be used in such a falsification process. Rather, all aspects of the 'real' world are constructed and there are different, and contested, views, 'narratives', of the 'world', and what we regard as 'real' within it. So, for an interpretivist, theories are no more, or less, than narratives about the world and how it works. At any given time, one narrative may be dominant, but it is not 'true'. Of course, such a narrative may shape and/or influence behavior, as people act as if it was true. However, the theory cannot be used to explain how the world operates in a way which is not narrative-dependent, because there is no world which is not narrative-dependent.

The claims an interpretivist would make on the basis of her research are much more circumspect than those that a positivist would make. For example, they would make claims about how the young people understand politics and their 'political actions', rather than about what caused them to act in the way they did. Overall, an interpretivist would not see ontology as prior to epistemology, rather ontological positions are themselves constructed. However, she would see a clear relationship between her epistemological position and the qualitative methodology which she would usually utilize.

3 QUALITATIVE METHODS FOR GENERATING DATA

Qualitative research is labor- and time-intensive, especially when it involves fieldwork. One particularly difficulty is that there is no clear-cut distinction between the data-generation and data-analysis phases of the research. Such research hardly proceeds in a neat and tidy way. Rather, qualitative research involves a constant meaning-making process that requires appreciation of the ambiguity that may arise from multiple interpretations of the same events/processes/actions (Hendriks 2007). The researcher has to be flexible, changing the research design in the face of 'research site-realities that the researcher could not anticipate in advance of the beginning the research' (Yanow 2003, p. 10).

This is a totally different process than that involved in the use of a quantitative methodology, which uses either existing data-sets, for example, those compiled by government or generated from prior research, or data-sets generated by the researcher. In contrast, qualitative research utilizes methods such as: participant observation; ethnography; individual or group interviews; focus groups; documentary analysis; and the examination of visual objects and artefacts.

Of course, the use of qualitative methods in social science research is far from new and is widely used in sociology and anthropology to provide in-depth understanding of the topic at hand. However, increasing attention is now paid to making the steps involved in qualitative data generation and analyses more transparent. As Yanow (2007, p. 405) notes, this both helps students to learn about 'how to' questions and shows critics and sceptics that interpretive methods can yield 'trustworthy analyses', are not impressionistic and have regularized procedures. Below we consider three common methods of generating data by using qualitative methods: ethnography; interviews and focus groups; and photo-elicitation.

Ethnography: an ethnography is a means to understand the culture, values and actions of a group through focusing upon the experience of members of the group in their natural context, often being involved as a participant observer. The emphasis is on exploring social phenomena, not testing hypotheses. Ethnographic fieldwork aims to produce fine-grained, 'thick description' (Geertz 1973), not causal explanations. While ethnography has usually been associated with small-scale and single-case studies, it can be applied in a variety of different contexts and at different levels of comparison (Bray 2008). Ethnography is common in anthropology, significant in sociology, but rarer in political science.

An exception is Rhodes's (2002, 2011) ethnographic work on policy networks. He argues (Rhodes 2002, p. 399) that: 'political scientists should spend more time observing policy networks, using ethnographic tools to capture the meaning of everyday activities'. Rhodes relies on different methods in the two contributions discussed here, although he sees all the methods he used as contributing to an ethnography. His 2002 article, which focuses upon the experiences of consumers, managers and senior officials of working in networks, utilizes: first, files produced by a UK local authority's social workers, which Rhodes edited and agreed with the authors; and, second, elite interviews with a dozen UK Permanent Secretaries (PSs), from which he produced 'an agreed construction of how the permanent secretary saw his world' (Rhodes 2002, p. 402). In his 2011 book, whose aim is summed up in its title, *Everyday Life in British Government*, he uses (Rhodes 2011, p. 8): interviews with ten PSs and 20 other officials; a variety of documentary material; 120 hours of observation in the offices of two Ministers and three PSs; and 300 hours of shadowing of two Ministers and three PSs.

Many would want to distinguish interviews and documentary analysis from the other more clearly ethnographic methods, but the point here is that all these methods are qualitative and designed to tease out the meanings that those involve attach to their experiences, allowing the researcher 'to get out there and see what actors are thinking and doing' (Rhodes 2011, p. 7). In Rhodes's case, these methods link very clearly to his constructivist/interpretivist position.

Individual interviews and focus groups: interviews are a key method in political science, particularly, although not exclusively, when dealing with elites, as in Rhodes's work. In most cases, such interviews are semi-structured, with the researcher having a clear idea of what questions or issues they want to raise, but allowing the interview to shape the order in which questions are asked, and the issues which are covered.

Focus group interviews are becoming increasingly common, often linked to follow-up, individual interviews. This method involves engaging small number of people in an informal group discussion 'focused' on a particular topic. This could be, for example, young people discussing the meaning of 'political' participation. The discussion is usually based on a series of questions and the researcher generally serves as a facilitator, keeping the discussion flowing. One advantage of the focus group interviews comes from their interactive and deliberative nature: rather than focusing on individual responses in isolation, focus group interviews help researchers to identify the common issues of concerns, as well as the points of agreement and disagreement among the participants. They also provide a way of generating data relatively quickly from a large number of research participants.

Marsh et al. (2007) combined focus groups with individual interviews, and photo-elicitation. Their research was rooted in a critical response to the mainstream literature which saw young people as increasingly apathetic, in large part because it operates with a narrow conceptualization of the 'political'. Their aim was to explore how young people understand, and 'participate' in, 'politics', rather than imposing their view of politics on their respondents through using a questionnaire, even one with open-ended questions.

The focus group interviews were conducted on five sites, which varied significantly in demographic composition, with, for example, some sites, such as the university, being 'privileged', while others, such as a homeless hostel, were disadvantaged. In addition, all respondents who were willing were subsequently interviewed individually, with the output from the focus groups being used to structure those interviews.

The focus groups, together with the photo-elicitation method discussed below, allowed the researchers to tease out the young people's own understanding of politics, rather than asking questions already informed by the understanding of politics which is dominant in the mainstream literature.

Photo-elicitation: this method is more rarely used than the others discussed, although its use seems to be growing. It is a method often linked to interviews or focus groups with the aim of making these more open and less controlled by the interviewer (Harper 2002; Clark-Ibáñez 2004; Padgett et al. 2013). Sometimes the images are provided by the researcher, but often the respondents provide or create the image. The type of images involved include photographs, videos, paintings, cartoons, graffiti and advertisements. This is a particularly useful method if dealing with sensitive or more abstract issues (such politics), but the main aim is to allow respondents more opportunity to speak for themselves.[2]

Marsh et al. (2007) used photo-elicitation as a means of uncovering their respondents' understandings and experience of politics. Given that their criticism of most extant literature was that it involved researchers imposing their views of 'politics' on young people, they could hardly ask direct questions about politics. Rather, they gave their focus groups a series of pictures, some of which were overtly political, but many of which were not. Each picture was discussed in the focus group and at the end of the session the group was asked to sort the pictures into 'political' and 'non-political' piles.

One feature of this research distinguishes it clearly from a more quantitative approach. The researchers treat class, gender and ethnicity, not as independent variable but, rather, as 'political' lived experiences and their methods are designed to uncover these experiences. However, they see these experiences as structured, which reflects their critical realist position, indicating that such methods are not only used by interpretivists.

4   METHODS FOR ANALYZING QUALITATIVE DATA

Here, we provide some examples of methods for analyzing qualitative data. There is a rich variety of tools that qualitative researchers use when analyzing their data, such as content analysis, discourse analysis, frame analysis and narrative analysis, and the different methods are usually associated with different theoretical positions.

Qualitative content analysis is one of the most frequently used methods of analyzing qualitatively generated data, and involves the researcher analyzing her data in relation to a series of questions she has posed. The raw material for content analysis may be any form of communication, such as interview transcripts, email messages, political speeches, or documents, such as parliamentary transcripts, newspapers and magazines. Historically, content analysis was seen as an 'objective' way of capturing the content of various texts or communications, so there was a focus on counting the number of mentions of specific items or terms (Berelson 1952, p. 18). As it has evolved, however, it has taken an interpretivist turn, and begun to be viewed as a method for interpreting qualitatively generated data. One of the early examples of this method is Shannon's (1954) analysis of the newspaper cartoon 'Little Orphan Annie'. Guided by a series of questions that sought to reveal the underlying values of the cartoon, Shannon examined 104 weekly appearances of the comic strip over a period of two years. Her analysis revealed how the editors of the paper used the cartoon to communicate conservative, middle-class American, anti-Roosevelt sentiments and values.

Discourse analysis (see Chapter 26 in this volume) is another key method of analysis used by qualitative researchers, albeit in different ways. Different approaches define the term 'discourse' differently and suggest different ways of analyzing it empirically. However, the general idea is that 'language is structured according to different patterns that people's utterances follow when they take part in different domains of social life' and discourse analysis is the analysis of these patterns (Jørgensen and Phillips 2002, p. 1). This form of analysis can be applied in different social domains, such as institutions or media; and used to depict the language associated with a particular domain (for example, political discourse or medical discourse), or as a way of defining aspects of the world associated with a particular perspective (for example, a 'neo-liberal discourse of globalization'; see: Fairclough 2013). From this perspective, discourses can help coordinate the actions of large number of people and organizations. The purpose of discourse analysis is usually to uncover the particular ways of viewing, talking about and understanding the world, or some aspect of the world, in the particular social domain.

For some scholars, most notably for the advocates of 'critical discourse analysis' (CDA) – a particular stream of discourse analysis utilized particularly in linguistics, the purpose of discourse analysis goes beyond mapping the ways of viewing the world or some aspects of it. Rather, CDA, in the words of Wodak and Meyer (2009, p. 7) seeks to 'produce and convey critical knowledge that enables human beings to emancipate themselves from forms of domination through self-reflection'.

The starting point of any type of discourse analysis is the acknowledgement that language matters; so, the way we talk, interpret and discuss issues have important consequences. It thus directs our attention to the importance of texts and talk, such as official documents, parliamentary transcripts and interviews, but also visual objects, such as photographs or stamps, for identifying the language patterns at play. Given its capacity to capture different ways of making sense of a particular issue, discourse analysis has usually been used by scholars of democracy, particularly in the empirical studies of deliberative democracy (for example, Dryzek 2012) or in the context of a deliberative policy analysis (Hajer and Wagenaar 2006).

Closely related to discourse analysis is *frame analysis*, which is often used in political science research, particularly in the study of public policy and social movements, and usually regarded as one approach within the broader family of methods of discourse analysis. In the context of policy analysis, frame analysis seeks to reveal how 'public policies rest on frames that supply them with underlying structures of beliefs, perceptions and appreciation' (Fischer 2003, p. 144). Although the concept of frame analysis is traced back to Goffman (1974), its introduction to the field of policy analysis can be attributed to Schön and Rein (1994). Differently from discourses, frames are usually employed intentionally and strategically by actors, such as political parties, government agencies or social movements (Poletta and Ho 2006). Each frame contains implicit representation of what is considered to be a problem (diagnosis), a solution to the problem (prognosis) and a call for action (who is responsible for solving the problem).

In the context of policy research, one particularly insightful tool for frame analysis is suggested by Carol Bacchi's (2012) '"What's the problem represented to be" approach'. This approach is empirically operationalized by way of engaging with a set of questions that seek to reveal particular 'problem definitions', as well as the underlying values at work. For example, if language training is recommended for migrants to improve their integration in the mainstream society, the implication is that their lack of language knowledge is the 'problem', responsible for their poor integration. Bacchi offers a pre-defined set of questions for qualitative researchers to map the 'problem definitions' contained in policy proposals (for examples of this framework in the qualitative analysis of various policy debates, see Murray and Powell 2009; Ercan 2014, 2015).

5   CRITICISMS OF QUALITATIVE RESEARCH METHODS

Many positivists avoid ontology or epistemology, which they put in the 'too-hard basket'; pursuing their empirical work, solving puzzles from within a positive paradigm. They often criticize qualitative approaches for being unsystematic or treat them as of secondary importance, suggesting they are useful if located within a positivist frame. King, et al.'s (1994) seminal work on designing social inquiry offers an excellent example here. They assert:

> In our view, however, science . . . and interpretation are *not* fundamentally different endeavours aimed at divergent goals. Both rely on preparing careful descriptions, gain deep understanding of the world, asking good questions, formulating falsifiable hypothesis on the basis of more general theories, and collecting the evidence needed to evaluated those hypotheses. (King et al. 1994, p. 37, emphasis added)

They continue: 'Yet once hypotheses have been formulated, demonstrating their correctness . . . requires valid scientific inferences. The procedure for inference followed by interpretivist social scientists, furthermore, must incorporate the same standards as those followed by other qualitative and quantitative researchers' (King et al. 1994, p. 38).

King et al. see interpretivism as a methodological orientation, which may have utility, rather than as an ontological/epistemological position. Interpretivism can be used to generate better questions to be utilized within a positivist framework. They seem to be advocating a major/minor methodological mix (see Read and Marsh 2002), where qualitative, interpretivist methods are used to generate better questions for survey research designed to test, and attempt to falsify, hypotheses.

The main point, however, is that the ontological and epistemological problems have not disappeared, rather they have been ignored. It is true that quantitative and qualitative methodologies involve different methods for generating data and, as such, can be incorporated into positivist, as well as interpretivist research. However, an interpretivist sees qualitative research methods as at the core of his or her research, because the aim is not to test hypotheses, but rather to explore people's experiences, practices and perceptions in depth in order to establish her understanding of their understanding of their actions.

It is often argued that researchers who utilize qualitative methods are unsystematic and that their results are not generalizable, reproducible or even reliable. Again, the key problem is that such judgments are usually made by scholars operating from within a different, positivist, epistemological position; so most qualitative researchers are being judged against standards they do not, and cannot, accept. In particular, ideas of generalizability and reproducibility as they are understood by positivists would not be accepted by interpretivists. The problem is that, if research is about developing understandings rather than discovering 'truth', then the methods utilized and the way they are used will be different.

As regards generalizability, a positivist wants to make generalizable, causal claims, but an interpretivist does not. Rather, the interpretivist wants to outline her understanding/interpretation of respondents' understandings of their experiences/actions. So, generalizability, and reproducibility are problematic for at least two reasons. First, different respondent's experiences will be different and the best we could hope for as researchers would be to discover patterns, although these patterns may be unlikely to hold across time or space. Second, the interpretations of researchers are likely to vary, as they are not objective observers, and their own values and experience effect their judgment.

However, none of this means that the output from qualitative work involves just opinions and assertions. While the flexibility required by a qualitative research design has been taken by positivists to mean that these methods are not systematic, but impressionistic, good qualitative research is reliable when judged against its own epistemological standards. Indeed, it needs to be both impressionistic and systematic. At one level, qualitative research within the interpretivist tradition is inevitably 'impressionistic'. Researchers are developing interpretations, not discovering 'truths'. These interpretations are affected by their own experiences, but this does not mean that they necessarily lack validity. This is where reflexivity comes in, because it means that the researcher is clear about how her values/ experiences may have affected her interpretation and, crucially, they give the reader (sometimes another researcher) information with which to assess that interpretation.

However, qualitative research can be systematic, and in this sense reliable. The requirements here are little different than in quantitative research. First, the researcher needs to be well-trained in the use of the methods. Anyone who thinks that conducting ethnographic research is easy is misguided. So, the methods used need to be appropriate and properly utilized. Second, the concepts used need to be well defined and clearly operationalized. Thirdly, the researcher needs to give sufficient detail about how the methods are used, so that another researcher could undertake the same research. Fourthly, the methods and techniques used to analyze the data need to be both clearly outlined and appropriate. Finally, the researcher needs to be circumspect about the conclusions drawn from the study, being particularly wary about making generalizability claims.

6 CONCLUSION

Political science is, or at least should be, a broad church. Any tendency to dismiss qualitative methods should be resisted. Qualitative methods can be used from within any epistemological position, although its use is different in each one. We have acknowledged this, but our main claim is that qualitative methods are useful in many contexts and particularly if we are concerned to *understand* the actions and experiences of actors. However, as with all methods, the crucial point is to use them well, acknowledging their limitations, as well as their strengths.

NOTES

1. One of the main reasons for the move towards big data is because it usually involves a population, not a sample, which removes all the issues involved with significance tests.
2. One of the early uses of this method can be seen in the work of Goffman (1979), who looked at how gender roles and expectations were reflected in magazine ads.

FURTHER READING

Schatz, E. (ed.) (2009), *Political Ethnography: What Immersion Contributes to the Study of Power*, Chicago: Chicago University Press.
Schwartz-Shea, P. and D. Yanow (2012), *Interpretive Research Design: Concepts and Processes*, New York: Routledge.
Wagenaar, H. (2011), *Meaning in Action: Interpretation and Dialogue in Policy Analysis*, New York: M.E. Sharpe.

REFERENCES

Bacchi, C. (2012), 'Introducing the "What's the problem represented to be?" approach', in A. Bletsas and C. Beasley (eds), *Engaging with Carol Bacchi: Strategic Interventions and Exchanges*, Adelaide: University of Adelaide Press, pp. 21–4.
Ball, T. (1987), 'Deadly hermeneutics; or sinn and the social scientists', in T. Ball (ed.), *Idioms*

of Inquiry: Critique and Renewal in Political Science, Albany, NY: State University of New York Press, pp. 95–110.

Berelson, B. (1952), *Content Analysis in Communication Research*, Glencoe: Free Press.

Bray, Z. (2008), 'Ethnographic approaches', in D. Della Porta and M. Keating (eds), *Approaches and Methodologies in the Social Sciences: A Pluralist Perspective*, Cambridge: Cambridge University Press, pp. 296–316.

Bryman, A. (1988), *Quantity and Quality in Social Research*, London: Routledge.

Clark-Ibáñez, M. (2004), 'Framing the social world with photo-elicitation interviews', *American Behavioral Scientist*, **47** (12), 1507–27.

Dryzek, J.S. (2012), *The Politics of the Earth. Environmental Discourses*, 3rd edn, Oxford: Oxford University Press.

Ercan, S.A. (2014), 'Same problem, different solutions: the case of "honour killing" in Germany and Britain', in A. Gill, K. Roberts and C. Strange (eds), *'Honour' Killing and Violence. Theory, Policy and Practice*, London: Palgrave Macmillan, pp. 199–217.

Ercan, S.A. (2015), 'Creating and sustaining evidence for "failed multiculturalism": the case of "honour killing" in Germany', *American Behavioral Scientist*, **59** (6), 658–78.

Fairclough, N. (2013), 'Critical discourse analysis', in J.-P. Gee and M. Hanford (eds), *The Routledge Handbook of Discourse Analysis*, Abingdon, UK: Routledge, pp. 9–21.

Fischer, F. (2003), *Reframing Public Policy: Discursive Politics and Deliberative Practices*, Oxford: Oxford University Press.

Furlong, P. and D. Marsh (2010), 'A skin not a sweater: ontology and epistemology in political science', in D. Marsh and G. Stoker (eds), *Theory and Methods in Political Science*, 3rd edn, London: Palgrave Macmillan, pp. 184–212.

Geertz, C. (1973), *The Interpretation of Cultures: Selected Essays*, New York: Basic Books.

Goffman, E. (1974), *Frame Analysis: An Essay on the Organization of Experience*, Cambridge, MA: Harvard University Press.

Goffman, E. (1979), *Gender Advertisements*, Cambridge, MA: Harvard University Press.

Hajer, M.A. and J. Wagenaar (eds) (2006), *Deliberative Policy Analysis. Understanding Governance in the Network Society*, Cambridge: Cambridge University Press, pp. 209–27.

Harper, D. (2002), 'Talking about pictures: a case for photo elicitation', *Visual Studies*, **17** (1), 13–26.

Hendriks, C.M. (2007), 'Praxis stories: experiencing interpretive policy research', *Critical Policy Analysis*, **3** (1), 278–300.

Jørgensen, M.W. and L. Phillips (2002), *Discourse Analysis as Theory and Method*, London: Sage Publications.

King, G., R. Keohane and S. Verba (1994), *Designing Social Inquiry: Scientific Inference in Qualitative Research*, Princeton, NJ: Princeton University Press.

Kritzer, H.M. (1996), 'The data puzzle: the nature of interpretation in quantitative research', *American Journal of Political Science*, **40** (1), 1–32.

Marsh, D., T. O'Toole and S. Jones (2007), *Young People and Politics in the UK: Apathy or Alienation?* London: Palgrave Macmillan.

Moses, J.W. and T.L. Knutsen (2007), *Ways of Knowing. Competing Methodologies in Social and Political Research*, New York: Palgrave Macmillan.

Murray, S. and A. Powell (2009), '"What's the problem" Australian public policy constructions of domestic and family violence', *Violence against Women*, **15** (5), 532–52.

Padgett, D., B. Smith, K. Derejko, B. Henwood and E. Tiderington (2013), 'A picture is worth . . .? Photo elicitation interviewing wit formerly homeless adults', *Qualitative Health Research*, **23** (11), 1435–44.

Pattie, C., P. Seyd and P. Whiteley (2004), *Citizenship in Britain Values, Participation and Democracy*, Cambridge: Cambridge University Press.

Poletta, F. and M.K. Ho (2006), 'Frames and their consequences', in R.E. Goodin and C. Tilly (eds), *The Oxford Handbook of Contextual Political Studies*, Oxford: Oxford University Press, pp. 187–209.

Read, M. and D. Marsh (2002), 'Combining quantitative and qualitative methods', in

D. Marsh and G. Stoker (eds), *Theory and Methods in Political Science*, 2nd edn, London: Palgrave Macmillan, pp. 231–48.

Rhodes, R.A.W. (2002) 'Putting people back into networks', *Australian Journal of Political Science*, **37** (3), 399–416.

Rhodes, R.A.W. (2011), *Everyday Life in British Government*, Oxford: Oxford University Press.

Schön, D.A. and M. Rein (1994), *Frame Reflection: Toward the Resolution of Intractable Policy Controversies*, New York: Basic Books.

Shannon, L.W. (1954), 'The opinions of Little Orphan Annie and her friends', *Public Opinion Quarterly*, **18** (2), 169–79.

Wagenaar, H. (2011), *Meaning in Action. Interpretation and Dialogue in Policy Analysis*, New York: M.E. Sharpe.

Wodak, R. and M. Meyer (eds) (2009), *Methods for Critical Discourse Analysis*, London: Sage.

Yanow, D. (2003), 'Interpretive empirical political science: what makes this not a subfield of qualitative methods', *Qualitative Methods*, **1** (Fall), 9–13.

Yanow, D. (2007), 'Qualitative-interpretive methods in policy research', in F. Fischer and G.J. Miller (eds), *Handbook of Public Policy Analysis. Theory, Politics, and Methods*, London: Taylor and Francis, pp. 405–15.

22 Multilevel regression analysis
Jan Kleinnijenhuis

1 INTRODUCTION

The central defining feature of *multilevel data* is that data are available for units of analysis that can be distinguished across different dimensions such as nations and years, classes and pupils, municipalities and citizens, sources and statements, or subject actors and target actors or target issues. These dimensions can be *hierarchically nested*. For example, citizens within municipalities within nations, pupils within classes, or statements within sources. In the absence of a hierarchy they are *cross-nested*, which means that data are available for all combinations of subject actors with target issues, or all combinations of territorial units like nations with time units like days, weeks, quarters or years.

Regression analysis of multilevel data aims at the explanation or prediction of dependent variables that are defined *at the lowest level*, which is *for each available combination* of the different dimensions; for example, which citizens in which municipalities within which nations are likely to be unemployed (hierarchically nested data). Why did specific nations face a high unemployment in specific years (cross-nested data)? Independent variables can be defined at the lowest level also (for example, consumer demand in the case of data about nations per quarter), but also at higher levels (for example, quarterly effects that vary between summer and winter). A single-level regression analysis of multilevel data would result in estimates of averaged regression coefficients that would hold equally for each nation, each quarter, and so on. The feature which distinguishes multilevel regression analysis from ordinary regression analysis is the ability to model the *variation of regression coefficients* between different nations, different times, different municipalities, different citizens, and so on, on top of the estimation of averaged (or fixed) effects. To put it differently, multilevel regression analysis enables the estimation of *regression parameter noise or causal heterogeneity*. From a statistical point of view multilevel regression analysis offers the proper tools to model multilevel data, whereas ordinary regression analysis does neither reckon with the lack of independence in multilevel data (for example, between subsequent periods in time, or between geographically nearby municipalities), nor with the limited variance across specific higher level units (for example, low variance of economic growth in the midst of an economic crisis).

This chapter presents two examples of multilevel regression models, one for hierarchically nested multilevel data, and one for cross-nested multilevel data with a time dimension (also labeled as 'pooled time series analysis'). These examples may serve as a snapshot guide to decide whether a research question should be answered by a single-level analysis of single-level data, or whether multilevel data are available that render a particular type of multilevel regression analysis more attractive.

2   AN EXAMPLE OF A HIERARCHICALLY NESTED MULTILEVEL ANALYSIS

Matthes et al. (2012) pose the question whether fear of social isolation (FSI) increases the willingness to self-censorship (WTSC). This question dates back to Elisabeth Noelle Neumann's theory on the 'spiral of silence' (Noelle-Neumann 1974) which in turn dates back to Alexis de Tocqueville who hypothesized that the availability of a free press had made Americans so aware of majority opinions, that on many issues holders of minority opinions would feel isolated and would therefore decide not to speak up anymore, which could eventually lead to apathy and a democratic tyranny of the majority (De Tocqueville 1835 [1951]).

2.1   Possibilities for Single-Level and Multilevel Analysis

Clearly the FSI–WTSC-relationship could be modeled with one-shot single-level data from a public opinion survey. Starting from the assumption that citizens vary in their personal FSI, two batteries of questions with regard to the FSI and with regard to the WTSC could be posed to respondents in the survey. The hypothesis can be tested better with multilevel data for various time points, various issues and/or various nations. It is worth discussing each of these three possibilities.

In principle the survey could be repeated at various time points, with the same respondents, to assess the causal order. Single-level regression coefficients per respondent per year would, however, still be based on a very limited variance in FSI, whereas a pooled correlation coefficient across all respondents and across all time periods would not take the possibility into account that the relationship could vary between respondents and between time periods.

Additional data on FSI and WTSC for a variety of issues could be used to test the relationship between FSI and WTSC per issue. The prediction would be that we like to talk about issues only when the majority supports our opinion, which comes close to the prediction on the basis of issue ownership theory (Budge and Farlie 1983; Petrocik 1996) that liberals address taxes because the majority agrees with them on the issue of taxes, whereas socialists address social services, because the majority agrees with them on that issue.

Matthes et al. (2012) gathered additional data to test the relationship between FSI and WTSC across various nations. They opted for survey research in nine nations that vary with respect to their individualism (for example, the US versus China) and with respect to democratic governance (for example, Germany versus Russia). In total 2215 respondents participated in a survey conducted in 2009, with a minimum of 236 respondents for the US and a maximum of 253 respondents for Mexico. Respondents were asked a battery of questions with regard to the FSI and the WTSC that were validated in earlier research.[1] Here we rescaled the two scales to the range of −1 to +1. The complete absence of fear of isolation and complete unwillingness to self-censorship is denoted as −1 and the presence of fear of isolation and of willingness of self-censorship as +1.

The key to understand multilevel regression analysis is that WTSC along the *y*-axis can be regressed on FSI across the *x*-axis both at the lowest level of respondents nested in nations (cf. Figure 22.1) and at the highest level of nations (see Figure 22.2).

In Figure 22.1 each respondent is represented with a dot, whereas in Figure 22.2 each nation is represented with a dot. The lines in the figures are the ordinary least squares (OLS) regression lines.

The regression lines from Figure 22.1 appear to show causal heterogeneity since fear of isolation amounts to WTSC, but not in China.

Figure 22.2 shows, however, that in China a high average level of WTSC is to be expected given the average level of FSI, which is indeed the case. A closer look at the variances in FSI across the *x*-axis in Figure 22.1 is required to see that, for example, US citizens vary enormously with respect to their FSI, whereas in South Korea and especially in China almost nobody is *not* afraid to become socially isolated. Thus, the explanation why a relationship between the 'fear of isolation' and the WTSC within China was not detected by ordinary regression in Figure 22.1 could be that the Chinese variation in fear of isolation is too small.

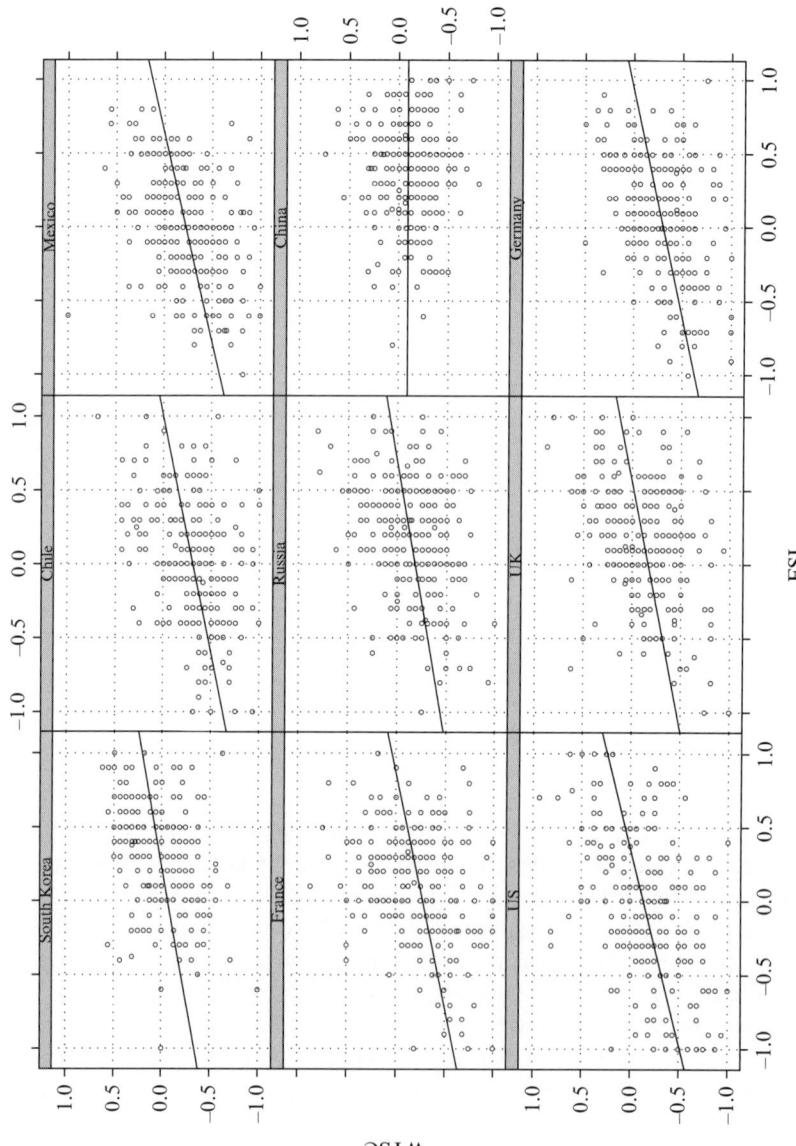

Figure 22.1   Data on FSI and WTSC per nation summarized by regression lines

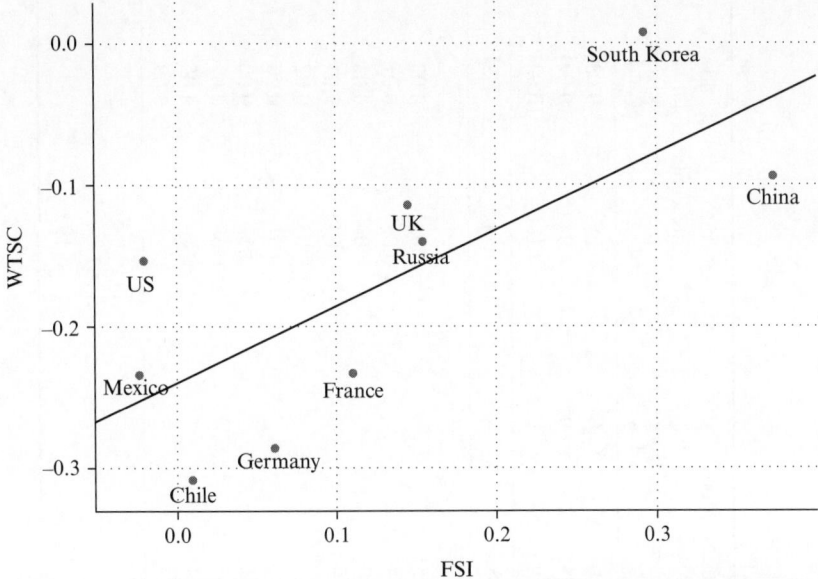

*Figure 22.2   Data on the mean FSI and WTSC of nations summarized by
                a regression line*

3   A MULTILEVEL MODEL FOR NESTED FSI–WTSC MULTILEVEL DATA

3.1   The Empty Model

The point of departure for a multilevel regression model of substantial interest is the *empty model*. In the empty model the variation in the dependent variable – here willingness to self-censorship – is explained from differences between higher level factors – here differences between countries – without delving into the variables between countries or within countries that account for differences between countries. The empty model is actually an analysis of variance (ANOVA) with the dimensions of analysis as factors.

The first column in Table 22.1 presents the estimates for the empty model for the dependent variable WTSC.

The intercept in the empty model shown in Table 22.1, which in the empty model is the only fixed parameter that is estimated, is known as the grand mean in the literature on ANOVA-models. It amounts to −0.17 on a −1 to +1 scale, with a standard deviation (SD) of 0.03. That is, on

Table 22.1 FSI–WTSC multilevel models for citizens nested within countries

Fixed part	Empty model		Random slopes model		Random slopes and intercepts model	
	B	(s.e.)	B	(s.e.)	B	(s.e.)
Fear of Social Isolation			0.30	(0.04)	0.28	(0.03)
Lack of civil liberties			0.04	(0.01)	0.04	(0.04)
Intercept	−0.17	(0.03)	−0.19	(0.01)	−0.18	(0.03)

Random part	Empty model	Random slopes model	Random slopes and intercepts model	
	Intercept	FSI	Intercept	FSI
Deviances				
US	0.02	0.05	0.07	0.08
UK	0.06	0.04	0.06	0.01
Germany	−0.11	−0.09	−0.08	0.03
France	−0.06	−0.10	−0.04	0.03
Russia	0.03	−0.05	−0.03	−0.02
China	0.08	−0.02	−0.03	−0.20
South Korea	0.17	0.01	0.01	0.00
Chile	−0.13	−0.03	0.12	0.02
Mexico	−0.06	0.04	−0.08	0.05
SD deviances	0.10	0.10	−0.04 / 0.08	0.09
Deviance IC	1429	1183	1119	
Akaike IC	1445	1233	1162	
R^2	0.076	0.163	0.199	

average, citizens in the nine nations are not inclined to self-censorship. The random part includes the deviances of the intercept for the separate nations, which are known as the group means in ANOVA models, as well as the standard deviances of the group means from the grand mean, or intercept. The score for 'SD deviances' amounts to +0.10, that is, the confidence interval of the country mean of WTSC ranges from roughly −0.17 + 2*0.10 and −0.17 − 2*0.10, and thus between 0.03 and −0.37. In tables in the research literature on the results of multilevel analysis only the *standard deviation* of group means is usually reported, although only the *actual deviances* provide substantial information about the higher level units. Willingness to self-censorship is remarkably high in South Korea (+0.17) and China (+0.08), and remarkably low in Chile (−0.13) and Germany (−0.11).

3.2 The Random Slopes Model

The random slopes model leaves out the random part of the intercept that was included in the empty model, but includes FSI as a fixed predictor, as well as *random slopes* for the effect of FSI in different nations. Fear of social isolation is a predictor at the lowest level, which varies between nations, but also between citizens within nations. In addition, we include a measure of the lack of constitutionally guaranteed civil liberties at the national level, since we expect that subjective FSI is partly rooted in an objective lack of civil liberties.[2] Civil liberties do not vary between citizens. The ability to include independent variables at different levels, in this case both at the level of citizens and of nation, is one of the advantages of multilevel models. Both measures are linearly transformed to the −1 to +1 value range, which holds also for the dependent variable WTSC. A common −1 to +1 value range greatly helps to make the sizes of the multilevel regression estimates comparable to each other (Gelman and Hill 2007; Hox 2010).

The random part shows the deviations of the fixed effect of FSI per nation. The total effect of FSI on WTSC, as measured by the sum of the fixed part and the random part of the slope coefficient, is relatively small for Germany (0.30 − 0.10 = 0.20) and France (0.30 − 0.09 = 0.21) and relatively large for the US (0.30 + 0.05 = 0.35), the UK (0.30 + 0.04 = 0.34) and Mexico (0.30 + 0.04 = 0.34). Interestingly enough the random slopes model does not show a particularly weak effect for China, although the regression lines per nation in Figure 22.1 suggested the absence of an FSI-effect in China. The reason why the multilevel random slopes model does not consider China as a deviant case can be seen already from Figure 22.2. The random slopes model starts from the total, 'pooled' variance of fear of isolation across citizens irrespective of their nations, and from this perspective the combination of a high FSI and a high WTSC in China is perfectly in line with the hypothesis that FSI affects WTSC.

3.3   The Random Slopes and Random Intercepts Model

The random slopes and random effects model differs from the previous model in one respect, which is the inclusion of random intercepts. This terminology may give rise to confusion, since the term 'random slope model' is often used in the research literature for models that include also random intercepts. Without random intercepts the regression lines for each country are forced to cross through the fixed intercept when FSI equals 0, which is an assumption that is reasonable when all variables share a (-1 to $+1$) value range, but which is easily relaxed by allowing for random intercepts. The random intercepts show that they are still not near zero. This means that FSI and the lack of civil liberties do not fully explain the variation between countries. For example, WTSC is much more prevalent among South Koreans ($+0.12$) than among Germans (-0.08), even when controlled for civil liberties at the national level and the personal FSI. No noteworthy diminishment of the explanatory power of FSI (0.30, 0.28) and the lack of civil liberties (0.04, 0.04) occurs when random intercepts are included. Note however that the standard error of civil liberties increases, apparently due to the collinearity with country specific intercepts. The coefficient of 0.04 is statistically insignificant in a random slopes model with random intercepts in addition. Since the size of the underlying regression coefficient remained 0.04, this shows that 'the difference between "significant" and "not significant" is not itself statistically significant' (Gelman and Stern 2006). The model with random slopes and random intercepts still shows for China a positive regression slope of FSI on WTSC ($0.28 - 0.20 = 0.08$). The inclusion of random intercepts does not radically alter the interpretations based on the random slopes model without random intercepts.

3.3.1   Goodness of fit

Which model is the best one from a statistical point of view can be assessed by measures for the goodness of fit in multilevel regression analysis. Akaike's information criterion (AIC), and the derived deviance information criterion (DIC), take the number of estimated parameters of each model into account. The starting point for model evaluations based on AIC and DIC is the AIC, respectively, DIC of the empty model. A subsequent model fits the data better if its AIC, respectively DIC, is lower. How much lower is a fairly technical matter, but at least five points lower is a crude rule of thumb. According to this rule of thumb, the random slope model is a much better model than the empty model. The goodness of fit of the model with random slopes and random intercepts is even better.

As long as we deal with a *linear* multilevel regression model it is still possible to use the explained variance R^2 as a measure of explained variance. R^2 amounts to 7.6 percent for the empty model. The random slopes model explains 16.3 percent of the variance, which is more than twice as high. The random slopes and random intercepts model explains 19.9 percent of the variance.

The results give rise to the overall conclusion that De Tocqueville's and Noelle-Neumann's theory about the influence of the FSI on the WTSC holds in each of the nations that were investigated, even when the objective lack of civil liberties at the national level and random effects per nation are taken into account. The multilevel regression analysis does not provide evidence that China is a deviant case, although this was suggested by a single-level regression analysis for China (cf. Figure 22.1).

4 AN EXAMPLE OF A CROSS-NESTED MULTILEVEL ANALYSIS: POOLED TIME SERIES

Changing issue positions of parties provide an example of cross-nested multilevel data, because for each combination of parties, issues and time points we can ask for a party's issue emphasis and a party's issue position. Parties may compete with issue emphasis only, with issue positions only, or with a combination of the two, similarly in party manifestos (Dolezal et al. 2014), in the media (Kriesi et al. 2006) and in public opinion (Sanders et al. 2011). Parties change their issue emphasis and their issue positions not only between elections, but also within election campaigns (Kleinnijenhuis and de Nooy 2013).

The analysis of issue positions during a single election campaign results in data on issue positions that are cross-nested within parties, issues and days. Our example is based on data for ten parties with regard to 13 issues on 60 days (ten weeks with Sundays excluded) before the Dutch national elections on 22 November 2006 (Kleinnijenhuis and de Nooy 2013). A content analysis of news items in national newspapers and television news programs resulted in 5636 quotes or paraphrases about issue positions of parties and 3995 statements on support and criticism (also labelled as cooperation or conflict) that are helpful to explain changes in issue positions. Reversely, issue positions are helpful to explain support and criticism of parties for each other (De Nooy and Kleinnijenhuis 2013), whereas both are helpful to attract voters (Kleinnijenhuis et al. 2007).

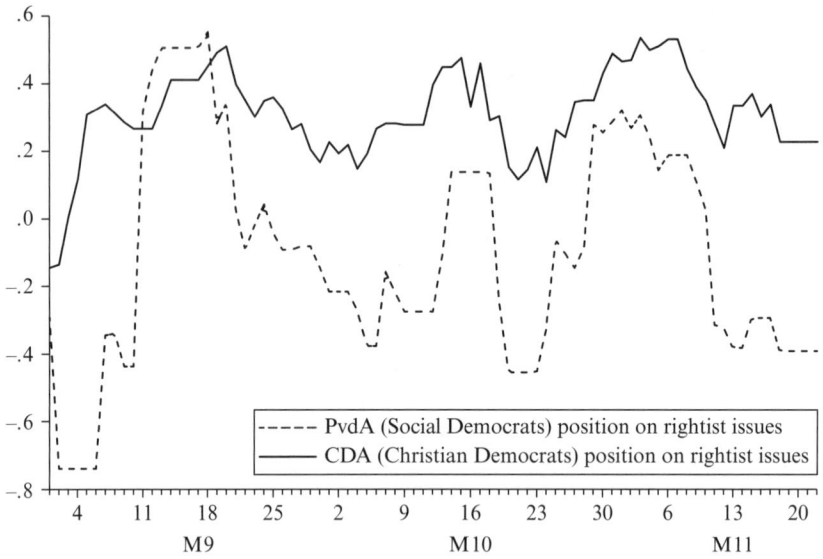

*Figure 22.3   Issue positions of PvdA and CDA on rightist issues in the
2006 election campaign*

Figure 22.3 gives a teaser by showing the changes in the issue positions
of PvdA (Labour) and CDA (Christian Democrats), which were the two
most newsworthy parties during the Dutch election campaign of 2006, with
regard to rightist issues (for example, cuts in government expenditures,
lower taxes and privatization). Pro-rightist statements are represented as
positive statements (values > 0 on the *y*-axis), and con-statements as negative statements (values < 0 on the *y*-axis). Figure 22.3 is based on a content
analysis of statements in newspaper and television news.

   The data show that the issue positions of the two parties tend to
move together, with the CDA somewhat more often as the first mover.
The PvdA is less rightist than the CDA, with as an exception the week
preceding 'Prinsjesdag'[3] on 19 September, in which the Labour Party
presented itself as a financially solid party. The Labour Party embraced
a more rightist issue position in the middle of October when the Labour
Party was surpassed in the polls by the Christian-Democrats, and in early
November when the Christian-Democrats unfolded their daily flip-flop
campaign targeted at the Labour Party, which was inspired by the flip-
flop campaign of Bush against Kerry. However, on 12 November senior
PvdA-politicians stated in a renowned television program that the Labour
Party leader should cooperate with parties to the left of the PvdA and that

the PvdA should attack the Christian Democrats rather than compromise with them. The PvdA followed this advice: the distance between the PvdA and the CDA increased enormously, with as a disastrous electoral effect for the Labour Party that it lost even more voters. The aim of the cross-nested multilevel model is to model the forces that systematically account for such changes in issue positions.

4.1 Towards a Dynamic Multilevel Network Theory of Issue Positions of Parties

To attract voters, it is essential for parties to persistently keep their promises by holding on to their former issue positions, especially with regard to their owned issues. Margaret Thatcher launched a famous speech with her principal statement 'the Lady is not for turning' to strengthen her reputation as the Iron Lady who was averse to flip-flop U-turn policies. Parties that do not succeed in raising media attention for the viewpoints with regard to their owned issues will lose at the elections. Therefore each issue position in the media is weighted with the number of times it is addressed, whereas the strength of a party's issue position decays exponentially unless it is repeated with equal or even greater force (Fan 1996). The *persistence hypothesis*, which is the first hypothesis displayed in Figure 22.4, is therefore that a party will persistently repeat its former issue positions. Note that the principle of exponential decay implies that a party still holds the same issue positions as before after many days without news about them, but that they count less and less as compared with issue positions that are reiterated.

Persistence becomes boring, however. To gain media attention for their issue positions, parties have to tune in to the latest events, frames, narratives and story lines in the media. Their issue positions must be perceived as newsworthy, valuable, and balanced or consonant responses to the latest news or to the latest questions. Concepts such as balance, cognitive consistency or consonance can be operationalized with the theory of signed graphs or networks (Cartwright and Harary 1956). The examples in Figure 22.4 suffice here to explain the hypotheses about consonant, balanced responses that are usually newsworthy (Galtung and Ruge 1965).

Newsworthiness owing to balance means that a politician who states he or she is pro or con an issue position is saying something that is potentially newsworthy because this statement creates one or more new *positive cycles* in a network that is comprised of the exponentially decaying news thus far. A cycle is positive if – regardless of the direction of its arrows –the product (or division) of all the positive and negative signs of its arrows is positive. The cycles of $-.9 * -1.0 * +.9$ for transitivity and ideological tit-for-tat are positive, for example.

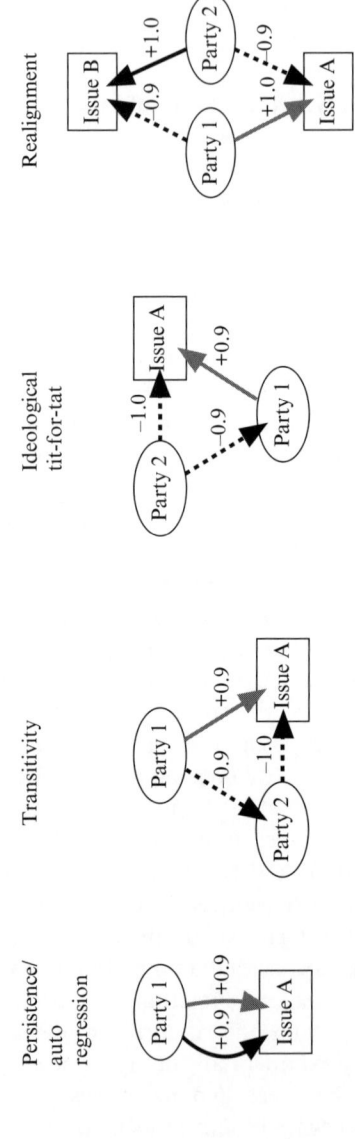
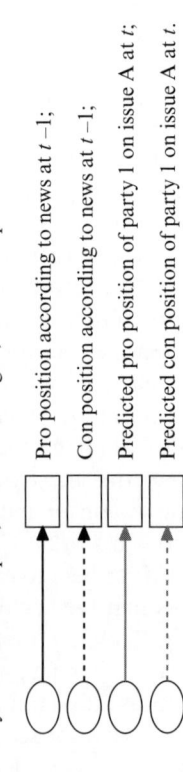

Persistence/ auto regression

Transitivity

Ideological tit-for-tat

Realignment

Key: Parties in ellipses, issues in rectangles, numbers = pro-con on a –1 to +1 scale;

Pro position according to news at *t* –1;

Con position according to news at *t* –1;

Predicted pro position of party 1 on issue A at *t*;

Predicted con position of party 1 on issue A at *t*.

Figure 22.4   Examples of four strategies to keep or adopt issue positions during an election campaign

334

The transitivity hypotheses predicts that party 1 in Figure 22.3 will speak in favor of A in case the news thus far maintained that party 2 was against A and that party 1 attacked party 2. The new statements of party 1 in favor of A would appear to be consistent with the earlier attacks of party 1 on party 2, because party 2 opposes A. Similarly, new statements of party 1 in favor of A would appear to be consistent with earlier support of party 1 for party 3 in case party 3 supported A.

The tit-for-tat-strategy, which comes down to reacting to rewards with rewards and punishments with punishments (Axelrod 1984), can be generalized to an ideological tit-for-tat hypotheses. An ideological tit-for-tat party 1 is predicted to state that it supports issue position A in case the news thus far maintained that party 2 that attacked party 1 opposed A. The ideological tit-for-tat hypothesis predicts that party 1 will support A in case party 3 supported both party 1 and issue position A, but will oppose A in case another party 4 either supported party 1 but not A, or A but not party 1.

The ideological realignment strategy predicts that party 1 will state to be in favor of A if A is opposed by party 2 in case party 1 disagrees with party 2 on other issues like B – and if A is supported by a party 3 in case party 1 agrees with party 3 on issues like B. On the other hand, party 1 is predicted to oppose A if either A was opposed by parties with whom party 1 agreed on other issues, or A was supported by other parties with whom A disagreed on other issues. Ideological realignment strategies of parties ultimately gives rise to Schattschneider's (1960) one-dimensional democracy in which parties line up their issue positions along a single ideological conflict dimension. Ideological realignment amounts to one-dimensional polarization.

4.2 A Cross-Nested Multilevel Regression Model

The hypotheses result in predictions of issue positions for each party for each issue on each day, given the network representation of the news thus far. The cross-level multilevel regression model entails that for each combination of a party i, an issue j and a day t, a party's issue position depends on persistence, as measured by persistence in holding their former issue position, transitivity, ideological tit-for-Tat and ideological realignment, all measured at $t–1$, and on a regression constant and a regression residual ε. Thus, the variance in issue positions from day to day is accounted for by the variance in the independent variables at previous days. The random slopes per day could be left out because they were too small to be meaningful. The cross-nested multilevel regression model with random slopes and random intercepts allows for causal heterogeneity, since each of the regression slope coefficients is allowed to vary systematically between parties i and issues j. If the focus is not on the precise nature of causal heterogeneity, but on the overall picture, then we could also resort to a pooled model for all parties, all issues and time periods with panel corrected standard errors (PCSE) (Beck and Katz 1995) to correct for the lack of statistical independence in the data.

Table 22.2 presents the regression estimates for the cross-nested multilevel equation.

The empty model maintains that issue positions simply differ systematically between parties and between issues. For reasons of space we do not present the random estimates per party, but the standard deviations of the regression coefficients per party (0.18) and per issue (0.26). These systematic, but theoretically unexplained, differences between parties and issues explain 23 percent of the variance in issue positions of parties.

The multilevel model with random intercepts and random slopes for the independent variables persistence, transitivity, tit-for-tat and realignment increases the explained variance to 70 percent, while reducing the amount of variation that is attributed to theoretically unexplained systematic differences between parties (from 0.18 to 0.03) and between issues (from 0.26 to 0.08).

The fixed regression slopes show that issue positions are primarily a mixture of persistence (0.46) and realignment (1.31). In the case of the 2006 Dutch elections realignment meant polarization along the left–right axis (see also Figure 22.3). Ideological tit-for-tat is overall a more popular strategy than transitivity. The relative popularity of tit-for-tat (0.18) as compared to transitivity (0.10) shows that it is somewhat more newsworthy to react to an opposed issue position taken by an adversary after this adversary attacked the party, than after a previous attack of the party on this adversary.

Table 22.2 presents also the standard deviations of the random slopes per party and per issue. The standard deviations are manifestations of interesting features of parties and of issues. For example, the PvdA and the VVD relied heavily on ideological realignment (polarization along the left–right axis) to the detriment of persistence. Both parties lost at the elections. Persistence is not only dependent on party strategies, but is partially conditioned by the nature of issues. Persistence was high for the valence issue of crime, but remarkable low for position issues, especially for rightist issues. The latter was already observed on the basis of the shifts in issue positions with regard to rightist issues of the CDA and the PvdA in Figure 22.2.

Table 22.2 Multilevel models for issue positions cross-nested within parties, issues and days

	Empty model				Network auto regression model with cross-nested random effects				
	Fixed part		Random part		Fixed part			Random part	
	B	SE(B)	SD(B) per party	SD(B) per issue	B	SE(B)		SD(B) per party	SD(B) per issue
Persistence (autoregression)					0.46	0.07	***	0.19	0.15
Transitivity					0.10	0.07		0.14	0.20
Ideological tit-for-tat					0.18	0.08	*	0.23	0.10
Ideological realignment					1.31	0.26	***	0.66	0.52
Intercept	0.31	0.09 **	0.18	0.26	0.09	0.03	**	0.05	0.08
Number of observation	2 800		10	13	2 800			10	13
Goodness of fit									
Deviance IC	12 736				5 767				
Akaike IC	12 749				5 832				
R^2	0.23				0.70				

337

5   PRIMARY LESSONS AND FURTHER REFERENCES

The examples in this chapter show that multilevel regression analysis is an attractive modeling strategy in case multilevel data can be made available. Multilevel regression analysis is especially useful when causal heterogeneity is plausible, and single-level data could be hampered by small samples or a limited amount of variation in the independent variables.

The key to understand how multilevel analysis deals with dependencies in the data is the concept of *partial pooling* (Gelman and Hill 2007, pp. 252–9). Figure 22.1 showed regressions per nation that provide examples of no pooling at all, with as a result that regression estimates still rest on the limited variance in the independent variables per nation. A complete pooling would entail that all cases would be lumped together, thereby disregarding how they were clustered. The notion of partial pooling entails that parameters for each higher level unit are estimated as a weighted average of observations within a higher level unit (the unpooled estimate) and observations over all higher level units (the completely pooled estimate).

A *nested* multilevel regression model can be perceived as a model for a staged random sample, on the basis of which the researcher wishes to generalize to populations at each level, for example, both to the population of nations, and to populations of citizens within nations. A multistage sample perspective gives rise to the demand that the number of units at each level should be high enough to warrant statistical generalization to the population, for example, at least 30 higher level units with at least 30 lower level units per higher level unit (Hox 2010, ch. 12). The pragmatic perspective is that multilevel regression models with random intercepts and random slopes are merely an efficient means to describe potentially heterogeneous relationships in the data at hand *for the units of analysis at hand*. This gives rise to less high demands: even with three higher level groups multilevel modeling outperforms 'no pooling' and precisely in the case of only a few lower level units within some of the higher level groups the group estimates will benefit greatly from partial pooling (Gelman and Hill 2007, ch. 12.9). This chapter is based on the pragmatic perspective.

To learn more about multilevel analysis and about the available software to apply variants of the technique (for example, R lme4/lmertest/winbugs/blme, Stata Xtmixed, SPSS Mixed Models, mlwin) the reader should consult one or more of the excellent articles (Steenbergen and Jones 2002; Hayes 2006) or books (Gelman and Hill 2007; Hox 2010; Snijders 2011) on the subject. The reader should realize that various other labels have been used in the research literature to discuss (specific types of) multilevel models such as mixed models, random effects models and models for pooled time series analysis. The difficulties in applying software for multilevel regression analysis are usually not in the syntax of the multilevel model itself,[4] but in the preparation of the data to an appropriate 'long' format, and in mastering estimation strategies and overcoming estimation problems. Ultimately we should acknowledge, however, that estimation problems with models that do not converge may signal that a more parsimonious theory is called for.

FURTHER READING

Gelman, A. and J. Hill (2007), *Data Analysis Using Regression and Multilevel/Hierarchical Models*, Cambridge: Cambridge University Press.
Hox, J.J. (2010), *Multilevel Analysis: Techniques and Applications*, Hove: Routledge.
Snijders, T.A.B. (2011), *Multilevel Analysis*, New York and Berlin: Springer.

NOTES

1. The author is grateful to Jörg Matthes, Andrew Hayes, Hernando Rojas, Fei Shen, Seong-Jae Min and Ivan Dylko for sharing their research data.
2. The Lack of Civil Liberties Index for the year 2009 from Freedom House (2015) was used to operationalize civil liberties, first because this index intends to measures precisely limitations on civil liberties, and secondly, because this index performed slightly better than related indices, such as Hofstede's individualism index.
3. *Prinsjesdag* is the annual occasion of the King's Speech from the Throne proclaiming the governmental plans for the coming year including the presentation of fiscal budget of the state.
4. The model with random intercepts and random slopes from Table 22.1 to estimate the influence of the lack of civil liberties (CL) and of FSI on WTSC, for example, can be estimated with the freely available lme4- and lmerTest-packages in R with a single statement:

$$lmer(WTSC \sim 1 + FSI + CL + (FSI\text{-}1|COUNTRY) + (1|COUNTRY))$$

in which $\sim$ is the sign to start the right hand side of the regression equation, and 1, FSI, CL, (FSI-1|COUNTRY) and (1|COUNTRY) represent respectively the regression intercept, FSI, CL, the random slope of FSI per country, and the random intercept per country.

REFERENCES

Axelrod, R.A. (1984), *The Evolution of Cooperation*, New York: Basic Books.
Beck, N. and J.N. Katz (1995), 'What to do (and not to do) with time-series cross-section data', *American Political Science Review*, **89** (3), 634–47.

Budge, I. and D.J. Farlie (1983), *Explaining and Predicting Elections: Issues Effects and Party Strategies in Twenty-Three Democracies*, London: George Allen and Unwin.

Cartwright, D. and F. Harary (1956), 'Structural balance: a generalization of Heider's theory', *Psychological Review*m, **63** (5), 277–93.

De Nooy, W. and J. Kleinnijenhuis (2013), 'Polarization in the media during an election campaign: a dynamic network model predicting support and attack among political actors', *Political Communication*, **30** (1), 117–38.

De Tocqueville, A.C.H.C. (1835), *De la démocratie en Amérique*, 1951 8th edn, Paris: Gallimard.

Dolezal, M., L. Ennser-Jedenastik, W.C. Müller and A.K. Winkler (2014), 'How parties compete for votes: a test of saliency theory', *European Journal of Political Research*, **53** (1), 57–76.

Fan, D.P. (1996), 'Predictions of the Bush–Clinton–Perot presidential race from the press', *Political Analysis*, **6** (1), 67–105.

Freedom House (2015), *Individual Territory Ratings and Status, FIW 1973–2015 (EXCEL-file)*, Washington, DC and New York: Freedom House.

Galtung, J. and M.H. Ruge (1965), 'The structure of foreign news', *Journal of Peace Research*, **2** (1), 64–91.

Gelman, A. and J. Hill (2007), *Data Analysis Using Regression and Multilevel/Hierarchical Models*, Cambridge: Cambridge University Press.

Gelman, A. and H. Stern (2006), 'The difference between "significant" and "not significant" is not itself statistically significant', *American Statistician*, **60** (4), 328–31.

Hayes, A.F. (2006), 'A primer on multilevel modeling', *Human Communication Research*, **32** (4), 385–410.

Hox, J.J. (2010), *Multilevel Analysis: Techniques and Applications*, Hove: Routledge.

Kleinnijenhuis, J. and W. de Nooy (2013), 'Adjustment of issue positions based on network strategies in an election campaign: a two-mode network autoregression model with cross-nested random effects', *Social Networks*, **35** (2), 168–77.

Kleinnijenhuis, J., A.M. J. van Hoof, D. Oegema and J.A. de Ridder (2007), 'A test of rivaling approaches to explain news effects: news on issue positions of parties, real world developments, support and criticism, and success and failure', *Journal of Communication*, **57** (2), 366–84.

Kriesi, H., E. Grande, R. Lachat, M. Dolezal, S. Bornschier and T. Frey (2006), 'Globalization and the transformation of the national political space: six European countries compared', *European Journal of Political Research*, **45** (6), 921–56.

Matthes, J., A.F. Hayes, H. Rojas, F. Shen, S.-J. Min and I.B. Dylko (2012), 'Exemplifying a dispositional approach to cross-cultural spiral of silence research: fear of social isolation and the inclination to self-censor', *International Journal of Public Opinion Research*, **24** (3), 287–305.

Noelle-Neumann, E. (1974), 'The spiral of silence a theory of public opinion', *Journal of Communication*, **24** (2), 43–51.

Petrocik, J.R. (1996), 'Issue ownership in Presidential Elections, with a 1980 case study', *American Journal of Political Science*, **40** (3), 825–50.

Sanders, D., H.D. Clarke, M.C. Stewart and P. Whiteley (2011), 'Downs, Stokes and the dynamics of electoral choice', *British Journal of Political Science*, **41** (2), 287–314.

Schattschneider, E.E. (1960), *The Semisovereign People: A Realist's View of Democracy in America*, New York: Holt, Rinehart and Winston.

Snijders, T.A.B. (2011), *Multilevel Analysis*, New York and Berlin: Springer.

Steenbergen, M.R. and B.S. Jones (2002), 'Modeling multilevel data structures', *American Journal of Political Science*, **46** (1), 218–37.

PART IV

RESEARCH TOOLS: QUANTITATIVE AND QUALITATIVE APPLICATIONS

23 Studying how policies affect the people: grappling with measurement, causality and the macro–micro divide

Staffan Kumlin and Isabelle Stadelmann-Steffen

1 INTRODUCTION

In a democracy citizens' attitudes and behavior should influence future public policies. However, in practice the reverse may frequently also be true: attitudes and behavior can be results of previous policies. This is the simple and powerful idea of *policy feedback*.

On the one hand, policy feedback is an 'oldsaw in political science' (Soss and Schram 2007, p. 111). It can, with some detective work, be traced through the history of political science and pinned to names such as Schattschneider (1935), Easton (1965) and Pierson (1993), to mention a few. On the other hand, it has been rather slow to reach the mainstream of empirical political behavior research. Only some ten years ago, Mettler and Soss (2004, p. 1) argued in a programmatic review article that 'aside from some notable exceptions, political science has had little to say about the consequences of public policy for democratic citizenship'. Quite such a harsh verdict is no longer fair. A more recent overview points to 'great strides in a few short years' at the same time as 'outstanding questions linger as to the mechanisms and conditions under which feedbacks emerge' (Campbell 2012, p. 334). As recently illustrated in Kumlin and Stadelmann-Steffen (2014), policy feedback is now broadly examined in empirical studies employing a host of dependent variables, ranging from political participation and party choice, to welfare state attitudes, to social and political trust.

While this is a positive development, a more general point made by Mettler and Soss is still entirely valid: in spite of its potentially broad relevance, policy feedback has rarely been recognized as a distinct 'category', 'mode' or 'paradigm' of research on citizens and politics. Instead, textbooks have traditionally divided this vast field into three, or possibly four, broad schools of thought. There is the 'sociological' tradition, focusing on group socialization and social communication; there is the 'psychological' tradition looking more to individual values and identifications; and there is the 'economic' tradition concentrating on self-interest and rationality.

As a possible fourth group one might discern a 'communication'-oriented tradition, analyzing concepts such as 'agenda-setting', 'priming' and 'framing'. Despite obvious differences these schools of thought have, at least in practice, conceived of causal processes and key variables in ways largely exogenous to actual public policies.

As a result, even very influential studies on policy feedback are typically pitched as contributions to these other traditions. Alternatively, researchers identify themselves in even more specific terms, for example, as contributors to ongoing research on certain dependent variables, pitching their work as contributions to 'voter behavior', 'political participation', 'trust', and so on, rather than as 'policy feedback research' or the like. Accordingly, findings on policy feedback are scattered over large and self-contained research communities essentially dealing with other research problems. Mettler and Soss tried to remedy this compartmentalization by discerning a more 'political' tradition concerned with institutions and policy feedback, which has actually long been alive and well in the shadows of the bigger paradigms, but was never quite recognized as a distinct mode of explanation.

Compartmentalization has probably slowed down progress. Moreover, and crucial for this chapter, it may have obscured common methodological challenges, which have become harder to spot and discuss. We attempt to remedy this, to some extent, paying particular attention to the policy domain where policy feedback analyses have probably been most frequently applied: the welfare state. We do not provide anything like a full literature review; for this, we refer to the suggested reading section at the end of the chapter. Rather, we seek to discuss generic methodological issues, problems, and solutions. These are related in particular to the 'macro–micro divide', that is, whether to conceive of policy feedback at the contextual or the individual level (or both), how to measure independent policy variables, and how causality can be studied in an area where the relationship between independent and dependent variables is inherently reciprocal.

We proceed as follows. First, we present an analytical framework that encapsulates the various generic factors and effects present in the field. We then introduce the methodological challenges we would like to highlight. Finally, we discuss four recent applications of the policy feedback perspective. These illustrate the breadth of the research field as well as partial solutions to methodological challenges. We close by summarizing the chapter but also make a plea for 'cross-level thinking', that is, a conceptual willingness to analyze policy feedback as a cross-level process.

2 A MULTILEVEL ANALYTICAL FRAMEWORK FOR RESEARCH ON POLICY FEEDBACK AND CITIZENS

Figure 23.1 defines the analytical terrain of research on policy feedback and citizens. Note first the coexistence of individual-level variables (ellipses) and contextual/macro-level variables (rectangles). The model conceives of 'policy' at both these levels, including both the policy context in which all citizens of a country (or region, municipality, and so on) live, as well as individual-level within-context variation in exposure to, and evaluations of, those policies. While this duality may seem reasonable, past research has often been marked by a divide between macro and micro designs. By example, some of the earliest research on policy feedback developed mainly along a *macro-comparative* track, examining correlates of country-level welfare state 'effort' and 'regimes' (Esping-Andersen 1990), or (more recently) area-specific variation (Svallfors 2003; Naumann 2014). Often the dependent variable here has been attitudinal welfare state support. A second track has involved investigating consequences of *individual-level* variation within one country in policy experiences and evaluations. Here, dependent variables have included mainly political participation and trust (for example, Soss 1999; Kumlin 2004; Campbell 2005; Mettler 2005).

In recent years, these two tracks have moved closer to each other. Many studies now operate at both levels of analysis. On the one hand, this has been the result of developments in data availability (comparative survey data), statistical modelling (multilevel analysis), and computational power, which allows for combining individual and contextual data. On the other hand, as we shall see, there have also been theoretical and conceptual advances, making it easier to integrate the two.

Let us look at the components of Figure 23.1. Beginning with the individual level, there is 'policy exposure' at the back of the causal scheme. Quite naturally, some individuals are exposed more than others to certain types of welfare state policies, transfers and services. This is true for current use of a single policy (that is, 'my kids are currently in a public kindergarten'), but also for probability to eventually encounter it (for example, risk of eventually becoming a recipient of unemployment benefits). Taking unemployment benefits as an example, this would translate into measuring the effects of people currently receiving a particular type of unemployment benefit, how long this has gone on, as well as information that can be used to predict variation in future usage (including the respondent's own perception of likely future use). A number of different conceptualizations and measures of exposure are present in the literature. Simple dummies registering current use are ubiquitous. However, there

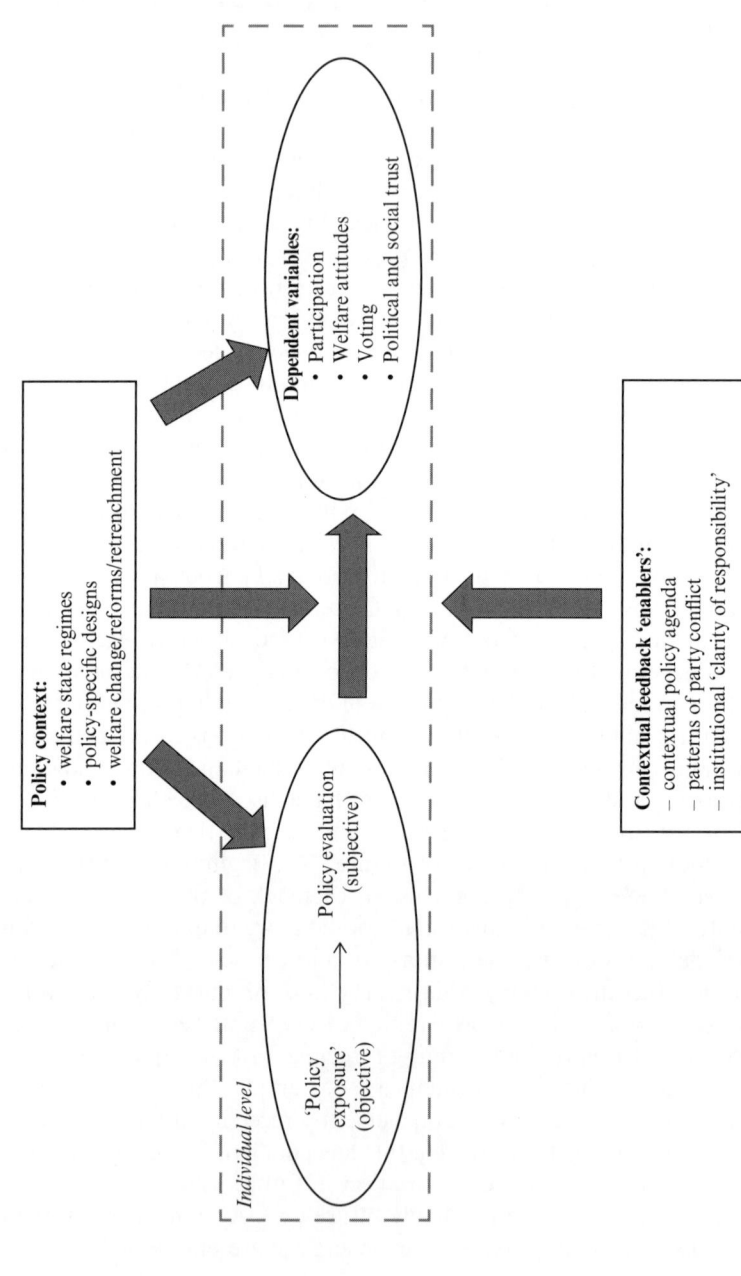

Policy context:
- welfare state regimes
- policy-specific designs
- welfare change/reforms/retrenchment

Individual level

Dependent variables:
- Participation
- Welfare attitudes
- Voting
- Political and social trust

'Policy exposure' (objective) → Policy evaluation (subjective)

Contextual feedback 'enablers':
- contextual policy agenda
- patterns of party conflict
- institutional 'clarity of responsibility'

Figure 23.1   An analytical framework for research on policy feedback and citizens

are also studies that conceive of exposure to particular aspects/parts of the welfare state (that is, to what extent/how often is the individual exposed to policies of *type* X) or even the extent to which an individual is somehow exposed to the entire set of welfare state policies (Kumlin 2004).

Moving a step to the right in the scheme, we find subjective 'policy evaluations'. Policy feedback hypotheses typically assume that effects not only depend on exposure in itself, but also on how exposure triggers subjective, evaluative reactions. Aspects of a benefit or service, and the processes through which they are delivered, is evaluated as good or bad, which may in turn generate some political conclusion or generalization about, for example, the incumbent government, politicians in general, the workings of a policy or the entire welfare state, and so on. Continuing the example of unemployment benefits, we may be interested in evaluations of whether the benefit itself is possible to live on, or whether encountered employees have done a good job.

A crucial research problem here concerns the yardsticks people use in policy perception and evaluation. The most commonly examined yardstick is probably material self-interest where evaluations, and ultimately political conclusions, depend on how much the individual evaluates social protection and public services to benefit him or her ('the more I get, the better'). However, consistent with social-psychological research on social justice (Tyler et al. 1997) subjectively evaluated 'distributive justice/deservingness' ('I get the level of protection and service that is right') and 'procedural justice' ('the process that led to the benefit was OK') have proven to be distinct from self-interest, and more important for some dependent variables. Procedural justice may become especially salient whenever a benefit application must be processed by a 'street-level bureaucrat' or when a service is delivered through repeated face-to-face contact with an employee.

The concepts of policy exposure and evaluation are intuitive enough. Less obvious, perhaps, is the fact that these are not necessarily the same as personal experience. Citizens may in theory be (unequally) exposed to information about (different parts of) the welfare state also through the media or via personal communication with family and friends (who may or may not have direct experiences themselves). Likewise, their evaluations may reflect personal experiences as well as 'sociotropic' or collective experiences (that is, evaluations of others' experiences or of how, for example, a service area functions overall in society). Still, Kumlin (2004) argued and found that personal experiences were more politically influential, as well as more correlated with sociotropic judgments, in the welfare state domain, compared with other domains, most notably the evaluation of macroeconomic performance.

Moving to the contextual level in Figure 23.1 (the rectangular boxes), first there is policy context; which policy, or set of policies, exist in society (regardless of whether and how the individual is exposed to and evaluates them). Thus, for unemployment benefits policy context can be about variables such as the benefit generosity in a particular country, or the size of retrenchment in such generosity in recent times. Further, note that policy context can in principle range from complex and highly institutionalized policy legacies (such as those captured by the concept of a welfare state 'regime') to very specific and short-term variables (such as, reductions in benefit generosity in the last year).

There are three ways for policy context to influence a dependent variable of interest (see the three arrows departing from the policy context). First, they can, at least in principle, directly influence citizens regardless of individual-level variation in policy exposure and evaluations. Such hypotheses have played a role in studies of whether cross-national differences and similarities in welfare state support are structured by the 'welfare regimes' (Esping-Andersen 1990). Building on 'historical institutionalism', one idea has been that slowly accumulating and eventually institutionalized policy legacies will generate norms, routines and established ways of thinking that affect citizens regardless of how they are individually exposed to and evaluate specific policies. Thus, scholars have looked for traces of attitudinal adaption to long-standing welfare state regimes (for an overview, see Mau 2003; Svallfors 2010).

Second, policy contexts may matter by influencing the distribution of individual exposure and evaluations (arrow on the left). Citizens of countries with more generous unemployment benefits may, for example, have more, and more long-lasting, individual exposure and potentially more subjectively satisfying evaluations. Taking another common hypothesis, citizens in the largest and most costly 'social democratic' welfare states, involving a greater number of more ambitious transfers and services, typically have more, and more long-lasting, experiences of welfare state policies, in particular services. Similarly, citizens of 'liberal' welfare states might have fewer and more short-term experiences in general, at the same time as more people encounter, for example, means-testing. 'Conservative' policy contexts, finally, may display more marked labor market 'insider–outsider' divides in the nature of social protection (see Marx and Picot 2014). These simple examples actually illustrate one of our main themes: the usefulness of simultaneously thinking about, and connecting, the macro and micro levels respectively.

This theme is relevant also for the final two arrows. Here, contextual factors are not only believed to impact the distribution but also the effects of individual-level variation in exposure and evaluation. This may, first, apply to policy context itself. Taking one example, the impact of individual experiences may become more politically and culturally recognizable, and thus easier to connect to politics, in a large, highly redistributive, and costly setting where the welfare state tends to follow citizens 'from the cradle to the grave'. Another example is that the policy setting may affect citizens' expectations such that identical individual experiences may instill very different degrees of dissatisfaction, as well as political reactions, in different policy contexts.

Second, the macro factors that moderate the impact of individual-level variables do not have to concern policies. This has proven to be true for macro-political circumstances such as the current policy agenda of the public sphere at large, patterns of party conflict, and institutional 'clarity of responsibility'. Such contextual factors seem to function as important 'enablers' – and sometimes also stumbling blocks – of policy feedback (see Kumlin and Stadelmann-Steffen 2014, ch. 15).

3 GRAPPLING WITH CAUSALITY AND MEASUREMENT

Two further issues need to be raised. First, almost always in feedback analysis, there is a risk of reciprocal causation. Causal inference problems are increasingly emphasized in empirical social science research (for example, Falleti and Lynch 2009), but in analyses of policy feedback these questions are endemic; policy-related independent variables can almost always be construed as both consequence and cause of attitudes and behavior. As we noted initially, attitudes and behavior should from a normative standpoint affect public policy in a democracy.

Causality issues manifest themselves both at the macro and the micro levels of analysis. At the macro level, for example, a justified but rarely addressed question is whether any uncovered relationship between policy 'regimes' and aggregate opinion, or group differences in opinion, simply reflects responsiveness of the political system to mass preferences and conflicts, or whether it (also) reflects policy feedback. At the micro level, a key question is whether policy evaluations are really, as Figure 23.1 has it, structured by policy exposure, or whether evaluations instead depend on deep seated predispositions like ideology, party identification or pre-adult socialization. It is possible that citizens self-select themselves to a menu of policy exposure, and develop evaluations, which are consistent with already existing political leanings. But if such processes are the only drivers of policy exposure and evaluation, it becomes hard to speak of policy feedback. When it comes to direct personal experiences, this problem is naturally greater for public services where several providers exist, or where it is possible, if not preferable, to get by without the service altogether. Interestingly, some panel analyses suggest policy evaluations can elicit subsequent change in political orientations, such as European Union (EU) support, left–right ideology and incumbent government voting (Kumlin and Haugsgjerd forthcoming). While more work is needed, these studies offer preliminary, though hardly final, evidence that policy evaluations and experiences can be more than simply results of self-selection.

A second major issue concerns the measurement of policy context, exposure and evaluations. This challenge is in many ways a continuation of a larger debate on how to measure welfare state variation at the macro level (Stephens 2010). While Esping-Andersen (1990) famously argued that aggregate social expenditures do not adequately capture the welfare state – especially not from the point of view of individual citizens – recent suggestions to disaggregate expenditures (Castles 2008) have to some extent resurrected the expenditure approach. A similar 'disaggregation' trend exists in research on citizens and policy feedback. This is probably driven by the difficulty in establishing overall welfare state regime-consistent country differences in welfare state support. Research on this topic has found much attitudinal variation and variation in group patterns, also within countries belonging to the same regime. In the face of such inconsistencies, Svallfors (2003) suggested that policy feedback might best be captured by 'unpacking' welfare regimes, that is, by analyzing policy effects and attitudinal reactions specific to well-defined key concepts and policy areas, with immediate relevance for attitudes and behavior linked to that area. The state-of-the-art examples discussed later illustrate this successful trend.

Measurement issues also exist for individual-level variables. Beginning with policy exposure, most surveys with a reasonable selection of political dependent variables provide little information on welfare state policy exposure and experiences. This can be a real problem especially when the research question concerns how welfare state interests broadly conceived affect general political orientations and cleavages. Kumlin (2004, ch. 7) describes how past research had drawn far-ranging conclusions, one way or the other, based on just a handful of indicators, and demonstrates that access to much more information can make a difference.

A similar data shortage exists for policy evaluations and perceptions. Most research on citizens and the welfare state has been preoccupied with normative support, whether for concrete policy areas or more generalized support for spending and redistribution. Less attention has been reserved for evaluations and perceptions of how policies function in practice. This imbalance is especially apparent in comparative datasets where normative support measures are available, or even abundant, whereas evaluations and perceptions are not. Thankfully, this has now begun to change, as evidenced by recent rounds of, for example, the European Social Survey or the International Social Survey Program. Still, whenever such measures exist questionnaire designers frequently ask evaluative questions only to those with direct personal experience of the policy in question. This is not very satisfactory as it assumes direct experience is the only relevant policy exposure. This restriction prohibits analysis of which exposure actually matters.

Overall, there is no general or simple solution to these methodological challenges. At the same time, the situation is anything but hopeless: by carefully conceptualizing and theorizing the phenomenon under investigation, at least partial solutions can be achieved. In the remainder of this chapter we illustrate this good news with a special focus on the causality problem, showing that causality in feedback research is not just an entirely intractable 'chicken and egg' problem. The examples illustrate that researchers have been successful in identifying situations and cases, and achieving results, that make causal feedback effects seem plausible. Additionally, the concluding section makes a plea for 'cross-level thinking' during all steps of the research process, which also help bring us closer to causality.

4 POLICY FEEDBACK RESEARCH IN PRACTICE: FOUR RECENT APPLICATIONS

A first example is Elias Naumann's (2014) 'Raising the retirement age: retrenchment, feedback and attitudes', which analyses peoples' adaption of preferences (that is, towards the retirement age) to a policy change (that is, a reform raising the retirement age). Naumann integrates all elements of the feedback process in Figure 23.1. Using multilevel analysis (see Chapter 22 in this volume) he is able to link the contextual and individual levels of explanation. He also engages in group-specific analyses accounting for the possibility that various population groups could react to these reforms differently. Finally, he implements a quasi-experimental difference-in-difference design to analyze whether reforms to increase the retirement age had an effect on aggregate support for further increases in the retirement age over time. This is possibly one of the best available possibilities in practice to apply a strict test of causality.

Naumann's main finding is twofold. On the one hand, Europeans seem to have moderated their retirement age preferences to the new reality produced by population ageing. On the other hand, after actual policy adjustments of the retirement age support for further increases of the retirement age decreased, demonstrating that people also adapt to the new policy environment. Naumann also shows that this is a general adaption pattern that can be observed across different groups and social classes. It seems to be something of a genuine policy context effect that does not interact all that much with individual-level self-interest.

Sara Watson (2015), in her article 'Does welfare conditionality reduce democratic participation', investigates the civic consequences of an emerging transformation of welfare states that includes a shift away from rights-based to conditional, work-centered social entitlements. Similar to Naumann, she uses a mix of methods and models to capture a potential causal feedback effect. In particular, her study is one of the rare examples using longitudinal data, giving her the opportunity to observe individuals before and after they enter conditional welfare programs in Britain between 1990 and 2010. She, moreover, enhances her research design by investigating various group differences, eventually also applying a so-called difference-in-difference analysis. Watson delivers strong support for the assumption that – especially in liberal welfare states – the movement to a more work-centered and obligations-oriented social policy may have detrimental effects on welfare state recipients' political life. Whereas traditional rights-based social programs even seem to increase individuals' active citizenship, conditional entitlements appear to generate political demobilization by hampering personal and political efficacy.

Among the most promising research designs to causal inference are natural experiments, which are however rare and difficult to identify. In this vein, Stefan Svallfors' (2010) 'Policy feedback, generational replacement, and attitudes to state intervention: Eastern and Western Germany, 1990–2006' is illustrative. He convincingly argues that the socialist policy context was almost randomly imposed on one part of the country, remained in place for some decades, and then suddenly changed again with reunification. This is a situation, in which the problem of reversed causality (that is, that attitudinal change led to institutional change) can almost be excluded. Svallfors finds that the arbitrary division and reunification of Germany and the subsequent changes in welfare state institutions had a decisive impact on peoples' attitudes to state intervention in the Eastern part of the country: by observing stability in attitudes in Western Germany (and most other countries), while attitudinal change occurs in the Eastern part, he provides convincing evidence for real policy feedback.

Finally, Anders Lindbom's 'Waking up the giant? Hospital closures and electoral punishment in Sweden' (2014) demonstrates that also a purely aggregate research strategy can be fruitful. He argues that previous research has underestimated electoral punishment in the face of retrenchment policies, because it has been too general in conceptualizing and measuring retrenchment and the conditions under which it may produce electoral punishment of incumbents. Lindbom exploits the fact that in Sweden three elections occur on the same day (for the national parliament, the county councils and local governments). Electoral punishment can be observed if the vote shares of the incumbent social-democratic party declines more in the county election than in the national election in counties that have proposed welfare state retrenchment (that is, hospital closures). This isolates feedback effects in regions that were strongly affected by welfare retrenchment. In so doing, Lindbom indeed finds clear evidence for electoral punishment in his particular example. However, he also shows that governing parties will only be punished under quite specific enabling contextual conditions: retrenchment needs to be visible and transparent (in this case, dramatic one-shot hospital closure decisions), at the same time as voters need a viable alternative untainted by past or future retrenchment plans of their own (in this case, newly formed regional healthcare parties). Like Svallfors, Lindbom shows that an important success factor in grappling with causality is not just complex modeling, but also careful attention to particular cases and situations that offer advantageous conditions in isolating policy feedback from other possible causal interpretations.

5   CONCLUSION: CROSS-LEVEL THINKING

This chapter has outlined a framework for studying policy feedback and citizens, discussed some generic methodological problems, as well as illustrated partial solutions. The main messages of this chapter can be summarized as follows.

First, while research on policy feedback has originated along two quite separate methodological tracks, one emphasizing aggregate comparisons of countries and concepts, the other focusing on individual level consequences of policy exposure, recent developments have involved something like a merger between these approaches. Individual and aggregate aspects of policy feedback can be integrated into one generic analytical framework, which in particular helps to be clearer about the various mechanisms behind feedback effects.

Second, thinking about policy feedback using one integrative framework should have substantive but also methodological payoffs. Among the latter would be making visible some generic challenges and problems in this line of work. These concern being aware of the micro–macro divide inherent in policy feedback, difficulties in measuring relevant variables, and how to handle reciprocal causality issues.

Third, while there are no perfect solutions to these problems, we have used four recent examples of feedback studies to illustrate that the challenges can be successfully addressed. Different research designs have unique sets of strengths and weaknesses with respect to measurement issues and the problem of potential reversed causality. Various research designs, including macro, micro and cross-level approaches, can all offer possible ways forward.

Against this background we want to conclude by arguing that we can possibly learn the most about policy feedback analyses by going beyond one or the other research strategy and apply what we may call 'cross-level thinking'. The approach we are after however entails more than simultaneously analyzing micro and macro implications. It involves a willingness to analyze policy feedback as a cross-level process as described in Figure 23.1. This is a contrast to the influential comparative studies in the 'regime' tradition, which largely limited analysis to the level of nation states, investigating the relationship between some welfare state indicators and some aggregate outcome measures, such as employment rates, or aggregate attitudes. However, cross-level thinking also goes beyond classical multilevel analyses, in which general contextual effects on individual behavior and attitudes have been studied. Both the regime tradition and the classic multilevel approach imply that there is something like *the* policy outcome and thus one overall and general policy effect. In reality, however, policies are typically targeted at particular groups or affect individuals differently (Schmid 1984; Scheepers and Te Grotenhuis 2005). To assess the impact of policies it is therefore often crucial to know how specific groups of individuals react to particular policy contexts (Elster 1998; Jones and Cullis 2003). Even though in political behavior research citizens have often been found to be 'sociotropic' (Kinder and Kiewiet 1981) and 'impersonal' (Mutz 1998) in their reactions to policy outputs and outcomes, there are theoretical and empirical reasons to believe that policy feedback in the welfare state domain is to a greater extent driven also by personal considerations and information sources (Kumlin 2004).

In the most general terms, cross-level thinking is valuable as it allows us to understand the individual-level processes generating aggregate outcomes. Several recent studies illustrate theoretically and empirically how modelling group-specific policy effects illuminates feedback mechanisms and opens the black box of how exactly a given policy produces observed outcomes.

The broader implication for comparative research on feedback and citizens, then, is that pure contextual effects cannot be assumed, but rather should be tested for. What in a multilevel analysis might seem to be a contextual 'level-2' effect frequently turns out to be driven by a particular group with a particular set of interests, experiences and informational sources. If so, the strength of the seeming contextual effect will actually depend on group composition. It is equally important to note that there may be situations in which such group-specific mechanisms do not matter, in which case a more 'sociotropic' characterization of feedback applies (Kumlin and Stadelmann-Steffen 2014: ch. 15). This conclusion should, however, still be the result of proper theoretical and empirical cross-level thinking.

SUGGESTED FURTHER READING ABOUT POLICY FEEDBACK AND CITIZENS

The reader may want to start with the existing general overviews. Suzanne Mettler's and Joe Soss's 2004 article might be the best starting point as it is something of a 'programmatic' statement, suggesting that there is a distinct 'political' mode of explanation emphasizing how the results of the political process (that is, policies and institutions) affect citizens and future political processes. Andrea Campbell's 2011 overview in *Annual Review of Political Science* (2011) takes stock of much of the empirical evidence accumulating in recent years, focusing mainly, but not exclusively, on the US, as well as on methodological challenges. Kumlin and Stadelmann-Steffens co-edited volume *How Welfare States Shape the Democratic Public* (2014) contains numerous comparative and European contributions analysing policy feedback on participation, voting behaviour, and political attitudes. Mettler and SoRelle (2014) discusses policy feedback on citizens but also on other actors and aspects in the political system.

Several distinct subtopics might then be of interest. One is the impact of personal experiences with public policies. For the US, this problem is studied in books by for example Suzanne Mettler (2005) and Andrea Campbell (2005), whereas Kumlin (2004) uses Swedish data.

If you have a particular interest in explaining attitudes towards the welfare state, three accumulations of studies might be of interest. One deals with the impact of policy context – often conceptualized in terms of 'welfare regimes' – and is discussed in books by Steffen Mau (2003) and Christian Albrekt Larsen (2006), as well is in the article 'Welfare regimes and welfare opinions' by Stefan Svallfors (2003). Second, a different approach is taken by researchers analysing how policy preferences may react 'thermostatically' against the previous policy direction. Here, the natural starting point is Stuart Soroka's and Christopher Wlezien's (2010) *Degrees of Democracy*. Third, scholars have examined the relationship between subjective evaluations of 'performance' and support for welfare state policies; a useful starting point here is the book chapter 'Welfare performance and welfare support' by Wim van Oorschot and Bart Meuleman (2012).

A final group of studies assess the impact of welfare state cutbacks and subjective evaluations thereof. Here, one question has to do with electoral accountability, that is, how retrenchment and dissatisfaction affect support for responsible actors such as incumbent governments. A thorough analysis of this problem can be found in Natalie Giger's book, *The Risk of Social Policy* (2011). A related, but distinct, 'twin literature' rather examines effects on *generalized* political trust, as discussed in the overview chapter 'Bringing performance back in: the welfare state and political trust' (Kumlin and Haugsgjerd 2017, forthcoming).

REFERENCES

Campbell, Andrea (2005), *How Policies Make Citizens: Senior Political Activism and the American Welfare State*, Princeton, NJ: Princeton University Press.
Campbell, Andrea Louise (2012), 'Policy makes mass politics', *Annual Review of Political Science*, **15**, 331–51.
Castles, Francis G. (2008), 'What welfare states do: a disaggregated expenditure approach', *Journal of Social Policy*, **38** (1), 45–62.
Easton, David (1965), *A Framework for Political Analysis*, vol. 25, Englewood Cliffs, NJ: Prentice-Hall.
Elster, Jon (1998), 'A plea for mechanism', in Peter Hedström and Richard Swedberg (eds), *Social Mechanism: An Analytical Approach to Social Theory*, Cambridge: Cambridge University Press, pp. 45–73.
Esping-Andersen, Gøsta (1990), *The Three Worlds of Welfare Capitalism*, Cambridge: Polity Press.
Falleti, Tulia G. and Julia F. Lynch (2009), 'Context and causal mechanisms in political analysis', *Comparative Political Studies*, **42** (9), 1143–66.
Giger, Nathalie (2011), *The Risk of Social Policy? The Electoral Consequences of Welfare State Retrenchment and Social Policy Performance in OECD Countries*, London: Routledge.
Jones, Philip and John Cullis (2003), 'Key parameters in policy design: the case of intrinsic motivation', *Journal of Social Policy*, **32** (4), 527–47.
Kinder, Donald R. and D. Roderick Kiewiet (1981), 'Sociotropic politics: the American case', *British Journal of Political Science*, **11** (2), 129–61.
Kumlin, Staffan (2004), *The Personal and the Political: How Personal Welfare State Experiences Affect Political Trust and Ideology*, New York: Palgrave Macmillan.
Kumlin, Staffan and Atle Haugsgjerd (forthcoming), 'The welfare state and political trust: bringing performance back in', in Sonja Zmerli and Tom van der Meer (eds), *Handbook on Political Trust*, Cheltenham, UK and Northampton, MA, USA: Edward Elgar.
Kumlin, Staffan and Isabelle Stadelmann-Steffen (eds) (2014), *How Welfare States Shape*

the Democratic Public: Policy Feedback, Participation, Voting, and Attitudes, Cheltenham, UK and Northampton, MA, USA: Edward Elgar.

Larsen, Christian Albrekt (2006), *The Institutional Logic of Welfare Attitudes: How Welfare Regimes Influence Public Support*, Aldershot, UK: Ashgate.

Lindbom, Anders (2014), 'Waking up the giant? Hospital closures and electoral punishment in Sweden', in Staffan Kumlin and Isabelle Stadelmann-Steffen (eds), *How Welfare States Shape the Democratic Public: Policy Feedback, Participation, Voting and Attitudes*, Cheltenham, UK and Northampton, MA, USA: Edward Elgar, pp. 156–77.

Marx, Paul and Georg Picot (2014), 'Labour market policies and preferences of fixed-term workers', in Staffan Kumlin and Isabelle Stadelmann-Steffen (eds), *How Welfare States Shape the Democratic Public: Policy Feedback, Participation, and Attitudes*,. Cheltenham, UK and Northampton, MA, USA: Edward Elgar, pp. 113–31.

Mau, Steffen (2003), *The Moral Economy of Welfare States: Britain and Germany Compared*, London: Routledge.

Mettler, Suzanne (2005), *Soldiers to Citizens: The G.I. Bill and the Making of the Greatest Generation*, New York: Oxford University Press.

Mettler, Suzanne and Mallory SoRelle (2014), 'Policy feedback theory', in Paul A. Sabatier and Christopher M. Weible (eds), *Theories of the Policy Process*, Boulder, CO: Westview Press, pp. 151–82.

Mettler, Suzanne and Joe Soss (2004), 'The consequences of public policy for democratic citizenship: bridging policy studies and mass politics', *Perspectives on Politics*, **2** (1), 55–73.

Mutz, Diana C. (1998), *Impersonal Influence. How Perceptions of Mass Collectives Affect Political Attitudes*, Cambridge: Cambridge University Press.

Naumann, Elias (2014), 'Raising the retirement age: retrenchment, feedback, and attitudes', in Staffan Kumlin and Isabelle Stadelmann-Steffen (eds), *How Welfare States Shape the Democratic Public: Policy Feedback, Participation, and Attitudes*, Cheltenham, UK and Northampton. MA, USA: Edward Elgar, pp. 223–43.

Pierson, Paul (1993), 'Review: when effect becomes cause: policy feedback and political change', *World Politics*, **45** (4), 595–628.

Schattschneider, Elmer Eric (1935), *Politics, Pressure, and the Tariff*, New York: Prentice Hall.

Scheepers, Peer and Manfred Te Grotenhuis (2005), 'Who cares for the poor in Europe? Micro and macro determinants for alleviating poverty in 15 European countries', *European Sociological Review*, **21** (5), 453–65.

Schmid, Günther (1984), 'The political economy of labor market discrimination: a theoretical and comparative analysis of sex discrimination', in Günther Schmid and Renate Weitzel (eds), *Sex Discrimination and Equal Opportunity: The Labour Market and Employment Policy*, Aldershot, UK: Gower Publishing Company, pp. 264–308.

Soroka, Stuart N. and Christopher Wlezien (2010), *Degrees of Democracy: Politics, Public Opinion, and Policy*, Cambridge: Cambridge University Press.

Soss, Joe (1999), 'Lessons of welfare: policy design, political learning, and political action', *American Political Science Review*, **93** (2), 363–80.

Soss, Joe and Sanford Schram (2007), 'A public transformed? Welfare reform as policy feedback', *American Political Science Review*, **101** (1), 111–27.

Stephens, John D. (2010), 'The social rights of citizenship', in Francis G. Castles, Stephan Leibfried, Jane Lewis, Herbert Obinger and Christopher Pierson (eds), *The Oxford Handbook of the Welfare State*, Oxford: Oxford University Press, pp. 511–25.

Svallfors, Stefan (2003), 'Welfare regimes and welfare opinions: a comparison of eight western countries' *Social Indicators Research*, **64**, 495–520.

Svallfors, Stefan (2010), 'Policy feedback, generational replacement and attitudes to state intervention: eastern and western Germany, 1990–2006', *European Political Science Review*, **2** (1), 119–35.

Tyler, Tom R., Robert J. Boeckmann, Heather J. Smith and Yuen J. Huo (1997), *Social Justice in a Diverse Society*, Boulder, CO: Westview Press.

Van Oorschot, Wim and Bart Meuleman (2012), 'Welfare performance and welfare support', in Stefan Svallfors (ed.), *Constested Welfare States: Welfare Attitudes in Europe and Beyond*, Stanford, CA: Stanford University Press, pp. 25–57.
Watson, Sara (2015), 'Does welfare conditionality reduce democratic participation?', *Comparative Political Studies*, **48** (5), 645–86.

24 Regression analysis
Uwe Wagschal

1 INTRODUCTION

Regression analysis is one of the best-known and most frequently used statistical methods of analysis in science. It is characterized by great flexibility and has a widespread use across many disciplines. The general idea of regression analysis is that the variance of a dependent variable could be explained by one or several independent (or exogenous, or explanatory) variables. They are usually denoted in an equation with an X. The dependent variable is usually labelled with a Y and is also called the endogenous variable, or regressand or predictand. It should be clear that the relation between the dependent and independent variables have to be causal. Usually theories and hypothesis are used to specify the causal mechanism between the explanatory variables and the variable that is to be explained. In a bivariate case, the independent variable X is the (only) cause that leads to the dependent variable Y.

Typical research questions for a bivariate regression might be: How strong is the influence of campaign expenditures (X) of a specific party on their election result (Y), that is, what is the effect of an additional euro spent during the campaign on the vote share? What is the effect of an increase of 1 percent unemployment (X) on the public debt (Y)? What is the effect of left party strength (X) on welfare state expenditures (Y)? How did a party's election results (Y) change over a period of 40 years (X = time)? What is the impact of an additional year of schooling (X) on an individual regarding his or her post-material attitudes (Y)?

An important assumption of (linear) regression is that the presumed causal influence of the predictor variable on the outcome variable is truly linear. This assumption about linearity is crucial. However, it is not always tenable. For instance the fourth question that deals with election-result outcomes over time is problematic, since a back and forth in election results is much more likely than a continuous linear trend. Here one should expect a non-linear relationship and therefore use other statistical methods. Linear regression is also often referred to as ordinary least squares (OLS) regression. This refers to the mathematical technique that attempts to find a mathematical function which best estimates the data. In a scatterplot diagram with all combinations of the X and Y values (see below) this regression line can be described as a line of best fit. In addition, regression analysis could be used for macro (aggregated) and micro (individual) data. However, some of the statistical tests can only be applied for micro data.

Regression techniques have become more complex over the past decades and new developments have enriched research possibilities. In general, regression techniques can be used for cross-sectional (between different units of analysis at the same time point) or longitudinal analysis, that is, over time. A major extension of the basic regression model were the pooled time series models (panel regressions) where both dimensions are combined (Beck and Katz 1995; Kittel 1999; Greene 2012). Logistic regression is a further innovation that is well suited for specific research questions in the social sciences. Whereas OLS regression requires interval scaled data for both the dependent and the independent variables, logistic regression is suited for categorical dependent variables. With these discrete choice models, we can answer research questions such as which factors determine whether a person votes or not, why a conflict occurs or does not occur and why budget consolidation happened or did not happen.

This book also deals with different regression techniques and aspects of the method. In Chapter 19 on quantitative data analysis, regression analysis describes a possible research technique with quantitative data. Chapter 22 is about multilevel regression, a new development which takes a specific data structure into account. Such a hierarchical linear model analyses employs data from a macro (for example, institutions) and micro level (for example, individual attitudes) simultaneously. The dependent variable is then analyzed on the lowest level (Snijders and Bosker 2012). Another reference to regression analysis as a possible model can be found in Chapter 20. From a general perspective, regression is also mentioned in Chapter 2 (on epistemology and approaches) with a focus on causation and explanation.

2   APPLICATION AND CAPACITY OF REGRESSION ANALYSIS IN POLITICAL SCIENCE

There are numerous examples of OLS regressions in political science. In this section, four different studies will be discussed briefly, two OLS regressions at the macro level and two at the micro level (individual level). The examples are selected in order to identify drawbacks and problems of the method.

One typical social science approach of the 1970s and 1980s was the bivariate correlation comparing nations at a macro level. Douglas Hibb's

(1977) seminal paper on political parties and macroeconomic policy was a stimulating paper for the partisan theory within comparative public policy research. Hibbs analyzed the relationship between government complexion and macroeconomic outcomes in advanced capitalist democracies. His correlations (Hibbs 1977, p. 1473ff.) and scatter plots supported his reasoning that strong left governments tend to reduce unemployment in exchange for higher inflation rates. For conservative parties this relationship is the other way around. Several critiques were raised in the following years. One concerned the correct theory and therefore the causal mechanism. Hibbs relied on the modified Phillips-curve approach, which suggested a trade-off between unemployment and inflation. Governments should be able to exploit this 'menu of choice'. However, economic theory later argued that this theory does not hold true. Besides, his findings were based on only 12 cases. Some important cases (for example, Austria, New Zealand and Switzerland) were left out. Furthermore, the analyzed periods for the dependent variable (1960–69) did not match with the periods for the independent variable (1945–69). Finally, Hibbs did not perform any statistical checks for outliers or other possible intervening variables. Especially other, omitted factors should have had an impact either on inflation (for example, central bank independence) or unemployment (for example, economic growth).

While Hibbs focused on the macro level Steven Greene (2004) analyzed voting at an individual level. He asked an important question about partisanship, a variable that has vexed voting researchers for decades: Is a person's longstanding tendency to prefer a certain party best understood as a summary judgment that rests on repeated positive experience with the party or is it a social identity, that is, a sense of belonging with the social group that forms the party's voter base? The question is highly relevant, because it has major implications for how voters and parties are related.

To find an answer, Greene conducted a mail survey in Franklin County, Ohio, in which 302 randomly selected residents completed a list of ten questions that psychologists had explicitly developed to measure whether someone identifies with a social group. The battery contained questions such as 'When someone criticizes the Democrats, it feels like a personal insult', or 'When I talk about Democrats, I usually say "we" rather than "they"' (party names were changed accordingly for those attaching to Republicans). Respondents had to indicate on a scale from 0 to 3 how much they agreed with the respective statement (with 0 indicating strong disagreement and 3 indicating strong agreement). To measure the degree of overall identification, Green averaged the answers across items so that a person's score ran from 0 to 3.

Based on the theory of social identity, Greene predicted that partisans would evaluate their party more positively than those merely holding a preference for it. To capture this idea, he asked respondents to rate their preferred party on an interval-scaled 'feeling thermometer' score that went from 0 to 100 and indicated how 'cold' or 'warm' they felt towards the party. To test his predictions, Greene estimated an OLS regression in which he took the respondents' feeling thermometer score as the dependent variable and their respective averaged identity score as the independent variable. Additionally, he included several other variables known to be associated with partisanship in general (for example, political interest or age), and variables which could also explain why a person would positively/negatively rate the party (for example, ideology and how strongly they felt about their partisanship).

Greene obtained a coefficient of 8.870 for the averaged identity score which was significant at the $p = 0.001$ level (with a standard error = 2.94). The value of the coefficient indicates that if a respondent moves up one point in his or her average identity score, the party evaluation rises by 8.870 points. Its significance means that it is safe to assume that the coefficient does not equal zero in the population from which respondents came, that is, the effect is present there, too. Greene's results indicate that identity must be regarded as an important aspect of partisanship. In his paper, Greene then goes on to estimate several other models which corroborate his main idea by showing that other effects predicted from social identity theory bear out as well, for example, that partisan identifiers vote more consistently and that they actively help their party by attending rallies or donating money.

Greene's results certainly are impressive and his data collection is a nice example of the standard approach to infer a parameter in a population by drawing a random sample from it and estimating a regression model. Yet, since he collected respondents only from a single county, his results, strictly speaking, only pertain to the population his respondents came from – although, to be fair, we are hard pressed to come up with an explanation why residents of Franklin County, Ohio, should be different enough from other US voters as to render his findings inapplicable elsewhere.

As the contribution by Stone Sweet and Brunell (1998) shows, even a simple regression model can yield results that significantly add to the coherence of a hypothesized mechanism. The authors use regression analysis to illustrate their theoretical argument about the role of the European Court of Justice in the process of European integration. The argument begins with the premise of existing transnational interactions between private actors. These actors are presumed to enter into private contracts, which can, however, become the object of conflicts because of (changing and) differing national rules. Therefore, there will be a demand for the resolution of disputes by national courts. In addition to national judges, the European Court of Justice (ECJ) enters into play when national judges pass on claims by private actors to the ECJ to give an interpretation of relevant European Union (EU) law. The ensuing so-called preliminary rulings by the ECJ should then be applied by the national courts. In theory, this procedure for preliminary reference could thus lead to a homogenization based on the consistent application of supranational law. The more of these references occur, the more transnational interactions should increase because of more predictability and lower contracting costs, which again leads to more such references. In their article, Stone Sweet and Brunell argue that this mechanism lies at the core of a growing constitutionalization of the European Union.

If their argument is to at least hold up against reality, we would have to prove that the number of preliminary references actually increases with the volume of trade between European Union – at the time, European Community – countries. Therefore, in order to test their argument, Stone Sweet and Brunell regress the number of preliminary references on the intra-European Community (EC) trade volume for 13 countries (11 cases, as the Benelux countries are treated as a single case). A scatter plot for this bivariate relationship already shows a clear correlation, with the explained variance for the regression amounting to 92 percent. Besides this cross-national dimension in their analysis, the authors also examine the time dimension and aggregate the data over the countries but distinguish by year. Moreover, they expect there to be an important effect on the number of preliminary references owing to an important previous constitution-alization and the prohibition of national restrictions regarding intra-EC trade by the beginning of the year 1970. This expected effect is accounted for by including a dummy variable in their regression model that is coded '0' for the time before 1970 and '1' for the time from the year 1970 onwards. For this regression model, they plot the predicted yearly values for the dependent variable, preliminary references, against the empirically observed values for this variable. This visualization of year-wise residuals illustrates the explanatory power of the model. R-squared is again relatively high with over 70 percent explained variance.

One issue that is not resolved with this kind of analysis, however, is the question of causality. Regression effects are not per se proof of causality. Stone Sweet and Brunell themselves presume that their dynamic of successive constitutionalization operates as a virtuous circle, that is, effects should go in both ways. However, their regression analysis at least serves to reinforce their argument with empirical data by mapping actual socio-economic and legal processes using suitable data.

Macro-level analysis like this it is often accompanied by the challenge of justifying the sample as representative of a larger population. At the micro level, linear regression is often used with survey data to explain citizen behavior or attitudes. When such survey data has been generated by means of random sampling techniques it allows the making of inferences about the sampling populations. Moreover, the merit of the micro-level approach is especially evident in multiple regression where several explanatory factors are studied and tested for their relative impact while taking all these variables into account at once. For these reasons, regression analysis has been extensively used as a tool in the field of political sociology.

A more narrow area of research on citizen attitudes and behavior is concerned with citizens' position toward European integration. Some of the first studies in this field dealt with the influence of economic performance evaluations. Soon, other authors added political and then identity-based variables to explain EU support to variables that had already been tested. This field thus offers a number of examples of how competing explanations and their corresponding variables are tested against each other. One explanation has been provided by Anderson (1998), who put forward the hypothesis that EU attitudes are largely projections of evaluations about national political objects. As the European level is relatively removed from citizens, who have little information about this political entity, their attitudes toward the EU are likely to be determined by proxies. These proxies take the form of domestic political evaluations: system support, government support, and established party support.

Anderson draws on a Eurobarometer survey to test his hypothesis for seven countries. For the dependent variable, he uses a question where respondents have to state whether they see the membership of their country in the EC as 'a good thing', 'neither good nor bad' or a 'bad thing'. As stated above, this clearly violates the requirement of interval scaled data. Therefore we could criticize that an ordered or multinomial logistic regression model should yield more robust results with this kind of dependent variable. Turning to the independent variables, Anderson tested personal and national economic performance evaluations, interest in EU politics, a post-materialism scale and several socio-demographic variables besides the three domestic proxy variables. He conducted the analyses separately for the seven examined countries, testing first only the economic and control variables, then political variables and finally all variables in a single model. This allowed Anderson to single out the relevant variables based on their partial effects, that is, each variable's effect while also taking into account all other variables respectively.

His results show a clear and statistically significant effect of satisfaction with the working of democracy in one's own country in almost all countries. Moreover, followers of established parties relatively consistently showed stronger support for European integration. However, he observed practically no evidence in line with the idea that support for the national government would transfer positively to EU attitudes. Therefore, his regression demonstrated that the political proxy variables had an independent effect even when economic performance evaluations and additional control variables are included in the model. Anderson (1998, p. 592) concluded that these results 'help resolve the incongruence of a coexistence of strong economic effects and widespread ignorance about the integration process by pointing to an alternative individual-level model of attitude formation'.

3   HOW TO APPLY REGRESSION ANALYSIS

3.1   The General Idea

Regression analysis is about the functional relationship between variables. Examining only two variables is called a bivariate regression, and using two or more independent variables is called a multivariate regression. The strength of a correlation between two metric variables can be measured with Pearson's correlation coefficient r. However, substantially meaningful correlations can only be ascertained if there is causality between the two variables. Causality is the relationship between an event and an effect, that is, a cause-and-effect-relation. This relationship has to be specified in advance, ideally derived from a theory. The cause is the independent variable (X) and the effect is the dependent variable (Y). Mathematically a bivariate regression as the simplest form of a linear regression model, can be expressed with the formula for a straight line (see equation (24.1)).

$$Y = a + b_1 \cdot X_1 \qquad (24.1)$$

The dependent variable Y is on the left hand side and the independent variable X is on the right hand side. The constant is denoted as 'a' and indicates the intercept (height) of the equation and b_1 stands for the slope (that is, the steepness) of the line. In regression analysis, the intercept is often of minor importance. It merely indicates the level of Y if the independent variable were zero.

Of more interest is the slope, which expresses the effect size. The slope b_1 indicates the number of units Y changes, if X changes one unit. Depending on the algebraic sign (positive or negative), it indicates the functional direction of the impact, that is, whether Y increases with X or

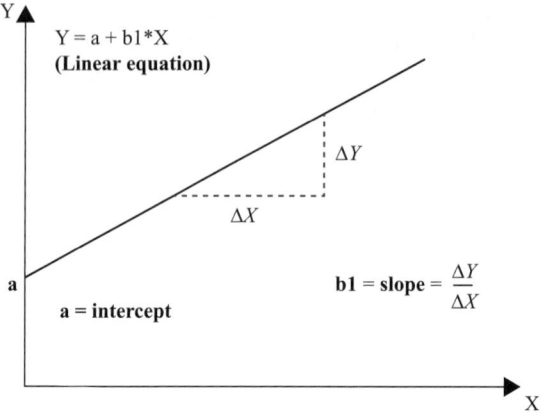

Figure 24.1   The linear equation

the relationship is inverse (in Figure 24.1 the effect of *X* on *Y* is positive). In addition, the absolute value of the slope is important, because it helps to determine whether the influence of *Y* on *X* is of actual substance or not.

Conventionally, in scatterplots the dependent variable is represented on the *Y*-axis and the independent variable on the *X*-axis. The intercept, also called the absolute term or the constant, is simply the point where the regression line crosses the vertical axis. It therefore takes the values a on the *Y*-axis for the value of zero on the *X*-axis. The slope determines the line's steepness. It indicates the amount of units to which *Y* alters, if *X* is altered by one unit. It can thus be expressed as the difference in vertical units (ΔY) divided by the corresponding distance in horizontal units (ΔX). By means of the point-slope form, the slope of a line can be easily determined if two points on the line are given (see Figure 24.1).

3.2   Modelling a Bivariate Regression

In case someone is only interested in the causal effect of a single independent variable on the dependent variable, the researcher applies a simple linear regression or a bivariate regression. Usually the researchers are dependent on questionnaires, observations, experiments or secondary statistics when they are investigating functional relations between two variables. As relationships analyzed in these kinds of data are generally not deterministic, it will virtually never occur in social science that all the points acquired from observation will lie on the exact same line. Rather, the points will more or less strongly scatter around this line. Regression analysis aims to find a line for which the vertical distances, that is,

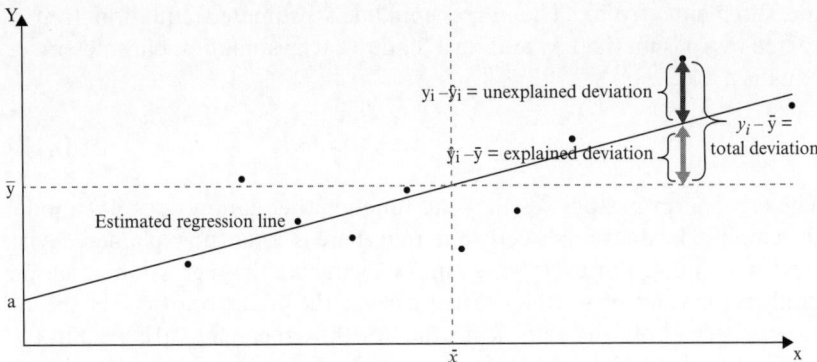

Figure 24.2   The regression line

deviations or residuals, to all observations are minimal. It does, however, not use the simple deviation but squared ones, thereby effectively giving larger deviations more weight. This criterion is known as the method of 'least ordinary squares' (OLS).

To illustrate the idea of minimizing the squared deviations, In general, bivariate regression analysis can be seen as 'fitting a straight line' for all $X - Y$ combinations in a two-dimensional scatterplot diagram (see Figure 24.2). Figure 24.2 shows a regression line that has been fitted into a scatter plot of observations that are charted based on their $X - Y$ coordinates. The OLS method is used to calculate the regression line, by minimizing the least squares we can find the slope and intercept for the line that yields the best possible adjustment in terms of total squared deviations. Mathematically, the minimization for determining the 'OLS estimators' is based on a partial derivation, which is not set out here. Rather, the exemplary calculations below will take the equations for the OLS estimators for granted and show how the regression line can be determined based on available data. Beforehand, the principle of regression shall be explained with the help of another figure (Figure 24.2).

One characteristic of the regression line is that it passes through the coordinate system's centroid. Although this condition applies to an innumerable number of lines, there is only one line (and therefore one slope b_1), for which the sum of squared deviations is the smallest. The observed values' deviations from the regression line $(y_i - \hat{y}_i)$ are called 'residuals'. These residuals are denoted by e_i and represent the equation that is to be minimized. The residuals can represent the actual, empirical variety of observations but they also can derive from unobservable errors, which includes all random and immeasurable influences (for example, measurement errors). The regression line's estimated equation (represented by $\hat{y}_i$) is marked by adding a 'hat' to each estimation parameter (see equation 24.2).

$$y_i = \hat{y}_i + e_i = (a + \hat{b}_1 \cdot x_i) + e_i \qquad (24.2)$$

The error term e expresses that the functional equation does not model the empirical values y_i perfectly and that there is some 'unexplained deviation' remaining. For every case i and its value x_i, the regression equation predicts the value of $\hat{y}_i$, which is hence called the predictor of y_i. The difference between both the empirical value for the dependent variable and the predicted value is the prediction error or what is left unexplained (residual, error of prognosis).

The larger this error term e the worse is the fit of the regression line. As stated above, the regression line minimizes this value and can be easily calculated. Because the sum of deviations from a fix value is always equal to zero (positive and negative deviations compensate one another), the squared expression is minimized instead. This means that the regression line is the one line which minimizes the sum of squared prediction errors (= OLS).

However, the error is not interpreted as an absolute value; it has to be set in relation to the original variation in the data. The idea behind this can be demonstrated by looking at the three distances delineated in Figure 24.2 for a single observation.

1. $(y_i - \bar{y}_i)$ = The total deviation between the observed value yi and the arithmetic mean value. The sum of these squared total deviations over all observations $\Sigma (y_i - \bar{y}_i)^2$ is called the total sum of squares (= TSS).
2. $(\hat{y}_i - \bar{y}_i)$ = the 'explained' deviation between yi and the arithmetic mean value (measured by the difference between the predicted value and the arithmetic mean value). The sum of these squared 'explained' deviations over all observations $\Sigma (\hat{y}_i - \bar{y}_i)^2$ is called the explained sum of squares (= ESS).
3. $(y_i - \hat{y}_i)$ = the 'unexplained' deviation between yi and the predicted value (measured by the error of prognosis). The sum of these squared 'unexplained' deviations over all observations $\Sigma (y_i - \hat{y}_i)^2$ is called the unexplained sum of squares (= USS).

If we did not have the variable X and the regression equation, the best estimation of values for the variable y_i would be the mean for that variable, which is defined as the value for which the sum of all deviations are zero. The sum of these squared deviations denominates the total variation $\sum(y_1 - \bar{y}_1)^2$, which can be explained by using other variables. Based on the regression equation, one can predict a value of the dependent variable for every observed value of X that is hopefully closer to the observed value of Y than its mean. For the example in Figure 24.2, one can see that the predicted value (the line) indeed lies closer to the observed value than the mean. The amount to which the line is closer represents the explained deviation. What is still missing is the unexplained deviation. These three kinds of distances – total, explained and unexplained deviation – can be calculated for every observation and summed up individually.

It can be mathematically shown that the resulting total variation is equal to the 'explained' and 'unexplained' variation (TSS = ESS + USS). The larger the explained sum of deviations, the smaller is the unexplained variation, making the modelled regression line more accurate with regard to the observations. This ratio is reflected in the coefficient of determination (R^2), which is the standard measure to judge how well the regression explains a dependent variable and describes a functional relationship. It is the ratio of the explained variation to the total variation.

Below, a numerical example is used to explain the calculation of the regression line. Subsequently, measures about the quality of the regression models and their statistical significance will be introduced, which becomes important when using data samples. The starting point for this example is the relationship between the unemployment rate and the debt-to-GDP ratio as shown in Table 24.1. As indicated previously, the calculation of correlations is closely connected to the calculation of regression lines. The slope b1 can be taken directly from the table of correlation, as it is the ratio between the covariance of X and Y and the variance of X:

$$b_1 = \frac{\text{Cov}(xy)}{S_x^2} \qquad (24.3)$$

The closelink to the calculation of correlations (in the case of a bivariate regression) is made obvious by the relationship between the correlation coefficient and the slope:

$$b_1 = r \cdot (Sy/Sx), \qquad (24.4)$$

with r = correlation coefficient, S_y = standard deviation of Y, S_x = standard deviation of X.

The y-intercept can be taken directly from the linear equation. The regression line always passes through the centroid point of the scatter plot $(\bar{x}; \bar{y})$. The y-intercept on the other hand is marked by the coordinates

Table 24.1   Working table for the calculation of the regression line

Country i	UNEM x_i	DEBT y_i	$(x_i - \bar{x})$	$(x_i - \bar{x})^2$	$(y_i - \bar{y})$	$(y_i - \bar{y})^2$	$(x_i - \bar{x})(y_i - \bar{y})$
A	12	120	4.2	17.64	53.2	2830.24	223.44
B	6	45	−1.8	3.24	−21.8	475.24	39.24
C	7	65	−0.8	0.64	−1.8	3.24	1.44
D	5	52	−2.8	7.84	−14.8	219.04	41.44
E	3	34	−4.8	23.04	−32.8	1075.84	157.44
F	10	86	2.2	4.84	19.2	368.64	42.24
G	4	70	−3.8	14.44	3.2	10.24	−12.16
H	8	40	0.2	0.04	−26.8	718.24	−5.36
I	9	56	1.2	1.44	−10.8	116.64	−12.96
J	14	100	6.2	38.44	33.2	1102.24	205.84
	Σ 78	Σ 668	Σ 0.0	Σ 111.60	Σ 0.0	Σ 6919.60	Σ 680.60
	$\bar{x}$ =7.80	$\bar{y}$= 66.80		S^2 = 11.16		S^2= 691.96	COV = 68.06
				Sx = 3.34		Sy = 26.31	

Notes: UNEM = rate of unemployment for country i measured as a multiannual average;
DEBT = public debt in percentage of GDP for country i in a specific year.

P (0; *a*). As the linear equation is given in the form of a straight line, we can calculate *a* by substituting the values $(\bar{x}\,;\bar{y})$ for the variables X and Y respectively in the regression line equation:

$$a = \bar{y} - b_1 \cdot \bar{x} \qquad (24.5)$$

In the following, a numerical example shall illustrate the calculation of a bivariate regression. The example refers to the hypothesized influence of an important socio-economic factor, unemployment (*UNEM*), on the dependent variable public debt (*DEBT*). According to the socio-economic school of thought in public policy research, higher unemployment should lead to a higher public debt (measured in percent of national gross domestic product, GDP). Table 24.1 displays the data for this relationship. For the sake of simplicity, only ten countries are selected. The average value for unemployment is 7.8 whereas the average public debt equals 66.8. In column 5 and 7 of Table 24.1, the standard deviation and the variance of the two variables are displayed. The operation in column 8 is required for calculating the co-variance between these two variables. For this purpose, the cross product of the deviations from both averages for the two variables has to be calculated and then averaged for all ten cases.

Using the values from the working table and equation (24.3) for the calculation of the slope, we get:[1]

$$b_1 = \frac{\text{Cov}(xy)}{S_x^2} = b_1 = 68.06/11.16 = 6.099.$$

The y-intercept, on the other hand, is calculated as follows according to equation (24.5):

$$a = \bar{y} - b_1 \cdot \bar{x} = 66,8 - 6,1 \cdot 7,8 = 19,22.$$

Therefore, the function of the linear bivariate regression in analyzing the effect of the average unemployment rate on the debt-to-GDP ratio is:

$$DEBT = 19.22 + 6.099 \; UNEM,$$

with DEBT = debt-to-GDP ratio for country i and ALQ = average unemployment rate for country i (that is, for 2000–2015)

The substantial interpretation of these numbers goes as follows: If the unemployment rate (measured as the average over a longer period) for a country is zero, the predicted debt-to-GDP ratio would be 19.22. If the unemployment rate was one percentage point higher, the model shows that the debt-to-GDP ratio would presumably rise by 6.1 percentage points (to 25.32 = 19.22 + 6.1).

One major purpose of using regression models is making predictions. Knowing the y-intercept and the slope of the regression function, we can estimate the value of the dependent variable even for cases that have not (yet) been observed or for which the value of the dependent variable is unknown. Assume that we add another country, K, to our sample of 10 western industrialized nations. Between 2000 and 2015, this country had an average unemployment rate of 11.0 per cent. Which debt-to-GDP ratio (*DEBT*) would we predict for country K based on our regression equation?

The answer is that we would expect a debt-to-GDP ratio of 86.32 for country K. The prediction is based on the regression equation, in which we enter the known value for the independent variable. This leads to:

$$\hat{y}_K = 19.22 + 6.099 \cdot x_K = 19.22 + 6.099 \cdot 11 = 86.32$$

In practice-oriented empirical research, it is often of much higher interest to make a prediction rather than give an explanation. In the field of electoral analysis, for example, researchers are interested in who will win the election and not by how many votes the candidate or party wins. Explanatory and predicting models are not necessarily different from one another. Usually, a model that explains something well will also manage to make precise predictions.

3.3 Assessing the Explanatory Power and Significance

Having simply calculated the regression equation, we still do not know how good our model is. From the inspection of the scatter plot it seems clear that the closer the empirical observations are distributed around the regression line, the better the fit. The best fit would be if all x–y combinations were on the regression line, which is either a perfect positive or negative correlation ($r = +1$ or $r = -1$). In such a case there is no unexplained variation left, the unexplained sum of squares (USS) is zero. On the other hand, since we have no deviation from the regression line, we explain all the variance with our model. The explained sum of squares (ESS) equals the total sum of squares in that extreme case (TSS). In general, it is possible to assess the goodness of fit of a regression model with the coefficient of determination R^2 (equation (24.6)):

$$R^2 = ESS\,/\,TSS \;(= \text{explained variance}\,/\,\text{total variance}) \qquad (24.6)$$

Since $TSS = ESS + USS$ also the following way of calculating R^2 is valid:

$$R^2 = 1 - (USS\,/\,TSS). \qquad (24.7)$$

For a bivariate regression, the coefficient of determination is simply the square of the correlation coefficient r:

$$R^2 = r^2 \qquad (24.8)$$

In Table 24.2, the calculation of R^2 is demonstrated step by step. First, the predicted value $\hat{y}_i$ has to be calculated from the regression equation. In the next steps the USS, ESS and TSS are calculated.

Inserting the numbers into the equations gives a R^2 equal to 0.60:

$$R^2 = \frac{\sum_{i=1}^{n}(\hat{y}_i - \bar{y})^2}{\sum_{i=1}^{n}(y_i - \bar{y})^2} = \frac{4150.32}{6919.60} = 0.60. \qquad (24.6')$$

$$R^2 = 1 - [USS\,/\,TSS] = 1 - (2768.92\,/\,6919.60) = 0.60. \qquad (24.7')$$

Since

$$r = \frac{\text{Cov}(xy)}{S_x S_y} = \frac{68.06}{3.34 \cdot 26.31} = 0.7745 \qquad (24.8')$$

Table 24.2   Working table for the calculation of R^2

Country	DEBT y_i	Pred. value $\hat{y}_i$	Residual $y_i - \hat{y}_i$	USS $(y_i - \hat{y}_i)^2$	$\hat{y}_i - \bar{y}$	ESS $(\hat{y}_i - \bar{y})^2$	$(\hat{y}_i - \bar{y})$	TSS[a] $(y_i - \bar{y})^2$
A	120	92.41	27.59	761.21	25.61	655.87	53.2	2830.24
B	45	55.82	−10.82	117.07	−10.98	120.56	−21.8	475.24
C	65	61.92	3.08	9.49	−4.88	23.81	−1.8	3.24
D	52	49.72	2.28	5.20	−17.08	291.73	−14.8	219.04
E	34	37.53	−3.53	12.46	−29.27	856.73	−32.8	1075.84
F	86	80.22	5.78	33.41	13.42	180.10	19.2	368.64
G	70	43.63	26.37	695.38	−23.17	536.85	3.2	10.24
H	40	68.02	−28.02	785.12	1.22	1.49	−26.8	718.24
I	56	74.12	−18.12	328.33	7.32	53.58	−10.8	116.64
J	100	104.61	−4.61	21.25	37.81	1429.60	33.2	1102.24
	$\bar{y} = 66.80$	1163		Σ 0.00 Σ 2768.92	Σ 0.0	Σ 4150.32	Σ 0.0	Σ 6919.60

Note: [a] = TSS = ESS + USS. Due to rounding error, there is a slight deviation.

the coefficient of determination[2] is:

$$R^2 = r^2 = (0.7745)^2 = 0.60.$$

There are further diagnostics to assess the quality of the regression. In Table 24.3 the computer output of the statistics software SPSS is displayed. We can easily identify the correlation coefficient, R^2, the explained (regression) and unexplained (residual) sum of squares. The last two rows display the constant term (a) and the slope for the independent variable unemployment (*UNEM*).

For further interpretation of the regression results four more parameters of Table 24.3 are of interest: the standard error of the regression, the standard error of the slope estimate (*SE B*), the beta value (Beta), the *t*-statistics (*T*) and the corresponding significance (Sig. T). Also, the *F*-statistics and its significance level are of importance when interpreting the overall fit of the model. These statistics are all relevant for the making inferences on a general population based on a given data sample from that population.

The standard error of the regression should not be confused with the standard error of the slope (*SE B*). The standard error of the regression concerns the overall goodness-of-fit. It estimates the average distance that the observed values fall from the regression line. In general, smaller values are better because they indicate that the observations are closer to the fitted line. The standard error of the regression is also used to assess the precision of the predictions. Approximately 95 percent of the observations

Table 24.3   SPSS output of the regression

MULTIPLE REGRESSION

Listwise deletion of missing data
Equation number 1. Dependent variable DEBT
Block number 1. Method: Enter UNEM
Variable(s) entered on step number

1. ALQ	
Multiple R	.77450
R Square	.59984
Adjusted R square	.54983
Standard error	18.60415

Analysis of variance			
	DF	Sum of squares	Mean square
Regression	1	4150.68423	4150.68423
Residual	8	2768.91577	346.11447

F = 11.99223
Signif. F = .0085

Variables in the equation					
	B	SE B	Beta	T	Sig T
UNEM	6.0986	1.7611	.7745	3.463	.0085
(Constant)	19.2312	14.9432		1.287	.2341

should be within a boundary of plus/minus two times standard error of the regression from the regression line $(= \hat{y} + 2.s_e)$.

The standard error of the slope estimate (*SE B*) is highly relevant in determining whether the results are statistically significant or not, that is, whether the slope or effect in the population – which we estimate with our sample – is different from zero. Knowing the slope of the linear relationship is not sufficient because the estimated slope is based on only one sample from a population and could very well differ if we drew another sample. It is therefore also important to know how much variability there is in the sampling distribution. Only with both pieces of information, is it possible to decide if the slope is significantly different from zero. It is also possible to calculate the boundaries which we would expect to contain the true slope parameter with a given possibility. Based on a theoretical distribution, we know which so-called *t*-value for a given probability we need to create these boundaries. Adding to and subtracting from the estimated slope this *t*-value times the standard error for the slope (its estimated variability) yields the confidence interval for the given probability within which we expect the true value for the slope.

We can also calculate the probability with which we can state that the slope estimated with our regression is in fact different from zero. For this, one has to divide the difference between the estimate (B) and zero, which is simply b_j, by the *SE B* ($t = b_j / S_{bj}$). We can then express the size of the estimated slope as a t-value and can look up the exact probability of getting a sample with that value if the actual slope in the population were zero by looking at a *t*-table, which is published in most statistical textbooks. As a rule of thumb, the *t*-value should exceed two for at least 30 cases, for being statistically significant at a 95 percent confidence level. In other words, we can posit that the slope is different from zero with a probability of at least 95 percent. SPSS automatically displays the *t*-statistics. The confidence level (*CL*) can also be immediately derived from the SPSS output: $CL = (1 - Sig\ T) \cdot 100$. According to social science convention this value has to be larger than 95.

Finally, the *F*-statistics checks for the overall significance of the regression. In regression analysis the *F*-value expresses the relative variance we explained with our model. As with the slope the calculated *F*-value is based on, a single sample and can be presumed to vary in certain fashion if we were to draw a large number of samples and calculate it again. We would then want to know whether the variance we have explained with our regression actually differs from zero or whether we just randomly explained some variance although there is no actual relationship in the population from which we took our sample. Here, again the *F*-value can be used to calculate or to look up the corresponding significance level. Common statistics software facilitates this step and routinely displays the significance level. The value should be lower than 0.05 indicating a confidence level of at least 95 percent.

3.4 Multivariate Regression

Multivariate regression is an extension of the simple bivariate regression. Instead of only one independent variable there are at least two independent variables. In general the equation looks like:

$$\hat{y} = \hat{a} + \hat{b}_1 x_1 + \hat{b}_2 x_2 + \ldots + \hat{b}_k x_k. \tag{24.9}$$

Although simply an extension of the linear model for the bivariate regression the multivariate model is far more powerful. It is now possible to test several theories and competing factors simultaneously. The estimation of the parameter follows the same logic as in the bivariate case. Also, the interpretation of the regression parameters and the statistical diagnostics are the same. The constant a is the expected value of Y when every independent variable is zero. The slope (for example, b_1) for a particular independent variable (X_1) can be interpreted as follows: A change of one unit in X_1 leads to a change of b_1 in the dependent variable Y under the assumption that all other factors are hold constant. Therefore, the slope is now called partial slope or partial regression coefficient. With the t-statistics, the significance of each partial slope is tested.

Suppose there are four independent variables in a multivariate regression. Which of these factors is most important and contributes most to the explanation of the dependent variable? The answer to this important question gives the BETA value of each independent variable. These beta weights are standardized values of the slopes, which control for the fact that the variables have different scales and differ in their empirically observable variability. The computer package performs a so-called z-standardization of all variables (including the dependent variable) and regresses these transformed values on the dependent variable. The larger the calculated (standardized) slopes (that is, the BETA-weights) the stronger is the impact of this variable.

However, it should be mentioned that assessing the specific importance via the BETA values is not undisputed. Achen (1982, p. 75) has criticized this traditional view and suggested an alternative measure: the level importance (LI). The level importance for a particular variable is derived from the product of the partial slope with the mean of this variable:

$$LI_j = \hat{b}_j \cdot \bar{x}_j, \qquad (24.10)$$

with LI_j = level importance for the independent variable j, $\hat{b}_j$ = partial slope for variable j and $\bar{x}_j$ = arithmetic mean of variable j.

Achen has demonstrated that ranking of the importance can change. The interpretation of the level importance is straightforward: The LI indicates the contribution of each independent variable in explaining the average of the dependent variable. Large values indicate a higher contribution.

3.5   Pitfalls and Problems

There are several pitfalls and problems, especially in multivariate regressions. Three substantial and relatively common problems are addressed in this section: multicollinearity, heteroscedasticity and the identification of outliers.

Multicollinearity is a problem arising in multivariate regression analysis and stands for the undesirable case of independent variables being highly correlated. Perfect multicollinearity exists whenever an independent variable is perfectly correlated with another independent variable ($r = \pm 1$). In this case, the regression equation cannot be determined. A first way to identify this problem is to analyze the correlation matrix of independent variables. If it shows any strong correlations, those indicate multicollinearity.

Multicollinearity means a loss of information because information is shared by two or more (highly correlated) variables and hence redundant. The consequence of multicollinearity is a lower precision of the estimation and a decreased significance of the regression coefficient, as the standard deviation of the regression coefficient (the standard error) increases and therefore the value of the *t*-statistic decreases. Nevertheless, the estimated regression coefficients are still 'BLUE' ('best linear unbiased estimators'), which means that, following the method of least squares, they provide the best estimated values. As a result, a prognosis is not affected by the given coefficients. For a study aiming at the explanation of phenomena, on the other hand, the loss of significance has a grave effect, because the explanatory power of the model decreases (Berry and Feldman 1985, p. 41).

Other diagnostic instruments to identify this severe problem are the so-called 'tolerance' values, which are based on the Klein test, and the 'variance inflation factor' (VIF). The Klein test consists of regression estimations for each independent variable, in which all other independent variables are included in the equation as predictor variables: 'Regress each independent variable on all the other independent variables' (Lewis-Beck 1980, p. 53). Subtracting the resulting coefficient from one yields the value of tolerance. Results close to zero indicate a high multicollinearity. The second diagnostics for high collinearity is the variance inflation factor, which is defined as the inverse of the tolerance. If the VIF is close to one, there is no collinearity. Furthermore, a high *F*-statistic (above 2.0) with a simultaneous insignificance of the partial regression coefficients, that is, small *t*-values of the slope parameters, can also be regarded as an indicator of multicollinearity.

A solution to this problem might be to leave out of the model one of the highly correlated independent variables. However, this may effectively negate the theoretical assumptions which guide the formulation of the model. Another possibility might be to create a common, combined indicator when it makes theoretical sense. A simpler solution would be to have more information by sampling more data, but this will hardly be tenable for a great number of practical applications.

The term heteroscedasticity denominates a second common problem in regression analysis, namely, the non-constant variation of residuals over the values of a predictor variable. In short, heteroscedasticity is the uneven variance of residuals. It also means a direct violation of one of the key assumptions of linear regression, which is the constant variance of error terms (homoscedasticity). Heteroscedasticity becomes apparent in a scatterplot of the residuals and the variable that is the cause of heteroscedasticity: the scattering of the residuals will appear wedge-shaped. A simple scatterplot will indeed often suffice to identify heteroscedasticity. Various phenomena can be the reason for its occurrence, which is mainly the case in cross-sectional regression. For certain independent variables, the variance will be higher if the measured value rises, while all other variables stay the same. A number of examples for this phenomenon have to do with data on income or expenditure components. The variance in expenditure will be larger for wealthy people than for poor people, whose freely available income is much lower. Also, with averages of grouped data, the variance decreases if the size of the group (or of the sample) increases (Wonnacott and Wonnacott 1990, p. 200). Finally, heteroscedasticity can be a result of measuring errors or inaccuracies. For instance, official statistics in wealthy countries are more accurate than in poor countries. This could influence measurements of the gross national product (GNP), as the GNP values in poor countries are usually based on basic surveys and estimations.

The consequences of heteroscedasticity are severe. The estimators are still unbiased, but not efficient anymore, which bears on the test of significance. An estimator, in this case the OLS estimator for the slope, is defined as efficient, if its variance in a given sample size is lower than the variance of all other conceivable unbiased estimators. Owing to heteroscedasticity in the data, the true variance (and standard error) for the slope will be underestimated, which means there are other ways of getting an unbiased estimator that are more precise, that is, with a lower variance of residuals. The OLS-estimator therefore becomes inefficient, with an important consequence for the practical application of regression. Underestimating the slope's variance causes its t-statistic to increase, thereby making it more likely to find an effect to be significant even when it is not.

Heteroscedasticity can be identified in various ways. One possibility is to inspect the residual plots or the regression equation, trying to find the typical wedge-shape of residuals looking at the graph. A formal test is the White test for heteroscedasticity (White 1980; Pindyck and Rubinfeld 1991, p. 136; Greene 2012, p. 315). The null hypothesis is H_0 = homoscedasticity, whereas the alternative hypothesis is H_1 = no homoscedasticity (= heteroscedasticity). The test performs a regression of the squared residuals on the independent variables of the original regression equation, on the squared independent variables, and on arbitrarily higher powers of the independent variables. The test statistic is chi-square and the value of the test results from $n \cdot R^2$ (of the estimated equation). The null hypothesis is rejected for any value greater than the critical value of the chi-squared distribution (95 per cent confidence interval). The test statistic has $k - 1$ degrees of freedom (with k = the amount of regressors without the constant).

Another possible test for heteroscedasticity is the Goldfeld–Quandt test, for which the observed values are first divided into two groups. Under the assumption of homoscedasticity, the variance of residuals in both groups have to be identical, whereas for a heteroscedastic distribution, the variance would be different in each group. As a part of the test, the values of the independent variable X are sorted in ascending order, enabling us to divide the set into two groups. If the number of cases and therefore the amount of degrees of freedom is large, the mid-level cases can be taken out of the sorted set. After this step, the regression equation is estimated for both groups separately. With these results, the sums of squared residuals from both groups can be put into relation. The null hypothesis is homoscedasticity, that is, identical variances. This is determined by means of an *F*-test, which, as already noted above, allows for the comparison of variances Large *F*-values lead to a rejection of the null hypothesis.

How can heteroscedasticity be handled? The method of regression analysis for eliminating this phenomenon is the so-called generalized least squares (GLS) regression. A description of this method would go beyond the scope of this introduction. Those interested can read the relevant publications (Assenmacher 1995; Johnston 1991; Pindyck and Rubinfeld 1991; Greene 2012). Furthermore, some statistical packages have implemented corrected (so called robust) standard errors, adjusting for heteroscedasticity.

Finally, outliers can influence a regression substantially. The easiest way to identify outliers is to look at the scatterplot graph. Observed values that are far from the regression line in terms of their residuals can be seen as outliers. A first clue can also be given by univariate statistics like stem-and-leaf or boxplot diagrams. Cases that can be identified as extreme values or outliers this way are most likely going to be outliers in the regression equation as well.

Outliers that have a big impact on the regression line can be identified by calculating so-called leverage values. These show the influence of single cases on the expected linear relation. The leverage value of a case describes the effect this case has got on the corresponding predicted value. Possible leverage values lie between 0 and $(n - 1) / n$, with an expected average of k / n (k = number of regressors, n = number of cases). Leverage values below 0.2 are not problematic; values between 0.2 and 0.5 should be handled with care and values greater than $2k / n$ or above 0.5 are critical. Cases with high leverage values should be eliminated from the study to ascertain the validity of the results, because these might be strongly influenced by a single case. When calculating a regression with a statistical software package, the leverage values can be automatically generated, for example using SPSS. The program SYSTAT even gives out warnings when there are large leverage values.

A third method to identify problematic outliers is the Mahalanobis distance, which is closely connected with the leverage value. Dividing the Mahalanobis distance by the factor $(n - 1)$ leads to the leverage value. It is based on a case's distance to the mean value for an independent variable. The greater this distance, the greater the Mahalanobis distance. Finally, there is another control statistic that can identify influential cases: the Cook's distance. This statistic can also be calculated by various statistics packages. A large value for Cook's distance indicates an influential case that has a large impact on the regression.

There are several ways of how to treat outliers and influential cases (outliers with a high leverage). First, we can eliminate the extreme value from the data set, although this is sometimes not justified. It is definitely better to model the outlier case (for example, with a dummy variable) into the model. Perform two regression analyses, one including the outliers, one excluding them. Transform the variables, for example by taking the logarithm and thereby turning a non-linear relationship into a linear relationship. Finally, gather more cases to get more stable results.

4   STRENGTHS AND WEAKNESSES OF REGRESSION ANALYSIS

In summary, regression analysis is one of the most powerful instruments in social science. Various new developments in past decades, such as logistic regression, panel regression or multilevel regression, show its strength, flexibility and widespread use. The most important application in social science is theory testing via hypotheses. These hypotheses are tested with regression models, that is, by the effect of the independent variables on the dependent variable in the regression model. Whether these hypotheses hold up to the data or have to be rejected can often easily be read from the regression coefficients and their significance levels. At the same time, we can assess the impact of different independent variables on the dependent variable and determine which variables are most important. The method can also be used for predictions and forecasts. Furthermore, some newer research strategies, for example, interaction effects, can expand the potential of regression analysis even further.

However, there are also some pitfalls when it comes to its application. Researchers often use inappropriate data, as it does not meet the requirement of only using at least interval scaled variables. A certain kind of data selection, namely random sampling, is also, strictly speaking, necessary for a meaningful interpretation of the *t*-values and the significances. Furthermore, severe robustness checks of the results are quite rare. A popular strategy is also to include as many independent factors as possible in a multivariate regression and not to report the adjusted R^2, which punishes the model for a larger number of explanatory variables. Sometimes it also seems that there is not much if any theoretical reasoning behind a regression model. Building and testing simple additive models in a trial and error fashion is clearly insufficient. Results from a regression analysis gain their greatest value when they can be tied back to a prior rigid theoretical discussion of causal relationships we expect to find.

NOTES

1. It should be noted that there are several other ways to calculate the slope.
2. See Table 24.1 for the numbers.

REFERENCES

Achen, C.H. (1982), *Interpreting and Using Regression*, Beverly Hills, CA: Sage.
Anderson, C.J. (1998), 'When in doubt, use proxies: attitudes toward domestic politics and support for European integration', *Comparative Political Studies*, **31** (5), 569–601.
Assenmacher, W. (1995), *Einführung in die Ökonometrie (Introduction into Econometrics)*, 5th edn, Munich; Vienna: Oldenbourg.
Beck, N. and J. Katz (1995), 'What to do (and not to do) with time-series cross-section data', *American Political Science Review*, **89** (3), 634–47.
Berry, W.D. and S.A. Feldman (1985), *Multiple Regression in Practice*, Beverly Hills, CA: Sage.
Greene, S. (2004), 'Social identity theory and party identification', *Social Science Quarterly*, **85** (1), 136–53.
Greene, W.H. (2012), *Econometric Analysis*, Boston, MA and Munich: Pearson.
Hibbs, D.A. (1977), 'Political parties and macroeconomic policy', *American Political Science Review*, **71** (4), 1467–87.
Johnston, J. (1991), *Econometric Methods*, 3rd edn, New York: McGraw-Hill.
Kittel, B. (1999), 'Sense and sensitivity in pooled analysis of political data', *European Journal of Political Research*, **35** (2), 225–53.
Lewis-Beck, M.S. (1980), *Applied Regression: An Introduction*, Beverly Hills, CA: Sage.
Pindyck, R.S. and D.L. Rubinfeld (1991), *Econometric Models and Economic Forecast*, New York: McGraw-Hill.

Snijders, T. and R. Bosker (2012), *Multilevel Analysis: An Introduction to Basic and Applied Multilevel Analysis*, 2nd edn, Los Angeles, CA: Sage.

Stone Sweet, A. and T. Brunell (1998), 'Constructing a supranational constitution: dispute resolution and governance in the European Community', *American Political Science Review*, **92** (1), 63.

White, H. (1980), 'A heteroskedasticity-consistent covariance matrix estimator and a direct test for heteroskedasticity', *Econometrica*, **48** (4), 817–38.

Wonnacott, T.H. and R.J. Wonnacott (1990), *Regression: A Second Course in Statistics*, New York: Wiley.

25 Configurational comparative methods (QCA and fuzzy sets): complex causation in cross-case analysis
Benoît Rihoux

1 INTRODUCTION

Qualitative comparative analysis (QCA) has gained quite some ground in various political science sub-fields over the past three decades, because it provides an original toolbox enabling one to handle multiple cross-case comparisons, to test models laying more emphasis on causal complexity, and to conduct formal/computer-run analyses while also keeping an eye on the 'qualitative' specificities of given cases. It was initiated by Charles Ragin (1987), who first presented it as a research approach seeking to reconcile case-oriented ('qualitative') and variable-oriented ('quantitative') perspectives. It was also gradually translated in a series of techniques, with attached protocols and software programs, now brought under the label of 'configurational comparative methods' (CCMs) (Rihoux and Ragin 2009) or 'set-theoretic methods' (STMs) (Schneider and Wagemann 2012).

This chapter first discusses the foundations of QCA as an approach and set of techniques. Next, some of the main critiques formulated via-à-vis QCA are presented, as well as the main responses and some of the innovations these critiques have stimulated. Further, the different types of uses of CCMs are laid out, including the main stages of a typical QCA protocol, using a simple empirical illustration. Next, this chapter examines the evolution and state of play of QCA applications in political science. Finally, some stakes of the current mainstreaming and diversification of CCMs are discussed.

2 FOUNDATIONS OF QCA

During the 1970s and 1980s, Charles Ragin, a junior scholar in the field of comparative welfare state studies, identified limitations of quantitative approaches, particularly the emphasis laid on the identification of the 'net effect' of each independent variable on the dependent variable: this did not enable the richness of historical cases in terms of causal mechanisms to be tapped, and the different techniques relying on interaction effects did not enable more complex forms of causality to be modelled (Marx et al. 2013). The search for alternatives to 'net effects thinking' has remained a core preoccupation of Ragin and other CCM developers ever since (Ragin 2006).

Ragin also questioned the 'qualitative' and 'quantitative' labels, which he replaced by 'case-oriented' and 'variable-oriented', as case studies can exploit quantitative data, and variables used for statistical treatment can also be apprehended qualitatively. He questioned, too, mainstream quantitative approaches for their emphasis on given populations and standard sampling procedures, following Przeworski and Teune's (1970) advocacy that populations, on the contrary, need to be carefully constructed. Therefore Ragin's early interest was in more qualitative case selection strategies and in the whole process of apprehension and definition of 'what is a case?' (Ragin and Becker 1992).

Hence Ragin's quest for tools enabling us to model and process cases as complex combinations of traits. The decisive impulse leading to the development of QCA was his intuition that other, non-statistical mathematical tools could suit that purpose: Boolean algebra and set theory. The first empirical QCA application was published in 1984 (Ragin et al. 1984), on the topic of employment discrimination in the US; it demonstrated some decisive advantages of QCA vis-à-vis logistic regression.

Ragin's ambition in his seminal volume was to 'integrate the best features of the case-oriented approach with the best features of the variable-oriented approach' (Ragin 1987, p. 84) as well as to develop an empirical analytical technique. As spelled out by Ragin in his 1987 volume, and still largely standing today with some refinements and nuances (Marx et al. 2013; Rihoux 2013), QCA is an approach and set of techniques which: (1) is case oriented, with each case being considered as a whole (holistic approach); (2) represents cases as configurations of 'conditions' and 'outcome' variables, with combinations of conditions being causally linked to the outcome; (3) systematically identifies similarities and differences across comparable cases through 'truth tables' (tables of configurations); (4) promotes frequent iterations to theoretical and case-based knowledge, so to enhance the 'dialogue between ideas and evidence'; (5) identifies, through minimization algorithms, the key combinations of conditions leading to the presence or absence of the outcome, framing complex causation in terms of 'multiple conjunctural causation'; (6) systematizes the analysis in terms of (combinations of) necessary and/ or sufficient conditions; (7) seeks to achieve some parsimony while also maintaining the complexity of each individual case; and (8) enables us to process more than a few cases ('intermediate-n', multiple cross-case

---

BOX 25.1   WHAT QCA IS ALL ABOUT

QCA

- is case-oriented and holistic;
- represents cases as *configurations* of *condition* and *outcome* variables;
- exploits *truth tables* (tables of configurations) to identify similarities and differences across comparable cases;
- requires frequent iterations to theoretical and case-based knowledge;
- identifies the key combinations of conditions leading to the presence or absence of the outcome;
- systematizes the analysis in terms of *necessary* and *sufficient* conditions;
- strives to achieve a balance between parsimony and case complexity; and
- enables us to process multiple cases and to engage into modest generalization.

---

comparisons), to move beyond the idiosyncrasies of single case studies and to conduct forms of 'modest generalization'. See Box 25.1.

The 'complex causation' side of QCA has been gradually elaborated, in different ways. It was first conceptualized as 'mutiple conjunctural' causation, which entails equifinality (different combinations of conditions may produce the same outcome), non-permanent causal direction and causal asymmetry. It has then been further refined in the form of more complex necessity/sufficiency statements combining multiple conditions, including 'quasi'-necessity and 'quasi'-sufficiency statements.

Together with criminologist and programmer Kriss Drass who also co-authored some of the very first applications, Ragin developed the first software program ('QCA'). The latter, conducting what is now referred to as crisp-set QCA (csQCA), was based on Boolean logic and therefore required that each variable be coded in a binary way (0 or 1), placing one clear dichotomization threshold for each variable and each case. The user thus had to establish fundamental distinctions – differences in kind, not in degree – in each variable (for example, revolutionary situation yes/no, low/high welfare state development, and so on).

3   MAIN DEBATES AND INNOVATIONS

Qualitative comparative analysis and the other developing CCMs have spurred numerous debates and critiques, especially vivid in the US. This probably stems from the fact that Ragin has increasingly framed QCA as an alternative approach to quantitative (read: statistical) approaches and techniques which are more predominant in the US than in Europe. Ragin and other CCM developers have increasingly framed CCMs as a toolbox also geared towards larger-n datasets (Ragin 2008; Schneider and Wagemann 2012; Fiss et al. 2013). In the process, Ragin also increasingly framed CCMs as a 'set-theoretic' approach, fundamentally distinct from the 'correlational' (mainstream statistical) approach (Ragin 2008). Indeed, the foundations of the set-theoretic approach (and related methods) are distinct from those of mainstream statistics: set-theoretic methods focus on membership scores of elements in sets (versus linear 'measurement'), causal relations are modelled as subset or superset relations (versus correlations), and so on (Schneider and Wagemann 2012, pp. 3–12).

It is beyond the scope of this chapter to list and discuss the numerous critiques and debates around QCA and CCMs (De Meur et al. 2009; Schneider and Wagemann 2012; Marx et al. 2013). A number of main critiques and responses are briefly examined here. First, QCA has been criticized for being too sensitive to cases, as the inclusion or exclusion of one case can significantly alter the QCA solution (Goldthorpe 1997). The response to this critique, from the side of case-based researchers, is that this precisely constitutes a richness of QCA, and that each case should be carefully selected. Second, (cs)QCA has often been criticized for the over-simplification of data through dichotomization. This has pushed other innovations through the development of finer-grained multivalue QCA (mvQCA) and fuzzy-set QCA (fsQCA); besides, some still make the argument for the great analytical strength of dichotomies (De Meur et al. 2009).

Next, several critiques have been voiced around 'measurement errors' in QCA, in addition to fundamentally questioning (fs)QCA's ability to produce meaningful results (Lieberson 2004; Hug 2013; Lucas and Szatrowski 2014). There have been forceful rebuttals to these critiques (for example, Fiss et al. 2014 as well as other pieces in the same symposium), arguing that the latter are largely invalid since they are forcing statistical and probabilistic reasoning on tools that are non-statistical and non-probabilistic. Along similar lines, some have pinpointed a strong omitted variable bias in QCA, especially since QCA requires a relatively limited number of conditions (Seawright 2005). Besides a rebuttal of this simplistic statistical critique (Ragin 2005), this has led to the development of more elaborate models in QCA, in particular 'two-step' QCA distinguishing 'remote' from 'proximate' conditions, that is, conditions more indirectly or more directly causally related to the outcome (Schneider and Wagemann 2006).

Other critiques have focused on limitations of QCA, for instance, on the non-explicit inclusion of the time dimension, on the assumption of cross-case independence, or on the difficulty to maintain within-case knowledge on multiple cases. All these critiques have led to further technical developments and to more elaborate designs, among which the sequencing QCA with 'thick' case studies.

Most of these critiques have thus forced QCA developers to further clarify the assumptions underpinning CCMs. They have also spurred many technical innovations. Among the main innovations, one could mention: (1) the development of fsQCA which enables richer measurement; (2) the development of multi-value QCA (mvQCA) as an extension of csQCA; (3) the development of software programs among which TOSMANA, FSQCA, as well as some increasingly powerful R modules (Thiem and Dusa 2012); (4) more sophisticated model-building strategies through the formulation of 'configurational hypotheses'; (5) more refined strategies for dichotomization of crisp sets and calibration of fuzzy sets; (6) robustness analyses of QCA results; (7) the development of coefficients in the QCA procedure, among which a relevance coefficient (enabling one, in particular, to separate genuine from trivial necessary conditions) (Schneider and Wagemann, 2012, p.139ff.) and a coverage coefficient (evaluating the empirical coverage of the QCA solution); (8) benchmarks in terms of the number of conditions/number of cases ratio; (9) more varied modes of data visualization, through Venn diagrams, scatterplots and 'decision trees'; (10) more varied strategies to obtain 'complex', 'intermediate' or 'parsimonious' QCA solutions – only the latter being causally interpretable; and so on.

There have also been numerous developments and innovations, still under way, in terms of research designs. Besides the manifold refinements in the QCA procedure itself, the main point is probably that QCA has been confronted with – or combined with – both quantitative and qualitative methods, in various ways. However a 'multi-method' or 'mixed methods' use of QCA has not increased over time, probably because QCA has gradually gained recognition and legitimacy as a stand-alone method (Rihoux et al. 2013).

With regards to quantitative methods, QCA has thus far been combined with several techniques: time series analysis, factor analysis and many variants of regression analyses. There have also been a number of combinations of QCA with other formal techniques such as event structure analysis, optimal matching, game theory, social networks analysis, and so on. On the qualitative front, many applications have combined QCA with 'thick' case studies. More recently, some protocols have been developed to sequence QCA with a process-tracing analysis of individual cases (Rohlfing and Schneider 2013).

4   USES AND PROTOCOLS OF QCA

There are at least five different types of QCA uses (see Box 25.2), some of which are used more frequently than others. The first type of use consists in exploiting QCA to describe cases in a more synthetic manner, without reducing complexity through minimization algorithms. The technical feature of QCA that is used to this end is the 'truth table' which groups cases into different configurations (that is, combinations of conditions associated with one given outcome value). This is a more exploratory use of QCA – it constitutes anyhow a core intermediate step in a more full-fledged application – and can be exploited for typology-building (for example, Kvist 2007).

The second use, which also constitutes a core intermediate step in a more complete analysis, consists in the exploitation of 'contradictory configurations', that is, configurations gathering cases with similar condition values but different outcome values (see also the empirical example in section 5). These logical contradictions enable one to re-examine the cases at hand, in a qualitative way – and thereby to discover more about the cases, to put into question the theoretical model or to re-examine the operationalization of the variables. Thus: a thorough exploitation of contradictory configurations constitutes a powerful heuristic tool for cross-case comparative analysis (Rihoux and De Meur 2009).

The three further uses are more full-fledged to the extent that they exploit a core QCA operation: minimization, that is, the reduction of complexity from full configurations to more parsimonious solutions containing key combinations of conditions leading to a certain outcome value. Among these full-fledged uses, by far the most frequent is the empirical test of some existing theories – QCA is a particularly powerful device to this end (Schneider and Wagemann 2012), with a (causal) hypothesis linking each condition to the outcome. Obviously the QCA results (the parsimonious solutions) do not by themselves establish 'causal' mechanisms linking the conditions and the outcome; this requires case-based and theory-based interpretation by the researcher.

The fourth use is the test of propositions or conjectures beyond existing theories. This is another facet of QCA use, more exploratory and to some extent more inductive. It is naturally possible to combine theory-testing and proposition-testing uses of QCA, by articulating hypotheses and propositions within the same model. The fifth and final exploitation of QCA consists in the elaboration of new theoretical propositions or segments of theories. The technical way to do this is to interpret the QCA solutions, in particular the combination of two conditions which were not yet linked up in the existing theory.

BOX 25.2   THE FIVE MAIN USES OF QCA

1. Describing multiple cases in a more synthetic manner.
2. Exploiting 'contradictory configurations' to re-examine the cases and/or the theoretical model.
3. Empirically testing some existing theories (most frequent use).
4. Empirically testing some propositions or conjectures beyond existing theories.
5. Elaborating new theoretical propositions or segments of theories.

Note: These uses may be combined in different ways.

In terms of practical protocol and the actual research being conducted, whatever the use of QCA, one should stress that the technical part of the QCA (the 'analytical moment' exploiting the software program) is only one stage of the research process. Taking a bird's eye view, the whole process can be summarized into three main stages: first an 'upstream' stage (gathering case knowledge, building a model, compiling data), then QCA proper, then the whole 'downstream' phase of case-driven and/or theory-driven interpretation (Rihoux and Lobe 2009). The goal of the QCA stage, which is often not so time-intensive, is simply to reach a more or less strong level of parsimony – whereas complexity is much more taken into account in the 'upstream' and 'downstream' stages.

5   THE MAIN STEPS OF A TYPICAL QCA PROCEDURE IN POLITICAL SCIENCE

The third, most frequent use of QCA, that is, theory testing (see above) is outlined here below along the main steps of a standard QCA procedure. The empirical example is taken from the 'Inter-War Project': an international research project examining the collapse or survival of democracies in greater Europe between the two world wars (Berg-Schlosser and Mitchell 2000, 2003). This is a typical intermediate-n most similar cases with different outcomes (MSDO) design, with 18 countries as cases (see Table 25.1), and a contrasted outcome (collapse or survival). Different QCA techniques can be exploited to analyze the data that is both numerical for the main conditions and non-numerical for the outcome (for more details on this empirical example, see Berg-Schlosser and De Meur 1994, 2009; Cronqvist and Berg-Schlosser 2009; Ragin 2009; Rihoux and De Meur 2009; Schneider and Wagemann 2012).

Table 25.1   Raw data table for the collapse or survival of democracies,
with the four Lipset conditions plus a fifth condition

Cases	GNPCAP	URBANI	LITERA	INDLAB	GOVINS	SURVIV
AUS	720	33.4	98.0	33.4	10	0
BEL	1098	60.5	94.4	48.9	4	1
CZE	586	69.0	95.9	37.4	6	1
EST	468	28.5	95.0	14.0	6	0
FIN	590	22.0	99.1	22.0	9	1
FRA	983	21.2	96.2	34.8	5	1
GER	795	56.5	98.0	40.4	11	0
GRE	390	31.1	59.2	28.1	10	0
HUN	424	36.3	85.0	21.6	13	0
IRE	662	25.0	95.0	14.5	5	1
ITA	517	31.4	72.1	29.6	9	0
NET	1008	78.8	99.9	39.3	2	1
POL	350	37.0	76.9	11.2	21	0
POR	320	15.3	38.0	23.1	19	0
ROM	331	21.9	61.8	12.2	7	0
SPA	367	43.0	55.6	25.5	12	0
SWE	897	34.0	99.9	32.3	6	1
UK	1038	74.0	99.9	49.9	4	1

The first steps are typical steps of a comparative research design, that is, formulating a research question in a comparative fashion and making sure that the concepts used can 'travel', defining the cases, defining the contrasted outcome of interest linked to the research puzzle, that is, the survival or collapse of democracies, and looking for 'candidate theories' that might account for this contrasted outcome. Thereby we also define, conceptually and empirically, the 'outcome' variable for the QCA, that is, what would be referred to as the 'dependent variable' in a statistical analysis.

A most frequent situation in political science as well as in social sciences more broadly is that there is a wealth of alternative theories to account for a given outcome – therefore we first have to rule out some theories and choose what would be the core theories – ideally one core theory that contains a set of clearly formulated directional hypotheses. Naturally there are many other ways to proceed, for instance, combining segments of various complementary theories and thereby obtaining a model to be empirically tested. In this example, a simple theory has been selected: Lipset's theory on the more general socio-economic preconditions of a stable democracy. Then, following each one of the four main dimensions suggested by Lipset (wealth, industrialization, education and urbanization), four directional hypotheses must be formulated. In order to then pursue with a QCA at later stages, we should strive to formulate each one of these hypotheses in terms of necessity and sufficiency. For instance, for the first dimension: 'high economic wealth is a *necessary* (but not *sufficient*) condition for the survival of democracy'. In the process, we also define, conceptually and empirically, the 'condition' variables for the QCA, that is, what would be referred to as the 'independent variables' in a statistical analysis. Note however that QCA conditions are absolutely not 'independent' variables; quite the contrary, a core QCA assumption is that conditions will operate as part of more or less complex combinations.

The next steps consist of operationalizing the variables and gathering the data; this is most often a challenging task, especially in cross-national comparison –even if one relies on secondary sources. Based on this, we obtain a raw data table. In this example, the data table contains (from left to right in Table 25.1), on the one hand, four Lipset conditions: GNP per capita, in US dollars (GNPCAP); urbanization, that is, the percentage of population in towns with 20 000 and more inhabitants (URBANIZA); the percentage of literacy (LITERACY); and the percentage of industrial labor force (INDLAB); and, on the other hand, a fifth condition that is not contained in the Lipset theory but that will be useful at a further stage (see below).

Before the QCA itself, we can already examine this raw data table and gain some first, albeit not systematic, insights on some patterns which seem to emerge across the cases. For instance, most collapsing democracies (outcome 0) display a low GNP per capita.

In the next steps, we engage in QCA proper, with specialized software. The first, crucial and often challenging operation consists in deciding on meaningful thresholds and cut-off or 'calibration' points on each one of the condition variables. For the purpose of demonstration, only the simplest form is presented here; dichotomization, that is, setting a single threshold between 1 and 0 values for each condition. This enables us to then engage in a csQCA. There are more elaborate options – mvQCA and fsQCA – that cannot be demonstrated here for reasons of space. The result of this dichotomization is a *binary data table*.

The table is then examined in two ways. On the one hand, a test of necessity is performed, through the computation of consistency coefficients for the respective conditions. On the other hand, we achieve a first 'synthesis' of the data by producing successive *truth tables*, that is, tables of configurations, in which several cases frequently occupy the same configuration (same combination of condition values and same outcome value). We can already exploit this in a more descriptive way, by interpreting the ways the various cases cluster in those configurations.

Table 25.2   Contradiction-free truth table (five conditions)*

Cases	GNPCAP	URBANI	LITERA	INDLAB	GOVINS	SURVIV
AUS	1	0	1	1	1	0
BEL, CZE, NET, UK	1	1	1	1	0	1
EST	0	0	1	0	0	0
FIN, IRE	1	0	1	0	0	1
FRA, SWE	1	0	1	1	0	1
GER	1	1	1	1	1	0
GRE, POR, SPA	0	0	0	0	1	0
HUN, POL	0	0	1	0	1	0
ITA, ROM	0	0	0	0	0	0

Note: * Thresholds used: respectively $550, 50 percent, 75 percent, 30 percent and 9.5 cabinets.

The most frequent difficulty at this stage is the occurrence of 'contradictory configurations', that is, configurations with similar condition values but different outcome values on different cases. There are multiple strategies to lift those contradictions – in particular switching to mvQCA or fsQCA. In this simple example, we choose to add a fifth, more political variable in the model: the level of governmental instability (GOVINS, the fifth condition in Table 25.1, operationalized by the number of different cabinets during the period under consideration), and to carefully examine the dichotomization of the GNPCAP condition. The result of this stepwise procedure is a 'contradiction-free truth table' (Table 25.2).

The final step within the computer-run part of QCA, at the core of the QCA protocol, is the 'minimization', using Boolean algorithms to obtain shorter expressions – shorter combinations of conditions, thereby gaining some level of parsimony – leading to a certain outcome value.

In practical terms, one must perform a sequence of four separate minimizations: (1) for the 1 outcome, without 'logical remainders'; (2) for the 1 outcome, with (some) 'logical remainders'; (3) for the 0 outcome, without 'logical remainders'; (4) for the 0 outcome, with (some) 'logical remainders'. We thus obtain at least four QCA solutions. Logical remainders are simply those configurations that do not contain observed empirical cases. Not using these produces a complex solution (little parsimony gained), whereas bringing logical remainders enables the software to formulate simplifying assumptions, that is, to allocate an outcome value to some of the logical remainders, which produces a much more parsimonious solution. However one caveat here is that some simplifying assumptions might not be plausible on theoretical or empirical grounds ('difficult' simplifying assumptions); therefore the researcher has the option of only enabling the inclusion of the 'easy' (more plausible) logical remainders, thereby obtaining an intermediate solution – that is, longer than the parsimonious solution with unconstrained inclusion of logical remainders.

For instance, the 'long' solution for the 1 outcome is expressed as follows:

GNPCAP * LITERA * INDLAB * govins + GNPCAP * urbani * LITERA * govins SURVIV
(BEL,CZE,NET,UK,FRA,SWE)   *(FIN,IRE,FRA,SWE)*

This solution contains two terms, with standard Boolean notation (uppercase = 1 value; lowercase = 0 value; * = logical 'AND'; + = logical 'OR'). The first term (combination of high GNP per capita, high literacy, high industrial labor and low governmental instability) covers six countries, whereas the second term (combination of high GNP per capita, low urbanization, high literacy and low governmental instability) covers four countries. This solution can also be further assessed in terms of the 'coverage' (proportion of cases covered) of its respective terms. Both terms can lead to some interpretations, but only a small level of parsimony has been achieved.

By contrast, the 'short' solution for the 1 outcome, with the inclusion of logical remainders, is expressed as follows:

GNPCAP * govins → SURVIV

This is much more parsimonious (combination of high GNP per capita and low governmental instability) and covers all eight countries with surviving democracies.

A major limitation of the use of csQCA in this example is that it has necessitated the inclusion of a fifth condition beyond the test of the Lipset theory proper. Opting for mvQCA would have enabled such a test, by bringing in a bit more complexity in the GNP per capita condition, with three values (low, medium, high) (Cronqvist and Berg-Schlosser 2009). Further, going for fsQCA and also infusing some theoretical knowledge would have produced an intermediate solution highlighting the important role of a high level of literacy (in conjunction with GNPCAP and GOVINS) in explaining the survival of democracies (Ragin, 2009).

Finally, after the computer-run part of the procedure, the researcher can engage in the interpretation of the various solutions. This can take multiple forms depending on one's priorities: 'deep' case-by-case interpretations of single case narratives, qualitative cross-case comparisons within clusters of cases covered by the same solution terms, further theoretical development based on observed intersections of conditions, 'modest' generalization towards neighboring cases not (yet) analyzed empirically, and so on.

6   QCA APPLICATIONS IN POLITICAL SCIENCE: MAIN TRENDS

In the early 1990s, shortly after the publication of Ragin's seminal volume, the number of empirical applications remained low and mostly confined to political sociology, the sociology of organizations and welfare state studies. The core substantive topics were, for instance: revolutions, social movements, trade unions and labor relations. Until the late 1990s, QCA had penetrated sociology (including top-tier journals such as the *American Journal of Sociology* and *American Sociological Review*) much more than political science. This is probably owing to the fact that some well-established US sociologists were regularly conducting research with intermediate-n designs and were relatively open to methodological diversity. By contrast, the top US political science journals were (and still remain) more 'mono-method' and quantitatively oriented (Marx et al. 2013; Rihoux et al. 2013).

As Figure 25.1 shows, the sheer number of applications began to increase significantly from the early 2000s onwards. Note that Figure 25.1 only considers peer-reviewed journal articles with a full-fledged QCA application, and not other types of publications such as books and book chapters. This increase was observed both in political science and in other disciplines, in a process of disciplinary diversification. In particular, one also notices an increasing number and variety of applications in the fields of management and organizational studies. Particularly in political science broadly defined, this growth of QCA applications is observed more in Europe than in the U.S. – during the 2000–2014 period, about 70 percent of all published applications have been produced by Europe-based scholars.

Considering the whole period, political science broadly defined amounts to roughly one-half of all empirical applications published so far. A closer look at the applications in political science shows that wide range of empirical topics and sub-fields have by now been covered, such as (non-limitative list): political regimes, party politics, public administration, policy analysis, governance, regulation, political sociology, conflict studies and so on (Marx et al. 2013). In European journals in particular, there has clearly been a mainstreaming of QCA, as many top-tier journals in the respective

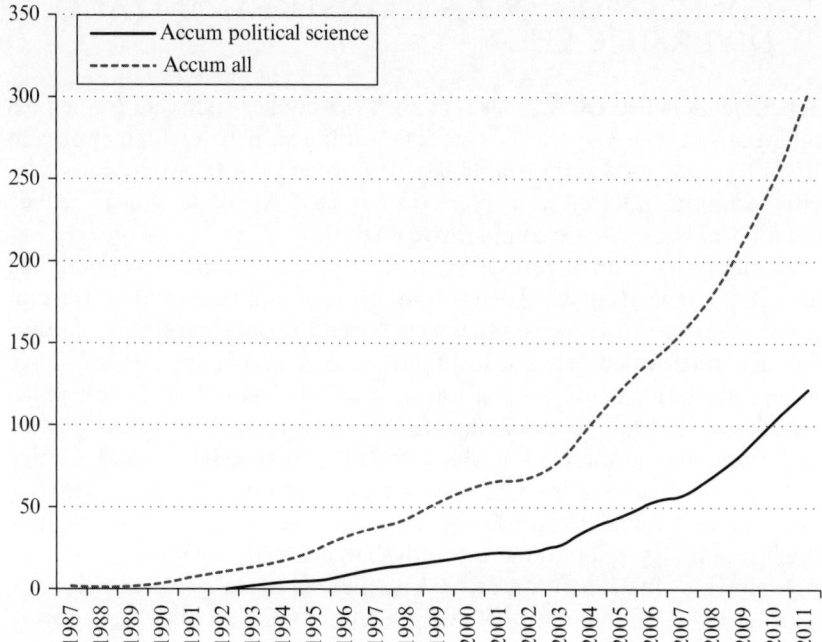

Source: Based on the COMPASSS bibliographical database: http://www.compasss.org.

Figure 25.1   *QCA applications (journal articles) in political science and other disciplines (taken from Marx et al. 2013)*

fields have published QCA articles – for example, *European Journal of Political Research*, *West European Politics* and *Journal of European Public Policy*. Other established US-based journals, such as *Political Research Quarterly* or *Comparative Political Studies*, have also opened up to QCA. Altogether more than 80 different political science journals have published QCA pieces.

With regard to political science applications, the most striking trend from the early 2000s onwards is the growing predominance of applications in the field of comparative policy analysis, including policy evaluation. This comes as no surprise, as there are strong connections between the features of QCA and the research goals and designs of many policy analysis researchers (Rihoux et al. 2011).

7 CONCLUSION: QCA'S MAINSTREAMING AND DIVERSIFICATION

When he launched QCA in his seminal 1987 book, Ragin had framed his intentions in relatively simple terms: developing a new research approach bridging case-based and variable-based approaches, and developing a specific technique (QCA – now referred to as csQCA) enabling us to reduce complexity in cross-case comparative analysis.

In slightly less than three decades, the CCMs or STMs that have developed around the initial (cs)QCA have become quite broadly used and accepted in political science as well as in other social scientific disciplines – though they still generate heated debates. Configurational comparative methods have also produced many useful empirical and theoretical results in the discipline. Altogether it is fair to assess that CCMs have been more mainstreamed in Europe than in the US – probably because intermediate-n comparative designs and cross-case comparisons are more commonplace in European political science, and because European political science is less dominated by 'high-technology' quantitative methods than in North America.

Following this expansion of CCMs, there is no longer one technique (rather, three techniques: csQCA, mvQCA, fsQCA). Other neighboring techniques are also being developed within the realm of CCMs, such as adding temporality to qualitative comparative analysis (TQCA) (Caren and Panofsky 2005) or coincidence analysis (Baumgartner 2009). Neither is there a single design anymore: even if intermediate-n applications are more frequent, there is an increasing proportion of larger-n QCA applications. More generally, the uses of QCA have diversified, with some researchers using more probabilistic procedures and benchmarks.

Thus, while some of Ragin's fundamental seminal points still hold (such as the formalization or necessity and sufficiency relationship or the ambition to combine within-case and cross-case analysis), some re-framings have been operated. The introduction of fsQCA, in particular, has shifted the emphasis from Boolean to set-theoretic logic. This shift also enables us to clarify one core point: although QCA does resort to variables at some point in the procedure, it is by no means a 'variable-oriented' method, as the variables are always considered part of combination or set relations (Schneider and Wagemann 2012).

The growing sophistication of the QCA techniques (including software programs) has coincided with a broader dissemination of QCA towards publics with varied prior methodological backgrounds. This also means that the usages of QCA are bound to become more diversified in the future, too, with more 'qualitative' and more 'quantitative' uses. Another recent trend, in domains neighboring political science, is that

---

BOX 25.3 MAIN ISSUES RAISED

- QCA, as part of configurational comparative methods (CCMs), is both a research approach and a set of techniques.
- QCA is case oriented, yet it resorts to mathematical treatment; it enables us to process multiple cases and to engage into modest generalization; it is geared towards causal complexity and set relations.
- Criticisms vis-à-vis QCA have spurred further innovations, among which are the development of fuzzy-set QCA (fsQCA) and more refined procedures.
- QCA can be exploited for different purposes, among which are theory- and model-testing; it requires frequent iterations with theoretical and case-based knowledge.
- QCA is being mainstreamed in different sub-fields, in particular comparative policy analysis.
- QCA and CCMs are being developed in various directions, including larger-n applications.

---

some non-academic analysts have begun to show interest in QCA: policy consultants, evaluators, analysts for non-governmental organizations or public administrations, and so on. Indeed QCA can prove very useful as a tool for the meta-analysis of case studies (projects, policy programs, and so on) which are frequently relatively small-n in some real-life settings. In parallel, numerous further technical as well as conceptual refinements are being developed in the CCMs epistemic community.

ESSENTIAL FURTHER READING

Essential further reading – in addition to various resources through the http://www.com-passs.org resource site:

Rihoux, B. and C.C. Ragin (eds) (2009), *Configurational Comparative Methods: Qualitative Comparative Analysis (QCA) and Related Techniques*, Thousand Oaks, CA and London: Sage.

Schneider, C.Q. and C. Wagemann (2012), *Set-Theoretic Methods for the Social Sciences: A Guide to Qualitative Comparative Analysis*, Cambridge: Cambridge University Press.

Thiem, A. and A. Dusa (2012), *Qualitative Comparative Analysis with R: A User's Guide*, New York: Springer.

REFERENCES

Baumgartner, M. (2009), 'Inferring causal complexity', *Sociological Methods & Research*, **38** (1), 71–101.

Berg-Schlosser, D. and G. De Meur (1994), 'Conditions of democracy in interwar Europe: a Boolean test of major hypotheses', *Comparative Politics*, **26** (3), 253–79.

Berg-Schlosser, D. and G. De Meur (2009), 'Comparative research design: case and variable selection', in B. Rihoux and C.C. Ragin (eds), *Configurational Comparative Methods: Qualitative Comparative Analysis (QCA) and Related Techniques*, Thousand Oaks, CA and London: Sage, pp. 19–32.

Berg-Schlosser, D. and J. Mitchell (eds) (2000), *Conditions of Democracy in Europe, 1919–39: Systematic Case Studies*, Basingstoke, UK: Macmillan and New York: St Martin's Press.

Berg-Schlosser, D. and J. Mitchell (eds) (2003), *Authoritarianism and Democracy in Europe, 1919–39: Comparative Analyses*, Basingstoke, UK: Palgrave Macmillan.

Caren, N. and A. Panofsky (2005), 'TQCA: a technique for adding temporality to qualitative comparative analysis', *Sociological Methods & Research*, **34** (2), 147–72.

Cronqvist, L. and D. Berg-Schlosser (2009), 'Multi-value QCA (MVQCA)', in B. Rihoux and C.C. Ragin (eds), *Configurational Comparative Methods: Qualitative Comparative Analysis (QCA) and Related Techniques*, Thousand Oaks, CA and London: Sage, pp. 69–86.

De Meur, G., B. Rihoux and S. Yamasaki (2009), 'Addressing the critiques of QCA', in B. Rihoux and C.C. Ragin (eds), *Configurational Comparative Methods: Qualitative Comparative Analysis (QCA) and Related Techniques*, Thousand Oaks, CA and London: Sage. pp. 147–66.

Fiss, P.C., A. Marx and B. Rihoux (2014), 'Comment: getting QCA right', *Sociological Methodology*, **44** (August), 95–100.

Fiss, P.C., D. Sharapov and L. Cronqvist (2013), 'Opposites attract? Opportunities and challenges for integrating large-n QCA and econometric analysis', *Political Research Quarterly*, **66** (1), 191–8.

Goldthorpe, J.H. (1997), 'Current issues in comparative macrosociology: a debate on methodological issues', *Comparative Social Research*, **16**, 1–26.

Hug, S. (2013), 'Qualitative comparative analysis: how inductive use and measurement error lead to problematic inference', *Political Analysis*, **21** (2), 252–65.

Kvist, J. (2007), 'Fuzzy set ideal type analysis', *Journal of Business Research*, **60** (5), 474–81.

Lieberson, S. (2004), 'Comments on the use and utility of QCA', *Qualitative Methods: Newsletter of the American Political Science Association Organized Section on Qualitative Methods*, **2** (2), 13–14.

Lucas, S.R. and A. Szatrowski (2014), 'Qualitative comparative analysis in critical perspective', *Sociological Methodology*, **44** (August), 1–79.

Marx, A., B. Rihoux and C. Ragin (2013), 'The origins, development and applications of qualitative comparative analysis (QCA): the first 25 years', *European Political Science Review*, **6** (1), 115–42.

Przeworski, A. and H. Teune (1970), *The Logic of Comparative Social Inquiry*, New York: Wiley-Interscience.

Ragin, C. (2005), 'Core versus tangential assumptions in comparative research', *Studies in Comparative International Development (SCID)*, **40** (1), 33–8.

Ragin, C.C. (1987), *The Comparative Method: Moving Beyond Qualitative and Quantitative Strategies*, Berkeley and Los Angeles, CA and London: University of California Press.

Ragin, C.C. (2006), 'The limitations of net-effects thinking', in B. Rihoux and H. Grimm (eds), *Innovative Comparative Methods for Policy Analysis*, New York: Springer, pp. 13–41.

Ragin, C.C. (2008), *Redesigning Social Inquiry: Fuzzy Sets and Beyond*, Chicago, IL: Chicago University Press.

Ragin, C.C. (2009), 'Qualitative comparative analysis using fuzzy sets (fsQCA)', in B. Rihoux and C.C. Ragin (eds), *Configurational Comparative Methods: Qualitative Comparative Analysis (QCA) and Related Techniques*, Thousand Oaks, CA and London: Sage, pp. 87–121.

Ragin, C.C. and H.S. Becker (eds) (1992), *What is a Case? Exploring the Foundations of Social Inquiry*, New York: Cambridge University Press.

Ragin, C.C., S.E. Mayer and K.A. Drass (1984), 'Assessing discrimination: a Boolean approach', *American Sociological Review*, **49** (2), 221–34.

Rihoux, B. (2013), 'Qualitative comparative analysis (QCA), anno 2013: reframing *The Comparative Method*'s seminal statements', *Swiss Political Science Review*, **19**(2), 233–45.

Rihoux, B. and G. De Meur (2009), 'Crisp-set qualitative comparative analysis (csQCA)', in B. Rihoux and C.C. Ragin (eds), *Configurational Comparative Methods: Qualitative Comparative Analysis (QCA) and Related Techniques*, Thousand Oaks, CA and London: Sage, pp. 33–68.

Rihoux, B. and B. Lobe (2009), 'The case for qualitative comparative analysis (QCA): adding leverage for thick cross-case comparison', in D. Byrne and C. Ragin (eds), *The Sage Handbook of Case-Based Methods*, London: Sage. pp. 222–43.

Rihoux, B. and C.C. Ragin (eds) (2009), *Configurational Comparative Methods: Qualitative Comparative Analysis (QCA) and Related Techniques*, Thousand Oaks, CA and London: Sage.

Rihoux, B., I. Rezsöhazy and D. Bol (2011), 'Qualitative comparative analysis (QCA) in public policy analysis: an extensive review', *German Policy Studies*, 7 (3), 9–82.

Rihoux, B., P. Álamos-Concha, D. Bol, A. Marx and I. Rezsöhazy (2013), 'From niche to mainstream method? A comprehensive mapping of QCA applications in journal articles from 1984 to 2011', *Political Research Quarterly*, 66 (1), 175–84.

Rohlfing, I. and C.Q. Schneider (2013), 'Improving research on necessary conditions: formalized case selection for process tracing after QCA', *Political Research Quarterly*, 66 (1), 220–30.

Schneider, C.Q. and C. Wagemann (2006), 'Reducing complexity in qualitative comparative analysis (QCA): remote and proximate factors and the consolidation of democracy', *European Journal of Political Research*, 45 (5), 751–86.

Schneider, C.Q. and C. Wagemann (2012), *Set-Theoretic Methods for the Social Sciences: A Guide to Qualitative Comparative Analysis*, Cambridge: Cambridge University Press.

Seawright, J. (2005), 'Qualitative comparative analysis (QCA) vis-à-vis regression', *Studies in Comparative International Development*, 40 (1), 3–26.

Thiem, A. and A. Dusa (2012), *Qualitative Comparative Analysis with R: A User's Guide*, New York: Springer.

26 Discourse analysis, social constructivism and text analysis: a critical overview
David Howarth and Steven Griggs

1 INTRODUCTION

Critical approaches to discourse analysis are distinguished by their desire to uncover issues relating to power, subjectivity and domination.[1] Alongside other species of critical theory, they are also concerned with emancipation in the sense of opening up spaces in which people can identify dominant ideologies and escape from such oppressive discourses (by deconstructing their meanings). They thus constitute alternative and qualitative approaches to probe how power is used to define the parameters of particular questions, set rules for particular practices and shape agendas. Critical discourse theorists question policies and practices in order to inquire into underlying issues of power and ideology, which are embedded in the very framing of policy problems and solutions. This chapter explores various models of discourse analysis, where questions are posed about the source, scope and pattern of policy, as well as the evaluation of policy in relation to the problem about how and to what extent the nature of relationships and organizations in political processes are (re)framed in texts and signifying sequences.

The past few years have brought a veritable 'discourse on discourse' in the social and political sciences. The initial focus on the role of 'talk and text in context', which includes various forms of conversation analysis, speech act theory, hermeneutical research and content analysis, has given way to a number of critical and interpretive approaches. Some have taken their lead from Michel Foucault's innovative conceptions of discourse. Proponents of critical discourse analysis (CDA) and historical discourse analysis (HDA), borrowing *inter alia* from aspects of the Foucauldian problematic, have developed a critical approach to the study of ideologies and social phenomena that focuses on the semiotic dimensions of social practice (for example, Fairclough and Wodak 1997; Wodak and Chilton 2005). By contrast, Laclau and Mouffe and others have developed a post-Marxist theory of politics, which builds upon a poststructuralist conception of discourse, and is applied mainly to the emergence, sedimentation and transformation of ideologies and social formations (for example,

Glynos and Howarth 2007). Finally, within the field of policy analysis, argumentative, discursive and interpretivist approaches have been at the forefront of deepening critical approaches to policy analysis (for example, Litfin 1995; Dryzek 1997; Fischer 2003). Notably, Maarten Hajer (1995) has elaborated a novel form of argumentative discourse analysis in his exploration of environmental policy and new types of governance.

Such discussion about the concept of discourse has led to contested definitions, competing theoretical assumptions and rival research strategies. However, it has also meant that the concepts of discourse and discourse analysis vary widely with respect to their scope and complexity, especially in the field of policy research (Glynos et al. 2009). Focusing initially on Foucauldian approaches, then the CDA and HDA perspectives, and finally on Laclau and Mouffe's poststructuralist discourse theory, this chapter clarifies some of these perplexing issues by developing a particular approach to political discourse analysis. Despite important theoretical advances and empirical applications, there remain persistent critiques of this influential approach, both because of its theoretical assumptions, which are alleged either to be too ideational or insufficiently attuned to the linguistic aspect of discourse analysis, and because there are difficulties in operationalizing their work and thus in generating effective research strategies (for example, Jessop 2009; Davies 2011; Wagenaar 2011; Connolly 2013).

2   THE FOUCAULDIAN PROBLEMATIC

Foucault's voluminous writings can be decomposed into distinct, though sometimes overlapping, phases. His earlier archaeological method drew upon developments in structuralist analysis, French philosophy of science, as well as advances in theoretical linguistics, to elaborate a complex study of knowledge and scientific discourse (Foucault 1972). His concept of discourse is nicely illustrated in his immanent critique of John Austin's idea of speech acts. While Austin (1986) focused on everyday linguistic performances – the performative act of naming a ship, for example, or getting married – where 'saying is doing', Foucault elaborates a theory of what might be termed serious speech acts. Serious performatives – or statements – are regarded as true or false depending on the particular set of rules which come into play on their utterance in a certain historical context. More precisely, Foucault explores those linguistic performances in which subjects are empowered to make serious truth claims because of their training, institutional location and mode of discourse. Assertions about the prospects of an economic recovery, for example, achieve the status of statements when they are uttered by suitably qualified economists or financial experts, who mobilize plausible theories and evidence to justify their arguments. Foucault's archaeological project is thus concerned with those groups of statements that are taken to be serious claims to truth by particular societies and communities at different points in time. His aim is then to describe their appearance, the different kinds of statements, as well as the regularities between statements in particular systems of discourse – or 'discursive formations' – and their regulated historical transformation.

Foucault's early program thus endeavors to locate and describe the rules that facilitated the generation of discourse in particular historical periods, such as the rules that enabled the production of statements about physics or biology in the nineteenth century. He thus accounts for the rarity of scientific discourse, while extracting the peculiar criteria that allowed scientific statements to be distinguished from non-scientific statements within particular periods. However, this endeavor to elaborate a quasi-structuralist theory of discourse, where the latter is comprehended in terms of a discrete corpus of statements, encountered a series of inconsistencies. At least one source of this tension arose because Foucault's purely descriptive intent pushed against the explanatory and critical potentials of his enterprise. Also, while his project infers the rules that allow some statements to be accepted as candidates for truth or falsity, while others are relegated to a 'wild exteriority', his approach does not put forward an explanation of such exclusions. Nor does he explicate the normative implications of his characterizations. Further issues concerned the precise relationship between the discursive and non-discursive dimensions of his enterprise – what is the relationship between discourse and material objects and practices? – as well as the role and status of the archaeological investigator in his program.

In response to such dilemmas, Foucault developed a more Nietzschean-inspired genealogical approach (Foucault 1984). Here he attempts to address the problems of his earlier work by broadening the notion of discourse to include a much wider range of social phenomena, including organizations, power and institutions. Indeed, the very distinction between the discursive and non-discursive dimensions is increasingly blurred, so that his new concept of discourse blends the two elements together. He also stresses the constitutive role of power in forming scientific knowledge and organizing its application. The upshot is that Foucault now stresses the interweaving of power and knowledge, where the latter is manifest in disciplines such as criminology or psychiatry, and he focuses on the way in which these discourses are used to construct and discipline social subjects like 'the criminal', 'the delinquent' or 'the insane' in different institutional contexts, such as prisons, schools or mental asylums. As against the ideal theory of discourse proposed by Habermas, his genealogical investigations explore the contingent and ignoble origins of knowledge systems, and he emphasizes the role of power, rhetoric and conflict in the forging of identities, rules, and social forms (for example, Habermas 1976, 1984, 1987).

Foucault's final set of writings is built around the methodological device of problematization, which as its name suggests investigates the way in which problems emerge and are constructed as problems by different and often competing discourses. Here he focuses on the role of ethics (understood as the way we comport ourselves in relation to others), the construction of subjectivity, the character of truth in modern societies, and especially what might be termed the political institutions and practices of contemporary bio-power. The latter emerges in the way governments become concerned with monitoring and regulating the population of those it governs – its size, composition and 'quality' – as well as the array of practices through which individuals are disciplined in particular institutional locations, such as schools, armies, hospitals, factories and so forth. More precisely, his reflections on governmentality have spawned a school of thinking in which government is understood as an art of doing politics – an activity of governing issues and individuals in particular arenas (including the family, the school or organizations) – which concentrates on the 'how' and 'what' of public interventions; what Foucault famously termed the 'conduct of conduct'.

3   CRITICAL AND HISTORICAL DISCOURSE ANALYSIS (CDA AND HDA)

Drawing on elements of this Foucauldian problematic, in CDA and HDA the study of social practices and political institutions presupposes an ongoing and complex relationship between specific discursive events, on the one hand, and situations, institutions and social structures on the other (Fairclough and Wodak 1997, p. 258). Discursive events are both constitutive of – and constituted by – particular social contexts (situations), as is the case for objects of knowledge (institutions) and the social identities of people and groups (social structures). By considering the discursive event in this interactive context, CDA stresses the way discourses are principally constituted through power relations, exclusions and the operation of social structures.

Critical discourse analysis and HDA have been used in studies of the emergence and impact of Tony Blair's New Labour project in Britain, the growth of right-wing populism in Europe and elsewhere, as well as different policy responses (in the fields of higher education for example) to the logic of globalization (for example, Fairclough 2000). According to one of its founding statements, CDA analyzes various social issues in the present by engaging in a detailed study of texts, interactions and other forms of semiotic material, with a view to rendering visible the continuities and discontinuities in different forms of governance, policy, education and democracy, while also detecting unrealized potentialities for changing the way social life is currently structured and organized (Fairclough 2001; see also Fairclough 2003). Critical discourse analysis thus focuses on the role and impact of ideology in policy-making, where the concept of ideology is not defined in terms of a comprehensive and coherent world view, but in terms of a discursive naturalization of contingently constructed meanings and identities (see Box 26.1).

A fundamental element of this perspective is the role of critique. Historical discourse analysts isolate three important aspects of critique within their approach. These are 'discourse-immanent' critique, 'socio-diagnostic' critique and 'prospective' critique. Borrowing from Adorno, immanent critique enables the analyst to discover contradictions, paradoxes and dilemmas in the text or discourse that is examined (internal validity). Socio-diagnostic critique understands ideology to be a property of everyday beliefs, and the task here is to identify the conceptual metaphors that conceal the ideological function of these everyday beliefs (conceptual validity). Finally, prospective critique is concerned with processes

---

BOX 26.1   APPLYING CRITICAL DISCOURSE ANALYSIS, FROM NORMAN FAIRCLOUGH, *NEW LABOUR, NEW LANGUAGE?* (2000)

Object of study: the political discourse of the 'Third Way', the communicative styles of New Labour leaders and the language of government.

Analytical focus: how New Labour and its 'Third Way' discourse excludes and marginalizes others forms of political discourse, naturalizes its own 'end of ideology' ideology, and transforms political issues into technocratic and managerial issues.

Illustration: 'The construction of the social relations of welfare is the mixture of bureaucratic/professional welfare discourse ("helping" etc.) and managerial/cultural ("promoting" etc.) with the latter predominant. . . . "personalized", "flexible" services are "delivered" through a single "gateway" for "customers" by "personal advisers" who develop "tailor-made actions plans" for individuals. There is a new discourse here which "re-lexicalizes" welfare services, gives them a new vocabulary' (Fairclough 2000, p.141).

Critical focus: how groups and elites have an interest in sustaining and propagating particular ideologies, which function to maintain, or enhance their political power.

of communication, and the possibility of improving such communication. Such prospective critique comes directly from critical theory and the belief that social theory should focus on exposing relations of exclusion and domination, and thus contributing to the transformation of social relations, rather than just describing or explaining them (cf. Habermas 1976).

Integral to this critical task is the process of delimiting particular objects of study, which in CDA and HDA is achieved by reference to four main criteria: discourse, text, genre and fields of action. At the outset, researchers working in this tradition seek to identify and distill singular patterns of knowledge in relation to social structures. Discourses are thus individuated and named. Secondly, its proponents identify text as a particular and singular accomplishment or product of a discourse. Thirdly, a genre is defined 'as a socially ratified way of using language in connection with a particular type of social activity' (Fairclough 1995, p. 14). In this context, genres subsume texts, so that the latter instantiate the former. The reference to fields of actions, which is the fourth criterion, is drawn principally from the work of Pierre Bourdieu. Fields of action capture the broader structural context in which discourses, texts and genres are located. Discourses are instantiated in specific texts, which are constitutive of – and constituted by – specific genres, and both are located within different fields of practices. For example, different ways of talking (discourses) about immigration in contemporary European countries can be observed in various government documents about immigration (texts), including policy statements, key speeches or policy guidelines. In turn, such discourses and texts comprise a delimited set of linguistic practices (policy genre) that function within a broader socio-cultural field of action or practice. The latter includes, for example, the actions of a particular government or the dynamics of a political campaign.

Working within a CDA perspective, Isabela Fairclough and Norman Fairclough have also elaborated a particular form of 'political discourse analysis', which focuses on the role of argumentation, especially 'practical argumentation', and includes practices of reflection and deliberation (Fairclough and Fairclough 2012, p. 4). Their approach is grounded in a view of politics that focuses on decision and action about different options in the context of disagreement, conflicts of interests and values, power inequalities, uncertainty and risk. In this perspective, various actors position themselves or try to impose their perspectives on others during policy exchanges and discussions. Arguments, specifically those with a problem-solution character, are thus crucial components of their approach; arguing is best characterized as what political actors 'do' when they 'do' politics. Fairclough and Fairclough suggest that arguments can

---

BOX 26.2   ANALYZING PRACTICAL REASONING, FROM
NORMAN FAIRCLOUGH AND ISABELA
FAIRCLOUGH, *THE UK GOVERNMENT'S
RESPONSE TO ECONOMIC CRISIS IN THE 2008
PRE-BUDGET REPORT* (2011)

Archive: British Pre-Budget Reports, 1997–2009, presented to House of Commons
by Chancellor of the Exchequer.
Illustration: forging arguments in support of action in the opening to the 2008 Pre-
Budget Statement to House of Commons.
Excerpts (Fairclough and Fairclough 2011, p.256)
Claim: [The right thing to do is] to 'take . . . steps', 'to put in place' a 'comprehensive
plan' of 'wide ranging measures'.
Circumstances: these are 'extraordinary, challenging times for the global economy',
'economic uncertainty not seen for generations', having an 'impact on businesses
and families'.
Goals: 'My central objective is to respond to the consequences of this global
recession on our country, both now and in the future' that is, short-term goals: 'to
protect and support businesses and people now' and 'maintain our commitment to
investing in schools, hospitals, key infrastructure'; 'medium-term' goals: 'to ensure
sound public finance', 'putting the public finances on the right path', 'live within our
means'; long-term goals: place Britain in a position to 'take full advantage from the
recovery of the world economy', 'benefit from a return to growth'.
Values/concerns: our [the government's] values are 'fairness' and 'responsibility'.
Our (implicit) concerns: people's well-being, people's 'needs' – we want to support
them 'when they need it most'.
Means-goal: (If we put in place this plan of action, then we will achieve the goals.)

---

be decomposed into more basic units, such as definitions, clauses and,
especially, statements. More precisely, an argument consists (explicitly or
implicitly) of a system of statements – a set of premises concerning values,
goals, circumstances and means and claims or conclusions – which are
logically connected (Fairclough 2013, pp. 183–4; see Box 26.2).

Fairclough and Fairclough's interest is mainly in the role of argumentation as a social activity that endeavors to justify or refute a certain
claim, while seeking to persuade an interlocutor – what they term a
'reasonable critic' – of the acceptability or unacceptability of a claim
(Fairclough and Fairclough 2012, p. 36). Importantly, a practical argument
can only be deemed 'reasonable' if 'it can stand up to the processes of critical
questioning which occur in the generic format of deliberation' (Fairclough
2013, p. 190). Such critical questioning investigates, for example, the existence of alternative courses of action, the relevance of alternative goals
or the negative consequences of proposed goals and means. However, as
Fairclough and Fairclough (2011, p. 259) recognize, in politics this process

of critical questioning is not 'straightforward' given the plurality of values and framings of problems, which can legitimize arguments on different sides of any issue in multiple ways. It thus follows that any critical evaluation of political action has to extend beyond the narrow focus on the arguments of specific political actors to the broader public debates and spaces in which arguments are challenged and critically assessed. This wider context could include the alternative practical arguments articulated by different actors at parliamentary questions, in newspaper editorials, across think-tank reports or at protests and demonstrations (Fairclough 2013, p. 190). Indeed, Fairclough and Fairclough (2011, pp. 261–2) highlight the importance of questioning circumstantial premises (whether, for example, understandings of the context of any action or decision are built upon a particular narrow ideology or set of interests), as well as assessing value premises (the extent, for example, to which values are compatible with the stated goals of policies and whether certain values are excluded). It is through such questioning that practical argumentation exposes potential explanations of policy and politics and generates critical assessments of power and domination.

Seen in these terms, Fairclough and Fairclough (2011, p. 244) present practical 'reasoning' and argumentation as best characterizing political discourse and its various genres. However, it also performs a determining role in the practice of sedimenting or structuring different political or policy regimes (see also Fairclough 2013, p. 183). More specifically, they claim that the focus on practical argumentation and deliberation offers four advances in critical explanations of politics and policy (Fairclough 2013). First, it grounds discourse in the actions of political actors, directing attention to the way in which specific discursive representations and interpretations are articulated as the premises of practical arguments which legitimate particular courses of action. Secondly, it offers a means to better capture the impact of semiotic and extra-semiotic factors in hegemonic struggles, shedding light at the same time on structural and agential selectivities. The practical arguments voiced by decision-makers, such as Chancellors of the Exchequer (see Box 26.2), are part of their causal powers as social agents. Yet these arguments are not constructed in the absence of any consideration of broader structural and institutional factors, whether they take the form of economic regulations, competition laws or business and financial dependencies. The likely impact of such factors are anticipated, acting to constrain or enable the recognition of particular reasons for action over others. Studying the practical arguments voiced by decision-makers thus brings to the fore the role of agents in articulating specific arguments. However, it also sheds light on the influence of social and institutional structures, and how such structures advance particular reasons for action, or fail to do so.

Thirdly, the focus on practical argumentation generates novel insights about the role of problematizations in policy change and hegemonic struggles. As with discourse, problematizations are intrinsically linked to action because they offer premises with which to forge practical arguments. At the same time, they are viewed as 'elements of problem-solution' structures (Fairclough, 2013), such that problematizations concern both existing situations and arguments for change. In fact, as a 'normal' component of the practical argumentation undertaken by multiple actors, problematization is part of evaluation in that political actors through problematization engage in the practice of 'problematizing the problematizations' or challenging established lines of argumentation (Howarth and Griggs 2012; Griggs and Howarth 2013). Finally, conceptualizing critique as a form of practical argumentation clarifies the relationships between explanation, critique and normative evaluation. On the one hand, critique – the practice of 'problematizing the problematizations' – cannot be divorced from normative evaluation, as norms and values are always mobilized in the process. On the other hand, it can be distinguished from evaluation by its focus on explanation and its concern with the way some political actors, and not others, construct particular problematizations (Fairclough 2013, pp. 192–3).

Much of the concrete empirical research in this tradition operates at the micro-level of analysis, focusing intensely on particular segments of text. For example, the detailed comparative analysis of newspaper advertisements for a lectureship position at two different British universities (Sheffield City Polytechnic and the University of Newcastle upon Tyne, respectively), where in the former promotional and corporate discourses are interlaced with traditional academic discourses, while traditional academic discourses are wholly predominant in the latter, is used to discern and highlight wider social logics and political tendencies, such as the marketization of higher education in keeping with neo-liberal policies. The stated requirements that a prospective candidate has to fulfill in order to get the job in the former – the need to generate external research funding, for example, or to build links with the private sector – casts him or her in a particular sort of role, namely, an enterprising or entrepreneurial subject, while also foregrounding the overall conception of the university that is invoked in the discourse (Fairclough 1995, pp. 143–4).

At the macro level, the detailed analysis of a singular piece of text, such as a newspaper advertisement, is then related in a dialectical fashion to the wider set of institutions and social structures within which it functions. In this approach, such structures strongly constrain human agency – both individually and collectively – thus setting limits on their possibilities. Nonetheless, despite the efforts to link the textual and linguistic components of discourse, on the one hand, to their structural and institutional conditions, on the other, this approach maintains a clear distinction between the semiotic and material dimensions of social practices. It is this assumption that has been challenged by those who adopt a 'thicker' conception of discourse. It is to such approaches that we now turn in our discussion of Laclau and Mouffe and poststructuralist discourse theory.

4   POSTSTRUCTURALIST DISCOURSE THEORY (PDT)

Some of the ambiguity surrounding recent discussions of discourse analysis concerns the scope, content and complexity of discourse, especially with respect to the distinction between the discursive, non-discursive or extra-discursive aspects of (social) reality. Even within the limits of Foucault's texts, for example, the concept of discourse varies between a narrow version of the term, where it refers to the historically specific 'rules of formation' that inform the discursive practices which constitute statements, and a much broader conception, in which discourse is equated with historically specific regimes of power/knowledge, as well as a strategic orientation in which discourses are understood to be 'tactical elements' or 'blocks' operating in a field of force relations (Foucault 1972). Yet, despite this variation, it is clear that in Foucault's writings – and in most other approaches – discourses are generally understood to be a particular subset of linguistic or symbolic practices, such as speaking, writing, representing or communicating. This subset of practices is then distinguished from other activities, such as striking or hitting an object on a court, as well as the objects and entities that compose such actions and practices, namely, the ball, court, and player.

Laclau and Mouffe (1985) have contested this interpretation by arguing that discourse is not reducible to the spoken word, the written text, or communicative actions. This approach is grounded upon a materialist conception of discourse, which deconstructs the sharp distinction between, on the one hand, a material world of structures and objects, and on the other hand, a realm of ideas and representations, as well as the traditional metaphysical dichotomies between thought and reality, linguistic and non-linguistic practices, and mind and matter. In Laclau's view,

'discourse' is not a topographical concept, but the horizon of the constitution of any object. Economic activity is, consequently, as discursive as political or aesthetic ideas. To produce an object, for instance, is to establish a system of relations between raw materials, tools, etc. which is not simply given by the mere existential materiality of the intervening elements. The primary and constitutive character of the discursive is, therefore, the condition of any practice. (Laclau 1990, p. 185)

Consider, for example, a forest that stands in the path of the building of a new road or airport runway. The meaning and import of this object depends on the way it is perceived and constructed in different discourses by various subjects or groups. The latter include, for example, the construction company, which hopes to profit by building the transport infrastructure, or the government, which is endeavoring to resolve a policy problem. On the other hand, for conservationists, environmentalists or scientists the forest is constituted and represented in radically different ways. Discourses thus represent objects in different ways. But proponents of PDT also argue that the objects themselves are radically contingent entities that admit of different discursive articulations; the 'form' or 'essence' of something does not exhaust its being or existence. Similar considerations apply to roads or airports, and the discourses that constitute their meanings (see Box 26.3)

More precisely, then, Laclau and Mouffe reject a purely linguistic, 'cognitive' or 'contemplative' approach to discourse analysis by defining discourse as 'an articulatory practice which constitutes and organizes social relations', thus constructing their pattern and meaning (Laclau and Mouffe 1985, p. 96). Discourse is articulatory in that it links together contingent elements – linguistic and non-linguistic, natural and social – into relational systems, in which the identity of the elements is modified as a result of the articulatory practice. However, secondly, it is also important to note that the outcomes of such practices are incomplete systems of meaning and practice, which include linguistic and non-linguistic components (Laclau and Mouffe 1985). Such outcomes are the product of political struggles in which opposed political forces – 'discourse coalitions' or 'hegemonic projects' – seek to 'universalize' their particular storylines and interests. This is accomplished by articulating a common discourse that can win the support of affected parties, while securing the compliance of others. Finally, a key condition of this approach is that all such elements are contingent and unfixed, so that their meaning and identity is only partially fixed by articulatory practices. In short, then, all objects and social practices are discursive, as their meaning and position depends upon their articulation within socially constructed systems of rules and differences (Laclau and Mouffe 1985; Howarth 2013).

BOX 26.3   AIR TRANSPORT POLICY, FROM STEVEN
GRIGGS AND DAVID HOWARTH, *THE POLITICS
OF AIRPORT EXPANSION IN THE UNITED
KINGDOM* (2013)

Assumption   Language, actions and objects are intertwined in what is called discourse.

The discourse of 'air transport policy' goes beyond the talk or language of policy guidance and ministerial speeches to include a diverse array of actions and practices, such as forecasting, noise measurement, planning rules and public inquiries, as well as airport regulations, air traffic management and even package holidays.

Assumption   Discourses are differential and relational configurations of elements, each element acquiring meaning only in relation to the others.

The discourse of aviation policy establishes systems of relations between different objects and practices (including airports, airlines, noise contours, flight paths, landing patterns). It provides subject positions or roles with which actors can identify ('business flyer', the 'leisure passenger', 'air traffic controllers', or the 'national carrier', 'BAA').

Assumption   The meaning and significance of different objects and practices is acquired only within a particular historical context.

Particular discursive regimes or appeals presuppose precise conditions of possibility. For example, 'jet-set' appeals to the luxury of flying were possible only in the particular conjuncture of the 1930s; they lacked credibility in the era of mass aviation consumption, which emerged in the 1980s and 1990s with the advent of low-cost carriers.

Assumption   Discourse installs a particular kind of coherence by bringing 'things named' into a 'composite whole' (borrowing from Rein and Schön 1993, p.153). Consequently, the identities of such elements are modified.

Attention is given to practices of articulation and specific moments of rhetorical redescription; examining for instance of the transformation of the understandings of 'aviation' and 'sustainable development' when they are articulated into the discourse of 'sustainable aviation'.

---

5   APPLYING DISCOURSE: LOGICS OF CRITICAL EXPLANATION

How do these basic ontological assumptions of PDT get used in conducting concrete research? What Glynos and Howarth (2007) have termed the 'logics of critical explanation', which consists of five connected steps, constitutes one possible response to this question (see Box 26.4).

Although, for analytical purposes, such steps can be separated and considered independently of one another, in the conduct of research they are closely intertwined. The practice of research consists, therefore, of a

BOX 26.4   *LOGICS OF CRITICAL EXPLANATION*, JASON
GLYNOS AND DAVID HOWARTH (2007)

Five Connected Steps

1. *Problematization.* Constructing the object of study as a problem, at requisite level of abstraction and complexity.
2. *Retroduction.* Form of explanation: production and testing of a tentative hypothesis to account for problematized phenomenon by a to-and-fro engagement with empirical data.
3. *Logics.* Content of explanation: capturing the rules that govern regimes or practices, as well as the conditions and objects that make such rules possible. Focus on: *social logics* that characterize a practice or regime; *political logics* of equivalence and difference that account for emergence of practice or regime and its contestation and transformation; *fantasmatic logics* that account for the way particular practices and regimes 'grip' subjects.
4. *Articulation.* Process of linking together a plurality of logics in order to account for problematized phenomenon. Involves linking different together theoretical and empirical elements so as to create a putative explanation. Each element is modified in the process.
5. *Critique.* Employing political and fantasmatic logics to explain and expose the contingency of processes and relations. Political logics reveal exclusions and foreclosures at moments of regime institution. Ideological closure is evident in fantasmatic narratives that naturalize relations of domination. Requires the recognition of values brought to the study by researchers and the identification of counter-logics in the analyzed practices.

constant relaying between each of the components. We consider each in turn.

Problematization. Following Foucault, this approach begins by problematizing a particular practice or regime of practices, both within the field of academic questions, and with respect to the social and political issues that confront social actors in a specific historical conjuncture (Foucault 1984). In most empirical cases, there is no single 'problem', but rather a range of ongoing problematizations, which vary according to the interpretations of different interests and stakeholders. Consider, for example, the tensions brought about by the attempts of various governments in the United Kingdom (UK) to formulate and implement a workable aviation policy, especially with respect to the expansion of airport capacity in the South-East of England, in the period since 1945 (Griggs and Howarth 2013). Of particular importance in this regard is the tension between, on the one hand, the role of airports and aviation as drivers of economic growth and prosperity and, on the other hand, their considerable and growing negative impacts on the natural and social environment. At the same time, while many citizens express concerns about the environmental consequences of air travel, and local residents protest about the noise impacts of aircraft, they still continue to fly in ever-increasing numbers.

This problem unfolds further questions about (1) the institution and installation of the particular regime of aviation expansion since the Second World War; (2) the struggle over the expansion or regulation of aviation at the start of the twenty first century; (3) the subsequent reframing of air travel and civil aviation by local campaigning and environmental movements, which presented the aviation industry as a major contributor to global carbon emissions; (4) the government's and industry's attempt to re-signify and ring-fence aviation as a necessary component of global connectivity in the wake of the financial crisis; and (5) the current UK policy stalemate, where parties are still contesting whether or not to build more airport infrastructure and where it should be located. Each problematization thus exhibits different dimensions, be it the distribution of power between agents, groups or institutions, structural and organizational limits, or the particular cultural traditions and belief-systems through which subjects acquire their identities and interests.

Retroduction. Drawing on the work of Charles Sander Peirce (1957) and Norbert Hanson (1961), the form of an explanation in this perspective is retroductive or abductive, rather than just inductive or deductive. The explanatory task begins with an anomalous or wondrous phenomenon, which must then be constructed as a tractable *explanandum*. Such anomalies and puzzles can be rendered intelligible, if and only if there is the elaboration of a credible *explanans* (Peirce 1957; Hanson 1961). Critical explanation thus proceeds by seeking to render a problematized phenomenon more intelligible by the proposal of plausible hypotheses. This involves the production of a hypothesis or hypotheses that is tested through a to-and-fro movement with the available empirical data, until the investigator is persuaded that the putative *explanans* clears away the confusion and properly fits the phenomenon under consideration.

Logics. The content of any putative *explanans* of a problematized event or phenomenon is couched principally in terms of logics, rather than laws, causal mechanisms or cultural interpretations. More precisely, the logics of a discourse capture the rules that govern a practice or regime of practices, as well as the conditions that make such rules possible and impossible. ('Impossible' because they also highlight their contingency and undecidability in certain contexts.) Three distinctive types of logics are distinguished – social, political and fantasmatic – which we discuss in more detail next.

Social logics enable the discourse analyst in PDT to characterize practices and regimes in different contexts by discerning the rules and norms that govern such practices in a particular historical context. However, this means that there are as many logics as the various situations that social and policy analysts explore. Such logics can capture economic, social, cultural and political processes. This may be a particular logic of competition or commodification, for example, or a specific logic of bureaucratization in a particular social context (Howarth 2009, p. 325). Consider, for example, the discourse of aviation policy that emerged in the UK since the end of the Second World War. Social logics capture the rules that informed the practices of this regime, including, for example, the logics of 'forecasting' and 'predict and provide' by which successive governments sought to meet the growing demand for new airport infrastructure, especially in the South-East of England. In general terms, the logic of aviation expansion is that demands for airport infrastructure were met in a haphazard and incremental fashion, despite calls for better planning or for the privileging of other ends, such as environmental protection and the development of alternative transport systems.

Political logics, by contrast, enable the researcher to critically explain the emergence and formation of a practice or regime by exploring how different practices and regimes engendered antagonisms between groups and demands. Seen in this light, different regimes are understood as 'sites' for political contestation, and the role of political logics is to characterize how a practice or regime functions to privilege particular actors, and thus leads to specific patterns of inclusion and exclusion in different sites or organizations. Political logics can thus help us to show other possibilities of social organization when the 'ignoble origins' of rules and norms are reactivated, contested and instituted.

In the case of UK aviation policy, for example, political logics are evident in the ongoing contestations about the precise location, character and amount of airport infrastructure required at different times and places. The struggles over the building of a third London airport in the 1960s and 1970s, the conflicts over the expansion of Heathrow airport in the mid-1980s and 1990s, and the current debates about the expansion of Heathrow and Gatwick, in which successive governments have deferred and vacillated, are indicators of this logic. Of particular importance in this regard are the interacting logics of equivalence and difference. In the former, different demands in various spaces are bundled together through the naming of a common enemy, so that the particular import and meaning of each is cancelled out in favor of a more universal appeal. In the logic of difference, by contrast, demands are expressed and negotiated one by one, so that they are either processed within the system (and thus addressed in various ways) or are marginalized and thus dissipated by the dominant logics of the system.

Completing the development of a putative *explanans* in a logics approach, the identification of fantasmatic logics enables the researcher to disclose the ways in which subjects identify and are gripped by a discourse or set of practices. That is, they allow the analyst to detect the particular narratives that provide ideological closure for the subject, thus masking the contingency of social relations and naturalizing the relations of domination in discourses or meaningful practices such that they appear to subjects as natural and 'given'. In any particular case, this would suggest, for example, an empirical investigation into the explicit role of the fantasmatic appeal of particular images or discourses, and their appeal in enabling new forms of action and being.

Fantasmatic appeals and narratives can be detected in the development and operation of UK aviation policy. Throughout the postwar institution of the regime of aviation expansion, the threat of foreign competition, in particular from the United States, operated as something akin to a horrific fantasy for British policymakers and manufacturers. If actualized, this fantasy carried the threat of destroying UK aviation and its drive to secure global markets in the postwar period. At the same time, politicians and policymakers repeatedly articulated fantasmatic appeals to the contribution of aviation to the UK's economic well-being, including the need to grow civil and military aircraft manufacturing and to develop more sophisticated and safer technologies. They also extolled the very experience of flying and the 'jet-set' and heralded the promise of mass tourism. All the above were intimately connected with a discourse of modernization and progress, which was an essential ingredient in countering Britain's (perceived) inexorable economic decline. More recently, in the run-up to the 2003 public consultation over the future of aviation, the Labour government and supporters of expansion sought (but ultimately failed) to rhetorically redefine the question of airport expansion in terms of 'sustainable aviation', thus articulating a beatific fantasy in which aviation expansion and environmental sustainability could be linked in a harmonious and mutually reinforcing fashion.

Articulation. Any putative *explanans* consists of a plurality of logics, as well as other causal mechanisms, which have to be linked together in order to render a problematic phenomenon intelligible. In order to account for this linking together, this approach stresses the practice of articulation, which involves linking together different elements in a logic that modifies each element. For example, in our illustration a full-fledged account of the problems that have been discerned would involve the pinpointing and connecting of multiple logics in various contexts. A successful *explanans* would thus require the production of a synthesis comprising 'a rich totality of many determinations and relations', and its testing would depend on the extent to which it rendered the various puzzles discerned in the problematization process less puzzling (Marx 1973, p. 100).

Critique. Finally, each of these logics enables the researcher to render visible the contingent character of a practice, policy or institution by showing the role of power, exclusion, and closure in its formation and reproduction. Constructed around different responses to radical contingency, social, political and fantasmatic logics endeavor to formalize these intuitions and tactics. The practice of critique is predicated on the centrality of political and fantasmatic logics, for their discernment enables us to highlight the contingency and undecidability of particular social relations and structures. The political is evident in those conjunctures when social relations are formed and challenged by the exercise of power, and where exclusions and foreclosures occur. They thus indicate the moments of the potential reactivation of moments of political institution, and thus the possibility of resistance against various forms of dominations. The ideological is evident in those fantasmatic narratives that function to conceal contingency and naturalize relations of domination.

6   CONCLUSION

The multiplication of discursive approaches to politics and policy is evident in the contemporary social sciences. In this contribution, we have focused on three main variants – Foucauldian approaches, critical discourse analysis, and researchers working in the field of poststructuralist discourse theory – where we have examined their underlying ontological underlying assumptions and methodological postulates. In general, discourse analysis adds a distinctive twist to other interpretive and qualitative approaches to political science by focusing on the meanings of phenomena for historically positioned social actors and subjects. On methodological grounds, attention is focused on close readings of particular texts or documents, and the latter are related to wider institutions and social structures. Here there are differences in the way in which discourse is understood, where some perspectives restrict discourse to the linguistic and semiotic dimensions of practices, while others extend the notion of discourse as an articulatory practice to include all aspects of social and political life. Although, as we have noted, there are incompatibilities and differences between these perspectives, especially their different ontological commitments, they share a concern with describing, criticizing and evaluating singularly problematized phenomena in a variety of historical contexts. What is more, for purposes of empirical research, if carefully negotiated, they can be rendered compatible with one another, thus offering a more comprehensive and multidimensional orientation for the study of pressing issues in the present (Jørgensen and Phillips 2002; Griggs and Howarth 2013).

NOTE

1. This chapter builds upon and reworks some of the arguments that we have advanced elsewhere, notably in our research monograph, *The Politics of Airport Expansion in the United Kingdom* (2013, Manchester University Press), as well as our 'Poststructuralist policy analysis: discourse, hegemony and critical explanation', in F. Fischer and H. Gottweis (eds), *The Argumentative Turn Revisited* (2012, Duke University Press). It also draws upon the collaboration between Jason Glynos et al. (2009), as well as the research monograph by Glynos and Howarth entitled *Logics of Critical Explanation in Social and Political Theory* (2007, Routledge).

FURTHER READING

Introduction to the Approach

Glynos, J. and D. Howarth (2007), *Logics of Critical Explanation in Social and Political Theory*, Abingdon, UK: Routledge.

Application of the approach

Griggs, S. and D. Howarth (2013), *The Politics of Airport Expansion in the UK*, Manchester: Manchester University Press.

Advanced Text

Howarth, D.R. (2013), *Poststructuralism and After. Structure, Subjectivity and Power*, Basingstoke, UK: Palgrave Macmillan.

REFERENCES

Austin, J.L. (1986), *How to Do Things with Words*, 2nd edn, Oxford: Oxford University Press.
Connolly, W.E. (2013), *The Fragility of Things*, Durham, NC: Duke University Press.
Davies, J.S. (2011), *Challenging Governance Theory: From Network to Hegemony*, Bristol: Policy Press.
Dryzek, J. (1997), *The Politics of the Earth*, Oxford: Oxford University Press.
Fairclough, I. and N. Fairclough (2011), 'Practical reasoning in political discourse: the UK government's response to the economic crisis in the 2008 Pre-Budget Report', *Discourse & Society*, **22** (3), 243–68.
Fairclough, I. and N. Fairclough (2012), *Political Discourse Analysis*, London: Routledge.
Fairclough, N. (1995), *Critical Discourse Analysis: The Critical Study of Language*, London: Longman.

Fairclough, N. (2000), *New Labour, New Language?*, London: Routledge.
Fairclough, N. (2001), 'Critical discourse analysis as a method in social scientific research', in R. Wodak and M. Meyer (eds), *Methods of Critical Discourse Analysis*, London: Sage, pp. 121–31.
Fairclough, N. (2003), *Analyzing Discourse: Textual Analysis for Social Research*, London: Routledge.
Fairclough, N. (2013), 'Critical discourse analysis and critical policy studies', *Critical Policy Studies*, **7** (2), 177–97.
Fairclough, N. and R. Wodak (1997), 'Critical discourse analysis', in T. van Dijk (ed.), *Discourse as Social Interaction*, London: Sage.
Fischer, F. (2003), *Reframing Public Policy*, Oxford: Oxford University Press.
Foucault, M. (1972), *The Archaeology of Knowledge*, London: Tavistock.
Foucault, M. (1984), 'Nietzsche, genealogy, history', in P. Rabinow (ed.), *The Foucault Reader*, Harmondsworth: Penguin Books, pp. 76–100.
Glynos, J. and D. Howarth (2007), *Logics of Critical Explanation in Social and Political Theory*, Abingdon, UK: Routledge.
Glynos, J., D. Howarth, A. Norval and E. Speed (2009), *Discourse Analysis: Varieties and Methods*, Economic and Social Research Council (ESRC) National Centre for Research Methods, accessed 23 August 2016 at http://eprints.ncrm.ac.uk/796/1/discourse_analysis_NCRM_014.pdf.
Griggs, S. and D. Howarth (2013), *The Politics of Airport Expansion in the United Kingdom: Hegemony, Policy and the Rhetoric of 'Sustainable Aviation'*, Manchester: Manchester University.
Habermas, J. (1976), *Legitimation Crisis*, London: Heinemann.
Habermas, J. (1984), *The Theory of Communicative Action (Vol. 1), Reason and the Rationalization of Society*, London: Heinemann.
Habermas, J. (1987), *The Theory of Communicative Action (Vol. 2), Lifeworld and System: A Critique of Functionalist Reason*, Cambridge: Polity Press.
Hajer, M.A. (1995), *The Politics of Environmental Discourse*, Oxford: Oxford University Press.
Hanson, N.R. (1961), *Patterns of Discovery*, Cambridge: Cambridge University Press.
Howarth, D. (2009), 'Power, discourse and policy: articulating a hegemony approach to critical policy studies', *Critical Policy Studies*, **3** (3–4), 309–35.
Howarth, D. (2013), *Poststructuralism and After: Structure, Agency and Power*, London: Palgrave.
Howarth, D. and S. Griggs (2012), 'Poststructuralist policy analysis: discourse, hegemony and critical explanation', in F. Fischer and H. Gottweis (eds), *The Argumentative Turn Revisited*, Durham, NC: Duke University Press, pp. 305–42.
Jessop, B. (2009), 'Cultural political economy and critical policy studies', *Critical Policy Studies*, **3** (3–4), 336–56.
Jørgensen, M.W. and L. Phillips (2002), *Discourse Analysis as Theory and Method*, London: Sage.
Laclau, E. (1990), *New Reflections on the Revolution of Our Time*, London: Verso.
Laclau, E. and C. Mouffe (1985), *Hegemony and Socialist Strategy*, London: Verso.
Litfin, K. (1995), *Ozone Discourse: Science and Politics in Global Environmental Cooperation*, New York: Columbia.
Marx, K. (1973), *Grundrisse*, London: Allen Lane.
Peirce, C.S. (1957), *Essays in the Philosophy of Science*, New York: Liberal Arts Press.
Rein, M. and D.A. Schön (1993), 'Reframing policy discourse', in F. Fischer and J. Forester (eds), *The Argumentative Turn in Policy Analysis and Planning*, Durham, NC: Duke University Press, pp. 145–66.
Wagenaar, H. (2011), *Meaning in Action*, Armonk, NY: M.E. Sharpe.
Wodak, R. and P. Chilton (eds) (2005), *A New Agenda in (Critical) Discourse Analysis: Theory, Methodology and Interdisciplinarity*, Philadelphia, PA: John Benjamins.

27 Case study analysis
Esther Seha and Ferdinand Müller-Rommel

1 INTRODUCTION

Case studies enjoy great popularity in political science and have decisively contributed to the discipline's knowledge about the world of politics. In the wake of the development and refinement of modern statistics, case studies have increasingly been considered as less than ideal solutions for drawing causal inferences and producing generalizations which are valid across space and time. As weaknesses of case study research have been disproportionally highlighted over their strengths, representatives of the qualitative position have recently engaged in emphasizing the merits of case studies while at the same time attempting to put them on a more rigorous methodological footing.

2 CASE STUDY ANALYSIS IN POLITICAL SCIENCE: BETWEEN SPECIFICITY AND GENERALITY

The social sciences do not embrace a single understanding of what case study research is and how it should be applied. While a common understanding is that case studies are intrinsically tied to qualitative methods of scientific inquiry and are set apart from other research strategies by analyzing cases in an in-depth fashion, it remains contested whether the objective of case studies is to contribute to empirical generalization or to uncover the uniqueness of a particular case (Platt 2007).

A multitude of notions about what a case study is and which purpose it serves can also be found in the realm of political science. However, the methodological discussion about case study research in this discipline has early on been linked with comparative analysis and has therefore been shaped by assessing case studies in the light of how they can contribute to the attainment of theoretical, generalizable knowledge (Lijphart 1971). Hence, while many conceptions of case study research exist, the understanding of case study research as an instrument for uncovering law-like generalizations following positivist suppositions is commonly given prevalence over interpretative approaches and the notion of studying cases for their singularity (Yanow et al. 2010, p. 109). Given the intention to make statements that are general as well as testable, practitioners of case study research in political science have commonly not confined themselves to studying a single case on its own terms, but have instead placed the study of cases under the umbrella of the comparative method as one of the three main research methods in comparative analysis (the other two being the experimental and the statistical method).

In comparative analysis a general distinction is made between *large-N* and *small-N* research designs (Della Porta 2008, p. 199). While the former study a large number of cases by means of statistical analysis, *small-N* research focuses on a few cases that are studied applying the comparative method. Based on this fundamental distinction, both the study of a single case and the study of a few cases are generally thought of as *small-N* designs. Both designs study a small number of cases in-depth and are therefore faced with the 'many variables, small N' problem which has been famously depicted by Lijphart as the overall weakness of the comparative method (Lijphart 1971, p. 686).

Regardless of the number of cases studied, both *small-N* and *large-N* research designs seek to uncover key patterns of similarity and differences between empirical cases and explain them by means of theory. Further, both research designs aim at drawing generalizations which hold true for a larger universe of cases. While *large-N* studies use quantitative data and aim for generalizable knowledge and the discovery of broad patterns across cases, *small-N* research utilizes qualitative data and intends to generate thick knowledge (Della Porta 2008, p. 199). Since the term 'case study' thus covers both the study of one and the study of a few cases, a generic definition may thus be as follows: 'A case study is a research strategy based on the in-depth empirical investigation of one, or a small number, of phenomena in order to explore the configuration of each case,

Table 27.1   Case studies in comparative analysis

Research design	Research strategy	Number of cases
Small-N (few cases, many variables)	Single case study	One
	Comparative case study	Few
	Qualitative comparative analysis (QCA)*	
Large-N (many cases, few variables)	Statistical analysis	Many

Note: * For a thorough account of qualitative comparative analysis see Chapter 25.

Source: Own illustration.

and to elucidate features of a larger class of (similar) phenomena, by developing and evaluating theoretical explanations' (Vennesson 2008, p. 226).

Case studies have been and continue to be a popular research strategy in political science. Nonetheless their role is somewhat ambiguous. While, on the one hand, they enjoy a reputation of being the repository of knowledge about the political world and have played a crucial role in the development of theory, they have on the other hand been the target of methodological criticism with regard to their ability to generate scientific explanation (Blatter and Haverland 2012, p. 1). Such objections are not new and have upon the refinement of statistical methodology been prominently expressed by Lijphart who in his seminal article 'Comparative politics and the comparative method' established a clear hierarchy of comparative analysis, in which both the comparative and the case study methods were ranked behind the experimental and statistical method (Lijphart 1971, p. 685).

More recently, case study scholars have again been admonished to place their approach to scientific inquiry on a more systematic foundation. Based on the assumption that the natural and social sciences share a single approach to scientific inference, it was once again stressed that case studies' heel of Achilles consists in their limit to draw causal inferences and make generalizable claims on the basis of one or a small number of cases. For the notion of applying the logic of quantitative research to qualitative research, the publication of King et al.'s treatise *Designing Social Inquiry* is emblematic and represents the main reference point of current endeavors on the part of qualitative researchers to theorize about case study methodology more systematically (King et al. 1994). More recently, there has been a visible increase in publications of articles and books, which seek to place case study research on a more rigorous footing, both seeking to clarify its nature and illustrate how it can contribute to the overall goal of scientific explanation (see, for instance, Brady and Collier 2004).

While the debate on the logics underlying *large-N* and *small-N* research is ongoing, political science has on principle retained a pluralist perspective. Rather than favoring one approach over the other, scholars commonly seek to mitigate the putative contradiction between *small-N* and *large-N* research by pointing out respective strengths and weaknesses each strategy is afflicted with. In that regard, the advantage of case study research is generally seen in its ability to deal with complexity and provide in-depth and holistic, context-sensitive knowledge about cases. Case studies offer extensive insight into the empirical relationship between variables in individual cases and are an appropriate means for uncovering multiple pathways to the same outcome ('equifinality'). Its greatest benefit is seen in its suitability to generate hypotheses, to study causal mechanisms and to achieve good concept validity (Gerring 2009, pp. 1139–41).

Notwithstanding this general consensus, case study methodologists do not share a unified notion of what case study research is and have multi-faceted conceptions of both the objectives of case studies and how they should be conducted. As the recent book-length contributions by Blatter and Haverland (2012) and Rohlfing (2012) have convincingly shown, case study research can be conducted in many different ways. It can be based on various ontological and epistemological suppositions, and lends itself to generating, testing, and modifying theory as long as methodological rigor is applied to the process of inquiry. The following sections will focus on providing some general advice for conducting case study research and will illustrate it with examples from existing research.

3   METHODOLOGICAL STANDARDS FOR DOING CASE STUDIES

Understanding case studies as a means to attain statements about empirical regularities entails paying attention to research design and methodological standards. While the methodological literature does not offer ready-made solutions to matters of defining and selecting cases, it nevertheless provides guidelines as to how these questions should be approached in the formulation of a research design.

4   WHAT IS A CASE?

The first issue concerns the term 'case'. Regardless of whether a case study deals with one or a few cases, researchers need to give an answer to the question, 'What is a case?' The response to this question is not self-evident and has been subject to intense debate, and hinges on how we choose to frame the object of investigation (Ragin and Becker 1992). A look into the literature reveals that a case is either defined as 'an instance of a class of events' (George and Bennett 2005, p. 17), 'a spatially delimited phenomenon (a unit) observed at a single point in time or over some period of time' (Gerring 2009, p. 1137) or 'a bounded empirical phenomenon that is an instance of a population of similar empirical phenomena' (Rohlfing 2012, p. 24). What can be derived from these definitions is that what constitutes a case is never a given. The demarcation of a case closely depends on choices made by the researcher whose obligation is to clarify what the phenomenon of interest is a case of. In sum, 'a case is a phenomenon, or an event, chosen, conceptualized and analyzed empirically as a manifestation of a broader class of phenomena or events' (Vennesson 2008, p. 226).

5   SINGLE AND COMPARATIVE CASE STUDIES

Single and comparative case studies share fundamental characteristics in that they seek to uncover detailed knowledge about a certain phenomenon or dimension thereof. While comparative case studies are generally set apart from single case studies by being less interested in the case itself rather than what it stands for, they can nevertheless be seen as following the same logic of research.

Single case studies can make different contributions to the generation of knowledge about the political world. The most widely known systematization of different types of case studies was presented by Lijphart (1971, p. 691ff.), who differentiates six ideal types of case studies: A-theoretical, interpretative, hypothesis-generating, theory-confirming, theory-infirming and deviant case studies.

An *A-theoretical case study* is merely descriptive and does not make reference to theory. It neither aims at formulating nor testing theoretical propositions but rather seeks to delve into the depth of the single case and capture it in great detail. While a-theoretical case studies are by all means a rich source of empirical information, they take no pains in making generalizations beyond the case of interest and are therefore of little theoretical value.

The same assessment holds true for *interpretative case studies* which make little effort at looking beyond the case of interest but which do, however, look at the case through the lens of an established theoretical framework. Although its contribution to general knowledge cannot be entirely denied, it nevertheless remains erratic.

Hypothesis-generating case studies aim at formulating hypotheses and therefore specifically look beyond the confines of the case under investigation. This type of case study is particularly useful in uncharted fields of study where no or little theoretical knowledge is on hand.

Theory-confirming and *theory-infirming case studies* are types of case studies which rather than generating hypotheses seek to contribute to existing theoretical propositions. The general problem with these types of case study is that one case alone is unlikely to either confirm or reject theory and underpin broader generalizations. A strategy to mitigate this drawback is generally seen in choosing cases that are either least likely or most likely to confirm or rebut the theoretical claim.

Finally, the *deviant case study* is the study of a case which has been proven to diverge from a well-established body of theory. An in-depth study of a deviant case can therefore be instructive in that it can help to uncover additional determining factors and can in turn help adjust previous theoretical statements and improve cross-case comparison.

As shown, the respective types of case studies vary in their conduciveness to comparative analysis. While the comparative merit of ideographically-oriented case studies is relatively low, nomothetically-oriented types of case studies are generally valued with regard to their contribution to building theory (Lijphart 1971, p. 691ff.). A single study of a deviant case that has been extremely influential in comparative politics is Lijphart's (1968) *The Politics of Accommodation*. In this study Lijphart sought to answer the question why parliamentary democracy in the Netherlands could succeed in the face of a profoundly divided society, thereby running counter to the main tenets of pluralist theory. Lijphart uncovered that Dutch political elites reconciled divisive matters and conflicts by means of specific rules which he called the 'politics of accommodation'. This study was crucial for developing the concept of consociational democracy and laid the groundwork for analyzing democracies in terms of their institutional structure and how it affects their overall performance. It played a key role in generating hypotheses and concepts for further study of institutional patterns of democracies.

While the issue of comparative merit is particularly crucial in the study of one case, the matter is less significant in the realm of comparative case designs. As Odell states comparative case designs 'add the analytical leverage that comes from comparison to the strengths of the case study' (Odell 2004, p. 167). By definition, comparative case studies aim at obtaining a general understanding of the phenomenon under study and at drawing causal inferences. They are among the most popular research designs in political science and lend themselves to both generating and testing theoretical propositions.

6   CASE SELECTION

Like all research designs, both single and comparative case designs are fraught with general methodological challenges. In the realm of case study analysis, this particularly applies to the selection of cases. As two prominent case study methodologists, George and Bennett (2005, p. 234) state, 'Case selection is arguably the most difficult step in developing a case study research design'. When selecting one or a few cases for intensive study, the overall goal is to avoid the pitfalls of selection bias that lead to producing findings that are either unrepresentative of the wider population of cases or that merely confirm a favored hypothesis. Therefore the deliberate selection of cases is an indispensable attribute of good case study research and always needs to correspond with the overall research objective that is being pursued.

As illustrated above, single case studies can serve multiple theoretical purposes. Therefore the selection of a case depends on the objective the case study is meant to fulfill. Surprisingly, however, the methodological literature says very little about the actual process of selecting cases for single case studies. While for instance Hague and Harrop (2010) distinguish single case studies that deal with *representative, prototypical, deviant, exemplary,* and *crucial cases,* they say little about how the character of a case can be determined. More recently, Seawright and Gerring (2008) have addressed this gap by offering techniques on how to select cases for in-depth case study analysis. They identify seven methods that allow the selection of one or more cases for in-depth investigation (*typical, diverse, extreme, deviant, influential, most similar* and *most dissimilar*). However, despite being sophisticated, the main limitation to Seawright's and Gerring's approach is that their technique is explicitly based on a previous large-N analysis. If this requirement is either not feasible or not favored, a deliberate selection of a case to be studied is not impossible, however it does presuppose familiarity with the population of cases from which a case is to be selected and an awareness of the theoretical contribution the case study is supposed to fulfill. In this context, cross-national research endeavors such as Dahl's *Political Oppositions in Western Democracies* (1966) or Berg-Schlosser's and Mitchell's edited volume on *Conditions of Democracy in Europe* (2000) can help identify cases that are theoretically interesting and merit in-depth analysis.

The problem of which cases to choose from a population of cases also holds true when selecting cases for a controlled comparison of two or a few cases. In order to be able to draw causal inferences from comparative case studies and approximate the logic of experimental research when studying a small number of cases, Przeworski and Teune (1970) have proposed two research designs for comparative case analysis: the *most similar systems design* and the *most dissimilar systems design.* Both research designs go back to John Stuart Mill's remarks in his treatise *A System of Logic* (1874) about systematically comparing social phenomena and aim at controlling variables in such a way that causal relationships can be isolated.

The *most similar systems design* is the design that is most frequently applied in actual research and has been prominently advocated by Lijphart (1975) as the 'comparable-cases strategy'. A *most similar systems design* aims at comparing cases that are similar with regard to important context and background variables. Yet they differ in that the outcome of interest (dependent variable) is absent in one case while it is present in the second. By attaining a wide measure of control both with regard to background variables and independent variables, the factor that caused the outcome of interest is sought to be uncovered. Since comparability of

Table 27.2   Illustration of most similar systems design

	Context	Dependent variable	Independent variable X1	Independent variable X2
Case 1	A	Yes	Yes	Yes
Case 2	A	No	Yes	No

Source: Own illustration.

two cases is not easy to determine, researchers generally resort to selecting cases that share typological characteristics (for example, presidential or parliamentary systems) or that belong to a 'family of countries', for instance, Westminster democracies. By way of example, Kitschelt (1986) has compared anti-nuclear movements in France, Sweden, the United States, and West Germany. These countries were similar in that they all experienced acute conflicts over nuclear technology. Yet, they differed with regard to both the strategies the respective nuclear movements pursued and their repercussion on energy policy. In his study 'Political opportunity structures and political protest' he sought to explain this variation by applying the concept of political opportunity structure while holding other determining factors constant.

In contrast to *most similar systems designs, most dissimilar systems designs* are less frequently used. In a *most dissimilar design* cases are analyzed that show the same outcome of interest but are very different in all other respects. The underlying notion is that both cases have one or a few factors in common and that are thus likely to have caused the outcome of interest. A prominent example for a study applying the *most dissimilar logic* is Skocpol's (1979) study *States and Social Revolutions* in which she studies social revolutions in France, Russia and China. While previous research has looked at the origins of revolutions from the viewpoint of purposive action, her focus lies on the structural prerequisites for these events which she seeks to uncover by analyzing three most different cases.

In conclusion, the matter of case selection is of crucial importance to the study both of single and comparative cases. While the above guidelines can by no means be applied one-on-one to all types of case study designs, they nevertheless represent the most common advice and are a reasonable reference point for all researchers who want to engage in the systematic study of cases and seek to make a contribution to building theory.

Regardless of studying one case or a few, case studies in political science on principle strive to speak to a larger theoretical interest and pursue a generalizing purpose. They are compatible with multiple research

Table 27.3   Illustration of most different systems design

	Context	Dependent variable	Independent variable X1	Independent variable X2	Independent variable X3
Case 1	A	Yes	Yes	Yes	Yes
Case 2	B	Yes	Yes	No	Yes

Source: Own illustration.

techniques such as text or document analysis. Thus there is no elaborate manual to be followed when actually devising a case study design, except that informed decisions have to be made about the selection of cases and the choice of research technique, all of which should be in accordance with the overall research objective.

7   CONCLUDING REMARKS

Case studies have been and will continue to be a prominent and widely used research design in political science. After having been marginalized as an appropriate means to obtain scientific knowledge, case study methodologists have in recent years made a good case for studying cases in their own right and have substantially helped to clarify its practice. The debate on case study methodology is extensive and has become increasingly hard to survey. Hence, recent contributions by Blatter and Haverland (2012) as well as Rohlfing (2012) are helpful in that they synthesize the debate by offering an overview of case study approaches.

They show that case study research is compatible with different ontological and epistemological conceptions as well as multiple research techniques and provide methodological as well as hands-on practical advice. While the main challenge lies in harmonizing theoretical and methodological parameters in the attempt to answer a particular research question, recent contributions to the methodological debate have been tremendously instructive in highlighting both benefits and weaknesses of case study research and how this tool can be applied in practice. Even though pitfalls such as drawing accurate generalizations and causal inferences remain, it is indisputable that case study methodology has in the past years gained in expertise and that case studies in both their single and comparative form are key instruments to build theory.

BOX 27.1   TOPICS HIGHLIGHTED

- Case study analysis has and continues to be a frequently employed approach in political science research.
- Vis-à-vis critics from the quantitative camp, representatives of the qualitative position have recently engaged in reflecting more systematically on how to do case study research.
- The label 'case study' encompasses the study of a single or a few cases and is compatible with multiple theoretical approaches and methodological techniques.
- In general, both single and comparative case studies aim at generating theoretical knowledge about the political world.
- Defining and selecting cases are the most challenging aspects in creating a research design.

SOURCES FOR FURTHER USE

David, M. (2007), *Case Study Research*, 4 vols, London: Sage.
This multi-volume compendium brings together key articles about case study research from all social science disciplines.
Mills, A.J., G. Durepos and E. Wiebe (eds), *Encyclopedia of Case Study Research*, Thousand Oaks, CA: Sage.
The encyclopedia provides articles on key topics in case study research and serves as an excellent introduction to the main methodological debates.
Qualitative Methods Newsletter, American Political Science Association Organized Section for Qualitative and Multi-Method Research (http://www.maxwell.syr.edu/moynihan/cqrm/Qualitative_Methods_Newsletters/Qualitative_Methods_Newsletters/).
The newsletter covers key debates in qualitative and multi-method research, and serves as a platform for novel methodological approaches.

RECOMMENDED READING

Blatter, J. and M. Haverland (2012), *Designing Cases Studies. Explanatory Approaches in Small-N Research*, Basingstoke, UK: Palgrave Macmillan.
Gerring, J. (2009), 'The case study: what it is and what it does', in R.E. Goodin (ed.), *The Oxford Handbook of Political Science*, Oxford: Oxford University Press, pp. 1134–65.
Lijphart, A. (1971), 'Comparative politics and the comparative method', *American Political Science Review*, **65** (3), 682–93.
Ragin, C.C. and H.S. Becker (eds) (1992), *What is a Case? Exploring the Foundations of Social Inquiry*, Cambridge: Cambridge University Press.

REFERENCES

Berg-Schlosser, D. and J. Mitchell (2000), *Conditions of Democracy in Europe, 1919–1939: Systematic Case Studies*, New York: St Martin's Press.

Blatter, J. and M. Haverland (2012), *Designing Cases Studies. Explanatory Approaches in Small-N Research*, Basingstoke, UK: Palgrave Macmillan.

Brady, H.E. and D. Collier (eds) (2004), *Rethinking Social Inquiry: Diverse Tools, Shared Standards*, Lanham, MaD: Rowman & Littlefield.

Dahl, R.A. (1966), *Political Oppositions in Western Democracies*, New Haven, CT: Yale University Press.

Della Porta, D. (2008), 'Comparative analysis: case-oriented versus variable-oriented research', in D. Della Porta and M. Keating (eds), *Approaches and Methodologies in the Social Sciences: A Pluralist Perspective*, Cambridge: Cambridge University Press, pp. 198–239.

George, A.L. and A. Bennett (2005), *Case Studies and Theory Development in the Social Sciences*, Cambridge, MA: MIT Press.

Gerring, J. (2009), 'The case study: what it is and what it does', in R.E. Goodin (ed.), *The Oxford Handbook of Political Science*, Oxford: Oxford University Press, pp. 1134–65.

Hague, R. and M. Harrop (2010), *Comparative Government and Politics: An Introduction*, Basingstoke, UK: Palgrave Macmillan.

King, G., R.O. Keohane and S. Verba (1994), *Designing Social Inquiry: Scientific Inference in Qualitative Research*, Princeton, NJ: Princeton University Press.

Kitschelt, H.P. (1986), 'Political opportunity structures and political protest: anti-nuclear movements in four democracies', *British Journal of Political Science*, **16** (1), 57–85.

Lijphart, A. (1968), *The Politics of Accommodation: Pluralism and Democracy in the Netherlands*, Berkeley, CA: University of California Press.

Lijphart, A. (1971), 'Comparative politics and the comparative method', *American Political Science Review*, **65** (3), 682–93.

Lijphart, A. (1975), 'The comparable-cases strategy in comparative research', in *Comparative Political Studies*, **8** (2), 158–77.

Mill, J.S. (1874), *A System of Logic, Ratiocinative and Inductive*, New York: Harper & Brothers.

Odell, J.S. (2004), 'Case study methods in international political economy', *International Studies Perspectives*, **2** (2), 161–76.

Platt, J. (2007), 'Case study', in W. Outhwaite (ed.), *The Sage Handbook of Social Science Methodology*, Los Angeles, CA: Sage, pp. 100–118.

Przeworski, A. and H. Teune (1970), *The Logic of Comparative Social Inquiry*, New York: Wiley.

Ragin, C.C. and H.S. Becker (eds) (1992), *What is a Case? Exploring the Foundations of Social Inquiry*, Cambridge: Cambridge University Press.

Rohlfing, I. (2012), *Case Studies and Causal Inference: An Integrative Framework*, Basingstoke, UK: Palgrave Macmillan.

Seawright, J. and J. Gerring (2008), 'Case selection techniques in case study research. A menu of qualitative and quantitative options', *Political Research Quarterly*, **61** (2), 294–308.

Skocpol, T. (1979), *States and Social Revolutions: A Comparative Analysis of France, Russia, and China*, Cambridge: Cambridge University Press.

Vennesson, P. (2008), 'Case studies and process tracing: theories and practices', in D. Della Porta and M. Keating (eds), *Approaches and Methodologies in the Social Sciences: A Pluralist Perspective*, Cambridge: Cambridge University Press, pp. 223–39.

Yanow, D., P. Schwartz-Shea and M.J. Freitas (2010), 'Case study research in political science', in A.J. Mills, J. Albert, G. Durepos, and E. Wiebe (eds), *Encyclopedia of Case Study Research*, Thousand Oaks, CA: Sage, pp. 109–15.

28 Cluster analysis
Uwe Wagschal

1 INTRODUCTION

Political science, and especially policy analysis, often relies on building typologies. Certain typologies have become a focus of interest in public policy research over the past decades.[1] One of these typologies is Esping-Andersen's *Three Worlds of Welfare Capitalism* (1990), which became a dominant approach in the analysis of welfare states in advanced capitalist democracies. Esping-Andersen identified Liberal, Conservative and Social-democratic worlds of welfare capitalism on the basis of two defining concepts 'stratification' and 'decommodification'.

A competing approach by Castles, Therborn and Schmidt (Castles 1993) sorted western democracies into four 'families of nations', arguing that historical traditions, language and neighborhood are the decisive factors shaping similarities between these countries. These four families are the English-speaking countries, the Nordic countries (Scandinavia), continental Western Europe and Southern Europe. Japan does not really seem to fit and appears to be an idiosyncratic case.

In the study of varieties of capitalism, Hall and Soskice's (2001) distinguished between liberal market economies (LMEs) and coordinated market economies (CMEs). They focused on several aspects of market economies including relations among enterprises, investors, trade unions as well as between enterprises and financial institutions and between them and the government. Major aspects besides this level of coordination were also state intervention, corporate financing and the apprenticeship system.

All three typologies have one thing in common: none of these authors have used cluster analysis to identify similarities between the countries. They attributed points (in the case of Esping-Andersen 1990) and used averages (Castles 1993) or scatterplots (Hall and Soskice 2001) to build more or less homogenous country groups. These basic grouping methods have several disadvantages: they do not use all the available information for the classifications, the selected methods can be influenced by thresholds and outliers and, finally, no absolute measure can be calculated to judge the overall fit of the selected allocation.

An empirical solution to this more or less arbitrary allocation is cluster analysis. The aim of cluster analysis is twofold:

1. The classification of the objects within clusters should be as homogenous as possible.
2. The heterogeneity between the clusters should be as large as possible.

Cluster analysis is a multivariate statistical procedure, which, over the past decades, has become increasingly sophisticated (Aldenderfer and Blashfield 1984; Bacher et al. 2010; Everitt et al. 2011; King 2014). Different approaches are used to cluster either objects (that is, cases such as countries or parties) or variables. Clustering techniques can be applied in different ways: either they are confirmatory or exploratory. The first – confirmatory – approach assumes that there is a given number of clusters, which is already known. Exploratory cluster analysis is used more often and aims to reveal an optimal number of clusters. The basic assumption is that the numbers of clusters are not known and the fit of the adaptation is maximized.

The remainder of this chapter is organized as follows: in the second section several articles employing cluster analysis will be discussed. The third section demonstrates the use of cluster analysis with the original data of Esping-Andersen's study on the worlds of welfare capitalism (1990). The strengths and weaknesses of cluster analysis are discussed in the final section.

2 APPLICATION AND CAPACITY OF CLUSTER ANALYSIS IN POLITICAL SCIENCE

Guy Peters performed one of the first cluster analysis in public policy (Peters 1991, p. 58ff.). He examined the patterns of taxation in 22 Organisation for Economic Co-operation and Development (OECD) countries in 1965 and 1987 with 11 different tax variables. His most notable result was the identification of four different clusters. Similarly, Wagschal (2005, p. 105ff.) also identified four 'families of taxation' in an analysis of 21 OECD countries (using 144 tax relevant indicators such as tax structure, tax-to-gross domestic product (GDP) ratios, and specific tax system features), on the basis of a hierarchical cluster analysis. These taxation clusters are to some extent similar to the 'worlds of welfare capitalism' (Esping-Andersen 1990) and the 'families of nations' concept (Castles 1993). The four families of taxation can be labelled as: (1) the liberal-conservative family, (2) the social-democratic-Scandinavian family, (3) the Christian-democratic-continental family and (4) a peripheral residual cluster. Further analysis shows that two factors are the decisive driving forces behind this classification: (1) the partisan complexion of government and (2) the religious structure of the society.

Cluster analysis can also be useful when trying to systematize parties from differing countries based on their programmatic positions. Ennser (2012), for instance, investigated the party families of 94 parties in 17 Western European countries. He argues that when drawing on conventional taxonomies for categorizing parties into party families, the radical right should be considerably more heterogeneous than other party families. To test his hypothesis, he first selects his cases based on an a priori classification of parties, drawing on existing research. The author then performs a cluster analysis on the parties in his sample using party position data from an expert survey (data from Benoit and Laver 2006) in order to compare the resulting cluster solution with the a priori categorization of cases. This allows him to ascertain the degree to which this categorization corresponds to the empirically located grouping of cases. Moreover, the cluster analysis provides an answer to the question of homogeneity of the identified party groups: 'Contrary to the assumptions made in the theoretical part of this article, the policy profile of the radical right parties not only distinguishes them clearly from other party families but also characterizes them as a party family of noticeable homogeneity' (Ennser 2012, p. 15). Looking more closely at the sources of this homogeneous cluster in terms of the input variables, Ennser can establish that it is the immigration issue which accounts to a large degree for the discovered homogeneity of radical right parties.

Gary Reich (2004) investigated whether there are typical developments in the first democratic elections of a country. While some studies hypothesize that high party-system fragmentation in the founding election is followed by a subsequent reduction, others assume there will be an increase in fragmentation due to the splintering of the pro-democracy block. To test these hypotheses, Reich uses a most similar systems sample of the Political Regime Change dataset comprising 23 transitions from autocracy to democracy. Four different party system characteristics are measured for each of the first four democratic elections: the effective number of electoral parties, the vote share of smaller parties and the vote shares of the strongest and second largest party in the founding election. Because paired t-tests reveal that only the vote share of the strongest party significantly differs in founding elections, multiple, different trajectories could exist. To track and distinguish several types of party-system development, the research applies a k-medians cluster analysis with the Euclidean distance. Because this type of clustering is sensitive to the initial setting of k by the researcher, Reich ran the cluster analysis for a wide range of k and then decided to set k = 4 to avoid clusters with only one case. Two of the four clusters represent relatively stable party systems, while the other two include highly decentralized systems in which the initially strongest party lost considerable support. In sum, the study shows that a uniform pattern of new party systems is hardly recognizable. Instead, there is more stability in new party systems than the existing theories predicted.

Lyn Ragsdale and Jerrold Rusk (1993) use cluster analysis to distinguish between different kinds of non-voters in the 1990 US midterm Senate election. Their model builds on the idea that the decision of whether or not to participate in an election springs from four different decision scenarios – political ignorance, indifference, dissatisfaction, and inactivity – all of which indicate different levels of attention for the campaign (Ragsdale and Rusk 1993, p. 724ff.). Also, demographic characteristics, political interest and the electoral context are hypothesized to affect the decision of whether to vote by moderating the effect of the four decision conditions (Ragsdale and Rusk 1993, p. 725ff.). Their clustering draws on respondents' issue awareness, recognition of the candidates' names, and knowledge of the incumbent's accomplishments (as measures of ignorance), respondents' agreement with the incumbent's past voting record, perceived ideological distance between the candidates, and the difference between respondents' feelings towards the candidates (to measure indifference), an indicator of dissatisfaction (constructed from party feeling thermometers), and respondents' past voting behavior (to capture inactivity; Ragsdale and Rusk 1993, pp. 728–30). Demographically, individuals are compared across education, income, age, residential mobility and unemployment (Ragsdale and Rusk 1993, p. 730). Interest in politics in turn is captured through campaign knowledge and the absence of partisanship, while the electoral context is assessed through candidates' campaign expenditures, the degree of competitiveness, the closeness of the gubernatorial election, the terms of voter registration, and respondents' perception of the economy (Ragsdale and Rusk 1993, pp. 731–3). The distance between two non-voters is calculated as the Euclidean distance from the z-transformed variables (Ragsdale and Rusk 1993, p. 734ff.). Clusters are formed through a 'hierarchical agglomerative method' (Ragsdale and Rusk 1993, p. 734), although the authors do not state which linkage criterion was used.

Wolfson and his colleagues (2004) apply a cluster analysis to the field of international conflict and peace studies. They assume that the relationship between politics, economics and conflict is so complex in terms of time-dependence, non-linearity and multicollinearity that classic regression analysis is, in most cases, unable to adequately cope with it in a single model. They argue that, 'when internal linkages are too complex to model under a single-equation regime assuming causal relations, it might be better to be guided by the data themselves rather than impose a test equation on them' (Wolfson et al. 2004, p. 608). This makes cluster analysis a perfect approach: its basic inductive idea does not assume any kind of causality between the variables but 'bidirectional and fully interactive effects upon each other' (Wolfson et al. 2004, p. 608).

Wolfson et al. constructed their dataset for five years (1967, 1974, 1981, 1988 and 1995) from a number of other macro-data projects such as Polity IV, the CIA *World Factbook* or the Uppsala Conflict Data. In the end they use 18 variables – six variables each from the three basic categories: politics (for example, the method by which chief executives are recruited), conflict (for example, number of conflicts in a country) and economics (for example, percentage of GDP spent on military) (Wolfson et al. 2004, p. 613). They z-standardize all variables using the year-specific mean for all countries, before including them in the cluster analysis. Applying the Ward-method to the data for each of the five years separately finds three relatively persistent clusters: (1) advanced, wealthy democracies with low conflict involvement, (2) poor, anocratic states with low conflict involvement, and (3) poor autocracies with low conflict involvement. All other clusters found in one year or another are less stable (Wolfson et al. 2004, p. 620).

By employing cluster analysis, Obinger and Wagschal (2001) analyzed welfare states with respect to their public policymaking. They showed that for two policy fields (social and economic policy) the Castles's families-of-nations concept was quite robust and stable over time. In addition, cluster analysis revealed two pairs of avenues towards modernity. On the one hand, there are more state-oriented and market-oriented models of public policymaking; on the other, there was a cleavage in public policymaking between rich countries located at the center and poorer countries located at the periphery.

Saint-Arnaud and Bernard (2003) performed a hierarchical cluster analysis to identify welfare regimes in advanced countries. The authors had three objectives: (1) they wanted to test whether a hierarchical cluster analysis verified the existence of welfare state regimes, (2) whether the regime types converge or stay resilient and (3) what the reasons for this resilience might be. The context of their analysis is the apparent weakening of the welfare state in relation to globalization. Starting with the assumption that different welfare regimes structure three types of systems (the market, the state and the civil society) in a distinct way, the authors presented the current state of research with special weight on Esping-Andersen's typology.

3   HOW TO APPLY CLUSTER ANALYSIS

3.1   The General Idea

In general cluster analysis seeks to discover groups within the data. The aim of cluster analysis then is twofold:

1.   The classification of the objects (or variables) within clusters should be as homogenous as possible.
2.   The heterogeneity between the clusters should be as large as possible.

Overall there are three different approaches to cluster objects (for example, countries and parties) or variables (see Figure 28.1): hierarchical, partitioning and probabilistic approaches. There are also widespread methods within these approaches. In what follows, only the hierarchical method, which is the most frequently used method, as well as only the clustering of objects, is discussed in detail.

The application of these different clustering methods depends on the sampling size, for example, hierarchical approaches are suitable for small to medium size samples, which is particularly useful for comparative politics. Other methods, such as the K-means approach and the probabilistic method, require a large number of cases. The latter provides probabilities for the cases to fit into one cluster, meaning that a case is – within a certain

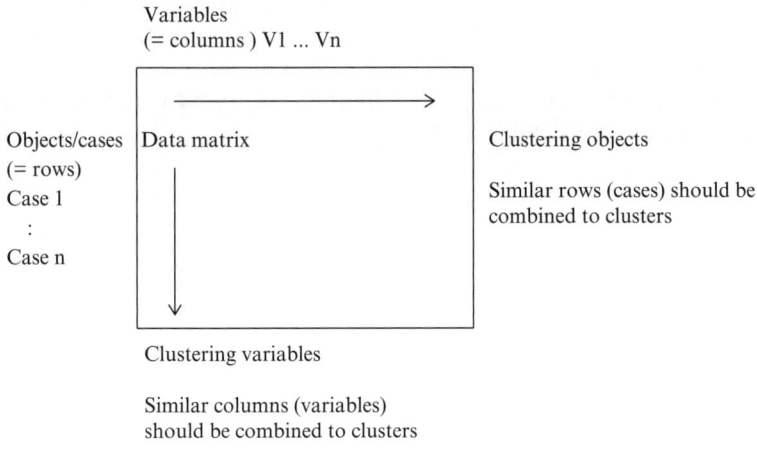

Notes: According to Bacher (1996, p. 7).

Figure 28.1   Possibilities of classification

percentage – part of each cluster. Cluster analysis can either be exploratory or confirmatory. In an exploratory cluster analysis, the number of clusters is unknown and the number of clusters has to be estimated. In a confirmatory cluster analysis the number of clusters is known and the classification is reassessed.

3.2   Proximity Measures

The closeness (proximity) of objects in a hierarchical cluster analysis can be measured by similarity or dissimilarity measures. Which measure is applied depends on the scale level. It has to be decided a priori which kind of measure is used. The most famous proximity measure for interval scaled data is the Pearson correlation coefficient. For binary data and frequencies, it is also possible to use phi or chi square as an association measure.

3.2.1   Similarity measures
There are several similarity measures for binary or nominal data. The calculation of these measures depends on whether a characteristic is present or not (see Table 28.1). However, the absence or presence of a characteristic is not a symmetrical relationship, since its absence can have different meanings.

In literature, as well as in statistical packages such as SPSS, many similarity measures can be found.[2] Table 28.2 displays the most common types. High values of the similarity measure indicate a high proximity of the objects (for example, countries, parties and individuals).

The decision regarding which of the similarity measures should be used depends on the content and has to be justified by the researcher. The scale level is also important. For ordinal and interval scaled variables distance measures are more suitable.

Table 28.1   2 × 2 table of binary outcomes for two objects

Object 1	Object 2		Sum Σ
	Characteristic present (1)	Characteristic not present (0)	
Characteristic present (1)	a	b	a + b
Characteristic not present (0)	c	d	c + d
Sum Σ	a + c	b + d	ΣΣ a + b +c + d (= S)

Table 28.2   Similarity measures for binary data

Similarity measure	Definition	Explanation
Russel and Rao (RR)	$RR = a / S$	Measures the share of conjoint matches. Conjoint absences (that is, both 0) are excluded from the nominator. The denominator uses all observations
Simple matching	$SMK = (a + d) / S$	Conjoint absence and conjoint presence have equal weights. The denominator uses all observations/combinations
Jaccard I	$JI = \dfrac{a}{a + b + c}$	Uses only combinations where at least one characteristic is present. Conjoint absences are ignored
Rogers and Tanimoto	$RT = \dfrac{a + d}{a + d + 2(b + c)}$	Mismatches are given a double weight in the denominator. Conjoint absence and conjoint presence have equal weights in the nominator

3.2.2   Dissimilarity and distance measures

For interval scaled variables, it is possible to calculate the proximities between the objects by dissimilarity measures or distance measures. In contrast to similarity measures, high values indicate a considerable diversity between the objects, as opposed to low values which indicate resemblance. Distance measures have no upper limit, and the magnitude depends on the number of variables (characteristics) and on the unit of measurement. Measuring the likeness of two objects (for example, countries) poses another problem, since the utilized variables have different units and scales and must therefore be standardized in advance. When the variables analyzed are all measured on the same scale there is no need to standardize.

There are different ways to standardize the variables; the most common is the z-standardization. The absolute value of z_i represents the distance between the raw score x_i and the population mean in units of the standard deviation s. z_i is negative when the raw score is below the mean, and positive when it is above the mean. All z-standardized variables have an average of 0 and a standard deviation of 1.

$$z_i = \frac{x_i - \bar{x}}{s} \tag{28.1}$$

where z_i = standardized score, x_i = raw value, $\bar{x}$ = mean and s = standard deviation.

In what follows, the original data from the stratification concept of

Table 28.3   Raw stratification data for the worlds of welfare according to Esping-Andersen

	Conservative welfare state		Liberal welfare state			Social Democratic welfare state	
	Corporatism	Etatism	Means tested social benefits	Private pension	Private health spending	Universalism	Generosity
AUS	1.00	0.70	3.30	30.00	36.00	33.00	1.00
AUT	7.00	3.80	2.80	3.00	36.00	72.00	0.52
BEL	5.00	3.00	4.50	8.00	13.00	67.00	0.79
CAN	2.00	0.20	15.60	38.00	26.00	93.00	0.48
CH	2.00	1.00	8.80	20.00	35.00	96.00	0.48
DAN	2.00	1.10	1.00	17.00	15.00	87.00	0.99
FIN	4.00	2.50	1.90	3.00	21.00	88.00	0.72
FRA	10.00	3.10	11.20	8.00	28.00	70.00	0.55
GER	6.00	2.20	4.90	11.00	20.00	72.00	0.56
IRL	1.00	2.20	5.90	10.00	6.00	60.00	0.77
ITA	12.00	2.20	9.30	2.00	12.00	59.00	0.52
JAP	7.00	0.90	7.00	23.00	28.00	63.00	0.32
NL	3.00	1.80	6.90	13.00	22.00	87.00	0.57
NOR	4.00	0.90	2.10	8.00	1.00	95.00	0.69
NZ	1.00	0.80	2.30	4.00	18.00	33.00	1.00
SWE	2.00	1.00	1.10	6.00	7.00	90.00	0.82
UK	2.00	2.00	(13.5)[a]	12.00	10.00	76.00	0.64
USA	2.00	1.50	18.20	21.00	57.00	54.00	0.22
$\bar{x}$	4.056	1.717	6.683	13.167	21.722	71.944	0.647
s	3.208	0.978	5.157	9.948	13.698	19.374	0.222

Notes: Data refer to 1980 (Esping-Andersen 1990, p. 70).
[a] = data in the original table of Esping-Andersen not available.
Data was taken from Eardly et al. (1996).
$\bar{x}$ = arithmetic mean; s = standard deviation.

Gösta Esping-Andersen's pioneering book *Three Worlds of Welfare Capitalism* (Esping-Andersen 1990) will be used to demonstrate the various steps of cluster analysis (see Table 28.3). In his book, Esping-Andersen identifies a liberal (Anglo-Saxon), a conservative (continental) and a social-democratic (Scandinavian) world of welfare capitalism. He uses a scoring procedure, rather than a cluster analysis, based on attributing points (1–3) for each terzile. In the end, he sorts all 18 countries (objects) into one of these three worlds.

To use a distance measure, the seven different variables have to be z-standardized by using formula (28.1). For Australia's corporatism variable one gets a z-score of:

$$Z_{AUS} = \frac{1-4.0556}{3.20794} = -0.9525 \qquad (28.1')$$

The computer does this calculation for all 18 countries. Table 28.4 displays the z-scores, for the sake of simplicity, for only Australia, Austria and Belgium.

The next step is to use an appropriate distance measure. Again, there are many possibilities (Everitt et al. 2011, p. 50). The most popular are the City Block distance, the Euclidean distance and the squared Euclidean distance.

$$d_{km}^{CITY} = \sum_{i=1}^{n} |x_{ki} - x_{mi}| \qquad (28.2)$$

$$d_{km}^{EUKL} = \sqrt{\sum_{i=1}^{n} (x_{ki} - x_{mi})^2} \qquad (28.3)$$

$$d_{km}^{QEUKL} = \sum_{i=1}^{n} (x_{ki} - x_{mi})^2 \qquad (28.4)$$

Where the subindexes k and m refer to the objects (countries) and the r subindex i refers to a variable (i = 1 bis n variables).

Calculating the City Block distance from Table 28.4 between Australia and Austria results in (see also row 4 in Table 28.4):

$$d_{AUS-AUT}^{CITY} = |-0.9525 - 0.91786| + ... + |1.58972 - 0.5699| = 12.023$$

Calculating the Euclidean distance and the Squared Euclidean distance for Australia and Austria results in:

$$d_{AUS-AUT}^{EUKL} = 5.444$$

$$d_{AUS-AUT}^{QEUKL} = 29.634$$

We have to calculate all distances between each object/country. For our example with 18 countries this means a total of 153 distances $(= ((n * n - 1)/2))$.

3.3   Hierarchical Clustering Techniques

The next step is to sort the objects into clusters. On the basis of the similarity and dissimilarity measures, we can use hierarchical clustering techniques to solve this problem. Hierarchical clustering is a generic term for different clustering strategies. It is possible to subdivide these techniques

Table 28.4   Z-scores for Australia, Austria and Belgium

	Corporatism	Etatism	Means tested social benefits	Private pension	Private health spending	Universalism	Generosity
AUS	−0.95250	−1.03938	−0.65604	1.69207	1.04236	−2.01015	1.58972
AUT	0.91786	2.12989	−0.75299	−1.02194	1.04236	0.00287	−0.56990
BEL	0.29441	1.31201	−0.42336	−0.51935	−0.63677	−0.25521	0.64489
ABS[a] (AUS– AUT)	1.87036	3.16927	0.09695	2.71401	0	2.01302	2.15962

Note:
Calculated from Table 28.3; the z-scores for the remaining 15 cases are not displayed.
[a] = absolute differences between Australia and Austria.

into agglomerative and divisive methods. Agglomerative methods start with the finest partition. Each object/country forms a single cluster in the beginning. Subsequently, these clusters are combined step by step. In each round, the number of clusters is therefore reduced by one. In each round, the two clusters with the lowest degree of dissimilarity or the greatest degree of similarity are merged. Finally, all objects/cases form a single cluster. In contrast, a divisive technique starts with one cluster where all the objects/countries are assembled. In further steps, this cluster is split into more clusters, increasing the number of cluster in each round by one. Finally, each object forms a separate cluster. In both approaches the researcher then has to decide about the optimal number of clusters.

In what follows, only agglomerative methods are used. Again, there are several approaches (for example, SPSS offers seven different options) and two of them are explained in detail:

1. The single linkage or nearest neighbor method.
2. The complete linkage or furthest neighbor method.

The clustering method follows a strict procedure, which consists of six steps (Wagschal 1999, p. 262):

1. Start with the finest partition. Each object is a single cluster.
2. Calculate the distance or similarity between the objects.
3. In the case of a distance measure, identify the clusters with the least distance (that is, the highest proximity). In the case of a similarity measure, identify the clusters with the highest degree of similarity.
4. Merge the two clusters with the lowest distance. The number of clusters decreases by one.
5. Recalculate the distance between the newly formed cluster and the remaining clusters. A reduced distance matrix has to be calculated with a merging algorithm.
6. Repeat steps three to five until all objects are merged into one cluster.

The merging algorithms (i.e. single and complete linkage) are only relevant for step five. These algorithms differ in the way the new distance matrix is calculated. Table 28.5a shows the distance matrix for seven selected cases (for the sake of simplicity and demonstration purposes) based on the City Block measure.[3] Table 28.5a shows that Norway and Sweden display the lowest distance. They form a new cluster, which means that one has to calculate new distances between the new cluster (NOR, SWE) and all the remaining clusters. Single linkage uses the smallest distance of any the new

Table 28.5a   Distance matrix for selected cases (CITY BLOCK)

	1:AUS	2:AUT	3:BEL	13:NOR	16:SWE	17:UK	18:USA
1:AUS	0.000						
2:AUT	12.023	0.000					
3:BEL	10.421	5.426	0.000				
13:NOR	10.734	9.046	5.695	0.000			
16:SWE	9.327	9.448	5.600	2.402	0.000		
17:UK	11.165	9.023	5.463	6.223	5.781	0.000	
18:USA	11.050	12.517	12.880	13.985	13.543	8.784	0.000

Note: Calculation based on Table 28.3 and Equation (28.2). For demonstration purposes only seven out of 18 cases are displayed (see note 3 for explanation).

Table 28.5b   Reduced distance matrix after round one (single linkage)

	AUS	AUT	BEL	{NOR;SWE}	UK	USA
AUS	0.000					
AUT	12.023	0.000				
BEL	10.421	5.426	0.000			
(NOR;SWE)	9.327	9.046	5.600	0.000		
UK	11.165	9.023	5.463	5.781	0.000	
USA	11.050	12.517	12.880	13.543	8.784	0.000

cluster members in comparison to all the others. Equation (28.5) is the calculation method of the single linkage algorithm:

$$D(A; B + C) = \min\{D(A, B); D(A, C)\} \qquad (28.5)$$

Applying single linkage (equation (28.5)) to the distance matrix produces Table 28.5b. Except for the distance to Austria, Sweden is closer to all other countries in Table 28.5a.

The next merger is between Austria and Belgium. They form a new cluster and the number of clusters is again reduced by one. Applying single linkage (equation (28.5)) leads to a new reduced distance matrix (Table 28.5c).

In round three the Austria/Belgium cluster is merged with the UK. This leads to a new reduced distance matrix (Table 28.5d).

In round four the Austria/Belgium/UK cluster is united with the Norway/Sweden cluster. This leads to a new reduced distance matrix (Table 28.5e).

Table 28.5c   Reduced distance matrix after round two (single linkage)

	AUS	{AUT;BEL}	{NOR;SWE}	UK	USA
AUS	0.000				
(AUT;BEL)	10.421	0.000			
(NOR;SWE)	9.327	5.600	0.000		
UK	11.165	5.463	5.781	0.000	
USA	11.050	12.517	13.543	8.784	0.000

Table 28.5d   Reduced distance matrix after round three (single linkage)

	AUS	(AUT;BEL;UK)	(NOR;SWE)	USA
AUS	0.000			
(AUT;BEL;UK)	10.421	0.000		
(NOR;SWE)	9.327	5.600	0.000	
USA	11.050	8.784	13.543	0.000

Table 28.5e   Reduced distance matrix after round four (single linkage)

	AUS	(AUT;BEL;UK;NOR;SWE)	USA
AUS	0.000		
(AUT;BEL;UK; NOR;SWE)	9.327	0.000	
USA	11.050	8.784	0.000

In round five the USA is merged with the large cluster. Finally, in round six all countries appear in one cluster after Australia is also merged.

The single linkage method (or nearest neighbor) has a negative property (see Everitt et al. 2011, p. 79), since it tends to produce unbalanced and straggly clusters ('chain effect'). Complete linkage (or furthest neighbor) is therefore better suited for merging the objects, since it has no chaining effect. Complete linkage tends to find compact clusters by using the maximum distance between objects (see equation (28.6)).

$$D(A; B + C) = \max\{D(A, B); D(A, C)\} \qquad (28.6)$$

Starting with the finest partition (see Table 28.5a for data) Norway and Sweden are merged again. However, instead of using the closest distance, one uses the furthest distance for recalculating the distance matrix (see Table 28.6a).

Austria and Belgium form the next cluster in round two, which results in a new distance matrix (Table 28.6b).

In round three we can observe the first difference between single and complete linkage, when using the maximum distance. The UK is now merged with Norway and Sweden instead of Austria and Belgium. This leads to the results in Table 28.6c.

The next steps combine Austria/Belgium with Norway/Sweden/UK

Table 28.6a   Reduced distance matrix after round one (complete linkage)

	AUS	AUT	BEL	(NOR;SWE)	UK	USA
AUS	0.000					
AUT	12.023	0.000				
BEL	10.421	5.426	0.000			
(NOR;SWE)	10.734	9.448	5.695	0.000		
UK	11.165	9.023	5.463	6.223	0.000	
USA	11.050	12.517	12.880	13.985	8.784	0.000

Table 28.6b   Reduced distance matrix after round two (complete linkage)

	AUS	(AUT;BEL)	(NOR;SWE)	UK	USA
AUS	0.000				
(AUT;BEL)	12.023	0.000			
(NOR;SWE)	10.734	9.448	0.000		
UK	11.165	9.023	6.223	0.000	
USA	11.050	12.880	13.985	8.784	0.000

Table 28.6c   Reduced distance matrix after round three (complete linkage)

	AUS	(AUT;BEL)	(NOR;SWE;UK)	USA
AUS	0.000			
(AUT;BEL)	12.023	0.000		
(NOR;SWE; UK)	11.165	9.448	0.000	
USA	11.050	12.880	13.985	0.000

(round four). Australia and the USA then merge into one cluster (round five) and, finally, all countries combine to form one cluster.

3.4   The Graphical Presentation of Cluster

The cluster membership of each object can be displayed in tables or in a specific graph, the dendrogram. A dendrogram (or tree diagram) shows the merging of clusters at the respective distance level. SPSS automatically rescales these levels of amalgation on a scale between 0 and 25 (see Figure 28.2).[4] The advantage of this standardization is a possible comparison between different dendrograms. With a dendrogram it is easy to identify the hierarchical structure of the objects. We can also see which objects/countries are close to each other and which objects form larger clusters. The number of clusters can be determined where a line cuts off the branches of the dendrogram.

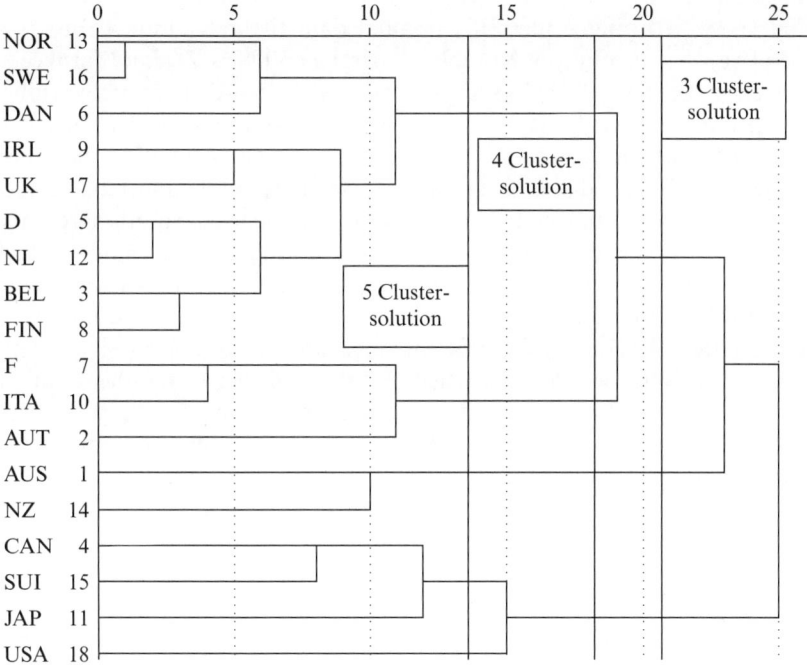

Note: Dendrogram is based on complete linkage as the amalgamation method; distance measure: Euclidean distance. All variables are z-standardized.

Figure 28.2   Dendrogram of clusters (complete linkage)

Table 28.7   Worlds of welfare as a result of a cluster analysis (replication study of Esping-Andersen's data)

Cluster 1	AUS NZ
Cluster 2	AUT BEL GER DAN FRA BEL FIN IRL ITA NL NOR SWE UK
Cluster 3	CAN JAP SUI USA

Note: Data sources in Esping-Andersen (1990, p. 70; see Table 28.3 above). Distance metric for calculation of distance matrix: Euclidean distance. Linkage (amalgamation) method: complete linkage. All variables are z-standardized. Only the seven variables measuring the "stratification" concept were used.

Esping-Andersen's remarkable study (Esping-Andersen 1990) suggested that there are three worlds of welfare capitalism. Though Esping-Andersen did not use cluster analysis he identified three different types of welfare state. Table 28.7 describes the clustering results derived from the data originally supplied by Esping-Andersen.[5] The results are very different to those produced by Esping-Andersen and as the dendrogram shows (see Figure 28.2) Esping-Andersen's original data fit better into a four (or even five) cluster solution. Notably, Australia and New Zealand form one cluster, as Castles (1993) has argued, and the Social-democratic world is grouped together with the Conservative welfare states in a single cluster.

A sensitivity analysis might combine different amalgamation methods as well as different distance measures to see how stable and reliable the results are. An initial comparison of the three-cluster solution reveals nine different classifications of clusters, depending on the choice of the distance measure (Euclidean versus City Block). However – as seen from Figure 28.2 – the four-cluster solution seems to be much more homogenous. In fact, the choice of the distance measure does not play a significant role. All 18 countries were classified into the same clusters. Other combinations of calculations of the distance matrix and linkage methods lead to similar or even identical results (for example, when the commonly used Wards method is employed).

3.5   The Optimal Number of Clusters

A simple way to determine the optimal number of clusters is by inspecting the dendrogram. However, this approach is unreliable and essentially untrustworthy, since someone decides which solution looks more 'homogenous'. A suitable heuristic is the inverse scree test (which is not a formal statistical test). For the inverse scree test we have to plot the number of clusters on the x-axis and respective amalgamation level (the distance for each merger) on the y-axis. The optimal number is determined by a

Table 28.8 *Four worlds of welfare as a result of a cluster re-analysis (replication study of Esping-Andersen's data)*

Cluster 1	AUS	NZ							
Cluster 2	AUT	FRA	ITA						
Cluster 3	BEL	DAN	GER	FIN	IRL	NL	NOR	SWE	UK	FIN
Cluster 4	CAN	JAP	SUI	USA						

Note: Data sources in Esping-Andersen (1990, p. 70; see Table 28.3 above). The results are identical for the City Block. Euclidean distance and squared Euclidean distance when the linkage (amalgamation) method is complete linkage. They are also the same for the Ward method (squared Euclidean distance). All variables are z-standardized. Only the seven variables measuring the 'stratification' concept were used.

sharp kink. This means a sharp decrease of the agglomeration levels, that is, increasing homogeneity of the clusters. For a kink the next decrease should be small.

Figure 28.3 displays the inverse scree test for our findings in Figure 28.2. Clearly a five cluster solution fits best (with the USA forming a single cluster), followed by the four-cluster solution.

3.6 Assessing the Homogeneity of Cluster Solutions

The aim of a cluster analysis was to identify clusters/groups of objects where the cases within a cluster are similar to each other and as dissimilar as possible to the other clusters. Therefore additional information about homogeneity and heterogeneity helps to assess which cluster solution is best.

To calculate an index for homogeneity, it is possible to calculate the homogeneity measure g, which is the difference between dissimilarity between all clusters $\bar{u}_{bt}$ and the dissimilarity within a cluster $\bar{u}_{in}$ (see equation (28.7)). The dissimilarity between all clusters is the mean of all distances (City Block or Euclidean or other distance measure) for all combinations and all clusters. Then the overall average is calculated as an unweighted average for all cluster combinations. To assess dissimilarity within a cluster, the means of all distances for the specific cluster members are calculated. Again the overall average is calculated as an unweighted average of all clusters (see Bacher et al. 2010, p. 249). Large values for g indicate a better solution. The aim of cluster analysis is of course that the dissimilarity within a cluster should be considerably smaller than between the clusters.

It is also possible to calculate the ratio of the dissimilarity within and the dissimilarity between all clusters (see equation (28.8)). Low values for

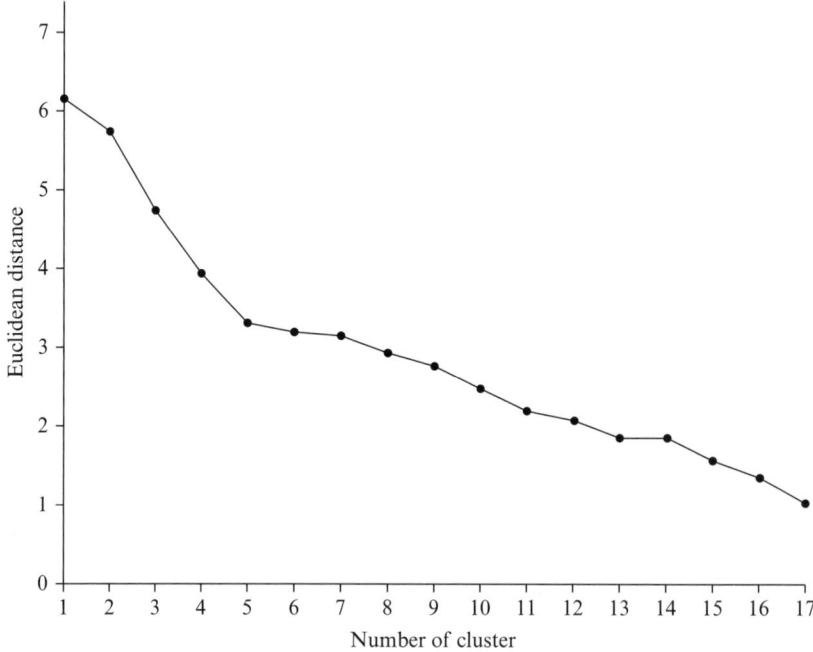

Note: The graph is based on the analysis displayed in Figure 28.2. On the y-axis the distance at the amalgamation is displayed. With 18 countries there are n – 1 mergers.

Figure 28.3　Inverse scree test for the worlds of welfare

the ratio h indicate a better solution, since a large denominator indicates a poor fit of the clusters.

$$g = \overline{u}_{bt} / \overline{u}_{in}. \qquad (28.7)$$

$$h = \overline{u}_{in} / \overline{u}_{bt}. \qquad (28.8)$$

Finally, it is also possible to construct a statistical test (Bacher et al. 2010, p. 249) using the homogeneity measure g:

$$z = \frac{g - E(g)}{s(g)}, \qquad (28.9)$$

where $E(g)$ is the expected value of the null hypothesis that g is zero and $s(g)$ is the corresponding standard deviation.

　Applying the homogeneity measures g and h to the Esping-Andersen data yields the following results. The most homogenous solution is the five-cluster-solution ($g = 1.65$; $h = 0.59$), followed by the four-cluster-solution ($g = 1.64$; h $= 0.62$). Esping-Andersen's own typology ('three worlds', that is, three cluster) is much worse ($g = 0.92$; $h = 0.75$) and not as good as the three-cluster solution as reported in Figure 28.2. Bambra (2007) discusses alternatives and similar research and supports these findings.

4 STRENGTHS AND WEAKNESSES OF CLUSTER ANALYSIS

Cluster analysis is a powerful instrument for joining objects into clusters/ groups. It is possible to compare the different outcomes and conduct a sensitivity analysis of the solutions. Cluster analysis can either be confirmatory or exploratory. In the present example, using Esping-Andersen's original data, the approach is clearly confirmatory. Furthermore, the outcome is striking: Esping-Andersen's data does not confirm his own three worlds of welfare typology. This finding also relates to another advantage of clustering: the computer does not calculate incorrectly. A major critique is Esping-Andersen's scaling procedure. If we use the same data and employ Esping-Andersen's scoring procedure for his stratification concept, the 'hand-coding' is error-prone. Esping-Andersen has misspecified ten cases (nearly 20 per cent of all his codings). Four countries have therefore been classified incorrectly according to his rules (see Wagschal 1999, p. 280).

Esping-Andersen's data transformation also significantly influences his result. He attributes according to the terziles (0, 2, 4 points) for each of the seven variables. If one assigns points for the rank ordering (from 1 to 18), one gets a different ordering. Adding up the ranks for each variable results in different cluster solutions. The boundaries for the terziles create further problems. Esping-Andersen has used arbitrary terzile boundaries. Employing the 'exact' statistical rules for terziles also changes the order of and classification for some countries.

Finally there is a non-consistent classification of countries into the worlds of welfare. For the measurement of the conservative and social-democratic type, Esping-Andersen only uses two variables. For the liberal world, three variables (see Table 28.3) are used. The range for the conservative and social-democratic worlds is between zero and eight points for both worlds. To be classified as conservative a country needs eight points and to be classified social-democratic a country needs at least six points. This is not congruent, and applying stricter rules would have meant that Finland (six points for the conservative world) would also have been classified as conservative. Esping-Andersen classified Finland and the Netherlands as social-democratic with six points. Therefore Finland belongs to both worlds. These problems and various mistakes show that deciding decisions can lead to different results.

Clustering with the use of a computer has clear advantages. However, as shown above, several other decisions have to be made. The first, and most important, is about the clustering technique. The user can choose between deterministic and probabilistic methods. Furthermore the deterministic methods can be differentiated in hierarchical and partitioning methods. This chapter focused especially on hierarchical cluster analysis, since they are most commonly used. There are several options to decide between standardization procedures, distance measures and linkage methods. Publishing the decisions and possible different outcomes should be the standard. The reader should be aware that there are other cluster techniques possible.

NOTES

1. There are many more typologies, especially a number of rival welfare state typologies that have been advanced in the aftermath of Esping-Andersen's seminal book.
2. There are several statistical packages for cluster analysis including CLUSTAN and ALMO.
3. It should be clear, that 'ideally' one has to recalculate the z-scores and the distance matrix, since both change with only seven cases instead of 18. However, for demonstration purposes we can make the assumption that the displayed distances are valid.
4. The standardized distance is calculated by multiplying the distance for each merger by 25 and then dividing by the maximum value.
5. It should be mentioned that including the decommodification data of Esping-Andersen would improve the results slightly in the hypothesized direction.

REFERENCES

Aldenderfer, M.S. and R.K. Blashfield (1984), *Cluster Analysis*, London, New Delhi and Newbury Park, CA: Sage.
Bacher, J. (1996), *Clusteranalyse: Anwendungsorientierte Einführung*, 2nd revised edn, Munich and Vienna: Oldenbourg.
Bacher, J., A. Pöge and K. Wenzig (2010), *Clusteranalyse: Anwendungsorientierte Einführung in Klassifikationsverfahren* (*Cluster Analysis. Applied Introduction into Classification Methods*), Munich and Vienna: Oldenbourg.
Bambra, C. (2007), '"Sifting the wheat from the chaff". A two-dimensional discriminant analysis of welfare state regime theory', *Social Policy and Administration*, **41** (1), 1–28.
Benoit, K. and M. Laver (2006), *Party Policy in Modern Democracies*, London: Routledge.
Castles, F.G. (ed.) (1993), *Families of Nations: Patterns of Public Policy in Western Democracies*, Aldershot, UK: Dartmouth.

Eardley, T., J. Bradshaw, J. Ditch, I. Gough and P. Whiteford (1996), *Social Assistance in OECD Countries: Country Reports*, London: HMSO.

Ennser, L. (2012), 'The homogeneity of West European party families: the radical right in comparative perspective', *Party Politics*, **18** (1), 151–71.

Esping-Andersen, G. (1990), *The Three Worlds of Welfare Capitalism*, Princeton, NJ: Princeton University Press.

Everitt, B.S., S. Landau, M. Leese and D. Stahl (2011), *Cluster Analysis*, 5th edn, Chichester, UK: Wiley.

Hall, P.A. and D. Soskice (eds) (2001), *Varieties of Capitalism: The Institutional Foundations of Comparative Advantage*, Oxford: Oxford University Press.

Kangas, O. (1994), 'The politics of social security: on regressions, qualitative comparisons and cluster analysis', in T. Janoski and A. Hicks (eds), *The Comparative Political Economy of the Welfare State*, Cambridge: Cambridge University Press, pp. 346–64.

King, R.S. (2014), *Cluster Analysis and Data Mining: An Introduction*, Dulles, VA: Mercury Learning Information.

Obinger, H. and U. Wagschal (2001), 'Families of nations and public policy', *West European Politics*, **24** (1), 99–114.

Peters, G.B. (1991), *The Politics of Taxation: a Comparative Perspective*, Cambridge, MA: Blackwell.

Ragsdale, L. and J.G. Rusk (1993), 'Who are nonvoters? Profiles from the 1990 Senate elections', *American Journal of Political Science*, **37** (3), 721–46.

Reich, G. (2004), 'The evolution of new party systems: are early elections exceptional?', *Electoral Studies*, **23** (2), 235–50.

Saint-Arnaud, S. and P. Bernard (2003), 'Convergence or resilience? A hierarchical cluster analysis of the welfare regimes in advanced countries', *Current Sociology*, **51** (5), 499–527.

Wagschal, U. (1999), *Statistik für Politikwissenschaftler* (*Statistics for Political Scientists*), Munich and Vienna: Oldenbourg.

Wagschal, U. (2005), *Steuerpolitik und Steuerreformen im internationalen Vergleich: Eine Analyse der Ursachen und Blockaden* (*Tax Policies and Tax Reforms in International Comparison. An Analysis of Causes and Veto Players*), Münster: Lit.

Wagschal, U. and P. König (2014), 'Alle gleich? Programmatische Unterschiede der Parteien in der Analyse' ('All equal? Programmatic differences between parties'), *Zeitschrift für Parlamentsfragen*, **4**, 782–801.

Wolfson, M., Z. Madjd-Sadjadi and P. James (2004), 'Identifying national types: a cluster analysis of politics, economics, and conflict', *Journal of Peace Research*, **41** (5), 607–23.

29 The logic of process tracing: contributions, pitfalls and future directions
Sherry Zaks

1 INTRODUCTION

Process tracing is a powerful inferential tool in social science research. It is defined as an analytic procedure for systematically evaluating pieces of (usually) qualitative evidence to explain an outcome of interest. With its focus on uncovering the underlying dynamics of social and political phenomena, process tracing makes two distinctive contributions. First, it contributes to our understanding of the causal sequence and mechanisms that give rise to a phenomenon. Second, it helps scholars adjudicate among competing explanations of an outcome. The utility and promise of process tracing has driven many scholars to refine this technique in order to impose rigorous standards for its use as well as for evaluating work that employs it.

Since its inception, scholars have proposed three major sets of innovations. The first set occurred in the realm of theory testing in which Van Evera (1997) demonstrated that different pieces of evidence can be classified along the dimensions of uniqueness and certainty. These dimensions gave rise to four tests to help researchers assess how evidence bears on different hypotheses: 'straw-in-the-wind tests', 'hoop tests', 'smoking-gun tests' and 'doubly-decisive tests' (Van Evera 1997; Bennett 2010; Collier 2011).

The second and third set of innovations represent divergent attempts to map the logic of process tracing onto more concrete epistemological and ontological foundations. One direction of innovation maps the logic of process tracing onto that of set theory (Mahoney 2011; Goertz and Mahoney 2012), the goal of which is to evince the distinct and crucial roles of necessity and sufficiency in qualitative research (Blatter and Haverland 2012). This approach has also brought to the table a discussion of how the logic of the process-tracing tests bear on case selection principles (Schneider and Rohlfing 2013; Rohlfing 2014). The other direction – and final set of advances – maps the logic of process tracing onto the procedures of Bayesian inference (Beach and Pedersen 2012; Bennett 2014).

This approach frames process tracing as a procedure in which evidence serves to update the researcher's prior confidence in the truth of a given explanation.

The methodology of process tracing is in a period of rapid innovation, yet some of the proposed advances have taken divergent and even contradictory paths. As such, it is an ideal moment to take stock of the recent innovations and map out the most productive directions for future work. This chapter proceeds in three parts. First, I outline the three major innovations in the process tracing literature. Next, I evaluate the three innovations. Finally, I highlight areas for future research.

2 PROGRESS WITH SYSTEMATIZING THE METHOD

As originally conceptualized, process tracing involved the use of historical narratives and within-case analysis as a means of evaluating complex causal processes (George 1979; George and McKeown 1985). Subsequently, scholars have introduced many advances in codifying the research procedure.

2.1 Developing and Advancing the Four Tests

Van Evera (1997) takes the first major step towards systematizing the method. He notes that different pieces of evidence contribute to different types of insights about the likelihood of a given hypothesis. Van Evera claims that any piece of evidence can be classified along two dimensions: uniqueness and certitude. Uniqueness captures the extent to which a given observation points to the validity of one specific hypothesis. Thus, when adjudicating between theories A and B, a piece of evidence that scores high on uniqueness for theory A represents an observation we would be likely to see only if theory A were true. The other dimension, certitude, describes a piece of evidence that suggests a requirement for a given outcome has been satisfied.[1]

Drawing on the extreme values of these two dimensions, Van Evera develops four tests that have been a crucial point of departure for much of the subsequent process tracing literature. His weakest test, the straw-in-the-wind, yields insight into the overall balance of evidence in favor of (or against) one hypothesis. However, it is not decisive. In his account, two additional tests yield stronger inferences. Drawing on the dimension of certitude, hoop tests must be satisfied for a given explanation to hold. Thus, while failing a hoop test decisively rules out a given hypothesis from consideration, passing only suggests that the hypothesis is still a contender. Smoking-gun tests are uniquely confirmatory in affirming the validity of the hypothesis. In contrast to hoop tests, passing the smoking-gun test suffices to accept an explanation, yet failing to find 'smoking-gun' evidence does not disqualify it. Finally, the strongest test scores highly on both uniqueness and certitude and is thus 'doubly-decisive' in that passing confirms the hypothesis and failing disqualifies it (Van Evera 1997).

Another important step in the development of this methodology is George and Bennett's call to critically assess alternative hypotheses (2005, p. 207). Motivated by the observation that any one case exhibits many potential causal paths by which the phenomenon could have occurred, George and Bennett enjoin researchers to map out the alternatives prior to assessing evidence. This recommendation both crystalizes the inferential contribution of each test and guards against 'cherry-picking' evidence that favors one hypothesis without regarding the role of alternative explanations.

Following from the logic of considering alternative hypotheses and keeping with Van Evera's conceptual distinctions (uniqueness versus certitude), Bennett's (2010) and Collier's (2011) refinements of the four tests encourage researchers to engage in a two-step evaluation for each piece of evidence. First, they should classify each piece of evidence based on whether it constitutes a necessary condition for a hypothesis to be true, a sufficient condition to accept the hypothesis, both, or neither. Second, researchers should consider how that piece of evidence bears on alternative hypotheses. The four tests, definitions of passing and failing, their implications for rival hypotheses and their proposed gradations in the strength of inferences they yield are illustrated in Table 29.1.

Moving beyond a systemization of just the procedures of process tracing, scholars in recent years have made varied attempts to map the logic of process tracing onto what they view as more concrete epistemological and ontological foundations. The goal with the latest innovations is to justify that process tracing as an analytic tool is consonant with an underlying view about how the social world works. Thus, the next two advances represent divergent attempts to tease out and make explicit the intrinsic logic of process tracing in order to further systematize the method.

2.2   Mapping Process Tracing onto Set Theory

One cohort of scholars argues that the method of process tracing maps clearly onto set theory and the logic of necessary and sufficient conditions. It is important to note the crucial difference between the use of 'necessity' and 'sufficiency' in this sense versus the refinement of the tests in

Table 29.1   The four process-tracing tests

Sufficient to affirm causal inference		
Necessary to affirm causal inference	1. Straw-in-the-wind Passing: affirms relevance of hypothesis, but does not confirm it Failing: hypothesis is slightly weakened, though not eliminated Implications for rival hypotheses: Passing – slightly weakens them Failing – slightly strengthens them	3. Smoking gun Passing: confirms hypothesis Failing: hypothesis is somewhat weakened, though not eliminated Implications for rival hypotheses: Passing – substantially weakens them Failing – strengthens them
	2. Hoop Passing: affirms relevance of hypothesis, but does not confirm it Failing: eliminates hypothesis Implications for rival hypotheses: Passing – weakens them. Failing – strengthens them	4. Doubly-decisive Passing: confirms hypothesis and eliminates others Failing: eliminates hypothesis Implications for rival hypotheses: Passing – eliminates them Failing – substantially strengthens them

Source: Collier (2011), who adapts the table from Bennett (2010).

section 2.1. According to this new view, set theoretic logic occupies two distinct roles in qualitative research. In line with the first advancement outlined above, they claim that we can interpret evidence as being either necessary or sufficient to confirm (or undermine) a hypothesis. Goertz and Mahoney, for example, maintain that the major process tracing tests are 'predicated on ideas of necessity and sufficiency' (Goertz and Mahoney 2012, p. 13).

The second role, however, exists at a more fundamental level: scholars in this tradition argue that causality in the social world works in a deterministic manner consistent with the logic of necessity and sufficiency (Mahoney 2008), and in response they re-conceptualize process tracing to reflect this view. Causality itself is redefined in set-theoretic terms: Mahoney for instance defines a cause as 'a variable value that is necessary and or sufficient for an outcome' (2008, p. 417). Drawing on this conception, scholars then argue that the primary task of process tracing is 'to find necessary, sufficient, and jointly sufficient factors for an outcome' (Blatter and Haverland 2012, p. 24). This aspect of the set-theoretic view suggests that social phenomena necessarily operate in deterministic, set-theoretic terms and that using this language the describe outcomes is desirable because it reflects the true nature of social reality. For scholars in this tradition, process tracing may either be used as a stand-alone method or as one component of a multi-method research project to complement broader quantitative component. Schneider and Rohlfing (2013), for example, set out to demonstrate that the set-theoretic conception of process tracing works in conjunction with qualitative comparative analysis (QCA) as both a tool for in-depth case analysis as well as a tool for case selection.[2]

2.3   Mapping Process Tracing onto Bayesian Inference

Other scholars turn to Bayesian inference to explicate process tracing's underlying logic (Bennett 2009, 2014; Beach and Pedersen 2012; Bennett and Checkel 2014). On this path, scholars frame the goal of process tracing to specify how much inferential weight researchers can give to particular observations based on their prior knowledge. Beach and Pedersen, for example, argue that researchers should give increased weight to evidence that is a priori expected to be less probable (2012, p. 77). Here, I provide a brief overview of Bayesian analysis and outline the application of Bayesian logic to process tracing.

Bayesian inference is based on what scholars refer to as 'subjective probabilities'. In assessing the likelihood of an event based on subjective probabilities, scholars must condition their expectation on prior contextual knowledge. For instance, the probability that someone has a PhD is quite different from the probability that someone has a PhD given that she is attending American Political Science Association (APSA). Since process tracing is inherently concerned with how context factors into analysis of evidence, Bayesian logic dovetails well with process tracing's underlying goals.

In a standard mathematical application of Bayesian inference, the procedure requires the specification of a three additional pieces of information: first, the prior probability represents the uncertainty regarding a given event before any new evidence is taken into account. Second, the likelihood function represents the set of parameter values given the observed outcome. Finally, the posterior probability represents the updated (and ideally, reduced) uncertainty about an event after the researcher incorporates new evidence.

As an example, Bennett suggests, 'let us assume we have an explanation of a case that we think is 40 percent likely to be true . . . let us assign [the likelihood of finding a certain type of evidence given the truth of the theory] of 20 percent . . . let us assign [the probability of a false positive] a probability of 5 percent' (2014, p. 47). He then goes on to insert these probabilities into Bayes's theorem to calculate the updated probability

---

BOX 29.1   SUMMARY OF ADVANCEMENTS

Three Advancements in Process Tracing

1. Four tests: the four process-tracing tests gave scholars a way of sorting different pieces of evidence according to their inferential leverage and the extent to which they supported or undermined both the main and rival hypotheses.
2. Set-theory: this is the first of two innovations that attempt to explicate the underlying logic of process tracing. Scholars in this tradition redefine process tracing as a search for necessary and sufficient conditions for the outcome of interest.
3. Bayesian approach: the Bayesian approach is the second of two innovations intending to make explicit process tracing's underlying logic. Bayesian scholars emphasize the need to consider the inferential weight of evidence given the researcher's prior expectations about the outcome.

---

that the proposed theory is true conditional on finding the evidence, which according to his assigned probabilities results in a probability of 0.73 of the explanation being true, and conversely, a probability of 0.36 of the theory being false (both in light of the evidence found).

3   THE STATE OF THE STATE OF THE ART

Do the four tests, combined with these refinements, provide an exhaustive account of the possible inferences and implications we can draw from evidence? While the innovations outlined above were crucial steps in developing this methodology, the framework remains incomplete. This section evaluates each development in terms of its overall contribution to employing process tracing as a research tool.

3.1   Evaluating the Four Tests

The development and further refinement of the four tests was beneficial to process tracing as it helped crystallize the nature of inferences that researchers can draw from different pieces of evidence. The advancements regarding the tests, however, have three important drawbacks and one additional problem that reveals itself later on. First, at least two of the four cells are difficult to fill given the nature of evidence in social science phenomena. Both cells in the right-most column of the chart require finding a piece of evidence that is so specific (and trustworthy in its source) that it is sufficient to confirm a hypothesis. Take, for instance, Skocpol's

(1979) seminal work on social revolutions: what type of evidence would she have needed to find to guarantee that social revolutions are in fact causal products of class-based upheavals and political change? Also, to a greater extreme what sort of evidence would have simultaneously guaranteed her theory of social revolutions and simultaneously eliminated all other possible causes from consideration? The likelihood of finding even a single piece of evidence that can be uncontroversially filed in either cell is quite low.

The second problem with the four tests is that one of the two remaining tests sounds too tenuous for researchers to be expected to take it seriously. As a metaphor, 'straws in the wind' refer to fleeting observations that slightly hint at future events. Consequently, any piece of evidence that does not meet the stringent standards of either being necessary to keep a hypothesis in the running or sufficient to ensure the hypothesis is true must be relegated to this label. By this narrow definition, a great deal of valuable evidence in support (or contest) of a hypothesis is left unclassified or misclassified as weaker than it may be.

The third and most exigent shortcoming borne out of this framework is a fundamentally incomplete treatment of rival hypotheses. In its current state, this process-tracing framework is built on the assumption that evidence in support of one hypothesis necessarily undermines alternative hypotheses (Collier 2011). That is, alternative hypotheses are treated as though they are mutually exclusive. While it is important to consider explanations in addition to the main hypothesis of interest, it is all the more essential to consider relationships among the rivals. An unjustified assumption of mutual exclusivity could lead researchers to hastily rule out explanations that may work in conjunction with the primary assumption. This assumption not only hinders, but works against a purported goal of process tracing: to help analysts critically adjudicate among alternative hypotheses.

Finally, a survey of the recent literature on process tracing reveals considerably uncertainty about where it stands vis-à-vis the four process tracing tests. The four tests, originally conceived by Van Evera (1997) and further formalized by Bennett (2010) and Collier (2011) served briefly as the benchmark for characterizing how evidence contributed to our knowledge of both main and rival hypotheses. More recently, however, the utility of the four tests has come under fire.

Collier (2014), for example, now argues that the tests (or pieces of evidence) are best understood as a continuum of strength, rather than discrete cells. This change was motivated in part by recognizing not only that tests have more than two levels of strength (between straw-in-the-wind and smoking-gun tests), but also that the likelihood of finding a true smoking gun – that is, a piece of evidence that is so unique as to unequivo-cally confirm the truth of a hypothesis – is small enough to be considered nearly impossible. Collier evaluates the Bayesian approach to process tracing as a step that moves beyond the rigidity of the four tests and com-mends Bennett for helping to devise an approach in which the 'ideas of necessary and sufficient are superseded' (2014, p. 5).

3.1.1   The verdict

The four tests are a valuable innovation in the process tracing literature because they call upon researchers to think critically about how differ-ent pieces of evidence bear on their hypotheses. Yet, this method is not without its drawbacks. The original four-bucket categorization of the tests is too blunt and slightly misleading since most evidence in social science research (whether qualitative or quantitative) will fit only into the left-hand column (either as a straw-in-the-wind test or a hoop test). On the flip side, although getting rid of some of the distinctions between the tests might help avoid an overly rigid categorization of evidence, dropping all of them would be a mistake as well.

I argue that retaining the hoop test is vital to maintaining a standard of falsification in our research designs. The hoop test captures the fact that for a theory to be correct, some empirical conditions must be satisfied – whereas their absence would render the theory unlikely or impossible. Put simply, this test represents a search for necessary conditions for a given hypothesis to be true.[3] As such, researchers could approach their work by classifying evidence in terms of either the conditions it satisfies (for a given hypothesis) or otherwise the amount of leverage or additional certainty it contributes.

3.2   Evaluating the Set-Theoretic Approach

The set-theoretic innovation is important in that it attempts to explicate an underlying logic of process tracing. This approach, however, comes at two costs that compromise the integrity and unnecessarily limit the scope of the method.

The most severe problems stem from a mistaken and poorly justified (re)definition of process tracing. Scholars advancing a set-theoretic con-ception of process tracing take what was previously defined as evaluating pieces of evidence to examine their inferential weight with respect to a set of hypotheses, and alter it beyond recognition as 'a search for necessary and sufficient conditions for an outcome'. Those who argue that process tracing inherently maps onto the logic of set theory mistakenly char-acterize all scholars who employ this method as adopting set-theoretic ideas. Goertz and Mahoney (2013, p. 237) argue this most explicitly when they claim that all verbal theory is inherently set theoretic. Goertz and Mahoney (2012, p. 11) echo this claim, arguing that 'qualitative scholars quite naturally use the language of logic', which they treat as synonymous with set theory, in formulating their theories.

The first problem with this redefinition is that it rests on false premises. Not all verbal theory is inherently set-theoretic in nature, nor does it necessarily stem from a deterministic ontological perspective. Take, for instance, the democratic peace theory, which is widely considered to be the closest thing to 'an empirical law of international relations' (Levy 1988, p. 662). Still, however, this theory is defined as 'the tendency for democracies to not fight one another' (Bueno de Mesquita et al. 2003). If any theory warrants formulation in set-theoretic and deterministic terms, it should be the theory exhibiting 'law-like regularity' and yet, scholars still err on framing it as a probabilistic trend.

The second problem with the redefinition is that it unnecessarily narrows the scope of phenomena to which process tracing may be applied. While process tracing certainly may be used to search for hypothesized necessary and/or sufficient conditions, nothing about the technique precludes it from finding other relationships as well. As such, this definition may guide researchers to either ignore certain phenomena, or to turn to different methods when outcomes do not conform to the rigid confines of necessary and sufficient conditions. If, for instance, an explanatory variable is present in nine out of ten instances of a phenomenon, how is a researcher supposed to characterize that variable? Do we omit the variable because it fails to satisfy the strict principles of necessity and sufficiency? Do we omit the tenth case on the grounds that it is fundamentally different from the other nine? It is one thing for a researcher to devise a hypothesis about either a necessary or sufficient condition for an outcome and conduct process tracing to find further evidence for that condition; it is another thing entirely, however, to argue that the search for necessary and sufficient conditions is what process tracing is all about.

3.2.1   The verdict

The set-theoretic innovation stems from the valuable goal of promoting verbal and analytic precision in specifying both how our theories are constructed and how our evidence bears on those theories. Scholars ought to be aware of the language we use to describe phenomena and what that language implies about the relationships between variables. This contribution is potentially useful for those wishing to specify and test a set-theoretic relationship, but ultimately, it is not suitable for adoption on a wide scale because process tracing is well suited for exploring a wider range of relationships than this literature suggests.

3.3   Evaluating the Bayesian Approach

Bayesian logic has three potential contributions to process tracing to enhance its analytic rigor. Bennett (2009) correctly observes that Bayesian inference focuses on updating degrees of belief in the truth of alternative explanations, and this aspect of Bayesian logic demonstrates its utility for being integrated with process tracing in terms of how researchers are thinking about evidence. Second, these same principles of updating give researchers a rigorous and precise language for framing how actors update their own beliefs and behave in the cases we study. Finally, the use of Bayesian procedures encourages researchers to be explicit and transparent about the inferences they make.

However, the use of Bayesian mathematical procedures (that is, filling in probabilities based on how likely we think an explanation might be) raises an important question: if a substantive researcher were to heed this advice and assign prior, likelihood and posterior probabilities to different pieces of evidence in a qualitative research setting and then send that research to a Bayesian statistician for peer review, would – or should – the reviewer let recommend it for publication? Can we reasonably expect this recommendation to meet the standards of Bayesian inference? It is well documented in the social-psychological literature that humans (scholars included) are remarkably bad at guessing probabilities of events (Tversky and Kahneman 1974). Worse yet, the biases are neither systematic, nor are they in the same direction. Consequently, any method that relies on an armchair prediction of an outcome's probability is bound to produce flawed estimates.

3.3.1   The verdict
I argue that the logical principles governing Bayesian inference – the importance of conditioning on context and updating given new information – have great utility for specifying a rigorous process tracing procedure. However, adopting the mathematical procedures of Bayesian inference is not only unnecessary to derive the benefits, it is potentially distracting and misleading.

4   FUTURE DIRECTIONS

As a methodology, process tracing has come a long way since its inception and the quest to institute more rigorous standards and procedures is ongoing. In this section I highlight two areas that could benefit from additional formalization. First, the process tracing literature is in need of a more explicit discussion of causality and the types of causal inferences that the method makes possible. Second, as I mentioned in section 3.1, methods scholars and practitioners alike would benefit from a more in-depth specification of how the relationships among rival hypotheses affect the causal inferences we draw.

4.1   Process Tracing and the Potential Outcomes Framework

The primary task of process tracing is to make unit-level causal inferences (that is, how a given cause affects a single unit – a country, a social movement, an actor). Indeed, any method that claims to perform causal inference must 'ultimately be concerned with the effects of causes on specific units' (Holland 1986). This phrase, however, is absent from nearly all of the process-tracing literature. Such an omission is problematic if process tracing is to hold its post as the standard for qualitative causal inference.

To address this omission, some scholars have begun exploring the connections between process tracing and the potential outcomes framework. The potential outcomes framework is held up in statistics as the paramount model of causation.[4] In short, a given unit (whether an individual or a country or something else) is interpreted as having different potential outcomes based on whether the unit is assigned a treatment or not (that is, assigned to the control group). If, for instance, the outcome of interest were heart rate, and the cause of interest were coffee, I have two potential outcomes: (1) my heart rate if I am assigned regular coffee, and (2) my heart rate if someone snubs me and assigns me decaffeinated coffee.

The problem, of course, is that we can never observe both potential outcomes for a single unit (especially when the causal factor is something like revolutions or democratization) – this problem is referred to as the 'fundamental problem of causal inference'. Although the difficulties of unit-level causal inference have driven many directed innovations in the field of statistical research, comparably little has been done to directly address this problem in qualitative research.

Waldner (2014) argues that using directed causal graphs to better understand the role of causal mechanisms can help get traction on this problem in process tracing. Paine (2014) is working on extending Waldner's work by situating the 'hoop test' in the potential outcomes framework to help formalize the causal inferences one can draw from passing or failing. This research is still in a nascent stage, but it promises to contribute needed insight into process tracing's capacity for causal inference.

4.2 Relationships among Rival Hypotheses

Another area in need of further development concerns the treatment of rival hypotheses. So prized is the ability to systematically assess alternative explanations that many scholars have built 'adjudication among rival hypotheses' into the very definition of process tracing (Bennett 2010). As I noted above, however, all of the current frameworks suffer from a fundamentally incomplete treatment of rival hypotheses. Current frameworks only provide explicit guidance on dealing with mutually exclusive explanations. This treatment can lead researchers to hastily rule out alternatives given enough evidence in favor of their own theories, thereby compromising the completeness generalizability of the explanation proposed.

5 CONCLUSIONS AND FUTURE DIRECTIONS

Process tracing has proven itself to be a powerful tool for qualitative inquiry and causal inference. Developments in the literature have highlighted the need for further refinements of the technique; each one, however, suffers from critical problems that must be rectified prior to wide adoption. The classical formulation must retain at least the distinction of hoop tests for the sake of constructing research designs around a standard of falsifiability. Furthermore, this framework must acknowledge that evidence falling short of the smoking-gun benchmark may nonetheless have more inferential leverage than is deserving of the 'straw in the wind' label.

The set-theoretic formulation should reframe their advancement as a subset of process tracing. This qualification would prevent scholars in this camp from unnecessarily inhibiting the scope of process tracing. By acknowledging process tracing's capabilities beyond finding necessary and sufficient conditions for outcomes, this advancement could be seamlessly incorporated into the wider repertoire of tasks for which the technique is well suited.

The Bayesian formulation requires further refinement it its recommendations and internal consistency for its adoption to be justified and for research to be guided. I maintain that Bayesian logic dovetails with the goals of process tracing; as such, a refined combination of the two has some of the greatest potential for a comprehensive and rigorous qualitative research method.

Finally, to best accomplish its two central goals of process tracing – causal inference and adjudication among rival hypotheses – future advancements ought to rely on a more formal understanding of causality and a more complete specification of the relationships among alternative hypotheses Understanding how evidence bears on a full set of hypotheses is possible only when a researcher knows how hypotheses relate to one another and whether they are capable of existing together or working in conjunction. Thus, while the literature on process tracing has come a long way and has included numerous advancements that increase the level of analytic rigor, there is more work to be done.

NOTES

1. If one commits a crime, for example, he must have been in the state in which the crime took place. And although evidence of his being in the state does little to prove that he did commit the crime, evidence that he was not in the state when the crime was committed is sufficient to exonerate him.
2. See Chapter 25 in this volume for a more comprehensive reference on QCA.
3. This position should not be confused with a search for necessary conditions for an outcome, which is an ontological standpoint.
4. For background reading on the potential outcomes framework see Rubin (1974) and Holland (1986).

FURTHER READING

For Introductions to Process Tracing

Brady, H.E. and D. Collier (eds) (2010), *Rethinking Social Inquiry: Diverse Tools, Shared Standards*, 2nd edn, Lanham, MD: Rowman and Littlefield.
Collier, D. (2011), 'Understanding process tracing', *PS: Political Science and Politics*, **44** (4), 823–30.
Schultz, K.A. (2001), *Democracy and Coercive Diplomacy*, Cambridge: Cambridge University Press.
Van Evera, S. (1997), *Guide to Methods for Students of Political Science*, Ithaca, NY: Cornell University Press.

For Set-Theoretic Applications of Process Tracing

Blatter, J. and M. Haverland (2012), *Designing Case Studies: Explanatory Approaches in Small-N Research*, New York: Palgrave Macmillan.
Goertz, G. and J. Mahoney (2012), *A Tale of Two Cultures: Qualitative and Quantitative Research in the Social Sciences*, Princeton, NJ: Princeton University Press.
Schneider, C. and I. Rohlfing (2013), 'Combining QCA and process tracing in set-theoretic multi-method research', *Sociological Methods & Research*, **42** (4), 559–97.

For Bayesian Applications of Process Tracing

Beach, D. and R.B. Pedersen (2012), *Process-Tracing Methods: Foundations and Guidelines*, Ann Arbor, MI: University of Michigan Press.
Bennett, A. and J.T. Checkel (eds) (2014), *Process Tracing: From Metaphor to Analytic Tool*, Cambridge: Cambridge University Press.

REFERENCES

Beach, D. and R.B. Pedersen (2012), *Process-Tracing Methods: Foundations and Guidelines*, Ann Arbor, MI: University of Michigan Press.
Bennett, A. (2009), 'Process tracing: a Bayesian perspective', in J. Box-Stefensmeier, H. Brady and D. Collier (eds), *The Oxford Handbook of Political Methodology*, Oxford University Press, pp. 702–22.
Bennett, A. (2010), 'Process tracing and causal inference', in H.E. Brady and D. Collier (eds), *Rethinking Social Inquiry: Diverse Tools, Shared Standards*, 2nd edn, Lanham, MD: Rowman and Littlefield.
Bennett, A. (2014), 'Process tracing with Bayes: moving beyond the criteria of necessity and sufficiency', *Qualitative and Multimethod Research*, **12** (1), 46–51.
Bennett, A. and J.T. Checkel (eds) (2014), *Process Tracing: From Metaphor to Analytic Tool*, Cambridge: Cambridge University Press.
Blatter, J. and M. Haverland (2012), *Designing Case Studies: Explanatory Approaches in Small-N Research*, New York: Palgrave Macmillan.
Bueno de Mesquita, B., J. Morrow and A. Smith (2003), *The Logic of Political Survival*, Cambridge, MA: MIT Press.
Collier, D. (2011), 'Understanding process tracing', *PS: Political Science and Politics*, **44** (4), 823–30.
Collier, D. (2014), 'Problematic tools: introduction to symposium on set theory in social science', *Qualitative and Multimethod Research*, **12** (1), 2–8.
George, A.L. (1979), 'Case studies and theory development: the method of structured, focused comparison', in P.G. Lauren (ed.), *Diplomacy: New Approaches in History, Theory and Policy*, Cambridge, MA: Free Press, pp. 43–68.
George, A.L. and A. Bennett (2005), *Case Studies and Theory Development in the Social Sciences: BCSIA Studies in International Security*, Cambridge, MA: MIT Press.
George, A.L. and T.J. McKeown (1985), *Case Studies and Theory Development in the Social Sciences*, Cambridge, MA: MIT Press.
Goertz, G. and J. Mahoney (2012), *A Tale of Two Cultures: Qualitative and Quantitative Research in the Social Sciences*, Princeton, NJ: Princeton University Press.
Goertz, G. and J. Mahoney (2013), 'Methodological Rorschach tests contrasting interpretations in qualitative and quantitative research', *Comparative Political Studies*, **46** (2) 236–51.
Holland, P.W. (1986), 'Statistics and causal inference', *Journal of the American Statistical Association*, **81** (396), 945–60.
Levy, J.S. (1988), 'Domestic politics and war', *Journal of Interdisciplinary History*, **18** (4), 653–73.
Mahoney, J. (2008), 'Toward a unified theory of causality', *Comparative Political Studies*, **41** (4–5), 412–36.
Mahoney, J. (2011), 'The logic of process tracing tests in the social sciences', *Sociological Methods & Research*, **41** (4), 1–28.
Paine, J. (2014), 'Process tracing and potential outcomes: conducting hoop tests with "invariant causal process assumptions"', working paper, University of California, Berkeley, CA.
Rohlfing, I. (2014), 'Comparative hypothesis testing via process tracing', *Sociological Methods & Research*, **43** (4), 606–42.

Rubin, D.B. (1974), 'Estimating causal effects of treatments in randomized and nonrandomized studies', *Journal of Educational Psychology*, **66** (5), 688–701.

Schneider, C. and I. Rohlfing (2013), 'Combining QCA and process tracing in set-theoretic multi-method research', *Sociological Methods & Research*, **42** (4), 559–97.

Skocpol, T. (1979), *States and Social Revolutions: A Comparative Analysis of France, Russia and China*, Cambridge: Cambridge University Press.

Tversky, A. and D. Kahneman (1974), 'Judgment under uncertainty: heuristics and biases', *Science*, **185** (4157), 1124–31.

Van Evera, S. (1997), *Guide to Methods for Students of Political Science*, Ithaca, NY: Cornell University Press.

Waldner, D. (2014), 'Aspirin, Aeschylus, and the foundations of qualitative causal inference', working paper, University of Virginia, Charlottesville, VA.

PART V

EVALUATION AND RELEVANCE OF RESEARCH OUTPUT

30 Political science research and its political relevance
Ben Crum

1   INTRODUCTION

Political science and political practice have different purposes. Political practice is to serve the realization of certain collective goals by making political decisions and producing public policies. Political science is to provide well-validated knowledge about the operation of politics. These two purposes are not necessarily aligned. In fact, political practitioners may at times consider well-validated knowledge as an obstacle rather than an asset, for instance, when it highlights that certain important interests have been disregarded in the preparation of a policy proposal. In turn, on the side of political science it is not uncommon to reach insights that do not chime with our generally established political preferences; the people themselves may, for instance, be much less enthusiastic about the institutions of democracy than we would expect them to be. Nevertheless the purposes of political science and political practice also connect. Particularly in a democratic society, political practice can be expected to base itself on well-validated knowledge and to justify its decisions in the light of it. In turn, I maintain that good political science has to address politically relevant questions, be it by providing knowledge that is of policy relevance in the short run or by opening up perspectives for political action in the longer run.

This chapter aims to give the political scientist insight in the ways we can maintain an autonomous but productive relation with political practice. For that purpose, I outline three positions on how political science relates to political practice, each offering a different vision on the kinds of problems the political scientist can and should address, the way these problems are conceptualized, and the ways they can be researched. Ultimately, the differences between these positions hinge on their views on the relation between political value statements and observational statements.

The overview departs from the classical position expressed by Max Weber in his methodological writings (especially Weber 1904 [1991]). Weber's view on social science was certainly motivated by a sense of political engagement. At the same time, however, he drew a strict distinction between facts and values, in which science holds the authority over statements of facts while politics is ultimately responsible for choices between values. As a consequence of this distinction, the politically relevant contributions that social science can make are limited and circumscribed. This view remains very instructive of what contribution political science can make to political practice, and of the limitations of its potential contribution.

The second position builds upon Weber's position in that it does separate the domain of political values from that of scientific observations of fact, but it recognizes that observations are informed by theories and, thereby, by values. As a consequence, scientific observations do take place against a given value background, and it is essential for the scientist to own up to that background. For this, different strategies can be adopted, ranging from a (minimal) declaratory approach to a foundational approach in which the value position adopted is subject to some kind of rational, though non-empirical, justification.

While the former two are well-established positions, the third position I add as a kind of counterpoint. This position takes issue with the strict distinction between facts and values and indeed with the assignment of the social sciences to the exclusive domain of facts. I develop this position on the basis of Richard Rorty's pragmatist vision of the vocation of the scientist. In Rorty's view, scientific theories should not so much be assessed on their compliance to certain discipline-internal standards but rather on their ability to yield insights that offer new lines of possible action on which people may come to agree (Rorty 1991).

2   MAX WEBER AND THE EMPIRICAL CHARACTER OF THE SOCIAL SCIENCES

'We all know that our science . . ., which concerns the institutions and events of human culture, was first motivated by practical considerations', Max Weber (1904 [1991], p. 23) wrote as he assumed the co-editorship of the *Archiv für Sozialwissenschaft und Sozialpolitik*. However, having recognized the origins of social science in practical concerns, he immediately proceeded by playing down any too grand expectations: 'it can never be the task of an empirical science to provide binding norms and ideals from which directives for immediate practical action can be derived' (Weber 1904 [1991], p. 24).[1] Crucially, for Weber the choices of norms and ideals lay beyond the domain of science. Such choices should be left to the political process. In contrast, the task of the social sciences is an empirical one: to make sense of social action and institutions on the basis of observation and interpretation.

BOX 30.1 THE THREE POLITICAL CONTRIBUTIONS OF
SOCIAL SCIENCE IDENTIFIED BY MAX WEBER

- Instrumental: identify the most efficient means towards a given societal end.
- Sociological: explicate the social conditions under which specific values and ideas emerge.
- Logical: scrutinize the internal consistency and logic of political positions adopted.

The crucial distinction underlying Weber's conception of the social sciences is the distinction between empirical claims and normative claims, between the choice of ends or values (which are a matter of faith or ideology) and the choice of means once an end is given (which can be subject to scientific analysis). As he writes: 'An empirical science cannot tell anyone what he should do, only what he can do and – under certain circumstance – what he wishes to do' (Weber 1904 [1991], p. 27). Importantly, however, the latter, scientific, questions are not completely unrelated to the former, practical, one. For anyone considering what he or she *should* do, it may be very instructive to know what he or she *can* do and what he or she *wishes* to do. It is exactly in these ways that social science can be politically relevant.

Thus, Weber defends a socially informed social science that can contribute to political questions in some specific ways, but only in these specific ways. Specifically, he distinguishes three ways in which scientific analysis can directly be of value for normative decisions (Box 30.1). The distinction between these three tasks for social science – which I label the 'instrumental', 'sociological' and 'logical' task, respectively – remains useful and relevant as most contemporary social scientists can probably identify with one or the other.

The first way in which scientific analysis can contribute to political decisions is essentially instrumental in character. It relies on a recasting of the distinction between normative claims and empirical claims in terms of ends and means. The choice of social ends is obviously a political choice. However, once a social end has been determined, social science can step in to analyze whether, in light of the actual conditions at hand, the means are available to attain this end in the first place (Weber 1904 [1991], pp. 24–5). Furthermore, if that question is answered affirmatively, social science can help to determine the appropriate means as well as the potential costs that their employment is likely to have.

This is, of course, a very recognizable role of social science. Consider, for example, the widespread social desire to reduce road congestion. Social scientific studies can draw on available evidence to estimate the impacts and costs of measures like road pricing or the promotion of public transport use. Or, to think of a more specifically political example, if political parties are keen to marginalize an extremist competitor, a political scientist may help in estimating whether a strategy of cooperation or one of ostracizing is more likely to be effective and, indeed, how such strategies may reflect on the parties involved themselves (for example, Downs 2001; Art 2007).

If the first task that Weber discerns for the social sciences focuses on the question of what actors can do, the second task that he identifies is more sociological in character, as it is concerned with the clarification of what an actor wishes to do and why she does so (Weber 1904 [1991], p. 26). Essentially, this task can be equated with the sociology of knowledge and values, which is concerned with tracking the ideational and sociological conditions from which given political convictions originate. As Weber puts it, such analysis offers an actor knowledge of the meaning of what he wants: 'We can teach him to think in terms of the context and the meaning of the ends he desires, and among which he chooses' (Weber 1904 [1991], p. 26). That is, the social scientist can trace patterns in the evolution of political preferences by identifying how similar conditions give rise to similar ideas and by demonstrating how certain ideas have come to be logically and sociologically related to each other (Box 30.2).

While the first two tasks that Weber discerns for the social sciences contribute to understanding and reflexivity, the third is of a more directly

---

BOX 30.2   EXAMPLES OF THE 'SOCIOLOGICAL' CONTRIBUTION OF SOCIAL SCIENCE

Gabriel Almond and Sydney Verba's *The Civic Culture* (1963) draws on extensive surveys of attitudes and values to compose integrated characterizations of the political cultures in the United States, the United Kingdom, Italy, Germany and Mexico, and to map these in relation to three ideal types of political culture: 'parochial', 'subject', and 'participant'.

Robert Putnam's *Making Democracy Work: Civic Traditions in Modern Italy* (1993) establishes a close relation between the density of voluntary social relations and organizations and the level of political engagement in different Italian regions. He explains this relation by submitting that social engagement creates 'social capital' that is conducive to political participation.

Other examples of research that explicates the social conditions under which specific values and ideas emerge can be found in: the history of political thought; public opinion research (for example, Dalton 2013); work on the evolution of political ideologies (for example, Keman 2011); and on the ideas of political elites and parties (for example, Adams et al. 2004).

**BOX 30.3   EXAMPLES OF THE 'LOGICAL' CONTRIBUTION
OF SOCIAL SCIENCE**

- *Conceptual analysis* seeks to clarify the meaning and use of specific political concepts by way of definition, logical analysis and analytical differentiation. For instance: what is liberty, and what is it not? How does it relate
  to competing values, like equality? What different kinds of liberty can be
  distinguished? (For example, Miller 1991; Carter 1999).
- *Ideology critique* assesses a set of viewpoints of an actor both in light of its
  internal consistency as well as in light of the underlying interests that may
  account for why certain viewpoints are adopted rather than others. This train
  of work originates in Marx's (for example, Marx and Engels 1848 [1967]) critique of liberal ideology and is continued in many strands of contemporary
  critical theory (Thompson 1984).

---

critical character as it involves the review of the internal consistency and
compatibility of the ends chosen and their underlying value-orientations.
This is a logical task as it assesses normative positions adopted by social
actors on their internal consistency and seeks to increase their reflexivity
by identifying the presuppositions and consequences that are logically
implied by them. Weber is particularly concerned to identify the 'final
axioms' underlying value-positions, which should help the actors involved
to attain greater clarity of what they stand for (Weber 1904 [1991], p. 27).
Of the three tasks distinguished, this last one relies eventually less on
empirically observed regularities and more upon the rules of logic and the
principles of good reasoning (see Box 30.3).

To sum up, being the godfather of the social sciences that he is, Weber
systematically separated the domain of social science from that of political practice. He delineated the practical contributions that social science
can make to three kinds of tasks: instrumental, sociological and logical.
He recognized that its very assignment to these particular niches would
be a precondition for social science to become more specialized and to
progress. Yet, in the end he was also confident that, whatever trajectory
social science will follow, sooner or later its 'viewpoint and conceptual
apparatus' will be called back to its original vocation of contributing to
the solution of practical problems (Weber 1904 [1991], p. 101).

3   BRACKETING VALUES IN SOCIAL SCIENCE

Eventually, Weber's vision aspires to a social science that operates in a
safely enclosed world of facts which can be neatly delineated from the

political world of values. This position assumes that the values will not impact on the scientific practice itself or, at least, that such influence will only be discernable to the extent that the scientist deliberately chooses to do so, as in the case of the instrumental scientist who puts his or her work at the service of a given political end. Even if value-judgments obviously inform *what* scientists choose to study, it is a fundamental conviction of Weber that they do not and should not affect *how* scientists proceed and hence what results they attain (Weber 1904 [1991], p. 65). Crucially, in his view, scientific findings have an autonomous foundation that does not rely on specific values but on scientific method. It is method that ensures the 'objective' character of social science and that sets it apart from any subjective value judgments.

Method has become ever more important with the progressive institutionalization and specialization of the social sciences (cf. Easton et al. 1991). It serves as the currency between specializations as well as the bulwark against subjective, non-scientific value-judgments. Yet, as much as contemporary scientists may rely on it, the objectivity of scientific method is far from uncontested. A fundamental challenge to the objective status of scientific method has emerged from Thomas Kuhn's depiction of scientific progress being premised on the establishment of a 'paradigm' (Kuhn 1962, 1963). Typical examples of such paradigms in the natural sciences are the wave theory of light, Newtonian physics and quantum physics. A paradigm offers a conceptualization of the key entities that are to be studied and the basic logic according to which they behave. It also informs the kind of scientific questions that are asked as well as indicating the techniques that can properly be used to answer them (Kuhn 1963, p. 359). At the same time, every paradigm forecloses a range of findings that can only come to light once a different paradigm is embraced. This is so because by its very nature of being an intellectual construction, no paradigm can ever be comprehensive and final. Indeed, '[b]ecause no paradigm ever accounts for all the facts or solves all its problems, anomalies can always be found and theories falsified' (Stokes 1998, p. 33).

Applied to the social sciences, the understanding of the practice of science by way of paradigms fundamentally challenges the objectivity of scientific method on which Weber relied. If all scientific observations are premised on a point of view (a paradigm) that is inevitably incomplete and partial, then these observations become inherently contingent. Also, to the extent that these observations suit certain value-positions better than others, method is no longer a convincing means for the scientist to eradicate the influence of values on them. Once the inevitable presence of a value background is recognized, there are roughly three strategies that

---

BOX 30.4   THREE STRATEGIES FOR DEALING WITH THE
VALUE-BACKGROUND OF SOCIAL SCIENCE
RESEARCH

- Declaratory: explicate values as given and assume scientific research to be self-contained against that background.
- Conformatory: engage in empirical research while adopting, and subscribing to, generally accepted values.
- Justificatory: provide an autonomous rational justification for the value position adopted and engage in empirical social research on that basis.

---

can be distinguished for dealing with it, which I label the declaratory, the conformatory and the justificatory strategy (Box 30.4).

The *declaratory strategy* fits, in a way, very well with the instrumental role for the social sciences as identified by Weber. It involves little more than that the social scientist from the outset declares the central values that inform her work. Thus, an expert in logistics may declare that her model is exclusively geared towards reducing road congestion and that hence any environmental effects are not within the purview of her work. Such a declaration of values may be facilitated by an official research assignment that already specifies the aims that the research is to serve. However, the declaratory approach is also a widely maintained heuristic strategy as most social scientists will not contest that scientific models inevitably involve a reduction of the complexity of the world, which is managed by the adoption of presumptions that help to delineate and frame the research from the start. From this heuristic perspective it is not even necessary that the researcher herself fully subscribes to the value position that is assumed in the research. For the declaratory strategy, the test is not that the value position adopted is comprehensive or fully justified, but only the marginal demand that the values invoked can be considered worthwhile and reasonable. In fact, by declaring its values squarely from the start, this strategy essentially leaves the choice to the reader: if he or she does not consider the values posited relevant, then he or she is free, and indeed justified, to ignore the findings.

The reference to the acceptability of the values invoked already anticipates the second strategy, which I label the *conformatory strategy*. This approach does not merely declare the values from which it departs, but it essentially identifies with them on the assumption that they are widely shared and engrained in the basic value positions obtaining in society (or even humanity) at large. Typical examples of this kind of research are work that concerns the adoption of human rights (for example, Risse-Kappen

---

BOX 30.5   A CLASSIC EXAMPLE OF THE PITFALLS OF THE
CONFORMATORY STRATEGY

Graeme Duncan and Steven Lukes (1963) famously take post-war election
studies (which they rubric under the label 'the new democracy') to task, arguing:
'The theorists of the new democracy, however, are less concerned to make the
competitive "democratic system" more democratic in the traditional sense than to
justify it as an efficient and stable system, depending on compromise, "pluralism",
and a general background of apathy and political incompetence. . . . The confrontation of classic democratic ideals with actual "democratic systems" ("what we
call democracy") has no other result than the acceptance of the actual systems
and their assumed conditions as entirely desirable' (Duncan and Lukes 1963,
pp. 168–9).

---

et al. 1998) or the level and scope of democracy around the world (for
example, Huntington 1991). Human rights and democracy typically are
overarching values that are little contested.

The big risk of the conformatory strategy is that political research
becomes the handmaiden of prevalent political positions (see Box 30.5).
The only more critical role it may play under these conditions is essentially
a negative one (along the lines of Weber's 'logical' contribution) of dispel-
ling myths concerning, for instance, unfeasible or incompatible policy
ends. However, to the extent that its value base remains indebted to the
prevailing political order, social science lacks any basis to offer constructive alternatives. This is only possible once political scientific research is
pursued on a normative foundation of its own, which is (at least partly)
autonomous from the values prevailing in society. That is, such a foundation cannot be established empirically but will have to be derived from the
precepts of reason or political philosophy.

This is what the 'justificatory strategy' aspires to: to engage in empirical
social research on the basis of autonomously justified normative foundations. As it happens, however, in contemporary political science we witness
a tendency for empirical research and normative foundationalism to grow
apart. Still, the pre-eminent example of a contemporary social thinker
who indeed covers the whole range from deep normative foundations to
concrete and original empirical observations is Jürgen Habermas. While
probably most widely known as a normative philosopher, Habermas has
always also styled himself as an empirical scientist who addresses concrete
political questions, ranging from European integration to the rise of the
Internet and the social adoption of new biotechnologies. However, whatever empirical issue Habermas turns to, his viewpoint is always anchored
in his normative philosophy which ultimately relies on the normative

BOX 30.6   AN EXAMPLE OF THE JUSTIFICATORY
STRATEGY: TOWARDS A EUROPEAN PUBLIC
SPHERE (BASED ON HABERMAS 1995)

Normative premises: (1) a functioning democracy requires 'a political public sphere which enables citizens to take positions at the same time on the same topics of the same relevance' (p. 306); (2) 'institutions of acting supranationally must be formed' (p. 305) to overcome the 'gap between the nation state's increasingly limited maneuverability, and the imperative of modes of production worldwide' (p. 304).
Theoretical knowledge: national identities in modern Europe were formed 'as the flowing contexts of a circulatory process that is generated through the legal institutionalization of citizens' communication' (p. 306).
Empirical observations: 'the EU exercises a supreme authority previously claimed only by individual states' (p. 303); but 'a European-networked civil society, a European-wide public sphere and a common political culture are lacking' (p. 304).
Constitutive and critical recommendations: 'Given the political will, there is no *a priori* reason why [Europe cannot] create the politically necessary communicative context as soon as it is constitutionally *prepared* to do so' (p. 307, original emphasis).

validity of what he calls the 'discourse principle', which stipulates that the validity of every social norm is ultimately subject to the test of being rationally acceptable to all people who are affected by it (Habermas 1992, p. 138).

In Habermas's approach the justificatory strategy implies that any theory of social action should aspire to yield generalizable knowledge that can both be anchored in normative foundations and is empirically consequential (Habermas 1983 [1990], p. 39; cf. Box 30.6). Note, however, that empirical effectiveness is not to be taken as a straightforward confirmation or falsification of theoretical claims by empirical observations. Rather, it involves a more active, productive relationship in which theories have a practical impact on the way we perceive or evaluate the social world. Social science theories may for instance be constitutive in that they constitute new meanings that enable people to discuss about, and coordinate in, the world (Habermas 1983 [1990], p. 39). An example of this would be the notion of the separation of powers between an executive, a legislative and a adjudicative power, which has prominently re-entered political practice in the way political institutions are maintained. Alternatively, a social theory may be critically effective in that it may help to identify and evaluate observations that deviate from the categories and regularities posited by it. Such a mismatch between theory and observations may point at a fallacy in the theory. However, to the extent that the theory is anchored in normatively validated principles, it might also point to a normatively deficient social practice.

In short, if we recognize that political science takes place against a value-impregnated societal background, the three strategies sketched essentially involve different conceptions of the division of tasks between society and political science. The declaratory strategy departs from the assumption that scientific practice cannot accommodate all relevant considerations and that, indeed, it can only be fruitful if it abstracts from some of them; leaving it for society to judge whether the research produced is relevant or not. In contrast, the conformatory strategy actively seeks to depart from values that are also taken to be widely supported in society, and puts its research at their service. Finally, the justificatory strategy takes it upon itself to ensure that the values that inform the research process are themselves the object of an autonomous process of rational justification.

4   THE SOCIAL SCIENTIFIC IMAGINATION

The one thing that all strategies sketched so far share is that they put the identification of empirical regularities at the heart of the scientific enterprise. It is through the exploration of such regularities that political scientific research can be of political relevance. At the same time, it is this focus on empirical regularities that also conditions and delineates the practical contribution political scientists can aspire to make. Before moving to the conclusion, I want to briefly reflect upon this focus and question whether it indeed captures all political science can practically contribute and whether it is indeed the right perspective for political scientists to adopt.

Weber already underlined that social science explanation differs from that in the natural sciences as it can depart from a reconstruction of the motivations of the agents under study. Yet, in his approach this interpretive (or even imaginative) dimension remains largely subservient to science's ultimate aim of causal explanation. Still, there remains a powerful strand in social science that suggests that its contribution is not restricted to the identification of causal regularities but also involves a distinctive capacity to put social experiences in an original light and indeed to open prospects for change (cf. Wright Mills 1959).

Such a line of argument has most provocatively been pursued by Richard Rorty. Rorty, in a way, brings Paul Feyerabend's famous creed 'against method' (which Feyerabend primarily targeted at the natural sciences) to the social sciences. As a pragmatist philosopher, he uncompromisingly insists that knowledge ultimately requires human judgment, without any '"outside" touchstone' (Rorty 1987 [1991], p. 42); such judgment is not to be pre-empted by an insistence on some conception of scientific method or on externally given 'facts'.

From this anti-methodical view on the social sciences emerges a distinctive perspective on the practical relevance of the social sciences, which is fundamentally at odds with the predominant focus on regularities. Most strikingly, Rorty (1987 [1991], p. 40) posits that 'prediction and control may not be what we want from our sociologists and our literary critics'. On the contrary, the (over-)reliance on regularities (on which prediction and control are premised) may rather inhibit our ability to offer rational answers to practical problems. Rorty (1987 [1991], p. 43) nicely illustrates his point by arguing: 'Suppose that for the last three hundred years we had been using an explicit algorithm for determining how just a society was, and how good a physical theory was. Would we have developed either parliamentary democracy or relativity physics?' In other words, a conception of science that is focused on regularities seems misplaced if we aspire it to yield innovative and useful ideas. Hence, in Rorty's view, scientific practice needs to be redirected so that there will be 'less talk about rigor and more about originality' (Rorty 1987 [1991], p. 44). That is, he aspires to a conception of science in which the 'image of the great scientist would not be of somebody who got it right but of somebody who made it new' (Rorty 1987 [1991], p. 44).

Rorty's position runs the risk that it dispenses with any standards that can differentiate scientific practice from other forms of reasonable deliberation. However, even for political scientists that do not want to go that far, Rorty's argument still has the virtue that it puts the generation of new ideas at the heart of scientific practice. What he does, in effect, is to (re-)elevate the scientific task of hypotheses generation (or, in Popperian terms, 'conjectures') to at least an equal plane as the task of hypotheses review (or 'refutations'). This is in contrast to most methodological textbooks in the social sciences that tend to focus on the latter task and have little or nothing to say on the former, exactly because it does not lend itself to any easily instructable recipes. Ultimately, Rorty regards the domain of science as a community for the unrestricted generation and assessment of original ideas on no other basis but open debate, curiosity and unforced agreement. The relevance of science lies exactly in its presence besides all other spheres within modern society in which the operation of human reason is compromised by other forces (like power, economic gain and tradition) and for which it can serve as a kind of critical mirror and provide new ideas to which they may, or may not, be receptive.

5   CONCLUSION

As Weber reminded us, social science was initially motivated by practical considerations. At the same time, however, he underlined that social science is subject to specific methodological standards that are internal to science itself and independent from any societal value judgments. With the progressive institutionalization of, and specialization in, the social sciences, such science-internal standards have become ever more important. They also imply that science can only make certain, rather tangential, contributions to political choices, which can be represented as the instrumental, the sociological and the logical tasks that were discussed in section 1.

In turn, we have seen that it has become common within the social sciences to bracket normative questions, either by assuming, with Weber, that the domain of empirical observations can be wholly delineated from that of value statements or by adopting (what I have called) a declaratory or conformatory strategy. However, the strict separation of the scientific domain from that of values is challenged by Habermas and, more directly, by Rorty.

When it comes to the relation between political science research and the values by which society will assess its relevance, we probably best seek to chart a middle course between the 'unconscious' and the 'overconscious' researcher – to borrow a distinction once made by Giovanni Sartori (1970). An 'overconscious' attitude towards the specter of values that haunts political science may well be a drag on the realization of any findings and risks paralyzing the researcher. At the same time, if anything, this chapter has sought to make the point that political scientists cannot simply adopt an 'unconscious' attitude and bracket the question of values. One way or the other, society weighs in on the choices they make in framing their research problems and in picking their theories. Political science research inevitably takes place, and is received, in a context that is informed by values and practical problems. In that context, political scientists need to have a sense of the values that motivate and inform the research that they do; and they have to be ready to justify their choices in this, if not on philosophical or political then at least on heuristic grounds.

NOTE

1. See Runciman (1972) and Ringer (1997, esp. ch. 5) for more extensive discussions of Weber's views on the relation between the domain of science and the domain of values.

FURTHER READING

The openness and directness with which Max Weber (1904 [1991]) addresses the practical challenges for the social sciences has rarely been matched since. Still, the style and composition of his methodological writings is somewhat dated, and interested readers may thus prefer to access his ideas through a secondary source like Ringer (1997). Habermas (1990, 2012) and Rorty (1987 [1991]) are compact statements of their respective views on the practical aspirations of the social sciences. For a related and possibly more accessible view, see the excellent discussion in Hesse (1978). As a general introduction, Baert (2005) offers a wonderful overview of the main positions discussed in this chapter, against a slightly broader philosophical background. Ultimately, however, the best insight in how political science can attain political relevance is to be found by closely studying successful examples (such as some that have been mentioned in this chapter).

REFERENCES

Adams, J., M. Clark, L. Ezrow, and G. Glasgow (2004), 'Understanding change and stability in party ideologies: do parties respond to public opinion or to past election results?', *British Journal of Political Science*, **34** (4), 589–610.
Almond, G. and S. Verba (1963), *The Civic Culture*, Boston, MA: Little Brown.
Art, D. (2007), 'Reacting to the radical right: lessons from Germany and Austria', *Party Politics*, **13** (3), 331–49.
Baert, P. (2005), *Philosophy of the Social Sciences*, Cambridge: Polity Press.
Carter, I. (1999), *A Measure of Freedom*, Oxford: Oxford University Press.
Dalton, R. (2013), *Citizen politics: Public Opinion and Political Parties in Advanced Industrial Democracies*, 6th edn, Washington, DC: CQ Press.
Downs, W. (2001), 'Pariahs in their midst: Belgian and Norwegian parties react to extremist threats', *West European Politics*, **24** (3), 23–42.
Duncan, G. and S. Lukes (1963), 'The new democracy', *Political Studies*, **11** (2), 156–77.
Easton, D., J. Gunnell and L. Graziano (1991), *The Development of Political Science*, London: Routledge.
Habermas, J. (1983), 'Reconstruction and interpretation in the social sciences', reprinted in J. Habermas (1990), *Moral Consciousness and Communicative Action*, Cambridge, MA: MIT Press, pp. 21–42.
Habermas, J. (1992), *Faktizität und Geltung (Between Facts and Norms)*, Frankfurt am Main: Suhrkamp.
Habermas, J. (1995), 'Remarks on Dieter Grimm's "Does Europe need a constitution?"', *European Law Journal*, **1** (3), 303–7.
Habermas, J. (2012), *The Crisis of the European Union: A Response*, Cambridge: Polity Press.
Hesse, M. (1978), 'Theory and value in the social sciences', in C. Hookway and P. Pettit (eds), *Action and Interpretation: Studies in the Philosophy of the Social Science*, Cambridge: Cambridge University Press, pp. 1–17.
Huntington, S. (1991), *The Third Wave: Democratization in the Late Twentieth Century*, Norman, OK: University of Oklahoma Press.

Keman, H. (2011), 'Third ways and social democracy: the right way to go?', *British Journal of Political Science*, **41** (3), 671–80.
Kuhn, T. (1962), *The Structure of Scientific Revolutions*, Chicago, IL: University of Chicago Press.
Kuhn, T. (1963), 'The function of dogma in scientific research', in A. Crombie (ed.), *Scientific Change*, London: Heinemann, pp. 347–69.
Marx, K. and F. Engels (1848), *The Communist Manifesto*, reprinted 1967, London: Penguin.
Miller, D. (ed.) (1991), *Liberty*, Oxford: Oxford University Press.
Putnam, R. (1993), *Making Democracy Work: Civic Traditions in Modern Italy*, Princeton, NJ: Princeton University Press.
Ringer, F. (1997), *Max Weber's Methodology: The Unification of the Cultural and Social Sciences*, Cambridge, MA: Harvard University Press.
Risse-Kappen, T., S. Ropp and K. Sikkink (1998), *The Power of Human Rights: International Norms and Domestic Change*, Cambridge: Cambridge University Press.
Rorty, R. (1987), 'Science as solidarity', reprinted in R. Rorty (1991), *Objectivity, Relativism, and Truth*, Cambridge: Cambridge University Press.
Rorty, R. (1991), *Objectivity, Relativism, and Truth*, Cambridge: Cambridge University Press.
Runciman, W.G. (1972), *A Critique of Max Weber's Philosophy of Social Science*, Cambridge: Cambridge University Press.
Sartori, G. (1970), 'Concept misformation in comparative politics', *American Political Science Review*, **64** (4), 1033–53.
Stokes, G. (1998), *Popper: Philosophy, Politics and Scientific Method*, New York: Wiley & Sons.
Thompson, J.B. (1984), *Studies in the Theory of Ideology*, Cambridge: Polity Press.
Weber, M. (1904), 'Die "Objektivität" sozialwissenschaftlicher und sozialpolitscher Erkenntnis' ('The "objectivity" of knowledge in social science and social policy'), in M. Weber (1991), *Schriften zur Wissenschaftslehre*, Stuttgart: Reclam, pp. 21–101.
Wright Mills, C. (1959), *The Sociological Imagination*, New York: Grove Press.

31 What's methodology got to do with it? Public policy evaluations, observational analysis and RCTs
Edward C. Page

1 INTRODUCTION

Are methodological choices critical to the success of an evaluation study? For policy evaluation research, the kind of research that governments and international organizations commission to find out whether policies or other interventions are working, we might expect methodology to play a more important role than for conventional academic research. If the questions evaluation research explores are relatively simple, empirical rather than theoretical issues – above all whether the program works or not, what is going wrong and how might it be fixed if not – and if governments make decisions committing huge public resources based on these evaluations, we might expect those who sponsor and conduct such research to be especially concerned with its scientific credibility as established through the empirical research techniques it uses (Box 31.1). This appears to be the reasoning behind those who advocate policy evaluation research adopting the 'gold standard' of randomized controlled trials (RCTs), which are especially popular among politicians and government officials since they are deemed to be 'the best way of testing whether a policy is working' (Cabinet Office 2012).

However, the activity of evaluating policies is rarely simply a matter of developing and applying a convincing methodology to guide policy by showing government what works and what does not. This chapter looks at the role of methodology in evaluations from the perspective of whether there is any evidence that policy-makers are more likely to pay attention to, or act upon, studies that are deemed to be methodologically superior, whether by virtue of being more sophisticated, rigorous or appropriate. The concern of this chapter is not with establishing the merits and demerits of different methodologies in evaluation studies, but rather with assessing the role of methodology in explaining the impact or lack of impact of any evaluation studies. In practical terms it seeks to answer the question: if a researcher makes additional efforts to increase the integrity or sophistication of the research methodology used to perform

---

BOX 31.1   COMMON BASIC DESIGNS USED TO EVALUATE POLICY

- Randomized controlled trials (also known as 'social experiments') in which participants are randomly assigned to groups; some to a 'control group' not exposed to the policy intervention and the rest to at least one other 'experimental group' that is. The effect of the policy can in principle be assessed by comparing the control and experimental groups. These have become especially important since the 1990s and are often claimed to be the 'gold standard' of evaluation design (for example, on the impact of different approaches to workfare on employment outcomes of those seeking work).

- Before-and-after studies that seek to derive an understanding of the effects of a policy by assuming that they are reflected in changes over the *status quo ante*. A simple and effective design that can help assess the impact of a significant event or intervention (for example, looking at changes in the re-use of shopping bags following a law mandating charges for single-use bags).

- Area-based comparisons that introduce an intervention in some locations but not in others and assess the impact of the intervention by comparing the outcomes in the different places. Where systematically conducted these may approximate randomized controlled trials. Often also used to 'pilot' programs to see if interventions have any effect at all or whether there are problems in implementing them (for example, proposed changes in unemployment benefit administration are tested in specific locations first).

- Ethnographic studies that trace through impacts of policies by close observation of how those receiving and/or delivering the service behave. Useful among other things for exploring the reactions of poorly understood groups and unanticipated consequences (for example, evaluating the impact of needle exchange programs on the behavior of injecting addicts).

- Case studies that seek to trace through the impact of an intervention by following through a selection of cases (for example, an evaluation of the value of evaluation studies based on tracing through the impact of a sample of such studies on policy).

- Reputational studies that base their assessments of an intervention or policy on the perceptions of those receiving or delivering them. Not invariably to be dismissed as 'anecdotal' (for example, where the policy seeks to change perceptions, such as in evaluations of programs about the treatment of victims of crime).

---

an evaluation, will the effort pay off in terms of increased influence for that research?

This chapter first considers what a successful policy evaluation might look like and then goes on to consider the contribution that the level of methodological sophistication might make to that success. The generally small role that methodology plays as presented in these first parts of this chapter contrasts with the big role claimed by those advocating the adoption of RCTs. The fact that RCT methodology has been influential has more to do with its reputation for accuracy rather than any superiority of results that it produces. In the conclusion I go on to look at the problems of setting out a 'gold standard' of evidence-gathering for public policy evaluations and offer an account of the importance of methodology that reflects the wider constraints involved in evaluating public policy.

2 SUCCESS AND THE UPTAKE OF POLICY RESEARCH

The common, if no longer entirely conventional, understanding of the success of policy evaluation research, here understood to be research commissioned by organizations with some view to shaping such policies (including terminating them), is related to its impact on policy-makers and policy. In principle we can look at the impact of methodology in two stages: first by examining whether policy-makers pay much attention to the research (uptake) and second by assessing whether this research actually improves the quality of policy or policy-making. As will be seen, in practice the character of the first stage makes it difficult to assess the role of methodology in the second.

Policy uptake comes in three broad forms. First, a 'linear' uptake where a specific piece of research has a discernable impact on a directly or indirectly related policy. This kind of uptake is extremely rare. While it is very hard to prove a negative, one can say that the most determined efforts to find evidence of specific pieces of evaluation research shaping directly the development of policy have long drawn a blank, irrespective of where and when they are sought. From the social research surrounding Great Society programs in the US in the 1960s (Aaron 1978) to British local government 'best value' and 'evidence based' initiatives around the turn of the twenty-first century and UK national government in the early twenty-first century (Sowden and Raine 2008; Monaghan 2012) significant traces of a direct role of research in policy-making have remained elusive. The literature on research utilization contains many convincing accounts of why research does not appear to be taken up by policy-makers in this linear way (see Beyer and Trice 1982 for a meta-analysis), including those based on differences in timescales (Jowell 2003, pp.9–10), professional environments (Martin et al. 2011) and modes of argumentation between the worlds of science and politics (Ritter 2009) and on institutional constraints on policy-making, such that this lack of direct or 'instrumental' influence can be described as overdetermined.

Many scholars seeking to assess the impact of social scientific policy evaluations on policy tend instead to emphasize a second, less direct, uptake route: research can add to cumulative knowledge and understanding about the characteristics of policy interventions and can at some unspecified time be brought into the policy-making process (Weiss 1995; for a review see Weible 2008). Research evidence does not have a direct 'instrumental' use but can have less direct 'conceptual' and 'symbolic' uses in policy-making (see Davies 2012). Carol Weiss's (1977, pp. 534–5) definition of research as having an 'enlightenment' function is, consequently, a widely accepted account of how social research affects debates about policy. It results from the 'diffuse, undirected seepage of social research into the policy sphere' which 'can gradually change the whole focus of debate' over a range of policy issues including education, housing, child abuse and legislative reapportionment (also Weiss 1995).

A third uptake route, a political route, can be identified if we consider that some evaluations are commissioned for reasons that have less to do with providing an evidential basis for policy-making than with politics. It is impossible to prove the *mens rea* issue of the intention behind commissioning evaluations, but we can point to evaluations that have served a range of political purposes including:

- *Endorsing the wisdom and foresight of the politicians who claim responsibility for a particular policy.* An evaluation of the 'Troubled Families' (Casey 2012) program, a form of 'payment by results' scheme for local councils making an impact on families with multiple social problems, was claimed as an example of 'this government' turning 'around the lives of thousands of troubled families'.
- *Advertising policies deemed to be successful.* An initiative to create 'Sarah's Law', with the aim of informing parents when convicted sex offenders have access to their children, was announced several times; including when a pilot was initiated, when it was extended several times over and when it reported that it had 'already protected more than 60 children from abuse during its pilot' (discussed in Goldacre 2010).
- *Showing that politicians are prudent people who pay attention to evidence.* The British Home Secretary sought to use the small matter of poor results from an evaluation to explain why she discontinued a widely ridiculed scheme to encourage illegal immigrants to 'go home' by a campaign which included sending vans decked out with the 'Go Home' message to advertise the scheme ('"Go home" billboard vans not a success, says Theresa May' in the *Guardian*, 22 October 2013).
- *Proselytizing.* Research has played a significant role in helping

persuade international organizations as well as other countries that a particular policy model should be adopted. Thus research evaluations helped make the case for international organizations supporting schemes such as the directly observed treatment shortcourse (DOTS) tuberculosis treatment program and conditional cash transfer (CCT) programs (see below).

Thus we have at least three broad mechanisms by which policy evaluations can be taken up, by: (1) directly shaping the policy which it is evaluating (or a policy that is closely related to it); (2) adding to the evidence illuminating how policies work and (3) having an effect on public perceptions of policy-makers or the policies they produce, an effect termed here 'political'. How important are methodological choices likely to be in each form of uptake?

3 DOES METHODOLOGY SHAPE UPTAKE?

What all three forms – linear, enlightenment and political – might appear to have in common is that they all rely on a significant degree of scientific credibility. This credibility might be bestowed on research by the application of conventional academic scientific rigor in developing and applying the methodology of the study. For the linear and enlightenment effects we have to have confidence that the results of the research are internally and externally valid to place any faith in them as a basis for discussing existing or proposed public policy measures. Moreover, using research for political cover or support will be less attractive if the methodology used to produce it is obviously full of holes.

The effect of methodology on linear impacts is hard to assess because of the sparsity of cases where such an impact is detectable. Education research has been one area that has generated sufficient studies for meta-analysis of research impacts. One meta-analysis (Cousins and Leithwood 1986, p. 346), which included impacts on instructors as well as policy-makers, noted that most of the empirical analyses took potential for impact, rather than actual impact, as a dependent variable, and moreover pointed out that 'increased methodological sophistication' appeared as likely to inhibit as increase the uptake of research.

We can point to an example of claimed linear impact where the UK government stated that it 'listened carefully' to, and acted on, the findings from the national evaluation of Sure Start, a program with diverse components aimed at improving child welfare and education (DCSF 2008, p. 2). Did methodology play a role in determining which parts of the research were taken up? It is impossible to say as the document supposed to put such research-based recommendations into effect is vague on the question of what particular research findings were listened to. The 'Sure Start' guidance (DfE 2006, p. 14) only mentions in general terms obvious points such as 'Research has shown that many parents are unaware of the services on offer. It is important that centers make every effort to . . . publicize the range of help they can give parents' (for a discussion of the limited impact of the Sure Start evaluation program, see Lloyd and Harrington 2012). Moreover, it is not clear which of the recommendations to remedy such shortcomings are backed by research and which are not, and nowhere is the empirical support for the recommendations discussed. Finding evidence of the linear uptake of policy research is hard enough; finding evidence that the uptake was at all affected by the methodological choices made in producing the research is harder still.

Moving on to the political uses of evaluations, we would not expect the influence of the methodological approaches used to produce the evidence on uptake to be strong, at least not above a basic level of credibility. Roberts et al. (2012) base their conclusion, 'sound methods ≠ useable findings', on interviews with ten policy advisors from six countries with experience of handling evaluation evidence in dealing with politicians. One advisor argued 'by and large, methodology is a weak influence in the sense that policy-makers don't really tend to weigh up research evidence in terms of the strength of the source, it's much more the signal that they're interested in' and suggested that policy-makers 'tended to prefer very small scale studies, pilots, rather informal evaluation evidence where it supports what they're interested in doing, and [they are] quite resistant to the much stronger evidence where it doesn't support what they think'. Greenhalgh and Russell (2006, pp. 36–7) endorse this view by suggesting that 'social drama, personal testimony ("anecdotal evidence") is a uniquely authentic and powerful force' that can overrule hard statistical evidence.

Even in proselytizing public policies cross-nationally, the quality of the research underpinning an intervention seems at best indirectly related to its uptake. For example, Walt shows how the research of Styblo, a Czech physician, in the 1970s, was crucial in developing a form of treating tuberculosis and other diseases – the directly observed treatment shortcourse (DOTS). But this research, important as it was in the community of technical healthcare specialists, did not reach the attention of World Health Organization policy-makers for nearly two decades. The research was only taken up after a policy entrepreneur (an economist with experience and contacts in international health organizations) managed to package and sell it as a 'broader, generalizable policy' (Walt et al. 2004, p. 199). Moreover, the research on DOTS was taken as a guide to international policy action only after changes in the political environment, when 'political elites in industrialized nations became fearful that the disease would penetrate the ranks of their own middle classes, spurring the creation of a transnational coalition to fight the disease globally' (Shiffman et al. 2002, p. 231). Methodology did play a significant part in this process, yet the policy environment played a far greater role.

Only in the illumination effect might we easily argue that the quality of the methodology matters, and this only by default. If the illumination effect is achieved in part by a piece of research standing the test of time – being remembered and used in subsequent deliberations about desired policy options – then it is at least a plausible hypothesis that scientific rigor will be related to the staying power of a piece of research. However, since there is no existing evidence to help us assess accurately how social research persists and shapes subsequent policy thinking or policy research, it must remain just a plausible hypothesis.

There is therefore overall little evidence to suggest that methodological choices affect the uptake of evaluation research. The notion that in linear models of impact (that is, where a specific evaluation can be used to develop, modify or end a particular program) uptake can be affected by methodological choices falls down in large part because evaluation research at best only rarely has such a direct impact. With more diffuse forms of uptake falling under the enlightenment model, the notion that methodological rigor will make the light from a good piece of research shine stronger and longer than that emanating from less impressive methodologies remains a plausible hypothesis, but a hypothesis which carries little more weight than wishful thinking. In both linear and enlightenment forms of uptake it is hard to establish whether research produces better policy, let alone whether some methodologies produce better research which produces better policy, so we cannot really establish the effect of methodology of research on the quality of policy it helps produce. If we consider that evaluation research might have some form of political uptake, methodological rigor is one characteristic that can help establish its general credibility, but its political use is more likely to be shaped by a range of other features including the support its findings give to the politicians and others who seek to use it.

4   IMPROVING UPTAKE: THE PROMISE OF RCTS

Given the generally low record of direct uptake of policy research findings, it is hardly surprising that many observers and policy-makers have questioned whether there might be a better way of linking research to policy.

It has become a widely shared view that better methodologies in evaluation research, specifically the use of RCTs, would lead to better outcomes by providing harder and more accurate assessments of how well or badly a policy is working that policy-makers would find harder to ignore. The basic idea of the randomized controlled trial is that we evaluate the impact of a policy intervention on the basis of comparing at least two groups to which those who are eligible to receive that intervention are randomly assigned. One group, the control group, does not receive the intervention, the other experimental group does. By comparing the outcomes for the control and experimental groups we can be confident of the precise impact of the intervention. This methodology is a conventional method of testing the efficacy of drugs and medical procedures. While the RCT has been used in social interventions for a long time (see Oakley 1998), it has become increasingly important as a method of evaluating government policies since the 1990s (Basu 2013; Cabinet Office 2012).

The literature challenging the 'gold standard' status of the method is now large and growing. Common criticisms include the expense of RCTs, difficulties in recruiting and maintaining reasonably sized samples, the ease with which treatment and control groups can become contaminated, the problems of external validity and the general criticism that methodologies must be designed to fit research problems rather than specified independently of them (for a discussion of problems of RCTs in a medical context, see Kaplan et al. 2011). Moreover evidence from medical trials suggests that observational studies do not necessarily produce results that differ from RCTs (see, for example, Benson and Hartz 2000). However, the concern in this chapter is not with the methodological questions themselves but whether the method can buck the apparent trend of evaluation research not to be taken up. While there may be reasons for thinking that RCTs produce results that are harder to ignore and thus more likely to be taken up by policy-makers, is there much evidence that this is the case?

The best evidence that this is the case comes largely through the proselytizing mechanism of uptake. In the discussion above on the spread of the DOTS tuberculosis program it was an RCT (on treating sexually transmitted diseases in Tanzania) which helped foster international interest in the scheme, even though it had earlier been highlighted through other forms of evaluation. The popularity of RCTs among policy-makers seems to have added weight to the findings of other studies (though subsequent RCTs of the scheme have been less encouraging about its efficacy, see Tian et al., 2014). Another social intervention in which RCTs played an enormous part in proselytizing was the development of conditional cash transfers (CCTs). Originally popularized through implementation of the PROGRESA program in Mexico, the scheme linked welfare payments to conditions such as parents enrolling children in school. An RCT evaluation conducted by the International Food Policy Research Institute was especially influential in securing support from international organizations, especially the World Bank, in encouraging CCT schemes in other countries (see Handa and Davis 2006). In the international policy environment the methodological approach used by evaluation research can be important in selling an intervention.

At the domestic level, however, the promise of a linear uptake of RCT evaluations appears not to be fulfilled. It is hard to find examples of RCTs that have had direct impacts on policy. One of the biggest and most elaborate RCTs in recent UK experience was the 'Employment Retention and Advancement' pilot scheme evaluated over a seven-year period (see Greenberg and Morris 2005). It has produced significant volumes of government reports, working papers and published research on the substance of the program, on issues relating to active labor market policy and on methodological issues in RCT evaluation. Yet a sympathetic appraisal of the impact of the evaluation on policy concluded that it had no 'immediate or direct effect on welfare-to-work policies' but rather had 'other effects in terms of informing and enlightening policy-making on welfare-to-work issues (i.e. a conceptual use of evidence)' (Davies 2012, p. R45). This finding, that well-constructed RCTs on key policy issues do not affect directly policy development, is also echoed in work conducted on welfare-to-work policies in the US (Greenberg et al. 2000).

In part this lack of uptake might be because of the general tendency for RCTs to be more likely to show small or no effects for policy interventions, especially when one looks for effects that last further beyond the immediate experience of the policy or program. This tendency, noted in a range of studies of social experiments might be a result of Rossi's (1987, p. 4) 'stainless steel law' of evaluation in general, that the 'better designed the impact assessment of a social program, the more likely is the resulting estimate of net impact to be zero', or it might be a result specifically of the limitations of the RCT method. Either way it suggests that the prospects for uptake of RCTs might just as easily be lower than those of other forms of research evaluation as higher. This cannot, however, rule out uptake through negative mechanisms which are hard if not impossible to detect; such as when policy-makers discard plans for a policy on reading an unfavorable evaluation.

Do we have any reason to think that policy based on RCTs is superior to policy based on observational studies? As uptake by policy-makers in both is limited we do not have sufficient clear examples of either to be able to make a comparison. Perhaps the biggest intervention that has been supported by RCTs is the CCT 'cash transfer' scheme, in which the

PROGRESA evaluation in Mexico discussed above played a large role, and which has become one of the most widespread development interventions of the past 20 years. Subsequent analyses of cash transfer schemes have certainly tended to find that their impact on a range of outcomes, above all in education, have been positive. That cash transfer schemes have an impact on the poor appears beyond doubt. How far can it be considered that it was the evaluation of the PROGRESA scheme that generated good policy is, however, not so clear.

While the known defects of the PROGRESA evaluation are not of such a scale as to undermine its results, one can question how far it conformed to an RCT model. Faulkner (2014) describes how much of the implementation of the research was 'murky'. Many – the evaluators, the Mexican government and international organizations among others – had a political stake in establishing the story that this was an effective RCT. In the event it was at best quasi-experimental, with evidence of non-random attrition rates as well as contamination across groups, the precise extent of which remains unknown. These problems aside, we can question what lessons policy-makers outside Mexico took away from the study as what has been borrowed is not a single policy, but a range of cash transfer schemes, some conditional and some not, and where the conditions vary enormously. This looks less like the direct learning from a policy intervention through its RCT evaluation than the borrowing of a 'label' or at best a broad idea of providing cash to very poor people, but for rather different purposes and implemented in a variety of significantly different ways and targeting different groups (see Sandberg 2015). This might be interpreted as policy-makers themselves compensating for the often cited problem of RCTs; their lower levels of external validity. RCTs are open to the charge that their findings only apply under conditions identical to those where the study was conducted, not elsewhere. With different CCT schemes policy-makers in different countries may seek to avoid external validity problems by devising their version of the policy based on the social, economic and political conditions prevailing in their jurisdictions (see Pritchett and Sandefur 2013). We will never know how CCT schemes replicating exactly the Mexican model directly in different contexts might have worked, assuming such replication were even possible. Yet we can say that it is at least likely that the policies' success in other jurisdictions is due to the non-RCT adaptation of the basic idea. The study helped spread what appeared and still appears to be a good idea, it did not itself provide much by way of guidance as to how it should be structured. We would need more than this to argue that the methodology itself produces good policy.

5 METHODOLOGY AND EVALUATION

As Lindblom and Cohen (1979) argue, if we regard policy-making as a problem-solving activity, the role for professional social science based on the application of empirical techniques of social inquiry is likely to remain limited. Problem-solving is generally based on 'ordinary knowledge'; basic understandings, ideas and beliefs about how the world works derived from 'common sense, casual empiricism or thoughtful speculation and analysis. It is highly fallible, but we shall call it knowledge even if it is false' (Lindblom and Cohen 1979, p. 12). Not only this, but professional social inquiry, of the kind covered by empirical evaluation studies using social science techniques, is only applied through the medium of such ordinary knowledge; ordinary knowledge helps define when professional social research is called for and how it is interpreted and used. It is illusory to see the role of social science in policy problem-solving as largely shaped by the sophistication of the methodology it uses, and there is no evidence supporting the proposition that better methodology, whether it be RCT or any other, produces better policy. In Lindblom and Cohen's terms, such propositions would reflect the quest to establish the 'independent authoritativeness' of social research as a guide to problem-solving. Social research might be, and often is, dependently authoritative because it supports or endorses ordinary knowledge. Emphasizing the methodological sophistication of social science contributions to problem-solving is seeking to give it a status and authority in the process that is independent of its relation to ordinary knowledge. All that we know about the utilization of research in policy-making tends to underline Lindblom and Cohen's conclusion that this is a vain quest.

The contribution of social science research to policy-making does not have to be limited to the quest for authoritativeness through methodological sophistication. As Lindblom and Cohen (1979) go on to argue, there is a range of other contributions that professional social inquiry can make to policy-oriented problem-solving. These include conceptualizing issues and shaping the intellectual frameworks of policy-makers, providing evidence and argument, documenting what has been done in the past and with what result and challenging and changing ordinary knowledge. Insisting that social science's contribution should be largely a matter of applying only methodologies deemed to be of a higher order to weigh up whether a particular social intervention works or not is problematic; in part because it hankers after an effect social science can never have and in part because it closes off the other possibilities for social science to make a contribution to problem-solving.

None of this means that methodology is irrelevant in policy evaluation.

By seeking to conform to high standards of professional social inquiry, through adopting appropriate empirical research methods that can be justified and accepted by others in the same or related fields, social scientists do two things. First, they establish their credibility as people with something to say that could be worth listening to about policy issues. Second, they help establish their *locus standi* in the policy process. Their advocacy of different courses of action can be shaped, at least in part, by what they interpret to be the conclusions of their research. Some social scientists may not need this *locus standi*: they may be advocates or zealots for particular policies, programs or approaches. For others their conviction that scientifically valid conclusions deserve to be respected and the policy implications they draw from them be acted upon, might make them advocates. However, even the greatest of methodologies will not guarantee that anyone will listen to them, and neither should it.

REFERENCES

Aaron, H.J. (1978), *Politics and the Professors: The Great Society in Perspective*, Washington, DC: Brookings Institution.

Basu, K. (2013), 'The method of randomization and the role of reasoned intuition', World Bank Policy Research, Working Paper No. 6722, December, accessed 16 February 2016 at http://www-wds.worldbank.org/external/default/WDSContentServer/WDSP/IB/2013/1 2/12/000158349_20131212090918/Rendered/PDF/WPS6722.pdf.

Benson, K. and A.J. Hartz (2000), 'A comparison of observational studies and randomized, controlled trials', *New England Journal of Medicine*, **342** (22 June), 1878–86.

Beyer, J.M. and H.M. Trice (1982), 'The utilization process: a conceptual framework and synthesis of empirical findings', *Administrative Science Quarterly*, **27** (4), 591–622.

Cabinet Office (2012), *Test, Learn Adapt. Developing Public Policy with Randomised Controlled Trials*, London: Cabinet Office, accessed 20 March 2015 at https://www.gov.uk/government/uploads/system/uploads/attachment_data/file/62529/TLA-1906126.pdf.

Casey, L. (2012), 'Listening to troubled families', July, Department for Communities and Local Government, London, accessed 12 September 2016 at https://www.gov.uk/government/publications/listening-to-troubled-families

Cousins, B. and C.K. Leithwood (1986), 'Current empirical research on evaluation utilization', *Review of Educational Research*, **36** (3), 331–64.

Davies, P. (2012), 'The state of evidence-based policy evaluation and its role in policy formation', *National Institute Economic Review*, **219** (1), R41–R52.

Department for Children Schools and Families (DCSF) (2008), 'The Sure Start journey. a summary of evidence', Department for Children Schools and Families, London, accessed 12 September 2016 at http://webarchive.nationalarchives.gov.uk/20130401151715/http://www.education.gov.uk/publications/standard/Surestart/Page1/DCSF-00220-2008.

Department for Education and Skills (DfE) (2006), 'Children's centres practice guidance', Department for Education and Skills, London, accessed 23 August 2016 at http://webarchive.nationalarchives.gov.uk/20100210152250/http://dcsf.gov.uk/everychildmatters/research/publications/surestartpublications/1854/.

Faulkner, W.N. (2014), 'A critical analysis of a randomized controlled trial evaluation in Mexico: norm, mistake or exemplar?', *Evaluation*, **20** (2), 230–43.

Goldacre, B. (2010), 'More than 60 children saved from abuse – small update', Bad science blog, 7 August, accessed 23 August 2016 at http://www.badscience.net/2010/08/more-than-60-children-saved-from-abuse/#more-1748.

Greenberg, D. and S. Morris (2005), 'Large-scale social experimentation in Britain what can and cannot be learnt from the employment retention and advancement demonstration?', *Evaluation*, **11** (2), 223–42.

Greenberg, D., M. Mandell and M. Onstott (2000), 'The dissemination and utilization of welfare-to-work experiments in state policymaking', *Journal of Policy Analysis and Management*, **19** (3), 367–82.

Greenhalgh, T. and J. Russell (2006), 'Reframing evidence synthesis as rhetorical action in the policy making drama', *Healthcare Policy*, **1** (2), 34–42.

Handa, S. and B. Davis (2006), 'The experience of conditional cash transfers in Latin America and the Caribbean', *Development Policy Review*, **24** (5), 513–36.

Jowell, R. (2003), *Trying It Out: The Role of 'Pilots' in Policy-Making*, London: Government Chief Social Researcher's Office, accessed 12 September 2016 at http://www.civilservice.gov.uk/wp-content/uploads/2011/09/Trying-it-Out_tcm6-36824.pdf.

Kaplan, B.J., G. Giesbrecht, S. Shannon and K. McLeod (2011), 'Evaluating treatments in health care: the instability of a one-legged stool', *BMC Medical Research Methodology*, **11** (1), 65.

Lindblom, C.E. and D.K. Cohen (1979), *Usable Knowledge: Social Science and Social Problem Solving*, New Haven, CT: Yale University Press.

Lloyd, N. and L. Harrington (2012), 'The challenges to effective outcome evaluation of a national, multi-agency initiative: the experience of Sure Start', *Evaluation*, **18** (1), 93–109.

Martin, G., G. Currie and A. Lockett (2011), 'Prospects for knowledge exchange in health policy and management: institutional and epistemic boundaries', *Journal of Health Services Research & Policy*, **16** (October), 211–17.

Monaghan, M. (2012), 'Cannabis classification and drug policy governance', in S. MacGregor, N. McKeganey, M. Monaghan and M. Roberts (eds), *Essays on the Governance of Drug Policy*, London: UK Drugs Policy Commission, accessed 23 August 2016 at http://www.ukdpc.org.uk/publication/essays-on-the-governance-of-drug-policy/.

Oakley, A. (1998), 'Public policy experimentation: lessons from America', *Policy Studies*, **19** (2), 93–114.

Pritchett, L. and J. Sandefur (2013), 'Context matters for size: why external validity claims and development practice don't mix', Center for Global Development, Working Paper No. 336, Washington, DC, accessed 23 October 2015 at http://www.cgdev.org/publication/context-matters-size-why-external-validity-claims-and-development-practice-dont-mix.

Ritter, A. (2009), 'How do drug policy makers access research evidence?', *International Journal of Drug Policy*, **20** (1), 70–75.

Roberts, H., M. Petticrew, K. Liabo and S. Macintyre (2012), '"The Anglo-Saxon disease": a pilot study of the barriers to and facilitators of the use of randomized controlled trials of social programmes in an international context', *Journal of Epidemiology & Community Health*, **66** (11), 1025–9.

Rossi, P. (1987), 'The iron law of evaluation and other metallic rules', in J. Miller and M. Lewis (eds), *Research in Social Problems and Public Policy*, vol. 4, Greenwich: JAI Press, pp. 3–20.

Sandberg, J. (2015), 'Transformative social policy in development? Demystifying conditional cash transfers in Latin America', development dissertation, Lund University, Expertgruppen för Biståndsanalys (EBA), March, accessed 23 October 2015 at eba.se/wp-content/uploads/2015/01/Johan-Sandberg.pdf.

Shiffman, J., T. Beer and Y. Wu (2002), 'The emergence of global disease control priorities', *Health Policy Planning*, **17** (3), 225–34.

Sowden, S.L. and R. Raine (2008), 'Running along parallel lines: how political reality impedes the evaluation of public health interventions: a case study of exercise referral schemes in England', *Journal of Epidemiology & Community Health*, **62** (9), 835–41.

Tian, J.H., Z.X. Lu, M.O. Bachmann and F.J. Song (2014), 'Effectiveness of directly observed treatment of tuberculosis: a systematic review of controlled studies', *International Journal of Tuberculosis and Lung Disease*, **18** (9), 1092–8.

Walt, G., L. Lush and J. Ogden (2004), 'International organizations in transfer of infectious diseases: iterative loops of adoption, adaptation, and marketing', *Governance*, **17** (2), 189–210.

Weible, C.M. (2008), 'Expert-based information and policy subsystems: a review and synthesis', *Policy Studies Journal*, **36** (4), 615–35.

Weiss, C.H. (1977), 'Research for policy's sake: the enlightenment function of social research policy', *Analysis*, **3** (4), 531–45.

Weiss, C.H. (1995), 'The haphazard connection: social science and public policy', *International Journal of Education Research*, **23** (2), 137–50.

32 Re-analysis, testability and falsification*
Jan-Erik Lane

1 INTRODUCTION

The re-analysis of data has been a most helpful tool in the growth of knowledge in political sociology, or the theory of mass attitudes in political, especially election behavior. Since the end of the Second World War, a number of huge data files have been established, focusing either on behavior or beliefs and values. Interpreting these large data compilations, a few much discussed theories have been launched. Re-analyzing these data is crucial for the further growth of knowledge in political sociology.

The aim of this chapter is to discuss the fruitfulness of re-analysis in political science. The example I focus on is the central theory of party systems by Seymour Martin Lipset and Stein Rokkan (1967). More specifically, I discuss the Lipset–Rokkan frozen party system hypothesis from the point of view of philosophy of science as well as outline a few steps towards a re-analysis of the relevant themes, adding new data to the evaluation. Thus, we may ask:

- Can the Lipset–Rokkan theory be re-analyzed? Is it at all testable?
- What are the theoretical assumptions that the theory is based upon?
- What are the empirical implications of this theory?
- If they were true in the 1970s, are they still valid today?

The famous frozen party system hypothesis is in reality a theory comprising several middle-range hypotheses. It received almost unanimous approval by scholars in political sociology when it was launched in the 1960s and 1970s, and it stimulated a lot of research into mass political behavior and attitudes. Time has come to make a re-analysis of this well-known theory, comparing at the same the old data with new, involving an enquiry into standard political sociology information about West European politics. First, we reject the position that the Lipset–Rokkan theory is not testable (Lybeck 1985; Mair 2002). Second, I compare politics around 1970 with politics around 2000–2010 to show that this theory is not tenable.

There is an abundance of data to draw upon when submitting the Lipset–Rokkan theory to a re-examination. Besides macro data for a long time period, micro data are available too. In a re-analysis of the data available to Lipset and Rokkan, we may contrast their information with data on recent changes. To understand the useful of re-analysis, we need to enter into the debate in the philosophy of science concerning confirmation, falsification and innovation, as well as how these meta-concepts relate to the re-analysis of theories and data. What does it mean to test a theory by reference to empirical information? Can scientific hypotheses by falsified? What does confirmation of a theory amount to?

2   TESTABILITY: CONFIRMATION, FALSIFICATION AND INNOVATION

The aim of re-analysis of a theory and its database is to study its truth claims. A social science theory consists of a network of hypotheses or general statements about human interaction (micro) and social systems (macro). To support its truth claim, a social science theory is in need of empirical backing by means of the examination of a set of data. Data can validate or falsify a theory, but with no access to empirical information, the theory is merely an intellectual guess that needs testing – a conjecture. Theory construction is half of scientific work and data analysis constitutes the other half. A re-analysis of established theories by existing or new data, informs us about the coherence of the theory with data. When there is a high degree of coherence between the implications of the hypotheses of the theory with the available data, then we may conclude that what the theory states corresponds to reality with a certain probability – the case of *confirmation*. However, little coherence between theory and data entails the case of *falsification*. A theory may be 'saved' by changing some of its hypotheses, or restricting its range of application. Finally, a re-analysis of the data pertinent to the evaluation may result in theoretical *innovation*, where a theory that is in more coherence with the data supplants the established theory – the growth of knowledge.

   Now, what about the principle of testability? Does the Lipset–Rokkan theory satisfy it? If not, this central theory in political sociology would be untestable. It could be the following:

- The theory contain key metaphysical concepts, like 'God', 'Savior' or 'Paradise'. This list may be extended to terms such as 'the unconscious' or 'class struggle', if not properly defined.
- The theory explains too much, meaning that whatever happens it can account for the event. For instance, the phrase 'party system' is conceptualized so that it always includes the left–right spectrum of

parties, however much these may have changed, leaving the party system always 'frozen'.

- The theory receives so many ad hoc hypotheses, saving it from falsification, that it ends up being an analytical theory, that is, a tautology.
- The theory is considered as a necessary or a priori theoretical framework without which the subject in question – parties and their electoral ties – cannot be analyzed. To abandon this tool of analysis does not amount to falsification of a theory but to suggest a paradigm shift or *gestalt switch* involving concepts with different meaning (Kuhn 1962).

Testability or falsifiability targets the possibility of coherence or non-coherence between theoretical statements and data or fact statement. A theory is not testable when it is phrased in such a manner that there could not be any fact that would contradict the theory, as it would be coherent with whatever fact is conceivable. We may make a distinction between actual testability and potential testability. A theory may be so abstract that its test implications are not observable currently, but that does not exclude that new facts may arrive that make the theory testable.

The notion of testability in principle is employed to make a demarcation between science and meta-physics, as in the philosophy of science of logical empiricists (Hempel 1965) or similarly the concept of falsifiability with the Popper school (Popper 1965). Is the Lipset–Rokkan theory of the West European party system untestable, as some have argued? We answer certainly 'No'. The set of non-testable theories include religious propositions, race theories, vulgar Marxism, animism and so on. The Lipset–Rokkan theory may be potentially confronted with data when its components are listed succinctly and its actual coherence with facts may be evaluated in a re-analysis.

It should be noted that the criteria of testability and falsifiability have aroused a large debate in methodology (Hesse 1980), some scholars expressing a disbelief in a linear growth model of scientific theory (Feyerabend 2010). It is often emphasized that a theory cannot be verified or falsified once and for all. In pragmatist philosophy of science, a theory is looked upon as a 'web of hypotheses', some very abstract and some more empirical (Quine and Ullian 1970). We may save a theory by changing some of its empirical hypotheses or adding ad hoc hypotheses, but when the core abstract hypotheses are questioned, then a Kuhnian scientific revolution may be initiated, resulting in the formation of new concepts making theories incomparable or 'incommensurable' (Kuhn 1962, 2000). Now, the central task is to specify the abstract core of hypotheses in the Lipset–Rokkan theory. This web of hypotheses would constitute a so-called research program in the dynamic philosophy of science of Lakatos (Lakatos and Musgrave 1970). A research program may be highly successful in directing research but it may also run out of strength. If they are susceptible to falsification, this theory must be testable. In fact, it is not only testable in principle but also actually.

To sum up, although modern philosophy of science does not harbor a unambiguous notion of testability (Hansson 2014), what emerges from the intense debate among various schools about science and pseudo-science is the importance of the test implications, derived from a set of hypotheses. No test implication, not testable. How about the Lipset–Rokkan model?

3 THE FROZEN PARTY SYSTEM THEORY

The Lipset–Rokkan theory was the most successful attempt to model the politics of the full industrial society in Western Europe, adhering to the regime of parliamentary democracy in societies with a high degree of economic modernization. Its core hypotheses focus upon the logic of election outcomes in a society with cleavages in the social structure, emphasizing the nature of the tie between the political parties and various social groups. Thus, it aims to account for the nature of West European democratic competition in regimes based upon the political parties as the 'agents' of the basic principal, via the '*demos*'. This theory was testable in reality already when launched and it can certainly be re-tested in a re-analysis of the world of West European politics today.

When interpreting the basic text by Lipset and Rokkan: 'Cleavage structures, party systems, and voter alignments: an introduction' (1967), we arrive at the following hypotheses:

- Micro: Voters tend to be loyal in one election to another.
- Micro: Voters frame their choice of party on the basis of their position on a cleavage line.
- Macro: The cleavages in society are finite and change very slowly, if at all.
- Macro: The central cleavages in the fully blown industrial democracy include class, religion and region or ethnicity.

Conclusion: the fully developed party systems in West European democracies are frozen.

Let me adduce a number of quotations, supporting our interpretation of the frozen party system theory, which implies low volatility, restricted fractionalization, party stable outcomes and only a few types of party kinds:

- Central questions: (1) *'the genesis of the system of contrasts and cleavages* with the national community' (Lipset and Rokkan 1967, p. 1, original emphasis); (2) *'the conditions for the developments of stable system of cleavage and oppositions* in national political life' (ibid., original emphasis); *'the behavior of the mass of rank-and-file citizens* within the resultant party system' (ibid., p. 2, original emphasis). We may interpret this list of key questions that the theory will attempt to answer as a search for stability in democratic party politics on the basis of social groups and individual voting behavior.
- Key aim: 'to throw light on . . . the "freezing" different types of party systems'(ibid., p. 3), 'we seek to assemble materials for comparative analyses of the *current alignments of voters* behind the historically given "packages"'(ibid., original emphasis).

These presuppositions and core assumptions, constituting the leading research program in political sociology, were highly applicable for theory construction about West European politics in the societies of the 1960 s and 1970s. Clearly, they are refutable, depending on the data availability of the world of facts. However, is the research program with the above mentioned hypotheses (1–5) suitable as the starting point for a new enquiry in the party politics of the now mature post-industrial society in Western Europe? I think not.

Despite the misunderstanding about non-testability, we may list a compact set of test implications that may certainly be confronted with data or factual statement. The accusation of non-testability rests upon different argument, such as the theory being only static or the theory containing a confused notion of 'frozen' party or party system. Disregarding this erroneous critique, we may focus upon a set of indicators to test the theoretical hypotheses above, both for society and the state around 1970 and in a re-analysis of state and society in the early decade of this new century.

To enquire into whether the Lipset–Rokkan theory is testable as well as coherent with basic facts about West European parties and their electorates, we must gather empirical information about the following events or trends in elections and party systems (Rokkan 1970):

1. Volatility, net and gross.
2. Party fractionalization.
3. Types of parties in each country.

4.   The occurrence of earth quake elections.
5.   The transformation of the cleavages in the social structure.

Deriving test implications from the Lipset–Rokkan model of the frozen party systems in Western Europe, we may employ indicators such as 1–5 above to compare West European politics between 1970 and 2010. The finding is the frozen party system theory holds for 1970 but is not true of politics in this century, which we show now. Democratic societies or capitalist democracies today are very different from full-blown industrial democracies to such an extent that we are inclined to agree with French social scientist Touraine when he writes of the transformation from a Durkheimian ('structure') to a Weberian world ('actor') in his *La fin des sociétés* (Touraine 2013).

   The Lipset–Rokkan model has several test implications, three of which are examined briefly below, namely, voter volatility, party system fractionalization and party coalition pattern. The model satisfies the conditions of testability with both Hempel and Popper.

4   SOME RELEVANT POLITICAL CHANGES FROM THE 1970S TO 2010

The Lipset–Rokkan model of West European politics identified certain salient features in how the electorate relates to the party system as well as how the political parties maneuver to form a representative government on the basis of the principles of parliamentarianism. Today we would speak of the principal–agent relationships in a democratic polity. According to the model, the interactions between voters, parties and governments are characterized by certain features, including:

- a stable structure of cleavages in the electorate;
- loyal voting behavior from one election to another;
- a stable pattern of government formation based upon coalitions in Parliament.

In order to make these hypotheses testable, one needs to develop a set of indicators to map the political realities of the 1960s and 1970s. Explicitly constructed indices may be employed for re-analysis of data that are pertinent to the existence of the three model features above, including the aim to find out whether the model conjectures still hold for West European politics in 2000–2010. We suggest the following indicators are central for the Lipset–Rokkan theory:

- volatility;
- fractionalization and types of political parties;
- coalition structure.

The Lipset–Rokkan model amounts to a middle-range theory, focusing upon electoral choice, the outcomes of elections, the parties making up a party system and how these parties create viable governments. The emphasis is definitely upon stability. So let us firstly focus upon electoral volatility and what the Lipset-Rokkan model implies.

4.1 Volatility

The enquiry into the links between voters and political parties was much enhanced through the distinction between net and gross voter volatility (Pedersen 1979). It allows us to examine in depth whether electoral behavior is 'frozen', meaning changing little. Table 32.1 states the scores for 1970 against 2000. The finding is that volatility has risen considerably, from 5–10 percent to 15–25 percent. Net volatility results from gross volatility, or party switching among voters, being usually twice or three times as strong as net volatility.

The rise in volatility is dramatic for some countries that used to be well known for their electoral stability: Sweden, Switzerland, Denmark, the Netherlands and Norway.

In Table 32.2, the correlations between the volatility numbers are stated, showing that volatility in 2000 is different from volatility in 1970 for both net and gross volatility.

Volatility 1970, net and gross, go together but deviate considerable from net and gross volatility 2000. The pattern of voter–party relations from one election to another has changed from the industrial society of the Lipset–Rokkan model to the post-industrial model true of the early twenty-first century.

Figure 32.1 and Figure 32.2 provide ample evidence for the changes in voter volatility. The more the empirical cases fall outside the 45-degree line, to the right or to the left, the more change is indicated by the data.

For most countries hold that net volatility is much higher around 2000 than 1970, although we find a few notable exceptions. In any case, the 2000 pattern is entirely different from the 1970 pattern. This is even clearer for gross volatility (Figure 32.2). The empirical cases fall off the 45-degree line to the right mostly, providing evidence of a sharp rise in gross volatility.

Table 32.1   Volatility 1970–2010: net and gross

Country	Net 1970	Net 2000	Gross 1970	Gross 2000
Austria	2.6	16.6		
Belgium	6.9	15.5		27.0
Denmark	15.6	10.8	23.0	29.3
Finland	7.7	9.9	22.0	24.0
France	17.7	20.6	28.0	42.0
Germany	5.0	9.9	12.0	25.5
Greece	23.1	13.6		17.0
Iceland	12.6	12.9		30.9
Ireland	8.5	21.2		24.0
Italy	6.1	13.4		32.0
Luxembourg	12.3	7.2		
Netherlands	13.2	22.7	20.0	39.8
Norway	15.2	14.2	22.8	33.3
Portugal	11.7	11.4		16.5
Spain	12.1	11.2		10.0
Sweden	6.3	13.5	17.3	33.5
Switzerland	7.7	8.9		27.7
United Kingdom	8.3	7.0	18.3	17.8

Notes:
Net volatility: the gains and losses of political parties participating at two elections as measured by the Pedersen index.
Gross volatility: measured as party switching by voters changing parties over two consecutive elections.

Sources: Net volatility, based on data presented in Ersson (2012); gross volatility, see Table 32A.1 in the Appendix to this chapter.

Table 32.2   Correlations among volatility measures

	net_1970	net_2000	gro_1970	gro_2000
net_1970	1			
net_2000	0.15	1		
gro_1970	0.85	0.45	1	
gro_2000	0.03	0.56	0.50	1

Source: See Table 32A.1 in the Appendix to this chapter.

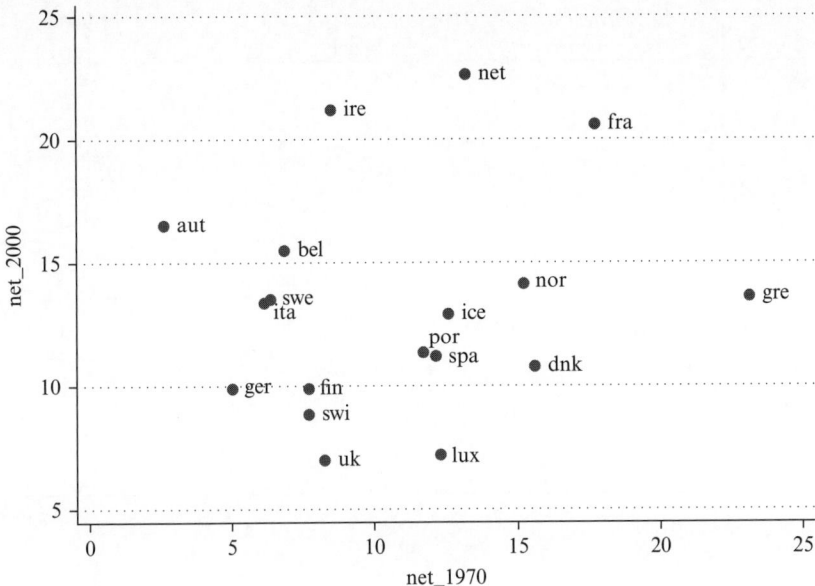

Source: See Table 32.1.

Figure 32.1 Net volatility 1970 and 2000

4.1.1 Summary

The concept of volatility, gross and net volatility, is a most powerful indicator on party system change. We may compare the pattern of volatility for 1970. Neither gross nor net volatility is especially high around the 1970s. Both kinds of volatility are sharply higher in the first decade of the twenty-first century. Secondly, let us look at indicators upon the parties in the party systems and what the Lipset–Rokkan model entails.

4.2 Fractionalization and Types of Parties

The growth in volatility has been combined with an increase in the number of political parties contesting elections. New parties have been created, some of them receiving enough support to survive a few elections. Others have operated like so-called flash parties, receiving much support at one election only to be phased out at later ones. As spectacular as flash parties is the slow death of a mass party such as the Communists as well as the sudden disappearance of the Italian Christian Democrats. Thus, we face the task of analyzing change of party systems between 1965 and 2005.

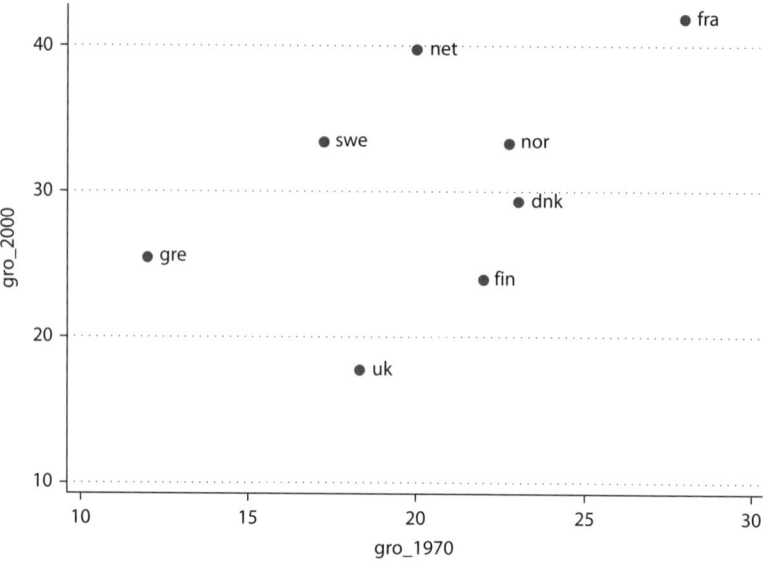

Source: See Table 32.1.

Figure 32.2   Gross volatility 1970 and 2000

To what extent can we speak of the same parties when comparing elections around 1970 with elections about 2005? According to the Lipset– Rokkan theory, the main parties would be mass parties responding to the basic cleavages in the social structure, that is, class, religion and region. These alignments would be frozen, meaning low volatility in election outcomes.

The postmodern condition is not one of huge mass parties. Party membership has declined significantly all over Western Europe, the parties finding financial support with the state instead. One mass party has disappeared entirely, the Communists who were a force to reckon with in, for example, France, Italy and Finland. The religious parties have survived but only as a Christian party. By regional parties, Lipset and Rokkan had in mind small parties fighting for autonomy or independence, such as the Scottish Nationalists. They did not envisage the rise of populist anti-system parties, such as the National Front in France or the Austrian Freedom Party. The populist party is to be found in many West European countries as an anti-immigration and anti-European Union party, such as in the Netherlands and Denmark as well as Norway, where they are sizable. Of course, there is also party continuity as with the Social Democrats, the Conservatives, Liberals and Agrarians. How to portray parties' change with quantitative numbers?

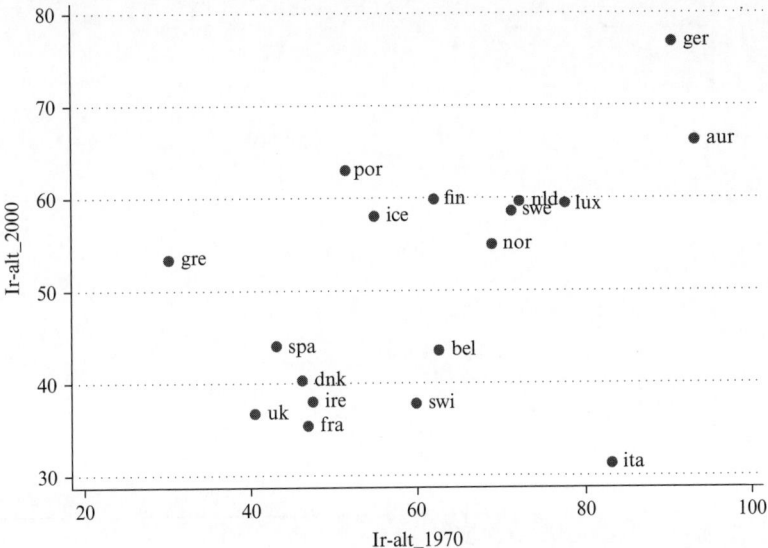

Source: Based on data available from Armingeon et al. (2013).

Figure 32.3   Mass parties: left + religious + agrarian

A few attempts have been made to map the existence and strength of various political parties that may be used for a re-analysis of the Lipset–Rokkan theory. One such classification targets the size of Left and religious parties or the mass or cleavage parties: socialist – left, socialist, communist, agrarian and religious parties. Figure 32.3 shows the combined size of the Lipset–Rokkan cleavage parties 1970 and 2000.

We can observe the decline of the cleavage parties in Figure 32.3, providing evidence of party system change. Most of these mass parties are below the 45-degree line.

Another indicator that may be employed to map party system transformation is to try to measure the size of new parties. In Figure 32.4, the category 'Others' designate political parties that are *not* socialist, conservative, agrarian, communist or liberals (Sundberg 1999). Again, we may note that these parties are mostly above the 45-degree line in Figure 32.4.

Another method for discovering changes in the party system over the last decades of the twentieth century and the first decade of the twenty-first century is to correlate the sizes of various aggregations of parties. Appendix Table 32A.1 contains such measures of associations. Finally, we look at indicators on government formation and what the Lipset–Rokkan model predicts.

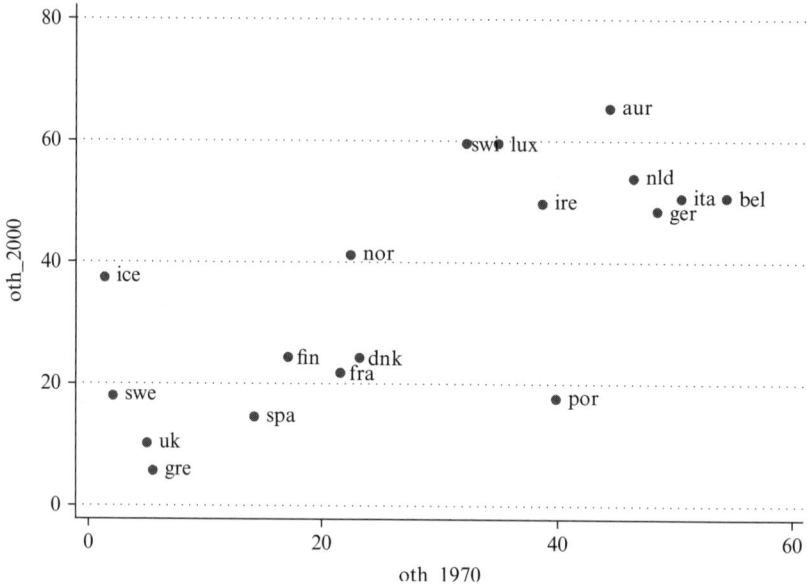

Source: Based on data available from Armingeon et al. (2013).

Figure 32.4   New parities

4.3   Government Coalitions

According to the logic of the Lipset–Rokkan theory, the pattern of government formation in a country must reflect the party alignments derived from the basic carpet of social cleavages. To them, electoral formulas do not establish governments, as with Duverger (1954), but are themselves endogenous to the cleavage structure. Thus, Western Europe will have predominantly proportional representation (PR) election systems that promote the creation or maintenance of multi-party politics. We would expect to find the following governments in a system of multi-party politics with fixed alignments and strong cleavages:

- several minority governments;
- fewer minimum winning coalition governments; and
- some oversized governments.

In Figures 32.5 and 32.6, I show that the patterns of government formation have changed, in a fashion typical of the transition from the politics of the industrial society to the politics of the post-industrial society.

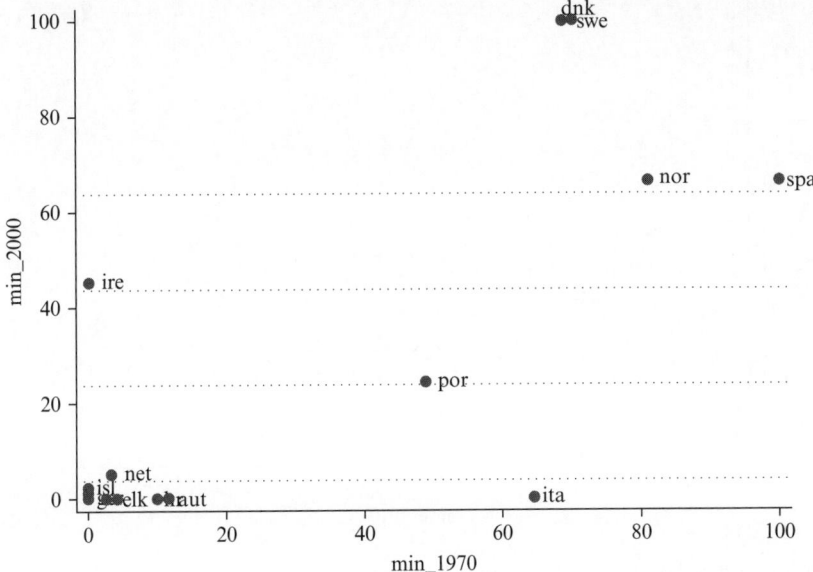

Source: Based on data in Andersson et al. (2014).

Figure 32.5 Minority governments

In a frozen party system harboring parliamentary democracy, PR is bound to result in minority governments. No political party receives a majority of seats in Parliament for itself, but a large party may still be reluctant to enter into a coalition owing to historically given animosities – a form of path dependency reinforced by the election system. Figure 32.5 shows that minority governments were more frequent around 1970 than 2000.

In a postmodern society, political parties are no longer constrained by cleavage legacies. They would thus be more willing to form majority coalitions like for instance the minimum winning coalition (MWC) that barely supersedes the 50 percent power threshold (Figure 32.6).

When historical patterns of voter alignments do not count as much, coalition making possesses more degrees of freedom (Karvonen and Kuhnle 2000). Majority governments are after all easier to run than minority governments, all other things equal.

In Western Europe, PR methods have in a few countries been used as the basis for so-called consociationalism (Lijphart 1968), meaning an effort to bring all players, or most of them, on board for consensus policy-making. The creation of grand coalitions would in a cleavage dominated

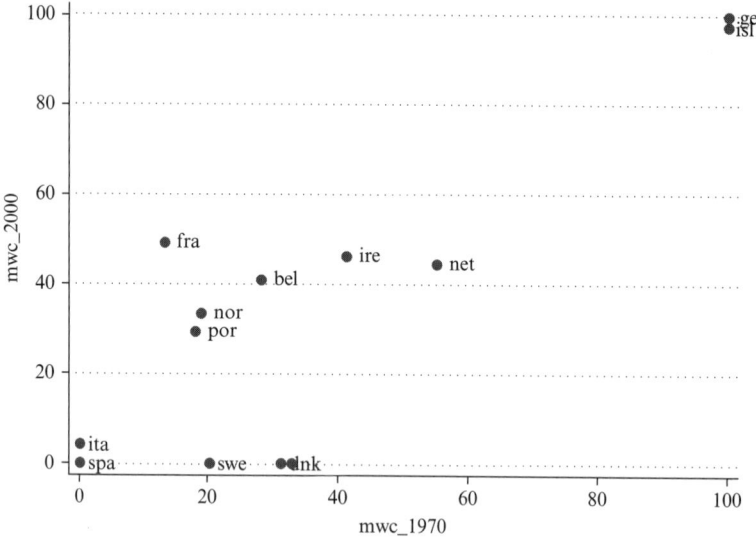

Source: Based on data in Andersson et al. (2014).

Figure 32.6   Minimum winning coalitions

society constitute a tool for the political elite to minimize conflict and avoid any tendency to civil war between the so-called camps (*zuilen*, pillars). However, in a postmodern society with border-less strata and communities, oversized or grand coalitions make little sense except for convenience. When a party system is dominated by two large parties that cannot form a simple majority government or a minimum winning coalition, then they may temporarily resort to the oversized format (Austria). Only Switzerland employs the *collegiado* as a matter of principle.

The simple majority coalition government is more prevalent around 2000 than 1970, which fits the theory that postmodern societies have a different form of democratic politics than the frozen industrial society. Political parties that can create a minimum winning coalition by means of a coalition with itself are not frequent in Western European parliamentary democracy.

5   CONCLUSION

The Lipset–Rokkan theory about the nature of democratic politics in Western Europe – the 'frozen party system' hypothesis, or better set of hypotheses – was the main theoretical tool for interpreting Western

Europe before the fall of the Berlin Wall, with the advent of many new democracies with an entirely different historical background. The theory seemed to fit the realities in the West European advanced industrial society, as alignments followed cleavages and election results produced stable government patterns (Sartori 1975).

However, when 'anomalies' started to crop up – flash parties, earthquake elections and new politics – scholars began to be inclined to regard the Lipset–Rokkan theory as more of a framework of analysis, or an approach that was indispensable but in principle not testable, like a Kantian a priori. It could always be saved by the addition of ad hoc assumptions, or the reinterpretation of key concepts, such as in the Kuhn story about scientific revolutions as concept switches and metaphors in his criticism of Popper's falsification methodology of falsifiability (Kuhn 1962, 2000). Yet, when anomalies pile up, such as gross volatility and fractionalization augmentations, then ad hoc hypotheses cannot save a basically flawed theory.

I have argued here that the position that the Lipset–Rokkan theory in comparative politics is in principle or in reality untestable is not at all tenable. One may point out that Hempel (1965) provided two requirements of scientific explanations: explanatory relevance and testability. According to criterion one the explanation must give good reasons to believe that the explained event occurred in time-space. Criterion two entails that the explanation must be capable of empirical test or confrontation with data. If a proposed explanation satisfies the requirement of explanatory relevance, it would satisfy the requirement of testability.

On the contrary, we argue that the Lipset–Rokkan model is not only testable against existing empirical information through re-analysis of data from around 1970 and data from about 2000, but it may also be rendered into a parsimonious quantitative model of the party system and its electoral politics. It is confirmable in Hempel's sense, its implications agreeing with data. Yet, and this is our second point: the Lipset–Rokkan model is false in relation to politics in the West-European postmodern society with its many features of instability.

In accordance with Lakatos (1978), the Lipset–Rokkan approach offered a successful research program in comparative politics for a time. However, the recent transformation of societies in Western Europe (Touraine 2013) has promoted the emergence of an entirely different kind of party politics and democratic contestation.

NOTE

* The author wishes to express his thanks and appreciation for Svante Ersson's assistance in collecting the data used in this chapter.

REFERENCES

Andersson, S., T. Bergman and S. Ersson (2014), 'The European Representative Democracy Data Archive, Release 3', main sponsor: Riksbankens Jubileumsfonds, accessed 1 February 2015 at www.erdda.se.

Armingeon, K., L. Knöpfel, D. Weisstanner, S. Engler, P. Potolidis, and M. Gerber (2013), *Comparative Political Data Set I 1960–2011*, Bern: Institute of Political Science, University of Bern.

Duverger, M. (1954), *Political Parties: Their Organization and Activity in the Modern State*, London: Methuen.

Ersson, S. (2012), 'Electoral volatility in Europe: assessments and potential explanations for estimate differences', paper presented at the 2012 Elections, Public Opinion and Parties (EPOP) Conference, September, Oxford University, Oxford, accessed 24 August 2016 at http://www.sociology.ox.ac.uk/materials/documents/epop/papers/Ersson_Svante_epop-paper_2012.pdf.

Feyerabend, P. (2010), *Against Method*, London: Verso.

Hansson, S.-O. (2014), 'Science and pseudo-science', *Stanford Dictionary of Philosophy*, accessed 1 February 2015 at http://plato.stanford.edu/entries/pseudo-science/.

Hempel, C.G. (1965), *Aspects of Scientific and Other Essays in the Philosophy of Science*, New York: Free Press.

Hesse, M. (1980), *Revolutions and Reconstructions in the Philosophy of Science*, Bloomington, IN: Indiana University Press.

Karvonen, L. and S. Kuhnle (eds) (2000), *Party Systems and Voter Alignments Revisited*, London: Routledge.

Kuhn, T. (1962), *The Structure of Scientific Revolutions*, Chicago, IL: University of Chicago Press.

Kuhn, T.S. (2000), *The Road Since Structure: Philosophical Essays: 1970–1993*, Chicago, IL: University of Chicago Press.

Lakatos, I. (1978), *The Methodology of Scientific Research Programmes: Philosophical Papers*, vol. 1, Cambridge: Cambridge University Press.

Lakatos, I. and A. Musgrave (1970), *Criticism and the Growth of Knowledge*, Cambridge: Cambridge University Press.

Lijphart, A. (1968), *The Politics of Accommodation*, New Haven, CT: Yale University Press.

Lipset, S.M. and S. Rokkan (1967), 'Cleavage structures, party systems, and voter align-ments: an introduction', in S.M. Lipset and S. Rokkan (eds), *Party Systems and Voter Alignments: Cross-National Perspectives*, New York: The Free Press, pp. 1–64.

Lybeck, J.A. (1985), 'Is the Lipset–Rokkan hypothesis testable?', *Scandinavian Political Studies*, **8** (new series) (1–2), 105–13.

Mair, P. (2002), 'The freezing hypothesis: an evaluation', in L. Karvonen and S. Kuhnle (eds), *Party Systems and Voter Alignments Revisited*, London: Routledge, pp. 27–44.

Pedersen, M. (1979), 'The dynamics of European party systems: changing patterns of elec-toral volatility', *European Journal of Political Research*, **7** (1), 1–26.

Popper, K. (1965), *Conjectures and Refutations: The Growth of Scientific Knowledge*, London: Routledge, Kegan Paul.

Quine, W.V.O. and J.S. Ullian (1970), *The Web of Belief*, New York: McGraw-Hill.

Rokkan, S. (1970), *Citizens, Elections, Parties*, Oslo: Scandinavian University Books.

Sartori, G. (1975), *Parties and Party Systems: A Framework for Analysis*, Cambridge: Cambridge University Press.

Sundberg, J. (1999), 'The enduring Scandinavian party system', *Scandinavian Political Studies*, **22** (3), 221–41.

Touraine, A. (2013), *La fin de la société*, Paris: Seuil.

APPENDIX   DATA ON GROSS VOLATILITY MEASURED AS PARTY SWITCHING COLLECTED BY SVANTE ERSSON (2012) FROM VARIOUS COUNTRY FILES

Table 32A.1   Data and sources: correlations among party types

	pole_1960	oth_1960	lr_1960	lralt_1960	pole_1970	oth_1970	lr_1970	lralt_1970	pole_2000	oth_2000	lr_2000	lralt_2000
pole_1960	1											
oth_1960	−0.81	1										
lr_1960	−0.25	0.68	1									
lralt_1960	−0.24	0.68	0.99	1								
pole_1970	0.92	−0.82	−0.36	−0.35	1							
oth_1970	−0.80	0.96	0.65	0.63	−0.87	1						
lr_1970	−0.30	0.70	0.96	0.96	−0.35	0.64	1					
lralt_1970	−0.28	0.67	0.93	0.95	−0.32	0.58	0.97	1				
pole_2000	0.65	−0.76	−0.53	−0.53	0.81	−0.76	−0.50	−0.48	1			
oth_2000	−0.61	0.83	0.74	0.75	−0.65	0.73	0.74	0.73	−0.84	1		
lr_2000	0.03	0.19	0.44	0.43	0.12	0.12	0.44	0.46	−0.12	0.16	1	
lralt_2000	0.11	0.14	0.43	0.44	0.18	0.08	0.45	0.49	−0.07	0.14	0.98	1

Notes:
N = 18.
POLE measure the support for socialist + agrarian + conservative parties.
OTH measures the support for new parties as 100 − (socialist + agrarian + conservatives + communists + liberals).
LR measures the support for socialist + left-socialist + communist + agrarian + religious + ethnic parties.
LR-ALT measures the support for socialist + left-socialist + communist + agrarian + religious parties.

33 The art of publishing: how to report and submit your findings
Richard S. Katz

1 INTRODUCTION

Although the satisfaction of personal curiosity is probably the primary reason why people do research, the real pay-off only comes with the publication of the results. The objective of this chapter is to review the most significant outlets for publication by political scientists, and to give some guidance in negotiating the publication process.

There are two primary audiences for political scientists, each with different needs, and consequently involving different standards and strategies for publication. First, political scientists write for other political scientists, contributing to the development of a professional scholarly literature. Second, political scientists write for non-academics. Aside from a desire to inform, these publications often aim to influence the course of political (as opposed to academic) debate.

There are a wide variety of venues in which political scientists can publish their work. Some, such as personal web-pages or blogs, have essentially no barriers to entry. The danger is that, with no peer reviewers or editors to satisfy, something intemperate, ill-considered or inadvertently mistaken will come back to haunt its author. Moreover, the absence of the external endorsement implicit in peer review or editorial acceptance may reduce the seriousness with which blogs are taken by their intended audiences.

Two additional non-academic outlets for political scientists are commentaries ('op-ed' pieces) in newspapers or other non-scholarly journals and expert testimony in court cases or before legislative or other public bodies. While these offer more opportunities for review and revision, both their purpose and their style differ from those of academic publications, and yet they become part of the overall corpus of work on which scholars ultimately are judged. Moreover, it is important to remember that the opportunity for these kinds of participation in the public arena, such as the probability that a blog will be taken seriously, generally are the result of academic standing based on scholarly publications, and not a substitute for those publications. Consequently, this chapter focuses primarily on academic publication.

2 ACADEMIC PUBLICATIONS

Broadly speaking, there are six classes of academic publications: conference papers; book reviews; journal articles; chapters in books edited or compiled by someone else; books edited or compiled by yourself; and books authored or co-authored by yourself. Within each category, there are several dimensions of variation – both with regard to strategy for publication and with regard to the 'return' to the author.

2.1 Conference Papers

The variety of conferences at which you might present a paper is virtually unlimited. Most, however, can be roughly categorized as being either large and general or small and focused. The primary examples of large and general conferences are the annual meetings of associations; small and focused conferences are more often organized by university departments (or individuals) interested in a particular subject or by groups like International Institute for Democracy and Electoral Assistance (IDEA), United States Agency for International Development (USAID) or the Inter-Parliamentary Union desiring to bring together a group of experts who will contribute to the organization's work. The European Consortium for Political Research's (ECPR's) Joint Sessions of Workshops represent a hybrid type – a large number of small and focused conferences taking place simultaneously at a single location.

Presenting a paper at a small conference is generally by invitation; even when applications are solicited, this is likely to be based on preselection by the organizers. Only people who are already directly or indirectly known by the organizers are likely to be included – although that recognition may be as a particularly promising student or as a young scholar doing particularly interesting and pertinent work, and may be based on informal networks as well as on objective criteria.

In contrast, opportunities to present papers at large conferences are more likely to be competitive. Large conference programs generally are constructed in two stages. First, a number of 'sections', each of which will include a number of panels, are selected. In some cases (for example, the ECPR General Conference), the selection is made from proposals submitted by would-be section chairs; in other cases (for example, the American Political Science Association – APSA), the sections correspond to the 'Organized Sections' of the association. Second, the section chairs receive proposals either for full panels (usually three to five papers on a related theme, often including a proposed panel chair and one or two discussants) or for individual papers, from which they select those to fill the slots allocated to them; the section chairs themselves will group papers proposed and accepted individually into panels. Often when the organizers allow whole panels to be proposed, a paper proposed as part of a pre-arranged panel has a greater likelihood of acceptance; recognizing this, some organizations have set quotas for pre-arranged panels. Before submitting a paper proposal, it is a good idea to find out what the dominant mode of acceptance is for the particular conference in question.

In applying to present a conference paper, you are promising to deliver a good that has not yet been produced. Although paper proposals are usually grounded in research in progress or recently completed, the paper itself very rarely is written before it is accepted. Those deciding which papers to accept are speculating on the quality of the paper that ultimately will emerge. A successful track record makes that gamble less risky, although conference organizers frequently see provision of opportunities for 'beginners' to be part of their mandate. Paper proposals are not enforceable contracts, and it is understood that the final paper may only loosely correspond to what was proposed. At the same time, remembering that for organizers to accept one proposal means that they must reject another, you do not want to develop a reputation for promising big and delivering small, and even less do you want to be known for taking a conference slot and then not delivering at all.

Beyond having the paper 'on the record', an important benefit for paper authors is receiving feedback, especially from formal discussants. This requires that the discussants be sent the paper well in advance. Paper authors should also be aware that as panels have become increasing crowded, the time allowed for presentation of each paper has shrunk, often to only 10–15 minutes. This means that beyond reporting the paper's principal findings or conclusions, the objective of the presentation should be to encourage people to read the paper rather than to summarize it so that they do not have to read it.

Particularly for large panel-oriented conferences, three other points should be borne in mind. First, the panels are only part of the point of these conferences; networking and informal discussions over meals and in the corridors and bars are at least as important for many conference participants. You should not be surprised, or offended, by an extremely small audience. Second, very few people in the room will have read the papers in advance. Third, although PowerPoint presentations can be very helpful, it is always risky to have to rely on someone else's hardware; paper presenters should be prepared for the system to be out of order.

2.2 Book Reviews

The initiative for book reviews usually comes from the book review editor of a journal. Publishers send copies of books to journals, and the book review editor invites reviews from people known to be working in the field. It is perfectly acceptable, however, to communicate with a review editor, offering to review a specific book or simply to express interest in reviewing books in a particular field: the problem for most review editors is to find qualified people willing to invest the time required to do a thoughtful review.

Book reviews have three primary functions. First, they give readers a summary of the book's contents that is more extensive than a jacket blurb but still far shorter than an article. Second, reviews give a critical evaluation of the book, pointing out its shortcomings as well as its strengths. In both of these respects, they aid scholars deciding which books to read, and which to skip. Third, and generally of most interest to the reviewer, they provide an opening for reviewers to make their own contribution to the debate.

A variant of the simple book review is the review essay, in which several books are dealt with in a single article. As with the review of a single book, these may originate on request by the review editor, but they may also be submitted (to some journals) in the same way as a 'normal' article. Because they deal with several books, review essays are longer than simple reviews, and because they compare and contrast the books reviewed, these essays give, and indeed demand, more freedom for reviewers to inject their own contributions – both in framing the terms of the debate and in suggesting how it should proceed.

In order to be useful, reviews must be honest – highlighting the negative as well as the positive. Reviewers should remember, however, that the academic world is quite small and that sooner or later the roles of reviewer and reviewed are likely to be reversed. Criticism should, therefore, be expressed as constructively as possible.

2.3 Journal Articles

By far the most common form of academic publication is the journal article. Although there are some institutions that give particular weight to monographs, journal articles are generally the most rewarding in terms of career development. In the most general terms, all journals operate in much the same way: authors send manuscripts to the journal, usually through its website, and the editor decides whether to publish them. While the author is free to send a rejected article to another journal, it is not permissible to send the same article to two journals at the same time.

2.4   Choosing a Journal

The first decision is to which journal a manuscript will be sent. Journals obviously differ in their subject focus, and will reject articles that are inappropriate for the journal in question; it will save everyone time and trouble if this is taken into account before submission. Moreover, an article is more likely to be noticed if it appears in a journal that is already known for publishing articles in the same general area. Similarly, most journals have guidelines concerning length; while an editor may be willing to stretch these rules for a particularly appealing article, it is again a waste of everyone's time to submit an article that is very far outside the limits – it is better to pare the article down, or even to split it into two separate articles, before submission. On the other hand, while journals nearly all have a 'house style' for references, section headings and the like, at the stage of initial submission adherence to these is far less important – meaning that if the article is rejected by one journal, these points of style generally need not be changed before submission to another journal (see below).

Beyond the question of subject matter, there are several dimensions of difference among journals to consider in choosing where to submit a manuscript. First, some journals are 'peer reviewed' while others are not; other things being equal, articles in peer reviewed journals are regarded as superior to those in other journals. Second, journals can be ranked according to their 'impact factor'; journals with high impact factors are usually considered superior to those with lower impact factors, and as a result are likely to have significantly lower acceptance rates, reinforcing the perception that they are the better journals. Third, although most journals are published on paper and made available on-line, an increasing number of journals are online only; other things being equal, the status of paper journals is higher. Fourth, some journals are simply quicker than others in making decisions, and in publishing manuscripts that have been accepted; if quick publication is important, for example, because of rules concerning promotion or departmental assessments, one may wish to take this into account. Finally, you may consult search machines to inspect a journal's (global) ranking within the social sciences as well as its impact factor.

2.5   Review

When a manuscript is received by a peer reviewed journal, the editor may decide to reject it out of hand on grounds either of low quality or of substantive fit to the journal; most submissions, however, are sent for 'double blind' review (meaning that identity of the author is not revealed to the reviewers, and their identities are not revealed to the author). This means

---

BOX 33.1   SOURCES

Web of Science – Source of Ranking Journals and Citations
This is a database containing various indicators regarding the reputation of journals: Science Citation Index Expanded covering more than 2400 journals since
1900.
Social Sciences Citation Index covering most journals within political science from
1956 onwards including Impact figures.
Conference Proceedings Citation Index containing presentations and Proceedings
of more than 100 000 academic gatherings.

See also:
Publish or Perish – Harzing.com/pop.htm.
www.harzing.com/pop.htm.
Site available to inspect individual research performance.

Google Scholar – https://scholar.google.com/citations?view_op=top.
Worldwide search machine, using individual and journal rankings.

---

that the version submitted to the journal should have references to the
author or to the author's own work removed. It also means that the editor
is captive to the reliability of the reviewers.

In submitting a manuscript, the author will be asked to provide an
abstract and four or five keywords. These can be important in providing
cues to the editor in deciding on the appropriate pool of potential reviewers. (Another significant cue is the work cited in the paper – if a particular
scholar's work appears quite prominently in the references, there is a good
chance that person will be asked to review the manuscript.) The abstract
should be short and concise (under 300 words). It should convey the main
points of the article in a way that is independently intelligible. In particular,
an abstract should not simply say that the article answers some question – it
should say what the answer is. While an abstract is an invitation to read the
article, for many readers it will be a substitute for reading it, and so it should
include any necessary qualifications or limitations to the findings as well.

Once two or three reviews have been received, the editor will make a
decision and inform the author. Generally, the editor will also send the
reviews (or at least summaries of the reviews), although it is important
for the author to recognize that the reviews are advice to the editor and
not dispositive votes; even three quite positive reviews can accompany a
rejection.

There are four basic decisions possible. The first, and most common
for highly regarded journals, is rejection; in some cases, the initial rejection rate can exceed 90 percent. Except in very rare cases, the only appeal

against an unwarranted rejection is to submit the manuscript to another journal. Editorial decisions are by their nature subjective; a different editor and a different set of reviewers may come to a different decision.

The second possible outcome is an invitation to 'revise and resubmit' ('R&R'). While this may strike a neophyte as a negative outcome, it is actually the most common initial response to articles that ultimately will be published. An R&R means that the reviewers and editor think that the paper has real promise if certain changes (which they identify) are made. It is not necessary to accept every suggestion, but neither should they be ignored; the reviewers represent a sample of the intended audience for the article – if they misunderstood something, that should be taken to be the fault of the author, not of the reviewers.

While you should respond to the criticisms of the reviewers, it is not generally a good idea to make more extensive revisions than they call for. On the one hand, this opens up new grounds for complaint; on the other hand, there is always another article, and no manuscript should be understood to be the author's final chance to contribute to the literature on a subject. The revised manuscript should be resubmitted along with a detailed statement to the editor explaining how the revisions have responded to the reviews – and why the revisions have not responded to suggestions that the author has rejected. Once the revised version has been received, the editor usually will send it for review again, with at least one of the original reviewers included among the referees. At this point, any of the possible outcomes from rejection to simple acceptance (including another R&R) is possible, although if the revisions have addressed the problems raised in the original reviews, the likelihood of acceptance is much higher.

The third possibility is acceptance subject to minor revisions. Ordinarily, the editor will decide independently whether the revisions are satisfactory, but one or more of the original reviewers may be consulted.

Finally, the paper may simply be accepted. This is extremely rare on the first round of review, but ultimately all articles that are published have to be accepted first. Even outright acceptance does not preclude further revision, however. It is likely that even very favorable reviews will contain some suggestions for improvement, and these should be considered carefully.

The same basic outcomes apply for journals that are not peer-reviewed. The only difference is that the editor, either alone or with advice, makes the decisions him or herself.

2.6 Production

Once the paper is accepted, the author is invited to send a final version, including 'camera ready' artwork (figures and so on). Authors should remember that figures that are perfectly clear in color may be unintelligible when translated into half-tones; publication will be significantly delayed if the publisher has to ask for better artwork. This is also when conformity to the 'house style' becomes important. Although most major journals employ professional copy-editors to make sure that the 'house style' is followed, every editorial change represents an opportunity for errors to creep in. Copy-editors will correct many errors of language (sometimes inadvertently changing the meaning), but are unlikely to catch errors in transcribing numbers into tables or other factual errors; it is important that the final manuscript be checked carefully before it is sent to the publisher.

After the final version has been copy-edited, it is sent to the compositor, after which page proofs will be sent to the author for correction. The proofs may be accompanied by a number of queries from the copy-editor. Generally, publishers expect very quick turn-around of page proofs, but while you should make every effort to meet the publisher's deadline, it is more important that the corrections are done carefully. If the deadline is not going to be met, notify the publisher early, lest silence be interpreted as approval of the proofs as they stand. This is the last chance for errors to be corrected, but you should not make substantive changes, especially if they would affect the pagination.

Once the corrected proofs are returned, the article enters a queue for actual publication. Because journals operate within page budgets fixed by their publishers, there may be a substantial backlog and wait. In response, many publishers now post on their websites 'pre-publication' versions of articles, exactly as they will ultimately appear except for page numbering; for most purposes, once this has been done the article can be listed by its author as 'published'.

2.7 Book Chapters

Edited books can develop in several different ways. Participants in a small conference may try to package their individual papers as a volume (or as a special issue of a journal). This requires that one or two participants take the initiative to serve as editors, both coordinating the project and presenting it to a publisher. For the individual paper author, this will probably require some revision in order to foster overall coherence, but otherwise it may represent a relatively low effort way to publish the paper. The choice for a paper author is whether to contribute his or her paper to the joint project, or to try to publish the paper as a stand-alone journal article.

The problem with 'conference paper' books, especially from the perspective of publishers, is that they often lack coherence of style, approach and, even, subject matter. These problems are reduced when the would-be book's editor begins with an outline and then recruits authors to produce the chapters. A hybrid version begins with conference papers, but rather than trying to revise those papers to impose coherence, the conference itself serves as a venue for its participants to define a coherent project, with new papers or chapters for the final book.

The advantage of a book chapter over a journal article is that the 'shelf life' of a book is generally longer than that of a journal article. If the book is well structured, its contribution may in effect be greater than the sum of its parts. The disadvantages are that the readership of a book is generally much lower than that of a journal (although a good edited volume may attract more notice by the relevant specialist community) and that the professional status of a book chapter is generally significantly lower than that of an article in a peer reviewed journal.

3   BOOKS

Proposing a book to a publisher is in a sense a cross between proposing a conference paper (the proposal is made before the book is finished) and submitting a paper to a journal (if the proposal is not dismissed out of hand, it will be sent for peer review). The stakes are higher, however, both for the author and for the publisher.

3.1   Choosing a Publisher

As with journals, not all book publishers are of equal status. There is a fairly definite 'pecking order', which affects not only the prestige of the publication, but also its likely sales, especially to libraries. At the top are the major university presses, followed by the smaller university presses. Next are the best known commercial presses. Then come the smaller commercial presses, and presses known for subsidized publications (these may not be the only things they publish, but they taint the entire list). Near the bottom are in-house publications (not necessarily a university press publication of a book by a member of that university's staff, but certainly publication of a dissertation by the department to which it was submitted). At the bottom is self-publishing (although some very prominent scholars have occasionally self-published when they could not reach a satisfactory understanding with a standard press).

While this ranking is valid in general terms, there are exceptions. Some commercial presses and some minor university presses have developed quite strong reputations within particular specialisms. If the book is intended for a wider-than-scholarly audience, a commercial press may the best choice; books intended for classroom use are often better placed with a publisher that has an extensive textbook list. Overall, would-be authors should ask themselves, 'If I wanted to buy a book of this type or on this subject, whose catalog or website would I search first?'

3.2   Book Proposals

Formally, the process of getting a book published begins with a written proposal to a publisher. Often, however, the process begins well before a proposal is drafted. One of the jobs of an editor is to identify promising projects with a view to encouraging an eventual submission. Potential authors can also initiate a relationship with an editor by asking about 'interest in principle'. When there is a book series into which the proposed book might go (for example, the Oxford University Press/ECPR series in comparative politics), an author may begin by approaching the series editors, who generally are scholars rather than members of staff of the press, for advice and an indication of interest. Large conferences at which publishers exhibit their books are a good venue at which to begin these conversations, but since the editors at these meetings are generally extremely busy, it is advisable to arrange an appointment in advance.

Regardless of how the conversation begins, the author's objective should be to profit from the editor's experience – and simultaneously to give the editor a personal interest in the project. Unlike journal manuscripts, which never should be sent to more than one journal at a time, it is permissible to have these preliminary discussions with several publishers at the same time. It is even sometimes acceptable to send a formal proposal to several publishers at once, but they should each be informed that they are not the only publisher to whom the proposal has been sent.

The formal proposal provides the basic information on the basis of which the editor will decide whether or not to recommend publication. It is also what will be sent to external reviewers. An effective book proposal needs six basic elements. The first is a statement of what the book will be about. This should lay out the background and aims of the project, and give a synopsis of the overall work. This section should be quite brief (it can be viewed as the 'executive summary' of the full proposal). The second section is a more detailed description of the proposed contents. This will generally run to several pages and include a table of contents for the book. The third section is an analysis of the likely market and readership. To whom (scholars, students or the general public) is the book addressed, and what other books are competing for the same readership or market? Fourth, how long will the book be, and what is the schedule for its production. Fifth, who is the author – and why is the author qualified to write the book and likely to attract readers. Finally, and especially for those who do not already have an established record, the proposal should include one or more sample chapters.

If the editor thinks the project has merit, the proposal generally will be sent to external reviewers. These are not double-blind: because the qualifications of the author are relevant to the marketability of the book, and because they are being asked to assess work that is not yet completed, the reviewers will know the identity of the proposed author. While the reviewers are asked to evaluate the scholarly merits of the proposal, they are also asked to evaluate the market potential; it is therefore important that the author's own assessment be realistic.

The results of a publisher's review are not as formalized as those for a journal, but the import is generally the same. The manuscript can be accepted (a contract offered), the author can be invited to revise the proposal in light of suggestions by the reviewers and the editor, or the author can receive a polite 'thanks, but no thanks'. Regardless of the outcome, the comments from the reviewers and editor should be taken seriously. If offered a contract or a chance to revise and resubmit the proposal, these demand a detailed response to the editor. Even if the proposal is rejected outright, you should remember that there are always other publishers – and that the proposal can always be improved.

3.3   Contracts, Revisions and Production

Book contracts often are issued on the basis of proposals rather than full manuscripts, but even when a full manuscript has been submitted, there are likely to be significant revisions suggested or required by the editor. Among these may be reasonably tight restrictions on length; while there may be some room for negotiation, the length restriction must be taken seriously. In any event, even what appears to be a firm contract will generally be conditional on the delivery of a final manuscript that is acceptable to the publisher.

After the final manuscript is agreed by the editor, it will be sent to a copy-editor. The quality of copy-editors varies enormously; every experienced author has stories of serious mistakes that have been caught by a good copy-editor notwithstanding that the author and friends had reviewed the manuscript many times – and stories of serious errors introduced by a not-so-good copy-editor (such as changing direct quotations to make them conform to a gender-neutral style). Well before a final manuscript is to be delivered, the publisher will give the author a copy of their style manual. The fewer changes the copy-editor makes, the fewer errors will be introduced, so it is worth the effort to submit a manuscript that already conforms to the house style.

In some cases, authors will be sent the copy-edited manuscript for review before it is sent to the compositor; in other cases only the proofs are sent. Minor changes can be made at the proof stage, but significant changes can be costly – and the cost is borne by the author, although generally charged against royalties so that the author is not immediately out of pocket. Again, care at the beginning can save significant trouble later on.

Preparation of an index (and academic books should have an index), is the responsibility of the author. Although it can be costly, it is generally worth the expense to have the index prepared professionally. Publishers will often provide an indexer as the default, but authors generally remain free to find their own indexer – or to do the index themselves.

3.4   Edited Books

Production of an edited book can be nearly as much work for its editor as simply writing a book is for its author, but most of the credit will (generally properly) go to the chapter authors. The apparent exceptions most often are books in which the editor's introduction or conclusion is itself a significant contribution. It is better to see the editing of books as a service to the profession than as an investment in one's own career.

It is becoming difficult to interest publishers in edited volumes – with the exception of 'handbooks', for which the intended market is the reference departments of libraries. Although it may appear that edited books could be very useful in teaching, the danger for the publisher is that each instructor will only assign one or two chapters, so that a single copy is purchased by a university library with the few chapters assigned made available to students electronically. This kind of collection is generally better suited to be a special issue of a journal, for which sales are part of an overall subscription, although this means that the number of papers or chapters that can be included will be more restricted.

4   WRITING FOR THE PUBLIC AND POLICY-MAKERS

Scholarly publications in the social sciences generally are written to address problems of enduring importance. While authors naturally are anxious to have their work appear and be read as soon as possible, the year or more that it often takes between submissions of a manuscript to a journal or book publisher and actual appearance in print will not affect its visibility and scholarly significance in any serious way.

In writing for the public or for policy-makers, however, relevance to current, and often fleeting, issues is important – and that means that speed in preparation is vital. As Harold Wilson is reputed to have said, 'A week is a long time in politics'. Good academic writing is nuanced, and often laden with qualifications and caveats. To be effective in writing for the public and for policy-makers, it is important to be straight-forward and relatively simple. Again a quotation from a politician, in this case Harry Truman, captures the point: 'Give me a one-handed economist! All my economists say, on the one hand on the other.'

When scholars write for policy-makers and the public, they inevitably find themselves on the horns of a dilemma. On the one hand, the purpose of this kind of writing is generally to support a politically contentious position, to support or oppose a particular line of policy. Even when ostensibly engaged to produce a 'background' paper, the work itself may only be taken seriously if it can be bent to support a particular position. From this perspective, contrary arguments may be anticipated and raised, but only to be pre-emptively countered. On the other hand, it is the author's standing as a scholar, with all that implies about non-partisan assessment of evidence that separates this kind of writing from 'mere' opinion – or justifies special interest in the opinions of its author. The ideal piece in this genre has the appearance of neutrality, and yet leads the reader ineluctably to the author's preferred conclusion.

The equivalent of an article abstract is the executive summary, although an executive summary may be one or two full pages rather than the 150–300 words of an abstract. Similar to an abstract, it should be written so that it can be a stand-alone statement of the argument that can be understood without reading the full document – since in most cases, it will in fact be all that is read by its intended target.

5   CONCLUSION

Regardless of intended outlet or audience, there are a few basic rules for all authors. Have someone else read the entire manuscript before submission; authors will see what they meant, but a third party will see what they wrote. Make the objective clear at the beginning; it is much easier for readers to follow an argument if they know where it is going. Communication depends on the receiver at least as much as the transmitter; if the reader is confused, it is almost always the author's fault. Do not become overly ego-invested in any one piece; everyone has submissions rejected from time to time – the successful authors and scholars are the ones who learn from the experience and move on.

FURTHER READING

Martin, F. and R. Goehlert (2001), *Getting Published in Political Science Journals: A Guide for Authors, Editors and Librarians*, Washington, DC: American Political Science Association.

.

Index

Note: titles of publications are in italics.

Aaron, H.J. 485
Aarts, K. 256
Achen, C.H. 376
Ackerly, B. 50
Adams, J. 472
Adorno, T.W. 42, 404
Alber, J. 68, 70
Aldenderfer, M.S. 431
Alesina, A. 104
Alexander, A.C. 122
Allan, J.P. 199
Almond, G. 26, 79, 80, 84, 91, 262, 472
Alvarez, R.M. 193
American Voter, The (Campbell et al.) 253
Amoretti, U.M. 105
Anderson, C.J. 364–5
Anderson, P. 72
Anheier, H.K. 141, 145
Ansolabehere, S.S. 252
Aristotle 9, 10, 12, 17, 19, 21, 22
Armingeon, K. 188, 220, 239, 241, 243
Ashley, R. 40
Assenmacher, W. 379
Atkeson, L. 262, 263
Austin, J.L. 401
Australia 439, 443, 445, 446
Austria 117, 145, 302, 361, 439, 442, 444, 506, 510
Axelrod, R. 304, 306, 335

Baccaro, L. 240, 242
Bacchi, C. 317
Bache, I. 97, 132
Bacher, J. 431, 447
Badie, B. 25, 30
Baert, P. 481
Ball, T. 311
Bambra, C. 449
Banks, A.R. 112
Bardach, E. 88, 91

Barker, D. 80
Barnes, S.H. 158, 159
Barrington Moore, G. Jr 68, 72–3, 74, 76
Barry, B. 204, 209, 210
Bartolini, S. 2, 67, 74, 75, 99
Basu, K. 490
Basutro, X. 130
bathtub 27–8, 30; *see also* Coleman, J.S.
Baumgartner, F. 150
Baumgartner, M. 396
Beach, D. 34, 452, 456
Beck, N. 336, 360
Becker, H.S. 384, 422
Becker, U. 105, 191, 193, 195, 198
Beishuizen, J. 249
Belgium 116, 138, 439, 442, 444
Bennett, A. 422, 424, 452, 454, 456, 458, 459, 461, 463
Benoit, K. 432
Bensen, K. 490
Bentham, J. 20
Bentley, A.F. 127
Benz, A. 101–2
Berelson, B.R. 253, 316
Berg, J. 249
Berg-Schlosser, D. 31, 32, 33, 34, 72, 73–4, 389, 393, 425
Bergman, M. 34
Berlusconi, S. 144
  and Fininvest 144
Bermeo, N. 105
Bernard, P. 434
Berry, W.D. 377
Bertelsmann Transformation index 111, 120–22
Best, H. 223
Bethlehem, J.G. 251
Beyer, J.M. 485
Beyme, K. von 222